third edition

the backpacker's HANDBOOK

CHRIS TOWNSEND

RAGGED MOUNTAIN PRESS / McGRAW-HILL

Camden, Maine | New York | Chicago | San Francisco | Lisbon | London | Madrid |
Mexico City | Milan | New Delhi | San Juan | Seoul | Singapore | Sydney | Toronto

DEDICATION

To Denise Thorn for her patience, love, and companionship.

The McGraw·Hill Companies

2 3 4 5 6 7 8 9 10 DOC DOC 0 9 8 7 6 5
© 2005 by Chris Townsend

Library of Congress Cataloging-in-Publication Data
Townsend, Chris, 1949–
  The backpacker's handbook / Chris Townsend.—3rd ed.
    p.   cm.
  Includes bibliographical references (p.   ) and index.
  ISBN 0-07-142320-6 (pbk. : alk. paper)
  1. Backpacking—Handbooks, manuals, etc.
  2. Camping—Handbooks, manuals, etc. I. Title.
  GV199.6.T69 2004
  796.51—dc22   2004017330

Questions regarding the content of this book should be addressed to
Ragged Mountain Press
P.O. Box 220
Camden, ME 04843

Questions regarding the ordering of this book should be addressed to
The McGraw-Hill Companies
Customer Service Department
P.O. Box 547
Blacklick, OH 43004
Retail customers: 1-800-262-4729
Bookstores: 1-800-722-4726

All drawings by Elara Tanguy unless otherwise noted. All photographs by the author unless otherwise noted. Bootprint courtesy arttoday.com.

Page	Credit
16	Map courtesy Natural Resources Conservation Service/USDA, from Hall: *The Essential Backpacker*
48	Christopher Hoyt drawing from Kestenbaum: *The Ultralight Backpacker*
71	Annie Getchell drawing from Getchell and Getchell: *The Essential Outdoor Gear Manual*
73	Christopher Hoyt drawing from Townsend: *Backpacker's Pocket Guide*
89	Ice ax courtesy Black Diamond Equipment, Ltd.
153	Mike Walsh drawings from Townsend: *The Backpacker's Handbook*, second edition
186	Christopher Hoyt drawing from Townsend: *Backpacker's Pocket Guide*
191	Christopher Hoyt drawing from Kestenbaum: *The Ultralight Backpacker*
192	Mike Walsh drawing from Townsend: *The Backpacker's Handbook*, second edition
199	Christopher Hoyt drawing from Townsend and Aggens: *Encyclopedia of Outdoor & Wilderness Skills*
259	Christopher Hoyt drawing from Townsend: *Backpacker's Pocket Guide*
260	Christopher Hoyt drawing from Townsend: *Backpacker's Pocket Guide*
266	Christopher Hoyt drawing from Townsend and Aggens: *Encyclopedia of Outdoor & Wilderness Skills*
269	Christopher Hoyt drawing from Townsend: *Backpacker's Pocket Guide*
279	Christophor Hoyt drawing from Townsend and Aggens: *Encyclopedia of Outdoor & Wilderness Skills*
290	Christopher Hoyt drawing from Townsend: *Backpacker's Pocket Guide*
338	Christopher Hoyt drawings from Townsend: *Backpacker's Pocket Guide*
339	Christopher Hoyt drawing from Townsend: *Backpacker's Pocket Guide*
346	Christopher Dowling drawing from Johnson: *The Ultimate Desert Handbook*
358	*Left:* Mike Walsh drawing from Townsend: *The Backpacker's Handbook*, second edition. *Right:* Christine Erikson drawing from Seidman: *The Essential Wilderness Navigator*
359	Christine Erikson drawing from Seidman: *The Essential Wilderness Navigator*
364	Mike Walsh drawing from Townsend: *The Backpacker's Handbook*, second edition
365	Mike Walsh drawing from Townsend: *The Backpacker's Handbook*, second edition
366	Mike Walsh drawing from Townsend: *The Backpacker's Handbook*, second edition
369	Craig Connally drawing from Connally: *Mountaineering Handbook*
370	Tools courtesy of maptools.com. These and other coordinate plotting tools are available from www.maptools.com
374	Christine Erikson drawing from Seidman: *The Essential Wilderness Navigator*
385	Christopher Hoyt drawing from Townsend and Aggens: *Encyclopedia of Outdoor & Wilderness Skills*
392	*Bottom two:* William Hamilton drawing from Hall: *The Essential Backpacker*
393	Christopher Hoyt drawing from Townsend: *Backpacker's Pocket Guide*
395	Christopher Hoyt drawing from Townsend and Aggens: *Encyclopedia of Outdoor & Wilderness Skills*

CONTENTS

Preface to the Third Edition v
Acknowledgments vii
Introduction: Into the Wilderness 1

1. Preparing for the Trail 5
   Fitness 5
   The Art of Walking 7
   Going Alone 10
   Slackpacking and Fastpacking 11
   Planning 13

2. The Load on Your Back: Choosing
   and Using Equipment 20
   Weight 22
   Checklists 29
   Choosing and Buying 31
   Final Thoughts 36

3. Footwear and Wilderness Travel 37
   About Footwear 37
   Footwear Types 40
   Fitting Boots and Shoes 45
   Footwear Materials and Construction 53
   Footwear Models and Choices 64
   Care of Footwear 67
   Foot Care 72
   Socks 73
   Gaiters 80
   Overboots 81
   Campwear 81
   Trekking Poles and Staffs 83

Ice Axes 88
Crampons 90
Skis and Snowshoes 93

4. Carrying the Load: The Pack 96
   Types of Packs 97
   Suspension Systems 102
   Fitting the Pack 108
   Packbags 113
   Materials 116
   Durability 118
   Packing 119
   Putting on the Pack 122
   Pack Care 125
   Pack Accessories 125

5. Keeping Warm and Dry: Dressing for the
   Wilderness 129
   Heat Loss and Heat Production 129
   The Layer System 130
   The Vapor-Barrier Theory 163
   Legwear 164
   Headgear 168
   Gloves and Mittens 172
   Bandannas 175
   Carrying Clothes 176
   Fabric Treatment and Care 176

6. Shelter: Camping in the Wilderness 179
   Bivouac Bags 180
   Tarps 184

Groundsheets 190
Tents 190
Pitches and Pitching:
Minimum-Impact Camping 210
Tent Care 217
Wilderness Shelters 218
Snow Caves 218
Sleeping Bags 220
Sleeping Pads 236
Other Comforts 241

7. The Wilderness Kitchen 243
Food and Drink 243
Water 263
The Campfire 277
Stoves 280
Utensils 315
Siting the Kitchen 323

8. Comfort and Safety in Camp
and on the Trail 325
Light 325
Health and Body Care 333
Equipment Maintenance and Repair 343
In Case of Emergency 346
Office 350
Binoculars and Monoculars 352
Photography 352
Entertainment 355

9. On the Move: Skills and Hazards 357
Finding the Way 357
Coping with Terrain 377
Minimizing Impact 381
Wilderness Hazards 383
Dealing with Animals 393
Hunters 396

10. Adventure Travel:
Backpacking Abroad 397
Information and Planning 399
Organized Trips 402
Immunizations and Health 402
Food and Supplies 402
Insurance 403
Different Cultures 403
Getting There 404

A Final Word 406

Appendixes
1. Equipment Checklist 407
2. Further Reading 409
3. Resources 415
4. Metric Conversions 432

Index 433

PREFACE
to the third edition

Seven years have passed since I wrote the previous edition of this book, years in which I've learned much more about backpacking and the wilderness—modifying some techniques, adopting new ones, and abandoning others. I've spent more time in the desert Southwest and also in the cold Far North. Much new equipment has appeared. The ultralight movement has boomed, LED lights have appeared, and electronic devices have become the norm. A new and better way of fitting boots is available. This new edition incorporates all these advances and much more.

As with the previous edition, I found more material I wanted to rewrite or change than I expected. Much of the book is new. My choices in gear have changed in many cases, and there are new kit lists showing what I carry on trips now. As before, this is a subjective book: I give my thoughts and describe how I operate. But the reasons for going into the wilderness haven't changed, nor has the simple activity of hiking. My memories of wilderness trips aren't about tents or boots or the weight of my load. They are about watching moose browse out in a shallow timberline lake below a dark forest topped by red rock cliffs; of striding along a rocky mountain ridge above a vast panorama of peaks and canyons dotted with blue lakes and deep green groves; of waking at dawn to watch the sun slice through the mist and light up a cliff-shadowed lake; of lying under the desert sky listening to the call of night birds and staring at the bright stars stretching into the infinite; of hearing the welcome sound of a trickling creek after a hot, dry climb. They are about, at heart, feeling part of nature. This is constant. This is what backpacking is.

ACKNOWLEDGMENTS

Far too many people have added to my store of knowledge and assisted on my walks to thank them all individually here, but some I must single out. As each edition of this book appears, the numbers grow. Although I travel solo more often than not, I've shared trails and campsites with many companions over the years, and I have many valued memories of these times. I've also spent many hours discussing backpacking with individuals and at hikers' gatherings. Many readers have written to me by e-mail and letter—a great encouragement—and I've had many discussions with other outdoor writers.

I can't mention everybody I've hiked with, talked to, or corresponded with, but I would like to thank Chris and Janet Ainsworth; Brad Allen; Judy Armstrong; Karen Berger; Brad, Karen, and Mark Buckhout; Georgina Collins; Mark Edgington; Ron Ellis; Lou Ann Fellows; Wayne Fuiten; Mick Furey; Franjo Goluza; Kris Gravette; Brice Hammack; Andrew Helliwell; Dave Hewitt; Pete Hickey; Andy Hicks; the late John Hinde; Tony Hobbs; Graham Huntington; Ray and Jenny Jardine; Jörgen Johansson; Alain Kahan; Dave Key; Larry Lake; Alex Lawrence; Paul Leech; Peter and Pat Lennon; David Lynch; Duncan MacDonald; John Manning; Cameron McNeish; the late Al Micklethwaite; Colin Mortlock; Eugene Miya; Tony Morfe; Joris Naiman; Tom Phillips; Dave Rehbehn; Jake Schas; Gary D. Schwartz; Todd Seniff; Pat Silver; Jane and Andy Smith; Clyde Soles; Wallace Spaulding; Scott Steiner; Douglas K. Stream; Ron Strickland; Lesya Struz; Graham Thompson; Fran Townsend; John Traynor; Steve Twaites; Stan Walker; Bill Watson; and Scott Williamson.

I'd also like to thank all those I've met at the annual gatherings of the American Long Distance Hiking Association–West and the Appalachian Long Distance Hikers Association and at meetings of the Backpackers Club (UK), plus all those I've guided on wilderness ski tours. I've had much-appreciated help and assistance from the Appalachian Mountain Club, the Arizona Trail Association, and the staffs of many national parks and national forests, especially Yosemite National Park.

Many equipment makers and designers have been generous with information and equipment. My thanks in particular to the late Chris Brasher of Brasher Boots; Nick Brown of Nikwax and Páramo; Allen Buckner of MSR; Rab Carrington of Rab; Gordon Conyers of Tor Outdoor Products; Demetri "Coup" and Kim Coupounas of GoLite; Coral Darby; Andrew Denton of Mountain Equipment (UK); Brian Frankle of ULA; Gordon Fraser of Anatom; Jeff Gray of Superfeet; Bo and Rolf Hilleberg and Peter Carati of Hilleberg; Ed Hueser of Grand Shelters (IceBox); Noeleen Keane of

Nikwax; Steve Laycock of Pertex; Julian Miles of Kathmandu Trekking; Phil Oren; R. Randall of Granger's International; Barry Robertson; Staffan Ronn of Optimus; Bob Rose, boot expert; Aaron Rosenbloom of Brasslite stoves; Christer Svensson of Silva Sweden; Aarn Tate of Aarn Designs; Glen Van Peski of Gossamer Gear; and Energizer, Lowe Alpine, Marmot, Montane, Mountain Hardwear, Nextec, Suunto, Tilley, and ZZ Manufacturing. Demetri Coupounas also kindly read through the first draft of the book and made many valuable comments.

The views expressed in this book are my own, of course. None of those mentioned above are assumed to agree with any of them.

Many thanks, too, to Jonathan Eaton, Tristram Coburn, Molly Mulhern, Janet Robbins, and Margaret Cook at Ragged Mountain Press, and to Alice Bennett, copyeditor, who have worked hard to make this book what it is.

Finally, I would like to thank my family, Denise and Hazel Thorn, for their love and their patience in listening to me rambling on about bootfitting, GPS, and more. Denise also read through the manuscript and made many valuable suggestions. Both of them posed for photographs and Hazel also took some of the photos of me.

THE CLEAREST WAY INTO THE UNIVERSE
IS THROUGH A FOREST WILDERNESS.

—*John Muir*

into the wilderness

This is a how-to book, an instructional manual on how to hike and camp in wild country safely and in comfort. Much of the book concerns techniques and equipment—factual stuff leavened with a little bias and opinion, but down to earth and functional nonetheless. The scope, theoretically, is worldwide, though you won't find much about tropical travel; my own experience has been mostly in the wild areas of North America and Western Europe, ranging from the hot deserts of the Southwest to the Arctic wastes of Greenland.

Over the years I have made several hikes lasting many months, the sort that refine your techniques and show you what equipment works. These include through-hikes of the Pacific Crest and Continental Divide Trails; 1,600 miles along the length of the Canadian Rockies; 1,000 miles south to north through Canada's Yukon Territory; 1,300 miles through the mountains of Norway and Sweden; 1,250 miles from Land's End to John o'Groat's in Britain; 1,600 miles over the 517 summits of 3,000 feet in the Scottish Highlands; and

the 800-mile Arizona Trail. These experiences, along with many shorter trips—more than twenty-five years of backpacking at least 20,000 miles—constitute my credentials for presuming to offer advice. Along the way I've made many mistakes; these are related for entertainment and with the hope that you can learn from them without having to experience them firsthand.

But my highest qualification is my enjoyment of backpacking, and the fact that, for me, it is a way of life, a reason for existing. I want to share that by pointing others in the same direction. The result is this book—an attempt to mesh the reasons for backpacking with the ways to do it.

Capturing the essence of backpacking in words —the joy of walking through the ever-changing, ever-constant natural world, the magic of waking to sunlight glinting on a mist-wreathed lake, the excitement of striding through a mountain storm—is difficult. At heart I suspect it is impossible to describe this experience to those not disposed to listen. How can one convey to a skep-

I

Rest stop, Sallie Keyes Lake, John Muir Wilderness, High Sierra.

experiencing only part of what the wilderness has to offer; it's like dipping your toe in the water instead of taking an invigorating swim. Only by living in the wilderness twenty-four hours a day, day after day, do you gain that indefinable feeling of rightness, of being *with* instead of *against* the earth, that gives the deepest contentment I have found.

I'm aware that this sounds mystical, but I make no apology. We are too prone to value only what can be defined in logical terms or assigned a cash value. Yet the natural, self-regulating earth cannot be quantified, calculated, and summed up—every attempt uncovers another mystery just beyond our grasp. And this pleases me. I'm content not to fully comprehend the joy I find in the wilderness; to try would be a fruitless task, like chasing the end of a rainbow; and the goal, if ever realized, would only disappoint.

The heart of backpacking lies in the concept of the journey itself, a true odyssey, a desire to explore a world beyond our everyday lives, and in doing so to explore ourselves. Not so long ago, all journeys were like this, because the known world extended little beyond one's hometown. Now, with modern communications and mass transportation, most "journeys" consist of nothing more than the mechanized moving of bodies from one place to another, a process so sanitized, safe, controlled, and so insulated from its surroundings that it precludes any sense of freedom, adventure, or personal involvement. Only when I shoulder my pack and set out into the wilderness do I feel a journey is really beginning, even though I may have traveled halfway around the world to take that first step.

A journey requires a beginning and an end, though what it is really about lies between those two points. Many journeys are circles, starting and finishing at the same place; others are point-to-

tic the liberating sense of living in the moment, free of thinking about tomorrow; the painful delight in the exquisite beauty of a fleeting cloud, a tiny flower in an ocean of rock, a butterfly's wing; the awe engendered by a mountain vista stretching unbroken beyond the power of sight; the fragile moment of identity when you stare deeply into a wild animal's eyes and just for a second connect? But then, it's not for skeptics that this book was written. If you are interested in my thoughts on backpacking, you are already responsive to the real world outside our technological shells.

Why backpack? Why forgo the comforts of home or hotel for a night under the stars or sheltered by a flimsy nylon sheet? Many people hike in the wilds but return to civilization at night. This is point, linear hikes that finish far from where they start; and still others are there-and-back-again routes where you retrace your outbound steps. All three are appealing, but I especially like circles, routes that take you through new country every day yet return you to your starting point. A circle emphasizes the primacy of the experience rather than the conclusion. Closing the circle finishes the journey, returning you to the same place, enriched by the wilderness you have hiked through.

Though being in the wilderness is what matters, and the real goal of any hike is to experience nature, a more specific purpose gives shape to a trip and provides an incentive to keep moving. Thus I always set a goal, even on day hikes—a summit, a lake, a distance to cover, a crag to visit, a vista to see. Once I'm under way, the overall goal is subordinated to the day-by-day, minute-by-minute events and impressions that are my reason for hiking.

Walking is the only way to really see a place, to really grasp what it's like, to experience all its aspects. This is true even for cities but applies much, much more to mountains and deserts, forests and meadows. Seen from a car, a train, or even a "scenic viewpoint," these are only pretty pictures, postcard images for the surface of the mind, quickly forgotten. By walking through a landscape, you enter into it, experience it with every one of your senses, learn how it works and why it's as it is. You become, for a time, a part of it. And once you stay out overnight and entrust your sleeping self to its care, a deeper bond is forged and, fleetingly and at the edge of your mind, you begin to grasp that we are not apart from but part of the earth.

This process of exploring the relationship between the self and the natural world grows and expands as you become more experienced and confident in wilderness wandering. It does not, I suspect, have limits. Perhaps it reflects a need to

return to or at least acknowledge our primordial roots, to recall the time, the vast time that covers most of human existence, when humans were nomadic hunter-gatherers.

I would not contemplate returning to such a state, even if it were possible. Civilization has good points as well as bad ones, but I do think we have gone too far toward a belief that we are superior to and separate from nature, that it exists for us to tame, control, and exploit. And in taming and controlling nature we tame and control ourselves, losing our freedom and the ability to live in and be part of the wilderness.

If backpacking has any validity apart from being an enriching personal experience (good enough in itself, of course), it lies in this. At a time when the balance of nature itself is threatened, backpackers in particular should understand that we have to change our ways, to acknowledge that our interests coincide with nature's. By experiencing the wilderness directly, by being in touch with the land, we can learn how valuable—how essential—it is, and that we must try to preserve and restore our still-beautiful world.

But what do we mean by *wilderness*, a magic word, redolent of mountain and forest, untamed nature and wild beauty? As defined by the Wilderness Act of 1964, wilderness is "an area where the earth and its community of life are untrammeled by man, where man himself is a visitor who does not remain." To be viable as a complete ecosystem, a wilderness needs to be large—huge, even—providing space for wildlife to survive and live free and for the landscape to be complete from valley bottom to mountaintop, from foothills to highest peaks. These vast, pristine areas are the prime places for backpacking, places of dreams and adventures. However, many areas backpackers hike are neither this size nor untouched. In Europe in particular, wilderness areas are small

Early-season snow in the White Mountains, New Hampshire.

and, if defined in terms of never having been touched by human hand, virtually nonexistent. I think that wilderness is as much an idea, a concept, as a physical reality. If there is enough land to walk into, enough room to set up a camp and then walk on with that freedom that comes when you escape the constraints of modern living, then it *is* wilderness, in spirit if not by definition.

All wilderness areas need defending, from the vast expanse of Antarctica to the small pockets that still exist even in heavily industrialized countries. That there are places you can reach only on foot, requiring effort and commitment to visit, is vital. It will be a sad day when the last such spot succumbs to the paved road and the hollow stares of detached tourists.

Ironically, wilderness also needs defending from those who love it. Damaging practices and an increasing number of hikers are turning many popular areas into worn-out remnants. Wilderness travelers traditionally lived off the land for shelter as well as for food; they built lean-tos and tepees, cut boughs for mattresses and logs for tables and chairs. Today this is irresponsible—and often illegal—in most wilderness areas. There is too little wilderness left, and every scar diminishes what remains.

Even with modern equipment, backpackers have more impact on the land than dayhikers and therefore have more responsibilities. No-trace, low-impact camping must be the norm if the wilderness is to stay intact. This book emphasizes these techniques, because there are only two solutions to the problem of hikers' damaging the wilderness: self-regulation and the practice of minimum-impact techniques by all, or bureaucratic regulation, which already is the norm in many parks worldwide. In some areas wilderness camping is allowed only on specified sites. In a few places in the Alps and elsewhere, wild camping is forbidden altogether, and people are required to use campgrounds or stay in mountain huts. Such restrictions are anathema to the spirit of freedom inherent in backpacking, but they will become common unless backpackers learn to respect the wilderness.

preparing for the trail

Backpacking isn't difficult, but it does require both physical and mental preparation. Every year, first-time hikers set off along the trail unfit, ill equipped, and with unrealistic expectations. Many of them never venture into the wilderness again. The better your planning, the more enjoyable your trip will be. You need not know exactly how far you'll walk each day, or precisely where you'll camp each night (though such detailed planning is useful for beginners), but you should know your capabilities and desires well enough to tailor your trip to them. Setting out to carry 65 pounds twenty-five miles a day through steep, mountainous terrain just about guarantees exhaustion, frustration, and disappointment unless you are extremely fit and know beforehand that you can do it.

FITNESS

Backpacking requires fitness. You need aerobic, or cardiovascular, fitness to walk and climb all day without having your heart pound and your lungs gasp for air. Without muscular fitness, particularly of the legs, you'll be stiff and aching all over on the second day out. Also, if you set out unfit, you're much more susceptible to strains and muscle tears.

Getting fit takes time. I know people who claim they'll get fit over the first few days of an annual backpacking trip. They usually suffer for most of the walk; yet with a little preparation, they could enjoy every day.

The best way to train for carrying heavy loads over rough terrain is to carry heavy loads over rough terrain—what sports trainers call *specific training*. Although this isn't always practical, you'd be surprised what you can do if you really want to, even if you live and work in a city. In *Journey Through Britain*, John Hillaby wrote that he trained for his 1,100-mile, end-to-end walk across Britain by spending the three months before the trip walking the six miles "from Hampstead to the City [London] each day and farther at the weekends. On these jaunts I carried weight lifters' weights sewn high up in a flat rucksack that didn't look too odd among people making their way to the office in the morning."

At the very least, spend a few weekends getting used to walking with a load before setting off on a longer trip. Walk as much as you can during the week—including up and down stairs. Brisk strolls or runs in the evening help too, especially if there are hills. In fact, trail running in hilly country is probably the best way to improve both your aerobic fitness and your leg power in a short time.

I trained at a fitness center once, before a through-hike of the Canadian Rockies. For six months I did hour-long circuit sessions on the weight machines three times a week and hour-long runs on the days between, with one day off a week. It helped, but probably no more than if I'd hiked

Looking across the Merced River Canyon to Red Peak, Yosemite Wilderness.

regularly with a pack and exercised in the woods and fields, which I prefer. I haven't followed an exercise program since. If you want to do so, however, The Outdoor Athlete, by Steve Ilg, is worth reading (see his Web site, wholisticfitness.com). The book includes programs for "mountaineering and advanced backpacking" and "recreational hiking and backpacking." The main thing I learned from fitness center training was that you need rest from strenuous exercise and that you need to pace yourself. I'd never heard of overtraining before, having never regarded backpacking or hiking as a "sport." But once I discovered that pushing yourself too hard results, unsurprisingly, in excess stress to the body and reduced performance, I understood why, after hiking all day every day for two weeks or more, I often felt tired and run-down instead of superfit. Now on walks longer than two weeks I aim to take a rest day every week to twelve days. I don't stick to a rigid timetable—a day off every week, say—but rather pay attention to my body and my mind. If I feel lethargic or uninterested, develop aches and pains, or find myself being clumsy and careless, I know I need to rest. Resting while training is important—if you force yourself to train hard every day because you've got a big trip coming up, you may burn out before the hike starts.

After my brief bout with the fitness center, I abandoned formal training and returned to short, brisk hikes in the local woods and fields, the occasional 5- to 10-mile cycle ride, and as an aim if not in reality, at least one full day a week walking or skiing in the mountains. This is apart from the two- to three-day backpacking trips I try to take once a month or so between longer walks.

If you haven't exercised for some time, return to it gradually, especially if you're over thirty-five. Preparing for a walk takes time anyway. You can't go from being unfit to toting a heavy load all day in a week or even a month.

THE ART OF WALKING

While the simple act of putting one foot in front of the other seems to require no instruction or comment, there are, in fact, good and bad ways to walk, and good and bad walkers. Good walkers can walk effortlessly all day, while bad ones may be exhausted after a few hours.

To make walking seem effortless, walk slowly and steadily, finding a *rhythm* that lets you glide along and a *pace* you can keep up for hours. Without a comfortable rhythm, every step seems tiring, which is one reason that crossing boulder fields, brush-choked forest, and other broken terrain is so exhausting. Inexperienced walkers often start off at a rapid pace, leaving the experienced plodding slowly behind. As in Aesop's ancient fable of the tortoise and the hare, slower walkers often pass exhausted novices long before a day's walk is complete.

The ability to maintain a steady pace hour after hour has to be developed. If you need a rest, take one; otherwise you'll wear yourself out.

The difference between novices and experts was graphically demonstrated to me when I was leading backpacking treks for an Outward Bound school in the Scottish Highlands. I let the students set their own pace, often following them or traversing at a higher level than the group. But one day the course supervisor, an experienced mountaineer, turned up and said he'd lead the day's walk—and he meant *lead*. Off he tramped, the group following in his footsteps, while I brought up the rear. Initially, we followed a flat river valley, and soon the students were muttering impatiently about the supervisor's slow pace. The faint trail

Mount Beulah and the West Fork Blacks Fork valley, High Uinta Wilderness, Utah.

began to climb after a while, and on we went at the same slow pace, with some of the students close to rebellion. Eventually we came to the base of a steep, grassy slope with no trail. The supervisor didn't pause—he just headed up as if the terrain hadn't altered. After a few hundred yards, the tenor of the students' response changed. "Isn't he ever going to stop?" they complained. One or two fell behind. Intercepting a trail, we turned up it, switchbacking steadily to a high pass. By now some of the students seemed in danger of collapse, so I hurried ahead to the supervisor and said they needed a rest. He seemed surprised. "I'll see you later then," he said, and started down, his pace unaltered, leaving the students slumping in relief.

This story also reveals one of the problems of walking in a group: each person has his or her own pace. The best way to deal with this is not to walk as a large group but to establish pairs or small groups of walkers with similar abilities, so people can proceed at their own pace, meeting up at rest stops and in camp. If a large group must stay together, perhaps because of bad weather or difficult route finding, let the slowest member set the pace, perhaps leading at least some of the time. It is neither fair nor safe to let the slowest member fall far behind the group, and if this happens to you, you should object.

The ability to walk economically, using the least energy, comes only with experience. If a rhythm doesn't develop naturally, it may help to try to create one in your head. I sometimes do this on long climbs if the right pace is hard to find and I'm constantly stopping to catch my breath. I often chant rhythmically any words that come to mind. When I can remember them, I find the poems of Robert Service or Longfellow are good. I need to repeat only a few lines: "There are strange things done in the midnight sun / By the men who moil for gold; / The Arctic Trails have their secret tales / That would make your blood run cold" (from Service's "The Cremation of Sam McGee"). If I begin to speed up, I chant out loud, which slows me down. It is of course impossible to walk for a long time at a faster-than-normal pace, but walking too slow is surprisingly tiring, since it is hard to establish a rhythm.

Once in a while all the aspects of walking come together, and then I have an hour or a day when I simply glide along, seemingly expending no energy. When this happens, distance melts under my feet, and I feel I could stride on forever. I can't force such moments, and I don't know where they come from, but the more I walk, the more often they happen. Not surprisingly, they occur most often on really long treks. On such days, I'll walk for five hours and more without a break, yet

with such little effort that I don't realize how long and far I've traveled until I finally stop. Rather than hiking, I feel as though I'm flowing through the landscape. I never feel any effects afterward, except perhaps greater contentment.

Distance

How far can I walk in a day? This is a perennial question asked by walkers and nonwalkers alike. The answer depends on your fitness, the length of your stride, how many hours you walk, the weight you're carrying, and the terrain. There are formulas for making calculations, including a good one proposed in the late nineteenth century by William W. Naismith, a luminary of the Scottish Mountaineering Club. Naismith's formula allows one hour for every 3 miles, plus an extra half hour for every 1,000 feet of ascent. I've used this as a guide for years, and it seems to work; a 15-mile day with 4,000 feet of ascent takes me, on average, eight hours including stops. Of course, 15 miles on a map will be longer on the ground, since map miles are flat miles, unlike most terrain. As slopes steepen, the distance increases.

The time I spend between leaving one camp and setting up the next is usually eight to ten hours, not all of it spent walking. I once measured my pace against distance posts on a flat, paved road in the Great Divide Basin during a Continental Divide hike. While carrying a 55-pound pack, I went about 3¾ miles an hour. At that rate I would cover 37 miles in ten hours if I did nothing but walk (and the terrain was smooth and flat). In practice, however, I probably spend no more than seven hours of a ten-hour day walking, averaging about 2½ miles an hour if the terrain isn't too rugged. That speed, for me, is fast enough. Backpacking is about living in the wilderness, not racing through it. I cover distance most quickly on

On Dead Horse Pass, High Uinta Wilderness, Utah.

roads—whether tarmac, gravel, or dirt—because I always want to leave them behind as soon as possible.

How far you can push yourself to walk in a day is less important than how far you are happy walking in a day. This distance can be worked out if you keep records of your trips. I plan walks based on 15 miles a day on trails and over easy terrain. For difficult cross-country travel, I estimate 12 miles a day.

When planning treks, it also helps to know how far you can walk over a complete trip. You can get an idea by analyzing your previous walks. For example, I averaged 16 miles a day on the 2,600-mile Pacific Crest Trail (PCT), a 1,600-mile Canadian Rockies walk, a 1,300-mile Scandinavian mountains walk, and an 800-mile Arizona Trail hike and 16¾ miles a day on the 3,000-mile Continental Divide, which seems amazingly consistent. A closer look, however, reveals that daily distances varied from 6 to 30 miles, and the time between

ADDITIONAL DISTANCE HIKED FOR SLOPES OF DIFFERENT ANGLES OVER ONE MILE ON THE MAP

Slope Angle	Height Gained	Additional Distance Traveled
10°	930 feet	1.5%/80 feet
20°	1,920 feet	6.5%/340 feet
30°	3,050 feet	15.5%/815 feet
40°	4,435 feet	31.0%/1,615 feet
45°	5,280 feet (1 mile)	41.0%/2,186 feet
50°	6,295 feet	56.0%/2,936 feet
60°	9,146 feet	100%/5,289 feet (1 mile)

camps varied from three to fifteen hours. All these walks were mainly on trails. My 1,000-mile Yukon walk was mostly cross-country, and on that my average dropped to 12½ miles a day.

One problem with a two-week summer backpacking trip is that many people spend the first week struggling to get fit and the second week turning the first week's efforts into hard muscle and greater lung power. By the time they're ready to go home, they're at peak fitness. The solution is to temper your desires. It's easy in winter to make ambitious plans for the next summer's hikes that fall apart the first day out as you struggle to carry your pack half the distance you intended. On all walks, I take it easy until I feel comfortable being on

Backpackers at a remote overlook.

the move again. This breaking-in period may last only a few hours on a weekend trip or a couple of weeks on a long summer trek. On two-week trips, it's a good idea to take it easy the first two or three days by walking less distance than you hope to cover later in the trip, especially if you're not as fit as you intended to be.

Pedometers

In theory, pedometers measure how far you travel during a specific time. But all pedometers work by converting the number of steps taken into distance, and this works only if your strides are regular. In the wilderness, with its ups and downs, bogs, scree, boulders, and logs, maintaining a regular stride hour after hour is difficult. I've tried pedometers, but they've never produced any reliable figures. (Note that a GPS unit—see pages 367–72—can measure how far you've traveled much more accurately than a pedometer.)

GOING ALONE

It's customary to advise hikers never to go alone, but I can hardly do that since I travel solo more often than not—I feel it's the best way to experience the wilderness. Only when I go alone do I achieve the feeling of blending in with the natural world and being part of it. The heightened awareness that comes with solo walking is always absent when I'm with others. Solitude is immeasurably rewarding. Going alone also gives me the freedom of self-determination. I can choose to walk twelve hours one day but only three the next, or to spend half a day watching otters or lying in the tent wondering if the rain will ever stop without having to consult anyone else. This is more than just freedom or what might seem self-indulgence, though. At a deeper level it's about finding your natural rhythm, the one where your body and mind work best and which is unique to you, and attuning it to the rhythms of nature. Your rhythm is most obvious when you're walking, but it is there when you eat, sleep, and rest. You can slip into this rhythm much more easily alone than with others, when it may not even be possible.

Of course, solo walking has its dangers, and it's up to you to calculate what risks you're prepared to take. When crossing steep boulder fields or fording streams, I'm always aware that if I slip there's no one to go for help. The solo walker must weigh every action carefully and assess every risk. In the foothills of the Canadian Rockies I once spent eight days struggling cross-country through rugged terrain. I was constantly aware that even a minor accident could have serious consequences, especially since I was also way off the trail. Such situations demand greater care than trail travel, where a twisted ankle may mean no more than a painful limp out to the road and potential rescuers may not be too far away.

The wilderness is far safer than civilization. Having a car accident on your way to the wilderness is more likely than getting injured while you're there.

Leaving Word

You always should leave word with somebody about where you are going and when you'll be back, especially if you're going out alone. The route details you leave may be precise or vague—but you must leave some indication of your plans with a responsible person. If you're leaving a car anywhere, you should tell someone when you'll be back for it. This isn't a problem in places where you must register a trail permit, but elsewhere a parked car could cause concern or even lead to an unnecessary rescue attempt if it's there for many days. Unfortunately, leaving a note on your car is an invitation to thieves.

Whenever you've said you'll let someone know you're safe, you *must* do so. Rescue teams have spent too many hours searching for hikers who were back home or relaxing in a café because someone expecting word didn't receive it.

SLACKPACKING AND FASTPACKING

Different hiking styles produce different outlooks —philosophies, even, if that's not too grand a word for a simple pleasure. Some hikers stride along the trail, aiming for the maximum mileage per hour, day, or week. Others dash up and down the peaks, bagging as many summits as possible. The more contemplative meander through forests and meadows, studying flowers, watching clouds, or simply staring into the distance when the spirit moves them.

The term *slackpacker* was first coined to describe Appalachian Trail (AT) hikers who, while intent on walking the entire 2,150 miles, nevertheless planned on doing it as casually as possible. Now it's often used to mean hiking without a heavy pack, which is accomplished by having gear and supplies transported to road crossings along the route. In this book I use the original meaning.

One of the walkers the description was first applied to holds the record for the slowest continuous Appalachian Trail walk: o.d. coyote (his "trail" name—an AT tradition—which has become his real name) took 263 days for his hike, an average of 8 miles a day.

In the September–October 1994 issue of *Appalachian Trailway News*, the journal of the Appalachian Trail Conference, o.d. coyote described slackpacking as an "attempt to backpack in a manner that is never trying, difficult, or tense, but in a slowly free-flowing way that drifts with whatever currents of interest, attraction, or stimulation are blowing at that moment" and wrote that slackpacking means escaping from "our culture's slavish devotion to efficiency" and banishing "the gnawing rat of goal-orientation" by relearning how to play.

The opposite of slackpacking is *fastpacking*, or *powerhiking*, which maximizes daily mileage by walking for long hours with only a few short stops. It can mean speed hiking, too, where you hike as fast as possible, but speed isn't the main aim—distance is. Fastpackers usually travel ultralight so they don't need to rest often. They can cover more miles and therefore see more in a weekend or hike long trails in half the normal time. Ultimately fastpacking merges into *trail running*, so I was interested but not surprised to hear from one fastpacker that he'd run sections of the Appalachian Trail while through-hiking. Fastpacking and trail running may sound like tough, painful work, but for devotees there are many rewards. Hearken to the words of long-distance runner John Annerino, who has run the length of the Grand Canyon on both the north and south sides of the Colorado River: "And so I run, run like the wind, the wind pushing me across a rainbow of joy that now extends from one end of the Grand Canyon to the other. The running is a fantasy come alive; there is no effort, nor is there the faintest hint of pain. It is pure flight" *(Running Wild)*. And British long-distance wilderness runner Mike Cudahy, who has run the 270-mile Pennine Way in England in under three days, offers this explanation for the "indescribable joy" that can occur on a long, hard run: "Perhaps the artificiality of a conventional and sophisticated society is stripped away and the simple, ingenuous nature of a creature of the earth is laid bare."

Fastpacking and slackpacking are extremes. Most backpackers do neither, but everyone tends toward one or the other. Is one better? No. Different approaches are right for different people. There's nothing wrong with walking the Appalachian Trail at 8 miles a day or running the length of the Grand Canyon in a week—as long as it satisfies and rejuvenates you and you respect nature and the land you are moving through. There's no need for hikers to criticize each other for being too fast or too slow, for bagging peaks or collecting miles, for going alone or in large groups, for sticking to trails or not sticking to trails—for being, in fact, different from the critic.

I've tried most forms of wilderness walking and running, including attempting 100 miles in forty-eight hours and more than one two-day mountain marathon race. I've also wandered mountains slowly, averaging maybe 10 miles a day. Overall, I prefer the latter approach, but I wouldn't call it superior. At times during long runs I've felt flashes of what Annerino describes, but these moments have never made up for my exhaustion and aching limbs. I gain the greatest fulfillment on backpacking trips lasting weeks at a time. How far I walk on such trips doesn't seem to matter. It's living in the wilds twenty-four hours a day, day after day, that's important to me. I still enjoy walking fast and am quite happy doing 25 to 30 miles a day in easy terrain with a light load, but I don't like *having* to do so. I like to know I can stop whenever I want, for as long as I want.

There are practical reasons for being able to cover long distances at times, though. Being able to travel fast if necessary can be important for safety. Having that ability in reserve means you are always hiking within your capabilities, so if a storm arises or you find your planned campsite a morass, you'll have the extra energy and strength to keep going. And if the weather or unforeseen hazards—difficult river crossings, blocked trails—slow you down, being able to hike fast for a day or two can mean finishing the trip when you intended without arriving exhausted and footsore.

To experience all that walking has to offer, it's worth trying different approaches. If you generally amble along, stopping frequently, try pushing yourself occasionally to see what it feels like. If you always zoom over the hills, eating up the miles, then slow down once in a while, take long rest stops, look around.

PLANNING

In its simplest form, planning means packing your gear and setting off with no prescribed route or goal in mind. This is what I sometimes do in areas I know well, especially when the weather might affect any route plans I did make. I've even done it in areas I've never visited before so that I could go wherever seemed interesting. Once, owing to an eleventh-hour assignment to attend and write about a mountain race, I found myself in the Colorado Rockies with ten days to spare and no plans. Having no route, no clear destination, worried me at first. Where would I go, and why? But there was freedom in not knowing. I didn't have to walk a certain distance each day. There were no deadlines, no food drops, no campsites to book in advance. I could wander at will. Or not wander. The Colorado Rockies are ideal for such an apparently aimless venture, because their small pockets of wilderness are easy to escape when you need to resupply or want a day or two in town.

Usually, though, a little more planning is

Contemplating the wild.

*Squaw Lake,
John Muir
Wilderness,
High Sierra.*

required. Guidebooks, maps, Web sites, DVDs, CD-ROMs, and magazine articles can all provide information on where to go. A Web search with Google is a good place to start. Once you've selected an area, you can obtain up-to-date information from the land managers—the National Park Service, the Forest Service, the Bureau of Land Management, or state forest or park services.

There is no such thing as too much information. The problem is sorting out what is useful from what is irrelevant. Information on water sources may be unnecessary in wet coastal mountains, but it's critical in the desert. The Internet can quickly overwhelm you with masses of information. Start to sift through it though, and you'll find that much is not of value for your hike. Consider whom the site is aimed at; often it's not hikers. Many Web sites are updated regularly, some daily. Up-to-date local knowledge is still important, however. Nothing beats talking to someone who

hiked over that ridge last week or drank from that spring yesterday. In really remote areas like the Yukon, local knowledge is invaluable. On my walk through that area, I changed my route several times based on information from locals.

For the initial route planning I use small-scale (1:250,000) maps covering large areas before purchasing the appropriate topographic maps and working out a more detailed line. DeLorme's Atlas and Gazetteer volumes—one for each state of the United States—and similar volumes are excellent for an overview of an area. Mapping software can be used too, though I find it easier to plan routes on a large paper map than on a screen, probably because I've had years of practice. When planning I'm always aware, however, that cross-country routes may be impassable or that a far more obvious way may show itself, so I don't stick rigidly to my prehike plans. It's easy to draw bold lines across a paper map, carried away by the excitement of anticipation, without considering the reality of trying to walk the route.

One of the big problems with planning a hike of more than a few days is resupplying. For popular trails like the Appalachian and the John Muir, there are regularly updated lists of facilities like post offices and grocery stores. There are even companies that will ship food parcels to you. Hikers may be rare or even unheard of in other places, however, so it's always best to write and ask about amenities.

Permits

Most areas don't require permits, but many national parks and some wilderness areas with easy access do. The number of permits issued may be severely restricted in the most popular places, making it essential to apply long before your trip. If you want to backpack popular trails in national parks like Grand Canyon or Yosemite, you need to apply for a permit many months in advance and must be flexible about your route. Whatever you think about limiting numbers by permit (I would rather see access made more difficult by long walk-ins in place

Backcountry advice, Inyo National Forest, California.

of entry roads and backcountry parking lots), it means that even in popular areas, you won't meet too many people. There remain vast areas of less-frequented wilderness where permits aren't needed, and even the trails most crowded in summer are usually quiet out of season, making permits much easier to obtain. On a two-week ski-backpacking trip through the High Sierra in May, my group encountered only two other parties, both on the same day. Where good campsites are rare, such as the Grand Canyon, you can camp only in certain spots and must have a permit for each site in the most visited areas, though wild camping is allowed elsewhere in the park. It's best to check whether permits are needed before making firm plans for an area.

Long-Distance Trails

Many backpackers dream of hiking a long-distance trail in one continuous journey. The big three National Scenic Trails, known as the Triple Crown, are the 2,100-mile Appalachian Trail, the

Advice to tread softly, Grand Canyon, Arizona.

2,600-mile Pacific Crest Trail, and the 3,100-mile Continental Divide Trail (CDT). Hiking such mammoth distances is a major undertaking. A few people have set off on one of these with no more than a hazy idea of the route or what to expect yet have completed the whole trail. But far more give up within the first few days or weeks—and this includes those who do some planning. The numbers succeeding have increased since the previous edition of this book, however. Then, just 15 to 20 percent of PCT through-hikers completed the trail. Now, of the three hundred or so who set off each year, some 60 percent finish (information from the Pacific Crest Trail Association). Figures for the much more popular Appalachian Trail aren't so good. Of the two thousand or so through-hikers each year, less than 20 percent reach the end (information from the Appalachian Trail Conference).

There are various reasons for failure. Heavy packs, sore feet, exhaustion, overly ambitious mileage goals, unexpected weather, terrain, and trail conditions are the most common. Detailed planning is advisable for a long-distance hike, especially one that will take several months. A surprising number of hikers set off each spring for Mount Katahdin, Maine (the northernmost point of the AT), having done no more than a few weekend hikes, if that. This in itself ensures a high failure rate. A gradual progression—an apprenticeship, in fact—should precede a multimonth trip.

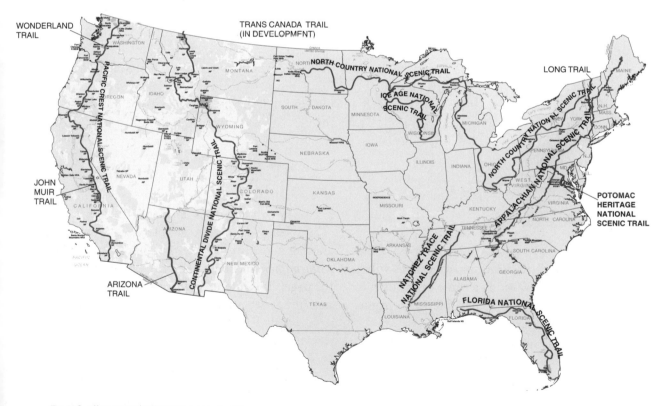

The U.S. offers many backpacking opportunities.

Before attempting one of the big three, try hiking a shorter but still challenging trail, such as the 211-mile John Muir Trail in California, the 471-mile Colorado Trail, or the 265-mile Long Trail in Vermont. My first solo distance hike, a seventeen-day, 270-mile trip along Britain's Pennine Way, followed several years of two- to five-day trips. Two years later, I made a 1,250-mile Britain end-to-end hike. Then, after another three years of shorter trips, I set out on the Pacific Crest Trail. I still made lots of mistakes, but I had enough knowledge and determination to finish the walk. If it had been my first distance hike, I doubt I would have managed more than a few hundred miles.

Preparation for a long trek doesn't mean just dealing with logistics—knowing where to send food supplies, where stores and post offices are, how far you can realistically walk per day—it also means accepting that at times you will be wet, cold, or hungry and the trail will be hard to follow. Adventures are unpredictable by definition. Every long walk I've done included moments when I felt like quitting, but I've always continued, knowing the moment would pass. If the time ever comes when the moment doesn't pass, I'll stop. If backpacking isn't enjoyable, it's pointless. Completing the trail doesn't matter—it's what happens along the way that's significant.

For me, the ultimate backpacking experience is to spend weeks or months in wilderness areas without long-distance trails, or sometimes without any trails at all. Walking a route of my own is more exciting and satisfying than following a route someone else has planned.

Planning such a walk can be difficult, however. Compiling information takes time, and there are always gaps. The easiest approach is to link shorter trails, as I did for the southern half of my walk the length of the Canadian Rockies. Even there, though, I had to travel cross-country on one trail-less section.

First, of course, you have to decide where you want to start and finish. This inspiration can come from the nature of the land, from the writings of others, and occasionally from photographs. My first long-distance walk from Land's End to John o'Groat's was inspired by John Hillaby's *Journey Through Britain*. Soon after that walk I read *Hamish's Mountain Walk*, by Hamish Brown, about the first continuous round of the Munros, Scottish mountains over 3,000 feet high. Brown's walk inspired a couple of 500-mile walks in the Scottish Highlands, but the idea of a *really* long walk there was put aside in favor of other ventures. A PCT walk was inspired by a slide show of the Yosemite backcountry and by Colin Fletcher's *The Thousand-Mile Summer*. On the PCT, I learned of the CDT, so it was that trail I hiked next. On a ski-backpacking trip in the Canadian Rockies I came upon Ben Gadd's *Handbook of the Canadian Rockies* and read that no one had hiked the length of the range. Another dream was born. A later Yukon trip was, in a sense, a continuation of this walk into an area I'd read about in the writings of Jack London and Robert Service.

I always thought that one day I would hike all the Munros in one go. The spur that turned a vague thought into a concrete plan came from another book, Andrew Dempster's fascinating *The Munro Phenomenon*, a sentence of which flew off the page: "It is interesting and almost strange that no one has yet attempted all the Munros and Tops in a single expedition." I knew instantly that I wanted to try this—a round of all 517 of Scotland's 3,000-foot summits. A year later I set off. (For the story of this walk, see my book *The Munros and Tops*.)

The thought of being the first to do something

lends excitement and adventure to an expedition. Yes, the heart of any backpacking trip is spending weeks at a time living in wild country, and it is the great pleasure and satisfaction of doing this that sends me back again and again. But a goal gives a walk focus—a shape, a beginning, and an end.

The initial buzz of excitement eventually gives way to a sober assessment of what is involved. This is the point at which ventures come closest to being abandoned. The planning often seems more daunting than the walk itself, but once begun, it's usually enjoyable.

The Scottish summits walk and the one that preceded it, a 1,300-mile traverse of the mountains of Norway and Sweden, both took place in mostly wet and windy weather. In between them I had spent two weeks hiking in the Grand Canyon. Having had enough of dampness and mist and loving the sharp clarity and burning sunshine of the Southwest, I decided my next long hike would be the 800-mile Arizona Trail, a route still incomplete in many places. On the Scottish and Scandinavian hikes I never carried more than a pint of water, and mostly I carried none. In Arizona I often carried a gallon and sometimes three gallons. (The story of that hike is told in *Crossing Arizona*.)

Spring backpacking by the Dubh Lochain, Beinn A'Bhuird, Cairngorm National Park, Scotland.

Moose, Kidney Lake, High Uinta Wilderness, Utah.

Water went from being an insignificant concern during the planning stages to the most important factor. (For more on long-distance hiking, see my book *The Advanced Backpacker*.)

Planning a hike, whether for a weekend or a summer, takes time and energy, and the adventure itself can vanish in a welter of lists, logistics, maps, and food. This is only temporary, of course. When you take that first step, all the organization fades into the background. Then it's just you and the wilderness.

TO EQUIP A PEDESTRIAN WITH SHELTER, BEDDING,
UTENSILS, FOOD, AND OTHER NECESSITIES, IN A PACK
SO LIGHT AND SMALL THAT HE CAN CARRY IT
WITHOUT OVERSTRAIN, IS REALLY A FINE ART.

—Camping and Woodcraft, *Horace Kephart*

chapter two

the load on your back

choosing and using equipment

Backpacking is about enjoying nature, about experiencing the wilderness—not about suffering. But many people are put off by the prospect of carrying on their backs everything they need for days, maybe even weeks. To the uninitiated the load looks backbreaking, a burden that will take all the joy out of walking, all the pleasure from a day in the mountains. For the uninformed novice, this may be true. It certainly was for me when I began. I am not a masochist, however; I don't like aching shoulders, sore hips, and trail-pounded, blistered feet. Nor do I like being wet or cold. After suffering all those conditions in my first attempts at backpacking, I developed a keen interest in techniques and equipment and learned that backpacking can be pleasurable and pain-free.

While experience and skill play a large part, no amount of technique will allow a poorly designed pack to carry 50 pounds comfortably or make a leaking rain jacket waterproof. Experienced backpackers are likely to avoid such problems, however.

The right equipment can make the difference between a trip you want to repeat and a nightmare that will make you shudder every time you see a pack. I've met walkers who recoil at the mere mention of backpacking, muttering about their one attempt on the Appalachian Trail—how their backs ached, their knees gave way, their tents leaked, and they suffered for weeks afterward. It doesn't have to be like that.

My interest in equipment was born from a couple of day hikes on which I got soaked (inadequate rain gear) and then lost (no compass), resulting in difficult night descents (no flash-light on the first occasion, dead batteries and no spares on the second) and near hypothermia. On my first camping trips I lugged a heavy canvas tent that leaked at the merest hint of rain in a pack that resembled a medieval torture rack. Not that I ever carried the tent into the wilderness—reaching a valley campground from a bus stop was exhausting enough. I used this equipment through ignorance; I didn't know anything better existed.

Two long-ago experiences showed me what was possible. Once, another hiker was horrified at the sight of my huge pack frame. "No hipbelt?" he exclaimed. "What's a hipbelt?" I replied. He handed me his pack, an even bigger one than mine. I put it on and tightened the hipbelt. The weight of the pack seemed to melt away. Ever since, I've viewed a hipbelt as the key feature of any pack designed for heavy loads. The other occasion was at a roadside campground when I was using a very heavy wooden-poled canvas tent. Sitting outside this monstrosity, I watched a walker with a moderate-size pack come down from the mountains and pitch a tiny green nylon tent. The next morning he packed everything up, shouldered his modest load, and headed—effortlessly it seemed—back into the wilderness. The realization that it was possible to backpack in comfort led me to visit outdoor shops, write away for equipment

PEACE IN THE WILDERNESS

It's good to be alone. I don't go far the first day, camping in a spruce grove above a cool, rushing stream after only a couple of hours. Miles traveled are irrelevant; I'm content just to be here.

catalogs, and read everything I could find about backpacking.

Later I worked in an equipment shop and started writing reviews of gear for outdoor magazines. I've been doing this since the 1970s and have acquired a fairly detailed knowledge of what to look for in equipment. It's important, though, not to assign gear a greater value than it deserves —it's only a tool. Backpacking is not about having the latest tent or trying out the new clothing system "guaranteed to keep you comfortable in all weather." If you know enough about equipment to select what really works, you won't need to think

A wild camp.

about your gear when you're in the wilderness. You can get on with what you're really there for—experiencing the natural world. Worrying about getting wet because you don't trust your rain jacket to keep you dry, or shivering through the night in your threadbare sleeping bag will come between you and the environment and may even dominate your walk. In extreme circumstances, inadequate gear could even be life-threatening. So it's worth taking your time when choosing equipment. It will be with you for many miles and many nights. Don't forget, though, that you also need the skills to use it

Weighing the pack at the start of a ten-day trip.

properly. No gear is magic, despite what many advertisements imply. Just having the latest jacket doesn't mean you can cope with a mountain storm, nor does having the fastest-boiling stove on the market necessarily mean you can produce anything edible.

WEIGHT

Three major factors govern choice of gear: *performance*, *durability*, and *weight*. The first is simple—an item must do what's required of it. Rain gear must keep out the rain; a stove must boil water. How long it goes on doing so efficiently is a measure of its durability. It's easy to make items that perform well and last for ages, but the backpacker's (and equipment designer's) problem is the weight of such gear. Backpackers probably spend more time trying to reduce the weight of their gear than on all other aspects of trip planning. Such time is well spent. Saving 2 pounds means you can carry another day's food; the difference between a 25-pound pack and a 35-pound pack is considerable, especially near the end of a long, hard day. Although your pack is supported by your shoulders and hips, it's your legs that carry the weight and will feel most tired with a heavy load. The heavier your load, the more often you need to stop and rest, the slower you walk, especially uphill, and the sooner you are likely to stop and make camp. Even if you aren't planning on high-mileage days or thousands of feet of ascent, the lighter your pack, the more comfortable you'll feel.

The total weight carried includes *everything*: everything you wear, everything hung round your neck, everything carried in your hands, and everything in your pockets as well as what's in your pack. Actual pack weight varies according to how much food, fuel, and water you're carrying, how much clothing you're wearing, and what's in your hands

GEAR FOR AN ELEVEN-DAY EARLY-SUMMER TRIP IN WET COASTAL MOUNTAINS

On this hike I expected rain and strong winds but relatively warm temperatures with only a slight chance of an overnight frost. In fact, the lowest overnight temperature was 40°F (5°C) and daytime temperatures were between 45 and 65°F (7 and 18°C), though the stormy weather meant it often felt colder. Rain- and windproof garments and a good tent were essential, while the fleece and insulated garments kept me warm at rest stops and in camp. It rained at some point on nine days. On four of those days it rained heavily all day. I risked taking ultralight rather than standard rain gear because the windproof jacket and nylon pants were very water resistant. I set off with two fuel cartridges, since I knew I could buy cartridges in stores during the second half of the hike. This, along with the expected above-freezing temperatures and the low weight, was why I chose to take a cartridge stove.

Gear	Weight in Ounces
PACK	
4,025 cu. in. internal frame	39.75
SHELTER	
solo single-hoop tent with stakes	54.5
7 oz. 750-fill-power down sleeping bag	16.0
three-quarter-length foam pad	9.0
KITCHEN	
cartridge stove	3.0
2 8 oz. butane-propane cartridges	28.0
0.9 qt. titanium pan	5.0
1.1 pt. titanium pan—doubles as mug	3.0
2 Lexan plastic spoons	1.0
dishcloth	0.5
matches/lighter	1.0
1 qt. collapsible water container	1.0
2 2.5 quart collapsible water containers	2.75
FOOTWEAR	
trail shoes	32.0
CLOTHING	
2 pairs merino wool midweight socks	6.0
waterproof-breathable socks	4.0
Supplex nylon zip-off leg pants	15.5
polyester wicking underpants	1.75
Lifa polypro long pants	3.0
long-sleeved merino wool base layer	7.0
Supplex nylon trail shirt	9.5
microfleece sweater	8.0
Primaloft sweater	12.5
Nextec EPIC wind shell	9.0
rain jacket	10.0
rain pants	5.5
fleece hat	2.0
sun-rain hat	5.75
fleece gloves	2.0
cotton bandanna	1.0
ACCESSORIES	
trekking poles	23.0
LED headlamp	2.5
compass	1.0
safety whistle	0.5
maps	4.0
first-aid kit	3.5
repair kit	4.0
altimeter-watch	2.0
Windwatch (see Chapter 9)	1.75
knife	1.0
8x21 binoculars	4.5
wash kit	2.0
toilet paper	1.0
toilet trowel	2.0
sunscreen	2.0
notebook and pens	5.0
paperback	8.0
TOTAL	**22.5 POUNDS**

Weight variations in the sidebars for similar items are due to different models worn (e.g., trail shoes) and different items carried (e.g., first-aid kits).

I was usually wearing or carrying about 6 pounds, so my pack weight without food and camera gear was about 16 pounds. I had 5 pounds of camera gear and started out with 12 pounds of food—enough for six days. That was my heaviest load—about 33 pounds (16 + 5 + 12).

or pockets. In the following discussion the weights mentioned are for all nonvariable gear, not just what's in your pack. To this must be added approximately 2 pounds a day for food and fuel plus a pound for each pint of water carried.

Equipment used to fall into two rough categories: *standard* and *lightweight*. There is now a third: *ultralight*. With standard equipment compromises are made between weight and durability; it is reasonably light but strong enough to withstand years of average use or the rigors of a multimonth expedition. With standard equipment, a load for a summer solo trip is likely to weigh about 25 to 35 pounds. If you're traveling with a group, sharing camping and cooking equipment will reduce this a little; specialized and warmer gear for winter conditions will add to it. With lightweight gear the weight can be reduced to 20 to 25 pounds; with the latest ultralight gear and a severe look at every item, 10 pounds or less is possible. Ultralight gear usually won't be as tough as standard gear (though there are exceptions), but the best is surprisingly durable.

To some extent, the way weight feels is subjective. If you set out deep into the wilderness with two weeks' supplies and a total pack weight of 70 pounds, the 40-pound load you emerge with feels amazingly light. But set off cold with 40 pounds for a weekend, and the burden can seem unbearable. There are limits, of course. Once, when I was young and foolish, I carried more than 110 pounds (including snowshoes, ice ax, crampons, and twenty-three days' food) through the snowbound High Sierra. I couldn't lift my pack; I had to sit down, slide my arms through the shoulder straps, then roll forward onto all fours before slowly standing up. Carrying this much weight was not fun, and I was exhausted by the end of every 12-mile day. I wouldn't do it again, though the hike through the Sierra was marvelous despite the load. Since then, I have started sections of long treks in remote wilderness with 80 pounds in my pack and found that too much. Only after the first week do such loads slim down to a bearable weight. I now try never to carry more than 50 pounds on any trip. Sometimes I have to break that intention—I had to carry three gallons of water and six days' food on one section of the Arizona Trail, pushing my pack weight up to 70 pounds—but the exceptions are rare. I find 50 pounds manageable as long as my pack can support the load and I'm not planning to cover more than 12 to 15 miles a day or climb thousands of feet. If I want to cover more distance or ascent, 30 pounds is my target pack weight, since I've found this to be the weight at which the load starts to slow me down noticeably. On one- or two-night trips, the average weight, including food and fuel, is now 20 to 25 pounds, a good 10 pounds less than when I started backpacking. The weight goes up for longer trips only because of extra food and fuel, not because I carry more equipment.

If the total weight seems excessive, I look for any item I can replace with a lighter option or even leave out—a lighter fleece jacket, say, or no extra socks. (It's a bit late to decide you could do with a lighter tent or sleeping bag when you're packing for a trip, though, which is the reason your original gear choices are so important.) When the only difference between two items is weight, I go for the lighter one every time. The big items—tent, sleeping bag, pack, stove—add weight most rapidly, but it all has to be carried.

I like to know the weight of *everything* I carry, down to the smallest item. I use a digital scale that measures to the nearest tenth of an ounce. If you can't decide between two items and the store where you're shopping doesn't have a scale, you might want to take yours along. Manufacturer's advertised weights are often inaccurate, and descriptions such as "lightweight" often bear little connection to reality. I also find that it helps to set maximum target weights and to disregard all heavier items. (See table, page 29.)

As an exercise, I once compiled two lists of gear from a mail-order catalog. The first consisted of standard items, chosen regardless of weight; the second contained the lightest gear in each category. The difference between items was small, often no more than a few ounces, yet the overall weights were 25 pounds for the lightweight gear and 35 for the standard.

I conducted a second exercise for a magazine feature on a spring weekend in wet coastal mountains with two hikers, one carrying his standard load, one an ultralight load that he was testing for a forthcoming Pacific Crest Trail through-hike (which he successfully completed). The standard hiker started with 33.5 pounds of gear and provisions, including clothes and footwear worn and two days' food; the ultralight hiker carried 19.5 pounds. They started out on a cool, breezy day, wearing a fair amount of clothing and with packs weighing 26 and 12 pounds, respectively. That's a huge gap. The packs themselves accounted for much of the difference: the ultralight pack weighed 14 ounces, the standard one 76 ounces, a difference of 3 pounds, 14 ounces. Shelter was significant too. The ultralight hiker had a tarp weighing 30 ounces including stakes and groundsheet, the standard hiker a tent weighing 68 ounces. That's another 2 pounds, 6 ounces. The variation in clothing was also startling. Leaving out clothing worn all the time (boots, socks, long pants, base layer), there was a difference in weight of 2 pounds, 4 ounces, with the standard load including 5 pounds, 6 ounces of clothing, the lightweight

one 3 pounds, 2 ounces. Together, pack, shelter, and clothing constituted two-thirds of the difference between the two loads. After the weekend the standard hiker became interested in reducing the weight of his load, feeling he could do so without affecting his comfort, while the ultralighter felt he couldn't reduce his load any more without compromising comfort too much.

The Ultralight Approach

In the past ten years ultralight hiking has boomed, though it's still a minority pursuit among most backpackers. A wealth of ultralight gear, books, and Web sites has aided its spread. As the name suggests, it involves using the lightest gear possible and carrying the absolute minimum. If you leave an item at home, you've cut its weight completely. Ultralight hikers modify gear too, shaving away every possible fraction of an ounce. Straps are trimmed and labels and even toothbrush handles are removed. When your total gear weighs only 10 pounds, removing ounces makes a difference. When it weighs 30 pounds, a few ounces here and there aren't so significant. Hiking styles go in cycles, and ultralight hiking has boomed before. Usually it's received with great enthusiasm; then, as the reality of hiking with minimum gear, especially in wet and cold weather, sets in, pack weights start to rise again. Gear designers can't help tinkering, either, adding extras here and there until their ultralight gear no longer merits the name, though it might be more comfortable or functional.

There's always been an interest in how little you need to carry, going right back to the early days of recreational backpacking. John Muir famously traveled with very little equipment or food. In the early twentieth century, Horace Kephart described in *Camping and Woodcraft* a summer

GEAR FOR A NINE-DAY SUMMER TRIP IN HIGH MOUNTAINS

This hike took place mostly at or above timberline—10,500 to more than 11,000 feet. I expected hot, sunny weather with occasional afternoon thunderstorms and cool but not cold nights. As it turned out, the lowest overnight temperature was 36°F (2°C), and most nights were in the upper 30s and lower 40s. The daytime temperatures were in the 60s and 70s, so I mostly hiked in a trail shirt, shorts, and sandals. I wore the trail shoes on the one rainy day; otherwise the sandals sufficed. A pair of waterproof-breathable socks instead of the trail shoes would have meant less weight and bulk to carry and would have kept my feet drier in the

rain. On the wet day I found the EPIC jacket and my wide-brimmed sun hat were enough to keep me dry. I never wore the rain jacket and pants. I wore the two wicking base-layer tops in camp, but they weren't really necessary. The synthetic sleeping bag was a test item. It kept me warm and comfortable, but a lighter, more compressible down bag would still be my first choice. There were no opportunities to resupply, so I carried all my supplies. The two fuel cartridges lasted the trip. There was just enough fuel left to make a hot drink and some soup while waiting for my ride at the end of the hike.

The author with gear for a nine-day hike in the Uinta Mountains, Utah.

load weighing 18 pounds, 3 ounces without food and a "featherweight" one of just 10 pounds including pack, tent, down sleeping bag, and spirit stove. The current surge in popularity can be

traced back to 1992 and the publication of Ray Jardine's *The Pacific Crest Trail Hiker's Handbook*. Ray and his wife, Jenny, hiked the PCT with packs averaging an astonishing 8.5 pounds without

Gear	Weight in Ounces
PACK	
4,500 cu. in. frameless	35.0
SHELTER	
7 ft. by 11 ft. silnylon (silicone nylon) tarp with stakes and cord	17.0
Polarguard sleeping bag	54.0
three-quarter-length self-inflating pad	17.0
KITCHEN	
cartridge stove	3.0
foil windscreen	1.0
2 8 oz. gas cartridges	28.0
0.9 qt. titanium pan	5.0
1.1 pt. titanium pan—doubles as mug	3.0
2 Lexan plastic spoons	1.0
dishcloth	0.5
matches/lighter	1.0
1 pt. water bottle	2.0
2 2.5 qt. collapsible water containers	2.75
FOOTWEAR	
trail shoes	36.0
hiking sandals	27.0
CLOTHING	
2 pairs midweight merino wool socks	5.0
nylon shorts	4.0
ripstop nylon trail pants	8.0
2 pairs polyester underpants	4.0
C-Thru polyester wicking T-shirt	3.0
C-Thru long-sleeved wicking polyester top	5.0
Supplex nylon trail shirt	9.5
Nextec EPIC wind shell with fleece lining in front	12.0
Polarguard 3D insulated jacket	18.0
rain jacket	13.0
rain pants	5.5
fleece hat	2.0
cotton sun hat	5.75
cotton bandanna	1.0
ACCESSORIES	
trekking poles	20.5
LED headlamp	2.5
compass	1.0
safety whistle	1.0
map	2.0
first-aid kit	4.0
repair kit	4.0
altimeter-watch	2.0
knife	2.0
8x21 binoculars	5.5
wash kit	1.0
sunscreen	2.0
insect repellent	2.0
toilet paper	2.0
toilet trowel	2.0
notebook and pens	4.0
paperback	8.0
TOTAL	**24.2 POUNDS**

To this must be added 5.75 pounds of camera gear and, at the outset, 18 pounds of food, giving an initial total weight of 48 pounds. Since I wore or carried at least 4 pounds of the basic load plus 3 pounds of cameras, my pack weighed about 41 pounds at the outset and 23 pounds at the finish. The ultralight pack had no padding in the hipbelt and was not comfortable with loads of more than 30 pounds. I reduced the discomfort considerably by threading a padded lens case and a padded compact camera case onto the hipbelt. When I got home I secured foam pads to the belt with duct tape.

food, and Ray described how he did this in that book and later in his influential and provocative *Beyond Backpacking*.

Lightweight hiking shades into ultralight hiking instead of being clearly separate. Arguably a pack weight below 20 pounds, including food and water, defines the ultralight hiker. Ultralight hiking works best in summer conditions on good trails in places with generally benign climates and is best suited to those who like to keep moving and spend as little time as possible resting or in camp. It also requires expertise and fitness—there's no backup gear to get you out of trouble. I've tried the ultralight approach on weekends when I wanted to cover high mileage, managing to get my total load down to 16¼ pounds including food for two days (see sidebar, page 30). I enjoyed the light weight, but I worried that any extended period of stormy weather would be unpleasant. I wouldn't want to travel with such minimal gear for long, but if you're interested in high daily mileage and stoic enough to endure minimal comfort in camp in bad weather, this could be the way to go.

Even though I don't try to reduce my pack weight to the absolute minimum—I like a pack with a hipbelt, a roomy shelter, enough warm clothing to sit outside in comfort, a proper stove, a paperback book, and more—my overall pack weight has come down because I've incorporated some ultralight items and because there's been a general reduction in weight of much standard gear. These days my average loads are a good 10 pounds lighter than those from several years ago; the ultralight movement has certainly benefited me and, I think, all backpackers.

Green Gear

Given our interest in unspoiled wilderness, it's not surprising that many backpackers and hikers are deeply concerned about the environment and involved with conservation groups. This concern spills over into outdoor equipment companies, and many of them are also involved in the environmental movement in various ways, usually by making cash donations. Companies often list the campaigns and organizations they support in catalogs and on Web sites. Some have environmental audits and do their best to minimize their impact on the environment. Many use recycled materials in both products and packaging. Whatever the companies' motivations (and the more cynical—or realistic—may have doubts about some of them), using recycled materials does less damage to the environment than using virgin materials and is therefore recommended. Patagonia was first on the market with recycled fleece garments way back in 1993, and it still makes these along with other environmentally friendly stuff. It also promotes various environmental and conservation causes through its catalog and Web site (patagonia.com) rather more strongly than most companies. Even some huge corporations pay attention to the environment these days. Nike, for example, has a Reuse-a-Shoe program whereby you can return old sports shoes (any make, not just Nike) for recycling. The rubber from old shoes, called Nike Grind, can be found on several of the brand's hiking shoes (see nike.com/nike biz).

Using gear made from recycled materials is only a first step, of course. What happens when you've finished with it? Donating it to a worthy cause, selling it, or passing it along to friends is preferable to sending it to a landfill.

Buying quality gear in the first place is a good idea too. Top-quality items usually last longest, covering the high initial cost, and perform best, making it less likely you'll want to replace them. Equipment lasts longer with proper maintenance, too. Annie and Dave Getchell's *The Essential Outdoor Gear Manual* covers repair and care of everything from packs to kayaks and is highly recommended. Repair centers exist, but unless you live near one or near an outdoor store that will forward gear, you will have to mail your gear to them, so they're worth using only for major problems you can't fix yourself.

TARGET WEIGHTS

Gear	Ounces
FOOTWEAR	
sports sandals	32
running shoes	32
trail shoes	40
three-season boots	48
winter boots (suitable for crampons)*	64
SHELTER	
groundsheet	10
bivy bag	20
tarp, solo	20
tarp, duo	32
bivy tent	40
solo tent, three-season	64
duo tent, three-season	96
duo tent, winter mountain	128
sleeping bag (summer)	25
sleeping bag (three-season)	48
sleeping bag (winter)	64
closed-cell foam pad	9
self-inflating pad	14
COOKING GEAR	
stove (cartridge)	7
stove (multifuel/white-gas)	16
stove (alcohol with solo cookset)	30
stove (alcohol with duo cookset)	44
1 qt. pot with lid	8
cookset with 1.5 and 2 qt. pans, lid	26
CLOTHING, WARM WEATHER	
synthetic T-shirt	6
trail shirt	10
fleece top	16
shorts	6
synthetic long johns	4
trail pants	12
windproof top	12
waterproof jacket	16
rain pants	8
warm hat	2
sun hat	4
CLOTHING, COLD WEATHER	
synthetic zip-neck shirt	8
fleece top	20
windproof fleece top (for wet/cold)	24
synthetic filled top (for wet/cold)	20
down top (for dry/cold)	24
synthetic long johns/pile pants	8
long pants	24
waterproof-breathable jacket	34
waterproof-breathable pants	30
windproof fleece-lined cap	4
liner gloves	2
warm gloves/mittens	4
shell gloves/mittens	8
PACKS	
loads up to 20 lb.	20
loads up to 30 lb.	30
loads up to 45 lb.	45
heavy loads	125

* These weights are for a pair, size 9½; scale up or down for different sizes.

CHECKLISTS

For any walk you have to decide exactly what to take. Here I find a checklist essential (see Appendix 1). No two hikes are the same, and I doubt I've ever taken exactly the same gear twice. When, where, and for how long you go will determine what you carry. You need to know about the weather, the terrain, and the environment. I work from a complete list of all my gear, then distill a shorter list for the walk at hand. Because I know what each item weighs, I can work out how much gear I'll be carrying. Adding about 2 pounds of food per day, plus the weight of my camera gear, tells me what the total load will be. At that point I review the list to see if anything can be left out or replaced with a

ULTRALIGHT OVERNIGHT SUMMER TRIP IN COASTAL MOUNTAINS

One purpose of this trip was to try a pack with no frame or hipbelt and an ultralight load. I covered 30 miles and 8,600 feet of ascent, mostly cross-country in rough, rocky terrain, and the light load made the trip seem like a day hike. The temperature was in the 60s during the day and the 40s at night with no rain and only light winds.

Gear	Weight in Ounces
PACK	
3,100 cu. in. frameless, no back padding, no hipbelt	14.25
SHELTER	
7 ft. by 11 ft. silnylon tarp with stakes	17.0
14 oz. 800-fill-power down sleeping bag	17.5
three-quarter-length foam pad	9.0
KITCHEN	
cartridge stove	3.0
foil windscreen	1.0
1 half-full 8 oz. gas cartridge	10.0
0.9 qt. titanium pan	5.0
1.1 pt. titanium pan—doubles as mug	3.0
2 Lexan plastic spoons	1.0
dishcloth	0.5
matches/lighter	1.0
1 pt. water bottle	2.0
2.5 qt. collapsible water containers	1.5
FOOTWEAR	
trail shoes	33.0
CLOTHING	
merino wool socks	2.5
running shorts—doubled as underpants	3.0
nylon trail pants	8.0
polyester long-sleeved top	4.0
Silmond polyester wind shell	7.5
Polartec 100 microfleece sweater	13.5
rain jacket	9.5
rain pants	5.5
fleece hat	2.0
cotton bandanna	1.0
ACCESSORIES	
trekking poles	18.0
LED headlamp	2.5
compass	1.0
whistle	1.0
map	2.0
first-aid kit	2.5
repair kit	2.0
altimeter-watch	2.0
Windwatch (see Chapter 9)	1.75
knife	2.0
wash kit	1.0
sunscreen	2.0
dark glasses	2.5
insect repellent	3.0
toilet paper	2.0
toilet trowel	2.0
binoculars	5.5
notebook and pens	4.0
paperback	5.0
TOTAL	**16.25 POUNDS**

I wore or held 4 pounds of the items above, so my basic pack weight was 12.25 pounds. My camera gear weighed 3.25 pounds, but this was all carried in a padded case slung across my body. I had 3 pounds of food at the outset, making a pack weight of 15.25 pounds and a total weight of 22.5 pounds.

lighter alternative. For a major trip that will last many weeks, I repeat this process obsessively, though this rarely makes much difference. With experience, you'll probably find that your first list needs only a little tinkering.

I keep a list of all my gear on my computer. Before each trip I make up a specific checklist, print it out, then check off each item as I pack it—and not before. (It's all too easy to remember that an item is hanging up drying somewhere, check it off, and then forget to go and get it. I know. I've done it.) You can list the gear on a database that adds up the weights for you. There's even a little program that does this, which I've used for a number of years now: the Backpacking Gear Weight Calculator, developed by hiker Chris Ibbeson. You add your gear in various categories along with the weights and any notes you want to remember. For each trip you check the items you want to take and the program computes the total weight. You can get further details at www.chrisibbeson.com/pages/Gear WeightCalculator.html.

CHOOSING AND BUYING

The highly competitive nature of the outdoor equipment market means that styles and names change rapidly—companies come and go, brand names are taken over, new materials emerge. While many changes are cosmetic and have more to do with fashion than function, some do involve new designs and practical improvements. There are basically four sources for the latest information on equipment: specialty stores, mail-order companies, manufacturers and importers, and outdoor magazines (see Appendix 3). All of these have Web sites, of course.

If you can find a good store with staff members who use the equipment they sell and know what they're talking about, give it your support. The employees in such a store can keep you well informed and advised. Popping in to chat and look at the latest gear can be enjoyable, too. Being able to handle gear and see it in three dimensions and talk face to face with real human beings beats cyberspace any day, in my opinion.

Paper catalogs still exist, of course, if you prefer them; however, Web sites are now the norm and arguably the best way to access information. If you don't have a good store nearby, buying through the Web is a good alternative. Equipment Web sites—from companies like Campmor, REI, Backcountry Equipment, and Mountain Gear—often feature equipment comparison charts and may have "house brand" items not available elsewhere. Many small specialty manufacturers whose products you may never find in a store have Web sites. Indeed, the Web has provided the opportunity for these companies to market their gear much more easily.

Gear manufacturers and retailers can hardly be expected to be objective about the gear they make their living from; for that you need to consult outdoor magazines and the plethora of hiking Web sites. Most test and review gear, often in great detail. They also carry news of the latest items and developments. (See Appendix 3.)

The leading specialty magazine for many decades has been *Backpacker*, which regularly carries detailed comparative gear tests and publishes an annual gear guide (March issue) listing specifications for thousands of items. *Backpacker* also publishes an Editor's Choice issue (April) of new gear. I find *Backpacker*'s gear reviews useful and informative. When the magazine's staff reviews gear I've tried, I usually agree with the findings, though not always. (I'd be worried if I always did!) *Outside* and *National Geographic Adventure* cover a much wider field of activities but often have features of interest to backpackers. In Canada, the same applies to *Explore*.

Of the many hiking Web sites, three stand out for their gear reviews. The site BackPackGearTest.org has masses of detailed reviews provided by readers. These vary in quality but can be interesting and useful. Ryan N. Jordan's Backpacking Light (backpackinglight.com) is more authoritative and has detailed comparative reviews as well as features on lightweight backpacking in general. As of June 2004, Backpacking Light is also a print magazine, published quarterly. The Lightweight Backpacker (backpacking.net) was one of the first backpacking sites and has grown to a vast size. It has both staff and reader reviews, backpacking philosophy, checklists for different types of trips, and much, much more. For general information on ultralight gear, Trail Quest (trailquest.net) has much useful stuff including gear reviews and details of how to make your own gear. Many of these sites sell gear too.

Quality

Today, outdoor companies are international. Globalization is the name of the game. Much high-quality equipment from reputable companies is made in the Far East, a region once known only for budget items. You may want to buy gear made at home for patriotic or environmental reasons, but you don't need to do so to ensure that you're getting good quality.

It's wise to check carefully and thoroughly every bit of gear you buy. However reputable the company, and however good the quality control, a faulty item occasionally slips through. It is better to discover that your tent door zipper jams or that the snaps fall off your jacket when you're home rather than when you're out in a raging blizzard. Check that stitching is neat and unbroken and that seam ends are finished properly. (With filled garments and sleeping bags, you can't see the interior work, but if the shell is put together well, chances are the insides are too.) All waterproof-breathable garments should have taped seams; check that the tapes are flat and run in straight lines. The same applies to tents with pretaped seams. You should be able to spot any gross manufacturing defects before they cause problems in the field.

Cost

Buy the best you can afford. During a mountaintop blizzard, a few dollars saved on a cheap jacket are meaningless. This doesn't mean you need to buy the most expensive items or that you can't go hiking if you can't afford top-of-the-line gear. There are huge price ranges—especially in clothing, where high prices often just mean the latest style, color, or fabric rather than better performance. Indeed, the most expensive gear is often too complex and heavy for backpacking. The simplest, lightest designs—not the most costly—are best. If you don't want the latest colors or styles (and why does this matter in the wilderness?), last year's models can often be had at knockdown prices. Cosmetic "seconds" can be good value too. Before I started testing gear for magazines, and therefore had an endless supply of the stuff pouring through the door, I looked for gear at sales and in surplus stores. My first down sleeping bag had a patch on the inside where it was torn in the factory. This didn't affect the performance, but the cost was half that of a perfect bag. I used to wear army surplus wool shirts—itchy next to the skin but fine if worn over another layer. I enjoyed sorting through piles of gloves, socks, hats, and other items in surplus stores—a sort of treasure hunt where I never knew just what wonderful bit of gear would turn up. I still occasionally go through the bargain bins in outdoor stores and have to remind myself that I really don't need another hat, however inexpensive. Web sites like eBay can provide bargains too, though I have never bought anything on them. As I write this, a quick look at eBay's Camping, Hiking, Backpacking section reveals an REI down sleeping bag for $9.99 "suitable for a youth or small adult" (no other specifications listed) and a new Arc'teryx Khamsin pack for $150 (list price $233) among a mass of car camping gear and some rather dubious "genuine black leather" packs (new, $7.95—for genuine leather!). Thrift shops may have hiking gear too, especially clothing. With care you can put together a top-quality backpacking outfit for very little money from sales, seconds, and secondhand stores. Doing this is certainly better than buying brand-new budget gear that probably won't last long.

Depending on where and when you plan to go, there are critical items for which money should be no object, but other items need not be expensive or even cost anything at all. You probably have clothing in your closet that will do for most hiking. Remember, too, that good gear isn't a substitute for skill. Equipment is no use if you don't know what to do with it. An experienced backpacker can function more efficiently and safely with a minimum of basic gear than a novice can with the latest high-tech designs. Many of us learned with gear that seems primitive now, but it let us get into the wilderness and survive there. Don't let a lack of gear keep you from getting out there. Just be careful to tailor what you do to your skill level and the gear you have.

Making Your Own

One way to cut costs is to make your own gear. This is also a way to design items the way you want. I've never made my own gear, but I've hiked with people who have and I greatly admire them. I can see that using an item you've made gives it a value and personal meaning that a store-bought item just cannot have.

Making complex items like geodesic dome tents is of course way beyond most people's skills, so home gear making tends to be the province of ultralight hikers who want very simple, basic gear. Ray and Jenny Jardine made their own gear for their ultralight long-distance hikes because they couldn't find what they wanted commercially. There are details of how to do this in *Beyond Backpacking*. There also are many Web sites about making your own gear, especially alcohol and solid fuel tablet stoves made from soda cans. The Lightweight Backpacker has a whole section on making gear, with instructions for everything from packs and shelters to stoves and headlamps. Trail Quest has a fair amount of information on making gear too, though it is scattered among the other topics.

Color

When I began backpacking, most items were green, brown, or blue, with an occasional splash of orange. However, the past two decades have seen an explosion of brilliant colors and multihued equipment that shows no sign of abating, to the point where some dully clad hikers—who don't go to the wilderness to see bright displays of nylon—mutter about "visual pollution."

Overall, I'm with the "dull crowd" rather than the peacocks. I prefer being inconspicuous when outdoors, blending in with my surroundings without broadcasting my presence like a neon sign. For a while, I was concerned I might be mistaken for someone using the outdoors as a backdrop for pseudomilitary games. At least one bright item of gear ensured this was unlikely (as would a Sierra Club or Greenpeace badge on my pack). Now, however, the outdoors is also used as a backdrop for "adrenaline sports," which seem to require tight, shiny, and very bright clothing. I don't like the idea of nature's being a backdrop to anything, but I no longer worry about being mistaken for those who use it as an adventure playground or a mock battlefield. If I'm going to worry at all, I'll worry about the future of wilderness.

GEAR FOR A TWO-MONTH ARIZONA TRAIL THROUGH-HIKE IN SPRING

Although this trip lasted two months, the same gear would be suitable for much shorter desert trips in spring or autumn. I took the large, heavy pack because I knew I would have to carry a great deal of water. I carried a gallon for a few hours most days, and three gallons on a few occasions. I took eight small water containers rather than a couple of large ones so that if any of them sprang a leak, most would still be OK. The rigid water container was for filling from trickles and shallow pools. The plastic coffee filter was for filtering visible dirt. Because I was resupplying in small towns along the way, I took a multifuel stove. Automotive gas was always available. Most nights were above freezing, but some were below, and the lowest overnight temperature was 21°F (–6°C).

Gear	Weight in Ounces
PACK	
5,550 cu. in. internal frame	109.0
SHELTER	
9.8 ft. by 9.8 ft. silnylon tarp	27.9
silnylon ground cloth	7.25
stakes and guylines	7.5
14 oz. 750+-fill-power down sleeping bag	31.5
three-quarter-length foam pad	9.0
KITCHEN	
multifuel stove and windscreen	17.75
2 20 fl. oz. fuel bottles	8.75
0.9 qt. titanium pan	5.0
1 pt. stainless steel cup—doubles as second pan	4.0
2 Lexan plastic spoons	1.0
dishcloth	1.0
matches/lighter	2.0
1 qt. water bottle	5.0
4 1 qt. collapsible water containers	4.0
2 2.5 qt. collapsible water containers	2.75
4 qt. water bag	3.0
chlorine dioxide water purification treatment	2.75
plastic coffee filter and filter papers	2.75
food stuff sack	3.5
FOOTWEAR	
ultralight leather boots	38.0
hiking sandals	23.0
CLOTHING	
2 pairs CoolMax liner socks	3.25
CoolMax midweight socks	3.5
Pertex nylon zip-off leg pants	8.75
polypro long johns	3.0
Capilene polyester underpants	1.5
DriClime polyester long-sleeved base layer	5.0
nylon trail shirt	12.0
Pertex wind shell	6.25
Polartec 100 microfleece sweater	13.5
down vest	14.5
Gore-Tex Paclite II rain jacket	16.0
polyurethane-coated rain pants	4.4
polypro liner gloves	1.0
fleece hat	2.0
cotton sun hat	5.75
cotton bandanna	1.0

A different visual issue is photography. When I hiked the Pacific Crest Trail, I wore dark blue and green clothing and used a sludge-brown tent. In the photographs, I look like a black smudge, and the tent blends neatly into the background. A bright garment, especially a red one, can give a splash of color that makes a striking photograph, assuming the wearer is meant to be prominent.

Why object to bright colors? There are many vivid hues in nature, but there's a difference between a field of flowers and a sheet of red nylon. I remember reaching a mountain pass and staring down on a beautiful green bowl dotted with green groves and blue pools and having my eye drawn instantly to a

ACCESSORIES

trekking poles	20.5
headlamp and spare AA batteries	9.5
2 candles	3.75
compass	1.4
safety whistle	0.5
maps	8.75
first-aid kit	2.5
repair kit	7.5
altimeter-watch	2.0
Windwatch (see Chapter 9)	1.75
knife	3.0
8x21 binoculars	5.5
wash kit	3.0
sunscreen	3.5
dark glasses and case	2.5
toilet paper	1.0
toilet trowel	2.25
umbrella	9.5
notebook and pens	7.5
paperback	8.0
TOTAL	**32.5 POUNDS**

On the Arizona Trail above Coyote Canyon.

Of this total, 5 pounds were worn or carried every day, leaving a basic pack weight of 27 pounds. I also had 6.25 pounds of camera gear; 3.75 pounds of it were normally in a case slung across my body. The remaining camera gear upped the basic pack weight to 29.5 pounds. The pack never actually weighed this little, however, since I always had food, fuel, and water as well. At one point I carried six days' food (12 pounds) and three gallons of water (24 pounds), which, with stove fuel and extra items like camera film and paperback books, made for a total pack weight of 70 pounds.

The basic pack weight was on the high side for a desert hike. On future trips in similar conditions I would take a smaller tarp, an LED headlamp (not available at the time of the hike), and a much lighter rain jacket. I wore the rain jacket for only a few hours. I would also take a pack weighing about 4 pounds or less rather than 6.8 pounds.

searing yellow tent pitched in the center of a meadow. On another occasion a line of orange- and red-clad hikers dominated a distant ridge, destroying any feeling of wildness and solitude. These are aesthetic reasons, but I think they're important, especially in popular backcountry areas where blending in helps make the place seem less crowded. Of course if the background is colorful, bright gear may not stand out. A red tent can disappear into the fall colors of a huckleberry-covered mountainside.

I don't stick strictly to my inconspicuous dogma. Sometimes I have bright items to test (sometimes I'm so embarrassed by them that I try them only in really remote or little-visited areas or, with clothing, when cycling on a road—highways are one place I really want to be noticeable). And in winter all colors tend to look black at a distance except for very pale ones. Against snow, green is just as conspicuous as blaze orange.

Testing

Many companies spend a great deal of time and money conducting laboratory tests on equipment and fabrics, and the results often appear prominently in their catalogs, Web sites, and advertisements. There are tests for everything from waterproofness to wind resistance, from heat output to tear strength. Test methods vary, however, so comparing results can be difficult, and each company seems to find a method that shows its products are better than its competitors'. Moreover, although these tests can *suggest* how a garment might work in the outdoors, they don't guarantee performance—and performance is often a subjective judgment anyway. This applies especially to warm clothing and sleeping bags—what keeps one person cozy may not stop someone else from shivering. Read and note laboratory test results by all means, but don't assume an item that works perfectly in a lab will perform perfectly in the real world.

FINAL THOUGHTS

The chapters that follow cover the intricacies of equipment and techniques. Technical details on gear and descriptions of techniques are interwoven because, as I've said, no equipment, however good, is of any value if you don't know how to use it.

The views here are my own, and experienced backpackers will undoubtedly find much to disagree with, which I hope will amuse and entertain them. Those who don't have enough experience to have strong views of their own should note that many of the techniques and items of equipment I describe are those that have worked well for me. No one can try out even a fraction of what's available, and there's plenty of undoubtedly excellent gear I've never tried. I've named names only to make it easier to illustrate details. So take the things I say as guides, not rules. I make no claim to objectivity. In putting my thoughts on paper, I've reappraised my views about gear and techniques. The general outline holds true even if the gear I describe changes form or name or even ceases to exist, as is bound to happen with some items. The reason for describing specific items is to illustrate types of gear and basic principles, not to say that a particular item is the only one to use.

chapter three

footwear and wilderness travel

Feet are marvelously complex, both flexible and tough, but if they are to carry you and your load mile after mile through the wilderness in comfort, they need care and protection. More backpacking trips are ruined by sore feet than by all other causes combined. Pounded by the ground and bearing the weight of you and your pack, your feet receive harsher treatment than any other part of your body.

This chapter covers the generic styles of hiking

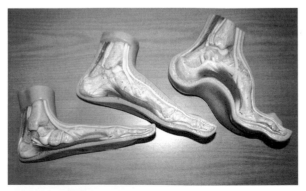

Feet come in different shapes as well as sizes.

boots and shoes, the critical process of fitting footwear, how and of what materials footwear is constructed, and finally models and brands. (A note on terminology: by shoes, I mean footwear that does not cover the ankles; anything that does is a boot.)

A variety of accessories can make walking easier and safer—from staffs to socks and, for snow travel, ice axes, crampons, snowshoes, and skis. Though snowshoes and skis aren't walking accessories per se, they make travel in deep snow much easier, especially with a heavy pack. The end of this chapter covers all these accessories.

ABOUT FOOTWEAR

The main purposes of backpacking footwear are to protect your feet against bruising and abrasion from rough wilderness terrain, to cushion your soles from the constant hammering of miles of walking, and to provide good traction on slippery, steep, and wet terrain.

WILDLIFE

Moving softly, I begin to meet local residents: fat black-and-gold marmots scuttling among rocks on the high passes, brown flickers swooping through trees, red-tailed hawks soaring overhead, and elk crashing through the undergrowth, antlers high. I hear the elk too—their weird bugling call heralds autumn.

On one steep trail I glance down to see a tiny mouse emerge from a hole in a log and prospect its way across a rill. Then it scurries back to take its even tinier offspring gently in its jaws for the journey across the water.

Protection for the sole of the foot comes from layers of cushioning; these layers must be thick enough to prevent stones from bruising the feet but flexible enough to allow natural heel-to-toe movement. Thick soles also insulate against snow and cold ground and the heat of desert sand and rock. The tread of the outer sole offers grip; the best soles not only give security on rough terrain but also minimize damage to the ground.

Footwear should also support your foot and ankle, though this is less important than some people think. Support comes from a fit snug enough to keep the foot from slipping around inside the shoe but not so tight that it won't allow the foot to swell. The ankle is supported by a stiff lower heel counter, or heel cup (see Heel Counters and Toe Boxes, page 56, and the illustrations on page 57), and not simply by a high-cut boot; some running shoes give more ankle support than some boots do.

Keeping your feet dry isn't a major purpose of footwear. Top-quality leather is fairly water resistant, but only boots with waterproof-breathable membrane linings can be considered waterproof. How long they stay so is open to question, however, and they have other disadvantages. Plastic and rubber boots are waterproof, of course, but they make your feet hot and sweaty except in snow.

Light versus Heavy Footwear

Once upon a time, virtually all boots were what we now call heavyweight—with leather inners and outers, leather midsoles, steel shanks, and heavily lugged rubber soles. A typical pair of size 9s weighed at least 4 pounds, and it took dozens, if not hundreds, of miles of walking to break them in. A few lighter boots were available, but they were neither very supportive nor very durable.

The introduction of lightweight leathers, synthetic fabrics, and running shoe features in the early 1980s revolutionized hiking footwear. Most

Lightweight boots mean less weight to lift with each step.

backpackers were won over, though some stayed—and still stay—loyal to the old heavyweights, and the lightweight versus heavyweight debate has rumbled on ever since. I am firmly on the side of lightweight footwear. My conversion came during a Pacific Crest Trail through-hike in 1982. I set off from the Mexican border in heavy traditional boots that soon gave me hot, sore feet. After just a few days, I ended up carrying them and wearing running shoes (brought along for campwear) much of the time. The heavy boots were more comfortable on my back than on my feet. Only in the snow of the High Sierra did I need them. After 1,500 miles, when the running shoes were just about worn out, I replaced both boots and shoes with a pair of the then-new fabric-suede hiking shoes, Asolo Approaches. These weighed less than half as much as my boots. The staff in the store where I bought the shoes were horrified to hear that I intended to backpack more than a thousand miles in them. But my feet rejoiced at being released from their stiff leather prisons, and my daily mileage went up. Although they were full of holes by the end of the trip, the shoes gave me all the support and grip of my old boots and vastly increased my comfort. I have never since worn heavy traditional footwear for summer backpacking.

That lighter footwear is less tiring seems indisputable. The general estimate is that every pound on your feet equals 5 pounds on your back. If that's correct, and it certainly feels like it, then wearing 2-pound rather than 4-pound boots is like removing 10 pounds from your pack. Boots weighing more than 3 pounds make my feet ache after about twelve miles, and after fifteen miles all I want to do is stop. Yet in shoes that weigh half as much, I can cover twice that distance before my feet complain. This isn't surprising when you consider that I lift my feet about 2,500 times a mile

WALKING STYLE

Heavy boots are bulldozers on the trail. Their rigidity forces a walker to stumble along, kicking rocks and gouging chunks out of the path.

Lightweight, flexible footwear encourages a better walking style. You can move faster and more gently, with less effort; you can step around and over rocks instead of banging into them. Gliding instead of trudging, you can cover more miles with the same effort simply because you are lifting less weight with each step.

(my hiking stride is about two feet long). That means I'm lifting 7,500 pounds per mile when I wear 3-pound boots but only 3,750 pounds when I wear shoes that weigh a pound and a half. Over fifteen miles that's 112,500 pounds lifted with the boots versus 56,250 pounds with the shoes, an enormous difference.

Heavier boots usually also mean thicker materials and more padding. In all but winter conditions this can give you hot, sweaty feet, which swell and ache and are more apt to blister.

The ultimate in weight saving is to wear no shoes at all. This might seem like a good way to hurt your feet, but in warm weather walking barefoot is perfectly feasible. I occasionally walk short distances barefoot when my feet feel hot and sweaty in my shoes, and I often wander around camp barefoot. Wearing sandals (as I do for most summer hiking) is close to going barefoot. If you're interested in this idea, Richard Frazine's *The Barefoot Hiker* is worth reading (see also barefoot ers.org/hikers).

The Ankle-Support Myth

One of the main arguments for heavy, stiff footwear is that you need it for ankle support when carrying a heavy pack or hiking on rough terrain. This is not true.

To begin with, most walking boots offer little ankle support, since their soft cuffs give easily under pressure. (Try standing on the outer edge of the sole of a standard walking boot and you'll feel the strain on your ankle.) Only boots with high, stiffened cuffs give real ankle support. My plastic telemark ski boots give good ankle support; I can balance on the edges without strain and traverse steep, icy slopes on my skis without my ankles' aching. But the stiff ankle support restricts foot movement so much that when I walk in these boots I loosen the clips to let my ankles flex fairly normally. Stiff-ankled boots and natural foot movement do not go together.

What actually holds your ankle in place over the sole of a shoe is a rigid heel counter, or heel cup, found in good-quality running shoes as well as most hiking footwear (see Heel Counters and Toe Boxes later in this chapter, page 56). I once tested a pair of high-top leather boots without heel cups. On rough terrain they were worse than useless—my foot constantly slid off the insole, and my ankle kept twisting sideways. I ended up using them only on good paths between campsites. For mountain ascents, I wore the running shoes I'd brought along as campwear—their heel cups made them more stable than the boots.

Some of the greatest strain on your ankles occurs when you run over steep, rough ground. Yet mountain runners, who do this regularly (sometimes for days on end), never wear boots. Try running in boots and you'll see why. For traversing steep, rugged terrain, you need strong, flexible ankles and lightweight, flexible footwear. Doing exercises to strengthen your ankles is better than splinting them in heavy, rigid boots.

The Stiffness Myth

The other argument in favor of heavy boots is that stiff soles protect your feet from rough terrain and help support heavy loads. I disagree. In my experience, restricting normal foot movement with stiff soles makes me feel unstable and insecure. Lateral stiffness—from side to side—is fine, though not required on most trails, since this stops the footwear from twisting under your feet when you traverse steep terrain. Heel-to-toe stiffness is what restricts natural foot movement.

Stiff soles can't flex enough to accommodate to the terrain. I find they prevent me from placing my feet naturally, leading to a slow and clumsy gait, which could lead to injury, since your feet are repeatedly forced into the same unnatural position. Also, straining against the stiffness requires energy and is tiring.

What really protects against rough terrain is footwear that cushions your feet and stops stones and rocks from bruising them. The best way to do this is with a hard but flexible thin synthetic midsole plus a shock-absorbing layer. Most lightweight boots and shoes have soles like this.

In flexible footwear you can place your whole sole in contact with the ground, even on steep terrain, rather than digging in your heels or boot edges, which jars your legs, can make you unstable, and often gouges holes in the hillside.

Sole stiffness is required only on steep, hardpacked snow. Then a bit of stiffness makes it easier to kick the boot toes and edges into the snow.

FOOTWEAR TYPES

Boots and shoes are complex constructions, and there are many ways of making them, using many different materials. You can buy and use footwear happily without knowing whether it has a "graded flex nylon midsole" or "EVA wedges" or is "Blake sewn." (I'll explore the more relevant terms in the Footwear Materials and Construction section later in this chapter.) What may be more important to you is whether the boots contain any recycled materials (many now do). The selection is enormous (a recent gear guide lists forty-two hiking footwear companies and more than four hundred models, and this isn't comprehensive). Choosing footwear can be daunting. But if you go to a store that has a good selection and a knowledgeable, helpful staff trained to fit boots, you can't go far wrong. Those who want to know more will find information about materials and construction below.

Running and Trail Shoes

Shoes designed for trail running and adventure racing make ideal lightweight backpacking footwear, as do the hiking shoes made by many boot companies, often described as cross-trainers, trail shoes, or multisport shoes, suggesting that the makers are not sure what they're actually for or whom to aim the marketing toward. Construction usually features suede-synthetic fabric uppers, often with large mesh areas for breathability, shock-absorbing midsoles, and strong heel counters. Because these shoes are not very warm, I wouldn't recommend them for snow or very cold weather, but for summer trails, dry or wet, they're a good choice. I wear them anytime I think sandals might be too cold or not quite protective enough.

Some trail shoes incorporate toe boxes, graded (for flex) nylon midsoles, and even half-length metal shanks (for explanations, see Footwear Materials and Construction later in this chapter). These weigh more than simpler designs but also give a little more protection.

Shoes weigh from 20 to 25 ounces a pair for the lightest running shoes to 40 ounces or so for the heaviest trail shoes. (Be wary of look-alike street shoes, which probably won't stand up to back-

A trail shoe (Merrell Exotech).

country use for long, and of road-running shoes without enough tread for good grip on rough, wet ground. To avoid these, buy from a reputable backpacking gear retailer.)

Trail shoes are usually designated as suitable for easy to moderate trails with light loads. I think this does them a disservice. I've carried heavy loads—50 to 60 pounds—over rugged mountain terrain in trail shoes without trouble.

Lightweight Boots

This is the most popular footwear category and has many names, including trekking, trail, off-trail, long-distance hiking, lightweight, and more. The designers hope one of these descriptions will catch your attention. Lightweight boots weigh from 2 to 3 pounds, the lighter end shading into the higher-cut trail shoes, the heavier end into midweight boots suitable for occasional crampon and snow use. The category includes most synthetic-suede boots and quite a few leather ones. The advantages of lightweights are comfort and weight. However, they are not usually waterproof because of the thin materials (except, for a while when new, those with waterproof-breathable linings), and some have many vulnerable seams. Lightweight boots reach the ankle or higher and have protective rands, or bumpers (either full or just at the toe and heel), cushioned linings, sewn-in tongues, graded flexible midsoles, and on some models, half-length shanks. When I wear boots they are usually light ones. They can cope with most terrain except steep, hard snow and ice. I wore a pair of 34-ounce leather lightweights for most of the Arizona Trail with a pack that weighed 70 pounds at one point (six days' food and three gallons of water). They lasted the 800-mile hike and were very comfortable except on the hottest days, when I wore sandals.

Medium-Weight Boots

Weighing from 3 to 4 pounds, medium-weight boots are good for mountain and winter backpacking where cold, wet weather is expected and crampons may be needed. The best models combine the durability and support of traditional boots with the comfort of lightweight designs. Although most have one-piece leather construction, a few models are fabric-leather combinations. Most medium-weight boots incorporate a sole stiffener—either stiff nylon midsoles or half-length shanks or both—and can be fitted with crampons for hard snow and ice. Generally these boots are designed to cope with rugged, off-trail terrain in any weather. The best ones are made on curved lasts and feature one-piece top-grain leather, padded sewn-in tongues, heel counters, toe boxes, and shock-absorbing midsoles or dual-density outsoles. Many also include waterproof-breathable sock liners.

The proper fitting of medium-weight boots is critical, and a short break-in period is advisable.

Heavyweight Boots

Heavy boots (4 pounds and up) are, in my opinion, too stiff and heavy for most backpacking, though some traditionalists prefer them. But they are good for *easy mountaineering*—trips that combine hiking with scrambling, easy rock climbing, or long periods of crampon use—the type carried out on easy alpine snow ascents in summer. Light- and medium-weight footwear may be too soft and flexible for these activities, especially crampon use. Even heavyweight designs have modern features, though, with synthetic cushioning midsoles, graded nylon midsoles, footbeds, synthetic linings, curved soles, and shock-absorbing heel inserts.

Heavyweights can require considerable break-

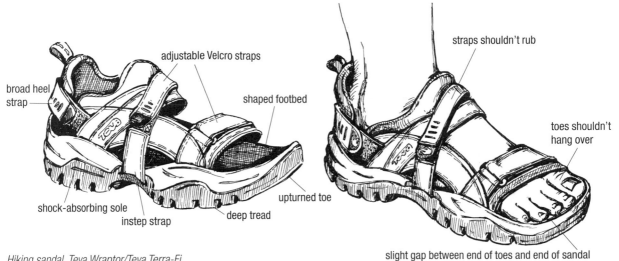

Hiking sandal. Teva Wraptor/Teva Terra-Fi.

slight gap between end of toes and end of sandal

ing in. I find them uncomfortable and tiring to walk in and wear them rarely—only when prolonged crampon use and step kicking in snow are likely. I can accomplish most of the very easy snow and ice climbing I do when backpacking using medium-weight boots that accept flexible crampons and are far more comfortable on easier terrain; on steep, rocky terrain where scrambling and easy climbing may be required, I find lightweight footwear perfectly adequate. The latest heavy boots are more comfortable than traditional models, though, because of rocker soles and carefully shaped uppers.

Sandals

Hiking or sports sandals are now my favorite footwear for summer hiking, and I'm using them earlier and later in the season too—whenever there's no snow—with waterproof-breathable socks for wet cold and wool socks for dry cold. I long ago overcame my first reaction: that they might be fine for leaping out of rafts in the Colorado River but that their only use to the back-

packer was as campwear and for river crossings. Once I tried a pair, I quickly became a convert. Not just any old sandals excel for hiking, of course. To be suitable for walking any distance, they have to support the feet, cushion against hard, rough, and hot surfaces, and grip adequately. The best of them do all of this very well.

Essential features are thick, shock-absorbing soles with a shaped platform that supports the foot; a deep tread for grip; and a strapping system

A hiking sandal (Teva Wraptor 2).

that holds the heel and forefoot firmly. Straps may be leather, synthetic leather, or nylon webbing. The last two materials absorb little moisture and dry quickly and would be my first choice for wet-weather use. They are usually fastened by hook-and-loop (e.g., Velcro) fabric, though some models use clip buckles.

A broad and fairly rigid heel strap is needed to keep the heel centered over the sole. Some models (Teva Wraptor, Chaco Z1) have instep straps that run over the foot, through the sole, and back over the foot. With these it's easy to get a very snug fit. I also look for curved or rimmed edges that protect the feet—especially the toes—from bumping against rocks and stones.

Like other footwear, sandals need to fit properly. Your foot shouldn't hang over the sole at the sides or at the toe or heel, and the straps should hold the foot snugly in place without rubbing. Try sandals on and walk around the store to see if they rub anywhere, just as you would with boots. If you're going to wear them without socks, you may need a size smaller than your boot size. Stabilizing footbeds like Superfeet won't stay put in most sandals, so if you need these, sandals may seem a poor choice. But footbeds will fit in Bite sandals such as the X-Trac and the Xtension. I tried the X-Tracs on a six-day, 115-mile hike with Superfeet fitted and found them comfortable, well cushioned, and supportive. Also many sandals have firm, shaped soles that mimic the effects of footbeds.

Although I haven't had any problems with sandals, they obviously have limitations. They're fine on trails and most rocky terrain but not so good in spiky vegetation. In deserts you need to take great care to avoid cacti; in forests, thorn bushes can be a problem. Though clearly best suited to warm or dry conditions, they can be worn with wool socks when it's cool and dry and waterproof-breathable

socks when it's wet. I first learned just how superior sports sandals are to other footwear in hot weather on a trek in the Himalaya, when I wore a pair for more than 75 miles on rugged, steep, stony trails. My feet stayed dry and cool and never felt sore or swollen, nor did I suffer any blisters. Sweaty socks weren't a problem—I wore socks only when it was cold and in camp. When streams crossed the trail, I sloshed straight through, unlike the others in the party, who had to stop to remove their boots and socks. Wearing sandals toughens your feet, too, as I found at the end of a Nepal trek, when I did a 2,000-foot scree run in them. The stones that slid between my feet and the sandals were irritating, but they didn't bruise or cut my feet. Really sharp tiny stones, like the pumice found in the Devils Postpile region of the High Sierra, are quite painful, but they would be if they got in your boots, too. An advantage of sandals is that usually you just need to tap the toe on the ground to shake out debris—much quicker than removing boots or shoes.

Since that Nepal trek, I've worn sandals for a 500-mile, five-week hike in the High Sierra; two-week trips in the Colorado Rockies, the Grand Canyon, and the High Uinta Mountains in Utah; and innumerable day and weekend hikes. Whereas sandals used to be my backup footwear, now I sometimes carry lightweight shoes for cool evenings in camp or the occasional cold, stormy day. Mostly, though, I make do with socks.

Five weeks is my longest hike in sandals. Others have gone much farther. Scott Williamson walked the Florida Trail and the Appalachian Trail in sandals, plus the country in between, and Hamish Brown hiked the 900-mile crest of the Atlas Mountains in Morocco in sandals. Ray and Jenny Jardine wore sandals over a significant portion of the Pacific Crest Trail, though Ray reported that the soles of his feet dried out on this trip and developed painful, deep cracks that took a long time to heal. On my 500-mile High Sierra hike, I had the same problem, with splits appearing in the tips of my big toes. Sunscreen kept the cracks moist and helped them heal, but one got so bad I ended up covering it with 2nd Skin gel, taped into place. Under this dressing it healed in about a week. It's wise to apply sunscreen to bare feet anyway. They don't usually see much sunlight. In sandals they are exposed and, just like any other part of your body, can get burned. Straps can rub, too. If they do, you need a patch of moleskin, Compeed, 2nd Skin, or other hot-spot treatment, just as with boots.

Hiking sandals weigh from 20 to 35 ounces, comparable to hiking shoes. If you just want a pair for campwear, simpler sandals like flip-flops are much lighter.

FITTING BOOTS AND SHOES

Take your time when choosing footwear—if the fit isn't right, you'll suffer. Nothing is worse than footwear that hurts. You need to consider the types of boots and shoes available, construction methods, and materials, but the most modern, high-tech, waterproof, breathable, expensive boots are worse than useless if they don't fit. Given the bewildering variety of foot shapes, good fit entails more than finding the right size. It's unwise to set your

heart on a particular model of boot or shoe before you go shopping, however seductive the advertising or the recommendation from a famous hiker, mountaineer, or even backpacking author. Since trying on footwear is essential, this is one item I wouldn't buy on the Internet or from a mail-order catalog.

All footwear is built around a *last*, a rough approximation of the human foot that varies in shape according to the bootmaker's view of what a foot looks like. Lasts sometimes are designated "American," "European," or "British," but these descriptions don't mean much in the real world and can be ignored.

Since women's feet are generally narrower and lower volume (less volume relative to the length and width) than men's, women's boots are made on different-sized lasts. Men with small, narrow feet may find that women's boots fit them best, just as women with larger, wider feet may prefer men's boots.

Curved lasts, which produce a boot with a "rocker" sole, make a big difference, especially in stiff-soled, heavy boots. The curve of the sole rolls with your foot, mimicking the flex of the forefoot and allowing a more natural gait.

Allow several hours for buying footwear, and try to visit a store at a quiet time, not on a busy Saturday afternoon. Feet swell during the day, so it's best to try on new footwear later in the day. Take your hiking socks with you, but if you forget

USA Men's	3.5	4	4.5	5	5.5	6	6.5	7	7.5	8	8.5	9	9.5	10	10.5	11	11.5	12	13	14	15	16
USA Women's	5	5.5	6	6.5	7	7.5	8	8.5	9	9.5	10	10.5	11									
European	35	35.5	36	37	37.5	38	38.5	39.5	40	40.5	41.5	42	42.5	43	44	44.5	45	45.5	47	48	49	50
British	2.5	3	3.5	4	4.5	5	5.5	6	6.5	7	7.5	8	8.5	9	9.5	10	10.5	11	12	13	14	15
Japanese	21.5	22	22.5	23	23.5	23.5	24	24.5	25	25.5	26	26	26.5	27	27.5	28	28.5	29	29.5	30	31	31

Boot size comparison chart.

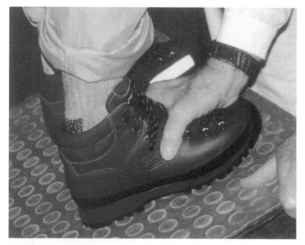
Phil Oren checking the fit on an incline board.

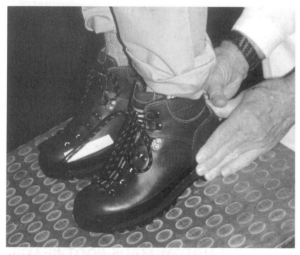
Phil Oren checking heel fit on an incline board.

them, most stores provide suitable socks to wear while trying on footwear. Use your normal shoe size only as a starting point; sizes vary from maker to maker and, just to make matters more confusing, there are different sizing systems. A store may stock footwear made in the United States, Italy, Austria, South Korea, and more, so you can't expect consistency.

Make sure you try on both shoes. One of your feet is almost certainly larger than the other,

perhaps by as much as half a size. *Make sure the larger foot has the best fit.* An extra sock or a volume adjuster can pad a boot that's slightly too large, but nothing can be done for one that's too small.

Lightweight boots and shoes are fairly easy to fit because they are soft and mold to the feet quickly. Medium- and heavy-weight boots tend to be uncomfortable at first, which makes finding a good fit in the store more difficult. But because they are so unforgiving, a good fit is essential, even though they should eventually stretch a little (in width, not length) and adapt to your feet. Even more care is needed when fitting traditional heavy leather boots.

I used to recommend the standard fitting method—put your finger down the back with the boots unlaced, wiggle your toes, lace the boots, walk around the store, kick something. It was, I thought, good advice. It is in fact totally inadequate. However just like everyone else, I didn't know any better. I do now. I know that with proper fitting you can get footwear that doesn't hurt your feet. If you're one of those lucky people—those lucky few—whose feet and legs don't hurt, whose boots don't rub, who don't get blisters, then you can ignore the next section. For those whose feet may give the occasional twinge, to those for whom blisters and aching feet are major problems, the next few paragraphs could be the most important part of this book.

Proper fitting begins with the feet, not the footwear. The system that has revolutionized boot fitting was developed by Phil Oren after he had problems finding footwear that fit properly for a 750-mile hike on the Pacific Crest Trail. His feet had been damaged by ill-fitting footwear in the past, so standard boots wouldn't fit him. After having his boots modified at a ski shop, he successfully completed his hike. Along the way he met many hikers with foot problems traceable to poorly fitting footwear, and he started searching for a better way to fit hiking footwear. Since then he has developed a sophisticated fitting system that really does work. Phil and his team train retail staff in boot fitting and run workshops for hikers (sponsored by *Backpacker* magazine and known as "Boot Camps"). He has also compiled a huge database of foot shapes and sizes and worked with manufacturers on producing better-fitting footwear. If you have any boot problems at all, I recommend finding a store with staff trained in Phil's FitSystem. (For more on this, see fitsystembyphiloren.com.) I've had footwear fitted by Phil Oren and I've taken the standard and advanced training workshops. I'm convinced that the FitSystem is the best way to fit hiking footwear.

Everyone's feet are different, so it's hardly a surprise that mass-produced footwear is unlikely to fit well without modification. I certainly had problems finding footwear that fit well until I used the FitSystem. These problems increased over the years as my feet appeared to get bigger. I was faced with a choice between footwear that hurt my toes, especially when hiking downhill, and larger sizes that allowed my toes room but didn't support my ankles or hold my heels in position, resulting in holes in the linings and in the heels of my socks. I went for the larger size, since this was less painful over a day's hiking, but it certainly wasn't ideal. Since having a proper fitting, I've gone back to my original size without sore toes, and I don't wear holes in the linings or my socks. Following is a description of the FitSystem and what you should expect from a boot fitter.

Foot Examination

A boot fitter should examine and measure your feet before you try on any footwear in order to find out whether you have any fitting problems and which footwear is likely to fit. Information from the examination should be entered on a foot chart, which you can do while being examined. This can be unnerving, as I discovered when Phil examined my feet and informed me I had (slight) hammertoes, Morton's toe, chubby toe, toe drift, calluses, and the beginnings of bunions. Ouch! Would I ever walk again?

Next comes the toe test, which is done standing, so the feet are bearing weight. The fitter tries to lift your big toe off the ground with a finger placed under its tip. If your feet are aligned properly, the toe should move easily. If, like mine, it seems glued

CUSTOM-MADE FOOTWEAR

Several companies offer a made-to-measure service for those who can't find a suitable pair of boots off the shelf. I once had the Swedish bootmakers Lundhags make boots for me by mail order (not something I recommend). Working from a sketched outline of my feet, they produced a well-fitting pair of their 3-pound Mountaineer boots, which I immediately wore on a two-week walk in the Pyrenees. They proved very comfortable. I had no problems with sore spots or blisters, though the lack of a heel counter made them unsuitable for off-trail travel. Peter Limmer of New Hampshire (limmer boot.com) is the best-known maker of custom boots. I know people who rave about theirs. It's not surprising that the wait for a pair can be long. Other makers include Mekan Boot in Salt Lake City, Utah (mekanboot.com), and Esatto (esatto.biz), which offers a kit for measuring your feet at home. Your local outdoor store may know of more.

If you have to order boots by mail, most companies have clear instructions for obtaining the right size. But nothing beats trying on boots in a store.

48

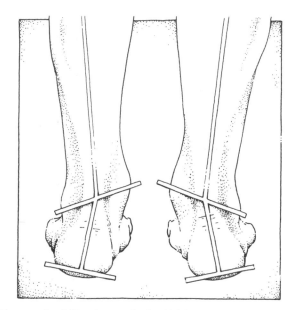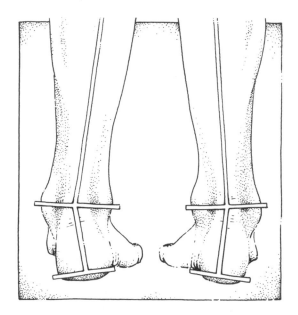

Overpronation (left) and oversupination (right).

to the ground, your foot is overpronated. To check this, the fitter twists your knee outward, putting the foot into the neutral position. The big toe should now be flexible.

The biomechanics of walking explains what the toe test tells us. As you walk, the shape of your foot changes constantly. All footwear interferes with this. When your foot is in midstride, with no weight on it, it's in the neutral position. When your heel hits the ground, your foot rolls to the inside and the arch flattens slightly. This *pronation* allows the foot to adapt to rough, uneven surfaces; remember that our feet were designed for walking on soil, grass, stone, sand, and other natural terrain, not flat, smooth, man-made surfaces. As your foot flattens against the ground, it should go into neutral and stiffen for stability and forward movement. As your heel lifts off the ground, your foot becomes a rigid lever with a high arch and instep so you can spring forward off your big toe. This is called *supination* (oversupination can occur but is

very rare). After years of wearing unsupportive footwear and walking on pavements and floors, instead of going into neutral and then becoming slightly supinated, the foot often just flattens out (overpronation). In this position your foot is locked to the ground with no spring in the toes (hence the toe test). To take your next step, you have to move from the inside of your foot rather than from your toes. When you do this the foot tends to turn slightly outward, which distorts the skeletal structure, twisting the ankle, knee, and hip when they should be aligned. This unstable posture can lead to joint problems. When your foot overpronates it also elongates, which makes boot fitting very difficult. Do you fit to the shorter, neutral position or the longer, overpronated one? That was my problem. This elongation can be shown by drawing around the foot while it is weighted and unweighted and comparing the two outlines. It's then easy to see that the same boot can't fit both shapes. Phil Oren's data show that overpronation affects about 80 percent of us, so it's a major boot-fitting issue.

Foot Measurement

The toe test shows whether you overpronate. But that in itself doesn't help much with boot fitting. Next you need to know what size your feet are and what difference overpronation makes. Each foot should be measured with the Brannock Device (an instrument for measuring foot length and width) for overall length (heel to toe) and for heel-to-ball length, which is important because boots should flex where your foot does. The measurements should be taken with the foot weighted and again with it unweighted and in the neutral position. The width of your feet should be measured too. Each of my feet varied by one size in total length and one and a half to two sizes from heel to ball. That explained why my feet appeared to be getting bigger. They weren't; they were overpronating and elongating when weighted.

Foot volume is important too, but this has to be estimated; the Brannock Device cannot measure volume. My feet are low volume, and I have narrow heels and very narrow Achilles tendons. However, my feet are also quite wide, so I need footwear that is wide across the metatarsals (the base of the toes) but low in volume and narrow at the heel.

Stabilization and Footbeds

If your feet overpronate, and chances are they do, they need stabilizing if your footwear is to fit properly. This can be done with footbeds that support the foot and hold it in position, which means junking the soft foam inserts found in most boots and shoes. These "footbeds" provide no support and don't stabilize the feet. Just try pushing your finger against the sides of the heel section while holding the center down with the other hand. With virtually all inserts that come in footwear, the sides collapse easily. They'll do the same under your foot. (Montrail footwear has the only half-way decent boot inserts I've seen. They're not as good as a proper footbed, but they're far better than most.)

There are several types of stabilizing footbeds (Conform'able and Sole Custom are two) as well as prescription orthotics. The ones I use are Superfeet footbeds. They have a hard plastic and cork rear and midsection that holds the heel in place, minimizing foot movement and overpronation. There are two types: off-the-shelf footbeds, called Trim to Fit, and Custom Fit. Trim to Fit footbeds can stabilize the foot 40 to 75 percent, and Custom Fit ones stabilize it up to 95 percent. Due to my level of overpronation, I wear Custom Fit Superfeet. To make these, the fitter holds the foot in the neutral position (footbeds made with the feet weighted will fit the overpronated foot, which you don't want). The footbeds, which are partially shaped already, are heated and then held under your feet in plastic bags. All the air is then sucked out of the bags—a slightly peculiar sensation—while the footbeds mold to your feet.

Since your feet are so firmly supported and no longer move in your footwear, stabilizing footbeds can feel strange and even uncomfortable at first. It may be a good idea to wear them for just a few hours at a time until you adjust, though I could wear them all day immediately. Once the footbeds are fitted they can be transferred from one pair of shoes or boots to another, and I now put them in all my footwear. I now take a smaller size because my feet no longer elongate much when weighted. I can stride off my toes too, rather than the insides of my feet, so I've lost that slightly splayed duck-footed walk I had. My feet ache less

BREAKING IN

Gone, thankfully, are the days when you had to wear boots for many short, gentle strolls before you dared subject your feet to them on a real walk. Today you can set off on a fifteen-mile walk the same day you buy a pair of lightweight boots and suffer not a blister; for medium-weight models a short break-in period is advisable, though not essential. Only if you have particularly tender feet or heavyweight boots (which I don't recommend) will you need to wear your boots for a long time before setting off on a major trek. Old-fashioned remedies like soaking your boots and then walking them dry or filling them with hot water were designed for old-fashioned stiff leather. This brutal treatment probably didn't do boots much good in the old days, and it would certainly harm modern boots.

because the footbeds prevent the cushioning fat pad under the heel from flattening and spreading sideways when weighted, and my knees ache less on long descents because my ankles, knees, and hips are properly aligned.

To test your alignment, stand with your feet slightly apart and your hands held out in front of you, one over the other. Have a friend slowly press down on your hands. If you overpronate you'll lose your balance quickly and feel very unstable. Next stand on a pair of stabilizing footbeds and repeat the test. With your joints properly aligned, you should be able to resist the downward pressure without much effort.

To demonstrate the fat pads, get a friend to push her fingers against the base of your unsupported heel. She should be able to feel the heel bone easily. Then have her squeeze the sides of the

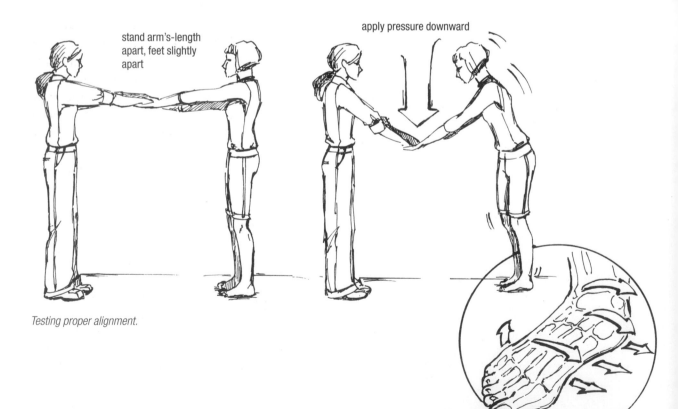

stand arm's-length apart, feet slightly apart

apply pressure downward

Testing proper alignment.

heel together with the other hand and press with her fingers again. This time the fat pad will prevent her from feeling the bone. Stabilizing footbeds do the same. If your feet don't overpronate, these tests won't show much difference, and you won't need stabilizing footbeds.

Volume Adjusters and Tongue Depressors

Stabilizing footbeds will have an effect only if your footwear fit properly. If they are too roomy, the footbeds alone won't stop your feet from moving in them. For that you'll need to reduce the boots' volume by wearing thicker socks; by putting a solid, noncompressible flat piece of neoprene, called a volume adjuster, under the footbed; or by placing a piece of soft rubber under the laces to push the tongue down on the foot when the laces are tightened (a tongue depressor). These methods can make boots and shoes with too high a volume fit better, but it's best to have a good fit to start with. Luckily that is easier than it used to be. Since Phil Oren's FitSystem came to prominence, some boot-makers have altered the shape of their lasts and reduced the volume of their footwear so they are more like most people's feet. Certainly I more often find footwear that fits well.

The Right Fit

Once your feet have been inspected and measured and the fitter has decided whether you need stabilizing footbeds or other accessories, it's finally time to try on some footwear. It's best to wear your hiking socks for this. Don't, even now, expect to find a perfect fit: as close as possible is what you're looking for, meaning a boot that approximates the shape of your foot in volume and width as well as length. Beware of boots that are too big.

These tend to feel comfortable because they don't press anywhere on your feet, but in use they'll rub and be unsupportive. Boots should fit snugly around the heel, ankle, and instep but have room for you to wiggle your toes. They should flex at the same point as your feet do so you don't have to fight them every time you take a step, which is tiring and may make your feet slip inside your footwear.

Incline Board

Once you've found a rough fit, you need to try the boots on a 20-degree ramp known as an incline board. Lace the boots firmly, then stand facing up the board while the fitter checks that the boot heels fit properly and sees whether there is any space or loose fabric around the instep and ankle, showing that the boot has too much volume. The fitter should also mark on the boots with chalk or a piece of tape the points where they flex and, by feeling for the first metatarsal head at the base of your toes, check whether your feet flex in the same place. Once this is done, you face down the incline board and jump up and down before the fitter again checks to see if your feet have moved much in the boots. If they have, the boots have too much volume. This can be solved as described earlier, but it is preferable to try lower-volume footwear instead.

Modification

The footwear that fits your feet best is still unlikely to fit exactly. A good fitter should be able to modify footwear to achieve a custom fit. Pressure points, often around the flex point, are the main problem. Boots can be stretched to remove them, using the blunt end of a bent metal *rubbing bar* to gradually ease out the leather or fabric. Just a

Right: Adjusting a boot-stretching device to the correct foot shape. Below: Jeff Gray of Superfeet placing a boot (without the footbed) in hot water to soften it for modification. Bottom: Jeff Gray stretching a boot.

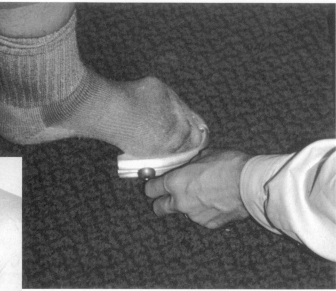

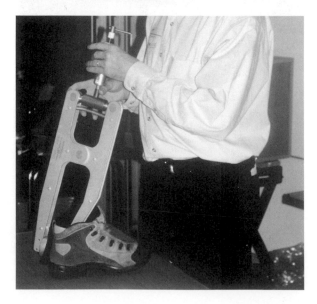

tiny modification can have quite an effect on the fit. Since I test boots for a hiking magazine, I have my own rubbing bar at home so I can stretch boots that are too narrow for me. This has let me test many boots that would otherwise have hurt my feet. Occasionally there may be tiny bumps inside footwear due to manufacturing anomalies. With the boot on the rubbing bar, these can be flattened with a convex hammer.

Although leather can be stretched on the rubbing bar, you can't stretch hard, synthetic toe boxes and heel counters or rubber rands (see under Footwear Materials and Construction below) without heating them first to soften the material. This can be done by sealing the boots in a plastic bag and dunking them in a large pot of boiling water. Various hydraulic devices can then be used along with the rubbing bar to stretch the boots.

For the fit that is closest to perfect, you can have casts made of the front or rear of your foot and then inserted into footwear to stretch it to the exact shape of your feet. Although initially expensive, the casts can be used for all your footwear.

A good boot fitter should make any required modifications when you buy footwear. If you already have footwear that doesn't fit properly, you can take it to a store to be modified. Phil Oren believes that most footwear needs modification of some sort to get the best fit.

I suggest going through the fitting process every time you buy new hiking footwear even if it is the same model. Manufacturing processes can change, and new lasts may be used. I've found that models that once fitted me well didn't do so a few years later. I discovered that a different factory was producing them and that the fit had indeed changed slightly. If you keep the details of your foot examination and measurements, this process doesn't need to be done every time, though it's worth an occasional check to see if anything has changed, especially if you have any foot problems. It's advisable to always fit footwear using any accessories you expect to use with them, such as stabilizing footbeds.

When you get your new footwear home, wear them inside for a few hours or even a few days just to check that they really do fit. A store should exchange footwear that haven't been worn outside. Once they're muddy and scuffed, they're yours.

FOOTWEAR MATERIALS AND CONSTRUCTION

There are two basic parts to a boot or shoe: the *uppers*, which are flexible and mold around the foot; and the *sole*, which is more rigid and lies under the foot. The sole is usually made up of a number of layers. The *insole* lies under the footbed and is usually quite thin. The *midsole* lies between the insole and the outsole and may itself

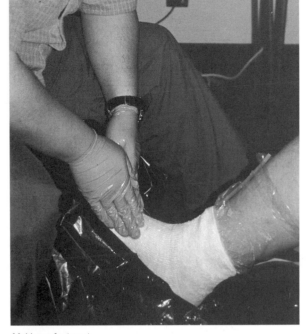

Making a foot cast.

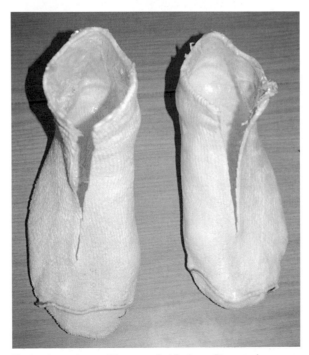

Foot casts can be used to ensure that footwear fits properly.

consist of several layers of shock-absorbing and stiffening materials. The *outsole* contacts the ground and has a tread cut into it. The uppers and the sole are made separately and then attached via the construction method.

Uppers

Leather

Leather is still the main material for uppers, though synthetics now dominate midsoles and linings and fabric-leather combinations are standard for running and trail shoes and common in the lightest boots. Leather lasts longer than other upper materials, keeps your feet dry longer, and absorbs and then disperses moisture (sweat) quickly and efficiently. It is also flexible and comfortable.

Although fancy names abound, there are two basic types of leather: *top-grain* and *split-grain*. Top-grain leather, made from the outer layer of the cow's hide, is tougher and thicker and holds water-repellent treatment and its shape better than split-grain leather, which is the inner layer of the hide. Split-grain leather is often coated with polyurethane or polyvinyl chloride (PVC) to make it more water resistant and attractive. However this shiny layer soon cracks and allows the leather to soak up water like a sponge, while the remaining coating impedes drying. Full-grain leather is the full thickness of the hide. It's very tough and water resistant but also thick and heavy, so it's rarely used in boots, although the term is often used for top-grain leather. Nubuck (also spelled *nubuc* and *nubuk*) is top-grain leather that has been sanded and polished to give it a smooth finish somewhat similar to suede. It's much tougher and more water resistant than suede, which is split leather with the inner surface turned outward and brushed. Nubuck is popular with bootmakers because it shows scuffs and scratches less than smooth leathers do and has a sensuous feel. Some top-grain leather boots have the rough inner surface of the leather facing out, though this is less common now that nubuck is available. Rough-out and nubuck leathers are easily distinguished from suede by their thickness and solidity. Suede is often used to strengthen the wear points of fabric footwear. Although it is not as durable, supportive, or water resistant as top-grain leather or the best split leathers, good-quality suede is still worth considering for lightweight footwear.

Leather comes in various thicknesses, always measured in millimeters—inches just aren't precise enough. Heavyweight mountaineering boots usually have 3-millimeter leather, light hikers 2-millimeter or less.

To make it usable in footwear, all leather has to be tanned—treated with chemicals or oils. With some leathers a water-repellent substance—usually silicone—is chemically bonded to the fibers during tanning. This leather goes by various names, such as HS12, Prime WeatherTuff, and Pittards WR100. I've found that this leather performs as advertised, especially when new, and is nearly waterproof. In time, though, the waterproofing breaks down and waxing (for more on this, see Waterproofing and Sealing later in this chapter) is required.

Fabric-Leather

Many lightweight boots and trail shoes copy the nylon-suede design of the running shoes they were based on. This works well in all but the coldest, snowiest conditions. Uppers are mostly fabric, often nylon mesh in shoes but usually textured nylon in boots (though sometimes polyester), reinforced with leather, suede, or synthetic leather. This design requires many seams, which are vulnerable

WET FEET/DRY FEET

One reason many people wear leather boots is to keep their feet dry. On weekend hikes, many boots will indeed do this, at least when they're fairly new. But on longer trips it becomes more difficult; on walks of several weeks it's impossible if the rain lasts many days. This is because leather boots need to be fully dried and then treated with a waterproofing compound after a few wet days if they are to keep your feet dry. Boots with waterproof linings need less care, but they have other disadvantages (see pages 56 and 58).

On a long walk in wet weather, completely drying any kind of boot material is very difficult. I walked 1,300 miles up the length of Norway and Sweden during a very wet summer. Because much of the route was over rough terrain, I wore lightweight leather boots. For most of the walk they were sodden, which doubled their weight, reduced the breathability, and softened the leather so it gave less support. I would have been far better off with fabric-leather shoes, which wouldn't have gained as much weight when wet, would have been much more breathable, and would have dried more quickly when

it wasn't raining. My feet would still have been wet, but they'd have been much more comfortable. I'd rather have cool, wet feet than hot, sweaty feet.

In warm weather, wet feet aren't a problem—as long as you can keep them dry overnight. When it's cold, the answer is thick socks, preferably with a high wool content, changed regularly. During a forty-day walk through wet, thawing spring snow in the High Sierra, my heavy leather boots were soaked most of the time. (If I did that trip again, I'd ski and wear plastic boots.) By the end of each day, my wool socks were soaked. To keep my feet as warm and dry as possible, I alternated two pairs of thick wool socks, hanging the previous day's wet socks on the back of my pack to dry each morning and wearing the pair I'd dried the day before. I kept a third dry pair for wearing in the tent. It worked—I had no blisters or other foot problems during the walk. An alternative for wet weather is a pair of waterproof-breathable socks (see pages 78–79). These will keep your feet dry and are, in my opinion, a far better choice than footwear with waterproof-breathable linings.

to abrasion and thus may not be durable in rough, rocky terrain, where boot uppers take a hammering. (I found this out the hard way many years ago while scrambling and walking on the incredibly rough and sharp gabbroic rock of the Cuillin Ridge on Scotland's Isle of Skye. After two weeks, my nylon-suede boots were in shreds, and virtually every seam had ripped open.)

Waterproofness is not a strong point of fabric-leather footwear either, unless they are lined with a waterproof-breathable membrane. This is again mostly because of the seams but also comes from the thinness of the materials. Grit and dirt can penetrate nylon much more easily than leather, however, so such membranes do not last as long in

synthetic boots as in leather boots, whether they are lightweight nylon or the much tougher Cordura. I like synthetic leather for trail shoes, but for lightweight boots I prefer all leather since I wear boots only in terrain I feel is too rugged for shoes.

So why consider fabric-leather footwear at all? Because it's cool in warm weather (as long as there's no membrane), it needs little or no breaking in, it's comfortable, and it dries more quickly than heavier footwear. It's also used on many of the lightest, most flexible shoes.

Synthetic Leather

Many sandals, some shoes, and a very few boots (such as the Garmont Vegan) use synthetic leather for the uppers, often in combination with nylon. Synthetic leather is flexible and mimics fairly well the performance of split-grain leather, though not top-grain. It has the advantage of being nonabsorbent and therefore quick drying, but it's not very breathable.

Plastic

Plastic is now the dominant material for mountaineering boots, alpine ski boots, and telemark ski boots because it's better than leather at providing the rigidity, waterproofness, and warmth such pursuits require. But hiking boots need to be flexible and permeable to moisture so that sweat can escape. I've hiked in plastic telemark and climbing boots, and I've never had such sore and blistered heels or such aching feet. With their rigid soles and outer shells, such boots work against your feet rather than with them. Now when I hike to the snow in my plastic telemark boots, I undo the clips on the uppers to allow my feet to flex. This isn't very stable, but it's less painful than keeping the boots done up. Plastic hiking boots have appeared in the past but soon vanished, since they were too hot and sweaty.

Heel Counters and Toe Boxes

Heels need to be held in place and prevented from twisting, and toes need room to move and protection from rocks and other natural protuberances. *Heel counters*, or heel cups, are stiff pieces of material—usually synthetic, though sometimes leather—built into the rear of boots or shoes to cup the heels and hold them in place. You usually can't see them, although some makers put them on the outside of some footwear, but you can feel them under the leather of the heel. Heel counters are essential. A soft, sloppy heel without a counter won't support your ankle, no matter how high the upper.

Toe boxes are usually made from similar material inserted in the front of a boot; some boots dispense with this construction in favor of a thick rubber rand around the boot toe.

Linings and Padding

Traditionally, linings were made from soft leather—as they still are in some boots—but lighter, less-absorbent, harder-wearing, quicker-drying, moisture-wicking, nonrotting synthetics are taking over. The main one is Cambrelle. I find these new linings superior to their leather counterparts (unless the boots have waterproof-breathable membrane linings, as discussed below, in which case leather protects the membrane better). Some wearers have found an odor problem with synthetic linings, but that hasn't occurred in the footwear I've used.

Many boots have a thin layer of foam padding between the lining and the outside, usually around the ankle and the upper tongue, but occasionally throughout the boot. Such padding does provide more cushioning for the foot, but it also makes boots warmer, something to be avoided in hot weather. Foam also absorbs water and dries slowly. I prefer boots with minimum padding; I rely on socks for warmth.

Many boots now feature linings, sometimes called *booties*, made from vapor-permeable waterproof membranes such as Gore-Tex and Sympatex. These certainly make the boots waterproof when they are new, but once the membrane is torn or punctured, it will leak. How long they keep water out varies. The membrane itself is fragile, and if your feet move in your boots, the membranes can wear out very quickly. Some people swear by them, others swear at them. My experi-

KEY FEATURES: THREE-SEASON BOOTS AND SHOES

- A good fit. This is more important than anything else. Regardless of the quality, badly fitting footwear means blisters and sore feet.
- Light weight. One pound on your feet equals five pounds on your back.
- Deep lugs for good grip on rough ground.
- A torsionally stiff insole that flexes at the right point.

- Shock-absorbing midsoles for cushioning and comfort.
- A solid heel counter to center your foot over the sole.
- A soft cuff to minimize rubbing (in boots).
- Speed hooks or pulleys for quick lacing.
- A sewn-in tongue to keep water out.

pull-on finger tab

tall foam-padded, sewn-in, gusseted tongue

combination of D-rings and speed hooks to adjust laces and fine-tune fit

foam padding around ankle support

combination of nylon and leather for light weight and breathability

A lightweight hiker (see details, left).

stabilizing footbed for fine-tuning fit

above-the-ankle height for support

heel cup (heel counter) for support and stability

protective toe rand

minimal seams for minimal leakage

fully gusseted tongue to keep water out

welt to accept clip-on crampons

deep-lugged outsole for good traction

locking hook

nylon lasting board (insole) for torsional support

A heavy-duty mountain boot.

molded polyurethane/EVA midsole for shock absorption

synthetic and suede for light weight and breathability

high-rubber-content lugged outsole for good traction

An approach shoe.

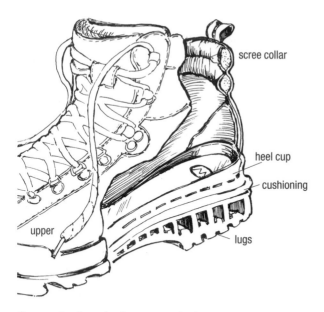

Cross section through a three-season boot.

scree collar

heel cup

cushioning

upper

lugs

ence suggests that such linings last longest and perform best in boots that have few seams and are made from leather rather than nylon and suede. Membranes laminated to leather are less likely to be cut by tiny specks of sharp grit than those laminated to more open-weave synthetic fabrics. The first membranes leaked fairly quickly, sometimes after only a few weeks' use, but newer ones do last longer. I have a pair of trail shoes several years old that have had months of use and are still waterproof. Even so, good-quality footwear should long outlast a membrane lining.

Waterproof-breathable membranes have another big disadvantage. Although they let some water vapor out, they are far less breathable than footwear without them. Thus they are hot and sweaty in warm weather, especially if the uppers get saturated—which is why water-repellent leathers are best for the outside. And if you do get them wet inside (say, by stepping in a deep pool or creek), they are slow to dry, because although vapor can

pass through the membrane, liquid cannot. There are better ways to keep your feet dry (see Waterproof Socks, pages 78–79).

A few boots have nonbreathable waterproof liners. These are suitable only for cold, wet conditions, and even then your feet can get quite wet from sweat. I'd avoid these boots.

The Tongue

Sewn-in, gusseted tongues with light padding inside are the most comfortable and water resistant, and they're found on most footwear; the only disadvantage of gusseted tongues is that if you're not wearing gaiters, snow can collect in the gussets and soak into the boots. *Oxford construction* is a better design for snow: two flaps of leather (basically extensions of the upper) fold over the inner tongue, which may or may not be sewn in, often held in place by small hook-and-loop tabs. Some heavier boots achieve the same purpose by a gusseted tongue with another tongue behind it, sewn in only at the base. On high-ankle and stiff leather boots, the tongue may be hinged so it flexes easily.

Lacing

Boots may be laced up using D-rings, hooks, eyelets, webbing, miniature pulleys, and speed lacing (tiny metal tunnels through which the laces can be pulled quickly). D-rings may be plastic and sewn to the upper (the norm on shoes and ultralight boots) or metal and attached to a swivel clip riveted to the upper. The easiest system to use combines two or three rows of D-rings at the bottom of the laces with several rows of hooks or speed lacing at the top. With this system you can open the boot fully at the top yet tighten the laces quickly. This advantage is not trivial when you're trying to don a stiff, half-frozen boot in a small tent while wearing gloves, with a blizzard outside. Boots with D-rings alone involve far more fiddling with the laces and are harder to tighten precisely. Some boots use tiny pulleys instead of D-rings. These make it very easy to adjust the fit evenly across the foot. Whatever the type of lacing, many boots have a locking hook offset at the ankle that holds the lace in place even when it's undone. The offset position allows you to tighten the boot around the instep to stop your foot from slipping.

Old-style eyelets are rare on boots now, though they are still found on some shoes. Although they are the most awkward system to use, eyelets are the least susceptible to breakage. Shoes often have webbing loops for laces, and these are starting to appear on boots.

My current winter boots (5-pound high-topped leather monsters, but good with crampons) have four rows of speed lacing, one set of metal D-rings, one set of offset webbing loops, and two rows of hooks. My lightweight hikers (2 pounds, 2 ounces, leather) have two rows of speed lacing, offset locking hooks, and two rows of hooks. And my trail shoes (1 pound, 11 ounces, mostly mesh with synthetic leather reinforcements) have one speed-lacing tunnel, a pair of synthetic leather loops, and three rows of speed lacing. The single lacing tunnel allows the lower lacing to run asymmetrically across the foot, following the flex line, rather than straight across, a sensible innovation first introduced by Garmont. All these lacing methods work well, enabling me to lace the boots quickly and adjust the tension so the footwear fits snugly.

Laces are usually made from braided nylon, which rarely breaks, though it may wear through from abrasion after much use. Round laces seem to last longer than flat ones, though not by much. I used to carry spare laces, but I gave it up long ago; it's been years since I had a lace snap, even on long walks. If one ever does, I'll replace it with a length of the nylon cord I always carry.

Whatever the type of lacing system, footwear must be laced properly if it is to support your feet. The laces should hold the footwear snugly around the forefoot but not be too tight across the instep, which can hinder the forward flex of the ankle. Loose laces allow the feet to move in the footwear; too-tight laces are painful.

Scree Collars

Many boots have one or more rolls of foam-padded soft leather or synthetic material at the cuff to keep out stones, grass seeds, mud, and other debris, but for this to work well the boots have to be laced up so tightly that they restrict ankle movement. The collars themselves don't seem to cause any problems, so their presence or absence can be ignored when choosing a boot.

Seams

Conventional wisdom says the fewer seams, the better, because seams may admit water and can abrade, allowing the boot to disintegrate; thus one-piece leather boots with seams only at the heel and around the tongue should prove the most durable and water resistant.

I agree. Having used quite a few pairs of shoes and boots made from several pieces of stitched fabric and leather, I've found their life expectancy limited by how long the seams remained intact. Side seams usually split first. (This can be postponed, but not prevented, by coating them heavily with a seam sealer or quick-setting flexible epoxy, which also decreases the likelihood of leaks.)

I don't rely solely on one-piece leather construction for footwear, however, as it's usually found only in medium to heavy footwear. But for long treks in cold, wet conditions, I still prefer one-piece leather boots. It's a difficult trade-off. I learned this the hard way. Walking the length of the Canadian Rockies, I used two pairs of sectional leather boots from different makers; they both split at the side seams after about 750 miles. I guessed that only a one-piece leather boot would have lasted the whole walk, so two years later, when I set off on a thousand-mile walk across the Yukon Territory, I wore one-piece boots. They lasted the whole trip.

However, it's debatable whether you should wear just one pair of boots or shoes for an entire long-distance hike. I now think you should change footwear after a while because the internal structure can begin to break down and the cushioning in the sole can compact. This is especially so with midsoles made from Evazote (EVA), a closed-cell foam, and similar materials. Heavier boots are generally more durable, but even they will change shape eventually and may no longer fit so well.

Removable Inserts

Most boots and shoes have a removable foam insert, sometimes incorrectly called a footbed or an insole. Some are made from dual-density foam or have pads of shock-absorbing material built into the heel and forefoot for cushioning. Thicker inserts made from shock-absorbing materials such as Sorbothane are said to improve cushioning. Some of these inserts are relatively heavy, adding up to 5 ounces to the weight of footwear, and they may also be hot in warm weather. I used to use such inserts but found they didn't last. Since they don't support your foot, the cushioning they give is mostly illusory, as your foot can still flatten out and overpronate. For real support, you need a stabilizing footbed (see Stabilization and Footbeds, pages 49–51).

If your feet tend to swell a lot (as is likely on long-distance walks and in hot weather), removing the inserts will make your footwear roomier. I've often done this toward the end of a long day. Inserts and footbeds get damp from sweat during the day, and moisture can accumulate beneath them, so taking them out each evening to let them and the boots dry is a good idea. Don't put them near a fire or other heat source, though—they melt very easily.

Insoles, Midsoles, and Lasting

The boot sole must support the foot, protect it from shock, and be flexible enough to allow a natural gait, but it doesn't need to be stiff. Extensive hiking over rugged terrain in sandals and flexible trail shoes has convinced me that flexibility is more important.

The upper layer of the sole is the insole, or lasting board, a flat, foot-shaped piece of material. Shoes with this layer are described as being board-lasted because the board is fixed to the last and the shoe built around it. The stiffness of a shoe or boot is in part due to the material the board is made from. A flexible fiberboard insole (which may be made from pressed wood pulp or may be synthetic) is common in running and trail shoes and the lightest boots. In inexpensive footwear, the insoles may be cardboard. (There are reports of cardboard insoles breaking up when wet, though this hasn't happened to any I've used.) Much hiking footwear now has torsionally stiff plastic or nylon insoles graded for flex according to the size of the boot. This means that small boots have the same relative flex as larger boots (other stiffening materials can make small boots too stiff and large ones too bendy). Many manufacturers vary the stiffness of the different insoles—the stiffest material is reserved for mountaineering boots, and the most flexible for what is usually described as "easy trail use" with a light load. You can judge flex by bending the boot: a stiff, hard-to-bend shoe is fine for kicking steps in snow but is tiring for most walking. A flexible shoe makes for easy hiking.

The lightest, most flexible shoes and boots may not have a lasting board at all. Instead, when the insole is removed, a line of stitching will be seen running round the edge of the sole or down the middle. This is known as *sliplasting*, in which the upper is sewn into a sock shape and then slipped onto the last. I prefer this construction for light-weight footwear, since it conforms to the natural shape of the foot and is very flexible. Sliplasted shoes are not usually as stiff as board-lasted ones, though there may be a flexible plate similar to a lasting board between the cushioning midsole and the outsole. Some shoes have *combination lasting* —the front is sliplasted, but there is a half-board in the heel. This gives a flexible forefoot but a more rigid heel.

The traditional sole stiffener is a half- or three-quarter-length steel shank, only half an inch or so wide, placed forward from the heel to give solidity to the rear of the foot as well as lateral stability and support to the arch while allowing the front of the foot to flex when walking. Full-length shanks are for rigid mountaineering boots, not for walking. Some boots combine a steel shank with a graded nylon insole.

Many boots incorporate a midsole of a shock-absorbing material. This is usually EVA in light-weight footwear and heavier but much harder-wearing polyurethane or microporous rubber in heavier boots. These midsoles are often tapered wedges, thickest under the heel. They absorb shock well, and I wouldn't consider footwear without them—the difference they make in how your feet feel at the end of a long day is startling. They are designed to protect against the shock of heel strike—the impact when your heel hits the ground—which jars the knees and lower back as well as the feet. Cushioning also is needed at the ball of the foot, and the best shock-absorbing wedges are quite thick under the forefoot as well as the heel.

Some boots also have a stiffening and support-ive synthetic plate under the cushioning midsole— this is a way to give some stiffness to a sliplasted shoe. Sometimes this plate—which is usually lat-ticelike rather than solid—combines with the shock-absorbing midsole and the rand, cradling the foot and providing cushioning as well as good side-to-side support and stability. Even the heel counter and the toe box may be incorporated into these units.

Outsoles

This is the bit of the boot that determines whether you stay upright or skid all over the place. Once there were only a few outsole patterns, with the Vibram carbon-rubber Roccia and Montagna lug outsoles as the standard tread; now they are legion. Vibram has become a whole extended family of sole patterns in itself, and there are many others (Skywalk is one of the most common). Having tried a wide variety of these, I've concluded that any pattern of studs, bars, or other shapes seems to grip well on most terrain. The key is a pattern that bites into soft ground so that the shoe doesn't slip and a sole made from soft enough rubber that when pressure is applied it grips rock and smooth surfaces by friction. I've had shoes with shiny out-soles that were just too hard to provide much fric-tion; they were dangerous on wet pavement. Once the surface of the lugs had worn away, they gripped better. Note that no rubber sole, whatever the pat-tern or stickiness of the rubber, will grip on hard snow or ice. For that you need metal.

Some footwear uses the "sticky rubber" that

revolutionized rock-climbing footwear. Soles with this material are ideal for scrambling and difficult rocky terrain, but the sticky, soft rubber that grips well on rock and other hard, fairly smooth surfaces doesn't bite into soft ground so well. It's also not very durable. Harder rubbers grip better on mud and wet vegetation and also last longer, so these are used for most boot soles. Some treads combine soft and hard rubber so that the edges grip well on soft ground while the center has good friction. Others are designed with different patterns and rubber densities for downhill braking and traction and uphill traction and push-off. I can't say I can tell any difference between these and traditional soles, but they sound good.

The type of sole footwear has depends on its purpose. Soles with the deepest lugs are found on mountaineering boots, those with the shallowest on sandals and trail running shoes—though some sandals now have surprisingly deep lugs.

There has been some concern about the damage that heavily lugged soles do to soft ground, and some manufacturers have designed soles said to minimize this damage by not collecting debris in the tread. Studded soles seem to work best in this respect, but unless all your walking will be done on gentle trails, grip is the most important quality of outsoles. Grip should not be compromised, especially if you're walking on steep, rugged terrain. Modern soles aren't quite as damaging as traditional ones, since they tend not to have the 90-degree angles at the edges and heels that cut into the ground so deeply. Instead, the edges are rounded and canted.

Many soles are made from a dual-density rubber—a soft upper layer for shock absorption and a hard outer layer for durability—and combine grip with cushioning.

Boot heel designs. Rounded (left) and right-angled (right).

In stiff-soled boots you have to come down steep slopes on your heels, so square-cut heels are best. In flexible footwear you can put your feet flat on the ground so rounded heels are fine.

square heels, stiff boots   round heels, flexible footwear

Heavier outsoles with deeper treads should outlast lighter soles, though it's hard to predict tread life. Wear depends on the ground surface—pavement wears out soles fastest, followed by rocks and scree. On soft forest duff, soles last forever. I have found that on long walks, lightweight soles last 800 to 1,000 miles, while the traditional Vibram Montagna lasts at least 1,250 miles. However, soft EVA midsoles last only about 500 miles (polyurethane lasts longer), so the life of the sole depends on more than the wear of the lugs.

There is little controversy over outsole patterns, but the shape of the heel has generated heated discussions. Indeed, some designs have been blamed for fatal accidents. The debate is over the lack of a *forward heel bar* under the instep, together with a *rounded heel* (derived from running shoe outsoles) and how these features perform when descending steep slopes, especially wet, grassy ones. Traditional soles have a deep bar at the front of the heel and a right-angled rear edge, which their proponents say make descents safe. Rounded heel designs, they say, don't allow you to dig in the back of the heel for grip or use the front bar to halt slips; instead, the sloping heel makes slipping more likely. To overcome these criticisms, some soles have deep serrations on the sloping heels and forward edges.

After experimenting with different outsoles and observing other hikers, I've concluded that it all depends on how you walk downhill. If you use the back or sides of the heel for support, you're more likely to slip in a boot with a smooth, sloping heel than in one with a serrated or square-cut edge. If you descend as I do, however, with your feet flat on the ground, pointing downhill, and your weight over your feet, heel design is irrelevant. I've descended long, steep slopes covered with slippery vegetation in smooth, sloping-heel footwear without slipping or feeling insecure. I've noticed too that many people who slip while descending steep slopes keep their boots angled *across* the slope and descend using the edges of the sole, without much contact with the ground. For this a stiff boot with a right-angled heel works best. Of course, if you descend hills flat-footed, you need fairly flexible footwear.

Rounded heels are said to minimize heel strike, because they allow a gradual roll from the heel to the sole instead of the jarring impact when the edge of a square-cut heel hits the ground, but I haven't noticed any difference in practice. A shock-absorbing midsole seems far more important for reducing heel-strike injury.

Rands

The most likely place for water to penetrate a boot is where the sole and the upper meet. Some boots have a rubber *rand* running around this joint, while others have just toe or toe and heel rands, or bumpers. Rands seal the joint against water and also protect the lower edge of the uppers from scuffs and scratches.

Stitching versus Bonding

Joining the soles to the uppers is a critical part of footwear manufacture. If that connection fails, the shoe or boot will fall apart. Stitching used to be the only way of holding footwear together but is now used mainly in leather boots made for mountaineering or Nordic ski touring rather than for walking. The most common stitched construction is the *Norwegian welt*, sometimes called *stitchdown construction*, in which the upper is turned out from the boot, then sewn to a leather midsole with two or three rows of stitching. These stitches are visible and exposed, but they can be protected by daubing them with sealant.

Currently, on most footwear the uppers are *heat bonded* (glued at high temperatures) or cemented to the sole. (Some are also *Blake* or *Littleway stitched*, which means the uppers are turned in and stitched to a midsole, to which the outsole is cemented.) Unlike the Norwegian welt, the quality of these construction methods cannot be checked. A bonded sole has failed me only once, many years ago. On that occasion, the sole started to peel away from the boot at the toe after only 250 miles. I was on a long trek and far from a repair shop, so I patched the boots with glue from my repair kit almost every night and nursed them through another 500 miles. I wouldn't like to repeat the experience.

FOOTWEAR MODELS AND CHOICES

Because fit is so crucial, I'm reluctant to recommend any specific models. I'm often asked to do so, though, so here are some hints. Over the years I've happily worn footwear from Adidas, Asolo, Bite, Brasher, Five Ten, Garmont, Hi-Tec, Lowa, Merrell, Montrail, Nike ACG, Raichle, Rockport, Salomon, Scarpa, Teva, The North Face, Vasque, and Zamberlan. That's a lot of boots, shoes, and sandals. Most of the specific models I've used are no longer available. Well-recommended brands I've never tried include Alico, Birkenstock, Boreal, Chaco, Danner, Dunham, Gronell, Kayland, La Sportiva, Limmer, Technica, and Timberland.

Of the footwear I've tried most recently and that therefore hadn't disappeared when I wrote this, here are my current favorites, described as examples rather than recommendations. Remember: my ideal shoe might be your worst nightmare.

Sandals

I've almost worn out a pair of Merrell Onos, which have a synthetic leather upper lined with stretchy neoprene and Spandex. They fasten with adjustable clip buckles. The rear section is stiffened at each side for support. The molded EVA footframe is soft and cushioning and shaped to support the foot. It has an antimicrobial treatment too, which works well, as I found after a sweaty nine-day hike. The tread is reasonably deep and made from sticky rubber. They weigh 27 ounces (all weights are for a pair of men's size 9½). I've hiked many miles in these sandals and found them supportive and comfortable, with a good grip on just about any terrain. But the Onos have been supplanted in my affections by Teva Wraptor 2s, the first sandal I've tried that holds the foot in place as well as the best lightweight shoes and boots. This is achieved by an ingenious design, a strap that runs across the instep, through the sole, and then back across the instep, completely encircling the foot. Tightening this strap pulls the sandal around the arch, heel, and instep for a very secure fit. Combined with the soft, deep footshaped top sole, this strap also helps prevent overpronation. The straps are padded nubuck, fastened at the forefoot, instep, and heel with Velcro. There's a dual-density EVA midsole and a deep tread on the outsole. They weigh 2 pounds, slightly on the heavy side for sandals but worth it for the support they give. Most recently I've been wearing Bite X-Tracs, which have a thick polyurethane footbed that can be replaced with Superfeet or other stabilizing footbeds. These have leather uppers with neoprene linings, a cushioning midsole, and an arch shank, and they weigh 29 ounces (without footbeds). The sole is torsionally flexible and quite wide, and the tread isn't very deep, so while they're

Bite sandal with Superfeet footbed fitted. The footbeds stabilize the feet and minimize overpronation.

fine on good trails, these sandals aren't that good on rough and steep terrain. Being able to fit Superfeet into sandals is a great idea, though, and I hope that sandals more suited to rough terrain will appear with this feature.

Trail Shoes

For low-cut shoes I like the sliplasted Salomon XA Pros, which are quite light at 27 ounces yet stable and well cushioned. They look like standard running shoes rather than trail shoes. I first tried these on a short adventure race and was impressed that after three hours or so of running and cycling on rough, steep terrain in very hot weather, my feet felt fine. The shoes are made from mesh backed with thin foam (which makes them quick drying and very breathable, though not at all water resistant), with synthetic leather reinforcements. There's a dual-density EVA midsole for shock absorption and an outsole made from three hardnesses of rubber. A synthetic plate between the midsole and the outsole gives lateral stiffness to the rear of the shoe while allowing the forefoot to flex easily. The laces are made of thin Kevlar with a cord lock at the top and speed-lacing hooks. One yank and they're tight, no knots required. They can't slip or come undone, either. The lower hooks are offset, so the shoes flex with the foot. I'd wear the XA Pros more often, except that in the weather for which they're most appropriate, I tend to choose sandals.

I've also been impressed with the sliplasted Blaze Low from The North Face, a suede-fabric shoe with a molded EVA midsole and a plastic plate for torsional stiffness. The shoes breathe well and dry fast, but the mesh means they're not very water resistant. The excellent tread has studs in the center, which help them grip on wet grass, and lugs round the edges. The cushioning is particularly good; thicker and softer than on most footwear. These shoes are excellent for long distances, and for hard terrain that pounds your feet. The heel counter is firm and the torsional stiffness means the shoes don't twist sideways much on rough terrain. Soft forward flex makes them very comfortable. Lacing is with eyelets and webbing loops. They weigh 29 ounces.

*My favorite lightweight leather boot,
the Hi-Tec Sierra V-Lite.*

Lightweight Boots

In theory, lightweight boots are my favorites, but I don't seem to wear them much these days, preferring trail shoes or sandals when there's no snow and slightly heavier boots when there is. Of the pairs I've tried in recent years, I like the Hi-Tec Sierra V-Lite Leather. These are made from nubuck leather with a synthetic CoolMax wicking lining. There's a thermoplastic lasting board for torsional stiffness and an EVA midsole for good cushioning. Lacing is with four sets of tunnels and two sets of hooks. They weigh just 34 ounces, very light for leather boots. Heel to toe the boots are very flexible but on rough, steep terrain these boots give me good support due to the torsional stiffness. On one occasion I descended 3,000 feet off trail on frozen turf, rock, scree, tussocks, and wet grass with no problem. I was surprised at how good the water resistance was for such light boots. They do leak eventually but drying time is fast. Overall these feel more like trail shoes than heavier boots, with the addition of a high ankle.

Midweight Boots

Montrail's 3-pound, 5-ounce Cristallo is a high-quality boot that does all that's required without any bells and whistles. The Cristallo is made from nubuck with a synthetic lining. The boots have a graded nylon insole with a half-length steel shank, microporous rubber midsole, and Vibram outsole. Torsionally they are quite stiff because of the shank, but they flex well at the forefoot. They have a fairly low volume, like my feet. I did have to stretch them slightly at the toes, however. The 3-pound, 10-ounce Scarpa Delta M3 is a similar boot, again made from nubuck with a synthetic lining. The leather is treated with silicone and oil and has proved very water resistant. There's a Vibram sole with an EVA shock-absorbing insert in the heel plus a polyurethane midsole. As with the Cristallos, I had to stretch them at the toes to get a good fit.

I wouldn't choose either of these boots for trail hikes in summer. They're too stiff, warm, and heavy. I wear them for mountain hiking when there's snow and I think I may need to use crampons or for off-trail hiking in steep, rugged, rocky terrain where I want some protection for my feet.

Heavyweight Boots

This is my least favorite category; I rarely wear boots this stiff and heavy. But I have been pleasantly surprised by the relative comfort of Scarpa Mantas. These 4-pound, 6-ounce rigid-soled boots have a rocker sole, a rigid nylon midsole with a steel insert, polyurethane cushioning, speed lacing, and a well-fitting, padded upper that makes them quite bearable, though I wouldn't want to do a long trail hike in them. However, if there's much hard snow and ice around and crampons are needed most of the time, they're my first choice. The uppers are made from rough-out water-resistant leather, and the sole is a deep-cleated Vibram M4 Tech with grooves at the toe and heel so clip crampons can be fitted. The polyurethane cushioning takes some of the sting out of rocks and hard surfaces, and the slight rocker in the sole makes walking on the flat easier than with a flat-soled boot. Although the ankles are held firmly in place, they can flex for-

A midweight leather boot (Montrail Cristallo).

ward thanks to a cutaway section below the top two lace clips, which also makes walking on the flat relatively comfortable. The overall quality of the boots is superb.

CARE OF FOOTWEAR

Waterproofing and Sealing

Although most footwear is fairly tough, it needs proper care to ensure a long life and good performance. This care can start before you wear the boots. Sealing any exposed stitching to protect it from abrasion will increase durability and make the seams waterproof. Urethane sealers like McNett Seam Grip work well, as do products specially designed for this use, like Aquaseal Stitch Guard. Some sealants come with an applicator; others are best applied with a syringe. Stitching should be sealed *before* you wear or wax the footwear so that the sealant has a clean, dry surface to stick to. I always used to seal the welts of my leather Nordic ski boots so that water didn't wick in through the stitching when the boots flexed. My plastic tele-

A winter-weight boot (Garmont Pinnacle).

mark boots don't have stitching, and I haven't bothered sealing the seams of other footwear.

Muddy, dirty boots need washing; if mud dries on the uppers, especially if they're leather, they can harden and crack. A soft brush (I use an old toothbrush) helps remove mud from seams, stitching, and tongue gussets, though you should be careful not to scratch leather. I find cold tap water adequate for cleaning hiking footwear, and I don't use soap. I'm not bothered if footwear is stained or discolored; indeed, this can add character. But if ingrained dirt is particularly stubborn or you want to remove any stains, there are specific cleaning products—Nikwax Cleaning Gel, Granger's New Technology Footwear Cleaner, and Aquaseal All-Purpose Footwear Cleaner. The first two have easy-to-use sponge applicators. You just rub them over the boots, then rinse off the foam, scrubbing with a soft nylon brush if necessary. A sink is the best place to do this.

The insides of boots can get dirty too, making them smelly and less breathable, so sweaty socks are more likely. In boots with waterproof membranes, tiny specks of grit may work their way through the lining and cut the membrane so it leaks. Just a wipe with a clean, damp cloth may be enough cleaning—it's all I ever do. However, Nikwax suggests filling boots with water and leaving them to soak overnight before emptying them out and rinsing them.

Excessive heat is very likely to make leather harden and split and may melt the glues that hold footwear together. Wet footwear should never be dried in a hot place such as next to a car heater, a house radiator, or a campfire. Leather should never become too hot to touch. Even midday sunshine can be too warm, and if you stay in a mountain hut or hostel with a drying room, you should keep your footwear out of there. Footwear should be left in a cool, dry place to dry slowly, with the

Water-based footwear products are easy to apply and produce no pollution, since they contain no solvents.

insoles removed and the tongues fully open. If shoes are really soaked, stuffing them with newspaper will help them dry. Replace the paper when it gets really wet. Fabric-leather shoes without internal padding dry quickly, but foam-lined leather boots can take a long time—at least several days for medium-weight ones.

Drying footwear can be a problem on long hikes, when it is tempting to dry sodden boots by a fire. I'm occasionally guilty of this. The second half of a Canadian Rockies walk was mostly cross-country in wet terrain, and my lightweight leather boots were soaked by the end of most days. I often helped them dry out by standing them a little too close to my campfire. I had to wear boots with cracked uppers and peeling soles for the last few snowy weeks of the hike.

When wet footwear has dried, it needs to be treated to restore suppleness and water repellency. Bootmakers recommend various products for this, sometimes proprietary ones. It isn't necessary to stick to the treatment specified. All footwear can be treated, including that with waterproof-breathable linings. Indeed, because such linings work well only if the outer of the boot is breathable, it is important that the water repellency of the outer is maintained. If it fails and the outer soaks up moisture, breathability will be impaired. Remove the laces and open the tongue fully so you don't miss any areas. The base of the tongue is a key leak point, so make sure you treat this area.

Once it's no longer part of a living animal, leather isn't waterproof. It's treated with waterproofing compounds during tanning, but this treatment will wear off after a few hikes, especially in wet conditions. Proper treatment increases water repellency and prolongs life by keeping leather footwear supple. What constitutes proper treatment depends in part on the type of leather. Virtually all leathers are now chemically treated

rather than oil tanned, and they must be dressed with wax or the new water-based treatments rather than oil. Traditional dressings like neat's-foot oil (made by boiling down cattle feet and shinbones) or mink oil can oversoften leather; I'd use them only for leather that has dried out and hardened. Even then I'd rather use a modern softening product like Nikwax Conditioner for Leather. Makers sometimes suggest not treating specially tanned waterproof leathers until they are scuffed, since they won't absorb proofing before then. Others say all leather should be treated before the first use. I have found that new boots won't absorb much treatment, so I don't bother applying any until the leather loses the initial sheen or water starts to soak into it rather than bead up.

The traditional way to proof leather boots is to apply a soft wax with a cloth or your fingers. Granger's G-Wax, Sno-Seal, and Biwell Classic are made from beeswax, while Nikwax Paste Wax is a synthetic mineral wax and Aquaseal Leather Waterproofing is silicone based. These waxes work best when applied to warm, dry leather and left to soak in overnight. Any residue visible on the surface should be wiped off. Several thin coats are more effective than one thick one. Too much can soften the leather anyway, so it's best not to slop the stuff on in dollops. Also, a thick layer of wax can prevent your boots from breathing and lead to sweaty feet. There is a trade-off between the amount of wax you apply, the degree of water resistance obtained, and the breathability of your boots. Several layers of wax will mean better and longer-lasting water resistance but less breathability. In hot weather I'd go easy on the wax, or your feet will get wetter from sweat than from the occasional summer shower. Even for desert hiking I still treat leather, though, to prevent it from drying out and cracking.

There's something sensuous about applying wax to warm leather with your fingers (I prefer fingers to a cloth because their heat helps soften the wax), but I rarely do this anymore because there are much better water-based products. It may seem odd that a waterproofing product's main ingredient is water, but it does work. Water-based treatments were first developed by Nikwax, which makes the widest range, and you can now get them from Granger's too. Others will follow, I'm sure. Nikwax water-based treatments consist of polymers made from EVA (the same material used for cushioning midsoles) and mineral wax. The active ingredients take the form of an emulsion—droplets of oil suspended in water. Nikwax treatments coat the fibers of leather and fabric with flexible water-repellent molecules. These molecules will stick only to fibers that aren't already water repellent, so you can't apply too much. The water soaks into areas that aren't water repellent, taking the active ingredients with it. Water-based treatments can be applied to wet leather; indeed, Nikwax says it's best to do so, since the active ingredients are then drawn into those areas that need them most. It's certainly convenient not to have to dry footwear before treating it. Water-based treatments don't block the spaces between the fibers, so footwear remains breathable. And because they can flex, they don't wear off quickly. Water-based products have other advantages. Nikwax says its products can deliver up to five times as many active ingredients per fluid ounce as solvent-based treatments. Water-based products are also environmentally friendly; they contain no petroleum solvents or propellant gases, which contribute to global warming and to the thinning of the ozone layer. The absence of solvents also means water-based products are non-flammable and don't give off noxious fumes, so they are safe to use indoors.

Nikwax Aqueous Wax, designed for use on smooth leather, has been my first choice for leather footwear for many years. It lasts longer than other treatments, doesn't soften leather, and is quick and easy to use. The treatment comes in black and brown as well as neutral if you want to restore color to your scuffed boot toes. Aqueous Wax will work on nubuck or suede, but these will look like smooth leather afterward. If you want to keep the rough texture, use Nikwax Nubuck and Suede Waterproofing. Or you can use a brush to raise the surface of the leather and return it to its original look, though I've never done this.

Granger's has developed its own water-based products, using fluorochemicals as the active ingredient, such as the New Technology (NT) Footwear Protector for all types of footwear and the NT Footwear Conditioner for smooth leather. My brief trials with these products suggest they work all right.

Fabric-leather footwear has poor water resistance unless there is a waterproof-breathable lining. It can be treated to keep the material supple and to prevent it from soaking up too much moisture, but no amount of proofing will make such footwear waterproof. The best treatment I've found is Nikwax Fabric and Leather Footwear Proofing, another water-based product. Another option is the silicone-based Biwell Trekking, which comes in a tube and can be applied with fingers or a cloth. On long walks I don't treat such footwear and have found it dries fairly quickly in warm weather, even when it hasn't been treated for weeks.

Most water-based treatments come with sponge applicators that make them very easy to use. They're also fine to use on footwear with waterproof-breathable linings.

There are a number of aerosol footwear treatments. I don't like them, though they seem effective when used correctly. I dislike the difficulty and hazards involved in using them, and the solvents usually used produce greenhouse gases. The propellants are flammable and poisonous too. As it says on one container: "Extremely flammable. Keep away from sources of ignition. Do not breathe spray. Avoid contact with skin and eyes. Use only in well-ventilated areas." I'd rather not use products hedged about with such warnings when far less hazardous alternatives work at least as well. (An additional warning is "Do not use in the same vicinity as pet birds," since birds are especially sensitive to airborne contaminants. I would not use them around other pets either.) Sprays are best used outside or somewhere with very good ventilation, which isn't appealing when it's cold and wet and may be very difficult when it's windy. I can apply water-based treatments in the warmth of my kitchen.

Pump-bottle sprays like Tectron Outdoor Leather Guard and Liquid Aquaseal are better than aerosols, but I'd still rather use water-based rub-on treatments.

Whatever treatment you use, polishing or buffing the leather produces a hard finish or shine that is more water repellent than a matte finish.

Repair

On lightweight boots the uppers often wear out at about the same time as the soles, so resoling is hardly worthwhile. Top-quality lightweights in good condition can be worth repairing, however; I have had trail shoes successfully resoled. Medium-weight boots should last the life of at least two soles, heavyweights even more (I had a pair that were on their fourth soles when I retired them). The key is to have boots resoled before the midsole needs replacing, which can be very expensive. However, EVA midsoles usually need replacing

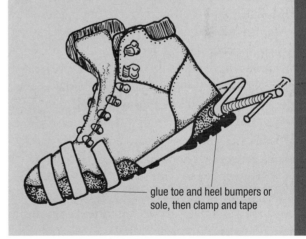

REGLUING A SOLE AT HOME

- Regluing any major boot part is essentially a surgical procedure—cleaning and preparing are key. Wash the boot with soap and water. Once it is thoroughly dry, lightly sand the gluing surfaces. Wipe down the clean, dry boot thoroughly with denatured alcohol before gluing.
- Stuff the boot with paper to provide structure.
- Use contact cement (Barge brand is the most popular footwear adhesive.) Spread a thin layer of adhesive on each prepared surface and let them rest until almost dry.
- Align and mate the parts carefully—you only get *one* chance with contact cement.
- Clamp the parts together with a C-clamp or wrap tightly with strong tape, and let dry. Secure clamping is important to the success and life of your repair.
- Finally, seal the joint with seam sealer.

glue toe and heel bumpers or sole, then clamp and tape

along with the soles, since they compress rather quickly (after 500 miles or so in my experience). For your own safety, don't let outsoles wear down too much.

Many outdoor stores accept boots for repair and send them to either a local cobbler or a national repair store. If you can't find a repair service, ask the manufacturer for advice.

Small holes or severe abrasions can be patched with a urethane seam sealant or a product like McNett Freesole Urethane Formula Shoe Repair. The latter can also be used for reattaching soles that are peeling away, as can Barge Cement. In the backcountry this is not easy to do, since you need some way of holding the sole and boot tightly together while the adhesive dries. Wrapping them with duct tape is probably the easiest way to do this. Don't expect such a repair to last long—just hope it gets you to the nearest trailhead. Duct tape and adhesive can also be used to patch torn seams, though again, such repairs don't usually last long.

FOOT CARE

Keeping your feet in good condition is a prerequisite to pain-free hiking. Toenails should be cut short and square; long nails can bruise, cut into the toes on either side, and inflict pain during descents. When possible, dry wet feet to avoid softening the skin too much. Some people try to harden their skin both before and during a trip with rubbing alcohol. I've never tried this, but I do go barefoot around the house and outside whenever I can. By going barefoot and wearing sandals as often as possible, I usually manage to keep my feet reasonably tough.

Blisters are the bane of many hikers, but too few take preventive measures. The moment you feel a hot or sore spot, stop and attend to it, covering the affected area with a dressing to prevent further rubbing. This may prevent a blister from appearing. This is easy to preach but hard to practice. All too often I ignore warning signs, telling myself that I'll have a look when I next stop. When I do, I invariably find a plump blister.

Blister remedies are legion. What is common to

all is that the blister must be covered to prevent infection and cushioned against further rubbing. You can cover a blister with ordinary adhesive tape, moleskin, micropore tape, or even duct tape, but I have found the most effective to be cushioning and friction-resistant dressings such as Spenco 2nd Skin Blister Pads, Spyroflex, and Compeed. These are easier to use than the original 2nd Skin, which had to be taped in place; they come with a thin sticky backing and border and so can be applied just like an ordinary Band-Aid. I carry up to half a dozen of these dressings, depending on the length of the hike.

Some experts advise against lancing a blister before covering it, but if you continue to walk after a blister forms, as you probably will, you need to remove the fluid built up inside to minimize the pain. To do this I sterilize a needle in a match flame, pierce the blister at one edge, then roll the needle over the blister until all the fluid drains out. A piece of toilet tissue can be used to absorb the fluid and wipe the area dry. Large blisters may need several holes to expel all the fluid. I know from painful experience that, however long it takes, the blister must be fully drained before being dressed, or your first steps will hurt so much you'll have to stop again. Antiseptic wipes can be used to clean the area, though gel dressings do this quite well.

Friction causes blisters, so try to find and remove the cause, which may be a tiny speck of grit, a rough sock seam, or more commonly, your foot moving in the boot and rubbing against it. Sometimes the cause isn't obvious, and you just have to hope that covering the blister will solve the problem. Mysteriously, footwear that has never given problems before can cause a blister one day yet be fine again on future trips. However, I would suspect footwear that repeatedly causes sore spots. Either it doesn't fit properly or something inside needs smoothing.

Treating blisters. Wash the area and treat it with antiseptic (1). Insert a sterile needle into the base or side of the blister (2). (If you don't have a sterile needle in your first-aid kit, you can sterilize a sewing needle by holding it in a match or lighter flame.) Roll the needle over the blister so all the liquid is squeezed out, wiping it up with a piece of tissue (3). (Squeeze out every drop, or the blister will be very painful when you start walking again.) If the blister is very large or under hard skin, you might need several needle holes. Once you've drained the blister, treat it with antiseptic (4), being careful not to break or move the loose skin covering it, as this protects the area while new skin forms. Cover the blister with a gel that will cushion and help heal the blister, such as 2nd Skin Blister Pads or Compeed (5).

I like to remove my footwear and socks several times during the day, weather permitting, to let my feet cool down and air. Pouring cold water over them provides even more relief on really hot days. Some people also apply foot powder to help keep their feet dry, but I've never found that powder makes a difference.

SOCKS

Buying whatever socks the store has on hand or making do with whatever is in your sock drawer is not the best way to treat your feet. I used to do that until I realized that socks do affect how your feet feel and deserve more careful consideration. Socks cushion feet, reduce abrasion from your footwear, wick away moisture, and keep feet at the right temperature. Good socks should fit snugly and stay in place. Poorly fitting socks, or socks with rough seams, can rub and cause blisters. Socks that are too thick can make your feet sweat; socks that are too thin let them get cold. People are different. Some have cold, clammy feet that need plenty of insulation even in warm weather. Others, like me, have warm feet that overheat easily.

On a backpacking trip you may not be able to wash your socks every day (or want to even if you can); you may end up wearing one pair of socks for days, even weeks, at a time, with just an occasional quick rinse in cold water to freshen them up. After a few days' constant wear, many socks mat down into a hard, sweaty mass, and rinsing them out in cold water doesn't do much to restore their fluffiness. Even repeated machine washings won't revive some types. Such socks provide little insulation or comfort underfoot—I relegate them to the spares box, which is crammed with dozens of pairs of test socks that may have had only two weeks or less of use.

For many years I wore traditional flat-knit ragg socks (ragg is a three-ply wool yarn); I found them vastly superior to the first terry-loop socks, which matted down very quickly. The more open structure of the ragg socks resisted matting better; when rinsed in cold water, they're almost as good as new. However, new construction methods and improved materials mean that the best terry-loop socks don't mat down fast and do fluff up when rinsed. Since they're far more comfortable than ragg socks, they're now my first choice. Ragg socks are very durable, though, and last longer than all but the best terry-loop socks. Companies like Fox River still make ragg wool socks.

Materials

Wool became the standard material for socks because wool socks cushion your feet, keep them warm in winter yet cool in summer, absorb and wick away sweat, and retain warmth when wet. Wool isn't very abrasion-resistant, however, so nylon is often added as reinforcement at the heel and toe. Wool has a natural crimp that makes it very springy, trapping air in its millions of tiny coils, so it's a good insulator. Because these coils stretch out when wool is stretched but spring back into shape once the pressure is off, wool holds its shape well.

Feet can give off a great deal of moisture, up to a pint in twelve hours when you're hiking. This liquid has to go somewhere, and only some of it can escape through your footwear. Wool socks will absorb this moisture until it can pass through your footwear or go out at the ankles. Good-quality wool also keeps its shape when damp. Socks that sag and wrinkle when wet feel uncomfortable and can cause blisters.

Synthetic socks, made from acrylic (Lumiza, Duraspun, Ginny Microfiber), polyester (CoolMax, Capilene, Hollofil, Dacron, Thermolite), polypropylene, and nylon are supposed to wick moisture faster than wool and dry more quickly. Certainly if you take a synthetic sock and drip water on it, the water will rapidly pass through the fabric whereas wool would absorb it. This property is fine when the socks are worn with sandals or very breathable shoes, but with most footwear the moisture still can't escape, so it stays on the sock's surface, making it feel clammy and sticky. Whereas wool can absorb up to 30 percent of its own weight in moisture and still feel dry and warm, nonabsorbent synthetics feel damp when only a small amount of moisture is present. I find synthetic socks don't feel as warm as wool when damp or keep my feet as comfortable over a wide range of temperatures. Synthetics mat down more quickly than wool, too, and don't wash as well in cold water. They also stink quickly, though silver fibers like X-Static, found in many socks, do reduce this noticeably. Wool is naturally odor resistant. After a week or so of wear there is a faint smell of wet sheep, but that's about it. I used to wear thin synthetic socks in hot weather because they seemed drier and cooler than thicker wool ones even though they needed rinsing out just about every day. But now I wear wool year-round—lighter socks in summer, heavier ones in winter.

The quality of the wool makes a huge difference,

and the best is merino wool, used by just about all the major wool sock makers in their top-end models. Merino has longer, softer, and finer fibers than other wool, making it more comfortable and more durable. Wool with thicker and coarser fibers can feel prickly or itchy next to the skin; merino wool just feels luxurious. It also fluffs up well when washed in cold water and holds its shape longer than other wool. Its durability is good too. And finally, merino wool socks smell less than any other wool socks I've tried, something I first discovered when a companion threw a pair he'd been wearing for a week at me saying, "Smell those!" I did, and they didn't, at least not much. Most merino wool comes from Australia and New Zealand, where merino sheep were brought from Spain in the late eighteenth century.

Blends of wool and various synthetics such as Isolwool, a fifty-fifty merino wool–polypropylene mix used by Fox River, are common and can work well. I find ones with at least 50 percent wool best. A few cold-weather socks are made with Outlast, an unusual material containing a substance that is supposed to regulate the temperature of your feet by absorbing heat when you are working hard and producing lots of it, then releasing it when you start to cool down. The theory sounds great, but I've tried socks with Outlast, and I can't tell any difference from socks without it. To test this I several times wore an Outlast sock on one foot and an ordinary sock on the other. By the end of a hike I couldn't tell which was which. However, others have reported that Outlast works for them.

Avoid cotton in socks; it soaks up sweat and then feels cold and clammy and takes a long time to dry. When wet it loses its shape and easily wrinkles and bunches up under the foot, which is uncomfortable and can cause blisters. Silk is a different matter. It absorbs moisture while staying warm and holds its shape pretty well. It's found in thin liner socks and as a component of cold-weather socks.

Whatever the material, sweat-soaked socks should be changed for dry ones or your feet will soften and are more likely to blister. If you have very sweaty feet you may need to change your socks once or twice a day, especially in hot weather. You can hang damp socks on your pack to dry.

Construction

How socks are made affects their comfort, performance, and durability. Densely knitted socks, with a high number of stitches per square inch, cushion better, feel more comfortable against the skin, and resist matting better than socks with fewer stitches per inch, which can feel rough against the skin. Terry loops on the inside, especially underfoot, are warmer and more comfortable than flat knits. The density of the terry loops makes a difference. Low-density loops will quickly collapse and become matted; high-density loops resist crushing, cushion more, and hold their shape better. For cold weather, terry loops throughout are worth having. In warmer weather, a flat knit over the foot and rib knit on the legs is cooler, with terry loops underfoot for cushioning. Some socks have different densities of material at different points for more cushioning or warmth. These look very complex and high-tech, but I haven't found that they feel any different from socks without them. Some socks have an elasticized section over the instep, which helps with the fit, though it isn't essential. Elastic fibers in the leg or at the top of the sock are more important, since they keep the legs from sagging and slipping down. Ribbed legs, with alternating thin and thick sections, also help socks stay up. Good socks are shaped at the heel for a good fit with no loose fabric. The best have stitching here in the shape of a Y rather than in a straight line, to conform better to the shape of your heel. Tube socks tend to have loose material around the heel that can slip and bunch up under your foot. They're best avoided.

Rough and bulky seams can rub, especially at the toe. The seam should be flat and smooth and set back from the toes, making it more comfortable and more durable. When buying new socks, you can turn them inside out to check the seams. You can also wear them that way if a seam does rub.

For a while I was impressed with double-layer socks. These usually are made from synthetics, though some have a wool content. They're actually two thin socks attached at the toe and ankle and can be awkward to put on if the layers become twisted, but once on they are comfortable, warm, and quick drying. I used to wear

them in shoes and lightweight boots when it was too cool for really thin socks. They weigh about 2.5 ounces a pair. But I found that they didn't remain as soft as terry-loop wool socks after repeated washings. Now that you can get lightweight terry-loop socks suitable for warm weather, I wear these rather than double-layer socks.

Choices

Thick wool socks go with boots and cool, wet weather. When wearing shoes rather than boots in warm weather, I prefer lighter, thinner, cooler socks, though still made from wool. Having tried dozens of different socks over the years, I've become a fan of SmartWool socks, since I find

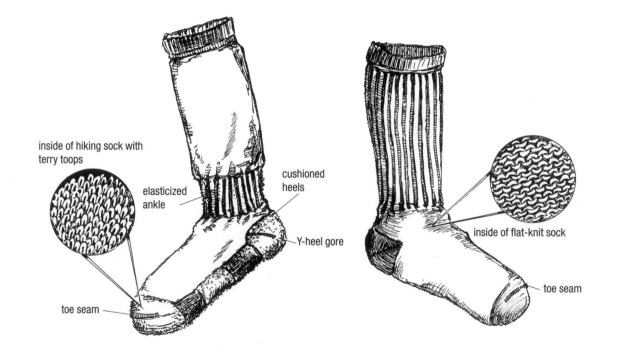

inside of hiking sock with terry toops

elasticized ankle

cushioned heels

Y-heel gore

toe seam

inside of flat-knit sock

toe seam

Terry-loop sock (left) and flat-knit sock (right).

them very comfortable even after many days of wear. In warm weather—expected temperatures above 50°F (20°C)—with light trail shoes, I like the SmartWool Light Hikers, which are 71 percent merino wool, 28 percent nylon, and 1 percent elastic. They have a medium-density terry-loop sole, a flat-knit instep with an elastic section over the arch, and a rib-knit leg. A large pair weighs 3 ounces. In moderate weather—30 to 50°F (0 to 20°C)—the SmartWool Hiking socks are a little warmer. These have a terry-loop foot with medium density on top and high density underfoot separated by a narrow, flat-knit side panel and a rib-knit leg. They're made from 70 percent merino wool, 29 percent nylon, and 1 percent elastic. A large pair weighs 3.5 ounces. I wear them with trail shoes or lightweight boots. If I'm wearing midweight or heavyweight boots, which means there is likely to be snow on the ground and below-freezing temperatures, I wear SmartWool Expedition Trekking socks, which are 77 percent merino wool, 22 percent nylon, and 1 percent elastic. These are terry loop throughout, high density underfoot, and medium density on the top and the leg, with a narrow flat-knit side panel and an elastic arch panel. They are very warm.

I don't wear liners with any of these socks. It seems a waste to me to put a barrier between the soft terry loops and my skin. I've also found that liners need rinsing every day if they are to stay comfortable—particularly synthetic liners. Silk is better and wool is best, but no liners can be worn for many days without being washed. The theory is that liners help reduce friction and remove sweat quickly, but I haven't found any increase in comfort over a single pair of socks, probably because modern socks are soft next to the skin and are efficient at wicking moisture. When socks were made from rough, scratchy wool, liners may have been more necessary. I sometimes carry liners, which

weigh 1 to 2 ounces a pair, to wear with sandals if it's cool. More often I carry the SmartWool Light Hikers. All these socks are crew (midcalf) height. Longer socks are hard to find, as are the knickers they were meant to reach. Socks that reach to or just above the ankle, designed to be worn with sandals or low-cut shoes, are becoming more common. I've tried them but returned to higher ones, because I can turn the cuffs down when they're not needed and pull them up if it gets chilly. They ensure a good overlap between long pants and sock tops, too, cutting out drafts around the ankles.

Although I prefer SmartWool, the company doesn't have an exclusive on good-quality socks. There are many excellent socks today. Other brands I've tried and liked are Bridgedale, Wigwam, Fox River, Thorlo, Rohner, Patagonia, Dahlgren, and X-Socks.

Fit

Whatever type of socks you choose, make sure they fit well. This is difficult to determine in the store because most socks come prepackaged and can't be tried on. Sock sizes bear no relation to shoe sizes, so you'll need to check the chart on the package to find the size that should fit. Nor are sizes standardized between makes—a good reason for sticking to the same brand once you've found some you like that fit well. Sock sizes often cover three or four shoe sizes, so you may find yourself at the junction of two sizes. Most socks, particularly wool ones, tend to stretch over time, so the smaller size is usually the better choice. There are women's socks, with narrower heels, slimmer ankles, and narrower feet than men's or unisex socks, but don't assume they'll fit just because you're female. My partner, Denise Thorn, found one brand's women's socks to be so broad at the toes that they bunched up uncomfortably inside her boots. Other women's socks fit her well, however, though her favorite socks are unisex merino wool.

Before you wear the socks it's worthwhile to check for loose threads, knots, harsh stitching, or bulky seams that might cause blisters and sore spots.

When putting on socks, make sure the heel pocket is in the right place and that the fabric is smooth and not too tight over the toes. There should be no loose fabric anywhere. If there is, the socks don't fit properly. Socks need to fit your footwear as well as your feet. Cramming thick socks into close-fitting boots won't make your feet warmer; they'll just be uncomfortable. Since the insulation will be crushed, your feet could end up colder. Thin socks in a roomy boot will let your feet slide around. When you fit your footwear, you should be wearing the thickness of socks you will always wear with it.

Waterproof Socks

Wet feet aren't a problem when wearing sandals or for short periods in boots and shoes. Lightweight shoes and boots without waterproof-breathable linings dry quickly when wet as long as the air is dry. However, in prolonged wet weather and in damp areas, your footwear can stay wet for days on end. This is unpleasant, especially when it's cold, and can lead to blisters and sore spots as the skin of your feet gets softer and softer. Boots and shoes with waterproof-breathable linings are one answer to this. I've already explained why I don't think it's a good one (see pages 56 and 58). Plastic bags are an emergency solution. I've used these at times, pulling one bag over my bare foot or a liner sock to act as a vapor barrier, then another over a thick sock. It works after a fashion, though it's not particularly comfortable, your feet can get sweaty, and the bags don't last

long. Companies like GoLite, Stephenson's Warmlite, and RBH Designs sell vapor-barrier socks that should last far longer, but except in extreme cold, these can be very hot and sweaty.

Waterproof-breathable socks are much better than waterproof lined boots because you need wear them only when it's wet. They give more protection than boots because they are much higher, some reaching to just below the knee. They're not sweaty either, except in warm weather.

Back in the mid-1990s, seven companies offered these socks in three materials. Now there are just three companies, each using a different material. Gore-Tex is found in Rocky Stretch Gore-Tex Socks, the Triad membrane in Cannondale's Ov'r'sox, and the SealSkinz membrane in the socks of that name. In all of these socks, a waterproof-breathable membrane is sandwiched between thin synthetic layers. (See Chapter 5 for fabric details.)

Years ago I tried some of the early Gore-Tex socks and wasn't impressed with any of them, since they lasted only a couple of weeks and weren't very comfortable. The Rocky socks are an advance on these and should last longer, though I haven't used them myself. I was more impressed with the first SealSkinz socks, and I have continued to use them. The latest ones are much more comfortable than the originals. There are three styles, all with nylon-Lycra outers and CoolMax inners. The All Season Socks and Over-the-Calf Socks are the same except for the height—11 inches for the first, 15 inches for the second. The Waterblocker Socks have a close-fitting seal at the top so, the maker claims, water won't enter even when you wade a stream. The socks are stretchy and quite comfortable against the skin. They're not as soft as wool socks and haven't got the same temperature range (they can be sweaty in hot weather), though they are quite breathable. Although I mostly wear

SealSkinz waterproof-breathable socks.

them for only a few hours at a time, I did once wear a pair for four days on a cold, wet fall hike in the White Mountains of New Hampshire. I was wearing trail shoes that were soaked the whole time, and I was in snow at higher elevations, but the SealSkinz kept my feet warm and dry. They work better than waterproof linings too, since they're closer to the skin, which keeps them warmer, so they transport moisture more efficiently. And if you don't need the socks or your feet start to overheat, you can swap them for an ordinary pair.

I often switch to my SealSkinz socks when I encounter wet ground or it starts to rain hard, then go back to wool ones as soon as it's dry again. If my feet get soaked during a stream crossing or in a swamp, I change the wet socks for waterproof ones and continue with dry feet even though my footwear is soaked. Doing this means I can wear trail shoes and ultralight boots all year round, since I don't have to worry about cold feet because of wet footwear. These socks dramatically extend the range of sandals, too; I find my feet are warmer in sandals and SealSkinz than in wet socks and boots. I now carry SealSkinz socks on any trip where wet weather or wet terrain is likely. Mine weigh 3 ounces. The closest of the current models are the All Season Socks. When I replace mine, it will be with the Waterblockers, so I can don them before fording a stream that would come over their tops.

Caring for Socks

On most trips I carry two or three pairs of socks. Usually I change them every couple of days, though on long trips I have worn a pair for as long as ten days. I like to keep one pair dry for campwear unless I'm carrying booties or fleece socks for that. Clean socks are warmer and more comfortable and wick moisture better than dirty ones. Whenever possible, I rinse socks in water taken from a stream or lake, using a cooking pot as a washbowl (and making sure to rinse it out well afterward). If using a cooking pot doesn't seem attractive, you can put socks in a plastic bag full of water and wash them by shaking the bag. Turning them inside out helps ensure that sweat is removed from the inside so the socks can fluff up again. I don't use soap for washing socks in the backcountry. If you do, make sure you dump the dirty water well away from water sources and rinse the socks well. Washed socks can be hung on a line in camp or just draped over a rock or branch to dry (don't forget them when you break camp, though—something I've done more than once). Thick wool socks take time to dry, so you often need to hang them on the back of your pack the next day to finish drying.

At home, socks should be either hand washed or put through the washing machine's delicate cycle (inside out), then line-dried. Pure soap and plant-based washing products such as those from Ecover and Gaiam's Seventh Generation are less harsh on fabrics than soaps derived from petrochemicals. They're also kinder to the environment. Fabric softeners are good for synthetic socks—you want them as soft as possible. I use them on wool only if the socks have become very matted and don't fluff up after washing. However, the wicking properties of some socks can be affected by fabric softeners, so check the washing instructions before you throw the packaging away. Too much heat can cause socks to shrink, especially those containing polypropylene. Most socks shouldn't be tumble-dried on a hot setting or draped over a hot radiator or near a fire—again, check the instructions.

GAITERS

In deep snow, neither waterproof-breathable lined boots nor waterproof-breathable socks will keep your boots and feet dry and, most important, warm for long. The waterproof socks may keep your feet dry, but your boots will fill with snow and your feet will be cold. Gaiters are a necessity. Some

people like them for keeping out dust and dirt as well. The lightest and simplest of these coverings for the lower leg are short (6 to 8 inches high) and are sometimes called stop tous (stop everything) or *anklets*. These are fine for keeping stones and bits of grass out of your boots and for snow that's only a few inches deep. I've tried a few pairs over the years but have always found even the ones made from uncoated fabric too warm. The most interesting I've seen, though I haven't tried them, are from Outdoor Research. The 4-ounce Flex-Tex Low Gaiters are made from uncoated Spandura (stretch Cordura), while the Terra Gaiters, made from uncoated Supplex nylon, weigh 3 ounces and will fit trail shoes. If I were to wear gaiters in warm weather, this is the type I'd choose.

Gaiters that come to just below the knee are the best choice for deep snow. They come in two types: those that cover only the upper part of the boot, and *supergaiters* that cover the entire boot. Gaiters may have zippers on the back, side, or front. Those with front zippers are easier to put on and let you adjust your laces without removing the gaiters. Those with zippers at the back are hardest to use—I avoid these. Zippers aren't waterproof, so a hook-and-loop (Velcro) flap is needed to keep out moisture. Some models dispense with the zipper and just use Velcro, which makes them very easy to get on and off as long as the Velcro doesn't become clogged with ice or mud. The lower edge of a gaiter may be elasticized or randed so it grips the boot. There may also be an elasticized section around the ankle. A drawcord tightens the gaiter below the knee.

In spite of their benefits, I don't like gaiters and wear them only when the alternative is wet, cold feet, which I like even less. However, when the snow lies deep, I often wear gaiters all day. I used to prefer supergaiters, which grip the lower edge of the boot with a tight-fitting rubber rand, sealing out snow and water. They keep boots dry and unscuffed for days on end. No other gaiters come close in terms of performance. They seem to be disappearing, though, probably because they are heavy and hard to fit and the rands are fragile and expensive to replace. The rise of plastic ski touring and mountaineering boots has probably hastened their demise. Without any conscious decision, I stopped wearing supergaiters and went back to lighter, easier-to-fit standard gaiters, and I guess many others did the same. The supergaiters that do remain tend to be insulated ones designed for extreme cold, like Outdoor Research's X-Gaiters, made from Gore-Tex with foam insulation and weighing 17 ounces a pair. Climb High does make the uninsulated Glacier supergaiters, which weigh 20 ounces.

Standard gaiters come in waterproof-breathable and uncoated fabrics. They have an adjustable cord, strap, or wire that fits under the instep. These straps fray and eventually break, so gaiters with attachment points for replacements are best. I'd avoid gaiters with fancy buckles that work only with the original straps. Gaiters range from 5 to 12 ounces a pair. The heaviest ones, made from fabrics such as Cordura, are the most durable. Since I abandoned supergaiters I've used two types of standard gaiters. Páramo gaiters are made from lined polyester and are extremely breathable (see Chapter 5 for fabric details). They have a front zipper, a stud-closed flap, a replaceable underfoot strap, and a front hook (which fastens to the boot laces to hold the gaiters down) that can be folded out of the way if not needed. I find them very comfortable and warm. They weigh 12 ounces a pair, as do the Mountain Hardwear Ascent Venti-gaiters, made from waterproof-breathable coated nylon with a Velcro-closed side flap and a zipped roll-back panel with mesh beneath it for ventilation. The vent works well, and these are good gaiters for spring conditions. There are plenty of other good gaiters available from companies like Outdoor Research and Black Diamond.

OVERBOOTS

Overboots are an alternative to gaiters if you want total protection for your boots and shoes. Basically they are gaiters with lug soles. Most overboots are insulated and are designed for high-altitude mountaineering and polar expeditions, but NEOS makes a few uninsulated pairs that are useful for backpackers. I have a pair of the Surveyors, which are knee high and have a thick sole with a good grip. They're made from nylon with a front zipper and a strap over the instep. You can wear them over running shoes and tramp around in snow without getting wet or cold feet. They're quite bulky and heavy, though, at 2.6 pounds, so I wouldn't want to carry them in my pack. The sole is soft, too, and wide and bulky to accommodate boots, so they're not very stable or precise on steep or rough terrain. I mostly use them for short hikes around home, but they could be an alternative to mukluks for long trips in the snow or mud.

CAMPWEAR

On most trips I don't bother with spare footwear. In the long-ago days when I hiked in heavy boots, I always carried spare footwear to relieve my hot, sore feet in camp. My morale got such a boost when I donned light, cool sandals or running shoes after a long day that it was well worth the weight of the spare footwear. However, I'm happy to forgo that pleasure in return for not having the initial pain that the heavy boots caused. Now I carry spare footwear only occasionally, usually on trips longer than a few weeks, when a change of hiking footwear can ease leg or foot pains. Light sandals or running shoes make good spare footwear for both hiking and camp use. If you do carry spare footwear for campwear in warm weather, simple sandals are the lightest choice. Basic flip-flops—no more than a slab of foam and a thin strap—weigh only about 3 or 4 ounces. You can make even lighter ones from pieces of closed-cell foam or old footbeds and bits of cord. It's easy; even I can do this. There's a description of how to make a pair on the Trail Quest Web site (trailquest.net), where they are called one ounce camp sandals or, more interesting, gram weenie sandals.

If the weather during a trip is apt to be very cold and snowy and I'm with a group and don't want to spend all evening in the tent, or if I plan to use huts or shelters, I carry insulated *booties*. These are very warm, and the mere thought of them is comforting when your feet are cold and wet, but many are useless on anything except flat ground because of their smooth soles—climbing down a bank to fetch water can seem like a major expedition. Booties come with down and synthetic fill and fleece linings. Although the synthetic and fleece ones are slightly heavier, I prefer them, since I don't have to worry about getting them wet in the snow. There isn't a wide selection, but features vary. If you're going to wander around camp, your booties need a closed-cell foam insole, preferably sewn in, to insulate your feet from the ground. For many years I've used REI Polarguard Booties, which weigh 11.25 ounces in the large size and have pack-cloth soles, closed-cell insoles, nylon outers, a warm polyester-cotton-nylon lining, and a front drawcord. These have been unavailable for quite a few years, but there are several similar ones, such as Campmor's fleece-lined Warm and Cozy Booties with "heavy-duty insulation," water-repellent outers, padded insoles, and no-slip soles, and the Parbat High Mountaineering Polarguard

Booties with fleece lining and nonskid patches on the Cordura soles. No weights are given for these, but they must be similar to the REI booties. Rather more robust and complex are the Mountain Hardwear Chugach Booties with Polarguard fill, a protective rand, a front zipper, and a ridged EVA traction sole. The weight is 15 ounces. Mountain Hardwear says they are for high-altitude mountaineering, but I'm sure they'll keep your feet warm on backpacking trips. Mountain Hardwear makes a similar bootie with a down fill, called the Sub Zero SL Bootie. This has a waterproof-breathable outer and also weighs 15 ounces.

There are lighter-weight down-filled models, such as Sierra Designs Hot Shooties, with a 2-ounce down fill, closed-cell foam insoles, nonskid nylon outsoles, and Velcro closures (9 ounces), Climb High Down Booties with reinforced soles (8 ounces), and Feathered Friends Down Booties (9 ounces), which have removable EPIC shell booties, removable foam insoles, and 4 ounces of 800-fill-power down. I particularly like the idea of the last ones, since you could wear them outdoors, then remove the shells and the insoles and wear them in a tent and in your sleeping bag. The shells could be used just over socks too.

On solo cold-weather trips when I'm likely to spend most if not all of my camp time in the tent (probably in a sleeping bag), I often carry pile or fleece socks, since they're much warmer for their weight than wool socks. For years I've used Helly Hansen fiber-pile boot liners, which just reach my ankle and weigh 3.5 ounces. The name suggests they could be worn in boots, but I wouldn't do this except around camp, because pile and fleece are nonabsorbent and don't wick moisture quickly, so they get sticky with sweat quite quickly, though you could wear them with sandals. They are, however, wonderful to pull on over cold, wet feet at the end of the day; great for sleeping in; and nice for wearing in the tent when you aren't in the sleeping bag. My Helly socks are no longer sold, but there are plenty of similar socks, usually made from 200-weight fleece and often promoted for wearing with sports sandals. Wyoming Wear is a major brand.

If you want to wear socks outside without putting your boots back on, a pair of mukluks (soft, weatherproof overboots that can be worn over pile socks, wool socks, or even insulated booties) are a good idea. Outdoor Research's Modular Mukluks are a lightweight example; they're made from Cordura—coated on the foot, uncoated on the legs—have removable closed-cell insoles, reach up to the knee, and weigh just 8 ounces. They come with removable 8-ounce pile socks, which makes them an alternative to insulated booties. Of course, for short excursions outside the tent, you could just pull stuff sacks or plastic bags over your socks.

TREKKING POLES AND STAFFS

When I started hiking, it never occurred to me to use a staff or trekking pole, and these aids were rarely used by anyone else. Using two poles was unheard of. When I started Nordic skiing, however, I discovered that when I had to carry the skis on my pack, using the poles improved my balance. After a while, I realized I didn't need skis on my pack for a staff to be useful, and I began picking up stout sticks to help me on steep slopes and when fording streams. Staff in hand, I found I could negotiate steep scree slopes, boulder fields, and tussocky tundra with much more confidence and less worry that my unwieldy burden would tip me over.

I soon found that a staff has even more uses. On level ground and good trails, it helps me maintain a walking rhythm. When crossing soft boggy ground or snow, it can probe for hidden rocks and deep spots as well as provide support. It can hold back bushes, barbed wire, stinging plants, and other trail obstructions and even fend off aggressive dogs. Perhaps most important, it takes some weight off my feet, particularly when I lean heavily on it as I climb steep slopes. Experts claim that using trekking poles can take between 10 and 18 pounds off the lower body with each stride, which adds up to a lot of weight over a day. Of course it's not a free ride—the strain is just moved to your arms and upper body, and you have to carry the weight of the poles. But sharing the effort does mean that my legs get less tired while my upper body and arms maintain their strength between ski seasons.

Most experts recommend using two poles, and this is what I now mostly do. All the advantages of a staff are more than doubled when you use two. Walking with two poles uses the upper body muscles and takes much of the strain off the legs and hips. Using one pole takes the strain off only some of the time and can make you feel unbalanced. If I don't swap the pole from hand to hand occasionally, I find that my shoulder starts to ache. On steep terrain, especially direct descents, you can always have three points of contact with the ground if you carry two poles, which gives much greater stability. When using two poles I can walk faster and farther before I begin to feel tired, and I no longer have aching knees at the end of days with long, steep descents. On long ascents, I can go faster with poles.

My poles have other uses. During rest stops, they turn my pack into a backrest. In camp they can turn a fly-sheet door into an awning, support a wash line or tarp, and retrieve bear bagged food.

When I began using a pole, it made me an oddity and other hikers used to stare at me; when I began using two, some people avoided me altogether and others asked where my skis were. Now poles are more common, and you get fewer strange looks and odd comments. Some people really dislike them, though, and can get quite worked up about them, which baffles me, since they hardly intrude on anyone else. For most hikers they're not essential, but if you suffer from sore knees, hips, or back, they can make a huge difference. They can also be useful if you hike infrequently. Demetri "Coup" Coupounas, president of GoLite, says, "[I find] dual poles *very* useful in allowing me to take on big-mileage days and weekends when I hike infrequently—the poles add so much stability in motion that I am not restricted to short, easy hikes when my ankles are not strengthened from frequent hiking on rough trails—i.e., gym fitness translates into trail fitness much more readily with dual poles than with none."

I also think a pole is a useful emergency item. If you injure a foot or leg, having a pole could make the difference between limping out of the backcountry and having to be rescued. And of course, having a pole makes injuries less likely anyway, since it can prevent stumbles from turning into falls. There are a few disadvantages to poles; for instance, your hands aren't free. But it's easy to dangle the poles from your wrists by their straps if necessary.

Materials and Designs

The obvious material for a staff is wood, and it's easy to find a suitable piece in any forest. As long as it's reasonably straight, solid, and at least elbow height (so you can hold it with the lower arm at a right angle to the body, the most comfortable position), any strong stick will do. Many tourist stores in popular mountain areas sell wooden staffs, usually inexpensive. But you can't always buy or find a

staff when you reach an area, and wooden staffs aren't easy to transport. You can't put them in your pack, and they're awkward to take on trains, buses, and planes.

The answer to this problem is the *adjustable metal staff*. Derived from (and sometimes identical to) adjustable ski touring poles, these staffs are lighter than wooden sticks yet stronger and can be carried in or on a pack when not in use. Many alpine ski pole manufacturers began to make them once they noted that mountaineers and hikers in the Alps often used ski poles. Indeed, a ski pole makes a perfectly functional staff if you don't need an adjustable one, and old ones are usually easy to find at any ski resort. Most poles are made from light aluminum; the lightest (and most expensive) are carbon fiber.

Trekking poles, designed to be used in pairs, are far more common than staffs meant to be used singly. One of the few staff makers is Tracks (part of Cascade Designs, more noted for its sleeping mats), which makes several models. I've used its Sherlock staff for many years. This two-piece staff adjusts from 42.5 to 57.5 inches by means of a locking button that clips into holes in the shaft. The upper shaft is covered with soft foam topped by a wooden knob that you can remove to reveal a camera monopod mount. Rather than a sharp carbide tip, the Sherlock has a blunter steel point. It comes with a removable rubber tip too. Mine weighs 17.5 ounces; current models are 16.5 ounces. The Sherlite staff is the same model without the foam sheath, which cuts the weight to 15 ounces. I find the sheath, which is warm and soft, well worth 1.5 ounces.

The Sherlock is fine when I use a staff, as I sometimes do with light loads and on day hikes, and when I don't expect to have to carry it on my pack, as it's a bit long for that. With heavier loads I usually use two trekking poles. These come in many models, and having tested quite a few, I can say confidently that there's not much difference between most of them. The ones I've used most are Komperdell Guides (20 ounces a pair, packed length 25 inches), because of the foam handles and the camera mounts on the top. Unfortunately these now come only with antishock springs, which I dislike (see page 86), though you can turn these off. Leki, Masters, Komperdell, Life-Link, Black Diamond, Garmont, Gabel, Tracks, MSR, and more all make a wide range of good models, and there are store-brand poles from places like REI, often made by Komperdell. Weights range from 14 to 32 ounces for a pair. Packed lengths range from 20 to 30 inches. The differences lie mostly in the handles and grips and the locking mechanisms. There are two-piece poles, but the packed length is quite long, so I prefer three-section ones, of which there are far more. Of course the more sections, the weaker the pole, at least in theory, but I've never broken a three-section pole.

What can fail, though, is the locking mechanism. Most poles have a twist-lock adjustment with an internal adjustable, expanding section that locks and unlocks depending on the direction you twist the shaft. This is fine when it works, but it can slip or jam. To help minimize the chance of its happening, dismantle the poles after use and make sure they are dry before you reassemble them to prevent corrosion. Some expanders are all plastic, some are plastic and metal. The expanding section can be replaced if it starts to slip repeatedly, as can happen. I haven't had serious failures with any of the poles I've used, but the most secure and strongest expanders look to be those from Masters and Leki. Most poles are circular. Life-Link poles, however, have oval sections, which are said to be more secure, since an oval can't twist inside

another oval the way two circles can. I use Life-Link Variant Carbon Fiber ski touring poles and have found them very secure. There are two alternatives to internal expanders. As I described previously, Tracks poles have locking buttons that can't slip. Black Diamond poles have external adjustable cam locks called Flicklocks that have large levers that are easy to use when wearing gloves. All of these methods work, and I haven't found any one to be superior to the others.

For grips, cork, soft foam, or soft rubber is more comfortable than hard rubber or plastic, though there's not a huge difference. I like poles with a long foam grip that I can hold lower down when I want a shorter length. I also like poles with a camera mount under a knob on the top, since poles make excellent monopods. Some poles have forward-angled grips that are meant to give a more relaxed wrist position.

This design is taken to radical extremes in British-made Pacerpoles, which have molded thermoplastic-rubber grips, acutely angled, that are shaped for each hand. These enable you to transmit far more power through the poles, since the angle is "calculated for optimum range of arm leverage." The grips are very comfortable, and the poles are a leap forward in design. They are the ones I use most now; they really do give me more power and take more weight off my legs than standard poles, especially on long climbs. They have only a short piece of cord as a security loop rather than a proper strap, which isn't needed—you hold the poles loosely in your hands rather than letting the loops take the weight. The poles come in three sections with an internal locking mechanism. There is a soft neoprene sleeve on the upper section, and Pacerpoles is developing a camera mount that will fit on the grip. A pair of Pacerpoles weighs 23 ounces. For more information, see pacer

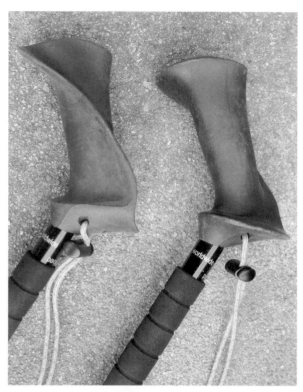

The unique Pacerpoles handles.

poles.com. Pacerpoles are distributed in the United States by Ultralight Adventure Equipment (ula-equipment.com).

Many poles have an antishock device, a spring built into the handle or the shaft that gives slightly when weight is applied. Antishock mechanisms add weight, increase packed length, and raise the price, all to no advantage in my experience. I've tried hiking with an antishock pole in one hand and a regular pole in the other, and I've noticed no difference. Antishock is supposed to absorb the shock of pole placements so your arm doesn't feel them, but my arms don't ache or feel any more tired whether I use them or not. On many poles, antishock can be turned off. I'd rather not have it at all.

Most poles come with small solid baskets. These are a hangover from skiing origins and aren't really necessary. If you're going to use your poles on snow, whether skiing or not, you do need to be able to fit large baskets to stop the poles from sinking in. Tip shafts are often synthetic and designed to break before the main shaft if they get caught in rocks, since they are cheaper and easier to replace. Some poles have blunt steel or alloy points, which are fine on everything except ice, but most have sharp carbide points. Poles can poke holes in trails and scratch rocks. I don't think this is a big problem, but you can put rubber or plastic covers over the tips. These covers are quite durable; one set lasted me for a five-week hike on the hard, rocky terrain of the High Sierra.

Using Poles

To gain the most benefit from hiking poles, you need to use them properly. I've seen many people letting poles dangle limply from their hands, ineffectually waving them around, rendering them just about useless, or else gripping them tightly and stabbing the ground, which is a good way to tire your arms and doesn't reap much benefit from the poles. Except with Pacerpoles, the straps should be used to support your hands and take the weight. To use the straps, put your hand up through the strap from below, then bring it down so the strap runs between the thumb and fingers and over the back of the hand. With the poles held like this, you can flick them back and forth without having to jerk your arms around or grasp them tightly. Place the poles by swinging one in front, placing the tip on the ground, pressing down on it, then walking past it while swinging the other pole forward. On even terrain you can get a good rhythm. You should feel the poles pushing you forward as you push down on them. On ascents you won't get as much of a forward swing, but you can really push down on the poles to help propel you upward.

To get the maximum benefit from poles, they need to be the right length. Many people use a pole that's too long, which requires more effort and can make your arms and shoulders ache. For hiking on the flat and gentle slopes, poles should touch the ground when held pointing straight down with your elbow bent at a right angle. On steep ascents a shorter pole is better. You can slip your hands out of the loops and grasp the shaft lower down or adjust the poles to a shorter length. When descending steep ground, you can plant a longer pole below you for greater support. On long descents, adjusting the pole length might be worthwhile; otherwise you can lengthen a pole by placing your hand over the top of the grip. When traversing steep slopes, you can slip your hand out of the strap on the upper pole and grasp it lower down on the shaft so it doesn't push you away from the slope. To make changing pole length

How to hold a trekking pole. Put your hand up through the loop so you can pull down on the strap. You don't need to grip the pole tightly.

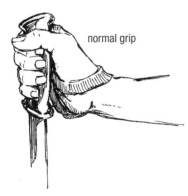

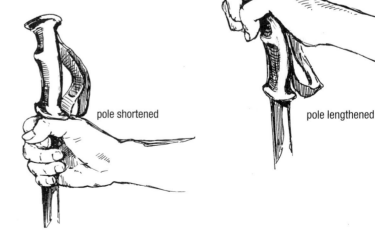

normal grip

pole shortened

pole lengthened

Holding the pole.

quicker, you can adjust the lower section to its full length and then just alter the middle section when you want to change the length. Overall, though, it's better to alter each section by the same amount, so that one section isn't overloaded.

ICE AXES

Whenever you're likely to encounter slopes of hard snow and ice, you need an *ice ax*. Winter might seem the obvious time to expect such terrain, but the snow then is often deep and soft. It's in spring and early summer, after the surface of the snow has melted and refrozen, perhaps several times, that ice axes are most often needed. An ax may be needed well into July for hikes above the timberline in some areas, and I've had to seek out an alternative route as late as September when a steel-hard bank of old snow blocked the trail to a high pass.

A trekking pole, very useful for balance in soft snow, is inadequate when crossing steep, hard-packed snow or ice. On such surfaces, a slip can easily become a rapidly accelerating slide. The only way to stop such a fall is by a method known as *self-arrest*, which requires an ice ax. For instruction, take a course in snow and ice skills at an outdoor center or learn from a competent friend. Cox and Fulsaas's *Mountaineering: The Freedom of the Hills* is a useful source for all aspects of snow travel other than skiing, but I'm not convinced that self-arrest can be learned from a written description. Practice is essential; in a real fall you have to react immediately and automatically, and you must be able to stop yourself whether you fall on your front or your back and with your head uphill or downhill. On slopes where you may have to self-arrest, carry your ice ax with the pick pointing backward so it's in position. On easier slopes I prefer to walk

BUT IT'S STILL SUMMER

An unexpected early September blizzard had blanketed the mountains with fresh snow—deep, soft, and wet. I struggled up to the 11,900-foot Farview Pass in the Never Summer range in the Colorado Rockies with the aid of a thick stick I'd picked up in the forest below. I had no ice ax, and this was in the days before I carried a staff or hiking poles. It was also in the days before I discovered waterproof socks, and my feet, in running shoes, were quickly sodden and chilled. At the pass, where the view was all of 50 yards, I wiped the snow off a trail sign, then followed the directions down into the Parika Lake basin, where I camped in the slight shelter of some stunted spruce. Once in the tent, I stripped off my wet shoes and socks, pulled dry wool socks over my frozen feet, and slid into my sleeping bag. After several hot drinks and a steaming bowl of curry, my feet began to warm up. The temperature in the tent was a damp 40°F (5°C). Thankfully, the next day arrived with sunshine and a clear sky, and my feet

felt only slightly cool as I followed the Continental Divide Trail across the snowy slopes of the White Cloud Peaks and into Rocky Mountain National Park.

With the rest of Colorado to cross in the next few weeks, however, I needed more than running shoes and a stick. In the little mountain resort of Grand Lake, I did a round of the stores. But it was still summer, and no one stocked gaiters or ice axes. (Outside, the mountains shone white with new snow.) They had boots, of course, and I continued my walk in a sturdy pair of midweight leather Pivettas, good for stomping steps in snow. But it was nineteen days and 320 miles of snowy trails later before I finally managed to find gaiters and an ice ax in the town of Creede—just in time to deal with a blizzard in the San Juans. The lesson from this is to have items I might need mailed ahead just in case. I can always send them on if they aren't required.

Using ice axes to safeguard a steep descent on hard snow.

with the pick pointing forward so that if I stumble I won't impale myself.

Ice axes also can be used to cut steps in ice and snow too hard to kick your boots into (though wearing crampons makes this unnecessary) and can replace a staff for balance on snow. If you do slip, thrusting the ax shaft into the snow will often prevent you from sliding down the slope. Other things I've found an ice ax useful for include pulling stakes out of frozen ground or hard-packed snow, chopping holes in frozen streams or ponds to get water, chipping ice off rocks so you can stand on them without slipping when fording streams, and digging toilet holes.

Ice axes come in many complicated and even bizarre styles; most are specialty designs for climbing frozen waterfalls and iced-up vertical cliffs. All a backpacker needs is a simple, traditional ice ax, usually described as a "walking" or "general mountaineering" ax. The head should have a wide adze, useful for cutting steps and possibly for self-arrest

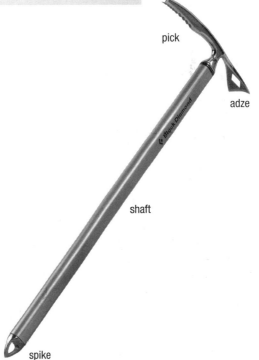

An ice ax. Always carry an ice ax and crampons if you're likely to encounter steep, snowy areas or ice.

in soft snow, and a gently curved pick with a few teeth at the end. Two-piece heads are perfectly adequate for walking use. They may be made from steel (strong but quite heavy), titanium (strong and light but expensive), or aluminum (light but not so strong and easily blunted). Shafts are normally aluminum, which is strong enough for most uses. Titanium shafts, found on a few axes, are stronger but expensive. Metal shafts are cold to touch and slippery when damp. Some form of tape or a rubberized sheath makes the shaft warmer and gives you a better grip. It shouldn't be very thick, though, or it can impede the shaft when you thrust it into the snow. A wrist loop is useful and worth attaching if your ax doesn't come with one. Length is a matter of debate; I like an ax whose spike is a half-inch or so off the ground when I hold the ax by my side with my arm hanging down. An ax this length will touch the snow on gentle slopes, which is good for security. On steeper slopes the shaft can be pushed into the snow, also good for security. On descents, it's easier to place a longer ax down the slope ahead of you without crouching or leaning forward. Climbers, who are used to being on very steep, icy slopes, often prefer shorter axes.

Axes weigh from 7 to 28 ounces. The lightest models are adequate for backpacking. Makes to look for include Climb High, Cassin, Salewa, Stubai, SMC, Mountain Technology, Petzl Moser, Omega Pacific, Camp, Stanley Alpine, Grivel, and Black Diamond. Since I don't do any alpine mountaineering or technical climbing, I don't need an ax designed for these pursuits; and since my ax spends most of its time strapped to my pack, weight is more important than technical design. For many years now I have used a 70-centimeter Camp HL250 ax that weighs just 12 ounces. It has a head made from alloy rather than steel and isn't

suitable for serious climbing—it even has "not for ice climbing" stamped on the pick—but for backpacking it's fine.

Ice axes are potentially dangerous implements and require care both in use and when being carried. Rubber head and spike protectors are useful when transporting the ax to and from the mountains—a wine bottle cork will do to cover the spike, and cardboard or foam can be wrapped around the head if necessary. On planes, trains, and buses I pack the ax inside my pack or duffel bag with the head and spike covered (on planes, the ax must be in your checked baggage).

CRAMPONS

If conditions warrant carrying an ice ax, *crampons* will probably be useful as well. These metal spikes strap or clamp onto the soles of your boots so you can cross ice and hard snow without slipping. I rarely use them, but when I do they are essential, so I carry them on any trips where ice or hard snow is likely. Flexible crampons—ones with a hinge or a sprung bar in the middle—can be fitted to most hiking boots, and some will fit trail shoes. Rigid crampons are strictly for climbers and rigid-soled boots.

The number of points on a crampon doesn't matter much for walkers; there are eight-, nine-, ten-, and twelve-point models. Points that angle out from the front of the boot are useful for climbing steep slopes because you can use your boot toes. I prefer crampons with angled front points to those with vertical points.

Crampons are usually made from steel, which is strong and stays sharp, though the lightest models are made from an aluminum alloy, which blunts quickly but is all right for occasional hiking use, and titanium, which holds an edge better but is

Crampons are needed for hiking on ice and hard snow. They need to be fitted properly. Charlet Moser (now Petzl Charlet) articulated 12-point crampon.

expensive. For most backpacking use, aluminum is fine. Weights for crampons range from 16 ounces to more than 2 pounds.

Fitting crampons to boots is a complicated business the first time, and finding the right size can be difficult. First-time buyers should take their boots to the store and have the salesperson demonstrate how to fit them. A properly fitted crampon shouldn't fall off when you pick up the boot and shake it with the crampon straps unfastened.

Crampons attach to boots by various methods; some are much easier to use than others, especially with cold fingers. Awkward systems may mean you don't bother to put the crampons on when you should or that you don't fit them properly, both of which can be dangerous. Practice attaching crampons until you can do it quickly. A blizzard isn't the place to work out what goes where.

The easiest system is the step-in with a wire bail at the front and a heel lever at the back. Unfortunately, these require boots with a pronounced lip at the heel and toe, which few hiking boots have anymore. Old-fashioned leather boots with external stitched seams and modern plastic climbing boots will take these crampons. To minimize the chance of the front bail's coming off, these crampons should have a strap linking the toe and heel pieces.

Almost as easy to fit are crampons with flexible plastic cradles at the front and back that wrap around the boot when tensioned with a single strap that runs from the heel to the front cradle and then back to a buckle at the rear. This is the system I prefer, since it will fit most hiking boots. Traditional systems use sets of straps. There are many variations of these. A common one has an O-ring linked by straps to the front of the crampons and a long strap at the heel that runs through this ring and then back to the heel. There are also mixtures of systems with O-rings and straps at the front and heel levers or cradles at the back.

The companies that make ice axes usually make crampons as well. For several years, when I've expected to need crampons for long periods I've used Grivel G10s, flexible ten-point steel crampons with plastic cradles that make them easy to attach to hiking boots. They're somewhat heavy at 29 ounces, though, and since I got them, Grivel has introduced an alloy version, the G10 Light, that weighs 23.7 ounces. However, for occasional use, which is most of the time, I use 21-ounce, twelve-point Salewa Alunal crampons with plastic cradles. If you want more strength and sharpness, the same design at the same weight in titanium is sold under the name Titan Ultra Walk. Some alloy crampons are even lighter than the Alunals, such as the 17-ounce, twelve-point Camp LCs, which unfortunately come only with step-in bindings, and the 20-ounce, twelve-point Stubai Ultralights, which have nylon cradles.

Like ice axes, crampons can be dangerous, so if you strap them to the outside of your pack, you should cover the spikes with rubber protectors.

The tangled rubber strands of these protectors can be a big nuisance, however; I long ago abandoned them and instead carry crampons inside the pack in a tough Cordura nylon pouch. The pouch I use hasn't been sold for years, but Outdoor Research makes a very similar one, the 11-ounce Crampon Pouch, which can be attached to the pack or carried inside. You can also wrap crampons in a length of tough cloth such as heavy-duty canvas, neoprene, or PVC. Some packs come with a pocket on the front designed to hold crampons.

Walking in crampons involves a change in gait and special techniques on steep slopes. You must take care not to catch the points on your pants or gaiters or the other crampon, so you need to spread your legs slightly wider than usual. On gentle slopes you need to keep your feet flat on the snow or ice so that all the points bite. On steep slopes you can kick just the front points into the snow and walk up on your toes, though this is tiring and difficult in

A ten-point flexible crampon.

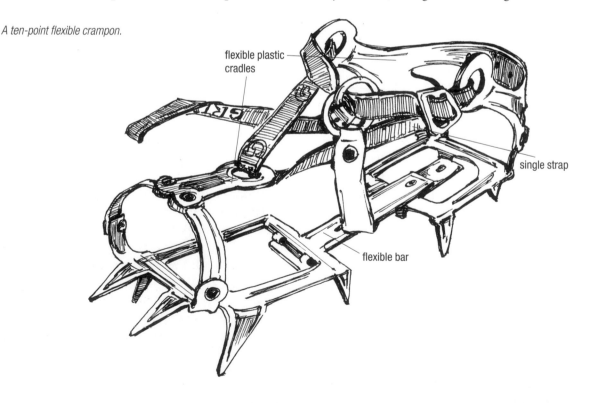

flexible plastic cradles

single strap

flexible bar

flexible boots. I find the least tiring way to climb moderately steep ground is to front-point with one foot while keeping the other flat on the ground, alternating feet as they start to ache. If you're going to venture onto really steep terrain, I suggest you take a mountaineering course.

SKIS AND SNOWSHOES

Walking through snow more than ankle deep can be very difficult; once you sink up to your shins and deeper, it becomes an exhausting and slow process, aptly known as *postholing*. The Scandinavians answered the problem some four thousand years ago: strap something to your feet that spreads your weight and allows you to ride on the snow's surface. After years of slogging through soft, wet snow, I discovered this for myself when I traveled with three hikers who used snowshoes in the San Bernardino Mountains on the Pacific Crest Trail in California. I bought a pair to use in the snowbound High Sierra, but then I watched enviously as two in our party swapped snowshoes for Nordic skis, swooped down snowfields, and slid through the forest, leaving the two of us on snowshoes to plod along in their wake. I became determined to learn to ski.

Snowshoes have their uses, though. They are more maneuverable than skis in thick forest, and the largest ones will keep you on the surface of deep, powdery snow, which the widest skis will sink into. You also can use them with ordinary walking boots. And it's much easier to learn to snowshoe than to ski. You can still get traditional wooden snowshoes, but they're heavy and need careful maintenance. Better and far more common are the more durable aluminum-framed ones with synthetic decking and pivoting bindings. The ones I used in the Sierra were Sherpa Featherweight Sno-Claw models that

weighed a little more than 3 pounds with straps. The Sno-Claw, a serrated edge that fits under the boot for grip on icy slopes, worked well on moderate slopes, but I changed to crampons for the steep slopes. Since I learned to ski a year later, I didn't use snowshoes again for many years. However, a few years ago I did get a new pair, which I've been using in the local woods where skis would be awkward to handle. My current shoes are the Baldas Matterhorn Treks, which have a metal frame with polypropylene decking, a pivoting binding with spikes, and an optional extension called a spatula. They measure 9 by 20.5 inches, weigh 4.5 pounds, and are designed to support more than 240 pounds. I've used them in moderate terrain with light loads, and for this they are fine. If I'd had them instead of the Sherpas for the hike through the High Sierra, I imagine they would have performed just as well.

Walking in snowshoes is slow work compared with skiing but far easier than walking in deep snow without them. Snowshoes have become popular for winter recreation, and there are now several good models with weights from 2 pounds upward. Besides Baldas and Sherpa, well-regarded brands include Atlas, Tubbs, Northern Lites, Redfeather, and Yuba. There are several books on the subject, of which the classic is *Snowshoeing*, by Gene Prater, now in its fifth edition.

I abandoned snowshoes for many years because skiing looked like more fun. Snowshoeing seemed functional but tedious by comparison. Crossing the High Sierra in May with a 100-pound pack was not the time to learn to ski, however. The next winter I took a Nordic ski course and have since been on ski backpacking trips most years in places as far afield as the High Sierra, Greenland, Spitsbergen (which lies in the Arctic Ocean north of Norway), the Yukon, the Alps, Lapland (in Arctic Scandinavia), the Norwegian mountains, and the

Ski backpacking is the ideal way to explore the wilderness in winter and spring. Sarek National Park, Arctic Lapland, Sweden.

Canadian Rockies. For nine seasons I worked as a ski touring leader, based in Norway.

Skiing is a complex subject. Alpine (downhill) skis are strictly for lift-served skiing and ultrasteep mountain descents. Even with alpine ski mountaineering bindings and boots, progress on the flat and uphill is painfully slow, and the weight of the gear is tiring. These skis are worth considering only if your aim is a long, steep descent. For most snow backpacking, they are unsuitable. The same applies to the heaviest telemark gear, which is again designed for resort skiing and steep descents. The lightest telemark gear is suitable for touring, however, especially in mountainous terrain. At the other extreme, light, skinny cross-country skis are designed for cut tracks and don't have much flotation or stability in untracked snow.

The best skis for ski backpacking are variously called *Nordic*, *backcountry*, or *mountain touring* skis. For carrying a heavy load and breaking trail in snow that ranges from deep powder to breakable crust, skis with metal edges are best. All skis are narrower at the waist than at the tip and tail. The difference between the waist and the tip is called the *sidecut*. More sidecut means a ski that is easier to turn going downhill, which is good for mountain skiing. I used to look for about 8 to 10 millimeters of sidecut, but this is now very little, since there has been a revolution in ski design and there are now many wide touring skis with plenty of sidecut. My current mountain touring skis, Tua Hydrogens, have 30 millimeters of sidecut and measure 102-72-92 millimeters, tip to tail yet, at 5.5 pounds, weigh no more than my old narrow skis, which measured 62-54-58 millimeters. The advantage of wide skis is in soft snow, where they have better flotation than narrow ones.

Whatever the skis, you need strong bindings, either cables or bindings with three pins that fit into the toe of your boots, since they'll have to undergo the stress caused by your body weight plus a heavy pack. Touring bindings haven't changed much over the past few decades; they've just become stronger. Boots have changed, however, and plastic has taken over. At first this was just for lift telemark skiing and steep mountain descents, and the boots were too stiff and heavy for ski backpacking, but now you can get excellent plastic touring boots from Scarpa, Garmont, and Crispi. I use Garmont Xcursions, which weigh 6 pounds. The plastic shell keeps my feet dry in wet spring snow while the inners make good hut and tent boots.

Poles are essential with skis (and a great help with snowshoes). Since lightweight fiberglass poles break easily (my first pair of poles shattered within a week), I use a metal pair. I like adjustable ones (long for the flat, shorter for uphill, shortest for downhill). There are many models—see the discussion of hiking poles earlier in this chapter (pages 83–88).

Climbing skins are long strips of "grippy" fabric that attach to the bottom of your skis. They make ascents much easier and are a worthwhile investment for mountain ski tours.

You need only moderate skill to travel the wilderness on skis, and the enjoyment of ski touring far outweighs the effort required. Beginners will benefit from a course at a ski school; I did. For more specifics on wilderness touring there are several good books, including Allen O'Bannon and Mike Clelland's entertaining *Allen and Mike's Really Cool Backcountry Ski Book*. For skiing skills I also like their *Really Cool Telemark Tips*. The classic book on skills is Paul Parker's superb *Free-Heel Skiing*.

chapter four

carrying the load

the pack

The heart of the backpacker's equipment is the pack. Tents, boots, stoves, and rain gear may be unnecessary at some times and places, but your pack is always with you. It must hold everything you need for many days' wilderness travel yet still be as small a burden as possible.

Ever since aluminum frames and hipbelts were introduced in the 1940s and 1950s, designers have tried to make carrying loads as comfortable as possible. Internal and external frames, adjustable back systems, sternum straps, load-lifter straps, side ten-sion straps, triple-density padded hipbelts, lumbar pads—the modern pack suspension is a complex structure that requires careful fitting. Only your footwear is as important to your comfort as your pack, so take the time to find a pack that fits.

The last decade of the twentieth century saw a huge change in pack design—a revolution even, though I'm wary of that word—with the advent of lightweight and ultralight packs weighing a small fraction of the weight of earlier packs. This shook up the pack world, and established makers scram-

WALKING BEFORE DAWN

Under a soft gray light, mountaintops lie black and brooding, draped in pale, wraithlike clouds. The last stars still shine in a dark sky, though far to the east a faint tinge of pink spreads along the horizon. As the light strengthens, the dark lines of peaks beyond the flat lake stand out as if etched onto the sky. The pink intensifies into red and orange, then a spot on the horizon darkens and flares; a shaft of light rushes from it, cutting the air. The spot becomes an arc, a bright curve that slowly edges above the horizon, turning into a hot white orb, the sun. The reeds on the tiny islet out in the lake are transformed from black shadows to green life. I must turn my eyes from the brightness.

bled to produce their own lightweight designs. Except for long cold-weather trips, there's now no need to carry a pack weighing even half what standard packs used to weigh. An added bonus is that these lightweight packs are usually less expensive than heavier ones.

TYPES OF PACKS

Walk into any outdoor equipment store and you'll be confronted by a vast array of packs. Any could be used for backpacking; the problem is to determine which are right for *your* kind of backpacking. Many people use one pack for all their hiking. If you do, then you need a pack with enough capacity for the bulkiest loads you're likely to carry. Overstuffing a too-small pack is not the way to achieve a comfortable carry. If you go on trips year-round, you may be better off with more than one pack, so you can tailor the load to their capacity and weight. I now regularly use three packs: a 21.5-ounce, 4,000-cubic-inch frameless pack for trips where the load will be less than 30 pounds; a more supportive 39.8-ounce, 4,000-cubic-inch internal frame pack for loads between 30 and 45 pounds; and a 115.6-ounce, 7,200-cubic-inch internal frame monster for even heavier loads. A pack designed to carry 60 pounds comfortably will be fine with 30 pounds, but the converse is not usually true. If I could keep only two packs, I'd drop the lightest one. If I could keep only one, it would be the heaviest. Of course if you do only short three-season hikes with light loads, then you'll need only a light, relatively inexpensive pack. You can always add a larger, heavier pack if you decide on longer or colder-weather hikes and an even bigger one for extended cold-weather trips.

Before I go into the details of pack design and construction, here's a brief overview of types of packs.

Ultralight Packs

The new ultralight packs weigh about a pound and are designed for loads up to 20 pounds. These packs have minimal features, with no frames and often no back padding or hipbelts. Once you'd probably have had to make such a pack yourself, but now several are sold by companies like GoLite, Lynne Whelden's LWGear, and Gossamer Gear (formerly GVP). The pack that started this revolution is the GoLite Breeze, designed by Ray Jardine based on the one he uses on his long-distance hikes. The Breeze is as simple as can be—just a large nylon bag made from tough Dyneema gridstop nylon with padded shoulder straps, mesh side and rear pockets, and a rollover closure. The medium size holds 2,900 cubic inches, plus another 850 if you use the extension,

An ultralight pack. GoLite Breeze.

CLOCKWISE FROM TOP LEFT: **(1)** *Ultralight pack with mesh pockets (GoLite Breeze), suitable for loads up to 20 pounds. Front view.* **(2)** *Lightweight pack with lightly padded back and unpadded hipbelt (GoLite Gust), suitable for loads up to 30 pounds. Back.* **(3)** *Lightweight pack with lightly padded back and unpadded hipbelt (GoLite Gust), suitable for loads up to 30 pounds. Side.* **(4)** *Lightweight pack with padded back, framesheet, and padded hipbelt (ULA P-2), suitable for loads up to 40 pounds. Front.* **(5)** *Lightweight pack with padded back, framesheet, and padded hipbelt (ULA P-2), suitable for loads up to 40 pounds. Back.*

and weighs 14 ounces. However, the title for lightest pack goes to the astonishing 7-ounce, 3,800-cubic-inch Gossamer Gear G5, which is made from 0.5-ounce ripstop nylon and has a webbing belt and mesh pockets. Gossamer Gear packs are designed to use a foam pad as a frame and to have small items of clothing stuffed into the shoulder straps and hip-belt as padding, though you can use small foam pads. The G5 is clearly a specialist pack that won't be very durable—Gossamer Gear describes it as for the "fanatic" ultralight hiker. Gossamer Gear's other pack, the Mariposa (formerly G4), has a similar design, weighs 18 ounces with all options and 15 ounces stripped, and has a capacity of 4,600 cubic inches. It's made from 2.2-ounce ripstop nylon, more durable than the 0.5-ounce but still not tough. The mesh used for Lynne Whelden's One Pound Pack, a 3,500-cubic-inch model that actually weighs 12.5 ounces, should be harder-wearing. I've tried the GoLite Breeze and the Gos-samer Gear Mariposa/G4 packs, and although they're fine with loads under 20 pounds, they're a little too minimalist for me. Using them reminded me why padded backs, frames, and hipbelts were developed.

Add a little more weight and a few more features, and there are plenty of day packs in the 1,800- to 2,500-cubic-inch range weighing 1.5 to 2.5 pounds that could do for ultralight back-packing.

Lightweight Packs

Not many people get their total loads below 20 pounds, but plenty carry no more than 25 to 45 pounds. For these weights you don't need a fully specified heavy, traditional backpacking sack, but you do need more support than you get from an ultra-light pack with no frame or hipbelt. Lightweight packs weigh from 1 to 4 pounds and have capacities

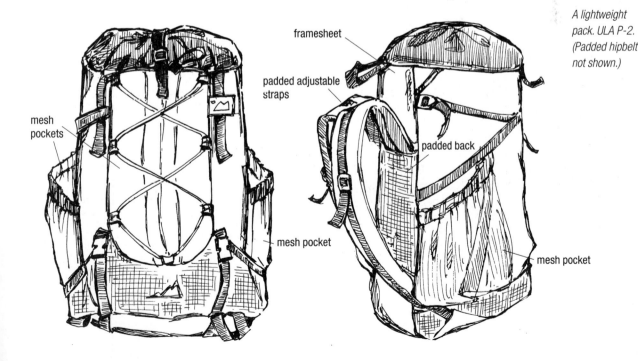

mesh pockets

framesheet

padded adjustable straps

padded back

mesh pocket

mesh pocket

A lightweight pack. ULA P-2. (Padded hipbelt not shown.)

from 2,500 to 5,000 cubic inches. The most basic have padded backs but no frames and simple unpadded hipbelts. Thirty pounds is usually the comfort limit for these. Add an internal frame and a padded belt, and that limit goes up to as much as 50 pounds. Until the first ultralight packs appeared, lightweight packs were hard to find. At first I couldn't find one I liked; now the problem is deciding which one to choose. The growing list includes:

- Dana Design Racer X—variable capacity (you strap on dry bags or stuff sacks), 34 ounces
- GoLite Jam—2,500 cubic inches, 23 ounces
- GoLite Infinity—2,750 cubic inches, 39 ounces
- GoLite Speed—3,400 cubic inches, 33 ounces
- GoLite Gust—3,900 cubic inches, 21 ounces
- GoLite Trek—4,800 cubic inches, 42 ounces
- Granite Gear Virga—3,400 cubic inches, 20 ounces
- Granite Gear Vapor Trail—3,600 cubic inches, 32 ounces
- Granite Gear Nimbus Ozone—3,800 cubic inches, 48 ounces
- Gregory G—2,900 cubic inches, 42 ounces
- Gregory Z—3,750 cubic inches, 50 ounces
- Kelty Cloud 4000—4,000 cubic inches, 40 ounces
- Kiskil Outdoors Mithril—4,400 cubic inches, 20 ounces
- McHale Spectra SUBPOP—3,500 cubic inches, 39 ounces
- Mountainsmith Auspex—4,200 cubic inches, 55 ounces
- One Pound Plus Pack—3,340 cubic inches, 23 ounces (available from both Lynne Whelden and Equinox)
- Osprey Aether 60—3,700 cubic inches, 56 ounces
- Six Moon Designs Starlite—4,100 cubic inches, 27 ounces
- Ultimate Direction WarpSpeed—3,000 cubic inches, 42 ounces
- ULA (Ultralight Adventure Equipment) P-2—4,025 cubic inches, 40 ounces
- ULA Fusion—3,500 cubic inches, 32 ounces
- Wild Things AT—5,000 cubic inches, 40 ounces

Weights and capacities are size-dependent, of course. Most of these packs come in several sizes. The figures quoted are mostly for large sizes.

Standard Packs

Despite the lightweight revolution, most packs still fall into the standard pack category, and there are dozens of models. I now use a standard pack only for loads of more than 45 pounds. I no longer carry that much very often, but when I do I still appreciate the comfort. These packs are sophisticated, complex, expensive, and marvelous. Without them, carrying heavy loads would be much more arduous. This category subdivides into two suspension systems based on frame type. Each system has its dedicated, vocal proponents.

First came the *external frame* of welded, tubular aluminum alloy; its ladderlike appearance was common on trails worldwide in the 1950s, 1960s, and 1970s. It's a simple, strong, and functional design, good for carrying heavy loads along smooth trails but unstable in rougher, steeper terrain. It's easy to lash extra items to the frame, making capacities enormous.

Although external frames have been to the summit of Everest, mountaineers found them unstable for climbing, generally preferring frameless "alpine" packs that hugged the back closely.

KEY FEATURES: PACKS FOR LOADS OVER 30 POUNDS

- A good fit. A poorly fitted pack can give you sore shoulders and hips and an aching back and is also unstable.
- A well-designed hipbelt. A good hipbelt should support 90 percent or more of the load without rubbing or making your hips sore.
- Curved, padded shoulder straps with top tension/load-lifter straps to take pressure off the top of your shoulders.
- A frame or framesheet to help transfer weight to your hips and prevent lumpy gear from poking you in the back.
- A capacity and design suitable for the gear to be carried. A pack for summer trails doesn't need ice-ax loops, ski slots, or room for a four-season sleeping bag—a pack for a winter ski-backpacking trip does.
- Light weight. The pack should be as light as possible for the weight to be carried—10 percent of the total load weight at most.

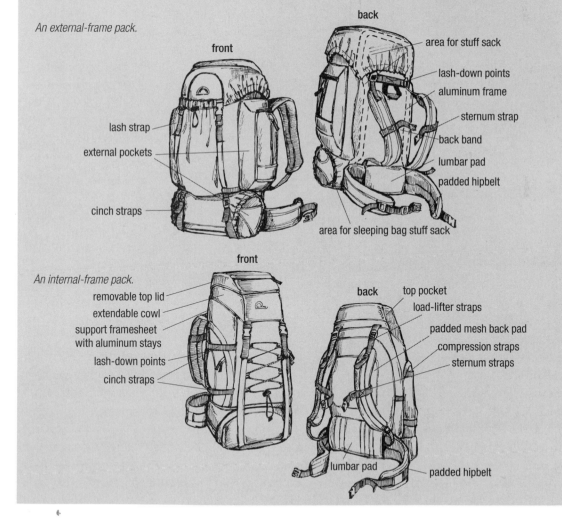

An external-frame pack.

front

back

area for stuff sack
lash-down points
aluminum frame
sternum strap
back band
lumbar pad
padded hipbelt

lash strap
external pockets
cinch straps

area for sleeping bag stuff sack

An internal-frame pack.

front

removable top lid
extendable cowl
support framesheet with aluminum stays
lash-down points
cinch straps

back

top pocket
load-lifter straps
padded mesh back pad
compression straps
sternum straps

lumbar pad
padded hipbelt

Standard pack with internal frame and thick hipbelt (Gregory Shasta), suitable for loads of 50+ pounds. Back.

However, these were uncomfortable with heavy loads. To combine stability with comfort, flat, flexible metal bars were added to the backs of the alpine packs, stiffening them and making it easier to transfer the weight to the hips. Thus, in the late 1960s the *internal-frame* pack was born. The design developed rapidly, and today most backpackers choose internal-frame packs. Ranging in capacity from 3,000 to a frightening 9,000 cubic inches, they serve just about any sort of backpacking, from summer weekend strolls to six-month expeditions. Internal-frame packs require careful fitting and adjustment, but if you're prepared to take the time for a proper fit, they're an excellent choice.

External frames seem to be fading away. *Backpacker* magazine's 2004 Gear Guide lists four companies that offer external-frame packs—and fifty that offer internals. And those four companies (Bergans, Coleman, JanSport, Kelty) offer more internal-frame packs than external-frame ones.

Travel Packs

Travel packs are derived from internal-frame packs and have similar suspension systems and capacities. The frame and harness can be covered by a zippered panel when they're not needed (or when you don't want to risk the suspicion that packs engender in some officials and in some countries) and to protect them from airport baggage handlers. With the harness hidden, travel packs look like soft luggage, with handles, zip-around compartments, and front pockets, and they can be used like suitcases when packing and unpacking. My limited usage of one Lowe Alpine model suggests that they're all right for the occasional overnight trip but don't compare with real internal-frame packs for comfort, which seems to be the general consensus. The larger ones with internal frames are probably adequate for moderate loads (40 pounds or so) as long as you don't mind the panel zippers.

SUSPENSION SYSTEMS

The suspension system is the most important feature to consider when choosing a pack; it supports the load, and it's the part of the pack that comes in contact with your body. A top-quality, properly fitted suspension system will let you carry loads comfortably and in balance. An inadequate or poorly fitted one can cause great pain. As with boots, it takes time to fit a pack properly. This applies even to frameless packs—they still need to be the right length for your back.

Frames

To hold the load steady and help transfer the weight from the shoulders to the hips, the back of the pack needs some form of stiffening. For loads less than 30 pounds, simple foam padding is adequate, but once the weight exceeds 30 pounds, a more rigid system is needed.

As I said earlier, there are two frame types: external, with the packbag hung on a frame by straps or clips or clevis pins, and internal, which fits inside the fabric of the pack, often completely integrated into it and hidden. The debate centers on which frame best supports a heavy load and which is more stable on rough ground; the answer used to be external for the first and internal for the second. Today, however, the best designs and materials have made the distinction less clear-cut.

For many years now my choice has been internal-frame packs. It's a couple of decades since I last used an external frame. Internals are more stable than all but a few externals, easier to carry around when you're not on the trail, and less prone to damage. Some are comfortable with any weight you're likely to carry. That said, I have a friend who has used a Kelty Tioga external-frame pack for decades and finds it just about perfect. His only complaint is that he can't replace it with an identical model. Since his stomping grounds are the Colorado Rockies and the Wind River Range and he likes challenging off-trail hikes above the timberline, he's clearly adapted to the rigidity of the frame.

External Frames

The traditional external frame is made of tubular aluminum alloy and consists of two curved vertical bars to which a number of crossbars are welded. Kelty introduced such frames back in the 1950s and still makes them in barely altered form for their Yukon and Trekker packs. Variations have appeared over the years, such as hourglass-shaped frames and frames made from flexible synthetic materials. External frames are usually not adjustable, though some have frame extensions for carrying larger loads while others telescope and come in different back lengths. Suspension systems are similar to those found on internals. With externals the weight transfers directly through the rigid frame to your hips, so they will handle very heavy loads comfortably as long as the hipbelt is well padded and supportive enough. Because of their rigidity, it's easy to keep the weight high up and close to your center of gravity, enabling you to walk upright. Also, because the packbag is held away from the back, they allow sweat to dissipate, unlike internal-frame packs, which hug the body. Even so I've always found that when I work hard carrying a heavy load, I end up with a sweaty back whatever the type of frame.

THE LIMITS OF EXTERNAL FRAMES

The trail was steep and rough, a direct line up the rocky mountainside. Just below the summit were two bands of rock I had to surmount. Climbing them wasn't difficult—just easy scrambling—but for a few yards the broken rock was very steep and I needed to steady myself with my hands. The only problem was that the tubes of my external-frame pack towered above my head and pushed my face forward into the slope so I couldn't look up to see where the trail went. The rigid frame made balancing difficult, too, and I lurched sideways when I took high steps. The situation wasn't dangerous, just awkward, but the experience was one of the main reasons I soon changed to an internal-frame pack, a design I've preferred ever since.

The disadvantages of external frames are balance and stability. External frames do not move with you; on steep descents and when crossing rough ground, they can be unstable and may make walking difficult or even unsafe. They also tend to be bulkier than internal-frame packs, making them awkward for plane, car, and bus travel and difficult to stow in small tents. Their rigidity also makes them more vulnerable to damage, especially on airplanes. My last external frame cracked during airplane baggage handling.

Externals are generally less expensive than internals, though, and some are lighter for similar capacity and load-carrying comfort.

A few external frames are designed to gain the advantages of internals without losing the advantages of externals. They have modified frame shapes, often made from flexible plastic instead of rigid alloy. Kelty makes an hourglass-shaped aluminum frame (Tioga, Super Tioga, and their 50th Anniversary models) that "allow gear to ride close and high," while the venerable JanSport frames have crossbars attached to the side bars by flexible joints, which, JanSport claims, allow the frames to twist and flex with body movement.

Not having used any of these frames, I can't comment on how effective they are, but it seems that the key to better balance with an external frame is the hipbelt's freedom of movement in relation to the pack, plus an increased curvature that molds the frame more closely to the body.

Internal Frames

The basic internal frame consists of two flat aluminum alloy stays running vertically down the pack's back. This original design, introduced in the late 1960s by Lowe Alpine, addressed the instability of external-frame packs on rugged terrain and the difficulty of designing a frameless pack to carry a heavy load comfortably. The bars, or stays, are usually parallel, though in some designs they form an upright or inverted V and in others an X.

Many internal frames now have flexible plastic *framesheets* in addition to or instead of stays to give extra rigidity to the pack and prevent hard bits of gear from poking you in the back. There are many variations on the framesheet/parallel stays theme, using aluminum, carbon fiber, polycarbonate, thermoplastic, Evazote, and polyethylene. Some packs have single stays down the center of the framesheet, and some have Delrin or titanium rods running down the sides to help transfer the weight to the hipbelt. One (McHale Bayonet) even has a two-part frame—remove the top for a smaller pack. Each pack maker has its own type of internal frame; all, of course, claim theirs can carry heavy loads more comfortably than anything else. The ones I've tested over the years—Aarn, Arc'teryx, Gregory, Dana Design, Lowe Alpine, The North Face, Osprey, Jack Wolfskin, and Marmot—all did a pretty good job with moderately heavy loads (45 to 55 pounds). Some—Dana Design, Arc'teryx, Gregory—will handle 60 pounds or more while some lightweight models (ULA P-2) will handle up to 40 pounds.

Whatever the style, internal frames are flexible and with use conform to the shape of the wearer's back, allowing a body-hugging fit that gives excellent stability.

Because internal frames move with your body and let you pack the weight lower and closer to your back, they are excellent where balance is important, such as when rock scrambling, skiing, and hiking over rough, steep terrain. A disadvantage of this is that you tend to lean forward to counterbalance the low weight. Careful packing with heavy items high up and close to the back is a partial answer when you are walking on a good trail but is no panacea if the pack is poorly designed (see Packing later in this chapter).

On many packs, the stays are removable; this is one way to lighten the pack for a side trip or an ultralight trip. In snow, the stays could be used as tent stakes or even an emergency snow saw.

Crude internal frames can be created for frameless packs with a foam pad by folding it to fit down the back of the pack or rolling it up, placing it in the pack, and allowing it to unroll. Pads take up a fair amount of room, however, and can still distort under heavy loads; I think 30 pounds is the upper limit. Some packs, like the Gossamer Gear models mentioned, are designed with sleeves in the back to use foam pads as frames; the pad takes up no room inside the pack. The best design I've seen like this is the ULA Fusion, which has a carbon fiber–composite rod hoop running around the edges of the back and a large, foam back panel. Your sleeping pad fits behind this panel and the pack itself and is held in place by straps, creating a much firmer support than usual with a pad. The Fusion is new (as of 2004) so I haven't used it much yet, but it looks like it will become a personal favorite.

The Hipbelt

Your back and shoulders are not designed for bearing heavy loads. In fact, the human spine easily compresses under a heavy weight—one reason back injuries are so prevalent. Furthermore, when you carry a load on your shoulders, you bend forward to counterbalance the backward pull of the load. This is uncomfortable and bad for your back, and the pressure on sensitive muscles and nerves can make your shoulders ache and go numb.

The solution is to lower the load to the hips, a far stronger part of the body. The *hipbelt* is by far the most important part of any pack suspension system designed for carrying loads of more than 20 to 25 pounds. It's the part of the pack I always examine first. A well-fitting, well-padded hipbelt transfers most of the pack weight from the shoulders onto the hips, allowing the backpacker to stand upright and carry a properly balanced load in comfort for hours. Some ultralight packs don't have hipbelts—indeed, some ultralight hikers seem to regard hipbelts as demonic symbols of submission to advertising hype. They argue that they are unnecessary with ultralight loads and restrict freedom of movement. Having tried hiking with the GoLite Breeze, which doesn't have a hipbelt, I can't agree. Even with less than 20 pounds in the pack, my shoulders could feel the weight by the end of the day, and I found not having a belt restrictive. Stability was poorer, too. Even with very light loads I like a hipbelt, though for loads under 30 pounds it doesn't need to be big and bulky or even have any padding at all.

The first hipbelts were unpadded webbing. On some ultralight packs they still are, but most of today's hipbelts are complex, multilayered creations of nylon, foam, plastic, and even graphite. A good hipbelt should be well padded with soft, thick foam that molds around your hips. Those designed for loads of more than 40 pounds should also have some form of stiffening to prevent twisting when loaded. This may be an outer layer of firm foam or stiff but flexible polypropylene or polyethylene plates. Many belts are made from thermal-molded foam that forms a belt with a firm conical shape that hugs the body without sagging.

As always, somebody disagrees with the prevailing wisdom. McHale, a custom pack maker in Seattle, claims stiff belts are uncomfortable and unnecessary; its soft belts, McHale says, made from Evazote foam with double buckles, wrap round the hips so well that they create their own firm structure. They are continuous, attached to the pack only at the bottom edge, and run outside the lumbar pad so they wrap around the body and mold to your shape. I haven't used a McHale hipbelt, but they look interesting. I haven't found any problems with conventional, stiffened belts, though.

In addition to being thickly padded, a hipbelt should be at least 4 inches wide where it passes over the hips, narrowing toward the buckle. Conical or cupped belts are less likely than straight-cut ones to slip down over the hips (though most belts eventually slip with ridiculously heavy loads, whatever the shape); most belts on top-quality packs designed for heavy loads are shaped. For the heaviest loads, continuous wraparound belts perform better than those sewn to the side of the pack; again, most top models have these. To support the small of your back, the lower section of the pack should be well padded. This can be a continuation of the hipbelt (as in most external-frame packs), a special lumbar pad (as in most internal frames), or part of a completely padded back. The lumbar pad is important for supporting the load and spreading the weight over your lower back and hips. A too-stiff or too-soft lumbar pad can lead to pressure points and sore spots. Continuous hipbelts run behind the lumbar pad and may be attached to it with Velcro.

Belts that are attached to the frame or the lumbar pad only at or near the small of the back need side stabilizer or side tension straps (also called hip tension straps) to prevent the pack from swaying. These straps pull the edges of the pack in around the hips, which increases stability. Most internal-frame packs have them. A few models also have diagonal compression straps, which run downward across the side of the pack to the hipbelt and

help pull the load onto the hipbelt. These work well.

Many hipbelts are nylon-covered inside and out. Although adequate, a smooth covering like this can make the belt slip when it's worn over smooth synthetic clothing, a problem that worsens as the load increases. Cordura or other texturized nylon is better; some companies use special high-friction fabrics. These may cover the whole inside of the belt or just the center of the lumbar pad.

Most hipbelt buckles are the three-pronged Fastex type or something similar. These are tough and easy to use, but they can break if you step on them, so be careful when the pack is on the ground. Carrying a spare on long trips, or putting one in a supply box, is a good idea. I had a buckle break at the start of a two-week winter trip. How, I'm not sure, though I suspect baggage handlers even though the pack was in a duffel bag. I didn't have a spare, and I was very glad that the mountain hut where I spent the first night sold them. Otherwise I'd have had to go out to a town to get one, since carrying a heavy winter load without a hipbelt was unthinkable. There are a few other buckle types around, such as the cam-lock buckles McHale uses.

Hipbelt size is important. The padded part of the belt should extend at least 2.5 inches in front of the hipbone, and after you tighten the belt there should be enough webbing left on either side of the buckle to allow for weight loss on a long hike and for adjustment over different thicknesses of clothing. Some packs come with permanent hipbelts, so you have to check the size when you buy. Packs that come in two or three sizes often have belts sized to the frame length (e.g., medium frame, medium belt), which is fine unless you are tall and thin or short and stout. Companies that make packs with removable belts often offer a choice of belt sizes. Such modular systems are the best way to achieve the optimum fit, especially if you're not an "average" size. Gregory, for example, makes hipbelts in four sizes—small, 22 to 28 inches; medium, 28 to 34 inches; large, 34 to 40 inches; and extra large, 40+ inches. My waist (measured around the top of the iliac crest, not the stomach) averages 34 inches (occasionally less, sometimes more), so I have a medium belt on my Gregory Shasta. There are different hipbelts for men and women, too, though since everyone is a different shape, it may be that one labeled for the opposite sex fits best. Keep an open mind! Rather than have belts for each gender, some makers, such as Gregory, have belts whose angle over the hips can be altered so it follows your shape.

How big a belt you need depends on the weight you intend to carry. The basic principle is simple: big loads need big belts. I've found that moderately padded belts handle loads up to 45 pounds adequately. Heavier loads, however, cause these belts to compress and press painfully on the hipbones or else twist out of shape, making it difficult to put most of the load on the hips. For heavy loads, wide hipbelts with thick layers of padding and stiffened flexible reinforcements on the outside are best. My favorite for many years has been the Dana Design Contour Hipbelt, a massive thick, stiffened belt. I've carried loads of 60 pounds or more for weeks at a time using this belt and never had bruised or sore hips. I'm also impressed with the Arc'teryx Bora hipbelt, made from four layers of laminated, thermo-formed foam in a curved, cupped shape that fits neatly around my hips.

Finally, consider what you wear *under* a hipbelt as well, because this will be pressed against your skin. Pants with thick side seams, belt loops, rivets, and zippered pockets can rub painfully. Wide, elasticized waistbands or bib styles are better. If you do find a sore point under a hipbelt, check to see if it's caused by your clothing before you curse the pack.

Shoulder Straps

Most of the time, shoulder straps do little more than stop the pack from falling off your back. But because there are times when you have to carry all or some of the weight on your shoulders (for example, river crossings when you've undone the hipbelt for safety and rock scrambles and downhill ski runs where for balance you've fully tightened all the straps to split the weight between shoulders and hips), these straps need to be foam-filled and tapered to keep the padding from slipping. This design is now standard on most good packs. Many straps are also curved so they run neatly under the arms without twisting. The key to a good fit is the distance between the shoulder straps at the top. Some straps are adjustable here so they will fit both broad and narrow shoulders. A few, like those on Gregory packs, adjust automatically. There are different shoulder straps for men and women, too. As with hipbelts, this isn't a strict division, however. Shoulder straps also come in different lengths—Gregory offers three for men and three for women, for example. Usually the length that corresponds to the frame length will fit, but if it doesn't you can change it for a different one.

Load-Lifter Straps

Packs designed for moderate to heavy loads (30 pounds and up) should have load-lifter straps (sometimes called top tension, load-balancing, or shoulder stabilizer straps) running from the top of the shoulder straps to the pack. These straps pull the load in over your shoulders to increase stability; they also stop you from feeling that the pack is falling backward and lift the shoulder straps off the sensitive nerves on top of the shoulders, transferring the weight to the collarbone. By loosening or tightening the straps, which you can do while walking, you can shift the weight of the pack between the hips and the shoulders to find the most comfortable position for the terrain you're on. Take a little time to adjust both the shoulder and load-lifter straps until the pack feels comfortable and stable. To work well, the straps need to rise off the front of the shoulders at about 45 degrees.

On most packs, the load-lifter straps are sewn to the shoulder straps, which means that altering the tension of one changes the other; so when you tighten the load-lifter straps for better stability, you also pull the shoulder straps down onto your shoulders. If they then feel too tight, you slacken them off, which also loosens the load-lifter straps and causes the pack to fall backward. To maintain stability, you tighten the load-lifter straps again. Repeating the cycle over and over can mean that by the end of the day the top tension straps are at their minimum length and therefore not as effective as they should be, while the shoulder straps have crept down your back and their buckles are pinching your armpits. I always try to get the adjustment about right at the start of the day and keep any alterations to a minimum. Even so, I end some days with a pack that is very badly adjusted. Though I haven't tried it, McHale seems to have found a simple solution with the Bypass shoulder system, in which the stabilizer straps aren't sewn to the shoulder straps. This means that the shoulder straps can slide along the stabilizers when they're adjusted without the latter's moving at all. The Bypass shoulder system has been around for a while, and I fully expected other makers to come up with their own versions. They haven't, however, presumably because they believe the conventional one works.

Sternum Straps

Sternum straps are found on most packs, attached to buckles or webbing on the shoulder straps. They pull the shoulder straps in toward the chest and help stabilize the pack. I don't use them much of the time, since they feel restrictive, but they can be helpful for stability when skiing or scrambling and for varying the pressure points of a heavy load during a long ascent. Most are simple webbing straps, but some have stretch sections that prevent overtightening. Fully elasticized straps can't be tightened at all and are useless. The position of sternum straps is important. They should sit high up, just below your neck, to reduce pressure on your chest.

Back Bands and Padding

In addition to a padded hipbelt and lumbar pad, most internal-frame packs have padded backs, some of them cushy panels of thermo-molded foam. If the entire back isn't padded, then the padding on the shoulder straps should run far enough down the back to protect the shoulder blades. Since much of the pack never touches the wearer's back directly, some of the padding is often unnecessary; too little, though, and sharp objects can poke you. Open-weave mesh over the foam helps moisture to disperse so your back doesn't get quite as sweaty as with plain nylon.

External frames need something to hold the crossbars off your back. On basic packs this is usually a wide band of tensioned nylon; mesh is better for ventilation than solid nylon. The tensioning cord or wire should be easy to tighten if it works loose. More expensive models sometimes have a pad of molded foam instead. The latter may be more comfortable, but it also reduces ventilation, lessening one of the advantages of external frames.

FITTING THE PACK

Modern packs are so complex that you can't just walk into a store, sling one on your back, and walk away. A good pack must be fitted, and it is important that this be done properly. A poorly fitted pack will prove unstable, uncomfortable, and so painful and inefficient that you may never want to go backpacking again. The best way to avoid this is to buy from a store with expert staff who can fit the pack for you. Allow plenty of time for this; it can take a while to get it right.

If you don't want to bother taking time to fit a pack—some people think having to do so means the pack is too complicated—a simple rucksack or a traditional external-frame pack would be the best choice. Even with these designs, you need to find the correct back length, though a precise fit isn't essential. A pack whose shoulder straps join the pack roughly level with your shoulders when the hipbelt, if there is one, is taking most of the weight comfortably on your hips should be fine. The first task in fitting a pack is to find the right back length. Your height is irrelevant here. The length of your legs, neck, or head makes no difference to the size of pack that will fit your back. I'm 5 feet, 8 inches tall, but I have a long torso. If I went by my height, as some pack makers still suggest, I'd end up with a pack that was too short. If a pack is too long, it will tower over your head and be very unstable; if it's too short, the hipbelt will ride above your hips and won't be able to take much weight.

The key measurement for finding the right size is the distance from the base of your neck to your upper hipbone, technically from the seventh cervical vertebra (a clearly felt knob) to the top of the iliac crest, which you can find by digging your thumbs into your sides. You can measure this yourself with a flexible tape measure, but it's much easier to get someone else to do it. Most frames come in two to five sizes. Dana Design's Arcflex packs, for example, come in five lengths—extra small, 14 to 16 inches; small, 16 to 18 inches;

medium, 18 to 20 inches; large, 20 to 22 inches; and extra large, 22 to 24 inches. My back measures 19.5 inches, so I have a medium Arcflex pack. However, I bought my Dana Design Astralplane by mail order and got the size wrong the first time, buying a large. The company quickly exchanged my pack, and the Arcflex is the most comfortable suspension system I've used.

Not all pack makers use the same back lengths for their sizes, though the variation is small; it partly depends on how many sizes they make. ULA P-1 and P-2 packs come in four sizes—small, 15 to 17 inches; medium, 18 to 20 inches; large, 21 to 23 inches; and extra large, 23 inches plus. Again I'm a medium, so that's the size of my ULA P-2. If

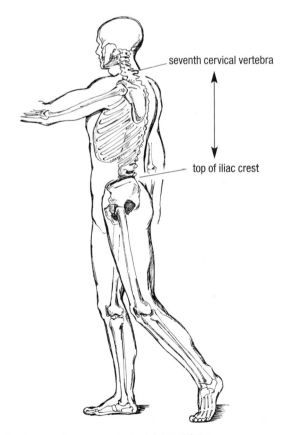

seventh cervical vertebra

top of iliac crest

How to correctly measure the back for pack fitting.

you're on the edge of two sizes, try on both and see which feels better.

When you have the right back length, check that the hipbelt and the shoulder straps are the correct sizes (see pages 105–7). The hipbelt should ride with its upper edge about an inch above your hipbone, so that the weight is borne by the broadest, strongest part of your hips. The top of the frame, if there is one, should then be 2 to 4 inches above your shoulders so that the load-lifter straps rise at an angle of about 45 degrees. Most pack makers tell you how to measure your back length and which of their sizes go with which back lengths. Some, like Gregory, provide stores with a fitting tool that makes finding the right size easy. All packs come with instructions for fine-tuning the fit, some more detailed than others. Instructions differ according to the specifications of the suspension system, but there are some general principles.

Once you have the right back length, it's time to fine-tune the pack for the greatest comfort. The most common way to do this is with an *adjustable harness*, which allows you to move the shoulder straps up and down the back of the pack. On a few packs the positions of both the shoulder straps and the hipbelt are adjustable. However, hipbelt adjustments change the position of the base of the pack in relation to your body, which causes the load to press on your backside when the effective back length is shortened and to ride too high on the back when it's lengthened. Both interfere with stability and comfort, so any hipbelt position adjustments should be very fine. I've found that the best position is with the base of the hipbelt level with the base of the pack.

Lowe Alpine was first with an adjustable shoulder harness system. In its much-copied Parallux system, the shoulder straps are fitted into slots in a

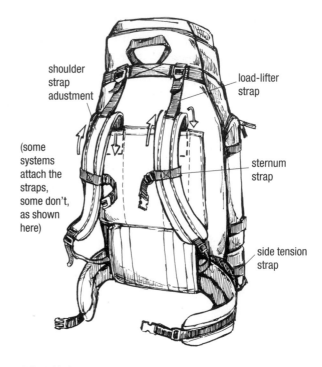

Adjustable harness systems.

webbing column sewn down the center of the pack's back. Variations employ Velcro straps or a slotted plastic adjustment "ladder." Others have plastic plates that attach to each other with Velcro. These systems demand some fiddling; easier are stepless systems that use a locking slider, screw, or similar device to slide the shoulder straps up and down the central column. Even simpler are systems in which the shoulder straps are attached to a stiffened plastic yoke that slides up and down the stays; you can adjust these while wearing the pack by simply pulling on two straps attached to the base of the plate. Some adjustment systems are easy to use; others are hidden under back padding and can be hard to find, let alone use. Losing your temper doesn't help, as I know from experience. Instruction manuals aren't always much use either.

Help from knowledgeable sales staff is the best bet. Whichever type you end up with, find the right position for your back and then forget about it. Obviously, any system has a limited adjustment range. At either end of this range a pack won't carry as well as it does if adjusted to a position nearer the middle. Packs that come in just one frame size will still fit only a narrow range of back lengths, however adjustable they are.

Before you try on a pack, load it with at least 25 to 30 pounds of gear. An empty or lightly loaded pack is impossible to fit properly and will of course feel fine. Most stores will fill the pack for you— sometimes with ropes—though you could take your own gear to check that it fits in the pack properly. Before putting on the pack, loosen all the adjustment straps. Then put the pack on and do up the hipbelt until it is carrying all the weight and the upper edge rides about an inch above the top of your hipbone. Next, tighten the hipbelt stabilizer straps, followed by the shoulder straps and load-lifter straps. The last should leave the shoulder straps at a point roughly level with your collarbone or just in front of it, at an angle of about 45 degrees. If the angle is smaller than that, the harness needs lengthening or the pack is too short; if it is larger, it needs shortening or the pack is too long. The aim is to have most of the pack weight riding on the hips while the pack hugs the back to provide stability. If the distance between the shoulder straps and hipbelt is too short, the load will pull back and down on the shoulders; if it's too long, although the weight will be on the hips, the top of the pack will be unstable and will sway when you walk. (See photos next page.)

Once you have the right size pack and have adjusted the harness correctly, most of your fitting problems are over. The shoulder straps themselves should curve over your shoulders a couple of inches before joining the pack. They shouldn't feel as though they are slipping off your shoulders or be so close together that they pinch your neck. The lower buckles should be several inches below the armpits so they don't touch you, but with enough webbing to allow for adjustment over different thicknesses of clothing.

Finally, make sure the sternum strap is in the correct position, above the part of your chest that expands most when you breathe but not so high that it presses on your neck. When you walk, the pack should hug your body as if it's stuck to you. If it feels awkward or uncomfortable, keep adjusting until you get it right or until you decide that this particular pack will never fit you comfortably.

Once I have the best fit I can obtain with an internal-frame pack, I usually bend over and stretch the pack on my back so the frame can start to mold to my shape, a process that is usually complete after the first day's walk. Some pack makers advise removing the stays of internal frames and bending them to the shape of your back before you start fitting the pack, but I've never been able to do this successfully, even with help from a friend, and prebent stays are the devil to reinsert in their sleeves. Some stores have staff trained to do this for you. However, a friend suggests that "the trick is to make lots of very fine adjustments, and to make each one by bending [the stays] around gentle curves such as one's upper thigh."

You have to make minute adjustments to the harness every time you use a pack. Loosening the top stabilizer straps, tightening the shoulder straps, then retightening the stabilizers cinches the pack to the body for maximum stability but also shifts some of the load onto the shoulders. This is useful on steep descents or when skiing or crossing rough ground—anywhere balance is essential. For straightforward ascents and walking on the

Altering the back length of an adjustable backpack (Vaude Astra 65 II).

Tightening the load-lifter straps.

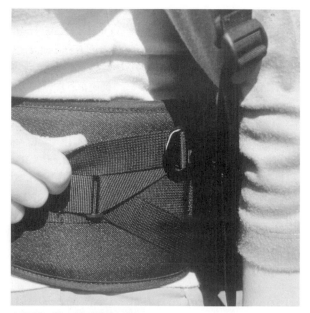

Adjusting the side tension straps.

flat, the shoulder and stabilizer straps can be slackened off a touch so that almost all of the weight drops onto the hips, then the stabilizers should be tightened a little again until you can just slide a finger between the shoulder and the shoulder straps.

Every time you put on the pack, you have to loosen the side stabilizer straps, then tighten them after you've done up the hipbelt—otherwise the latter won't wrap around the hips properly. While you're on the move, whenever the pack doesn't feel quite right or you can feel a pressure point developing, adjust the straps to shift the balance of the load slightly until it feels right again. I do this frequently during the day, almost without noticing it.

If you want or need a custom fit, McHale, which sells through its own store in Seattle and its Web site, will make a pack to your measurements. If you always seem to be between sizes with fixed-length packs or at the ends of the adjustment systems of adjustable ones, a McHale pack might be the answer.

Gender-Specific Packs

Although makers don't usually say so, packs that don't come labeled as "men's" or "women's" are usually designed for the "average" man. But women often have shorter torsos, narrower shoulders, and wider hips than men do. This means men's packs may have frames that are too long (leading to an unstable carry and too much weight on the shoulders), overly wide shoulder straps that slide off and have to be held in place by a tight sternum strap, and hipbelts that dig in at the lower edge and don't touch at the top.

The past twenty years have seen a big change, with many packs now specifically designed for women. Modular packs for which you can select different hipbelts and shoulder straps are an alternative. We're all different, so being able to choose components that fit your shape or else to vary the fit of those that come with the pack means everyone should be able to find a pack that fits well.

PACKBAGS

Compared with the intricacies of frames and suspension systems, packbag design is straightforward. The choice is purely personal—the type of packbag has little effect on the comfort of your pack. How many pockets, compartments, and external attachment points you want depends on how you like to pack and the bulk of your gear. Tidy folk like packs with plenty of pockets and at least two compartments so they can organize their gear. Those who are less neat tend to go for large,

single-compartment monsters so they can shove everything in quickly.

There are a couple of points to consider, however. To maintain balance and comfortable posture, the load needs to be as close as possible to your center of gravity. This means keeping it near your back and as high up as is feasible without reducing stability. While a good suspension system is the key to this, it helps if the packbag extends upward and perhaps out at the sides but not away from the back. For this reason, if your pack has large rear pockets, you should pack only light items in them. My Dana Design Astralplane has such pockets. I find that if I pack them with light items such as hats, gloves, and windshirts they don't affect the carry, but if I put full water bottles in them I can feel the pack pulling backward. Many packs have a strap at the top running from front to back across the packbag. When tightened, this strap pulls the load in toward the back. They work well, and I look for one on a large pack.

The packbag is an integral part of an internal-frame pack. The frame may be embedded in a foam-padded back, encased in sleeves, or just attached at the top and bottom of the bag. Whatever the method, the frame and pack work together and cannot be used separately. Packbags may be attached to external frames in various ways, but the most common is with clevis pins and split rings. One frame conceivably could be used with several different packbags or with other items such as stuff sacks.

Size

How large a packbag you need depends on the bulk of your gear, the length of your trips, and how neatly you pack. I've always preferred large packs. I like to pack everything inside (including my insulating mat when possible), and I like to know I can cram everything in quickly and easily, even in the dark after the tent has just blown down in a storm. (Paranoia? Maybe, but it has happened to me.) Those who favor small packs say that a large pack is a heavy pack because you'll always fill it up. I say this applies only to the weak willed! If I had only one pack, it would be a large one. A large pack cinched down when half full is far more comfortable than an overloaded small one.

Now that there is lighter, more compact gear, I generally use a smaller pack. A pack of 4,000 cubic inches or so is now enough for most three-season trips, however long. I still use a 7,200-cubic-inch monster for cold-weather trips, but it doesn't get as much use as it did, and my 5,500-cubic-inch pack hasn't been used for a few years, being too small for the cold-weather trips but too big and heavy for the rest of the year.

A minor problem is that different manufacturers seem to have different ideas of what constitutes a cubic inch, so one maker's 5,000-cubic-inch pack may hold less than another's 4,500-cubic-inch model. (GoLite and some other top makers use a standard approved by the American Society for Testing Materials. If every maker used it, the problem would disappear.) When choosing a pack, think about whether your gear will all fit in with room left for food. You could even take your gear to the store and pack the sack to be sure.

Internal-frame packs usually have *compression straps* on the sides or front that you can pull in to hold the load close to the back when the pack isn't full. Traditional external-frame packs lack these, though they do appear on some new designs. Packs with compression straps and removable *extendable lids* are often specified with maximum and minimum capacities; to achieve maximum volume, you may have to raise the lid so high that

the top of the pack becomes unstable, so it's wise to check this before you buy.

External-frame packbags that run the length of the frame tend to be very large. The more common three-quarter-length bags can have capacities as small as 2,500 cubic inches, though most average about 4,000 cubic inches. Extra gear (sleeping mat, tent, sleeping bag) can be strapped under the packbag without affecting how the pack carries, and if necessary, even more gear can be lashed on top. However, if you strap extra gear, other than light items like foam pads, under or above an internal-frame pack, you might ruin its balance and fit. If you need to carry a really awkward load, you can remove the packbag from an external frame and strap the load directly to the frame.

Internal Compartments

Most large packs come with zippered lower compartments, though you can get packs with one huge compartment. Compartments with long zippers that run right around the packbag or curve down to the lower edges are the easiest to use. With large packs—5,000 cubic inches or more—I prefer two compartments because they provide better access to my load. On most packs the divider separating the two compartments is held in place by a zipper or drawcord and can be removed to create a single compartment if needed. A few pack makers offer packs with more than two compartments. I suspect this might make packing difficult. I'm not that organized! With smaller packs I find a single compartment adequate. Not having the divider or zipper saves a little weight and expense, too.

Lids and Closures

Lids keep the contents of your pack in, prevent things from moving around, and protect the pack opening from rain. Most packbags have large lids, sometimes with elasticized edges for a trimmer fit, that close with two straps fastened by quick-release buckles. Ultralight packs often have no lid at all, just a rollover top that closes with buckles or a couple of drawcords and a buckle and strap.

Many packbags have a *floating lid* that attaches to the back of the pack by straps and can be extended upward over a large load or tightened down over a small one. These lids can be removed when not needed to save weight. A similar, though less effective, design is a lid that is sewn to the back of the packbag but extends when you release the straps at the back. When such a lid is fully extended, it tends to restrict head movement, interferes with easy access to the lid pocket, and fails to cover the load. Many detachable lids contain large pockets (500+ cubic inches) and can be used as lumbar packs or even small day packs by rearranging the straps, using extras provided for that purpose or by using the pack hipbelt. They can be useful for carrying odds and ends (film, hat, gloves, binoculars) on short strolls. I've used a detachable pack lid as a day pack for daylong hikes away from camp, managing to pack in rain gear, warm clothing, and other essentials.

The lower compartments of packs are always closed by zippers. Straps that run over the zipper take some of the strain and reduce the likelihood of its bursting. Since I've had problems with lightweight zippers on day packs, I like large zippers, whether toothed or coiled; lightweight zippers, protected by straps or not, worry me. Top compartments usually close with two drawcords, one around the main body of the pack, which holds the load in, and one on the lighter-weight extension, which completely covers the load when pulled in. If the only access to the load is through the top opening, items packed at the bottom of the top compartment cannot be reached easily. Verti-

cal or diagonal zippers in the main body are found on some large packbags. I find these useful, especially in bad weather, when I can extract the tent, including the poles, through the open zipper without unpacking other gear, opening the main lid, or letting in much rain or snow.

Zip-around front panels for suitcase-type loading, giving easy access to the whole interior of the packbag, have fallen out of popularity, probably because the pack had to be laid down to pack and unpack—not a good idea in the rain or on mud or snow. The pack couldn't be pulled tight around a partial load, either, so items would move around. Panel loading is now primarily found on travel packs.

Some large packs, however, have both top- and panel-loading main compartments. This has the advantages of both and is an alternative to the main-compartment zippers. I look for one or the other in any pack of more than 5,000-cubic-inch capacity.

Pockets

Pockets are useful for stowing small, easily mislaid items and things you may need during the day. Lid pockets are found on most packs except traditional external-frame models and some of the newer lightweight packs. The best lid pockets are large and have either curved zippers or zippers that run around the sides for easy access. Some packs also have a second flat security pocket inside the lid for storing documents, wallets, permits, and similar items.

External-frame packs normally come with one, two, or (rarely) three fixed pockets on each side. Internal-frame packs, often designed for mountaineering as well as backpacking, don't usually have fixed side pockets, since these can get in the way when climbing. Instead, optional detachable pockets can be fastened to the compression straps. These add 500 to 1,000 cubic inches per pair to the pack's capacity and 4 to 12 ounces to the weight. They can be removed to reduce the capacity of the pack or when using the pack for skiing or scrambling, when side pockets are a nuisance. Some side pockets have backs stiffened with a synthetic plate, which makes them slightly easier to pack but also heavier. A few makers also offer large pockets that can be attached to the back of a pack.

An alternative to a detachable pocket is an integral bellows side pocket with side-zipper entry, which folds flat when not used. I find bellows pockets more difficult to use than detachable pockets. They are narrow at the top and bottom, can be obstructed by compression straps, and when full can impinge on the volume of the main compartment. And you still have to carry the weight of the material when you don't need the pockets. On the other hand, they are always there when you need them—you can't forget one.

Many packs have open pockets at the base of each side. These *wand pockets* were originally designed to hold the thin wands that mountaineers use to mark routes and caches on glaciers and snowfields. They are useful for supporting the ends of long, thin items such as tent poles, trekking poles, or skis. Wand pockets are usually permanently attached, though some, like those from McHale, are detachable and can be replaced with a larger open pocket that will hold a quart or liter water bottle. Some wand pockets have elasticized edges and can be stretched to take a small water bottle. I often carry a map in the wand pocket for easy access.

With the new ultralight packs came ultralight pockets made from rugged mesh. These may have open tops with drawcord closures or else zippers. They are now my favorite pockets. You can stuff

wet gear into them—tarps, flysheets, rain clothing—and it will slowly drain and dry and not soak other items. The side pockets can hold water bottles so you can reach them while wearing the pack. You can also use them for snacks, a toilet trowel, fuel bottles, and other items you want to have outside the main pack. Detachable mesh pockets are sold, so you can add them if your pack doesn't have them.

I also like pockets on the hipbelt. I have these on my ULA P-2 pack, and they are great for a compass, a whistle, snack bars, and other small items.

Many packs have internal hydration sleeves or pockets designed to hold water bladders, with an exit hole for the drinking tube. If you use a hydration system, these are useful—though you can just put the bladder in an external pocket—otherwise they can be used for storing items like maps and small items of clothing.

Straps and Patches

Side compression straps can be used to attach skis and other long items (trekking poles, tripods, tent poles, foam pads). Most packbags come with one or two sets of straps for ice axes and straps (and maybe a reinforced panel) for crampons on the lid or the front. If straps don't come with the pack, there are often patches so you can thread your own. Many packs come with far too many exterior fastenings, but you can always cut off those you'll never use.

MATERIALS

Modern packs are made from a variety of coated nylons and polyesters. These fabrics are hardwearing, nonabsorbent, and flexible. *Texturized nylons* —made from a bulked filament that creates a durable, abrasion-resistant fabric—are often used for the pack base or bottom, sometimes with a layer of lighter nylon inside; some makers use this fabric for the whole packbag. The most common is Cordura, though a few companies have their own proprietary fabrics. *Packcloth* is a smoother, lighter nylon often used for the main body of the pack. All of these materials are strong and long-lasting.

One way to keep the weight of a pack down is to use lightweight fabrics. Packcloth and 500-denier Cordura are lighter than 1,000-denier Cordura, but not by enough to make a big difference in weight. (The *denier* is the weight in grams of 9,000 meters of yarn. Thus 500-denier Cordura is made from yarns that weigh 500 grams per 9,000 meters. The lower the denier, the finer the yarn.) There are some *really* lightweight fabrics, though. For ultralight packs where weight is more important than durability, ripstop nylon is sometimes used. Silicone ripstop nylon is the strongest lightweight nylon and companies like GoLite use it in packs like the Speed (32 ounces, 3,400 cubic inches). DSM's Dyneema and Honeywell's Spectra cloth are very light polyethylene fibers that are ten times stronger than steel, pound for pound, more durable than polyester, and very abrasion- and ultraviolet resistant. Kelty's 5,250-cubic-inch internal-frame Spectra pack, the Cloud, weighs 71 ounces, while McHale's 3,500-cubic-inch internal-frame pack, the Spectra SUBPOP, weighs 39 ounces.

Unfortunately, there are penalties for these low weights. These fibers are very expensive and come only in white and gray—they can't be dyed. However, they can be woven with ordinary nylon to produce a fabric with ripstop threads made from polyethylene fibers filled in with nylon. This produces a colored fabric with a white grid imposed on it that looks far less conspicuous than pure Spectra or Dyneema and also costs less. It's used in many lightweight packs from companies like GoLite, McHale, and ULA and is very tough. I've used Spectra and Dyneema gridstop packs extensively, including on a five-week hike, and haven't yet damaged the fabric. Even airport baggage handlers have failed to harm it—and in the interests of testing, one pack has been through several airports unprotected. I now consider these the best fabrics for packs.

While most of these fabrics are waterproof when new, the coating that makes them so is usually soon abraded. The seams will leak in heavy rain anyway. Some manufacturers advise coating the seams with sealant, but the process is too complicated and messy for me to even contemplate. I rely on liners and covers (see pages 125–26) to keep the contents of the pack dry.

Weight

For many years I used a large, heavy pack for all my backpacking on the rationale that the pack was the one item of gear whose weight wasn't significant because comfort came first. I'm less convinced about the weight now. Comfort still comes first, and for loads of 50 pounds or more, a pack with a sophisticated suspension system is certainly far more comfortable than one with a more basic design, despite the extra weight. With loads over 30 pounds, I still find a framed pack more comfortable than a frameless one, but it doesn't have to be heavy. For loads under 30 pounds, ultralight packs without frames can be perfectly comfortable. Comfort doesn't have to equal weight anymore. Indeed, a lighter pack means a lighter load, which means your legs get less tired.

Despite the increasing number of lightweight and ultralight packs, most packs are still pretty heavy, weighing at least a pound for every 1,000 cubic inches of capacity—about 62 cubic inches per ounce. Many packs are heavier, with as few as 45 cubic inches per ounce. Yet a standard 6,000-cubic-inch internal-frame pack I have that dates back to 1982 weighs less than 5 pounds, giving 77 cubic inches per ounce.

For two decades—right up until the late 1990s—the weight of packs kept increasing. More complex frames, thicker padding, heavier fabrics—which most packs are still made from—detachable pockets, detachable lids, more straps, zippers, and buckles all piled on the weight. Eventually there had to be a reaction. Other gear—tents, sleeping bags, stoves, clothing, footwear—had gotten lighter. The change came with the increased popularity of long-distance hiking and the rise of adventure racing. Fast movers and light hikers didn't want heavy packs, so lighter models began to appear on the market. The old heavyweights still dominate, but for light loads there's no longer any need to carry a heavy pack.

A good rule of thumb for estimating pack weight is that the pack shouldn't weigh more than 10 percent of the maximum total load: for a 70-pound winter load, a 7-pound pack is acceptable, but for a 30-pound summer load, a 3-pound pack would be better. Of course, if you use the same pack year-round, as many backpackers do, the 7-pound pack would carry the 30-pound load. Another way of thinking about pack weights comes from ULA, which suggests that a lightweight pack should be able to support in pounds the same figure as its weight in ounces. Thus my 40-ounce ULA P-2 pack should be comfortable with 40 pounds, which it is. ULA also says that an ultralight pack should support in pounds 150 percent of its weight in ounces. Thus, at 14 ounces, the GoLite Breeze should support 21 pounds, which it will do—just barely.

Acceptable weight can also be roughly determined by the volume-to-weight ratio, found by dividing the capacity by the weight in ounces. Since the average ratio for most modern packs is 60 to 65 cubic inches per ounce, any figure lower than this means the pack is heavy for its capacity (the Astralplane comes in at 58 cubic inches per ounce), and any higher figure means it's lightweight. Quite a few packs that should be fine with light to moderate loads come in the range of 70 to 90 cubic inches per ounce. Some are even lighter. The ULA P-2 has 100 cubic inches per ounce, the GoLite Gust an astonishing 192 cubic inches, the GoLite Breeze 206 cubic inches, and the Gossamer Gear G4 285 cubic inches.

I still regard comfort as the crucial factor for carrying loads. When you're lugging 60 pounds or more, a pound or two of additional pack weight is worth it if you get a more comfortable carry. But for lighter loads, especially those under 40 pounds, I now like packs with a volume-to-weight ratio of at least 100 cubic inches per ounce.

DURABILITY

Top-quality packs are very tough, but many won't last for a walk of several months. I've suffered broken internal frames, snapped shoulder straps, ripped-out hipbelts, slipping buckles, and collapsed hipbelt padding on long hikes. On my first long solo hike back in 1976, the hipbelt tore off my new external-frame pack after just 200 miles. But I've also had packs last 2,000 miles and four and a half months of continuous use with loads averaging 60 to 70 pounds. My old Gregory Cassin, a discontinued model, survived a three-month Yukon walk with a heavy load when it was five years old and had already had many months of use. The only damage was to the top of one framestay sleeve, which ripped out. (Duct tape held it in place for the rest of the walk.) This degree of use is comparable to years, if not decades, of backpacking for those who go out for several weekends a month and perhaps a couple of two- or three-week trips a year.

Of the three people I know who hiked all or most of the Pacific Crest Trail the same year I did, each broke at least one pack. After months of constant use and harsh treatment, it seems that something is almost bound to fail, considering how complex a modern pack is and how much can go wrong. The heavier the load, the more strain on the pack—another reason for keeping the weight down.

Crude repairs can, and often must, be made to equipment in the field, but I'm loath to continue backpacking in remote country with a pack that has begun to show signs of failing, at least not before it's had a factory overhaul. After replacing broken packs at great expense in both time and money on my Pacific Crest Trail and Continental Divide walks, I had a spare pack ready and waiting when I set off on a Canadian Rockies through-hike. On that walk I replaced my pack early because it wasn't able to carry the weight (the makers had changed the style of the hipbelt from earlier models). The replacement pack broke two weeks before the end of the trek, and I had to nurse it to the finish, bandaged with tape. Perhaps I'm unlucky or particularly hard on packs, but for future lengthy ventures I plan to have a spare pack, and I'd advise anyone else to do the same.

Reputable pack makers stand behind their products, and most will replace or repair packs quickly if you explain the situation, though that isn't much comfort if you're days away from the nearest phone when your pack fails. Even a spare pack is no good until you can pick it up. It's important to be able to effect basic repairs; in Chapter 8, I cover the items to carry in a repair kit.

PACKING

How you pack gear depends on the sort of hiking you're doing, which items you're likely to need during the day, and the type of packbag you have. For hiking on level ground on well-maintained trails, heavy, low-bulk items should be packed high and near to your back to keep the load close to your center of gravity and enable you to maintain an upright stance. This is how I pack all the time, regardless of the terrain. In theory, however, for any activity where balance is important, such as scrambling, bushwhacking, cross-country hiking on steep, rough ground, or skiing, the heavy, low-bulk items should be packed lower for better stability, though still as close to your back as possible. Women tend to have a lower center of gravity than men and may find packing like this leads to a more comfortable carry for trail hiking too. Whatever your packing method, it's important that the load is balanced so the pack doesn't pull to one side. The items you'll need during the day should be accessible, and it helps to know where everything is.

I normally use a packbag with side or rear pockets and, with heavy loads, a lid pocket, so my packing system is based on this design. I don't like anything on the outside except winter hardware (ice ax and skis) and a closed-cell sleeping mat; everything else goes inside, and I pack most items in stuff sacks to keep everything organized.

With ultralight packs with no back padding, a sleeping pad can be used to cushion your back. Standard foam pads can be placed vertically in the pack and then unrolled so you can pack gear in the middle of the pad. A Z-Rest pad (see page 237) can

PACKS: CHOICES AND MODELS

My ideal pack for heavy loads would have a suspension system that enabled me to carry 75 pounds as though it were 30; would be superbly stable for skiing and crossing steep, rough ground; and would allow me to walk upright on the flat. Internal or external frame? It doesn't matter. It's the performance, not the type of frame, that matters.

I would like a packbag with a capacity of at least 6,000 cubic inches; two compartments; mesh side pockets; an extendable, detachable lid with a large pocket; and straps for ice axes and skis. The total weight shouldn't be more than 4 pounds. This pack would also see me through a three-thousand-mile, six-month walk without anything breaking!

Not everyone would want my ideal pack, however. I have friends who don't like side pockets or lower compartments and others who never use skis or ice axes. One friend swears that traditional external frames carry heavy loads better, despite his having used top-quality packs for snow travel, where he concedes internals are better for balance.

I haven't yet found my ideal large pack, but the Dana Design Astralplane comes close. It's certainly more comfortable with a heavy load than any other pack I've tried and is also very stable. It's a bit heavy, but I have no other complaints. It has a 7,000-cubic-inch capacity, two compartments, vertical zippers in the top compartment, two front pockets, a detachable lid with a large pocket, and wand pockets. The frame consists of a polyethylene framesheet with a single aluminum stay down the center plus carbon-fiber rods at the side that help transfer the weight to the hipbelt. The belt itself is massive and supportive. My medium size weighs 7 pounds, 2 ounces, and current models are listed as 7 pounds, 12 ounces. Ultralight it's not! But I've had my Astralplane for twelve years, and it's been everywhere from the High Sierra to Greenland, Spitsbergen, Lapland, and the Yukon and it's still in good condition.

The wealth of lightweight and ultralight packs that has appeared in recent years means it's no longer true that I haven't found anything approaching an ideal ultralight pack in the 3,000- to 4,000-cubic-inch range. In fact I've found two, and there are many that look good that I haven't tried. For loads in the 30- to 45-pound range, I like the ULA P-2, a 4,900-cubic-inch pack made from tough Dyneema gridstop nylon with ripstop nylon panels. It has a foam framesheet with an aluminum stay in the center, a padded back, and a lightly padded hipbelt. There's one compartment and two huge mesh side pockets plus side compression straps. There's no lid, just two drawcords and a strap. There are other optional extras, and my pack has zipped pockets on the hipbelt, a large front mesh pocket, a front shock cord, and an internal security pocket. The total weight is 40 ounces, about a third the weight of the Astralplane. With 40 pounds inside, the P-2 feels fine. It's now my most-used pack.

Even lighter at just 21 ounces (large size) is the GoLite Gust. This 3,900-cubic-inch pack has no frame, just a lightly padded back, and an unpadded hipbelt. It's also made from Dyneema gridstop nylon, and there's just a zipped pocket on the front, a few front attachment straps, and a roll-top lid. Given the basic harness and lack of padding in the hipbelt, it's astonishingly comfortable with loads up to 30 pounds. The reason lies in the curved back, which flares at the base and directs the weight onto your hips. For light loads the Gust is now my first choice. Overload it, though, and it quickly feels uncomfortable, as I found when I took the GoLite Trek, which has the same back system, on a five-week walk in the High Sierra. At one point I had at least 45 pounds in it—and sore hips. I solved the problem by duct taping foam drink can holders to the hipbelt. My Trek has mesh pockets on the front and sides plus a lid. The capacity in the large size is 5,350 cubic inches, and the weight is 42 ounces. The latest model has been slimmed down a little—4,700 cubic inches, 32 ounces—but is still easily big enough for 45-pound loads. The extra features are useful, but for loads under 30 pounds I'd rather have the much lighter Gust, and for loads over that, the much more supportive P-2. A Trek with a stiffer back and more padding in the hipbelt would be excellent.

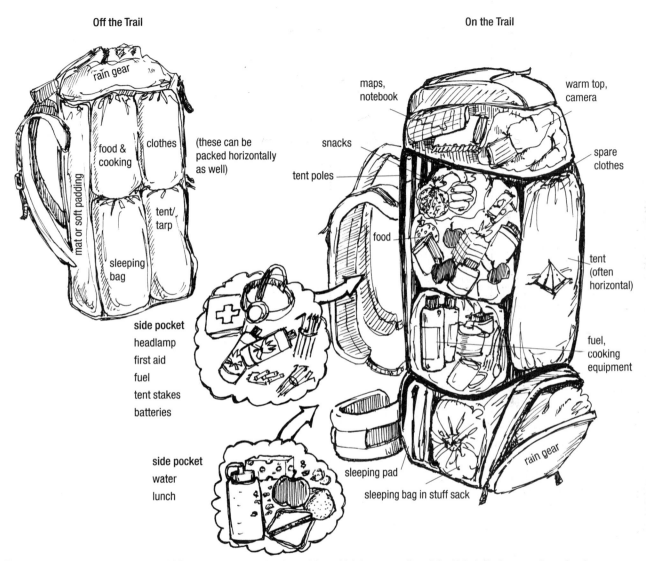

Off the Trail

rain gear

food & cooking

clothes

(these can be packed horizontally as well)

mat or soft padding

tent/ tarp

sleeping bag

side pocket
headlamp
first aid
fuel
tent stakes
batteries

side pocket
water
lunch

On the Trail

maps, notebook

warm top, camera

snacks

spare clothes

tent poles

food

tent (often horizontal)

fuel, cooking equipment

sleeping pad

sleeping bag in stuff sack

rain gear

There are many ways to pack your pack! For trail hiking, carrying the weight up high lets you walk upright. Light bulky items such as sleeping bags and clothing go low in the pack; heavy items such as food go in the middle, near the back. Keep heavy items close to your back to prevent the pack from pulling backward, forcing you to lean forward. For off-trail hiking on rough ground, where balance is especially important, place heavier items in the middle rather than at the top, still as close to the back as possible, as this makes for a more stable pack.

be folded flat and put down the back of the pack, as can a self-inflating mat. All these are effective but do take up a fair amount of the capacity of the pack. If you don't use a pad, gear can be packed into two long stuff sacks that you stand vertically side by side in the pack. Make sure there are soft items next to your back. If you layer gear horizontally, the back of the pack is likely to fold at the junctions between layers.

If the pack has a frame or padded back, the first

thing to go into the bottom of the pack, or the lower compartment if there is one, is my self-inflating mat, folded into a square and placed against the back of the pack so it's well protected. In front of this goes the sleeping bag (in an oversized stuff sack inside a pack liner); when I put weight on top of the sleeping bag, it fills out the corners and helps the hipbelt wrap around the hips. Next in are my spare clothes (in another oversized stuff sack). If there's space and the pack has a lower compartment, my rain gear goes in next to the zipper for quick access. If I'm carrying a bivouac bag, it too goes in the base of the pack. This means that the bottom of the pack is filled with soft items that are bulky for their weight.

I then slide tent poles down one side of the pack next to my back and if there is one, through the cutaway corner of the upper compartment floor. Next to go in are cooking pans, stove and fuel canisters, empty water containers, and small items such as candles and repair kit, with the heaviest items (such as full fuel containers) close to my back. Except for my lunch and the day's trail snacks, food bags go on top of the cooking gear, close to my back because of the weight. In front of the food bags go the tent or tarp and any camp footwear. At the top of the pack I put books, spare maps, spare camera, and the windshirt or warm top I've been wearing to ward off the early morning chill while packing. If I can't fit this in the top of the pack, I squeeze it into the lower compartment or into the front mesh pocket if there is one.

The lid pocket is filled, in no particular order, with hat, neck gaiter, gloves, mittens, sunscreen, camera accessories bag, insect repellent, camera lenses, dark glasses, and any small items that have escaped packing elsewhere. If there's no lid pocket these go in a small stuff sack at the very top of the pack. One side pocket holds a water bottle, lunch, and snacks; the other holds fuel bottles if I'm using a white-gas or alcohol stove, plus tent stakes, headlamp, and first-aid kit. Any items that didn't fit into the lid pocket or that I've overlooked also go in an outside pocket. Map, compass, mini binoculars, and writing materials go in a jacket or shirt pocket or hipbelt pocket. My camera, in its padded case, is slung across my body on a padded strap so it's both well protected and accessible. Then, once I've shouldered the pack, tightened up the straps, and picked up my poles, I'm ready for the day's walk.

Of course this system varies according to conditions. If I have a foam pad rather than a self-inflating mat, it goes on the outside of the pack. Rain gear can end up buried in the pack on days and in areas where it's unlikely to be needed. Items can move from pocket to pocket at times. The aim is convenience and comfort, not tidiness and organization for their own sake.

PUTTING ON THE PACK

Putting on the pack, repeated many times daily, requires a great deal of energy and more than a little finesse. With loads under 25 pounds, you can simply lift the pack and swing it onto your back. With most loads, though, the easiest way is to lift the pack using the shoulder strap (or the nylon "haul loop" attached to the top of the pack back on nearly all models), rest it on your hip, and put the arm on that side through the shoulder strap. You can then slowly swing the pack onto your back and slip your other arm through the shoulder strap.

With heavy loads (50 pounds or so), I swing the pack onto my bent leg rather than my hip, then from a stooped position I slowly shift, rather than swing, the load onto my back. Heavy loads make me aware of how much energy putting on a pack

Putting on a heavy pack.
(1) Grab the pack by the shoulder straps. **(2)** Lift it onto your bent leg. **(3)** Swing it slowly onto your shoulder and then . . . **(4)** . . . onto your back. **(5)** Adjust the straps for a good fit.

requires; whenever I stop on the trail, I try to find a rock or bank to rest the pack on so I can back out of the harness, and later back into it again. Such shelves are rare, though, so with really heavy loads (65 pounds or more) I usually sit down, put my arms through the shoulder straps, and then slowly stand up if I feel I haven't the energy to heave the pack onto my back. I also try to take the pack on and off less often when it's heavy; I keep items I need for the day in my pockets and rest the pack against something when I stop.

In camp I sometimes keep the pack in the tent—if I'm not in bear country and there's room—but usually I leave it outside, propped against a tree or rock or lying on the ground. I leave the items I won't need overnight in the pack, whether in or outside the tent.

During rest stops on the trail, the pack can be used as a seat if the ground is cold or wet. One advantage of an external frame is that it can be propped up with a staff and used as a backrest—its rigidity keeps it from twisting out of position and falling over, as can happen with internal-frame packs. This backrest is so comfortable that I've tried to make an internal-frame pack perform the same function. I've had some success wedging the staff into the top of the pack, but it's much easier with two trekking poles, since then you can form a tripod. Unexpected collapses still occur, however.

Using a pack as a backrest in camp.

PACK CARE

After a trip, I empty the pack, shake out any debris that has accumulated inside, and, if it's wet, hang it up to dry. You can try to remove stains with soap or other cleansers; I regard such marks as adding to the pack's character, and I'm also wary of damaging or weakening the fabric in any way, so I don't bother.

Before a trip, I check all the zippers. I also look for signs of any stitching failure if I didn't do so the last time I used the pack.

PACK ACCESSORIES

Covers, Liners, and Stuff Sacks

Most packs aren't waterproof, whatever claims the manufacturer makes about the fabric. Water trickles in through the zippers, wicks along drawcords, seeps through the seams, and when the waterproofing has worn off, leaks right through the fabric. The few packs that are totally sealed are designed for canoeing and other watersports rather than backpacking. These have welded seams and waterproof zippers and are made from vinyl. A few—such as the 5-pound, 6,940-cubic-inch SealLine Pro Pack and the 5-pound, 6,600-cubic-inch Gaia Pack—are big enough for backpacking and might be worth considering if you expect to spend a long time in the rain.

Water-sensitive gear (down-filled items, spare clothes, maps, books) is best stored in waterproof bags. Pack covers can be used to keep rain out of the pack, but these are easily torn and can blow off. When my last one ripped I stopped using them. You have to remove them to get into the pack, too, which can let rain in. If the items inside the pack are in waterproof bags, it doesn't matter if water enters. Some packs have built-in covers contained in the base or the lid, and a poncho can cover both you and the pack. Even if I had one of these, I'd still keep my gear in waterproof bags in wet country. The best covers are adjustable and hug the pack closely so they don't flap in the wind. Many pack makers offer them, and they are also sold by companies like Outdoor Research, whose Hydroseal Pack Cover comes in five sizes and has daisy-chain webbing so ice axes can be attached when the cover is on.

I don't use a single large liner that fills the pack because often there are wet items in the pack (such as the tent fly sheet and rain gear) that I want to keep separate from dry items. Instead, I put my sleeping bag and spare clothes in separate stuff sacks inside a large waterproof stuff sack and use another large sack for other items. For many years I used neoprene pack liners combined with seam-sealed Black Diamond Sealcoat stuff sacks. Both of these have long disappeared from the stores, however, and the coatings have long peeled off my most recent ones.

Dry bags with sealed seams and roll-top closures designed for watersports are a possibility but tend to be heavy and a bit stiff for stuffing in a pack. I have the XS size Ortlieb PS17 dry bag. It weighs 4 ounces, holds 793 cubic inches, and is completely watertight. The long, thin shape isn't convenient for storing in the pack, but it does make a good cover for a foam pad in wet weather. The larger Ortlieb bags are wider and could be used as pack liners. The 4,760-cubic-inch XL Short bag weighs 12.3 ounces. Pacific Outdoor's Pneumo Dry Bags are a bit lighter and also have a unique compression valve that allows you to squeeze out most of the air to reduce the volume. This is an exciting concept, since it could drastically reduce the packed bulk of sleeping bags and clothes. The

Pneumo bags come in four sizes—305, 915, 1,525, and 3,050 cubic inches, at weights of 3, 5, 7, and 9 ounces. I haven't tried them, but I intend to do it soon.

Nylon stuff sacks are the standard for packing gear, and many items, including sleeping bags, come with one. They're also available separately in a wide range of shapes and sizes. However, very few are fully waterproof. They leak at the seams even if the fabric is coated. They're fine for dry weather and when only light rain is likely. It's in continuous rain and downpours that waterproof stuff sacks are needed, although I always carry my sleeping bag in one.

Of course, you can just use heavy-duty plastic bags and trash bags, but these don't last very long, and when I used them I became concerned about how many I was throwing away. Bags designed for garden trash are tougher than those for indoor use. Of the few waterproof stuff sacks, Outdoor Research Hydrolite bags are very light (1 ounce for the 300-cubic-inch one), as are Exped Dry Bags (0.8 ounce for the 6-by-10-inch XXS Cord Dry Bag). Both types look excellent, though I haven't tried them. That's because I discovered silicone-nylon (silnylon) stuff sacks, which are very light, very durable, and waterproof. Equinox and GoLite make these; mine are by GoLite. They come in six sizes ranging from 125 to 3,200 cubic inches and weigh from 0.5 to 2 ounces in the Landlubber's Stow Sack range, which have a drawcord closure. Paddler's Stow Sacks have a twistable top seal as well as a drawcord and come in four sizes, from 500 to 3,200 cubic inches at weights of 1 to 3 ounces. The SiLite fabric is very thin, but I've used these stuff sacks for several years now, and they've proved tougher than standard coated nylon sacks, since the silicone can't wear off and the slick fabric is surprisingly tear-resistant. The large stow sacks make good liners, while the smaller ones hold sleeping bags, clothing, maps, and more. I was dubious at first about the water resistance of such light, thin bags but was convinced they worked after hanging one with food in it during a night of heavy rain and finding the inside bone-dry in the morning. The seams aren't sealed, but I haven't found this a problem unless they're pressed against a wet surface. If the base of your pack leaks and you have a silnylon stuff sack in it, moisture may come through the seams if it's next to the wet fabric. This can be solved by sealing the seams of your sack with McNett SilNet, which I've done with the large Stow Sack that I use to line the bottom of my pack.

For some items, like books and maps, zip-closed plastic bags are convenient. Standard ones aren't that strong, however, and need replacing quite often, which is a waste of resources and can also be a problem if one splits during a trip and you haven't a spare. Aloksak bags from Watchful Eye Designs are much tougher. They're made from 6-millimeter transparent polymer film and come in the following sizes: 4.5 inches by 7 inches; 6 inches by 6.75 inches; 9 inches by 6 inches; and 12 inches by 12 inches. I use the smallest bag for cash, documents, and other paper items, since it's compact enough to be carried in a pocket as a wallet when traveling to and from the trail or at town stops. It's survived a year of regular use, including one five-week trip, and is still waterproof and easy to seal. I'm impressed enough that I plan on buying some of the larger bags for items like maps, notebooks, and paperbacks.

I don't use waterproof stuff sacks for items that water won't harm, like cooking pots. For these, mesh stuff sacks are fine. They weigh an ounce or less, depending on size, and have the advantage of being see-through.

Lumbar Packs

For many years I wore a small lumbar pack (or fanny pack, as it's also known, though *lumbar* is more accurate, since the pack sits in the lumbar area when worn correctly) the wrong way around in order to reach small items without taking my pack off. I stopped doing this quite a few years ago for several reasons. One was the lightening of my load, which made it easier to take the pack off, but more important, I started using hipbelts with pockets attached and shirts with large chest pockets that would take all the items that I used to carry in my lumbar pack. I find this new system more efficient. However a light lumbar pack could be used with an ultralight pack with no hipbelt to take some of the weight.

Lumbar packs range from tiny models consisting of a pouch on a strip of webbing to complex models with frames and padded hipbelts. Capacities run from 50 to 1,250 cubic inches or more. The largest will hold up to 20 pounds and could conceivably be used for ultralight overnight trips. I don't like having that much weight so low on my body, however. Even with the firmest hipbelt, it feels as though it's pulling downward. I sometimes use a small basic lumbar pack for short day hikes when I want to carry binoculars, a rain jacket, and maybe a few other items, but it's been years since I took one on a backpacking trip. The lids of many packs convert to lumbar packs, and I do occasionally use those on my Dana Design Astralplane and Gregory Shasta packs for side trips from camps. They're OK for loads of 4 or 5 pounds but sag with much more.

Belt and Shoulder Pouches

Most pack makers and many other companies offer small zipped pouches and bags designed to be fit-ted to the pack hipbelt or shoulder straps. I've tried some such as the Dana Design Wet Rib that attach to the shoulder straps, but I find that they impede putting on and taking off the pack and feel clumsy. I'm not fond of belt pouches either, since they interfere with hipbelt adjustments. I prefer pockets built into the hipbelt for small items or else garment pockets. However, there are plenty of small pouches, with capacities of a few hundred cubic inches and weights from 2 to 8 ounces, and many people seem to like them.

Duffel Bags

Transporting packs by car usually isn't a problem—you just sling them in the trunk and set off. If you fly, however, your pack is at the mercy of airport baggage handlers, and it can easily be damaged. For a time some airlines made passengers sign waivers for unprotected packs, though this practice seems to have stopped.

If you fly regularly, remember that internal frames are less prone to damage than externals. (When I flew home after one hike, my external-frame pack came off the luggage carousel with a permanent bend and a couple of cracks in the frame.) You can minimize the chance of damage by tightening all straps, tucking away loose ends, and wrapping the hipbelt around the front of the pack and threading it through the ice ax loops or lower compartment compression straps to keep it in place. A long strap or a length of thick cord can be wound around the pack and then tied into a loop to give the baggage handlers something to grab. Make sure you have nothing fastened to the outside of the pack.

A duffel bag offers much more protection than these measures. But you'll need a very large duffel if you have a large pack. Duffels don't have to be heavy; mine, from Dana Design, is called a Travel Pocket. It even doubles as a pack cover, though I wouldn't want to carry it on a hike. Made of coated Cordura, the Behemoth model has an 8,000-cubic-inch capacity and weighs 28 ounces. I've transported my pack in it many times, along with other items, including several ice axes, and nothing has suffered any damage.

You can get duffels that are fully waterproof, ideal for canoeing trips but unnecessary for getting gear from airport to airport, and ones that are padded, which is necessary only if you carry fragile items inside. (I always put items like cameras, binoculars, and headlamps in my carry-on luggage.)

A duffel needs a couple of top compression straps, a grab handle, and perhaps a shoulder strap, but that's it. Many pack makers make duffels, as do travel-focused companies like Eagle Creek.

chapter five

keeping warm
and dry

dressing for the wilderness

When the clouds roll in, the wind picks up, and the first raindrops fall, your clothing should protect you from the storm. If it doesn't, you may have to make camp early, crawling soggily into your tent and staying there until the skies clear. At the worst, you could find yourself in danger from hypothermia. Besides keeping you warm when it's cold and dry when it's wet, clothing should also keep you cool when the sun shines. In other words, clothing should keep you comfortable regardless of the weather. Choosing lightweight, low-bulk clothing that does all this requires care. Before looking at clothing in detail, I'll try to give some understanding of how the body works when exercising and what bearing this has on clothes.

HEAT LOSS AND
HEAT PRODUCTION

The human body evolved to deal with a tropical climate, and it ceases to function if its temperature falls more than a couple of degrees below 98.4°F (37°C) or rises more than a couple of degrees above that. In cool climates, the body needs a covering to maintain that temperature, because the heat it pro-

Hiking in a synthetic-insulated top, fleece-lined cap, and gloves on a cold, windy fall day in the North Cascades.

ENTERING THE WILDERNESS

The switchbacks ease. Suddenly we're in the notch on the ridge, surmounting the pass, gazing on a wild new horizon. Below sprawls a tangle of bare rocky spurs and lake-strewn benches, split by curving valleys that gradually darken into green forest as they sink toward the black slash of a deeper, wider canyon. Beyond that, waves of rugged peaks are dotted with small white glaciers and remnants of snow. There is no mark of a human hand. This is what we've come to find.

duces is lost to the cooler air. Ideally, clothing should allow a balance between heat loss and heat production, so that we feel neither hot nor cold. It's hard to maintain this balance when we alternate sitting still with varying degrees of activity in a range of air temperatures and conditions: when we're active, the body pumps out heat and moisture, which has to be dispersed; when we're stationary, it stops doing so.

The body loses heat in four ways, which determine how clothing has to function to keep its temperature in equilibrium:

- ■ *Convection*, the transfer of heat from the body to the air, is the major cause of heat loss. It occurs whenever the air is cooler than the body, which is most of the time. The rate of heat loss increases in proportion to air motion—once air begins to move over the skin (and through your clothing), it can whip body warmth away at an amazing rate. To prevent this, clothing must cut out the flow of air over the skin; that is, it must be windproof.
- ■ *Conduction* is the transfer of heat from one surface to another. All materials conduct heat, some better than others. Air conducts heat poorly, so the best protection against conduc-

tive heat loss is clothing that traps and holds air in its fibers. Indeed, the trapped air is what keeps you warm; the fabrics just hold it in place. Water, however, is a good heat conductor, so if your clothing is wet, you will cool down rapidly. This means that clothing has to keep out rain and snow, which isn't difficult —the problem is that clothing must also transmit perspiration to the outer air to keep you dry, known as breathability, or moisture vapor transmission (MVT).

- ■ *Evaporation* occurs when body moisture is transformed into vapor—a process that requires heat. During vigorous exercise, the body can perspire as much as a quart of liquid an hour. Clothing must transport it away quickly so that it doesn't use up body heat. Wearing garments that can be ventilated easily, especially at the neck, is important, as is wearing breathable materials that water vapor can pass through.
- ■ *Radiation* is the passing of heat directly between two objects without warming the intervening space. This is the way the sun heats the earth (and us on hot, clear days). Radiation requires a direct pathway, so wearing clothes— especially clothing that is tightly woven and smooth-surfaced—mostly blocks it. Very little heat is lost by radiation anyway. Reflective radiant barriers built into clothing really don't make any difference.

THE LAYER SYSTEM

As if keeping out rain, expelling sweat, trapping heat, and preventing the body from overheating weren't enough, clothing for walkers must also be light, durable, low in bulk, quick drying, easy to care for, and able to cope with a wide variety of weather conditions. The usual solution is to wear several light layers of clothing on the torso (legs require less protection), which can be adjusted to suit weather conditions and activity. The *layer system* is versatile and efficient if used properly, which means constantly opening and closing zippers and fastenings and removing or adding layers. In severe conditions I also use layers on my legs, hands, and head in severre conditions.

A simple layering system consists of an inner layer of thin wicking material that removes moisture from the skin, a thicker midlayer to trap air and provide insulation, and a waterproof-breathable outer shell to keep out wind and rain

WORST-CASE PLAN

Many years ago I came close to finding my own worst-case plan inadequate when I spent a week battling the high winds, lashing rain, and melting snow of an Icelandic June. I wore a wicking synthetic T-shirt; a thin wicking synthetic shirt; a thin synthetic-filled top; a thin synthetic windshirt; and a light waterproof-breathable rain jacket. I was barely warm enough when walking, because the rain jacket wasn't breathable enough and I was permanently damp. Luckily I'd taken a vapor-barrier suit as backup, so I was able to stay warm in camp, but a thicker warm layer would have been a welcome addition.

Dressed for cold, stormy weather in New Hampshire's White Mountains. Warm, waterproof hat, fleece-lined waterproof gloves, and waterproof-breathable shell jacket over windproof jacket and lightweight fleece top.

Base layer

Midlayer

long underwear top
(zipper neck)

lightweight fleece
top (zipper front)

wicking
underwear,
not cotton

wicking long
underwear
bottoms

noncotton
wicking socks

A base-layer top may be adequate on its own in warm weather. Add a thin fleece when the temperature drops. Wicking long underwear can be worn under trail pants in cold weather.

Outer layer

fleece hat

wind and
waterproof top

underarm
vents

pockets

Velcro cuffs

gloves with
rain shells

trail pants

side zippers

trail shoes/lightweight boots

Rain wear

rain jacket with hood

rain pants

Clothing for wet, windy weather.

bandanna or
sun hat

long-sleeved
solar shirt

wicking
sport shirt

trail shorts

don't forget the
sunscreen!

sandals

Hot-weather wear.

while allowing perspiration to pass through. This neat three-layer system won't cope with a wide range of conditions, however. Additional layers could include one or two more midlayers such as a wind shell or soft shell and a thick, insulated garment for camp and rest stops in cold weather. I often carry six layers—a thin base layer, two thin midlayers, wind shell, rain shell, and insulated top (see the trip sidebars in Chapter 2 for lists of clothing I've carried on actual trips). Several thin layers are more versatile than one thick one, which is either on or off, often leaving you either too hot or too cold. The boundaries of the different layers have always been a little fuzzy—thick inner layers can be used as midlayers, and windproof midlayers are also outer shells when it's not raining—and this is getting fuzzier with garments claimed to function as all three layers. But nothing beats the versatility of having separate garments that you can combine differently according to the conditions.

How much clothing you plan to take on a particular hike depends on the conditions you expect. I take enough to keep me comfortable in the worst likely weather. If I'm in doubt as to what is enough, I sometimes take a light insulated vest just in case.

I don't carry clothing that can't all be worn together if necessary. If it's cold, I want to be able to wear everything. The only spare items I carry are underpants and socks.

The Inner Layer

Although it's sometimes described as "thermal" underwear, the main purpose of the inner layer (also known as the next-to-skin or base layer) is to keep the skin *dry* rather than *warm*—often called moisture management. If perspiration is removed quickly from the skin's surface, your outer layers keep you warm more easily. If the layer of clothing next to your skin becomes saturated and dries slowly, your other clothes, however good, have a hard time keeping you warm. No fabric, whatever the claims made for it, is warm when wet.

While you're on the move, as long as your outer layer keeps out rain and wind and your midlayer provides enough warmth, you generate heat and stay warm even if your inner layer is damp. But once you stop, wet undergarments will chill you rapidly, especially if you've been exercising hard and producing a great deal of moisture. After a climb to a pass or a summit, you often want to stop, both for a rest and to enjoy the view you've worked so hard to reach. Once you stop, however, your heat output drops rapidly, just when you need that heat to dry out your damp base layer. But that damp base layer conducts heat away from the body, producing *after-exercise chill*. The wetter and slower drying your clothing, the longer such chill lasts and the colder and more uncomfortable you'll be. Thus the inner and outer layers are important because they can minimize after-exercise chill by wicking moisture away from the skin and stopping rain from soaking your clothing; what goes on between these layers matters less, and this is where compromises can be made.

The one inner material to avoid is cotton, since it absorbs moisture quickly and in great quantities. It also takes a long time to dry, using up a massive amount of body heat. To make matters worse, damp cotton clings to the skin, preventing a layer of insulating air from forming. I haven't worn cotton next to my skin for years—not even on trips in sunny weather when some people like light cotton or cotton-blend garments because they're cooling when damp. I find thin synthetics or wool more comfortable than cotton in the heat, and I don't

need to change my top if the weather turns damp or cold.

Base-layer fabrics remove body moisture by transporting or *wicking* it away from the skin. Synthetic fibers are hydrophobic—they repel moisture—and tend to wick quickly. Natural fibers like wool and silk are hydrophilic—water loving—and absorb moisture into their fibers before passing it more slowly to the outside.

Synthetics can wick moisture by being nonabsorbent and having an open weave through which the moisture quickly passes, and having hydrophilic (water-attracting) outer surfaces that "pull" moisture through the fabric and away from the skin. In both cases, body heat pushes the moisture through the fabric.

Although synthetic wicking fabrics are very good, they can become overloaded with sweat and end up very damp on the inside. An important factor is the time they take to dry when you're not producing enough body heat to push the moisture through the fabric. The best are those with brushed or raised fluffy inner surfaces that have a minimum of material in contact with the skin, letting it dry quickly. If the inner surface is smooth and tightly woven, moisture passes through it more slowly. Oddly, both tightly woven and open-weave *outer* surfaces can speed moisture movement. In the first case moisture can spread out over the surface of the fabric and evaporate or pass into the next layer; in the second case the open weave allows moisture to pass through very quickly. Fabrics with different materials on the inside and outside are known as bicomponent fabrics. Examples include Polartec Power Stretch, Polartec Power Dry, and Páramo Parameta S.

Most fabrics come in several weights. The lightest—sometimes called silkweight—are very thin and fast wicking, ideal for aerobic pursuits such as trail running but also good for backpacking, either on their own in the heat or under other layers in cold weather. Midweight underwear is slightly heavier and thicker and usually has a tighter weave. It's warmer but often wicks more slowly, which is fine in cool weather. The heaviest and thickest fabrics are labeled *expedition* or *winter weight*. Most of these don't wick moisture or dry as fast as the lighter fabrics and are better suited for midlayers. A few, like Power Stretch and Parameta S, wick as well as or better than thin fabrics.

Designs are usually simple; most tops come with either a crewneck or a turtleneck with a zipper, buttons, or snaps at the neck. You can get short or long sleeves; I prefer short-sleeved crewneck T-shirts for warm weather and long-sleeved zippered turtlenecks for colder weather. The latter are good as midlayers too. Close-fitting garments are much more efficient than baggy ones. My partner, hiker Denise Thorn, says she didn't realize how effective base layers could be until she wore women's styles that fitted properly rather than loose "unisex" tops. Most makers now offer women's and men's base layers, while some companies like Wild Roses (now called OR Women) and Isis make only women's clothing. There are also bras made from wicking fabrics.

Figure-hugging "tights" are the norm for long underpants. Underpants made from wicking synthetics are far superior to cotton. Close-fitting garments help trap air and wick moisture quickly and also fit easily under other garments. Long pants should have a particularly snug fit to avoid the discomfort of baggy long johns sagging down inside other layers; elasticized waists are essential. Long backs stop tops from riding up at the waist. Stretchy fabrics often wick fastest because of their close fit. They're generally more comfortable, too. Seams should be flat sewn to avoid rubbing and abrasion. Dark colors show dirt and stains less, but white or pale colors reflect heat better when worn alone in warm weather.

Choosing a wicking synthetic fabric can seem hard because there are so many, each with a fancy name and claiming to work better than the others. Actually there are only a few base fabrics, and they're all derived from petrochemicals. Polypropylene was the original fiber used, but most base layers are now made from polyester. Other fibers like chlorofiber, acrylic, and nylon have just about disappeared.

The Smell Factor

Synthetic base layers are notorious for smelling bad, sometimes after only brief use. Ironically, the hydrophobic properties that make them effective at wicking moisture are the main reason for this. Your body moisture contains oils that stick to the fabric as the liquid evaporates or moves into your next clothing layer. These oils attract bacteria and can also undergo oxidation, both leading to nasty smells. Like the fabric, the oils are hydrophobic. Washing in cool water doesn't remove them. Hot water does, but not all fabrics can be washed in hot water without shrinking, making it hard to get the smell out. Hanging clothes in the sun and wind can help, as can repeated washing in plenty of detergent and soaking in cold water with a little dissolved soap. It's best, though, to choose garments that can be washed and dried at hot temperatures. This is also useful for long hikes when you want to chuck all your dirty clothes into a washer and dryer at town stops without worrying about the temperature.

Many fabrics have antimicrobial treatments. Most work a little but don't stop garments from smelling for very long. Fibers such as X-Static that contain silver—a natural antimicrobial that contains no chemicals and is safe next to the skin—

work best. Odor Resistant Polartec Power Dry contains silver fibers. Silver can't wear out or be washed out, so it lasts the life of the garment. It's said to remove 99 percent of bacteria in an hour and to work best in warm, humid environments. To test this, I wore an X-Static top for chopping firewood, day hikes, and cycle rides as well as backpacking trips. After two weeks' wear, my unwashed top smelled faintly musty, but nothing worse. My family didn't tell me to change it and take a shower. Synthetics incorporating silver fibers seem to be the answer to stinky synthetic underwear.

Fabrics

POLYPROPYLENE "Polypro" is the lightest and thinnest wicking synthetic. Introduced by Helly Hansen in its Lifa line back in the 1970s, it dominated the market for a while but is now found mostly in budget garments. Polypro won't absorb moisture but quickly passes it along its fibers and into the air or the next layer. It wicks away sweat and dries so fast that after-exercise chill is negligible. However, it's the worst synthetic fabric for stinking, producing a stench that can be hard to get rid of. Apart from the odor, if you don't wash it at least every couple of days, polypro ceases to wick properly, leaving your skin clammy and cold. On long trips you have to carry several garments or rinse one out regularly and learn to live with the smell of stale sweat.

Polypro's drawbacks are mostly overcome in Helly Hansen's Lifa range. Helly's polypro has a softer, less "plastic" feel than standard polypro, and it can be washed at 140°F (60°C), a heat that rids it of the noxious aroma. It's also said to be resistant to the bacteria that cause smells. Lifa polypro comes in three types: thin, stretchy Lifa Sport; midweight Lifa Active; and Prowool, which has an outer layer of merino wool. I've worn a Lifa Sport crewneck top for several days without washing it, and though

it smells faintly musty, I can bear to have it in the tent, something I wouldn't do with the old polypro after even one day's wear. It wicks moisture efficiently and, I suspect, faster than standard polypro. My crewneck Lifa Sport top weighs 5 ounces; my bottoms, which I mostly carry for campwear or unexpected cold weather, weigh 3.75 ounces.

POLYESTER Polyester repels water but has a low wicking ability—not ideal for underwear, since sweat just stays on the skin. However, it can be treated with chemicals or mechanically altered so that it becomes hydrophilic, resulting in moisture being drawn through the material to the outer surface, where it spreads out and quickly dries. The drawback is that after repeated washings chemical treatments wear off, though this isn't the problem it once was. When this happens the material stops wicking.

There are many wicking polyester fabrics. Some are proprietary like Patagonia's Capilene, GoLite's C-Thru, REI's MTS, and Lowe Alpine's DryFlow. Others, like Polartec Power Dry, CoolMax, Thermolite Base, and Akwatek, are used by many companies, though they may appear under names like Marmot's DriClime, which is Power Dry. Over the years I've tried many polyester base layers and concluded that they all work pretty well and there's not much difference between them.

Of the expedition-weight polyester fabrics I've used, two stand out. Polartec Power Stretch and Páramo Parameta S both wick moisture faster than any other materials of similar weight and better than many lighter-weight fabrics. Both materials have soft, brushed inner surfaces that wick moisture rapidly and smooth, tightly woven outers that spread the moisture so it evaporates quickly. Power Stretch is used by many companies; my zip-neck top and tights are made by Lowe Alpine and weigh 10 and 7 ounces, respectively—

less than some expedition-weight fabrics that aren't as warm or as efficient at removing moisture. As the name suggests, the fabric is very stretchy and hugs the body. Parameta S doesn't stretch and is exclusive to Páramo. I have the Trail Shirt, a conventional design with a collar, two chest pockets, and a snap-fastened front. It weighs 14 ounces. All Parameta S and some Power Stretch garments (such as Mountain Hardwear's Zip T) can be reversed so the smooth side is on the inside. This is meant to make them cooler and thus increase the temperature range over which the garment is comfortable. It works to some extent, but I still find the Trail Shirt a bit warm in hot weather. I've had my Power Stretch and Parameta S garments for many years, and they've proved very durable. I now mostly wear them as midlayers.

Weights for base-layer tops and bottoms range from 3 ounces in light garments to 14 ounces for expedition-weight ones. Briefs start at about 2 ounces.

WOOL Wool, the traditional material for outdoor underwear, has had a remarkable revival and is now regarded by many as the best choice for base layers. I tend to agree. Though it might seem that wool wouldn't fit into a layering system with high-tech synthetics, it does. Wool is excellent at drawing moisture into its fibers and leaving a dry surface against the skin. It can absorb up to 30 percent of its weight before it feels wet and cold, so after-exercise chill is not usually a problem. I've worn wool next to my skin on many winter ski tours and have always felt warm, even in camp after an energetic day. On those tours I've also worn the same top for two weeks with no odor problem. Because wool is hydrophilic and absorbent, body oils go into the fibers rather than staying on the surface and attracting the bacteria that cause smells. Wool's limitations used to be its

warmth, which made it useful only for cold weather, and the need for careful washing, often by hand. Now, however, there are very fine tops that work well in the heat and that can be machine-washed without shrinking. Wool does stretch slightly, though it usually regains its shape when washed. It is pretty durable, too.

What puts many people off wool is its reputation for being itchy. Old-style wool with coarse fibers could irritate the skin, though fine knits have always been available. When I began backpacking I wore a thin lambswool sweater I bought from a department store as my base layer in cold weather. I don't remember it's being itchy. The best wool base layers are made from fine, soft merino wool, which feels luxurious next to the skin, far more comfortable than any synthetic I've ever worn. SmartWool began the return to wool with its merino garments. Many others have followed as people learn just how wonderful wool is to wear, but of the garments I've tried, SmartWool still has the edge on softness and comfort. As a final plus, wool is a good material to wear around fires, since it doesn't burn easily or melt like synthetics, making it much safer and less liable to be damaged by sparks.

Wool is also relatively light; I have an Icebreaker long-sleeved crewneck merino wool top that weighs 7 ounces and a SmartWool Aero short-sleeved merino wool T-shirt that weighs 6 ounces, only a little more than equivalent synthetic ones. Both are light and cool enough for warm weather. Thicker, warmer garments weigh more, of course. My SmartWool Traditional Long Sleeve Crew and Traditional Relaxed Tights weigh 12 ounces and 9 ounces, respectively. These are warm garments, however. I wear them only when I expect temperatures to be below freezing. The top makes a good midlayer. Terramar has some good merino wool base layers, too. Its long-sleeved crew weighs 10.5

ounces. Terramar also makes polyester-wool mix and polyester-wool-Outlast acrylic garments (for my opinion on Outlast, see page 75). Wool-synthetic garments work quite well in my experience, though they're not quite as comfortable as pure wool. Ibex also has a good reputation for its wool base layers (and other wool clothing), though I haven't tried any of it, and Arc'teryx has a new line of merino wool base layers.

SILK Silk is the other natural material used in outdoor underwear. Like wool, it can absorb up to 30 percent of its own weight before it feels damp. Silk's best attribute, however, is its luxurious texture; it's light, too—a long-sleeved top weighs 3 to 4 ounces. A silk top I wore on a two-week hike in damp, cool weather kept me warm and dry, and at the end the odor was negligible. It was badly stained with sweat and dirt, though. When I rested after strenuous exercise, the top felt clammy for a few minutes, but then it warmed up. I probably won't take silk on a long hike again, though, because it demands special care; it has to be hand washed and dried flat, and it won't dry overnight in camp unless the air is very warm. Among those offering silk garments are Terramar, SilkSkins, and REI.

The Traditional Shirt Alternative

Cotton or cotton-synthetic shirts have always been popular for warm weather, though I find a light wool or synthetic top better because it gets less clammy and dries more quickly. And if the weather turns cold or wet, a noncotton top doesn't get cold and uncomfortable under other layers.

However, there are now a large number of synthetic shirts designed specifically for hiking in warm weather. Most are traditional in style, with collars, snap or button closures, and breast pockets. The fabrics feel nice against the skin, wick a little, though not as well as wicking base layers, and

dry quickly. A loose fit is more comfortable than a close one, since it allows moisture to disperse and cool air to move inside the shirt. Unlike most base layers, these shirts resist light winds. I now wear one on any trip where I expect it to be sunny and warm much of the time. I particularly like shirts with large pockets, in which I carry maps, a notebook and pens, binoculars, a whistle, a compass, and other items. Long sleeves are more versatile: roll them up in the heat, roll them down when it's cool or you want to keep the sun off your arms. Most shirts have buttoned tabs to keep the sleeves from falling down when rolled up. If the weather is a little too chilly for the shirt alone, I wear it over a base layer.

My favorite is the Mountain Hardwear Canyon, which is made from soft Supplex nylon and has one zipped pocket and one vertical Velcro-closed pocket. There are mesh ventilation panels under the arms and down the sides plus mesh across the back and stretch panels in the shoulders, though I can't say the shoulder panels make much difference. The collar has an extra panel at the back, so when turned up it really protects your neck from the sun. The Canyon weighs 10 ounces. As shirts go it's expensive, but it has proved durable, though it's somewhat stained from sweat and dye that has leached out of pack harnesses. You could of course just wear a nylon or polyester casual shirt, as a few people I know do. These are much less expensive and don't have all the features, but they seem to work well in the heat, though they can get a little sweaty.

A shirt I've had for many years that does better duty than most shirts of this type as a base layer in the cold and wet is Sequel's Solar Shirt, which has a wicking mesh body and, in current models, a nylon-polyester-cotton mix yoke. My original version has a CoolMax yoke, and I do wonder if the new mix will wick quite as well. The big advantage, though, is that it's a firmer fabric, so there's a stand-up collar and two breast pockets that look as though they'd be more comfortable with stuff in them than the soft mesh ones on my version. The Solar Shirt is a pullover design with a deep front opening. Mine is the long-sleeved version and weighs 8 ounces; current models are listed as 9.6 ounces. I first wore my shirt for a two-week hike in the Grand Canyon and found it superb in the heat; it never felt sticky or clammy, and it dried very quickly. At the end of this late-fall trip, the weather turned cold and windy, with frequent rain and hail; despite its accumulation of ten days' sweat, dust, and sunscreen, the Solar Shirt performed well as a base layer under a microfleece top and light rain jacket.

Windproof Underwear?

An unusual development is W. L. Gore's Windstopper N2S fabric. The N2S stands for "next to skin," yet this is a windproof fabric, since it contains a Windstopper membrane. Gore says that N2S can function as a wicking base layer, a light insulating layer, and a windproof and showerproof shell. The membrane is sandwiched between two thin, soft layers, and garments feel flexible and comfortable.

I've tried two garments, the Mountain Hardwear Transition (11 ounces) and the Marmot Evolution (11.5 ounces), both pullover designs with high collars and deep front zippers. (A lighter one is the GoLite Stealth Wind Shirt, at 9 ounces.) However, the Evolution has Power Stretch panels down the sides, while the Transition is 100 percent N2S. Both garments are stretchy, comfortable to wear, and windproof, and they wick moisture well. But I found they are comfortable on their own only over a narrow temperature range. If it's above 50°F (10°C), I am too warm and start to feel sweaty unless there's a very strong wind. If it's below 40°F (5°C), I start feeling chilly unless it's calm. This is not very versatile. The garments also smell a fair bit after a day's wear—I hate to think what they'd be like after a week. Once I'd discovered the performance limits for me, I started wearing the N2S tops as midlayers and found them far more functional and far less smelly. I think keeping the windproof and base layers separate is more practical, but if you want windproof underwear, it does exist.

The Midlayer

The midlayer keeps you warm by trapping air in its fibers. It also has to deal with body moisture that has passed through the inner layer, so it needs to let that moisture through or else absorb it without losing much warmth. Some midlayer garments are windproof and will resist a fair degree of rain, but they're not a substitute for a rain jacket in a real downpour.

Midlayer clothing can be divided into two types: *trailwear* and rest wear or *campwear*. The first category includes wool tops, light- and medium-weight fleece, soft shells, and wind shells. In warm weather, one or two of these garments may be all you need for campwear as well. Mostly though, I carry a down- or synthetic-filled top or

BASE-LAYER CHOICES

After years of wearing synthetic base layers for all my hikes, I now use them infrequently, mostly for day hikes. However, I often carry a very light top and long pants—GoLite C-Thru, Helly Hansen Lifa Sport, Capilene Silkweight—for campwear and as spare clothing. If the weather is cool I like merino wool—Smartwool's Aero T-Shirt is my favorite—and in the heat I prefer a shirt like the Mountain Hardwear Canyon or the Sequel Solar. In very cold weather I still wear Power Stretch and Parameta S tops, though often as midlayers over a wool base layer.

a thick fleece top to keep me warm when stationary. Of course you can wear these while hiking if necessary.

Midlayers come in every imaginable style of shirts, sweaters, smocks, vests, and jackets. Garments that open down the front at least partway are easier to ventilate than polo or crewneck styles—and ventilation is the best way to get rid of excess heat and prevent clothing from becoming damp with sweat. Far more water vapor can escape through an open neck than can wick through the fabric. Conversely, high collars keep your neck warm and hold in heat. I used to avoid pullover designs for fear I'd overheat, but as long as I can open up the top 8 or 10 inches, I've found I can cool off when necessary. Pullovers tend to weigh less than jacket styles, so I now use them regularly.

The traditional midlayer fabrics are wool and cotton, though they aren't so popular anymore. With cotton, this is for good reasons: it's heavy for the warmth provided, soaks up moisture, and is slow to dry. Many years ago I wore a thick brushed cotton (chamois) shirt on a two-week hike to remind myself how cotton shirts perform. Worn over a silk inner layer, it was comfortable and warm; worn under a waterproof-breathable shell, it never became more than slightly damp, despite wet and windy weather. I suspect that this was partly because the silk inner layer took up much of my sweat and the cotton shirt might have become damper with a synthetic inner layer. The performance then was OK, but the shirt weighed 17.5 ounces, more than twice the weight of a fleece top of equivalent warmth, and was bulky when packed. I've never hiked in a heavy cotton shirt since. I hadn't worn wool in many years either, not since discovering fleece more than two decades ago, but recently I have used the 12-ounce Smart-Wool Traditional Crew as a sweater and found that it works very well, though it's heavier than fleece of

equal warmth. SmartWool and Ibex both make wool sweaters, cardigans, jackets, and vests that look good and should be functional alternatives to synthetic garments. And of course if you have some wool sweaters in your closet, they should do fine. The traditional wool shirt in check, plaid, or tartan is still around too, from traditional companies like Woolrich and Pendleton. I have an ancient one I used to hike in back in the 1970s. It weighs 15 ounces, which makes it heavy for the warmth compared with fleece.

Fleece

Cotton and wool shirts and sweaters mostly disappeared from the backcountry with the advent of fleece, for many years now the standard fabric for warm garments. Fleece insulates well, moves moisture quickly, and is light, hardwearing, almost non-absorbent, and quick drying. These properties make fleece ideal for outdoor clothing. Most fleece is made from polyester, though you may find nylon, polypropylene, and acrylic versions.

Fleece, or pile as it used to be called, was first used in clothing by Helly Hansen and tested in Norway's wet, cold climate, for which it proved ideal. In North America it became popular after Malden Mills made a smoother version called Polarfleece for Patagonia in 1979. In 1983 this was replaced by the first of the Polartec fleeces, introduced by Patagonia as Synchilla, and the takeover of outdoor warm clothing by fleece was under way. There are other manufacturers of fleece, including Dyersburg and Draper, but in my opinion Malden Mills still leads the way.

Fleece isn't just one fabric, of course; it comes in a wide variety of weights and finishes. The more loosely knit, thicker, furrier fabrics are sometimes called *pile*; *fleece* is often reserved for denser fabrics with a smoother finish. But makers use both terms for the same fabrics, so they are in effect interchangeable. Malden Mills grades its classic Polartec fleece fabrics as 100, 200, and 300 weight, and other makers have similar weights. The higher the number, the warmer and thicker the fleece. Not all fleece fits easily into this system, but it is a useful guide.

Worn over a wicking inner layer and under a waterproof-breathable shell, fleece can keep you warm in just about any weather while you are on the move and is particularly effective in wet, cold conditions. Fleece moves moisture quickly: at the end of a wet, windy day, I've often found that the outside of my fleece top is damp from condensation inside my rain jacket but the inside is dry. If you feel cold, nothing will warm you up as fast as a dry, fluffy fleece top next to your skin.

Of course, fleece has drawbacks, albeit minor ones. It's not windproof—you can easily blow through it—which means you need a windproof layer over it even in a cool breeze. Although this is a disadvantage at times, the lack of wind resistance means that garments are very breathable and comfortable over a wide temperature range—without a shell when it's warm or calm, with one when it's cold or windy. There is windproof fleece clothing (see pages 143–44), but it's heavier, bulkier, and less breathable than ordinary fleece. Another drawback is that fleece clothing doesn't compress well, so it takes up more room in the pack.

Fleece garments should be fairly close-fitting to trap warm air efficiently. They are prone to the *bellows effect*—cold air is sucked in at the bottom of the garment, replacing warm air—so the hem should be elasticized, have a drawcord, or be designed to tuck into your pants. Cuffs and collars keep warmth in best if they fit closely. A high collar helps keep your neck warm and stops warm air from escaping.

Most fleece garments are hip length, which is just about right to keep them from riding up under your pack hipbelt. Pockets are useful, especially hand-warmer pockets, for around camp and at rest stops, but they are not essential. Hoods can be nice in cold weather, though they're not found on many garments. In light fleece I like pullover tops with zippers or snaps at the neck. Fancier designs simply add more weight.

I wear fleece garments most days, since I live in a mostly damp and cool rural area in the hills and I'm outdoors almost every day. I don't like overheated houses, so I wear fleece indoors much of the year too. Over the years I've accumulated a whole wardrobe of fleece garments, from old Helly Hansen nylon-fiber pile ones—now relegated to outdoor tasks like gathering wood—and early Patagonia Synchilla Snap Ts and Retro Cardigans to much newer Polartec Windbloc and Gore Windstopper jackets. Though fine for day-to-day wear, most are not versatile enough for backpacking; they are too warm when I'm walking and bulkier than alternatives for carrying. However, for hiking in cool weather and for campwear in warm weather, I find the lightest 100-weight fleece provides all the insulation I need. Sometimes called microfleece, this material is comfortable, soft, dense, nonstretchy, and thin. It can be worn next to the skin, though it doesn't wick very well. However it's excellent as a midlayer. When worn over a Power Stretch base layer, it's all the insulation I need while hiking in freezing weather. Garment weights run from 8 to 16 ounces. I've had several 100-weight fleece tops over the years, and they've all worn well. My favorites are two pullover designs with short neck zippers. One is a Lowe Alpine Polartec 100 top that weighs 11 ounces and has a small breast pocket. The other is a Jack Wolfskin Gecko, made from the company's own Nanuc microfleece. This is my most used fleece because it weighs just 8 ounces. Just about every maker of fleece garments has a thin microfleece top in its range, and there are plenty of choices. It takes up little room in the pack, so I carry a light fleece year-round. Expedition-weight base layers give similar warmth and make good alternatives. Besides the Power Stretch and Parameta S tops described earlier, I have a Patagonia R1 Flash Pullover, made from a thick version of Polartec Power Dry with a smooth outer face and raised fleece pillars on the inside that trap warm air and aid wicking. It weighs 12 ounces and is more comfortable next to the skin than microfleece because it wicks well. Another alternative for windy weather is one of the Gore Windstopper N2S base layers described previously.

I used to consider midweight 200-weight fleece the most versatile, wearing it as campwear on cool summer evenings and as a midlayer while on the move in very cold weather. I rarely use it anymore, however; it's been squeezed out by better alternatives. If I want warmth when hiking I prefer to wear two lighter fleeces or, if it's really cold, a light top filled with synthetic insulation, while for camp I prefer something warmer than midweight fleece. There are plenty of midweight fleece tops, in weights from 12 to 25 ounces, with Polartec 200 being the standard fabric.

The warmest fleece, like Polartec 300, is too warm to wear while hiking except in extreme cold unless you feel the cold a great deal. It's useful as a warm layer when you're resting and in camp, especially in wet, cold weather. Most of these fabrics are quite heavy and bulky, though. There is one exception, 6.5-ounce high-loft Polartec Thermal Pro, a shaggy, furlike fleece that is very warm for the weight. It has an open weave and is very breathable and fast drying, though it has no wind resistance at all. It's also very soft and flexible and feels wonder-

ful next to the skin. Indeed, it feels so nice and looks so soft that people often come up and stroke it—which may or may not appeal to you. Patagonia uses it in its Regulator R2 garments. I have an R2 jacket that weighs 14.5 ounces. It has Power Stretch side panels, a full-length front zipper, and two zippered hand-warmer pockets. Other companies making 6.5-ounce Thermal Pro garments include Cloudveil, Mountain Hardwear, Marmot, Lowe Alpine, and Arc'teryx.

There are other types of Thermal Pro that are heavier, warmer, and less fluffy, such as the 9.5-ounce fabric used in Patagonia's 20-ounce R3 Radiant Jacket (which I'm wearing as I write this), but I think the R2 version is the best for backpacking. Thermal Pro is expensive, but it should last—Malden Mills says it's the most durable fleece. My R2 jacket is several years old and has had much use, and it's still in good condition. I most often use it on day hikes, but I do occasionally take it backpacking when the weather may be cold and wet.

WINDPROOF FLEECE The most wind-resistant fleece is probably Polartec Wind Pro, said to have four times the wind resistance of other fleece (which is not saying much) because of its tight construction. Wind Pro will keep out cool breezes, but that's all. To make fleece fully windproof you have to add a windproof layer. This can be a thin nylon or polyester shell or lining or a membrane. Shelled and lined fleece garments are bulkier and heavier than standard fleece. They are very warm but not very versatile, since you can't separate the layers. The fabric actually called windproof fleece has a thin windproof membrane sandwiched between two layers of light fleece and looks like conventional fleece. There are two major windproof fleece fabrics: Malden Mills' Polartec Windbloc and W. L.

Gore's Windstopper fleece. Fabrics come in different weights, and garments weigh 18 ounces or more. Windproof fleece isn't as breathable as standard fleece or as fast at moving moisture. It's far warmer than standard fleece in any sort of wind but not as warm weight-for-weight in still air. It will also keep out showers, though not continuous heavy rain. If you do get it wet, it doesn't dry fast. I've tried several garments, and in all of them I've quickly overheated when walking uphill, even in cold, windy weather. There are some backpackers—like my partner, Denise—who can walk all day in windproof fleece without getting sweaty, so if you run cold rather than hot, it could be the answer for cold-weather backpacking. For me an ordinary fleece top and a separate wind shell are far more comfortable and versatile. That said, I have a Mountain Hardwear Windstopper Vest that I sometimes pack when I want an extra warm garment just in case the weather is cooler than expected. It weighs 11 ounces and packs quite small. Slipped on over a base layer at rest stops, it's just enough to stop me from cooling down.

WATER REPELLENCY Even though fleece is nonabsorbent and quick drying, moisture can be trapped between the fibers, especially in thicker and windproof garments, which slows the drying time and makes them feel damp. Some fleece fabrics have water repellency applied during manufacture; these quickly shed light rain and snow and don't hold moisture in the fibers, which speeds drying. You can improve the water repellency of any fleece by treating it with a wash-in waterproofing agent such as Nikwax PolarProof or Granger's Extreme Wash In.

RECYCLED FLEECE Some fleece is made from recycled polyester and plastic soda bottles, which reduces the use of oil and natural gas (used in manufacturing polyester) and keeps plastic bottles out of landfills. Dyersburg ECO Fleece, Draper's EcoPile, Wellman's EcoSpun, and some Polartec Classic fleece are all made from recycled polyester. Patagonia was the first company to use recycled fleece, back in 1993, and it's found in the Retro Cardigan and some of the Synchilla clothing such as the Synchilla Vest and the Synchilla Marsupial top.

Soft Shells and Wind Shells

For many years waterproof-breathable garments were promoted as being the only shells needed, able to protect from both wind and rain. While this is true, even the best waterproof fabrics are far less breathable than those that are windproof but not waterproof. Wind shells are also softer, more flexible, more comfortable, and more durable than waterproof-breathable shells. I've always carried a wind shell as well as a rain jacket. Indeed, a wind shell is the piece of clothing I use most. It may appear as extra weight given that you still have to carry a rain shell, but it needn't be. A light rain shell is all that's needed, even in severe storms, because you can wear it with your wind shell for greater protection. It's the layering principle again. A wind shell and a light rain shell are more versatile than a standard-weight rain shell. The warmth a thin wind shell provides is surprising. Pull one over a base layer or a fleece garment and you'll notice the difference even in still air.

Wind shells—simple garments with few features, made from a single layer of untreated fabric—were too basic and low-tech to attract much attention from the marketing people until the turn of the twentieth century. Then, spurred by some new high-tech fabrics, outdoor clothing designers suddenly discovered that waterproof-breathable garments weren't suitable for all conditions and that much of the time water-resistant, windproof, highly breathable clothing was more versatile and more comfortable. The marketers called this supposedly new clothing *soft shell* and called rain gear *hard shell*. The exact meaning of soft shell is disputed. The debate seems arcane and rather unhelpful, but overall the term is applied to fairly thin windproof garments with varying degrees of water resistance.

Soft shell, then, is a new name for an old idea. Having praised wind shells for years, I'm happy to see them suddenly become the in thing, even if it took a new name to achieve it. The benefit for backpackers not concerned with the latest fashions is that there are far more garments in different styles and fabrics than there used to be. The most basic are old-style wind shells, made from a single layer of uncoated nylon or polyester. Worn over a fleece top, they keep out a surprising amount of rain. They can be extremely light. Montane's Aero Smock, made from Pertex Quantum nylon, weighs an astonishing 2.68 ounces. It has a mesh pocket on the chest plus a short zipper at the neck. I have Montane's Featherlite Smock, made from Pertex Microlite and weighing 3 ounces. It has no features other than Lycra cuffs and hem and a short neck zipper, but it keeps out the wind and packs down small enough to hold in my fist. Patagonia's Dragonfly and Marmot's Chinook, made from ultralight nylon, weigh 3 ounces and have hoods and pockets. My favorite wind shell weighs slightly more, 5.29 ounces. This is the Montane Lite-speed, made from Pertex Microlite nylon. It's a bit longer than the lighter garments, and has a full-length front zipper, a double-layer hood, and a chest pocket. Wind resistance and breathability are both excellent, and water resistance is surprising for such a thin garment. Note that ultralight garments like these don't have great abrasion resistance and so aren't ideal for scrambling or bushwhacking. Most garments weigh a little more than these, but anything over 12 ounces is unnecessarily heavy.

Pertex is an excellent material for wind shells, but there are others, such as Supplex, Versatech, Clima-Guard, Silmond, and Tactel, plus proprietary ones such as The North Face's Hydrenalite. Some makers just use unbranded nylon and polyester. Many of these fabrics are made from microfibers, which have a denier less than 1: that is, each fiber weighs less than a gram per 9,000 meters, which is a hundred times finer than human hair. Microfibers are soft, supple, strong, and very comfortable. Because more fibers are packed into each thread, microfibers are very windproof and water resistant, since air spaces are fewer and smaller than in higher-denier fabrics. There are two variants on the original wind shell idea: shells treated to increase water resistance and shells with a wicking lining that increases warmth and means they can be worn next to the skin. Once you apply a coating to a fabric, however, you reduce the breathability even if it still isn't fully waterproof. Garments that don't keep out heavy rain yet aren't very breathable seem a bad compromise to me, and I've never liked them. The purpose of a wind shell is to resist wind and be highly breathable, not to be a poor imitation of a rain jacket. However one company, Nextec, has come up with a way to increase a fabric's water resistance without affecting the breathability much. This is done by encapsulating the individual fibers in silicone rather than applying a coating. This leaves microscopic gaps between the fibers through which body moisture can escape. Fabrics treated like this are highly water resistant and won't absorb moisture, making them very quick drying. The treatment, called EPIC (encapsulated protection inside clothing), can't be washed out, and there's no coating to wear off or membrane to tear (don't wash the garment in detergent, though—it ruins the water repellency). I've been impressed with the GoLite Flow jacket, made from EPIC-treated polyester. It's not fully waterproof, but it will resist heavy showers and prolonged light rain.

Breathability is far better than with fully waterproof fabrics, and I've had very little condensation. The Flow is no longer available but Wild Things makes a hooded EPIC jacket/windshirt weighing 8 ounces that appears to be a good substitute.

Line a wind shell with a thin base-layer fabric and you have a garment that can be a base layer or a midlayer and that is windproof, fast wicking, and surprisingly warm for the weight. There are many of these garments; the classic is Marmot's DriClime Windshirt, made from nylon with a brushed DriClime wicking lining. It has a full-length zipper, a large chest pocket, and weighs just 10 ounces. Slightly heavier at 13 ounces is the Patagonia Stretch Zephur Jacket, made from polyester with a brushed polyester lining. I've tried both, and they are comfortable next to the skin, wick moisture fast, dry quickly, and keep out brief showers and light rain. Slightly heavier but also a touch warmer is the hooded Rab Vapour Rise Trail Smock. This is made from Pertex Equilibrium, a polyester-nylon bicomponent fabric that wicks moisture really fast, with a brushed polyester lining. This easily replaces a fleece top and will cope with all but the worst weather without need of a shell. Even so, I find two separate layers more versatile so I mostly wear these tops on day hikes or in dependably cool and windy weather.

The fabrics that have stirred such interest in wind shells are stretch nylons with smooth outsides and brushed insides such as those from the Swiss company Schoeller and laminated stretch fabrics with a windproof membrane such as Gore Windstopper and Polartec Power Shield. The last two are really thin versions of windproof fleece. Although they come in different weights, all these fabrics are thicker, warmer, and heavier than simple nylon and polyester. The lightest and thinnest garments are roughly comparable to a midweight base layer plus a wind shell, the heaviest to a 100-weight fleece plus a shell. The laminated fabrics are more wind and water resistant but less breathable than the nonlaminated ones. None of them are fully waterproof, though Windstopper and Power Shield come close. To find out how they perform and how they might fit into a hiker's wardrobe, I tried four of these garments: the 19-ounce Mountain Hardwear Velocity, made from Schoeller Dryskin Extreme; the 21-ounce GoLite Path, made from Schoeller 3XDRY Extreme; the 16-ounce North Face Apex 1, made from stretch nylon; and the 20-ounce Arc'teryx Gamma MX Hoody, made from Polartec Power Shield Lightweight. They all coped with wet and windy weather, they all felt comfortable, and they all wicked moisture quickly. Yet I wouldn't take any of them on a backpacking trip. They're just too heavy and bulky for the warmth they provide. They're also expensive. Proponents—and there are many—say they keep you warm with fewer layers, increasing freedom of movement and comfort. Maybe so, but they're not as versatile or as warm as three separate layers: a simple wind shell, a base layer, and a 100-weight fleece. They're probably fine for cold-weather climbing and mountaineering, but they're not ideal for backpacking. Designers have fallen in love with them, though, and are having great fun combining fabrics and building garments that look beautiful and feel sensuous. The 19-ounce Marmot Super Hero Jacket, for example, is made from five fabrics—Windstopper Triton across the shoulders for water resistance, Power Shield under the arms for breathability, Polartec Wind Pro and Windstopper N2S on the body for warmth, and Windstopper Fitzroy on the arms and sides for reinforcement. Impressive! But do you need it?

I haven't rejected stretch soft shell fabrics totally, though, and I do sometimes carry a Windstopper N2S base-layer top (see page 140) or a thin stretch nylon North Face Apex Zip Shirt instead of a 100-weight fleece when the weather looks reliably windy. At 11 and 12.5 ounces, respectively, these simple pullover tops weigh less than fancier soft shells. Slightly heavier at 13.8 ounces but more rain resistant and more versatile is the GoLite Kinetic jacket, made from the lightest version of Power Shield with Power Stretch panels over the shoulders. The Kinetic has zip-off sleeves, leaving a 9.5-ounce vest that makes a good backup garment in cool damp windy weather. I treat these soft shells as alternatives to light fleece and sometimes wear a thin wind shell over them, which adds quite a bit of warmth and water resistance.

Many wind shells are pullovers, which are usually lighter than jackets and often more comfortable when worn as a shirt in camp. They're usually short, so they won't extend below a rain jacket worn over them. The size should be adequate for wearing over other midlayers. Useful though not essential features are hoods, map-sized chest pockets, and adjustable cuffs. Even unlined wind shells can be worn next to the skin, although they may feel a little clammy when you're on the move.

Insulated Clothing

While several thin layers are best when hiking, since you can add and subtract layers to suit the conditions, one thick, warm garment for camp and rest stop wear is worth carrying in all but the mildest weather. This garment could be a thick fleece such as Thermal Pro or Polartec 300, which are especially good in cold, wet weather. However, garments filled with down or synthetic insulation are warmer, weigh less, and pack smaller. They are breathable and windproof, too, so you don't need a shell over them except in rain. I find they warm me psychologically as well as physically. Just knowing I

The GoLite Kinetic jacket is a versatile soft shell.

have a thick, puffy garment stowed in my pack helps me feel warm on a cold day. Simple designs are best, since they weigh least. The only features I look for are insulated hand-warmer pockets. Hoods are nice, but a hat does just as well.

Vests make good insulating garments because they keep your core warm and are light and low in bulk. On Pacific Crest Trail, Continental Divide, and Arizona Trail hikes, I carried insulated vests—down on the PCT and AZT and synthetic on the CDT. In combination with a fleece top when the temperature occasionally fell well below freezing, these were just enough to keep me warm in camp. If weight isn't critical, I often carry a jacket or a sweater, which weighs more than a vest but provides more warmth.

Down from ducks and geese is still the lightest, warmest insulation, despite all attempts to create a synthetic that works as well. Garments filled with down pack small and, weight-for-weight, provide much more warmth than fleece or synthetic fills. They're too hot to wear when walking unless it's extremely cold, but they're ideal at rest stops and in camp. Down is very comfortable, and its thickness is reassuring. It looks and feels warm. There's nothing like snuggling into a down garment in freezing weather. Down is expensive, but it's also very durable and will long outlast any synthetic

fill. However, it *must be kept dry*: when sodden it loses its insulating ability, and it dries very slowly unless you can hang it in the hot sun or put it in a machine dryer. Down can absorb vast amounts of water, so a soaked down garment is also very heavy to carry. But keeping down dry isn't difficult if you carry it in a waterproof stuff sack and wear it only in a tent or under a tarp if it's raining. Despite this, I still carry a down top only when rain isn't likely, since I may want to wear it outside. If you really want to use a down top in wet weather, you can get down jackets with water-resistant shells like Dryloft or EPIC. They're more expensive than standard shells and in my experience slightly heavier and not quite as breathable. Also, if the weather

A down jacket, a fleece hat, and a hot drink keep the author warm on a frosty fall morning.

is wet it won't be freezing, so a down top isn't needed; a light synthetic one will be adequate.

The thickness of an insulated garment is the best guide to its warmth. This is known as the *loft*. Down comes in different grades, measured by how many cubic inches an ounce of down will fill. This is known as the *fill power*, and the higher the number, the more loft a given weight of down will provide. For example, 750-fill-power down is warmer weight-for-weight than 550-fill power.

For backpacking, a light down garment with sewn-through seams (where the stitching goes right through the garment—see the sleeping bag section in Chapter 6 for more on this) is all you need. Complex constructions, vast amounts of fill, and heavy waterproof-breathable shells are for Himalayan mountaineers and polar explorers. Garments suitable for backpacking need weigh no more than 25 ounces. For years I've used a Marmot Down Sweater filled with 650-fill-power down. This weighs 21.5 ounces and has an average loft of 2.5 inches (measured by placing a ruler across the garment in several places and reading off the height above the ground). The Down Sweater has a nylon shell, hand-warmer pockets, a down-filled baffle behind the front zipper, and a stand-up collar. This top has kept me warm in freezing temperatures for many years now, and until recently it seemed quite light for the warmth provided. But I'm being seduced away from my old friend by the delightful Western Mountaineering Flight jacket, which weighs an astonishing 10.5 ounces yet has the same loft (though the sweater is several years old while the Flight has been worn only a few times; the sweater may have had more loft when new). The design is the same as the Down Sweater too, except that the pockets don't have zippers and it's a little shorter, reaching just below the waist. It's the materials that differ. The Flight has an ultralight 0.9-ounce taffeta-nylon shell stuffed with

Down garments are excellent in cold, dry weather.

WATERPROOF FABRIC TERMS DEFINED

- *Microporous:* a material with microscopic holes that allow water vapor through but keep out liquid water (rain).
- *Hydrophilic:* a solid waterproof material with chains of water-attracting molecules built in, along which water vapor can pass through to the outside.
- *Membrane:* a very thin breathable waterproof film. *Gore-Tex* is a microporous membrane; *Sympatex* is a hydrophilic membrane.
- *Laminate:* a membrane stuck to a more durable fabric, usually a form of nylon. In *two-layer laminates*, the membrane is glued to the outer fabric and the lining hangs free. In *three-layer laminates*, the membrane is glued between an outer fabric and a light inner scrim, so the finished material looks like just one layer. In *lining laminates*, the membrane is glued to the lining and the outer layer hangs free. In *drop liners*, the membrane is bonded to a light scrim and hangs free between the inner and outer layers.
- *Coating:* polyurethane applied to the inside of a fabric, usually nylon or polyester. Many makers have their own coatings, though they may come from the same source and there is often little difference between them.

The Helly Hansen Thin Air Vest filled with Primaloft One is warm and light.

800-fill-power down. Western Mountaineering also makes a vest (and the company actually does make its products rather than importing them) called the Reactor that has the same fill and shell and weighs just 8 ounces. By contrast, Marmot's Down Vest, which I took on the Arizona Trail, weighs 14.5 ounces. There are many other good down garments from companies like Feathered Friends (especially the 16-ounce Helios), The North Face, Mountain Hardwear, Patagonia, Nunatak, GoLite, Rab, and PHD (Peter Hutchinson Designs), but none is as light as the Flight.

For wet-cold conditions, synthetic-filled garments are a good choice. They don't absorb much moisture, keep some of their warmth when damp, and dry quickly, so they perform better than down when wet. They're not as warm for the weight when dry, however, and they're bulkier when packed. They're warmer and lighter than heavy fleece garments, though. The best synthetic fills have good durability, but they still won't last as long as fleece or down. Although not as thick as down garments, they're soft and comfortable. You can choose from several fills. Primaloft and Polarguard are generally regarded as the best, with Thermolite Micro not far behind. Polarguard is well established as a warm, durable fill. It's a continuous polyester filament rather than a mass of short fibers. The filaments are hollow and trap air for greater warmth. Both materials come in several versions, of which Polarguard Delta and Primaloft One are regarded as the best. Primaloft is a very soft hydrophobic microfiber. Both materials are more compressible than other synthetic fills and resist moisture well. Primaloft is the softer of the two and drapes around the body better, but there's not much difference between them. The jacket I've used most is the hip-length GoLite Coal, which is filled with Polarguard Delta, has a ripstop nylon shell (Polarguard Delta and Pertex nylon-polyester shell in the latest models), and weighs 19 ounces (16.5 ounces without the detachable hood). The loft is 1 inch, less than half that of the down tops described earlier. The Coal is comfortable, will resist a fair amount of rain, and has kept me warm in temperatures down to 25°F (–4°C). The Coal has been replaced by the Belay parka, which weighs the same but is shorter and has an attached hood. If it's not likely to be that cold, I carry a lighter garment, the Rab Photon Primaloft One smock, which has a Pertex Quantum shell and weighs 12.5 ounces, with a loft of just under half an inch. The Photon is a pullover with a long front zipper and hand-warmer pockets that are accessible when you're wearing a pack hipbelt. It's very soft and comfortable, and I have occasionally hiked in it when the weather has been colder and windier than expected. If it's unlikely that I'll need an insulated garment but I want something just in case, I often carry a Primaloft One–filled Helly Hansen Thin Air Vest, which weighs 10 ounces and has a polyester microfiber shell and hand-warmer pockets. The loft is 0.67 inch. Patagonia makes a similar vest, the Puffball, filled with Thermolite Micro and also weighing 10 ounces. There are many others.

Synthetic insulated garments don't compact as well as down garments, but they do pack down much smaller than equivalent-warmth fleece. However, compression is bad for synthetic fills, and repeated or prolonged compression can flatten the fill so it loses its loft. To get the maximum life out of my synthetic garments, I pack them at the top of the pack, using them to fill out any remaining space. I don't stuff them into the small stuff sacks usually provided with them or load heavy items on top of them.

The Outer Layer

Keeping out wind, rain, and snow is the most important task of your outer clothing. If this layer fails in heavy rain, it doesn't matter how good your other garments are—wet clothing exposed to the wind will chill you, whatever material it's made of. In wet clothes you can go from feeling warm to shivering and being on the verge of hypothermia very rapidly, as I know from experience. Rain clothing must be waterproof; it's more comfortable if it also lets out at least some body moisture.

Don't, however, expect too much from rain gear. In heavy showers you can expect to remain pretty dry. At the end of a day of steady rain you'll probably be damp, even in the best waterproof-

breathable rain gear, because the high humidity will restrict the fabric's breathability. In non-breathable rain gear you'll be wet from condensation. If rain continues nonstop for several days so that you can't dry anything out, you'll get progressively wetter, however good your rain gear. This is where wicking inner layers and fleece mid-layers make a difference—they are still relatively warm when damp, and they dry quickly. A wind shell worn under your rain gear will help protect inner layers from condensation on the inside of the rainwear.

Rain jacket worn for protection on a damp, misty day.

If rain keeps up for more than a few days, it's a good idea to head out to where you can dry your gear. The wettest walk I've ever done was an eighty-six-day, south-to-north trek through the mountains of Norway and Sweden. It rained most days, and on several occasions it rained nonstop for a week. The only way I could get my gear and myself dry was to spend an occasional night in a warm mountain hut or a village hotel.

Waterproof-Breathable Fabrics

When the water vapor your body gives off eventually hits your outer layer, it will condense on the inside unless it can pass through the fabric or escape through vents. Over time, this condensation can eventually soak back into your midlayers, leaving you feeling damp and chilly.

The first waterproof fabric that allowed inner moisture to escape with any success was Gore-Tex, which started the waterproof-breathable revolution back in the 1970s. Since then a host of waterproof fabrics have appeared that transmit water vapor to some degree, though Gore-Tex still leads the market. These fabrics work because of a pressure differential between the air inside the jacket and the air outside; your body heat pushes the vapor through the fabric. The warmer the air, the more water vapor it can hold. Since the air next to your skin is almost always warmer than the air outside your garments, it contains more water vapor, even in the rain. Condensation forms on the inside of shell garments when the air in your clothing becomes saturated with vapor that cannot escape. This vapor hits the inside of your shell and condenses on the cool surface. But a breathable fabric lets at least some vapor pass through as long as the outside air is cooler than the inside air. (Theoretically, waterproof-breathable fabrics can work both ways, but when rain clothing is needed the outside air temperature is always lower than

your body temperature.) Breathable garments need to be relatively close-fitting to keep the air inside as warm as possible so the fabric can transmit moisture more effectively. However, ventilating any garment by opening the front, the cuffs, and any vents and lowering the hood is still the quickest and most efficient way to let moisture out.

Breathable fabrics aren't perfect, of course, and they won't work in all conditions. There's a limit to the amount of moisture even the best of them can transmit in a given time. When you sweat hard, you won't stay bone dry under a breathable jacket, nor will you do so in continuous heavy rain, despite makers' claims. When the outside of any garment is running with water, breathability is reduced and condensation forms. It's hard for water vapor to be pushed through a sheet of water. With the best fabrics, once your energy output slows down and you produce less moisture or once the rain stops, any dampness will dry out through the fabric. In very cold conditions, especially if it's also windy, condensation may freeze, creating a layer of ice inside the garment. The easiest way to get rid of this is to take the garment off and shake it.

In wet-cold weather, you need warm clothing between your base layer and your shell. How much depends on your level of activity. Clothing that is too thick compromises breathability. Nick Brown of Páramo has calculated that more than $\frac{1}{5}$ inch of insulation will significantly reduce breathability. Many heavy fleece garments are thicker than this. It's best to wear only enough clothing to keep you just warm while moving rather than trying to feel toasty.

There are two main categories of breathable materials: polyurethane coatings and membranes (see sidebar, page 149). From all the fancy names, you'd think there were vast numbers of coated

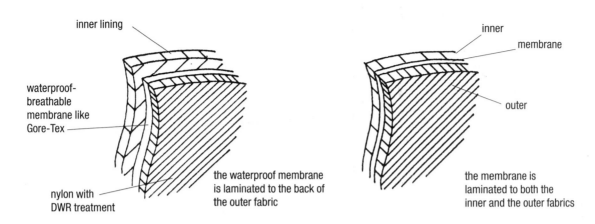

Waterproof (two- or three-ply laminate) (left) and three-layer laminate (right).

fabrics. Actually there are only a few, since many garment makers assign their own names to the same fabrics. Proprietary names include Triple-point Ceramic (Lowe Alpine), Helly Tech (Helly Hansen), H2NO (Patagonia), HyVent (The North Face), PreCip (Marmot), Elements (REI), Microshed (Solstice), Texapore (Jack Wolfskin), Omni-Tech (Columbia Sportswear), and Camp-Tech (Campmor). Many makers use Entrant, though not always under that name.

Coatings are as waterproof as membranes, but just as they started approaching membranes in breathability, new membranes came along that are definitely superior. I get damp more quickly in even the best coated fabrics (such as Marmot Pre-Cip) than I do in membranes like eVENT and Paclite. However, there is a new polyurethane coating from Toray called Entrant G2 XT that is designed to be almost as breathable as the best membranes. I haven't tried this yet but it sounds promising.

Membranes are arguably the most effective (and most expensive) waterproof-breathable fabrics. There are far fewer membranes than coated fabrics, with just one generally available—Gore-Tex. Sympatex is still around but is used by only a few mak-

ers. However, a new one, called eVENT, looks very promising. Pearl Izumi, Jagged Edge, Montane, and Rab all make eVENT garments. There are a few proprietary membranes, such as Alchemy (GoLite) and Conduit (Mountain Hardwear). An unusual membrane is 3M's Propore, a microporous polypropylene membrane laminated to nonwoven polyurethane to produce a very soft fabric used in Rainshield clothing made by ProQuip. A similar polypro membrane and nonwoven polypro fabric are used by Frogg Toggs.

Gore-Tex and eVENT are microporous membranes (see sidebar, page 149) made from expanded polytetrafluoroethylene (ePTFE). Sympatex is a hydrophilic membrane made of polyester. Gore-Tex has become a family of fabrics, with the original version joined by XCR (extended comfort range), which is more breathable, and Paclite, which is lighter and more breathable though not as tough as XCR. First-generation Gore-Tex was very breathable, but once contaminated with oil, whether from sweat, sunscreen, or some other source, it leaked—as I found out most unpleasantly on a cold, wet, windswept mountain pass. In second-generation Gore-Tex a thin layer of polyurethane was put over the membrane to

THE PICK OF THE BREATHABLES

Which breathable fabric is best? It depends on the membrane or coating and the materials used for the inner and outer layers, so there is no easy answer. There's also a big trade-off between breathability and durability. Based on my extensive use of many garments, I've found eVENT the most breathable of the barrier fabrics, followed by Paclite, though neither is as breathable as Páramo Directional Waterproofs. Surprisingly, I've found that three-layer laminates breathe better than two-layer constructions, despite laboratory tests showing the opposite. The tests are done on a two-layer laminate without a lining, but actual garments always have a lining, which impedes breathability. There are still times, of course, when condensation will occur whatever the construction.

In the past I found Sympatex to be the most durable fabric. I twice wore out Gore-Tex three-layer garments on walks lasting several months, and three Gore-Tex jackets failed during heavy rain. I gave Sympatex garments more use than the Gore-Tex jackets that failed and never had one leak. That was in the 1980s, though, and Gore-Tex has improved substantially since then. XCR is considered the most durable Gore-Tex, but I prefer Paclite for its lower weight. I have a first-generation Paclite jacket that has had many weeks of wear and is still waterproof. The third generation of Paclite and eVENT are still so new that I haven't been able to test their durability yet, though I expect both to be pretty tough.

For durability Páramo is way ahead anyway, since there's no coating or membrane to puncture or peel off. If a garment starts leaking, wash it in Nikwax TX-Direct and it will keep the rain out again. If a garment is torn, you can sew a patch on and the repair won't leak. (Try that with a laminate!) Páramo fabric is also far more breathable and comfortable than coatings or laminates.

Coated fabrics have the advantages of lower cost and, in some cases, lower weight, but none compares in performance with laminates, let alone Páramo. I would choose a coated fabric only if I didn't expect to wear rain gear very often. Of the coatings I've tested, Marmot PreCip and Lowe Alpine Triplepoint Ceramic perform the best.

My choices are Páramo for cold weather and eVENT or Paclite for warmer conditions or where weight is critical. Garments made with eVENT aren't quite as light as those made with Paclite but the breathability is better.

---

protect it. This solved the oil problem but reduced the breathability. However, BHA Technologies claims its eVENT membrane is oil repellent so that a polyurethane coating isn't needed and water vapor can pass through the pores in the membrane without having to be absorbed into the polyurethane first, a process BHA calls "direct venting." I've tried eVENT garments from Rab, Montane, and Lowe Alpine, and they are noticeably more breathable than any other membrane or coated fabric I've worn. Paclite, which has an inner layer consisting of carbon and an oleophobic (oil-hating) substance, is the most breathable Gore-Tex material.

Membranes can be laminated to a variety of nylon and polyester fabrics. The thicker the fabric, the more durable the garment. In three-layer laminates, the membrane is glued between two layers of fabric to produce a material that is hardwearing but slightly stiff. Because the membrane is protected by fabric on both sides, three-layer laminates are the most durable constructions. Less durable but softer are two-layer laminates, in which the membrane is stuck to an outer layer while the inner lining hangs free, and drop liners, in which the membrane is left loose between the inner and outer layers. Finally, there are lining laminates, also described as laminated to the drop, where the membrane is stuck to a very light inner layer. This design minimizes the number of seams, which is a bonus. Drop liners and lining laminates are now rarely used in hiking clothing.

Páramo: Soft Shell or Waterproof-Breathable?

The disadvantages of coatings and membranes are that the barriers aren't very durable, can't be reproofed when they start to leak badly, and transmit only water vapor, not liquid sweat. However, Páramo Directional Waterproofs, from the company that makes Nikwax proofing products, are very durable, can be reproofed, and allow sweat through to the outside. There are no coatings or membranes. Instead, Páramo mimics the way animals stay dry—a unique waterproof-breathable system that inventor Nick Brown calls the Nikwax biological analogy. This system requires a two-layer material.

The inner layer of a Páramo Directional Waterproof is a very thin polyester fleece, called the Nikwax Analogy Pump Liner, whose fibers are tightly packed on the inside but become less dense toward the outside, like animal fur. To replicate the animal oils that keep fur water repellent, Parameta is coated with Nikwax TX.10. Like fur, Parameta pumps water in one direction only—away from the body. It does this more quickly than rain can fall, so moisture is always moving away from the body faster than it arrives, keeping you dry.

To be effective on its own, the Pump Liner would have to be very thick, however. To keep it thin (and therefore not too warm or heavy), Páramo garments have an outer layer of windproof polyester microfiber that deflects most of the rain. The combination of these two fabrics allows more moisture to get out, including condensed perspiration, than any membrane or coating. It's not dependent on humidity levels outside the garment or on the temperature inside. The whole garment, including zippers and cords, is treated with TX.10, so it won't absorb moisture or wick it inside.

I've been using Páramo waterproofs since they first appeared in the early 1990s, and I've found them very comfortable and efficient. Because there is no coating or laminate, they are very soft and comfortable, feeling more like a soft shell than a waterproof. Reproofing works, and the garments last a long time. There are two limitations. The two-layer construction makes them rather warm and fairly heavy—the lightest Páramo jacket, the Cuzco, weighs 25 ounces. Effectively, you are wearing a wind shell and a base layer. This makes them too warm for me in summer, although some people find them comfortable year-round. From fall to spring, however, I find Páramo jackets and pants comfortable and have never gotten wet or suffered condensation in them. Because the garments are very soft and the lining wicks moisture, you can wear them next to the skin, so you need only one layer instead of three. They are far more effective than any of the new and much touted soft-shell fabrics because they are fully waterproof while being just as breathable and comfortable.

Nonbreathable Rain Gear

Nonbreathable waterproof clothing is made from nylon or polyester, usually coated with polyurethane or polyvinyl chloride (PVC), though occasionally with silicone. Its greatest advantage is that it's far less expensive than waterproof-breathable fabrics. Polyurethane is much more durable than PVC, though both eventually crack and peel off the base layer. Cheap vinyl rain gear lasts about as long as it takes to put it on and isn't worth considering, despite the price. Because moisture can't escape through the fabric, condensation is copious if you wear nonbreathable garments for long. The only way to remove that moisture is to ventilate the garment, hardly practical while the rain is pouring down. One way to limit the dampness is to wear a windproof layer under the waterproof one, which traps some of the moisture between the two layers.

While you're hiking you'll still feel warm, even if you're very damp with sweat, because nonbreathable rainwear holds in heat as well as moisture. When you stop, though, you'll cool down rapidly unless you put on dry clothes. It's far better to get damp with sweat than wet from rain, however. Until the late 1970s all rain gear was nonbreathable, and people still hiked the Appalachian Trail in the rain and slogged through the wet forests of the Pacific Northwest.

Weights of nonbreathable rain tops start at 6 ounces. Few name brands offer nonbreathable rainwear. Two that do are Sierra Designs, whose polyurethane-coated Backpacker's Jacket weighs 11.3 ounces, and Stephenson's Warmlite, whose silicone-coated nylon rain jacket weighs 6 ounces.

Garment Design

Material alone is not enough to ensure that a garment will perform well—design also matters. The two basic choices are jackets with full-length zippers and pullovers. I've tried both, and I much prefer jackets, since they are so much easier to get on and off. That old standby the poncho is still popular with some backpackers. Ponchos are versatile; they can double as tarps or ground cloths. They have good ventilation, too, but they can act like sails in strong winds, making them unsuitable for windy places. Ponchos are usually made of nonbreathable fabrics. Examples are Stephenson's Warmlite poncho and GoLite's Ultra-Lite Poncho, both made from silicone-coated nylon, which

weigh 8 ounces. Hilleberg makes a curious waterproof-breathable garment called the Bivanorak (18 ounces). It's a poncho-style garment that covers you and your pack but has sleeves and can also be used as a bivouac bag or sleeping bag cover.

Length is a matter of personal choice. I like hip-length garments because they give my legs greater freedom of movement, but many people prefer longer ones so they don't need rain pants as frequently.

Seams are a potential leak point in any waterproof garment. Only Páramo garments have seams that don't leak without being sealed, because they are treated with TX.10 and are water repellent. In waterproof-breathable garments and the more expensive nonbreathables, seams are usually taped, the most effective way of making them watertight. In cheaper garments, seams may be coated with a special sealant instead. If you have a garment with uncoated seams, you can coat them yourself with urethane sealant. You also can do this when the original sealant cracks and comes off—as it will. Taped seams can peel off, though this is rare. Even so, the fewer seams, the better. The location of the seams is important, too. The best garments have seamless shoulder yokes to avoid abrasion from pack straps.

The front zipper is another possible source of leaks. Standard zippers should be covered with a single or, preferably, double waterproof flap, closed with snaps or Velcro. The covering flap should come all the way to the top of the zipper. Many garments now have watertight zippers, first introduced by Arc'teryx, which are coated with urethane and have flaps that close over the zipper teeth. In my experience these are near enough to being waterproof, though driving rain can sometimes work its way in. I've never had much rain enter, though, and I like not having to fasten double flaps. The lack of bulk and slight weight reduc-

KEY FEATURES: RAIN GEAR

- Waterproof-breathable fabric to allow some body moisture out.
- Taped seams: the fewer seams, the better.
- An adjustable hood with a peak that gives protection and allows side-to-side vision.

- Adjustable cuffs.
- A full-length front zipper with a storm flap.
- Zippered chest pockets big enough for maps.
- Low weight and bulk. (I always hope my rain jacket will spend most of its time in the pack!)

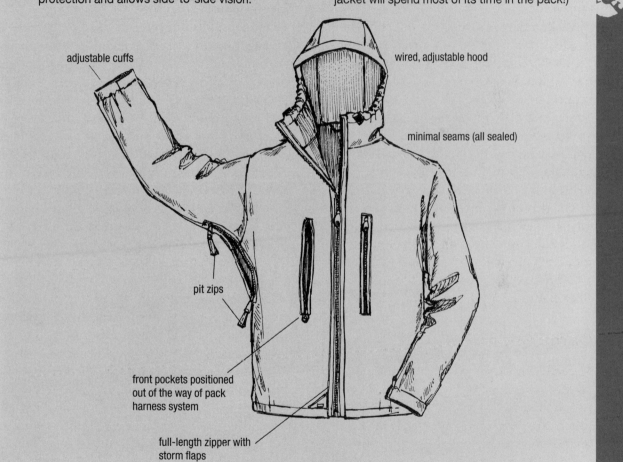

adjustable cuffs

wired, adjustable hood

minimal seams (all sealed)

pit zips

front pockets positioned out of the way of pack harness system

full-length zipper with storm flaps

tion is welcome too. Most zippers open from the bottom as well as the top. These are slightly more awkward to use than single-direction zippers and have no advantages that I can see except perhaps to allow ease of movement and access to pants pockets in very long garments.

To keep rain out, hoods should fit closely around your face when the drawcords are tightened, without leaving a gap under the chin. Hoods that roll into the collar seem pointless in the back country. They're designed to look neat in town, but often you can't easily get them out while wearing the jacket. Detachable hoods need to have a large overlap of material to prevent rain from running down your neck; most are very difficult to attach while wearing the jackets. I've been wary of them since I found a faded detachable hood in a gully high in the mountains. Had it been ripped off by the wind or dropped by fumbling cold fingers? Either way, someone had to function without a hood. A wired or otherwise stiffened peak or visor helps keep hail or driving rain off your face. People who wear glasses say this is essential. The best hoods move with your head so you can look to the side without staring at the lining, a problem with too many hoods. The best way to check is to try the hood on, though you can make a quick assessment by looking at the seams. A single vertical seam running back to front over the hood generally means it won't move with you; if there are two seams, or a single seam that runs across the hood from one side to the other, the hood is more likely to allow good visibility. Unfortunately, the hoods that limit vision most are the ones that give

A good hood should turn with the head and have a stiffened peak to keep rain off the face. GoLite Phantom.

the best protection. I prefer protection to visibility, especially when the rain drives down for hours and swirling mists hide the view.

In cold weather I usually wear a fleece-lined waterproof-breathable cap with a large brim instead of a hood during light showers, and I wear it under a hood in storms and blizzards for better protection than any hood alone can give. This combination is too warm outside the snow season, though baseball caps work reasonably well. Whether or not you wear such a cap, your jacket hood must be big enough to fit warm headwear underneath, from a full balaclava to a light knitted hat. Many hoods now have a drawcord or adjustable tab at the back so they can be expanded to cover a bulky hat or shortened so the peak doesn't flop in your eyes when you take the hat off. Most of these work well. Front hood draw cords can lash your face in strong winds, so many jackets have tabs to hold them down or have cords that tuck into the jacket at each end. These can be fiddly to use but are welcome in storms.

Sleeves need to be cut full under the arms to allow for free movement. Trying on a garment is the best way to find out how well the sleeves are cut. *Articulated sleeves* with a built-in curve at the elbow may be useful for mountaineering but don't have any advantages for backpackers.

Many garments have underarm zippers or "pit zips," which are great for ventilation, though they can leak in heavy rain. However, jackets with double Velcro flaps to protect the zippers can be extremely hard to use. I wonder if designers have ever stood on a mountaintop in a blizzard with one arm in the air while the other hand gropes under pack straps trying to do up a zipper? Double flaps over pit zips are also bulky and can feel uncomfortable. Watertight zips with no flaps over them are much easier to use. I rarely use pit zips and don't regard them as essential. Wide

RAIN JACKETS: MY CHOICES

The light rain jacket I favored in the last edition weighed 19 ounces. Now I wouldn't consider that particularly light. My affections are currently split between the 13-ounce GoLite Phantom jacket, made from Gore-Tex Paclite, and the 14-ounce Montane Superfly, made from eVENT. Both have hoods with wired visors. The Phantom has two large mesh chest pockets and pit zips; the Superfly has two hand-warmer pockets and a chest pocket. Overall, the Phantom has the best design and ventilation but the Superfly is more breathable. If a rain jacket is not likely to be needed, I carry neither of these, however, preferring the much lighter Montane Hydralite. The breathability of this coated anorak is only moderate, there are no vents, and it has elasticized cuffs and a hood that rolls into the collar, which are features I dislike. However, it weighs just 7.7 ounces, making it probably the lightest waterproof-breathable jacket that's capable of coping with the worst storms. It has a hood with a wired peak, a single chest pocket, and a watertight half-length zipper.

In cold weather, I wear a Páramo Alta II jacket that weighs 29 ounces. This has a snap-closed flap inside the front zipper that you can leave fastened with the zipper undone for ventilation, a hood with a wired peak, wide cuffs you can roll up, sleeve vents, and five pockets. It deals easily with the worst winter storms and is very comfortable. Because of the weight, I use this jacket only when I expect to wear it all day every day. A wind shell or a light fleece is unnecessary with it, which saves some weight.

The Montane Superfly eVENT jacket.

cuffs and mesh chest pockets are easier to use for ventilation.

Cuffs need to be adjustable if they're to be any use for ventilation. I like simple external, Velcro-closed ones rather than the neater but more awkward internal storm cuffs, and I abhor nonadjustable elasticized cuffs because my arms often overheat in them and run with sweat. Wide sleeves and cuffs provide the most ventilation and can even be rolled up when it's warm. They're also easy to pull over gloves or mittens.

Pockets are useful for maps, compasses, hats, gloves, and other small items as well as your cold hands. But pockets aren't always waterproof, and even if they are, water will get in when you open them in the rain or stick a wet hand inside. It's best to keep anything you want to stay dry inside a plastic bag. Páramo pockets are totally waterproof, as are some of those with watertight zippers. Pockets with standard zippers should always have covering flaps. The most water-resistant pockets hang inside the jacket, attached only at the top. My preference is for chest pockets, which are accessible when you're wearing a pack hipbelt. Hem pockets are usually inaccessible then, but I don't carry anything in them anyway, because they then flap irritatingly against my legs.

For chest pockets, the best compromise between waterproofness and accessibility is a vertical zippered entrance under the jacket's front flap but outside its zipper. (Pockets inside the jacket stay dry, but you let in wind and rain when you open the jacket front to use them.) Zippers that close upward are best because small items in the pocket are less likely to fall out when you open them. Pullover garments usually have a single large "kangaroo" pouch on the chest, which is the easiest to use and very water resistant.

Pockets don't need to be made from waterproof-breathable material. Indeed, breathability is reduced significantly if there are two or more layers of waterproof-breathable material on top of each other. Plain nylon is fine, but mesh is better, especially for chest pockets, because it adds minimum weight and you can ventilate the garment by opening the pockets. Mesh is particularly effective on a garment with two angled chest pockets on the outside, because with both pockets open but protected by their flaps, you can ventilate the whole chest and armpit area.

Mesh is also the best material for the inner lining found on most two-layer laminates and some coated garments, again because it's light and helps moisture reach the breathable layer as quickly as possible. If the mesh is made from a wicking fabric, as many now are, all the better. Mesh can get damp with condensation, but solid linings, even nylon ones, can get quite wet, however breathable the outer layer.

Drawcords are needed at the collar for tightening the hood. They are also often found at the waist, but these are unnecessary, since the pack's hipbelt closes off the jacket anyway. Self-locking toggles that grip until they are released are a boon on drawcords; trying to untangle an iced-up tiny knot with frozen fingers so you can lower your hood is not fun.

Finally, a note on shell garments with extra zippers for attaching a fleece inner layer: I hate them. The zippers add weight for no practical purpose and increase the cost. I've used such garments only briefly, but as far as I can see, they're designed purely so that the combined garment can be worn as a warm town coat. I don't find the effort of donning two garments too great to manage.

Weight and Fit

If you don't wear rain shells very often, then a light one is all you need. The lightest practical jacket I've come across is Montane's Hydralite at 7.7 ounces. There are plenty of good jackets between 10 and 16 ounces that should prove reasonably durable, including many made from Gore-Tex Paclite and a few made from eVENT. Above 16 ounces you find jackets that are tough and protective for severe mountain weather and regular use but a little heavy for carrying in the pack.

Rain jackets are more comfortable if they fit properly. A jacket should be roomy enough to fit over a fleece top without feeling restrictive. A close-fitting jacket will have better breathability, but slightly large is far better than slightly small. I also like sleeves that are long enough to pull over my hands if the weather turns unexpectedly cool.

Rain Pants

Rain pants used to be uncomfortable, restrictive garments that sagged at the waist, bulged at the knees, and snagged at the ankles. Some still are. Like most hikers, I wore them only during the heaviest downpours.

The introduction of waterproof-breathable fabrics made rain pants slightly more comfortable, but it was only when designers got to work on them that they really changed. In part this is related to changes in legwear in general. Traditional rain pants needed to be big and baggy because they had to fit over heavy wool or cotton pants, which were also big and baggy. Modern legwear is made from lighter, thinner fabrics and is closer fitting—a big improvement. Softer fabrics have helped, too. The changes have been so dramatic that the best waterproof legwear is comfortable enough to be worn next to the skin.

There are two basic designs: simple pants and bibs with a high back and chest and suspenders. For most hiking, pants are best, since they weigh less, are less bulky, are easier to get on and off, and cost less. Bibs, however, are excellent in cold weather, especially for ski touring, since they're warmer than pants, leave no gaps at the waist when you stretch, and minimize the chance that snow will get into your clothes. Putting them on in cold and windy weather is unpleasant, to say the least, because you have to remove other layers. For that reason, and because of their weight and bulk, they're best worn all day rather than carried.

Base-layer long pants or, in really cold weather, fleece pants are the best garments to wear under rain pants, since they feel comfortable when damp. Synthetic trail pants work well too, but cotton-nylon and cotton trousers absorb moisture and tend to feel damp and cold.

Features worth having on rain pants are adjustable drawcords at the waist and knee-length zippers to allow you to get the pants on over boots. Pockets, or slits to allow access to inner pants pockets, are useful. If you wear rain pants frequently, consider full-length side zips that can be opened at the top for ventilation; they also allow you to put on rain pants over crampons or skis,

RAIN PANTS: MY CHOICE

I often don't bother wearing rain pants at all in summer. Shorts are fine in warm rain—legs dry fast! If it's cool, synthetic long pants are reasonably warm when damp and dry quickly. However, I always carry an ultralight pair of GoLite Reed waterproof-breathable pants (weight 5.5 ounces) just in case it's colder than I expected. These are rather fragile and wouldn't stand up to continuous use, but because they spend most of their time in the pack, weight is my main concern. On the few occasions I've worn them, they've kept my legs adequately warm and dry. On winter and cold-weather trips, I wear Páramo Alta pants (current equivalent is the Páramo Aspira) that have full-length zippers for ventilation, suspenders, and reinforced knees and seat. They weigh 30 ounces, but they replace both insulating and shell layers. Mostly I wear them next to my skin, wearing base-layer pants under them only in extreme cold (below 10°F [–12°C]).

though it can be hard to handle long zippers in a strong wind. Keep in mind that it's very difficult to make full-length side zippers fully waterproof. Velcro-closed flaps help, but they make it even harder to put the pants on. Watertight zippers are a better choice. I prefer full-length zippers for pants I'll wear all day; I'd rather have good ventilation and suffer the occasional leak. Gussets behind knee-length zippers help keep rain out, but they tend to catch in the zippers. For men, rain pants with flies are worth considering. I don't like elasticized hems; I find they ride up over your boot tops, letting water in. Nonelasticized hems with drawcords or Velcro-closed tabs are better. Ultralight pants like the GoLite Reed omit zippers to save weight; when they'll spend most of the time on my back, I'm happy with this.

Rain pants run from 5 to 40 ounces, depending on design and fabric. As with rain jackets, heavier garments will outlast lighter ones. Rain pants suffer more hard wear than jackets, though, so if you're likely to wear them much of the time, I'd put durability above weight. But if they'll spend most of their time in your pack, the lighter the better. The heaviest garments might be a little hot in summer, while the lightest, thinnest rain pants don't give adequate protection in severe winter weather.

It's best to try rain pants on before you buy, preferably over the pants you'll wear under them so you can check that they don't bind anywhere when you move. Length is important, too. Unfortunately, few makers offer different lengths. Alterations are possible, though zipped legs make this

An umbrella makes a great sunshade. GoLite Dome.

difficult (if the zippers start a little way above the hem, pants are easier to shorten). It's better to find a pair that fits to begin with.

Umbrellas

Although they're not clothing, this seems an appropriate time to discuss umbrellas. I'd never considered carrying an umbrella or seen anyone else doing so until I met a hiker using one on a rainy day back in 1988 on the North Boundary Trail in Jasper National Park. It was much more comfortable than a rain jacket, Stu Dechka told me. His Gore-Tex jacket was draped over his pack to keep it dry. I was surprised but thought no more about it until five years later when Ray Jardine extolled the virtues of umbrellas in *The Pacific Crest Trail Hiker's Handbook*. My hiking apprenticeship took place in the windy, treeless British hills, and I'd never given umbrellas serious consideration. People on city streets seemed to have enough problems when it was windy; in the hills umbrellas would be impossible to handle. However, on reflection I could see that for hiking in forests and areas where gales are unusual, they could have advantages.

Then I had the opportunity to hike for a few days with Ray Jardine in the Oregon Cascades, and we took umbrellas. I soon discovered that in the woods they're excellent. It was wonderful to stride through the forest in heavy rain with my hood down and my jacket wide open and stay dry. The closed-off feeling of being sealed in a rain jacket was absent. At stops, the umbrella provided shelter and protected the pack. But above timberline a gusty wind was blowing. Ray showed me how to point the umbrella into the wind and close it down slightly to protect it and also keep the rain out of my face. But as we climbed higher the wind grew stronger and gusted from every direction; eventually both our umbrellas turned inside out and ripped. (Ray thought they could be modified to prevent this.) This was late October; such severe conditions would be unusual during the summer hiking season, but I'm too cautious to hike without rain clothing even with an umbrella. (Ray and Jenny Jardine have hiked both the Appalachian and Pacific Crest Trails with umbrellas and without rain gear, but Ray does recommend carrying a light rain jacket.) When I hiked the Arizona Trail several years later, I brought a 9-ounce GoLite Dome umbrella, designed by Ray. It made a great sunshade in the desert (though covering it with Mylar would have made it even better; GoLite now makes the Chrome Dome, which has a metallic canopy), and I used it to fend off one heavy shower. However, while it was easy to hold on good trails and open terrain, it was awkward on rough ground and in dense vegetation. You can't use two trekking poles and hold an umbrella, and overall I've decided the poles have more benefit for me, so the Dome doesn't get much use.

THE VAPOR-BARRIER THEORY

As always, there is a view that challenges accepted wisdom, in this case the concept of "breathability." Our skin is always slightly moist, however dry it may feel; if it really dries out it cracks and chaps, and sores appear. Our bodies constantly produce liquid—either sweat or, when we aren't exercising hard, insensible perspiration. The aim of breathable clothing is to move moisture away from the skin as quickly as possible and transport it to the outside air where it can evaporate. This inevitably causes heat loss. And as I have said, breathable shells may not work in severe weather conditions.

The vapor-barrier theory says that instead of trying to remove this moisture from the skin, you

should try to keep it there so no more will be produced and the attendant evaporative heat loss will cease. You'll stay warm, and your clothing will stay dry because it won't have to deal with large amounts of liquid. To achieve this, you wear a *nonbreathable waterproof layer* either next to or close to the skin, with insulating layers over it. Because heat is trapped inside, you need less clothing.

Vapor barriers are most efficient in dry cold—in temperatures below freezing—because when humidity is high, heat loss by evaporation lessens anyway. By preventing moisture loss, vapor barriers also help stave off dehydration, a potentially serious problem in dry-cold conditions.

When I first read about vapor barriers, I thought that anyone using one would be soaked in sweat. But various reputable outdoors people said vapor barriers worked, so I decided to give the idea a try rather than reject it out of hand.

Apparently, if you have a hairy body, waterproof fabrics feel comfortable next to the skin. I haven't, and the vapor barriers I've tried make me feel instantly clammy unless I wear something under them. Thin synthetic base layers are ideal for this. Initially I tried old nonbreathable light rain gear as a vapor-barrier suit. It was not a success for hiking, since I overheated rapidly and started to sweat even when the temperature was several degrees below freezing. It was superb as campwear, however. I was as warm wearing my vapor-barrier top under a fleece jacket as I was when wearing a down jacket over it. Wearing the vapor barrier in my sleeping bag added several degrees of warmth to the bag, and since the barrier was thin and had a slippery surface, it didn't restrict me or make me uncomfortable.

I was impressed enough with these first experiments to buy a lighter, more comfortable vapor-barrier suit made from a soft-coated ripstop nylon that weighs just 7 ounces. The shirt has a zippered front and Velcro-closed cuffs; the trousers have a drawcord waist and Velcro closures at the ankles. Although the suit performs well, I haven't used it for many years, even for sleeping in. Although I know it will keep me warm, I somehow don't have real confidence in it. A down jacket looks warm, and carrying one is psychologically reassuring; two thin pieces of nylon just don't have the same effect. I used to carry the vapor-barrier suit as an emergency backup in winter, but I haven't even done that for many years.

Plastic bags, or thin plastic or rubber socks and gloves, can be worn on your feet and hands as vapor barriers. If your feet become very cold and wet, an emergency vapor barrier worn over dry thin socks with thicker socks over that does help them warm up. I used this combination near the end of my Canadian Rockies walk, when I had to ford a half-frozen river seven times within a few hours and then walk on frozen ground in boots that were splitting and socks with holes. Dry inner socks and plastic bags made a huge difference. Today, though, I prefer waterproof-breathable socks.

Few companies make vapor-barrier gear. The main one is Stephenson's Warmlite, which offers shirts, pants, gloves, and socks in a fabric called Fuzzy Stuff, a stretchy, brushed nylon glued to a urethane film. The inside is said to feel like soft flannel and be far more comfortable against the skin than ordinary coated nylon. It wicks moisture and spreads it out for rapid drying. It sounds as though it should be far better than simple coated fabrics, and it's probably the stuff to try if you want to see what vapor-barrier clothing is like.

LEGWEAR

What you wear on your legs is not as important as what you wear on your upper body, but comfort and protection from the weather still matter. Leg-wear needs to be either loose-fitting or stretchy, so that it doesn't restrict movement.

Shorts

Shorts are my favorite legwear. Nothing else provides the same freedom and comfort. If you keep your upper body warm, you can wear shorts in surprisingly cold conditions. Any shorts will do, as long as they have roomy legs that don't bind the thighs. Many people wear cutoff jeans, a good way to use up worn-out clothing. Some people like close-fitting Lycra shorts, which can prevent rashes caused by your thighs' rubbing together. Running shorts are the cheapest and lightest types (my 100 percent polyester shorts weigh just 2 ounces), but they're flimsy and don't stand up well to contact with granite boulders, rough logs, and other wilderness seats. I sometimes carry them on trips when I doubt I'll wear shorts but want a pair in case the weather is gentler than expected. Shorts with liners can double as underpants.

When I'm planning to wear shorts, I prefer more substantial ones, preferably with pockets. For years I used polyester-cotton blend shorts (8 ounces) with lots of pockets and a double seat. They are very hardwearing—mine survived through-hikes of both the Pacific Crest Trail and the Continental Divide Trail. There are dozens of models; some are made from pure cotton, some from cotton and nylon, and some from 100 percent synthetics. Weights range from 4 to 16 ounces. Most shorts don't feature built-in briefs, so you have to wear underpants or at least carry them for wearing under long pants. Most shorts also feel bulky and uncomfortable under trousers, which is further complicated by pockets and fly zippers. This is a minor point, but I like to be able to pull long pants on over my shorts when the weather changes. Having built-in briefs lets me keep my shorts on under long pants and saves the snippet of weight of underpants.

Back in 1988, at the start of my Canadian Rockies walk, I found some nearly ideal hiking shorts. Browsing in the outdoor stores in the town of Waterton, on the edge of Waterton Lakes National Park, I bought a pair of Patagonia Baggies shorts (5 ounces). I wore them for most of the next three and a half months and found them comfortable and durable. The wide-cut legs made them easy to walk in, the mesh liner meant underpants weren't needed, and the nylon material dried quickly when wet. I went on to wear Baggies for a 1,000-mile Yukon walk and a 1,300-mile Scandinavian mountains walk, and over the years I've worn out several pairs. Baggies are still around and still excellent, but there are other good shorts. On a 500-mile hike in the High Sierra, I wore GoLite Terrain shorts (4 ounces), made from quick-dry nylon with a polyester crepe liner. These were just as comfortable as the Baggies.

Long Pants

Unfortunately, the weather is not always conducive to wearing shorts. During some summers I've hardly worn them at all. I always carry long pants in case the weather changes or insects or bushwhacking make wearing shorts masochistic. Around camp and in cold weather, you can wear synthetic long underwear under shorts. It doesn't repel wind or insects, though, and I rarely wear it, since I have to remove my shorts to put it on. It's much easier to pull pants on over shorts for extra warmth—and easier to take them off when you warm up. Long underwear is best for trips so cold that you wear it all day long.

Long pants fall into two categories: those that will be worn mostly in mild conditions but occasionally in storms, and those strictly for cold,

Hot-weather clothing: sun hat, shirt, shorts, sandals. Squaw Lake, John Muir Wilderness, High Sierra.

stormy weather. Many people hike in jeans, even though they're cold when wet and take ages to dry. These are potentially dangerous attributes in severe conditions, but wearing rain pants minimizes them. Other objections to cotton jeans are that they are heavy, tight, and not very durable. I find them so uncomfortable that I haven't owned a pair for years.

For three-season use, there are masses of *trail pants*. Depending on the fabric and the design, these weigh from 4 to 25 ounces. Features may include double knees, double seats, and multiple pockets, many of them zippered. Some versions, often called *wind pants*, have full-length side zippers so they can be pulled on over boots and vented in warm weather. A few, like Marmot's Dri-Clime Side Zip Pants (12 ounces), also have wicking linings. The traditional and heaviest material for trail pants is 100 percent cotton. Cotton-polyester and cotton-nylon blends such as 65/35 are better; best are 100 percent synthetics, especially microfibers, because they are much lighter and faster drying, though just as hardwearing, windproof, and comfortable. I've worn trail pants on all my long walks, switching from polyester-cotton blends to microfibers when they became available.

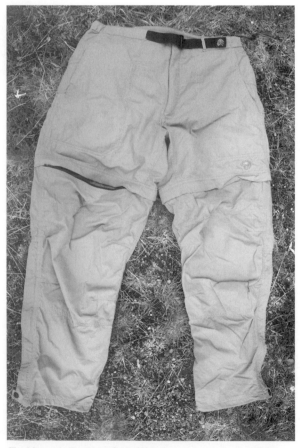

The Mountain Hardwear Convertible Pack Pants with zip-off legs.

When I expect to wear shorts most of the time, I carry a very basic light pair of nylon pants. My favorites, the now-discontinued GoLite Trunk, weigh 8 ounces and have no features except hand-warmer pockets and elasticized ankles to keep out insects. The current equivalent are the nylon Valmont Pants with five pockets, which also weigh 8 ounces. If you really want to keep the weight down, Montane's Featherlite Pants, made from Pertex Microlite nylon, are probably the lightest, at 3.8 ounces.

When buying a pair of pants, the main thing to check is the fit. Some pants are styled for fashion rather than function and can be uncomfortable to hike in, especially uphill. I like elasticized waistbands rather than conventional belt loops because I don't like wearing a belt under a pack hipbelt and I appreciate the stretchy waist when I feast in a restaurant after a long trip. I like to have at least one pocket with a snap or zipper for my wallet and money when traveling to and from the wilderness; large thigh pockets are good for carrying maps.

Trail pants with zip-off legs to convert them into shorts have become very popular. For years I viewed these as curiosities, but eventually I tried a pair and decided that, strange or not, they made sense, so I wore a pair on the Arizona Trail. I appreciated being able to simply zip on the legs when it got cool in the evening and then unzip them in the morning when it warmed up. However, if zip-offs are to be comfortable they need to be well designed and to fit properly. The big problem is that the zippers can rub. I tried on eighteen pairs and could feel the leg zippers on all but four. Only one pair was really comfortable—Mountain Hardwear Convertible Pack Pants. These seem to have actually been designed for hiking, unlike the others I tried. They're made from a tough wind-proof and fast-drying nylon with a synthetic wicking waist lining and lower leg zippers so they can be pulled on and off over footwear. They allow great freedom of movement, with a crotch gusset and articulated knees, and the large pockets can be reached when wearing a pack hipbelt. They're not that light at 16 ounces, though of course they replace both pants and shorts, and they're quite expensive. They fit me, though, and look as though they'll last a long while. I wear them if I'm not sure whether it will be too cool for shorts. On a fall trip to the White Mountains in New Hampshire they coped with snow, gale-force winds, rain, and below-freezing temperatures for a week before temperatures rose and the sun shone and I was able to zip the legs off. (The Pack Pants come without zip-off legs at a weight of 15 ounces.) There are plenty of other zip-offs, most of them less expensive than the Convertible Pack Pants. Remember, always check the fit.

Light pants are generally warm enough for moderate temperatures, those times when you're just a little chilly in shorts. They're not warm enough when the mercury drops toward freezing, however. If the weather turns really cold or mornings are frosty, I wear long underwear under them. With rain pants on top, the pants-base layer combination can cope with all but the worst winter weather while I'm on the move. Three layers are more versatile than one thick pair of pants when large variations in weather can be expected. In *really* cold conditions, you can wear thicker long underwear or fleece pants under long pants.

An alternative to trail pants and long underwear is a separate single pair of warm pants. I prefer these for constant wear in reliably cold conditions, since two or more layers are more restrictive and less comfortable than one. The obvious material is fleece, which is warm, light (typically 8 to 24 ounces), nonabsorbent, and quick drying. I don't like thick fleece pants, however, because they're not windproof, aren't very light, and are bulky to pack.

I've owned a pair of Helly Hansen nylon pile Polar Trousers (17 ounces) for many years but rarely use them because they require a pair of windproof pants over them in even the gentlest breeze, which then makes them too hot. Power Stretch tights are far better. My Lowe Alpine pair weighs 6.8 ounces. They're very warm, very comfortable, repel breezes and light rain or snow, and can be worn under rain pants in cold, wet weather or under trail pants in strong winds. They function well over a wider temperature range than any other fleece pants I've tried. I've worn them on spring ski tours, but mostly I carry them for campwear in winter, preferring Páramo waterproof-breathable pants when moving.

Pants made from thick stretch nylon such as Spandura (a mix of Cordura and Lycra) or the various Schoeller fabrics are a good alternative to fleece. They repel snow, rain, and wind and are extremely hardwearing. I wore these for years for winter backpacking and ski touring until Páramo came along. They disappeared for a while but have had a resurgence of popularity under the guise of soft shells. Although I think these fabrics are too heavy and bulky for tops, they are ideal for cool-weather legwear. Some are light enough to be used in all but the hottest weather—when you can wear shorts anyway. Of the various types I've tried, I like the Mountain Hardwear Velocity pants, made from Schoeller Dynamic, one of the lighter softshell pants at 14 ounces. I wear them when it's too warm for the Páramo pants but too cool for light trail pants or shorts. Pants made from stretch Gore Windstopper or Power Shield are totally windproof, almost waterproof, and pretty warm. They make a good alternative to Páramo pants. An excellent example are Mountain Hardwear's Alchemy Pants (10.5 ounces), which are made from Windstopper with Power Shield panels. They have watertight side zippers for ventilation. Windstopper N2S pants are available too, but these don't stretch, which I think is necessary in pants like this.

Wool or wool-blend pants used to be common; my first winter hiking pants were made of Derby tweed. They were warm but heavy, itchy, and very absorbent. When wet, they rubbed my inner thighs raw, and they took days to dry out. After my first weekend in stretch nylon pants, I never wore wool trousers again. Perhaps it's no wonder wool pants are now hard to find.

For severe weather, you can get insulated pants. I've never been out in conditions cold enough to warrant even considering these (even at −30°F [−34°C] my Páramo trousers worn over Power Stretch tights were warm enough while I was moving), but you might like to know they exist. Not surprisingly, there isn't a wide choice; Mountain Hardwear makes the Polarguard 3D-filled Chugach Pants (21 ounces); down pants include the light Nunatak Kabuk Pants (9 ounces with Pertex Microlite or EPIC shell) and the Marmot 8000

A light fleece hat is useful year-round.

Meter Pants (34 ounces with a DryLoft shell). The latter have as much goose down in them as the lightest down sleeping bags! Vapor-barrier trousers worn over long johns and under fleece or pile and shell trousers would probably prove as warm as down ones.

HEADGEAR

Warm Hats

"If your feet are cold, put on a hat." This adage was one of the first pieces of outdoor lore I ever learned. It's also one of the most accurate.

When you start to get cold, your body protects its core by slowing down the blood supply to the extremities—fingers, toes, nose. However, your brain requires a constant supply of blood in order to function properly, so the circulation to your head is maintained. In cold weather, you can lose enormous amounts of heat through your head— up to 80 percent, according to some figures. The capillaries just below your scalp never close down to conserve heat like the ones in your hands and feet, *so you must protect your head in order to keep your body warm.*

But which hat? Long ago the choice was simple: the only material was wool, and the only styles were watch caps and balaclavas. Then came synthetic fabrics—nylon, polyester, acrylic. Designs didn't change, though, until fleece became the main material for warm clothing and outdoor companies began employing designers to make their clothing more stylish.

Now outdoor hats come in a wild variety of colors and styles and every sort of material, including fleece, wicking synthetics, wool, and mixtures of everything. All these fabrics are warm and comfortable. I particularly like Power Stretch hats because the fabric is soft, comfortable, stretchy, very light, and quick drying. It resists light winds and rain and wicks moisture quickly.

Whatever the style, hats can be divided into two categories: those that are windproof and those (the majority) that aren't. Windproof hats are made from windproof fleece such as Polartec Windbloc or Gore Windstopper or have an outer shell made from a waterproof-breathable or windproof fabric. In a really cold wind, any hat that isn't windproof won't keep you warm unless you put your hood up. Hats that aren't windproof are more breathable and comfortable over a wider temperature range, though, making them better for milder weather than windproof hats.

The warmth of a hat is determined by both thickness and style. Whether it can be pulled down over the ears is important, since ears get cold easily. As with other clothing, the warmest hat isn't always the best; one that will keep your head warm in a blizzard may be too hot for a cool evening at a summer camp. How much you feel the cold matters, too. I know people who are happy bareheaded when I need a hat; others wear balaclavas in what feels to me like warm weather.

The basic watch cap, stocking cap, or tuque is still the standard design. Add earflaps to it and you have a Peruvian or Andean hat. Most watch caps can be pulled down over the ears anyway. Balaclavas give more protection than other designs. Some neck gaiters have a drawcord so one end can be closed when they're worn as a hat, while others are long enough to be worn as a balaclava. The best protection against wind and rain comes from the peaked cap, with earflaps and a fleece lining, sometimes known as a bomber cap. These protect the face from rain, snow, and sun and can be used in place of a jacket hood. There are also warm headbands, useful when a full hat isn't needed but your

A thick fleece hat with earflaps is excellent in cold weather.

ears feel chilly, and face masks or ski masks that cover all but the eyes and nostrils to give more protection than I've ever needed. Presumably they're good in bitter cold and severe high-mountain blizzards. If necessary, a neck gaiter can be pulled up to cover the mouth and cheeks, something I've done on occasion.

Some hat styles come in several sizes, though many don't. Because most fleece doesn't stretch the way knitted wool or acrylic does, it's important to get a good fit if you choose fleece headgear. Hats that are a bit tight are very uncomfortable after a few hours' wear, but a hat that is too loose may blow off in a breeze. Chinstraps are useful to prevent this, especially for hats with peaks or brims that can catch the wind.

Sun and Rain Hats

For many years I never wore a sun hat, even when hiking across the desert regions of Southern Cali-

WARM HATS: MY CHOICES

Over the years I've collected a variety of warm hats for different weather conditions and times of year. In warm weather I carry a light fleece hat for campwear and in case of a cold snap. My current one weighs 2 ounces. It's warm and comfortable and fits well under a hood in the rain. In cool weather I carry a second hat, partly in case I lose one, which could be serious in the cold. I've twice lost hats after foolishly tucking them into my hipbelt when I couldn't be bothered to take off my pack and put them away. I try not to do this anymore, though I sometimes forget. I also like to have a hat that is wind- and waterproof as well as warm so that I don't need to put up my rain jacket hood except in the worst weather. Fleece-lined waterproof-breathable caps with stiffened peaks keep rain off the face and have flaps that keep the ears warm. There are many such hats. I regularly use two: a 2.8-ounce Lowe Alpine Mountain Cap with Triplepoint Ceramic outer and fleece lining that is very warm and that I wear only in wintry conditions and a 2.5-ounce Páramo Cap, made from the same fabrics as the Páramo jackets, which isn't as warm and therefore gets more use. Both hats work very well.

An interesting and versatile cap is the Hat for All Seasons from Outdoor Research, which makes a large range of hats of all types. This has a removable fleece inner layer and a Gore-Tex shell with a large stiffened peak and a wicking synthetic lining. Effectively it's three hats in one: a fleece hat, a waterproof cap, and a fleece-lined waterproof cap. The total weight is 6.5 ounces. I bought one of these several years ago and took it on a couple of long winter trips and then for some reason never wore it again. To check the weight and remind myself what it's like, I just fished it out of the hat box. It looks and feels good. I must use it again.

Down hats exist, too. Many years ago I bought one, but it's too hot and the earflaps cut out sound, so I never use it while hiking, though every so often I consider taking it on cold-weather trips to sleep in. It weighs 4 ounces. I also find windproof fleece hats hot and far less breathable than lined waterproof caps. They cut out sound too.

In cool weather I often carry one of those light fabric tubes known as neck gaiters to replace one hat. This can be pulled over the head to form a thick collar or scarf and also worn as a balaclava or rolled up to make a hat. Over the years I've collected three of these made from polypro (2.5 ounces), Power Stretch fleece (1.5 ounces), and wicking microfiber polyester (1.5 ounces). I used to have a wool one,

fornia and New Mexico in baking temperatures. I thought my thick head of hair shaded my head from the sun. However, though I still have the hair, I now find that a sun hat adds greatly to my comfort in hot, sunny weather. I was simply ignorant of the benefits of a hat. I used to wear a bandanna headband to keep sweat from dripping into my eyes, and I discovered that when soaked in cold water, it helped keep me cool. You can do the same with a hat, of course.

Oddly enough, it was in the Far North on a 1,000-mile Yukon walk that I learned how useful a sun hat can be. I discovered the Canadian-made Tilley Hat, a cotton duck hat with a wide brim and a fairly high crown, reminiscent of an Australian bush hat. The instructions (it comes with a detailed leaflet!) say the fit should be loose—the double cords for the chin and the back of the head hold it on in windy weather. I bought a Tilley Hat, and it not only kept off the very hot summer sun but also repelled light rain, kept leaves and twigs out of my hair when I was bushwhacking, and held my head net in place when the bugs were bad. I liked wearing the Tilley Hat so much that I wore it when I didn't really need to. The Tilley weighs 5.75 ounces and comes with a lifetime guarantee. Mine has now had more than a decade's regular use. It's faded and rather shapeless, but it's a favorite piece

LEFT: Waterproof-breathable hats with fleece linings and earflaps are excellent in storms and cold weather because they keep your head warm and protect it from wind and rain. Lowe Alpine Mountain Cap. RIGHT: A neck gaiter such as this Buff model is very versatile. Here it's worn as a simple hat.

but it was too warm, so I passed it on to someone who felt the cold more. The stretchy microfiber neck gaiter is made by Buff, which makes more than 200 versions. Mine was a promotional item and has Buff written all over it in orange, which has limited my use of it—I'd prefer a boring dull-colored one. My stepdaughter uses it regularly, however. Someday I must get around to buying a plainer one, since it's very useful. I sometimes carry a neck gaiter instead of my fleece hat in summer—it all depends on which I find first in my gear pile. A neck gaiter plus a hat provides almost the protection of a balaclava without the restrictiveness. Neck gaiters are also made in silk, which is probably excellent, and thick fleece, which will be very warm. Some balaclavas, like Outdoor Research's Power Stretch Balaclava, can be pulled down to make a neck gaiter or rolled up to make a hat.

of equipment because it carries so many memories. Tilley Hats come in different brim sizes. I have the standard one. The Ultimate Hat is very similar and is also available in synthetic fabrics, including Gore-Tex. I have one of those that I use for short hikes in wet, windless conditions. It's quite light at 4 ounces, but it doesn't make a good rain hat when it's windy, since the rain just comes in under the brim and runs down my neck—when the hat doesn't blow off. I've never taken it backpacking. Other companies also make synthetic brimmed hats, sometimes with reflective foil in the crown. Examples are Sequel's cotton-mesh-foil Desert Shield (4 ounces) and Outdoor Research's Supplex nylon Sahara Sombrero and Gore-Tex Seattle Sombrero. Wide-brimmed hats are great as long as it's not too windy. A neck cord is essential to stop gusts from whipping them away. Many hats are white or light colored to reflect the sun. They need a dark underside to the brim to absorb reflected light so it doesn't dazzle you. My Tilley's brim is (or was) dark brown.

The alternatives to brimmed hats are caps with large visors and neck capes. Tucking a bandanna under the rim of a baseball cap gives much the same protection, though it's difficult to keep in place unless you pin it there. The advantages over wide-brimmed hats are complete protection for the neck regardless of the angle of the sun and good wind resistance, though a neck cord is still a good idea. One of the first and best of these caps is the Sequel Desert Rhat, which is made from breathable mesh lined with a reflective foil, with a cotton front and a terry sweatband. The extra large, stiffened visor has a black underside to absorb reflected light. The cape is made from cotton and attaches with Velcro. It's now my alternative to the Tilley Hat—it's lighter (at 4 ounces) and easier to pack, so I carry it when I may not need a sun hat. I take the Tilley when I expect to wear it every day. There are masses of hats of the Desert Rhat style. Outdoor Research alone makes three. Some capes are permanently attached, some are detachable. I prefer the latter; it can get warm under the cape, so I often remove it. And a cape can be awkward if you wear the cap under a hood, as I sometimes do.

For rain there are caps made from waterproof-

A sun hat with large peak and neck cape protects your face and neck from the sun. Sequel Desert Rhat.

breathable fabrics like Gore-Tex. These are useful when fleece-lined waterproof caps are too warm, though you could just wear the Hat for All Seasons (see sidebar, page 170) and remove the fleece liner. Hats with earflaps stay on best in the wind and give more protection. I tried a Marmot PreCip Cap, which has no earflaps or neck cord. It was fine when there was no wind and the rain came straight down but blew off quickly in a breeze. Of course, in heavy wind-driven rain, nothing beats a jacket hood.

GLOVES AND MITTENS

Not only are cold hands painful and unpleasant, they can make the simplest task, like opening your pack or unwrapping a granola bar, very difficult. Whether to wear gloves or mittens depends on how cold your hands get. Gloves aren't as warm as mittens because your fingers are separated, but mittens decrease dexterity, and you have to pull them off for all sorts of fine tasks. Those who suffer from cold hands usually prefer mittens. I like gloves because I can do most things with them on. (If your hands do get very cold, a good way to warm them up is to swing your arms in circles as fast as possible—this sends blood rushing to your fingertips and quickly, if a little painfully, restores feeling and warmth.)

Gloves or mittens have either gauntlet-type wrists designed to go over jacket sleeves or elasticized cuffs designed to go inside sleeves. Gauntlets are best if you use trekking or ski poles because snow and rain can't be blown up your sleeves. If you don't use poles, cuffs are better, since water running down your sleeves can't run into your gloves. Check too that gloves fit neatly over or under your jacket sleeves. Some types don't match up.

Except in reliably warm weather, I carry at least one pair of liner gloves. These are thin enough to

Thin windproof gloves (top left), waterproof shell gloves (top right), and pile liner gloves (bottom).

wear while doing things like pitching the tent or taking photographs. At 1 to 2 ounces a pair, they're hardly noticeable in the pack. They don't last long if worn regularly, though. Gloves with reinforcements on the fingers and palms are the most durable, though slightly heavier than plain ones. There are wool, silk, and synthetic versions. The natural fabrics are good for handling hot pots and stoves and putting wood on a fire because they don't melt as synthetics do. Most of these gloves aren't very water resistant and don't dry fast. If you want to wear liner gloves in the rain, SealSkinz makes thin waterproof ones (3 ounces) from the same fabric as its socks (see pages 78–79). These are useful when handling wet gear like trekking poles or tents, and I carry them in mild weather if rain is likely.

In cold temperatures, thicker mittens or gloves are essential. For many years I used gloves made from boiled wool. Boiling shrinks the wool fibers to make a dense fabric that increases wind and water resistance so a shell glove isn't needed. Once wet, they're slow to dry, however. Austrian-made Dachstein Mitts (6 ounces) are the classic example. Climb High's Himalayan Mitts, also from Austria, are very similar. There are plenty of other wool gloves and mittens, both boiled and not. I stopped wearing boiled wool gloves when my last pair wore out between the thumb and forefinger, a major wear point if you use trekking poles, ski poles, or an ice ax. Just to try a new fabric, I replaced them with windproof fleece gloves, which I found more windproof but not as warm. I could do much more with my hands while wearing them, though, because they were thinner. However, they wore out at the base of the fingers and thumb even faster than the wool gloves did. Fleece gloves that aren't windproof are just as fragile. Fortunately, plenty of wool and windproof fleece gloves and mittens now come with reinforcements on the fingers and palms that make them much more durable. I mostly use windproof fleece gloves made from Gore Windstopper or Polartec Windbloc. The thinnest are very light (2 to 3 ounces) and allow excellent dexterity. They're not especially warm, though, and they make a good windproof alternative to liner gloves. The thickest ones with plush pile inside and a smooth fleece outside, such as Mountain Hardwear's Windstopper Windshear Gloves (4 ounces), are very warm. Some fleece and wool mittens have a flip-back cover that lets you use your fingers without taking your mittens off.

Although they're synthetic, fleece gloves don't dry very fast, so it's best to keep them dry by wearing waterproof-breathable shell mittens over them in the rain. These weigh from 1.5 to 8 ounces. You can't do much with them on, but they do keep your inner gloves dry and your hands warm. Reinforcements on the palms increase durability.

While you can put together your own glove systems, many companies offer two-layer systems consisting of wool or fleece inner gloves or mittens and waterproof-breathable shells. The great advantage of these is that the two layers are designed to fit together, but some soft fleece inner gloves wear out quickly if worn without the shell.

When severe cold is expected, I wear Black Diamond Shell Gloves with thick Retro Pile inner gloves. I bought them because the inner gloves are the thickest I've seen. Together, they weigh 9.5 ounces (shells 5.5 ounces, inner gloves 4 ounces) and have long, gauntlet-type wrists. They have kept my hands warm in temperatures as low as −30°F (−34°C). I use them mainly in short stints of up to an hour or so if my hands are feeling very cold, changing to lighter gloves once my hands warm up. The outers of the Black Diamonds are waterproof but not breathable, which means they can get a bit damp; however, because you can pull out the inner gloves, they dry quickly. The nearest current model is the 9.5-ounce Black Diamond Stratos with a waterproof shell with stretch fabric on the fingers for dexterity and a Polartec Thermal Pro fleece inner glove.

Combining the shell and the insulation in one glove or mitten is the alternative to a glove system. The insulation may be down, wool, fleece, or a synthetic fill. Primaloft One is probably the best of the synthetics, being very soft and comfortable and quite water resistant. The shell may be a waterproof-breathable fabric like Gore-Tex or a water-resistant windproof material. These gloves are usually very warm and great for real cold. They're not very versatile, however. A separate shell can be worn over a lighter inner glove in mild conditions, a useful advantage. I have a pair of Mountain Hardwear Exposure Gloves with Primaloft One insulation. As you'd expect from Mountain Hardwear, they are not a simple design. They have a waterproof-breathable Conduit shell and a Gore-Tex insert plus tough reinforcement material called Duraguard on the palm and fingers, curved fingers with no seams over the tips, a wrist leash, and a chamois nose wipe on the thumbs. They're about as warm as heavy fleece gloves but also totally waterproof. They weigh 8 ounces. Mine came with removable fleece inner gloves. The current model, the Exposure II, doesn't have these and weighs an ounce less. It's not a loss, since the fleece gloves wore out very quickly. The Exposure gloves are excellent in wet cold, and I carry them when I think the Black Diamond ones will be too warm. They are expensive, though.

To sum up, I carry liner gloves year-round, supplementing them with windproof fleece gloves and waterproof-breathable shells in cool weather. If it's very cold I carry shells with removable pile inner gloves or Primaloft-insulated gloves, the windproof fleece gloves, and the liners, leaving the shell mittens behind. There are many makers of excellent gloves. Manzella and Outdoor Research have large ranges, and SmartWool makes some good-looking wool ones.

Losing a mitten or a glove in bad weather can have serious consequences. Once long ago, while getting something out of my pack, I dropped a wool mitten that I'd tucked under my arm. Before I could grab it, the wind whisked it away into the gray, snow-filled sky. Luckily I was about to descend into the warmth of a valley a short distance away. Even so, my hand, clad in just a liner glove, was very cold by the time I reached shelter. Since then I've adopted two precautions. One is to attach loops ("idiot loops") of thin elastic shock cord to my gloves so that they dangle from my wrists when I take them off. Many gloves now come with D-rings or other attachments for wrist loops; others come with the loops already attached. My second precaution is to carry a spare pair of mittens or gloves on any trip where cold weather is likely.

In an emergency, you can wear spare socks on your hands. I used this ploy at the end of a Canadian Rockies walk during a bitterly cold blizzard, when my hands weren't warm enough even in wool mittens and liner gloves. With thick socks added, my hands went from achingly cold to comfortably warm, almost hot. Unfortunately, if your feet are cold, the reverse isn't possible!

BANDANNAS

Although not really clothing, a bandanna is quite useful. This 1-ounce square of cotton can be a headband, brow wiper, handkerchief, potholder, bandage, dishcloth, washcloth, towel, napkin, or cape for protecting your neck from the sun. I usu-

Warm and waterproof Mountain Hardwear Exposure Gloves.

ally carry two, keeping one threaded through a loop on my pack shoulder strap so I can wipe sweat off my face whenever necessary. I rinse them out frequently and tie them to the back of the pack to dry.

CARRYING CLOTHES

Stuff sacks are ideal for storing clothing in the pack. They weigh from 0.5 to 8 ounces, depending on size and the thickness of the material—thin ones are fine for use inside the pack. My preference are GoLite silicone-nylon sacks (see Covers, Liners, and Stuff Sacks in Chapter 4). I usually carry spare clothing in a stuff sack in the lower compartment of the pack. If I carry a down jacket, it has its own stuff sack for extra protection. Dry dirty clothing usually languishes in a plastic bag at the very bottom of the pack. Rain gear and clothing I may need during the day (windshirt or warm top) moves around according to how much space I have, sometimes traveling at the very top of the pack, other times at the front of the lower compartment. I don't put these garments in stuff sacks, since they can more easily fill out gaps when packed loose. Headgear and gloves go in a pack pocket, usually the top one.

FABRIC TREATMENT AND CARE

You need to be careful when washing outdoor garments. Many fabrics that are tough in the field can be damaged by detergents, softeners, and too much heat. Most fabrics function best if they're kept as clean as possible, but a few materials can be worn out by too much washing. Down in particular will lose some loft every time it's washed, and wool loses natural oils. I sometimes sponge stains and dirty marks off the shells of down garments, but I

have never washed one. I'd rather send my down jacket away for professional cleaning than risk damaging it by doing it myself. Your local outdoor store should know of companies that do this. If not, ask the garment maker. If you do wash a down top yourself, you need to use a product that won't harm the down, like Nikwax Loft Down Wash.

The other items that need special treatment are those with durable water-repellent treatments (DWR), such as all waterproof-breathable garments, most wind shells and soft shells, and some fleeces. Dirt impairs water repellency, so it's best to sponge or wipe it off as soon as possible. When water-repellent garments need washing, don't use detergents, not even mild, environmentally friendly types like Ecover, since they can damage water repellency and also leave a residue in the fabric that attracts moisture. (That's why detergent is so effective at cleaning, of course—it pulls water through fabrics.) Instead, garments should be washed with a soap such as Nikwax Loft Tech Wash, Granger's Extreme Cleaner Plus, Blue Magic Tectron Pro Wash, Dri-Pak soap flakes, or Dr. Bronner's liquid soap. These can all be used in washing machines, though you need to remove and clean the detergent dispenser and run a rinse cycle or two to make sure there's no detergent left in the machine. If you do wash garments in detergent, rinsing them is not enough to get all the detergent out, no matter how many times you do it and no matter what the labels on the garments say. I no longer wash any garment with a water-repellent finish in detergent. Unfortunately, some garment washing instructions say detergent is OK. If you use detergent, you then need to wash the garment in liquid soap to remove detergent traces. The DWR may still be damaged and need reviving or replacing. Don't have water-repellent garments dry-cleaned either—the solvents strip off all DWR.

Even if you use soap, DWR treatments will cease to work in time—after about ten washes, according to Granger's. When this happens, dark, damp patches appear on the outside of the garment as it starts to absorb moisture, a process known as *wetting out*. Moisture absorption adds to weight and drying time and impairs breathability; condensation makes many wearers think their garments are leaking. Much work has gone into creating better DWR treatments. They certainly last much longer now than when they were first introduced, but they're not permanent.

Water repellency can be revived with heat, which melts the original DWR and spreads it over the fabric. You can put the garment in a dryer, iron it, or even run a hair dryer over it. Keep the heat settings low so you don't melt the fabric as well as the DWR. If you tumble-dry clothing, make sure all zippers are done up and flaps closed to minimize damage. One test showed that tumble-drying often damages coatings and membranes, leading to eventual leakage. Using an iron or a hair dryer

ABOVE: Garments with water-repellent finishes should be washed in soap products like these, not detergent, since detergents can damage the water repellency. LEFT: Care products for hiking garments can enhance and restore water repellency.

is much safer. If applying heat doesn't restore the DWR, then it needs replacing, which can be done with a wash-in waterproofing treatment like Nikwax TX, Granger's Extreme Synthetics, or Blue Magic Tectron Wash-In Waterproofer. Check that you have the right treatment product for your garment. Nikwax makes TX-Dircct for waterproof-breathable garments; PolarProof for fleece, synthetic insulation, and wool; and Cotton Proof and Soft Shell for those materials. Consult the label before treating garments. With some products that have wicking linings—lined rain gear and wind shells—only the outer should be treated, as DWR treatments can affect the wicking properties. For these garments you need a spray treatment such as Granger's XT Water Repellent Spray, Granger's Extreme UV Spray-On and Nikwax TX-Direct Spray-On.

During a trip, garment care is minimal; in cold and wet weather, it's nonexistent. On walks of a week or less, I never wash anything; on longer ones, I rinse out underwear, socks, and any really grubby items every week or so, as long as it's sunny enough for them to dry quickly. I don't wash laundry in a stream or lake, of course; I fill a cooking pot (and clean it well afterward!) or even a waterproof stuff sack, using water from my large camp water container. The aim is to get rid of sweat, rather than stains and marks, so the garment functions again rather than looks smart. I don't use soap for washing, since it can pollute. If you do, biodegradable soap is best and soapy wastewater should be poured into dry ground well away from streams or lakes. You can dry garments on a length of cord strung between two bushes or on the back of the pack as you walk. On walks lasting more than a few weeks, I try to find a laundromat when I stop in a town to pick up supplies. I don't carry fabrics, like silk, that require special care, because I want to do one load and then tumble it dry on a hot setting. Because of the effect detergents can have on water-repellent treatments, I don't wash any garments with a DWR finish in a laundromat unless I can find some soap powder.

Most outdoor clothing can be stored flat in drawers, but down- and synthetic-filled garments should be kept uncompressed on hangers so they maintain their full loft; even slight prolonged compression may permanently affect the loft of synthetic fills. Check zippers and fastenings before you put garments away, and make necessary repairs. It's irritating to discover that a zipper needs replacing when you're packing hastily for a trip.

chapter six

shelter
camping in the wilderness

Silence. A ragged edge of pine trees, black against a starry sky. Beyond, the white slash of a snowy slope on the distant mountainside. A cocooned figure stirs, stretches. A head emerges from the warm depths, looks around in wonderment, then slumps back to sleep. Hours pass. The stars move. An animal cry, lonely and wild, slices through the quiet. A faint line of red light appears in the east as the sky lightens and a faint breeze ripples the grasses. The figure moves again and sits up, still huddled in the sleeping bag, then pulls on a shirt. A hand reaches out, and the faint crack of a match being struck rings around the clearing. A light flares, then a soft roar breaks the stillness and a pan is placed on the stove's blue flame. The figure draws back into its shelter, waiting for the first hot drink and watching the dawn as the stars slowly fade and the strengthening sun turns the black shadows into rocks and, farther away, cliffs, every detail sharp and bright in the growing light. The trees turn green again as warm shafts of golden sunlight illuminate the silent figure. Another day in the wilderness has begun.

Nights and dawns like that—and ones when the wind rattles the tent and the rain pounds down—distinguish backpacking from day walking and touring from hut to hut, hostel to hostel, or hotel to hotel. On all my walks I seek those moments when I feel part of the world around me, when I merge

DAWN

My campsite is near a lake backed by pale talus slopes and steep cliffs. The night sky is alive with stars and edged by the deeper blackness of surrounding forest and silhouetted mountains. I awake to the first rays of sunlight catching the highest peak. The lake shines green and gray, reflecting rocks and trees in its cool depths. How many other mornings have I waited for the sun, warm in my sleeping bag? The joy does not diminish.

with the trees and hills. Such times come most often and last longest when I spend several days and nights living in the wilderness.

We need shelter from cold, wind, rain, insects, and sometimes sun. It's a necessary evil. I use a shelter only when I have to, which admittedly is much of the time. But if I can sleep outside reasonably comfortably with no barrier between me and the world except a sleeping bag, I do.

The kind of shelter you need depends on the terrain, the time of year, and how spartan you're prepared to be. Some people like to sleep in a tent every night; others use one only in the worst conditions. Polar explorer Robert Peary never used a tent or a sleeping bag but slept outside in his furs, curled up beside his sled. Most mortals require a little more shelter than that. In ascending order of protection, shelters include bivouac bags, tarps, tents, and huts and lean-tos, with snow shelters as a snow country option.

BIVOUAC BAGS

Sleeping out under the stars, known as *bivouacking*, is the ideal way to spend a night in the wilderness. The last things you see before you fall asleep are the stars and the dark edges of trees and hills. At dawn you wake to the rising sun and watch color and movement return to the world. These most magical times of day are lost to those inside a tent.

Of course, since the weather can be unkind and is often changeable, instead of sunlight you may wake up to cold raindrops on your face. The simplest way to cope with weather changes is to use a waterproof *bivouac bag*, also called a *bivy bag* or a sleeping bag cover. This is a waterproof "envelope" you can slip your sleeping bag into when the weather turns wet or windy. More sophisticated (and usually heavier) designs have short poles or stiffened sections at the head to keep the bag fab-

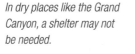

In dry places like the Grand Canyon, a shelter may not be needed.

ric off your face. (Bags with poles at each end are really minitents, so I'll explore them later, in the Tents section.)

Bivy bags made from nonbreathable fabric are now rare. Sleep in one of these and you'll get damp pretty quickly. Waterproof-breathable fabrics are much better, though some condensation is still possible in humid conditions. Gore-Tex is the standard fabric, though there are proprietary ones like Bibler's ToddTex and Integral Designs' Tegraltex as well as coated fabrics like Triplepoint (used by Exped). The extremely breathable eVENT fabric, which seems ideal for bivy bags (see pages 153–54) is starting to appear. Exped makes a 25-ounce eVENT bag. Highly breathable but not fully waterproof fabrics like Nextec's EPIC are also used. These are less prone to condensation than waterproof fabrics and will keep off dew and light rain but not heavy rain. Most bivy bags have non-breathable, coated undersides. The idea is that your sleeping pad goes inside the bag and on top of the base, so there's no point in making the bot-tom breathable. Some bags have straps inside to hold your pad in place. I prefer bags made wholly from waterproof-breathable fabric, however, since I like to put my pad under the bivy bag so the bag can move with me. I don't want a nonbreathable layer above me, which can happen if I turn over with the bag while asleep or if I deliberately turn it over to put the leak-prone zipper under me, which is the best way to stay dry when it rains. Placing the pad under the bivy bag also protects the bag against abrasion and sharp stones and thorns. A bivy bag needs to be roomy enough to allow your sleeping bag to expand fully. If it compresses the sleeping bag, you're likely to feel cold and uncomfortable. If the bag is too big, however, pockets of cold air can form where it doesn't touch the sleeping bag, which is likely to lead to more condensation. All bags have hoods of some sort, closed with a zipper or drawcord and often backed by no-see-um netting—essential in bug season. The bigger bivy bags can hold some of your gear such as clothing. Weight depends on the fabric and the design but generally runs from 8 to 32 ounces.

Straight-across zippers or entrances closed by drawcords are adequate for occasional use and bags that will mostly be used as sleeping bag covers in shelters. More complex entrances with vertical, diagonal, or curved zippers that make getting in and out easier and allow you to sit up with the bag partly undone are worth considering only if you intend to bivouac regularly, since these features add weight and cost. Many models have bug netting behind the zippers so you don't have to close the bag fully against biting insects. Hooped bivies keep the fabric off your face, but I find them claustrophobic because there's so little room. I spent a night in one once, and that was enough. I prefer simple bags, which I close fully only in heavy rain, so my face is out in the air most of the time. If you need more space, a good nonclaustrophobic option is to combine a small tarp with a bivy bag. This isn't as stable as a bivy bag with integral poles, but the setup can allow you room to cook under cover and doesn't shut you into a tiny, dark space. Some people use a bivy bag under a full-sized tarp to protect their sleeping bags against any rain that might blow in.

Bivouac bags are light and convenient for places where pitching a tent might be difficult, such as in the lee of a boulder or under a spreading tree. However, while a good bivy bag will keep out rain and wind, you have to cook outside whatever the weather or the biting insects. Unless the night is calm, dry, and insect-free, I prefer to sleep in a tent or under a tarp and cook, eat, read, write, and contemplate the world in comfort. This doesn't mean I never carry or use a bivy bag; there are situations, even when tent camping, when one comes in handy.

My first bivy bag was a 19-ounce Gore-Tex model with a horizontal zippered entrance covered by a flap. It once kept me and my down sleeping bag dry during several hours of heavy rain. That was many, many years ago, and that bag long ago started to leak. Because I don't carry a bivy bag much anymore—I just sleep out in my sleeping bag and move into a shelter if the weather changes—I replaced it with a lighter-weight waterproof-breathable coated Pertex nylon bag, the Rab Survival Zone, which weighs just 8.5 ounces (though the current catalog weight is 12 ounces). The fabric is very thin and probably not that durable, but since I mostly carry it in winter as an emergency item and have slept in it on maybe a dozen occasions in eight years, it'll last me a long while. I've also tried bags made from Tegraltex, ToddTex, and Sympatex. They all work much the same.

Even on calm, dry nights, condensation can be a problem with bivy bags. I once tested a bivy bag high on a bare mountainside on a clear and starry summer night. There was just a slight breeze, which I avoided by sleeping in a small hollow. By dawn, a thick, damp mist covered the ground. The outside of my bivy bag was wet, and there was a lot of condensation inside and on the outside of my sleeping bag. Turning the bivy bag inside out and draping it over a boulder along with the sleeping bag soon cleared the moisture as the mist faded and the sun rose. On colder nights I've awakened to find a layer of ice inside the bivy bag. Even if it doesn't seem damp, it's advisable to air your sleeping bag as soon as possible after a night in a bivy bag to get rid of any moisture it may have absorbed. Condensation is a reason for using bivy bags only on short trips or in mostly fine weather. It's hard to keep your sleeping bag dry if the weather is damp for several days.

In winter I usually carry a bivy bag as a backup shelter and sometimes use it inside my tent or a snow shelter for extra warmth and to protect against dripping condensation. A bivy bag adds several degrees to the range of a sleeping bag.

Outdoor Research, Bibler, Exped, and Integral Designs all offer a range of bags in waterproof-breathable fabrics. I especially like the look of the Bibler Winter Bivy, made of EPIC and weighing just 9 ounces. Although not fully waterproof, this would be fine for use in tents and snow shelters and outside for dew and drizzle. Oware also makes an EPIC bivy bag, which has a silnylon base and weighs 10.5 ounces without bug netting and 12 ounces with it. Oware makes Gore-Tex bivy bags too, and there are many design options so you can customize your bag.

The most interesting bivy bag I've come across is the Hilleberg Bivanorak. This 18-ounce bag is made from waterproof-breathable coated ripstop nylon and has sleeves and a hood so you can keep your arms and head protected when you sit up in it. There's a drawcord at the foot too, so you can open it up, stick your legs out, and wear it as a rain jacket. The Bivanorak is very roomy and will fit over a medium-size pack. The material does flap a little and breathability isn't that good when walking. I wouldn't want to walk far in it, but as an emergency item it's excellent. I have used it at rest stops in stormy weather and enjoyed the extra protection. As a bivy bag it's very roomy, easily big enough for a full-length mat and a bulky sleeping bag. However the fabric is quite thin and it's awkward to sit up with a mat inside, which negates one of the advantages of the design, so I prefer to keep the mat outside. I haven't used it in prolonged or heavy rain but the drawcord closures at the cuffs and foot and the hood opening mean it can't be 100 percent waterproof, though I wouldn't expect much leakage. The hood and sleeves can be tucked under the bag but the foot will always be exposed to the weather.

Carrying an emergency shelter on day hikes and side trips away from camp is a good idea, especially in winter or when you're going above timberline.

The Hilleberg Bivanorak, a bivy bag that becomes a rain jacket.

An expensive waterproof-breathable bivy bag is unnecessary for this purpose, however, as well as a little heavy. Nonbreathable plastic and foil bags, sometimes called *survival bags*, are fine for emergency use. They're inexpensive and take up little room in the pack. The comfort isn't great—I once slept out in a plastic bivy bag and got extremely damp—but if you ever need one, you'll be grateful. For emergency shelter in summer I usually carry an MPI Space Brand Emergency Bag, made from polyester foil with an aluminum reflective surface.

It weighs 2.5 ounces and measures 3 by 7 feet when unfolded. This is a very thin bag that will keep off the wind and rain but won't provide much warmth by itself. The MPI Extreme Pro-Tech Bag has a sealed corrugated pattern of the same fabric that traps air and is meant to be much warmer. There are elastic fibers in the construction that allow the bag to hug the body, cutting out dead air space. It weighs 12 ounces. An alternative is a plastic survival bag like one from Coghlan's that weighs 9 ounces. I've often carried one of these on day hikes.

TARPS

Tarps almost disappeared as backcountry shelters during the last third of the twentieth century as hikers turned to the seductive attractions of curving flexible poles and smooth, taut nylon tents. In the previous edition I wrote that "constructing your own shelter from sheets of plastic or nylon and cord is something hardly any backpacker does these days." Since then there's been a big and somewhat astonishing resurgence in the popularity of tarps because of both the ultralight revolution and the use of trekking poles, which make good tarp supports, although most backpackers still use tents.

First, though, a definition. A *tarp* is a sheet of fabric that can be suspended from poles or trees to make a shelter. Once you add doors it becomes a tent, or at least a fly sheet. Such designs will be considered below under Tents. Here I'm talking about basic tarps only.

I first used a tarp as a cooking shelter in areas where the presence of bears made eating and cooking in or near my tent unwise and where the likelihood of rain meant that eating and cooking outside could be unpleasant. On long walks in both the Canadian Rockies and the Yukon, I carried an 8-by-9-foot silicone-coated ripstop nylon tarp, with grommets for attaching guylines along each side, to use as a kitchen shelter. On the many occasions when I made camp in cold, wet, windy weather, the protection it provided while I cooked and ate was welcome and certainly justified its 16 ounces of weight. I usually pitched it as a lean-to, slung between two trees on a length of cord. Occasionally I made more complex structures, using my staff plus fallen branches as makeshift poles. At sites with a picnic table, I found I could string the tarp above the table and create a sheltered sitting and eating area.

However, I'd never used a tarp in place of a tent on a long walk until I hiked the Arizona Trail in 2000, when the almost certain prospect of dry weather made a tent unnecessary. Since then I've used a tarp frequently, including on a 500-mile hike in the High Sierra, and it's become my favorite shelter. I now reserve tents for dependably wet, windy, or buggy places.

Another use for a tarp is as an awning for your tent, which provides a large undercover cooking, storage, and drying area that also lets you leave your tent door open in rain with no danger of leakage. I drape the tarp over the tent door, peg out the sides, then use a trekking pole or poles to support the front.

The advantages of tarps are low cost, low weight, space, views, adaptability, good ventilation, and an element of creativity in how you pitch them. Cooking under a tarp is easy because there's no sewn-in groundsheet and you can raise a corner or side for safety. With each side raised high, you have a 360-degree view yet are still protected from precipitation. With a tent you're either inside it or outside.

The disadvantages are that tarps can be difficult

Tarp pitched as a lean-to.

to erect in storms, need careful pitching to keep out wind-driven rain, and—worst of all in my view—don't keep out bugs. Condensation can occur, but it's never the problem it can be in a tent: a breeze usually prevents it. If there's no wind, then you can pitch the tarp to allow plenty of ventilation.

Lightweight tarps, weighing 5 to 32 ounces, used to be hard to find but are now widely available. Companies like GoLite, Hilleberg, Bozeman Mountain Works, Integral Designs, MSR, Equinox, Campmor, Crazy Creek, and Oware offer a wide selection, as do some of the small specialist companies that have sprung up as part of the ultralight hiking movement, such as Lynne Whelden Gear, Dancing Light Gear, and Moonbow Gear. Most tarps are made from silicone-coated nylon (see Tents below for fabric details), some from standard polyurethane-coated nylon. Sheets of plastic from building and hardware stores can be used as tarps, but they're not very strong and can tear. Plastic is inexpensive, and some people leave torn sheets of it in the wilder-

Tarp pitched high off the ground for good headroom and ventilation. GoLite Cave.

ness. I know; I've packed a few of them out. Disposable equipment isn't environmentally friendly whether you pack it out or not, so overall I think it's best not to use plastic for shelters.

Most tarps are flat sheets, though some have graceful shapes with curved sides—the MSR Moss HeptaWing (25 ounces) has seven sides; the Dana Design Hat tarp (24 ounces) has six and can also be

Clockwise from top left: A lean-to tarp; an open-ended ridge using trees; an open-ended ridge using two sticks or poles; and an open-ended ridge using four sticks or poles.

zipped up to make a two-person bivy bag. The shaped tarps may be more wind-resistant, but they're also heavier and more costly. Sizes vary enormously. For solo use, 5 feet by 8 feet is probably the smallest feasible size. I tried the 7-ounce 5-by-8-foot Integral Designs Siltarp and found it just big enough to protect me if I pitched it carefully. I prefer more space, however, and the tarp I use most measures 7 feet by 11 feet, big enough for two and roomy for me and my gear. It's a silicone-nylon GoLite Cave 1, a Ray Jardine design. It weighs 14 ounces; stakes add another 4 to 6 ounces. The Cave has a small awning at each end, known as a "beak," that gives greater protection against rain than open ends. The beaks can be pitched down to the ground

to seal off the ends in severe storms. There are plenty of stake points and guylines, including some on the sides that can be tied to poles to create more interior space and prevent sagging. The larger Cave 2—8 feet, 9 inches by 11 feet, 7 inches and 18 ounces—sleeps two or three. There are two GoLite tarps with a beak at one end only: the Lair 1 (8 feet by 8 feet, 8 inches, 12 ounces) and Lair 2 (8 feet by 11 feet, 4 inches, 16 ounces).

Netting

I don't use a tarp in bug season because I haven't yet found any netting that I'm happy with. I want to be able to sit up and move around under a tarp,

LEFT: Tarp with bug-netting inner. GoLite Cave and Nest. RIGHT: Tarp pitched as a pyramid with a single pole.

not feel trapped in a mesh enclosure. Once a tarp gives less space and freedom than a tent, I'd rather have a tent. If bugs are out only when you're sleeping, you could just drape a piece of no-see-um material over your head or the hood of your sleeping bag. That doesn't solve the problem of bugs in the evening and morning, however. GoLite has a new bug tent that could be the answer. It comes in two sizes, the solo Lair 1 Nest with a front height of 33 inches (21 ounces) and the two-person Lair 2 Nest with a front height of 45 inches (25 ounces), and will fit inside the Lair and Cave tarps. The Nests have zipped doors and polyurethane-coated nylon floors and look far better than the original Nest, which didn't have a zipped door; you had to crawl in under a flap, an awkward maneuver that brought in insects too.

Some tarps have mesh panels at the ends and mesh strips around the perimeter. These probably help, but my experience is that when biting insects swarm, you need a totally closed, insect-proof shelter to keep them out. When the bugs are bad, I like a down-to-the-ground fly sheet with a zippered door and a vestibule where I can burn a mosquito coil or insect-repellent candle and an inner tent with mesh doors.

Pitching a Tarp

Tarps can be pitched in so many ways that the best advice is to experiment and practice—you don't want to be trying to figure out how to erect a stormproof shelter in the rain at the end of a long day's hike. Try different shapes and profiles. If you have a trekking pole or poles, these can be used as supports. You can easily lower the profile of the tarp if the weather becomes stormy by shortening the poles and then restaking the tarp from inside. You can also fit poles inside a tarp and pull the fabric over the handles without danger of damaging the tarp, as can happen with a stick. Having supports inside adds to wind resistance and stability. If you don't have poles, you'll need to find a stout stick or two or else tie the tarp to trees, which means camping only below timberline. You could carry tent poles, but this adds weight. You need enough stakes to hold the tarp down plus some cord for guylines unless your tarp comes with guylines attached. Most tarps have grommets or loops for attaching guylines. If yours doesn't or you want extra stake points, you can wrap a smooth stone in the fabric and tie a loop of cord around the neck between the stone and the rest of the tarp. I've

Top: Tarp pitched as a low-profile ridge with a storm approaching. *GoLite Cave. ABOVE: Tarp pitched as a pyramid with a trekking pole. A second pole is being used to hold the front of the tarp open.*

always found this method satisfactory, but there's a device called the Grip Clip, from Shelter Systems, that does the same job with perhaps less likelihood of tearing the fabric. Grip Clips come in various sizes; the smallest 0.08-ounce Micro and the 0.2-ounce Light Fabric clips are recommended for lightweight tarps. For silicone nylon, Shelter Systems recommends fitting pieces of a balloon as gaskets because the fabric is so slippery. To use Grip Clips, you push the two open-centered halves together with the tarp fabric between them. The pieces snap together and cannot come undone. Guylines can be attached to the clips, and they come with 11 inches of cord attached.

The most common tarp shapes are the lean-to, the ridge, and the pyramid. For the first, tie the corners at each end of a long side of the tarp to

Tarps can be pitched in unusual shapes using trees, both standing and fallen, as supports. GoLite Cave.

trees or poles, several feet above the ground. If you use poles, they'll need guying out to keep them from falling over. The other side of the tarp can be staked to the ground or, for better ventilation if there's no wind, loops of cord can be attached to the stake points and the tarp can be pitched with an air gap between the lower edge and the ground. Lean-tos are roomy and reasonably condensation-free, but they protect you on only one side, and they can flap in the wind.

Ridges give more protection. An open-ended ridge can be pitched by attaching lines to the centers of the short sides of the tarp and tying them to trees or trekking poles. Again, you'll need guylines to stake the poles out. If it's windy, one end of the ridge can be staked down close to the ground, which is most easily done with a tarp with a shaped end like the GoLite beak. This produces a sloping ridge that is more wind and rain resistant than one with both ends at the same height.

For a pyramid, stake out one side, then pull the center of the tarp over the handle of an upright trekking pole and tie it off with a bit of cord before staking out the other two corners with the tarp slack between them to leave space for a door. The center of this loose side can be pulled taut with a guyline or, more effectively, by tying it to a pole. Pyramids are quite wind resistant but are best suited to large tarps. Small tarps may not give you enough room to lie down.

These three basic shapes can be varied according to terrain and available supports. I've tied tarps to fallen trees to make unusual shapes and fitted them into awkward spots with one corner at ground level and the one diagonally opposite high in the air. Experiment. That's one of the joys of tarp camping.

With any shape, a low profile with the edges of the tarp at ground level is the most storm resistant but also the most prone to condensation.

GROUNDSHEETS

A *groundsheet*, or *ground cloth*, is useful when sleeping under the stars or under a tarp, especially if the ground is wet. I also carry a groundsheet if I'm planning on using a snow shelter or wilderness huts or lean-tos, because their floors may be wet and muddy. Unlike many people, I don't use one under my tent. I find tent groundsheets durable—I have some that have had more than a year's use and are still waterproof—and I don't want to carry the extra weight.

Cheap plastic sheets are lightweight but don't last long, and they can't be staked out, which is necessary when it's windy. Nylon groundsheets are much better, especially those that come with grommets or stake points. Tent-footprint groundsheets, designed to be used under tents, work well and weigh 8 ounces or more, depending on size. Many tent makers offer them. Silicone nylon makes for a very light, strong groundsheet, though it can be a little slippery. I have one that measures 54 inches by 84 inches and weighs 8 ounces. Dancing Light Gear makes a sheet 72 inches long that tapers from 36 to 22 inches and weighs 4.5 ounces. GoLite's Ultra-Lite measures 42 inches by 90 inches and weighs 5 ounces. The lightest ground cloths come from Gossamer Gear. The Spinnsheet, made from spinnaker ripstop nylon, comes in two sizes: the 27-by-84-inch size weighs 1.7 ounces; the 54-by-84-inch size weighs 3.4 ounces.

Of course, tarps can be used as groundsheets—and vice versa. I once used a groundsheet as a tarp during a thunderstorm in Yellowstone National Park. I didn't want to cook in my tent because of bears, nor did I want to sit outside in the cold storm. So I slung my groundsheet, carried for when I slept under the stars, between two trees as a lean-to and used my pack as a seat while I cooked, ate, and watched the lightning flashes illuminate the forest and the rain bounce off the sodden earth.

An alternative to coated nylon is polyethylene, which comes in two forms, DuPont's Tyvek and Space Brand aluminized fabric, and is much more durable than ordinary plastic. Tyvek is used in the construction industry and can be bought in rolls and cut to size (it's also used for waterproof maps). Tyvek is very light and has become popular with ultralight hikers. Six Moon Designs sells Tyvek in lengths of 3 feet or more (84 inches wide, 1.6 ounces per square yard; 59 inches wide, 1.75 ounces per square yard for aluminized Tyvek). Lynne Whelden Gear sells ready-cut Tyvek groundsheets measuring 42 inches by 90 inches and weighing 5.5 ounces with a foot pocket in the end for your sleeping bag to protect it from rain blowing in at the end of a tarp. I haven't used Tyvek, but it's recommended by many experienced long-distance hikers. I have used MPI Outdoors' Space Brand All Weather Blanket. Current versions are made from a four-ply laminate of clear polyethylene film, aluminum coating, reinforcing fabric, and colored polyethylene film. The blanket measures 60 inches by 84 inches and weighs 10 ounces. One side is silver, the other is blue, red, or olive. With the silver side out, these blankets make good sunshades in the desert. One drawback is that if you fold them for carrying, they tend to crack and then leak at the creases. I now roll mine, and this does seem to prolong the life. I don't use it much anymore anyway, preferring lighter-weight silicone nylon.

TENTS

A good tent provides complete protection from the weather and insects and also space to sit, cook, eat, read, make notes, sort gear, play cards, and watch the world outside. A tarp provides more space ounce-for-ounce, of course, but it doesn't give the same protection against windy weather or, especially, biting insects.

Choosing a tent can be confusing. They come in a wide variety of shapes and sizes, and few stores have the space to display many. There are limited opportunities to see tents pitched and to crawl in and out of them to assess how well they suit your needs. However, a good store should be prepared to erect a tent you're considering buying so you can have a look at it.

Condensation

A tent's primary purpose is to keep out rain and snow. Luckily that's easy to do. Ideally, a tent should also let out moisture vapor. This is not so easy. Bodies give off a fair amount of vapor, and there may be more from wet clothes, cooking, steaming drinks, wet hair, drips, and spills. Moisture from damp ground and vegetation in the vestibule and around the edges of the fly sheet can also condense on cold, impermeable tent walls. If you brush against those walls, you'll get damp too. In my experience the standard two-skin (or double-skin or double-wall) tent design with a breathable, nonwaterproof tent (nowadays sometimes called a *canopy*) and a nonbreathable, waterproof *fly sheet* or rainfly is the best solution

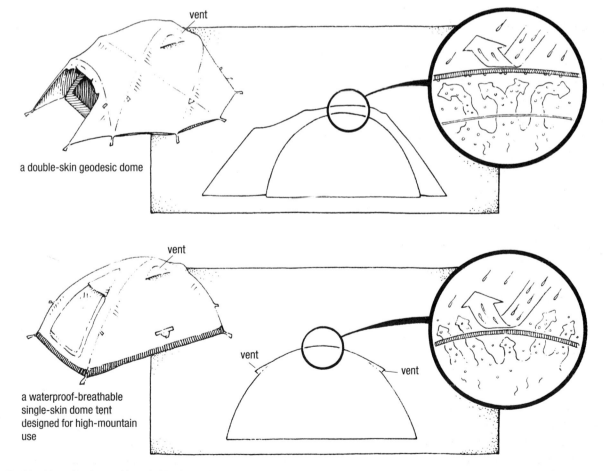

vent

a double-skin geodesic dome

vent

vent

vent

a waterproof-breathable single-skin dome tent designed for high-mountain use

Double-skin and waterproof-breathable single-skin tents.

KEY FEATURES: GEODESIC DOME TENTS

- Easy pitching. Check for minimum number of stakes or freestanding design.
- Shock-corded poles that can be quickly fitted to the tent by clips or wide sleeves.
- Waterproof, UV-resistant fly sheet.
- Uncoated inner tent to allow condensation to escape.

- Good space-to-weight ratio.
- Insect net doors. (When the mosquitoes or black flies are abundant, this is more important than any other feature.)
- A roomy vestibule.

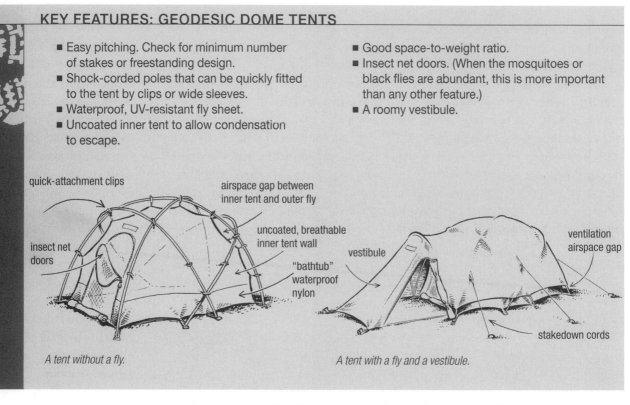

quick-attachment clips

airspace gap between inner tent and outer fly

insect net doors

uncoated, breathable inner tent wall

vestibule

"bathtub" waterproof nylon

ventilation airspace gap

stakedown cords

A tent without a fly.

A tent with a fly and a vestibule.

to condensation, but it's nowhere near perfect. In theory, moisture passes through the inner fabric and is then carried away by the air circulating between the two layers. Any condensation that forms on the fly sheet can run down to the ground, with stray drips repelled by the inner wall. To prevent condensation from reaching the inner tent, the gap between the tent and the fly sheet must be large enough that wind cannot push the two together. And you need to be careful not to press the inner walls against the fly sheet.

To some extent the double-layer system works. However, moist air is carried away only if there is a breeze and if it can escape. Since warm air rises and warm air holds more moisture than cold air, a vent high up on the fly sheet can create a chimney effect, drawing cool, dry air in under the bottom edge and expelling warm, damp air through the vent. Vents are more common than they used to be, but many tents still don't have them.

Two-way fly sheet door zippers are also useful for ventilation. I leave at least the top few inches open unless rain starts coming in through the gap.

Condensation is worst in calm, humid conditions. Then nothing—not even leaving all the doors open—will prevent the fly sheet from becoming very wet. One misty night I was awakened by drips falling from the tarp I was under, which was pitched as a lean-to. In a much more enclosed tent, condensation is unavoidable. I have even left tents empty in calm, humid conditions and found the fly sheets wet with condensation in the morning.

Where bugs are a problem, I've sometimes felt my tent turning into a sauna while I cooked inside the vestibule with all the doors shut tight, producing clouds of steam that promptly condensed on the fly sheet. But being warm and damp is preferable to being eaten alive!

Condensation is a more serious problem in freezing temperatures, when the inner tent can become so cold that moisture condenses on it and then drips back on the sleeper below. If temperatures drop even more, the problem may be solved, because the moisture will freeze on the tent. But when you wake in the morning and start to move around creating heat, the ice will melt, and it can seem as though it's snowing inside the tent. Ventilation is a partial answer to this.

If you camp regularly in damp, humid climates—on the Olympic Peninsula or in the Maine woods, say—it's worth looking for a tent with plenty of ventilation options, such as hoods over door zippers and covered vents. Tents that have sloping inner doors or large mesh panels without covers are poor designs for humid areas. Condensation can drip through the open door or the mesh panels and onto the groundsheet or your sleeping bag. The best design for keeping condensation out of the tent has solid inner walls, a vertical door, vents at the high point of the fly sheet, and outer doors with two-way zippers. Any mesh panels should have covers.

Fabrics

Polyester and nylon are excellent fabrics for backpacking tents, being strong, light, quick drying, and durable. Canvas, the traditional tent material, is not strong enough to make lightweight tents. Polyester stretches less than nylon when wet and resists ultraviolet light better. (Whatever the fabric, it's still best not to leave tents up for long in bright sunlight.) However, nylon has a much higher tear strength weight-for-weight.

Inner tents are usually made from nonwaterproof-breathable nylon that absorbs little moisture, dries quickly, and allows moisture vapor through. Most have a light fluorocarbon finish to repel drips of condensation from the fly sheet. Tents designed for warm weather often have large mesh panels for ventilation to keep out insects and provide views of the stars when the fly sheet isn't in use. However, mesh can let in cold breezes and drips of condensation. Some tents have mesh panels with covers for cool and damp conditions. In my experience, while mesh panels do make a tent cooler, they don't decrease condensation.

Fly sheets may be coated with polyurethane or impregnated with silicone. Silicone nylon, often abbreviated to silnylon, is the lightest fabric yet has a much higher tear strength than polyurethane-coated fabrics. It also has the best resistance to ultraviolet light. Silicone encapsulates the fibers completely rather than just lying on the surface, so it can't wear or peel off, making it very durable and permanently water repellent. Even after years of use, rain still beads up on silnylon, so it dries very quickly. Polyurethane is applied to only one side of

Seam sealant for silnylon.

WATERPROOF-BREATHABLE TENTS

I used a Gore-Tex tent on the Pacific Crest Trail, a walk that lasted more than five months, which gave me a good idea of how such tents work in different conditions. In the snowbound High Sierra, where the temperature fell below freezing most nights and the humidity was low, I had no problems with condensation, whereas my companions in two-skin tents found their fly sheets frozen solid each morning. However, in humid weather in September in the Cascades, condensation was a real problem, with moisture running down the taped seams and forming pools on the groundsheet. On too many rainy mornings I had to pack a wet tent and then pitch it, still sodden, in the evening, by which time the moisture had spread all over the groundsheet. I kept my down sleeping bag dry by sleeping in a Gore-Tex bivy bag inside the tent.

In theory, the efficiency of waterproof-breathable fabrics depends on a variation in pressure between the inside of the material and the outside, but I found that levels of condensation were related solely to the outside humidity, not to whether I closed or opened the tent doors. I also found that ventilation was the best way to minimize and clear condensation. If I were to buy another waterproof-breathable tent, I'd look for a good vent system.

But even then, I would use such a tent only where prolonged wet weather and high humidity were unlikely. On a spring ski crossing of the vast Columbia Icefield in the Canadian Rockies, our group of four had two similar-sized tunnel tents—one a two-skin model, the other Gore-Tex. Instead of four days, our crossing took eight because of blizzards, and we spent several days in the tents waiting out storms. The temperature never dropped below 24°F (−5°C); most of the time it was a degree or two either side of 32°F (0°C). This made for damp conditions with the air full of wet spindrift. The two of us in the two-skin tent stayed warm and comfortable, if bored. The condensation that formed on the fly sheet and in patches on the inner tent at night dried out during the day. The pair in the Gore-Tex tent had a rough time. Their tent was soaked inside and dripped on them constantly from the first night on, and their down sleeping bags became wet with condensation, severely reducing their warmth.

a fabric; it's put on the inside of the fly sheet to protect the coating from wear. Once the original durable water-repellent treatment (DWR) wears off, the outside can absorb moisture, making it heavy and slow to dry. Some fly sheets are coated inside and out with silicone, while others have silicone on the outside but polyurethane on the inside so the seams can be taped.

Weights for tough inner and outer nylons are about 1 to 2 ounces per square yard (usually stated in the form 1.5-ounce nylon); the lighter ones need slightly more care than the heavier materials. Deniers (see page 117) range from 30 to 75. To prevent leaks, fly sheet seams may need sealing with a seam sealant like SeamGrip unless they come with taped seams. Neither tapes nor standard sealant will stick to silnylon. You'll need McNett's special silicone sealant, SilNet. That said, I've been using silnylon tents and tarps for well over a decade, including months at a time in wet climates, and I've never sealed any seams or had any leaks.

An intriguing alternative to the breathable tent–waterproof fly sheet norm comes from Stephenson's Warmlite, whose tents have two layers made of coated fabric that are permanently linked. The inner layer also has an aluminized coating on the inside to block radiant heat. There are low and high vents to create a chimney effect. This design minimizes condensation, according to the makers, because the inner tent is warmer than in standard designs. I haven't tried a Warmlite tent, but it makes theoretical sense and has gotten positive reviews.

Friends who have one speak highly of it. For more on Warmlite tents, see page 209.

Some tents now come with plastic windows in the doors or the roof so you can look out without opening the tent—at least in theory. In my experience these mist up with condensation very quickly or else are covered with rain and are actually only useful at those times when opening the door isn't a problem. These windows used to be found only in budget tents, since they were brittle and cracked easily. Now they are made from flexible and tough materials and are more widespread.

Waterproof-Breathable Tents

Tents made from waterproof-breathable fabrics are easy to pitch and quite light for their size because they have a single skin. Wind can't get in under the edge of the fly sheet because there isn't one, so they can be warmer than two-layer tents. The chief makers of these tents are Bibler and Integral Designs, each using its own proprietary fabrics, ToddTex and Tegraltex, respectively. Gore-Tex tents seem to have mostly disappeared.

Waterproof-breathable tents work well in dry conditions, but they aren't breathable enough to cope with much moisture vapor in humid conditions, and then condensation is likely; moreover, the condensation can't escape by running into the ground because there is a sewn-in groundsheet (see sidebar, opposite).

Nonbreathable Single-Skin Tents

My first true backpacking tent was a single-skin (or single-wall) nonbreathable coated nylon ridge tent.

LEFT: Low-profile, single-skin bivy tent of waterproof-breathable fabric. Bibler Tripod.
BELOW: Low-profile single-skin tunnel tent of waterproof-breathable fabric with vestibule and trekking poles used to pull out the sides for more space inside.

Single-skin waterproof-nonbreathable tunnel tent. GoLite Den 2.

It was lightweight, easy to pitch, waterproof, and low in bulk when packed. However, in wet or humid conditions, to call the condensation copious was an understatement. It ran down the walls and slowly flooded the groundsheet. I replaced that tent with a double-layer model as soon as I could and wasn't surprised when single-skin tents disappeared shortly afterward. The lightweight revolution has seen them reappear, on the basis that cutting out the inner tent and sewing the groundsheet to the fly sheet saves weight. These modern nonbreathable tents often have vents and door configurations said to reduce condensation. These might help a little, but the inside of a fly sheet in a double-layer tent can be soaked with condensation in humid weather even with vents and doors open and an air gap right around the perimeter, so there's no way a single-skin tent, without that lower air gap, will have less condensation. I'd be very wary of nonbreathable single-skin tents with sewn-in groundsheets unless I camped only in places with low humidity. And then I would probably just carry a tarp anyway. A brief trial with the single-skin silnylon GoLite Den 2 (3 pounds, 9 ounces) showed that a good design with vents at each end does help, but when there's no wind much condensation still forms. GoLite says

the Den is for "areas with low humidity and/or with ample breezes." I'd say this applies to all tents of this type, and I'd drop the *or*.

There are also single-skin tents without ground sheets, basically just fly sheets. These are still prone to condensation, but it can run into the ground rather than onto the groundsheet, so they're more practical for conditions where a tent is most needed. Most pyramid tents are floorless single-skin models, as are many of the new ridge designs. The key when using these tents is to avoid touching the walls when they're damp.

Floors

Tent floors are usually made from 2- to 4-ounce polyurethane-coated nylon. Long ago nylon floors didn't stay waterproof very long and ripped easily, so people usually used a groundsheet under them, a habit that has remained even though the nylons used today are tough enough to make a groundsheet unnecessary. The tent I used on my Canadian Rockies walk back in 1988 was still waterproof after eighty nights with no protection under it.

The best floors are the "bathtub" type with no ground-level seams. Short sidewalls keep out rain splashes that come under the fly sheet. Tiny punctures are the most likely damage to occur to floors. To prevent further leaks, cover them with spots of sticky nylon tape. Better yet, check the ground for sharp twigs and stones before pitching the tent to minimize the chances of puncturing the floor.

If you do use a groundsheet with your tent, make sure it doesn't extend beyond the edge of the fly sheet, or rain can collect between it and the tent floor. This can happen even when it's tucked well under the tent, though it's much less likely if you fold up the edges of the groundsheet. On the few occasions when I've used a groundsheet with a tent, I've put it inside the tent.

Poles

Most tent poles are made from flexible aluminum, though those on less expensive models may be made from fiberglass. Pyramid tents often come with rigid aluminum poles. I've never used a tent with fiberglass poles, but the general view is that they're not as strong as aluminum. Aluminum comes in different types; DAC Featherlite and Easton 7075 are regarded as the highest quality. The diameter of the tubing also affects the strength. Most backpacking tents have 8.5- to 9.5-millimeter poles. Tents designed for severe high-mountain weather may have thicker poles, such as 11.5 millimeters.

Carbon fiber is stronger, lighter, and more expensive than aluminum. A new pole material is Easton's Ultralite A/C, carbon fiber bonded to an aluminum core. The poles are 30 percent lighter than standard Easton poles and are used by Sierra Designs. If you want to save a few ounces, you can—for a price—buy carbon-fiber poles for your tent from Fibraplex. These are half the weight of Easton 7075 poles. The pole on my favorite solo tent weighs 5.5 ounces. Since the shock cord linking the sections would weigh the same, I'd save maybe 2 ounces if I changed to carbon fiber. Of course, with a large geodesic dome tent with four or five long poles, the weight saving would be more significant, as would the increased cost.

Some flexible poles come prebent. If they are not prebent, they often develop a curve with use. This is not a problem as long as you don't try to straighten them, because then they may break. Pole sections are normally linked by shock cord, which makes it easy to put them together and almost impossible to lose sections (though I managed it once after a shock cord snapped).

Poles may run through nylon or mesh sleeves or attach to the tent with clips or shock cord; some have flexible hubs at pole intersections. Pole ends fit into grommets, plastic pole cups, or webbing. Clips theoretically allow better airflow between the inner layer and the fly sheet than sleeves, but I don't think they make much difference. What's more important is that poles are marked so you know where each one should go. Many poles come already marked. If not, it's worth sticking different-colored tape on each one.

Poles are strong when the tent is pitched but vulnerable when lying on the ground—especially long, thin, flexible poles. Take care not to step on them. And don't use them as handholds when entering and leaving the tent. A companion once broke a flexible pole by putting all his weight on it as he left the tent during a winter gale in a remote mountain area. I had to scramble out of my sleeping bag, throw on some clothes, and repair it before the storm caused any more damage. I fixed it by slipping a short alloy sleeve over the break and binding it in place with duct tape. Such sleeves are supplied with most flexible-pole tents. I always carry one, though that's the only time I've used it.

After I'd been using trekking poles for a few

years it occurred to me that carrying tent poles as well was a little superfluous, especially since trekking poles are stronger than most tent poles. However, you can't pitch a flexible-pole tent with trekking poles. Now, though, tents designed to be used with trekking poles are appearing, which makes good sense. I use mine with tarps and the GoLite Hex 3 pyramid tent.

Stakes

Every tent must be staked to hold it down in wind. Fifteen to twenty stake points are plenty; more increase the weight you're carrying and the time it takes to pitch the tent. Many tents need only eight to twelve stakes. Most stakes are made of steel or aluminum (I've found plastic too fragile for wilderness use), and they come in a variety of shapes. Thin ones work best in hard ground, wide-angled or curved ones in soft ground. For sand or soft snow, you need really wide snow pegs. I have a set

of 12-inch hardened aluminum stakes for snow camping. They weigh 1.8 ounces each and are drilled with holes to save weight and to attach guylines so they can be buried horizontally for maximum holding power. Hilleberg, MSR, and SMC make snow stakes. Hilleberg's come with a line and a hook for attaching them to guylines or stake points. Much lighter are fabric "stakes" with short lengths of cord attached that you fill with sand or snow and then bury, such as Bibler's 1-ounce Soft Stakes and Exped's 0.6-ounce Snow and Sand Anchors. I suspect it would be easy to make your own version of these.

Outside of snow country, I use 7-inch hardened aluminum pins (0.33 ounce each), which hold in most soils. For softer ground, I carry two or three 6-inch hardened aluminum V-angle stakes (0.5 ounce each). Y-shaped stakes are considered the strongest alloy ones, though I don't like them because they are harsh on the hands. If you want very strong stakes that weigh very little, you can get

A selection of tent stakes. From left: plastic I-beam for soft ground, C-curve for soft ground, short pin with loop end for hard ground, Y shape for soft ground, long pin with hook end for hard ground, thick pin for hard ground, snow stake for sand and snow.

titanium stakes, both pins and angles—at a price—from Stanley Alpine, Snow Peak, Vargo Outdoors, Bozeman Mountain Works (which paints them bright orange), and Simon Metals. Titanium pins are very thin and apparently can be driven into hard, rocky soil without bending or breaking. However, reports suggest that the thinness means they pull out of anything less hard too easily. Although I occasionally bend stakes, I've never felt the need for stronger ones. If you regularly camp on rocky ground or hardened tent platforms, titanium stakes might be worth using. In hard ground stakes can be tapped in with a small rock or pushed gently with the sole of your boot. Don't hit them too hard though, or they might bend or break. If stakes are hard to pull out by hand, use another stake by hooking it into the end of the stuck stake and using it as a lever.

Stakes are easy to misplace, so I carry a couple of extras. However, on many occasions I've finished a hike with more stakes than I started with, finding ones others had lost. I keep stakes in the small nylon stuff sack supplied with most tents and carry them in a pack pocket so they're easy to find when I pitch the tent.

Guylines

Depending on the design, tents need anything from two to a dozen or more guylines to keep them taut and stable in a wind, though more than ten is too many for one- and two-person tents. Most tents come supplied with a full set of guys, but some have only the main ones plus attachment points for others. It pays to attach these extra guylines before they're needed or at least carry some cord with you. I'd rather have plenty of guylines and leave them tied back when it's calm than not have enough.

To avoid confusion and to help when sorting out tangles, different-colored guylines are useful,

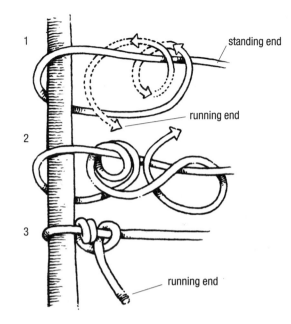

Tautline hitch. Wrap the rope around an object to create a loop. Feed the running end of the rope over the standing end and through the loop at least twice (1). Bring the running end out of the loop and over the standing end. Secure the running end as shown (2). Tighten the wraps so they lie flat and close together (3).

especially when several are attached to the tent at the same point. If the guylines are tied back in loops when you pack your tent, they're less likely to tangle. I always try to do this, though when packing in a hurry during a storm, I often forget and end up cursing myself the next night as my numb fingers undo knots. Metal locking or plastic friction adjusters come with most guylines, but you can also buy them separately. It's useful to know how to tie the tautline hitch (see illustration) in case you need extra guylines and have no extra mechanical sliders. This knot will slide up and down the guyline when the line is slack but lock when it's tightened. Nylon stretches when wet, so guylines should be staked out tightly. If it's wet and windy, I generally retighten them before going to sleep.

Size and Weight

The weight of a tent depends on its size and the materials it's made from. Tents come in a wide range of sizes—from tiny bivy tents barely big enough for one person to monsters that will accommodate half a dozen Himalayan mountaineers and all their gear. At a minimum, you need enough space to lie down and stretch out without pushing against the walls or either end. This is all the space the smallest tents have. There's no room to sit out a storm in comfort (for which you need enough headroom to sit up), nor space to lay out gear inside, nor a vestibule big enough for safe cooking. They are light, though. Most of these tiny tents are designed for one occupant. The amount of space two people need depends on how cramped they're prepared to be and how friendly they are. Many tents described in catalogs as sleeping two assume very close friendships!

Most tent makers give the floor areas of their tents, as do some retailers, and they all give length and width so you can compare sizes. As a rough guide, I'd look for at least 30 square feet of floor area in a three-season tent for two (excluding the vestibule), and 35 square feet or more in a winter tent. For solo use, 18 to 20 square feet is enough. The width for two should be at least 54 inches at the widest point; for one, 36 inches will suffice. Length should be at least 7 to 8 feet. Backpackers over 6 feet tall need to consider the length of a tent carefully; in many tents, they'll find their feet pushing against the end.

In mostly dry areas where storms are unlikely and you just want a bedroom to keep out bugs or the occasional shower, the smallest, lightest tents may be fine. In wet areas or in winter, you need more room because you're likely to spend more time in your tent and in winter you'll have bulkier sleeping bags and clothing.

Being able to sit up in a tent makes a huge difference to how spacious it feels. I don't like tents, however lightweight, that don't let me sit up, because they make me feel uncomfortably confined. The key factor here is the distance between the floor and the top of your head when you're sitting cross-legged. If you measure that, you can determine from catalogs which tents will be roomy and which will give you a crick in the neck. I always look for a tent with at least 35 inches maximum inner height.

The size of vestibule you need depends on whether you intend to cook and store gear in it. For cooking, a vestibule must be high enough and wide enough to prevent the fabric from catching fire or melting. Tents for two sometimes have double vestibules, and although they're heavier, they make tent living much easier. For areas where you usually live outside and use the tent only for sleeping, vestibules don't need to be large. Indeed, it doesn't matter if there isn't one at all.

I like vestibules with large zippered door flaps that can be rolled out of the way. It's not quite the same as bivouacking, but having a wide-ranging view is far better than being encased in a nylon cocoon. I close the doors only if forced by the weather or bugs.

Many tents weigh more than they need to, as designers add excess features and "improvements." It's easy to be impressed by fancy designs. I know; I've done it. I started out using solo tents in the 4- to 4.5-pound range (weights include stakes and stuff sacks—the actual weight when carried), but a decade later my tents weighed 5 to 6 pounds. Wanting to cut that weight, I decided on 4.5 pounds as the maximum I would carry in the future. With the latest materials, that has come down to 4 pounds. Except when I'm testing heavier tents for review, I've stuck to that rule. Keeping the weight down when you share a tent is easier. I've used a 5.5-

pound tent for snow camping with two and not felt cramped, and there are plenty in the 5- to 8-pound range that provide ample room.

Tent makers usually list two weights for tents. The minimum weight covers just the tent, fly sheet, and poles. The packed weight includes stakes, stuff sacks, spare parts, and instructions. The weight you'll carry is likely to be closer to the packed weight than the minimum.

Stability

The stability of your tent becomes a matter of great concern once you've struggled alone in the dark, cramming gear into a pack under a thrashing sheet of nylon after the wind has snapped one of your tent poles—which happened to me many years ago. It was pouring rain and I had to make a long night descent to the trailhead. Had it been a more remote location in winter, I could have been in serious trouble.

In the distant past, three tents collapsed on me—two because of wind and one because of a heavy, wet snowfall. On two other occasions I've camped with others whose tents have been blown down. I've also slept peacefully in a well-designed, properly pitched tent during a gale that blew down less stable tents nearby and shook others so hard that the occupants got little sleep. If you spend the night expecting your thrashing tent to collapse any minute, you'll be too exhausted to enjoy the next day.

The importance of tent stability depends on where and when you use your tent. For three-season, below-timberline forest camping, it's not a major concern. For high-level, exposed sites and winter mountain camping, it's very important.

Tent design and materials both contribute to stability. The most stable designs don't have large areas of unsupported material that can catch the wind. Many makers describe their tents as three- or four-season models. However many three-season tents are as stable as four-season ones. What they lack is often snow-shedding ability, extra space, and large vestibules. High winds can occur above timberline and in exposed areas at any time of year anyway.

Stability is relative. Hurricanes that strip roofs off buildings and blow down trees can certainly shred even the strongest four-season mountain tent. In strong winds, your experience and ability to select a sheltered site are as important as the tent you have. If pitching the tent in a storm seems impossible, it's better to go on, even after dark, in search of a more sheltered spot. You'll rarely have to camp in storm-force winds, but if you do, seek out whatever windbreaks you can—piles of stones or banks of vegetation—and consider sleeping out in a bivy bag, if you are carrying one, or even wrapped up in your tent. It may be uncomfortable, but it beats having your tent destroyed in the middle of the night.

Careful pitching is important, too. A taut tent with no loose folds of material will resist wind much better than a saggy mass of nylon. The best mountain tents will still thrash around in a storm if badly pitched. When pitched properly, a stable tent should feel fairly rigid when you push against the poles.

Inner or Outer Pitching

Traditionally the fly sheet was an extra layer thrown over the tent to protect it from rain. Originally both layers were needed to keep rain out, since neither was fully waterproof. When nonbreathable coated nylon was introduced for fly sheets, it made sense for inner tents to be breathable rather than water resistant. This can present a problem when you pitch the tent in the rain. Unless you pitch it very fast, which depends on both your skill and the design, it can get very wet. To counter this, some tent makers—mostly in wet Northern European countries—began building tents that pitched fly sheet first. Since the poles are often on the outside, these are sometimes known as exoskeleton tents. Many of them also pitch as a unit; that is, the fly sheet and inner tent go up together. If the fly sheet is damp inside with condensation, you can then detach the inner tent when packing up so it doesn't get wet from being packed with the fly. With many inner-first-pitching tents you can now pitch the fly sheet separately if you want, often with a separate groundsheet. You can't usually then add the inner tent, though.

For very wet areas where having to pitch in the rain is likely, I prefer exoskeleton tents. For drier areas either design will do, while for very dry areas inner-first pitching is probably best, since you may not need the fly at all much of the time. But in those areas, why do you need a tent at all?

Color

Dark tents can be gloomy inside in dull weather. Pale tents let in much more light. Warm colors—red, orange, yellow—give a warm light, which can be psychologically appealing in cold weather. Gray, blue, and green feel cooler; maybe too cool in dull weather but pleasant when it's hot. In most environments bright, hot colors stand out and can be an eyesore. At high latitudes where it barely gets dark during the summer, dark tents can be soothing and more conducive to sleep. Overall I prefer inconspicuous greens, browns, and grays for fly sheets (and tarps) but a warm color such as yellow for inner tents. That's except for snow camping, when I like bright yellow or orange tents. Any colors other than shades of white and pale gray look black at a distance against snow anyway, so the problem of visual pollution doesn't apply in the same way.

Tent Designs

Since the advent of curved poles in the early 1970s, designers have created a bewildering array of tent shapes, some of them bizarre. Overall, though, these developments have led to a superb range of tents that are lighter, roomier, tougher, and more durable than ever before. Some tents are hard to classify, but most fit into the categories of ridge, pyramid, dome, tunnel, and single-hoop.

Ridge Tents

Before flexible poles appeared, most tent designs were variations on the standard ridge tent, a solid structure that has had a bit of a renaissance as hikers have discovered that trekking poles make good upright tent poles. The simplest, but the least stable and most awkward to use, are those with upright poles at each end. A-poles make a far more stable tent, known as an A-frame, and leave entrances clear. It's not easy to use trekking poles as A-poles, though. Ridge tents don't have good space-to-weight ratios, and the angled walls mean a lack of headroom compared with curved pole designs. However if you use trekking poles, then ridge tents that can be erected with them are worth considering. These are usually single-skin tents, often with a bug netting inner tent as an option. The only one of these tents I've tried, albeit briefly, is the silnylon GoLite Trig 2. This has a sewn-in floor, a large vestibule, and retractable flaps. Mesh panels along the base of the sides and the internal mesh door keep out insects and provide ventilation. It weighs 2 pounds, 15 ounces without stakes, which add another 3 to 6 ounces depending on the type. Its area is 33 square feet plus 13 square feet in the vestibule. There's a smaller version, the Trig 1,

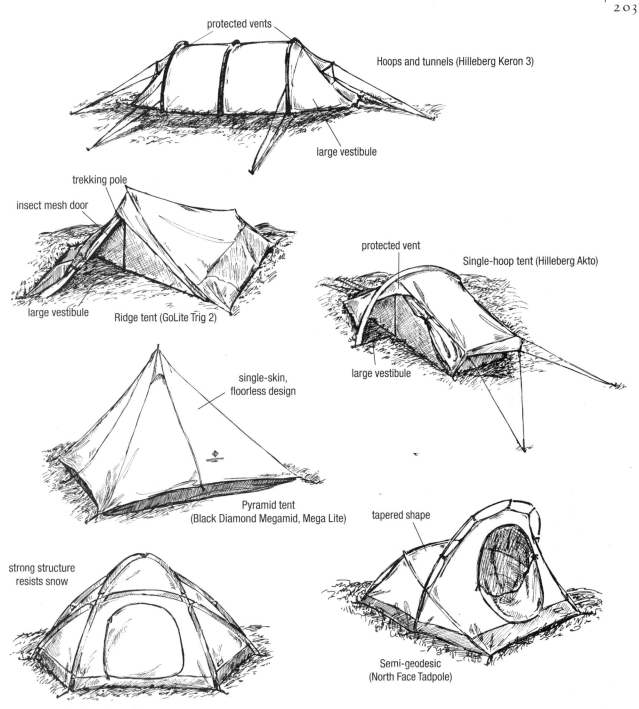

protected vents

Hoops and tunnels (Hilleberg Keron 3)

large vestibule

trekking pole

insect mesh door

protected vent

Single-hoop tent (Hilleberg Akto)

large vestibule

Ridge tent (GoLite Trig 2)

large vestibule

single-skin,
floorless design

Pyramid tent
(Black Diamond Megamid, Mega Lite)

tapered shape

strong structure
resists snow

Semi-geodesic
(North Face Tadpole)

Geodesic dome (North Face VE 25)

Basic tent designs.

RIGHT: A single-skin ridge tent pitched using trekking poles. GoLite Trig 2. BELOW: Tarp pitched as a tapered ridge to keep off the wind at a cool, breezy timberline camp. GoLite Cave.

that weighs 2 pounds, 3 ounces, and has an area of 24 square feet plus 5 feet in the vestibule. The Trig is easy to pitch with two trekking poles, is fairly roomy, and quite stable. I like the look of it but I need to try it in really wet weather to see what the condensation is like. The polyester MSR Trekker

Tarp (4 pounds) with optional mesh 40-square-foot Trekker Tarp Inner (2 pounds) sleeps two and can be used as a two-door tent or a three-sided tarp. Lighter is the side-opening MSR Missing Link at 3 pounds. This has a sewn-in groundsheet and a total area of 51 square feet. Much lighter again at 1 pound, 3 ounces is the 34.7-square-foot silnylon Black Diamond Beta Light. An optional floor weighs 1 pound, 5 ounces, and a mesh inner tent, the Beta Bug, weighs 1 pound, 14 ounces. Other ridge tents that can be pitched using trekking poles are sold by Dana Design, Oware, and Lynne Whelden Gear. There are also slightly modified tapered ridge tents that have a small hoop at the rear and a single pole at the front, available from Six Moon Designs and Henry Shires' Tarptents—the latter come with optional Tyvek groundsheets or sewn-in groundsheets. Transverse ridge tents, where the ridge runs across rather than along the tent, are sold by Dancing Light Gear and Dana Design. The 40-square-foot silnylon Dancing Light Tacoma-for-2 Shelter looks interesting. It weighs 2 pounds, 6 ounces and has

Velcro closures rather than zippers on the doors, a sewn-in groundsheet, and doors on each side. Dana Design's Javelina tapers sharply to one end, has an area of 31 square feet, and weighs 3 pounds, 5 ounces.

There are few tents left with A-poles, though this is a stable, easy-to-pitch design that is less expensive than domes. Eureka's Timberline tents are the classic A-frames and have been around since the 1970s. These have A-poles at each end and a curved ridgepole. They're freestanding, and the lightest two-person model weighs 5 pounds, 13 ounces.

Pyramids

Long before the current lightweight revolution, Chouinard made a floorless tent called the Pyramid. Chouinard became Black Diamond, and the Pyramid became the Megamid and, in lighter form, the Mega Lite. These have an area of 81 square feet and can sleep four. The coated nylon Megamid weighs 3 pounds, 13 ounces; the silnylon Mega Lite weighs 2 pounds, 8 ounces. There's an optional floor weighing 1 pound, 13 ounces. The tents come with adjustable shock-corded aluminum central poles, but the Mega Lite also has a pole converter that enables you to use two trekking poles instead.

The Pyramid/Megamid became popular with ski tourers, since the snow inside could be dug out for more space, something you can't do with a floored tent, and it's very light with lots of headroom. Other makers followed, and there are now several pyramid and tepee tents. I've used the 75-square-foot six-sided silnylon GoLite Hex 3, which has a canopy weighing 1 pound, 12 ounces, an 11-ounce pole, and 5-ounce stakes and stuff sacks for a total weight of 2 pounds, 12 ounces for a shelter that will sleep three and is very roomy for two. A floored mesh inner tent called the Hex 3 Nest weighs 2 pounds, 6 ounces. The Hex 3 proved a stable design when pitched for two nights in storms at 11,000 feet. The wind ensured that little condensation built up inside, though in calmer conditions there has been quite a bit. I've also used the Hex 3 on a two-week spring ski tour where the space was welcome. Cooking inside is no problem, and I really like being able to stand up to get dressed. Other makers of pyramid tents include Mountain Hardwear, Dana Design, Oware, and Kifaru, whose Tipis can incorporate a wood-burning stove (2 pounds, 5 ounces). The Ultralight 4 Man Kifaru Tipi weighs 4 pounds, 11 ounces.

Not quite a pyramid but similar enough to mention here are the Wanderlust Nomad silnylon tents. These are designed to be pitched with trekking poles as either A-poles or central uprights and have a groundsheet and huge mesh panels overhung by coated nylon. They look quite innovative, being neither single skin nor double skin. The 28-square-

Single-skin pyramid tent. GoLite Hex 2.

Geodesic dome with fly sheet.

Geodesic dome.

foot Nomad Lite weighs 1 pound, 11 ounces, and the 45-square-foot Nomad 2-4-2 weighs 1 pound, 15 ounces.

Domes

Domes have two or more flexible poles crossing each other at one or more points. Many are free-standing—they don't need staking down. This is often pushed as a huge bonus. It does indeed make pitching domes quicker and easier—if there's no

wind. But I've heard stories of domes taking off like giant balloons, never to be seen again. I would always stake down a tent. I have to say that although I've owned a few over the years and tested many more, I'm not particularly fond of domes. I prefer simpler designs that give more space for the weight and are generally easier to pitch. I seem to be in the minority here, however, since dome tents are by far the most popular design. *Backpacker*'s 2004 Gear Guide lists twenty-three companies offering over 160 models.

The two most common dome shapes are the *geodesic* and the *crossover pole*, though there are many variations. Geodesic domes are complex structures in which four or more long poles cross each other at several points to form very stable tents that are popular with mountaineers because they can withstand high winds and heavy snow loads. Crossover pole domes are simpler: two or three poles cross at the apex to make a spacious tent that is lighter than a similar-sized geodesic, though nowhere near as stable—in strong winds the poles can invert, and the whole tent can wobble like a gelatin mold. Weights run from 4 pounds for solo two-pole domes (sometimes called wedge tents) to 12 pounds for multipole tents that will sleep three or four.

A typical example of a simple wedge tent is North Face's Roadrunner 2, at 5 pounds, 13 ounces. This has a tapered shape with two poles that cross toward one end rather than in the center. Pitch the narrow end into the wind, and the Roadrunner is quite stable for a crossover pole tent. The floor area is 33 square feet, and there are vestibules on both sides that add 9 square feet each. The fly sheet is made from ripstop polyester. There are two vents near the apex of the tent and two-way protected fly sheet door zippers, and the top half of the inner tent is made of mesh so ventilation is excellent, though condensation can drip through. The North Face also made one of the original geodesic domes, the VE24. This has become the silnylon VE25, with an added pole to create a larger vestibule at one end. It weighs nearly 11 pounds, but it has a floor area of 48 square feet and will stand up to almost anything.

Geodesics are very stable but not very light. Almost the same wind resistance can be obtained by adding a third pole across the front of a two-pole wedge and tapering the back of the tent to the ground to create a semigeodesic or geo-hybrid shape. On the Continental Divide Trail I used a 6-pound tent of this design (a long-gone model called the Wintergear Voyager) and found it roomy, durable, and stable in storms. For the first month of the hike I shared the tent with a companion. After that I used the tent solo, relishing the space but not the weight. One of the most popular semigeodesics for many years has been North Face's Tadpole. The latest version weighs 4 pounds, 15 ounces, and has a 27-square-foot floor and 8-square-foot vestibule. The fly sheet is coated nylon, and there are mesh panels in the sides of the inner tent. I've used the Tadpole and found it a stable tent for two, though not very roomy because of the low rear and small area.

Hoops and Tunnels

Rather than crossing, in tunnel tents the poles form parallel hoops. Tunnels have a better space-to-weight ratio than any other design. They're also very easy to pitch, though they're not freestanding. This category includes the tiniest tents, weighing about 2 pounds. For years I never tried one of these because they are so low and narrow that I felt claustrophobic just

Double-layer tunnel tent with poles on the outside—the exoskeleton design. Hilleberg Nallo 2.

Timberline camp with tarp pitched as a tapered ridge and two tapered tunnel tents.

looking at them. This is hardly objective, however, so I did eventually brace myself and try a 2-pound, 5-ounce Bibler Tripod, which appeared to have slightly more headroom than most. The Tripod is made from waterproof-breathable Toddtex and has a tiny hoop at the foot and two poles at the head, one forming the main hoop, the other running at right angles to it and holding up the fabric at the end of the tent. This does give slightly more room than in tents with just two small hoops. (It also makes it debatable whether this is a hoop tent—it fits best here in my opinion, despite the third pole. Tent classifications are often fuzzy anyway.) With the doors closed the Tripod is very dark, but it didn't prove quite as claustrophobic as I feared. Condensation was minimal—just a small amount on the groundsheet. I could prop myself up on my elbow and read inside, but there's no room for any gear other than some clothes. It's awkward getting dressed and undressed inside, too. In the conditions where I want a fully enclosed tent, I'd like more space—much more space. If I don't need an enclosed shelter, I'd prefer a tarp. These minitents are light, but in my opinion they have more disadvantages than advantages.

Morning after a night of snow. Tunnel and geodesic dome tents.

Single-hoop solo tent, the Hilleberg Akto—my favorite solo tent.

The simplest models that can be called real tents weigh from 3 pounds upward for double-skin (or double-wall) models and 2.25 pounds for single-skin ones. The latter can be as light as mini-tents, but being made from nonbreathable fabrics they're much more prone to condensation, as I found when I tried the GoLite Den 2, a 3-pound, 9-ounce, two-pole model. The key to stability with tunnel tents is the distance between the poles. Large areas of material between the poles can flap and shake badly, so those with the poles close together are the most wind resistant. I used the 4.75-pound, two-pole silnylon Hilleberg Nallo 2 on a 1,300-mile Scandinavian mountains walk and found it very stable as long as I pitched the rear into the wind. Crosswinds shake tunnels, though, and one night the tent was thrashing about so much I got up about midnight and dashed out into the lashing rain to turn the tent 90 degrees into the wind. The difference was astonishing. Like all Hilleberg tents, the Nallo 2 pitches as a unit or fly first. It's roomy enough for two and very spacious for one. I now use it on midwinter trips when more space is welcome on

long dark nights and on trips where weight isn't too significant.

The lightest tunnel tents, indeed the lightest tents for the size of any design, are made by Stephenson's Warmlite. These are made of silnylon, and the weights are astounding—the smallest model, the single-skin 2X, weighs 2.3 pounds, yet it's 60 inches wide at the front, 48 inches wide at the rear, 134 inches long, and 40 inches high at the apex, with an area of 42 square feet. There are inside stabilizer straps for use in high winds—Warmlite tents are said to be extremely storm resistant. The lightest double-skin model, the 2R, weighs 2.7 pounds. Both layers are made from silnylon, and they are permanently linked and pitched together.

There are several tunnel tents suitable for solo use, including the popular Sierra Designs Clip Flashlight at 3 pounds, 13 ounces. Larger tunnel tents often have three poles, sometimes of different sizes, with the largest placed in the middle to give more headroom. These are excellent for two or more people. I've had great success using large three- and four-person Hilleberg Keron three-pole

MAKING CAMP AFTER DARK

One day toward the end of the Canadian Rockies walk, I picked a small lake on a watershed for a camp, only to find when I reached it a half hour or so before dark that the area around it was a quagmire surrounded by steep slopes. Circling the lake, I saw there was no place to camp, so I continued down into the forest, my headlamp picking out the trail ahead. For some time I descended a steep hillside where it would have been a waste of time to even look for a campsite. Eventually the trail, which was not marked on my map, reached the valley bottom, crossed a creek, and started up the other side. There was no flat ground, but there was water—the first since the lake—so I stopped and searched for a site. I found one between two fir trees. There was barely enough room for the tent, but the ground was flat enough for me to sleep comfortably. In the morning, my site looked as makeshift as you could imagine—the sort of place no one would dream of selecting in daylight—but it had served its purpose.

tunnels (8 pounds, 9 ounces and 9 pounds, 11 ounces) for group snow camping.

Tunnel tents are the most popular tents after domes. *Backpacker*'s 2004 Gear Guide lists twenty-one makers and sixty-three models.

Single-Hoop Tents

The problem with solo tents is that weight and size are related. Length has to remain constant, of course—one person needs the same space to stretch out as two—which means that width and height have to be reduced to cut the weight. In a slimmed-down version of a ridge, dome, or tunnel tent usually you can barely sit up. The solution is the single-hoop tent, a style that really works only for solo tents. As the name suggests, this design features one long, curved pole that may run across the tent or along its length. Single-hoop tents can be remarkably stable for their weight if the guying system is good.

My favorite tent is a single-hoop model, the Hilleberg Akto, that weighs 3 pounds, 7 ounces. I've been using this little tent since the early 1990s, and it's stood up well to many nights of wild weather. Made from silnylon, it has a huge vestibule that stretches the length of one side, a protected vent above the door, and two lower vents at each end. A problem with single-hoop tents is that the fabric can be close to your face when you lie down, especially if you're tall. Hilleberg has solved this with tiny corner poles permanently attached to the fly sheet that lift the ends of the tent a little.

PITCHES AND PITCHING: MINIMUM-IMPACT CAMPING

One of the pleasures of backpacking is sleeping in a different place every night. This can also be one of the horrors if you're stumbling around in the rain looking for a campsite long after dark. In popular areas there are plenty of well-used sites. Take the time to look at such places and work out why they've been used so much, and you'll soon learn what to look for when selecting a site.

There are both practical and aesthetic criteria for a good campsite. A site with a good view is wonderful, as long as it's also comfortable. For a good night's rest you want as flat a site as possible. Often, however, you must make do with a slight slope; most people then sleep with their heads uphill (if I don't, I develop a headache and can't sleep). Sometimes the slope can be so gentle that it's unnoticeable—until you lie down and try to sleep. I like to check sites by lying down before I pitch the tent. That way I also find any sharp stones or pinecones my eyes have missed. Beware of camping in hollows in wet areas, however, since rain may collect there.

If it's very windy, a sheltered spot makes for a more secure and less noisy camp, though I often head uphill and seek out a breeze if bugs are a problem. Cold air sinks, so valley bottoms are often the coldest spots. Where possible I like a site that will catch the early morning sun, making for a warm and cheerful start to the day, so I look for sites on east-facing slopes and on the west side of valleys.

Water nearby is useful, though in dry areas like deserts I often carry enough for the last few hours of a day and the next morning and have a dry camp. It's best not to camp right next to water; you could damage the bank and you may deter wildlife that needs access to the water. In many national parks and wilderness areas, the regulations forbid camping within a few hundred feet of water or trails. Camping well away from water and trails is best.

In popular areas there are usually many regularly used campsites, so finding one isn't difficult (finding one that you don't have to share can be harder). When I'm in country where such sites are rare or nonexistent, each morning I generally work out where I'm likely to be that evening and use the map to select a possible area for a site. Usually I find a reasonable spot soon after I arrive. If an obvious one doesn't present itself within minutes, I take off my pack and explore the area. If this doesn't produce a spot I'm happy with, I shoulder the pack and move on. At times, especially when daylight hours are short, this can mean continuing into the night.

When a possible spot turns out to be unusable and I have to keep walking, sometimes tired and hungry, I remind myself that a site always turns up; it may just require a little imagination to make the most of what seems unsuitable terrain. Perfect pitches are wonderful, yet many of those I remember best are the ones, like that in the northern Rockies (see sidebar, opposite), that were snatched almost out of thin air.

The most important aspect of selecting a site is to minimize your impact and leave the wilderness fresh and untouched, both for itself and for the next hikers.

All sites, whether previously used or not, should be left unmarked, which means no trenching around tents, no cutting of turf, and no prepara-

Tarp pitched in snow on a windy forested ridge.

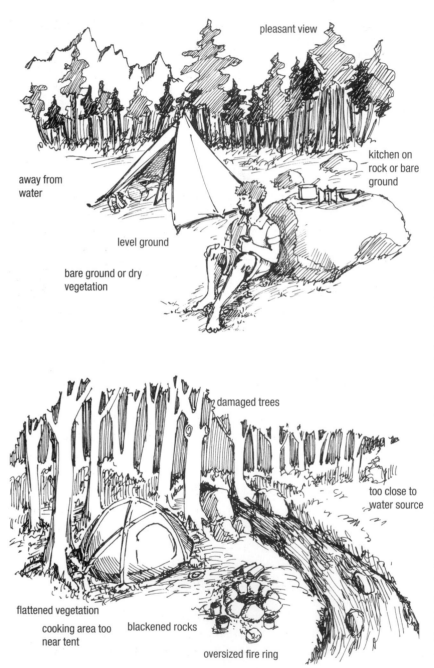

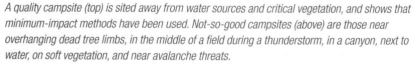

A quality campsite (top) is sited away from water sources and critical vegetation, and shows that minimum-impact methods have been used. Not-so-good campsites (above) are those near overhanging dead tree limbs, in the middle of a field during a thunderstorm, in a canyon, next to water, on soft vegetation, and near avalanche threats.

tion of the tent site. Previously unused sites should always—*always*—be left with no sign that anyone has been there. Camp on bare ground, forest duff, or dry vegetation such as grass that will be least damaged by your stay—which shouldn't be longer than one night. Avoid damp ground and soft, easily crushed vegetation. If you'll be staying more than one night on any site with vegetation, move your tent or tents each day to allow the plants to recover. Paths from tents to water, tent to tent, and tents to kitchen site are easily created if you're not careful. You can reduce the number of trips by carrying a water container big enough to hold all the water you'll need for overnight. Siting the kitchen so there is bare ground or rocks between it and the tents also cuts down the impact. Wear light footwear, not heavy boots, or go barefoot.

Light fires only if you can do so without leaving any sign of them when you depart (see Chapter 7). If you use rocks to hold down tent stakes—rarely necessary, though often done, especially above timberline—return them to the streams or boulder fields where you got them; I've spent many hours dismantling rings of stones on

Pitching camp on a forest site in spring.

regularly used sites. When you leave a wild site, make sure to obliterate all evidence that you've been there, fluffing up any flattened vegetation as a last chore.

Of course you'll often camp on sites that have been used before. If possible, I pass by a site that looks as if it's used only occasionally, perhaps stopping to further disguise the signs of its use. A well-used site, however, should be reused, because doing so limits the impact to one place in a given area. You should still try not to add to the damage, of course. Use bare patches for tents and an existing fire ring for a fire—if there are several, dismantling all but one is a good idea. Tidying up the site may encourage others to use it rather than make new ones. As with every site, leave nothing, and don't alter the natural surroundings.

In some areas, particularly in the eastern United States, land managers have provided wooden tent platforms at many sites. Use them, since they are

there to reduce impact. I first came across these in the White Mountains, New Hampshire. To stake tents down you need either very sharp, strong stakes that can be hammered into the planks or, preferably, long lengths of cord that can be attached to stake points, then run off the platforms and staked down or tied to trees. Freestanding tents would be ideal for tent platforms, but I had the Akto, which requires eight stakes. On the advice of a friend, I carried 50 feet of nylon parachute cord, and I used it all.

Safe Camping

Wilderness camping is generally safe as long as you have the right gear and the necessary skills. However, there are some external dangers that you need to consider.

In forests, dead trees and branches can fall on your tent; it's always wise to look up when selecting a site and not camp under dead limbs. If there are dead trees nearby, I like to be sure they're leaning away from the tent. Trees don't fall only in storms, either—the only time I've seen a tree come down was on a calm day. I heard a loud crack and looked up to see a large pine topple over and crash to the ground.

Lightning is a hazard at certain times of the year. Camping out in the middle of a large open area or above timberline isn't advisable during summer thunderstorms; you don't want to be the highest object around. On one two-week trip in the Colorado Rockies there were thunderstorms every evening, often lasting well into the night, and on several occasions I reluctantly passed up scenic timberline campsites and descended into the security of the forest. When a deafening crack of thunder right overhead woke me up and the flashes of lightning lit up the tent, I was glad to be deep in the trees.

Big storms can cause a different and potentially serious problem in desert areas: flash floods. Heavy rainfall in mountains far away can cause walls of water to roar down desert canyons, sweeping away everything in their path. If there are signs of distant storms, I'd be very careful about camping in narrow canyons or at the bottom of drainages that are regularly swept by floods. In many desert areas, summer brings storms that sometimes make camping in any canyon bottom hazardous. I've never seen a flash flood, though I've seen the destruction these floods can cause. There is a dramatic and sobering description of a flash flood in George Steck's *Grand Canyon Loop Hikes II* that is well worth reading if you're going backpacking in desert canyons. Steck narrowly escaped when his camp was overwhelmed by floodwater. He lost his tarp, groundsheet, pad, sleeping bag, boots, spare clothing, eating utensils, and walking stick, though he found many items downstream the next day. This book, with its companion, *Grand Canyon Loop Hikes I* (now combined in one volume, *Hiking Grand Canyon Loops*), is entertaining and informative and recommended reading for anyone venturing off the main trails in the Grand Canyon.

Camping on a tent platform in the White Mountains, New Hampshire. The Hilleberg Akto is not ideal for this! A freestanding tent would be better.

In mountain areas with permanent snowfields and glaciers, avalanches are a hazard. This isn't usually much of a problem except in winter and spring, but some canyons may be swept by avalanches even in summer. Signs to watch for are treeless corridors below snowfields, bent and flattened vegetation, and large areas of willows and alder—the latter often called "slide alder" because it occurs so often in avalanche zones. These shrubs are flexible enough to survive repeated avalanches.

Making Camp

Compared with finding a site, setting up camp is easy. I don't have a definite routine—it all depends on the time and the conditions. In cold or wet weather, when I'm tired or if darkness is imminent, I pitch my shelter as soon as I stop and chuck in the gear I'll need overnight. I then fill my water bottles, crawl into the shelter, change into warm or dry clothes if necessary, set up the stove, and sort out my gear in comfort while the water boils for a hot drink. (This assumes I'm not in an area where bears could be a problem, of course.) By the time the water has boiled, I'm comfortable in my sleeping bag. The whole operation from unpacking the shelter to taking the first sip can be done in less than ten minutes, though I usually like to do it in a more leisurely fifteen or twenty. The key is knowing your shelter so well that you can pitch it even when you're too tired to think. For greatest weather resistance and strength, pitch your shelter very taut and tighten guylines until you can play a tune on them. This also minimizes flapping and noise. Stakes should be at a 45-degree angle—sloping away from the tent—and pushed right into the ground. If you can't get them all the way in, make sure that the stake loop is at ground level and not around the top of the stake, where it might lever the stake out of the ground if the wind gets up.

When there's plenty of daylight and it's warm and sunny, I may just sit and relax for half an hour before I do anything.

In some places and at certain times, though, setting up camp is not so easy. In rocky terrain where stakes won't go in, you may have to attach loops to the staking points and tie them and the guylines to rocks to hold the tent down. I've done this only a few times, but then it's been essential—it's one reason I always carry a length of cord. In soft snow, tent stakes are nearly useless, but ice axes, crampons, skis, and ski poles can all be used to support the tent, through extra guylines tied to the stake points if necessary.

In snow, I first use skis or snowshoes to stamp out a hard platform; a snow shovel is also useful for this, especially for the final leveling of the site. If you use stakes, loop the guylines around them, then bury them lengthwise and pack the snow down on top. Once the temperature falls below zero, they'll freeze in place. Come morning, you'll probably need an ice ax to dig them out. You could use sticks instead of stakes. An alternative, which I've never tried, is to fill stuff sacks with snow, attach guylines to them, and bury them. Don't set small items down on the snow when making camp; they could easily get buried. If snow falls during the night, bang the roof of the tent occasionally to make any buildup slide off so the tent doesn't get buried. Make sure there's ventilation high up—open the top of the fly sheet door zipper if there isn't a vent—in case snow seals the gap around the edge of the fly sheet. Brush off snow before getting into the tent, and leave any snow-encrusted garments in the vestibule.

Whatever the surface, pitching a tent is easy—except in wind. You just follow the instructions that come with it. With a new tent, do a practice run first to see how it goes up and to check that all the pieces are there. There are so many ways of

It's always better to camp on clear ground than on snow. A spring camp with pyramid and geodesic dome tents.

putting up tents that detailed advice is impossible. If it's windy, I generally stake out the end of the inner or outer tent (whichever pitches first) that will face into the wind, then thread or clip the poles into position before raising the tent off the ground. In a strong wind, you may have to lie on the tent while you do this. The more the tent thrashes in the wind, the more vulnerable it is to damage, so speed is important. Once the basic shape is established, the rest of the staking can be done in a more relaxed manner. If the site allows, pitch rectangular or tapered tents with the tail or end into the wind; keeping the door away from the wind is a good idea for cooking, too.

Rain is not as much of a problem as wind, though you'll want to get a tent that pitches inner first up fast. If your tent is at the top of your pack you can get it out quickly without letting too much rain into the rest of your gear. You can stand packs up under a tree while you pitch the tent. Once the tent is up you can bring the pack into the vestibule and then unpack items you need for overnight

straight into the dry inner tent. You can sort them out once you're inside too. Remember to fill water containers before taking off your waterproof clothing and getting into the tent. It's a pain to have to put it back on to get water. Once the tent is up you need to keep the inside as dry as possible, so leave all damp gear in the vestibule or outside. You can strip off your wet jacket while squatting in the vestibule and then sit at the front of the tent with your legs in the vestibule while you remove wet pants, socks, and boots. Once you're in the tent, put on warm clothing or slide into the sleeping bag so you don't get cold. If your sleeping bag has gotten a little damp, getting into it will help dry it out.

For various reasons—late starts, unforeseen difficulties, a planned site's being full or unsuitable or having a bear around, even by choice—you may occasionally have to make camp in the dark. For this you need a good flashlight or, preferably, a headlamp, especially on dark nights or in dense forest. To avoid losing things, try not to put any gear on the ground where it could be overlooked or kicked aside. Keep everything in the pack that isn't needed in the tent. If you're setting up a kitchen away from the tent and when going to the toilet, make sure you know the way back to your tent. I've sometimes spent rather longer than I would have liked finding the tent again. From a distance in the dark, a tent can easily look like a boulder or a tree stump. Take your flashlight with you and make sure you remember the direction back.

When striking camp, I usually pack the tent last so that it can air out and any condensation can dry. In rain, I pack everything under cover. In very heavy rain you can collapse the inner tent, leaving the fly sheet staked out, withdraw the poles, and then stuff the inner tent into its bag under the fly so it stays dry. Push the poles out of their sleeves; if you pull them, they're likely to come apart. In very cold conditions, pole sections may freeze together—don't try to force them apart or they may break. Instead, rub the joints with your hands until the ice melts. In bitter cold, I wear liner gloves for this so the metal doesn't stick to my skin. If poles are frozen together, chances are that any condensation will have frozen to the fly sheet. If the fly sheet is coated with ice on the inside and frost on the outside, shake off as much of it as you can before you pack it. If the day is sunny and you have time, you could wait for it to thaw and evaporate. Wet tents can be strapped on top of the pack or stuffed into a mesh pocket.

Once you've packed everything, check the site for anything you've overlooked, such as bits of trash, clothes hung over a branch to air, or small items like tent stakes or cutlery.

TENT CARE

Tents look after themselves when you're out walking. On sunny mornings, I try to dry off any condensation, spreading the tent over bushes or on dry ground or hanging it over a length of cord or branch. If the stakes are particularly dirty, I wipe

Camping on snow with pyramid and geodesic dome tents. Be sure stakes are buried firmly, with snow packed down on top.

Airing and drying a geodesic dome tent.

them clean. Most tents come with two stuff sacks for poles and stakes but only one for the fly sheet and inner tent. I always use an extra stuff sack for the fly, because two small units are easier to pack and it keeps a dry inner tent separate from a wet fly sheet. The easiest way to pack tents is, appropriately enough, to *stuff* them into their stuff sacks rather than fold them—if you habitually fold the tent the same way, the waterproofing may crack along crease lines. I always put my tent near the top of the pack so it's accessible for quick pitching the next night. I slide the poles down one of the corners of the pack between the side and the back. Some people strap poles to the outside of the pack, but I'm afraid they might be damaged there or even fall off and be lost. Stakes tend to work their way down to the bottom when kept in the main pack, so I put mine in a pocket.

After a trip, I hang the tent up to dry before storing it in its stuff sacks. Nylon won't rot, but a tent stored wet will mildew, which leaves stains and an unpleasant, musty smell and may damage the waterproofing. Single-skin waterproof-breathable tents need plenty of drying time; they often

appear dry while still damp, since moisture can remain in the slightly absorbent inner material. If you want to wash your tent, use mild soap and warm water, never detergent, which can damage the proofing. Poles will corrode if not dried before storage. Salt corrodes poles very fast, so if you've been camping near the sea, wipe them down before you dry and store them.

WILDERNESS SHELTERS

Many wilderness areas have unlocked shelters for walkers to use. These usually provide shelter from the elements but no more, so you'll still need a sleeping bag, pad, stove, and warm clothing. On some long-distance routes, such as the Appalachian Trail, walkers can use shelters almost every night. I generally prefer the freedom and solitude of a tent or tarp, but in bad weather such shelters can be a blessing. I always like to know where they are in case I need them. It's best not to rely on them, though; they may be full.

SNOW CAVES

In deep snow you can build a shelter rather than pitch a tent. Snow is a good insulator and cuts out all wind; inside a snow shelter it's calm and quiet even when a blizzard rages outside. To build a proper one takes a few hours. Ice axes, cooking pans, and toilet trowels can all be used as digging tools, but a proper snow shovel speeds things up considerably.

Whatever tool you use, digging snow is hot work, so it's best to strip off your warm clothing so it doesn't get soaked with sweat. There are various forms of snow shelters—caves, domes, trenches, and igloos. Which you build depends on the terrain. Caves can be dug into steep snowbanks. Start by digging a vertical slot a bit more than shoulder width that goes in at least 6 feet. Then dig out the area around the slot to form sleeping platforms with a lower area in the center that leads to the entrance to act as a sink for cold air. A curved, smooth roof will minimize drips. How big you make the cave depends on how many it must shelter, how much time you have, and how much snow there is. The entrance should slope downward out of the cave and be kept small to prevent snow and wind from blowing in. Make sure you include an air inlet to prevent carbon monoxide buildup when you're cooking. It's a good idea to mark the cave too. A ski pole poked through the roof does this and acts as a vent. Wiggle the pole every so often to keep the hole open.

Where there are no steep banks, you can build a snow dome. Simply pile up a huge mound of snow, leave it a short while to harden, then dig out the center, leaving walls about a foot thick. Snow domes superficially resemble igloos, but igloos are

Using the IceBox to build an igloo.

A snow trench is the quickest type of snow shelter to build.

much stronger and more complex and require more skill and time to build. There is a tool that makes building igloos easy—the IceBox, a curved form into which you pack snow, and a long handle you use to determine the radius of the igloo and to ensure the snow blocks are positioned correctly. Using the form, you build a circle of snow blocks, each fitting next to the other, until the igloo is complete. The lightest IceBox weighs a touch over 5 pounds and can easily be strapped to a pack. With an IceBox, you can build an igloo in a couple of hours. If you're going to set up a base camp in the snow, it could be worth carrying one.

In a storm the quickest shelter to build is a snow trench. Mountaineers high in the Himalaya have survived for several days and nights in body-size "snow coffins." A simple trench can be roofed with tilted snow blocks or with a fly sheet or tarp spread over skis or ski poles and the edges held down with snow. The aim is to get out of the storm as fast as possible. If heavy snow is falling, make sure the roof of your snow trench isn't completely buried and that there is ventilation.

SLEEPING BAGS

Keeping warm at night is essential for enjoyable backpacking. Nothing destroys the pleasure of a trip like shivering through the night in an inadequate sleeping bag. Some people just pile on extra clothes at night, but I've never met anyone who does this by choice (a forced bivouac when you aren't carrying a sleeping bag is another matter), and it sounds both uncomfortable and inefficient.

A sleeping bag traps warm air, which keeps you from feeling cold. To prevent dampness from condensation, a bag must allow the moisture vapor given off by your body to escape, so both fill and shell should be breathable. If you intend to sleep under the stars, a bag with a quick-drying or even a waterproof-breathable shell is best. Even if it's dry, dew or frost may dampen your bag. (For more information on insulation and how to keep warm, see pages 120–30.)

Fill

Choosing a sleeping bag is much easier than choosing a tent. There are far fewer designs, though there are many models. The biggest decision is the kind of insulation or fill, followed by how warm a bag you need. The ideal material would be lightweight but very warm, low in packed bulk, durable, non-absorbent, quick drying, warm when wet, and comfortable. Unfortunately, this ideal doesn't yet exist, so compromises have to be made in terms of which properties are most important—determined in part by when and where you'll camp and what shelter you'll use. The basic choice is between synthetic fibers and waterfowl down.

Synthetics

Since the mid-1970s when DuPont launched Fiber-fill II, many synthetic fills have appeared; they all attempt to mimic down by being light and fluffy in order to trap warm air but low in bulk when compressed. There are two basic types of fiber. As you'd expect, *short-staple fibers* consist of short sections of fill while *continuous filaments* are endless strands of fiber. KoSa's Polarguard is the best-known continuous-filament fill. There are well-regarded proprietary versions too, like Wiggy's Lamilite. Polarguard comes in four types, of which 3D and Delta are the lightest and most efficient. Polarguard HV, 3D, and Delta are made from hollow polyester with a triangular cross section, which cuts down on weight and increases the insulation, since warm air can be trapped inside the fibers. Original Polarguard and Lamilite are solid polyester. Continuous filament is generally reckoned to be the most durable fiber. I've certainly found Polarguard tough in insulated jackets (see page 150). It's comfortable, too.

There are many versions of short-staple fibers, with new ones appearing frequently. The ones regarded as the best for sleeping bags are DuPont's Thermolite Extreme and Thermolite Micro and Albany International's Primaloft. Older fibers like Quallofil and Hollofil, both from DuPont, are less compressible and less durable and appear mainly in low-cost bags. Proprietary short-staple fills are mostly found in budget bags too. I've found Primaloft the most comfortable of the short-staple fibers. This microfiber is very soft and drapes around the body well. There are three types of Primaloft. Primaloft One is surprisingly water resistant, far more so than other synthetic fills, while Primaloft Two and Sport are similar to other synthetics in water resistance.

Synthetic fills cost less than down, are easy to care for, and resist moisture. But they are not "warm when wet," as some manufacturers claim—nothing is. What matters is how fast something dries, and synthetic fills dry fairly quickly, since they are virtually nonabsorbent. Because the fill doesn't collapse when saturated, it retains much of its warm-air-trapping thickness, too. A wet synthetic-filled bag will start to feel warm in a comparatively short time compared with a wet down-filled bag, as long as it's protected from rain and wind. You can't sleep outside in a downpour in a synthetic-filled bag and stay warm, however.

The disadvantages of synthetic fills compared with down are shorter life, less comfort over a wide temperature range, more packed bulk, and greater weight for the same warmth. The latest synthetics are lighter, more compressible, and more durable than earlier ones, but they still don't compare with down. In the long run, down costs less too. One company that makes both down and synthetic bags estimates that with average use, a down bag will last at least twelve years (I have bags much older than this, as do many other people), but a synthetic bag will last only four years. Because down is expensive, awkward to handle, and needs to be kept dry, if a synthetic that performs as well ever does appear it will probably replace down. That day isn't here yet, though.

Down

Down is the lightest, warmest, most comfortable and most durable sleeping bag fill. No synthetic yet comes near down for packability, low weight, and warmth. Down is the fluffy underplumage of ducks and geese and consists of thin filaments that trap air and thus provide insulation. Down recovers well from compression and goes on doing so for a long time, hence the good durability. Unlike feathers, in down there are no quills to poke through the fabric. A single piece of down is called a cluster and consists of a solid point, called a quill point, surrounded by a tangle of fine filaments. Large clusters with long tendrils fill more space and trap more air for less weight than small clusters. Large birds have large clusters, so down from geese is generally warmer than down from ducks. The more volume a given amount of down can fill, the higher its quality, because the thickness, known as *loft*, determines the warmth. Measuring the volume filled by an ounce of down determines the *fill power*. Down of 500 to 550 fill power (500 to 550 cubic inches of down per ounce) is the least expensive but provides less warmth for the weight than down with higher fill power. The warmest, lightest, and most expensive bags are filled with down of 750 to 900 fill power. Before being tested, down is stored for five days in a large screened box and regularly mixed and blown with a warm dryer. This "conditioning" stabilizes samples for consistent results. An ounce of the down is then placed in a measuring cylinder and a 68.4-gram weight is placed on the down. (One bag maker points out that the weight is more than twice the weight of the down and that this testing procedure ignores the fact that some bag manufacturers use extremely lightweight shells—such as DP Airnet and Pertex Quantum—and also that others unduly compress their super-high-fill down with overly beefy shells.) This process means the down is in just about perfect condition when measured. Even so, the results have a margin of error of plus or minus 5 percent. Western Mountaineering, from whose catalog I culled this information, calls the resulting fill power rating "optimistic" rather than "practical" and says that its fill power figures are the lowest its down would produce. In practice the figures can be taken as comparative rather than absolute. Down with higher fill power will be warmer for the weight than down with lower fill power, but it almost certainly won't loft as much in the wilds as under laboratory conditions.

People worry about down's lack of insulation when soaked. Down can absorb a great deal of moisture, and it takes a long time to dry. Drying a sodden down bag outside in wet weather is practically impossible; it takes dry heat. But keeping down dry need not be difficult or a chore, and it's harder to get down wet than many people think. I use down bags most of the time, including in wet places, and I haven't yet had one get more than a little damp. Packing a down bag in a waterproof stuff sack and sleeping in a tent or under a tarp when it rains are the best ways to keep it dry. It's also wise to air down bags occasionally to remove any moisture picked up from humid air or from your body.

If you want the warmth and comfort of down and the water resistance of synthetics, Marmot makes bags with down inside and Primaloft outside. The 30°F (−1°C) Fusion bag weighs 2 pounds, 4 ounces, and the 15°F (−9°C) weighs 3 pounds, 3 ounces. I've tried the 30°F; the rating is certainly accurate, and the bag is comfortable. The one problem I can see is that the down is likely to long outlast the synthetic fill. Using a light synthetic bag as a cover for a light down bag is probably a better idea.

There's currently no legal standard, but sleeping bags labeled as "down" should be at least 75 percent down, the rest being small feathers, which it's impossible to totally separate from the down. Many bag makers use a higher percentage of down. The figures are often expressed in the form 85/15 or 85:15 for 85 percent down, 15 percent feathers. "Down-and-feather" fills should be at least 50 percent down, but "feather-and-down" fill is less than 50 percent down. Feather-and-down and all-feather fills have just about vanished, since they offer no advantages over synthetics, which are easier to care for. The more quills you feel in down fill, the higher the percentage of feathers.

Down is a by-product of the food industry, and most down comes from places where waterfowl are eaten in large quantities, such as China and Eastern Europe.

Owing to the cost of the fill, virtually all down bags are high quality, since it isn't worthwhile to cut costs.

Shell Materials

Sleeping bag shells need to be lightweight, hardwearing, breathable, resistant to wind and water, nonabsorbent, quick drying, and, for down fills, downproof (so the fill doesn't leak out). Some modern synthetic fabrics have all these properties and feel comfortable next to the skin, making them suitable for the lining as well as the outer shell. Cotton and cotton-polyester shells have just about disappeared, since they're heavier, more absorbent, slower drying, and harder to keep clean. After several months of continuous use, a polyester-cotton inner lining feels sticky and unpleasant—I speak from experience—but because a synthetic liner won't absorb sweat or dirt, it stays fairly fresh as long as it's aired occasionally.

The lightest fabrics allow the fill to loft fully and mold themselves around the body, maximizing the warmth of a bag. Many nylon and polyester fabrics are used, often ripstop versions, and there really isn't much to choose between them. A typical high-quality nylon taffeta is 30 Max from Western Mountaineering, which weighs 1.4 ounces per square yard and has a denier of 30 (9,000 meters of fiber will weigh 30 grams). Some shells are made from microfibers (which weigh less than 1 gram per 9,000 meters of fiber). Although the denier is less than 1, this doesn't mean microfibers are lighter than other fabrics; it means that more fibers are packed into a thread, making a fabric that is very windproof and water resistant because air spaces are too small for wind and rain to enter easily. The thread count of a fabric—the number of threads per inch—matters too. Good fabrics have a thread count of 300 or more.

My favorite shell fabric is 20-denier Pertex Quantum nylon, which weighs just 0.9 ounce per square yard yet is hardwearing, downproof, breathable, and very soft and comfortable. It's not waterproof, but moisture quickly spreads out over its surface and dries. Quantum is used by a growing number of makers including Marmot, GoLite, Western Mountaineering, The North Face, Exped, and Rab.

Nonwaterproof shells are highly breathable, allowing body moisture through very quickly, which keeps the fill dry and ensures good loft. They are moisture resistant and dry quickly, but they won't keep rain out for long. Waterproof-breathable shell fabrics are waterproof, but bags made from them usually aren't, since water can enter through the seams unless they are sealed, which is rare. However, new construction methods make waterproofing seams possible, and fully waterproof bags are likely to become more common. The Swiss company Exped makes down bags with high-frequency-welded seams, while Mountain Hardwear makes down bags with baffles that are glued to the shell fabric. In both cases there are no stitch-holes through which water can enter, so these bags are waterproof.

There are several breathable waterproof or water-resistant shell fabrics, including Pertex Endurance, Gore Dryloft, and eVENT, plus proprietary ones like Mountain Hardwear's Conduit and Sierra Designs' DryDown. eVENT is new and so far is used only by Feathered Friends. Given how well it works in rain gear (see pages 153–54) it might well make the best waterproof-breathable sleeping bag shell. I've tried Endurance and Dryloft, and both are pretty good, keeping condensation drips from wetting the insulation of the bag. However, these shells add a little weight (they weigh from 1.7 ounces per square yard upward) and a lot of cost and don't breathe as well as nonwaterproof fabrics, as you'll quickly find out when you try to pack one into a stuff sack—starting at the foot is essential, so air can be forced out the top opening. When damp, bags with these shells take longer to dry, too—it's best to turn them inside out. In really damp conditions, I'd rather use a bivy bag over my sleeping bag. Any moisture is likely to occur between the sleeping bag and the bivy bag, leaving the insulation in the sleeping bag dry, and it's easier to dry a bivy bag. Mostly, though, I find a nonwaterproof shell fine, since when it's raining I always sleep under a tarp or in a tent. An interesting compromise would be a shell of EPIC by Nextec (see pages 145–46). This silicone-treated fabric is breathable and very water resistant but not fully waterproof. I haven't tried a sleeping bag with it, but I imagine it would work very well. EPIC is used by Feathered Friends and Nunatak.

The color of your sleeping bag may seem to have no practical relevance, unless you want to sleep out unobserved. However, dark colors absorb heat and dry more quickly than light ones, and any moisture in the fill will dissipate faster. This heat absorption is noticeable to the touch. A black bag feels much warmer than a pale one when both are aired in the sun. Since light colors also show dirt more—one with a white lining looked unpleasantly grubby after a five-week trip—I prefer bags with dark linings.

Shape and Size

The most efficient sleeping bag is the one that traps warm air closest to your body. A bag with lots of room is a bag with lots of dead air space to heat. Most bags reduce this dead space by tapering from shoulder to foot. Most also have hoods to prevent heat from being lost through the head and at the neck. The resulting shape is called a *mummy bag*. It's the standard shape for high-performance, lightweight sleeping bags and is very efficient at heat retention. Some warm-weather bags dispense with the hood and have a tapered shape sometimes called semirectangular. Actual rectangular bags are fine for warm-weather camping, though heavier than tapered ones. Because they usually have a zipper that runs down one side and across the foot, they can also be used as quilts on a bed. I don't think they're really a serious choice for backpacking though. If you find a close-fitting mummy bag restrictive, a broader mummy is a much better choice than a rectangular bag.

A sleeping bag that is too wide or too long won't keep you as warm as one that fits properly, and the weight will be more than you need to carry. But a bag that is too small will be uncomfortable and won't keep you warm in spots where you press against the shell and flatten the fill.

For these reasons, bags come in different lengths and shoulder, hip, and foot girths. Many companies offer two sizes in each model, while GoLite's SmartFit bags come in three lengths and three girths. Finding a reasonable fit isn't difficult, although very tall and very broad people may find their choices limited, and short people may end up with a bag that's a little too long and slim ones with a bag that's too wide. It's worth climbing into a bag in the store to see how it fits before you buy it, even if you do feel conspicuous. A slightly roomy bag is better than a slightly small one, for both comfort and warmth. Make sure you can toss and turn and lie comfortably in the bag. Check too that the bag will accommodate any clothing you intend to wear in it, such as an insulated jacket in a cold-weather bag.

There's a theory that most sleeping bags are designed for men and may be too roomy at the shoulders and too tight at the hips for many women. An increasing number of bags are now made for women, some with narrower shoulders, wider hips, shorter lengths, and more fill at the foot and across the chest, where many women report feeling the cold. EMS, Feathered Friends, Lafuma, Marmot, Outbound, REI, Sierra Designs, and The North Face all make women's bags. However, when GoLite designed its SmartFit bags it measured a number of people and found no significant difference between men and women within girth categories—there were just more women in the trim category and more men in the wide. Wide men and wide women resembled each other in all girth characteristics, as did trim and regular ones. The conclusion was that women tend to sleep colder because their bags are too wide for many of them throughout their length. Close-fitting bags are warmer than wide ones, so this makes sense. The best approach is to find a bag that fits well, ignoring whether it's labeled male or female.

A problem with a close-fitting bag is that it can feel restrictive. Some people like to be able to turn over inside a bag rather than with it and bend their knees and elbows. A good solution to this problem is stretch elastic seams and baffles, as found in MontBell bags and Sierra Designs' Flex Bags. These bags hug the body closely yet give when you move so they don't feel restrictive. Because the stretch baffles pull the fabric inward, bags with them have a somewhat strange wrinkled look, but they work really well, cutting out cold air spots and reducing air movement in the bag. I've used bags that stretch made by the British company Mountain Equipment, and they are very warm for the weight and very comfortable.

An alternative and less effective method is to add a zipped panel to a bag so that the volume can be varied—roomy when it's not too cold, close fitting when it is. Some bags, like Mountain Hardwear's Quantum Expander series, have these panels built in. In other cases, as with North Face's Polarguard 3D-filled Expander Panel, they're separate and can be zipped into a bag when required. Such panels add weight, though. North Face's weighs 9.5 ounces, which seems rather a lot for something that reduces the warmth of a bag.

Construction

The method used to hold fill inside affects the warmth of a sleeping bag. Down fill has to be held in chambers, which give the familiar ringed or ribbed look, to keep it evenly distributed through-

A mummy-shaped sleeping bag.

KEY FEATURES: SLEEPING BAGS

- A good fit. One that is too tight will be uncomfortable, and compressed loft will reduce its insulation; too much room can lead to cold spots.
- An adjustable, shaped hood.

- A tapered shape for efficient insulation.
- A shaped foot box.
- A two-way zipper for ventilation (optional).
- A filled draft tube behind the zipper to prevent heat loss.

Key features of sleeping bags.

out the bag. To create these chambers, the inner and outer fabrics are attached in sections. The simplest and lightest way of doing this is with *straight-through* or *sewn-through* stitching (also known as quilting). This method is adequate only for bags designed for above-freezing temperatures because heat escapes through the stitch lines and cold air can blow in through them. Most of the lightest bags use sewn-through stitching.

To cut this heat loss, the inner and outer shells can be connected by short walls of fine netting, called baffles, to make rectangular boxes—hence the name *box-wall construction.* If the walls are angled (offsetting the top and bottom stitches), it is called *slant-wall construction;* if they're angled away from each other it's *trapezoidal construction.* In *V-tube* or *overlapping-tube construction* the baf-

fles form triangular compartments. All cold-weather down bags use some type of walled construction. Chambers should have enough down in them so they bulge slightly, creating that familiar well-padded look. If the down can move much in the chambers, it may migrate to the corners or to one side, leaving a cold spot.

Synthetic-fill bags can't use baffle construction because the fill is fixed in layers known as batts. Continuous fiber synthetics can be used in single sheets in a bag, so no stitching is required. For cold-weather bags two or more continuous fiber sheets may be layered on top of each other. Batts of short fibers need stabilizing, so stitching is necessary. Sewn-through construction, as in down bags, is all right for warm weather bags, but for most conditions *double-layer* or *shingle construction* is better. In the first, two or even three sewn-through layers are layered, with the seams offset to avoid cold spots—an efficient method, though it produces a rather heavy bag. In shingle construction, slanted layers of overlapping fiber are sewn to both the inner and outer shells. Some bags are made with a combination of methods—a shingle layer over a quilted one, for example. Whatever the construction method, synthetic insulation should be stitched firmly to the shell at the edges to stop it from tearing away and leaving a cold gap. Down bags also usually have baffles along the sides that prevent all the fill from ending up on the top or the bottom. Some bags dispense with these on the principle that it might sometimes be useful to shift the fill to the top or bottom of the bag to give more or less warmth. I distrust such a construction because the down could move even when I don't want it to. Another construction method I don't like, used in both down and synthetic bags, places side baffles at ground level so that more of the fill is in the upper section. Other makers simply put more fill in the upper half of the bag. The rationale is that the fill under you is crushed anyway, so there might as well be less of it.

The problem with bags that have more fill in the top is they don't account for sleepers who don't keep their bags the "right" way up. The designers seem to assume that all users sleep on their backs and don't move during the night, although studies suggest that most people turn over many times during the night. I often wake to find the hood above me because I've turned the bag completely over during the night. Just turn on your side, and you can lift part of the base of a bag off the ground. If it has less insulation than the top, you may then feel a chilly line down your back. I prefer to have the fill equally distributed.

The outer shell on most bags is cut larger than

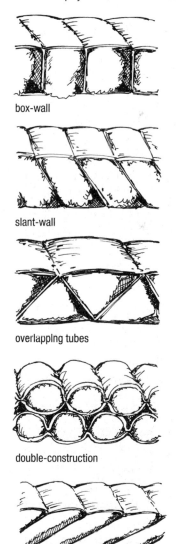

down-filled/polyester-filled sewn-through

box-wall

slant-wall

overlapping tubes

double-construction

shingle

Sleeping bag construction.

the inner; this *differential cut* means that the inner shell has a smaller circumference than the outer shell to allow the fill to loft fully, to cut out cold spots caused by loose extra fabric on the inside, and to stop the fill from being compressed by knees or elbows pushing against the inner fabric. The idea makes sense, but I have to say I've used bags both with and without it and not noticed any difference. These days virtually all mummy bags come with differential cut whereas rectangular ones don't so they can be opened out and used as quilts.

Bottomless Bags, Topless Blankets, Covers

If the fill under you is useless because it's compressed, the logical thing is to do away with it altogether. Bags such as the down-filled 35°F (2°C) Big Agnes Horse Thief (1 pound, 8 ounces) do just that, having nothing more on the bottom than a sleeve for you to slide your sleeping pad into. Bags like this are usually meant for above-freezing temperatures because the design has inherent problems. Cold can creep in between the bag and the pad, as it has with all three bags of this type that I've tried. I also didn't like not being able to sit up in the bags and pull them up around my chest. Sleeping on my side was awkward too. For low bulk and weight these bags can't be beaten, but I find a full sleeping bag much more comfortable and psychologically reassuring. I like being totally enclosed in cold weather.

Blankets or quilts are even lighter than bags with no insulation in the base. Ray Jardine promotes these in his books, and for a while you could get his quilt designs from GoLite. Insulated quilts have no zippers and no hoods, just shaped footpieces. You spread them over you and tuck in the edges. They're light, but to my mind—after, admittedly, only one very brief trial—they're inefficient compared with a sleeping bag. Some people like them, however. A hiker I met on the Arizona Trail had made his own quilt by simply removing the zipper from a sleeping bag. Jake Schas was perfectly happy with his quilt and went on to use it on a Pacific Crest Trail through-hike. Nunatak, Integral Designs, and Lynne Whelden Gear make blankets. Nunatak's 1-pound, 32°F (0°C) Ghost Blanket has 800-fill-power down and either a Pertex Microlight or an EPIC shell. Of course, a rectangular sleeping bag can be used as a blanket for two people. Integral Design's 50°F (10°C) Primaloft-filled Prima Blanket is really one of these, since it has a zipper for conversion to a bag. There are instructions on how to make a quilt in Jardine's *Beyond Backpacking* and on various ultralight Web sites.

Bottomless bags can be used as lightweight covers to boost the performance of a sleeping bag on trips that are colder than usual. Some companies offer zip-on covers for this purpose, and some bags even come with them. They have the same problem as having more fill in the top of the bag, however—they need to be kept above you to be any use. I should mention Stephenson, which introduced this type of bag back in the 1960s. Its Warmlite Triple bags come with either a 2-inch foam pad or a down-filled air mattress and two removable down tops of 820 to 890 fill power, a thin one rated to 25°F (−4°C) and a thick one to −10°F (−23°C). Combined, they are rated to an astonishing −60°F (−51°C). The tops attach to the bottom with double zippers, so there are no cold spots. I haven't used one, but the bags look roomy, come in four sizes, and are designed so you turn over in them rather than with them. The lining is a soft vapor-barrier fabric. Weights for the total system run from 91 to 123 ounces depending on the size and the type of pad, but you need only the thin top (16 to 20 ounces) in temperatures above 25°F and only the thick one (26 to 33 ounces) between −10 and 25°F.

Half Bags

An alternative to getting rid of the bottom of a bag is to get rid of the upper half and wear an insulated jacket. This type of bag, sometimes called an elephant's foot, was first developed by Alpine climbers for bivouacking on narrow ledges. One of the few half bags is the 14-ounce 20°F (−7°C) Akula from Nunatak, filled with 800-fill-power down and made with a variety of shells. Shock cord runs over the shoulders to keep the bag up around your rib cage. I've never used one of these bags, but I imagine you'd want a thick insulated jacket with a hood and a good seal between the two items.

Design Features

Hoods

Because of the massive amount of heat you lose through an unprotected head and at the neck, a hood is very useful in all but the warmest weather. A good hood should fit closely around your head and have a drawcord with self-locking toggles that permit easy adjustment from inside the bag. Most hoods fit reasonably well, though few are easy to adjust from inside. Some have two drawcords so they can be adjusted from both sides. This seems unnecessarily complicated to me, especially when I'm trying to get out of a bag and can't find the toggles. Some toggles and drawcords dangle in your face, which is irritating. Bag makers seem to assume that sleepers will lie on their backs staring upward with their hoods neatly framing their faces.

(Sierra Designs is an exception; its designers actually picture people in different positions.) Most people don't sleep like this (I often sleep on my front), and chances are you'll end up with your face pressed into the side of the hood much of the time. If it's badly designed, this will strain the fabric and feel uncomfortable. Getting into a sleeping bag and trying the hood is the way to find out if you can live with it or if it will drive you crazy.

Bags for use in below-freezing temperatures should have large hoods in which you can bury everything but your nose. Bags for warmer conditions sometimes have smaller hoods, or even no hood at all, to save weight. In above-freezing temperatures, I often find the hood too warm and fold it under the bag.

Draft Collars

A filled, drawcord-adjusted collar or neck baffle to prevent drafts is a feature of many bags, especially those designed for cold weather. It lets you close the bag around your shoulders while leaving the hood open. The most basic, lightest bags don't have draft collars. You can drape a shirt or warm top around your shoulders if necessary. Baffles usually have a drawcord adjustment and snap fastenings on the zipper side. I find them restrictive, so I do them up only when it's really cold. Some makers—GoLite, Marmot, Western Mountaineering—have a smaller filled tube in some of their bags that seals around the face rather than a large collar. This saves a bit of weight, since it requires less material than a draft collar.

Boxed Feet

To keep your feet warm, a sleeping bag should have a shaped or boxed foot section. If the two halves of the bag are simply sewn together at the foot, your feet will compress the fill when they push on it, reducing loft there. A boxed foot has an extra circular section, which could be made either in channels or as a single unit. Cold-weather bags may have an offset double layer of fill in the boxed foot. In down bags, some boxed feet have internal box walls.

Zippers

Almost all bags, except for the lightest down ones, now have zippers, usually on the side, occasionally on the top. For years I distrusted zippers—they added weight, leaked heat, and had the potential for disaster if they broke. I've now developed a grudging acceptance of them, since the latest ones are pretty tough, though I still can see no real advantages. In theory, zippers allow you to regulate temperature and make getting in and out easier. Some bags can be zipped together to make a double bag.

Most bags have full-length side coil zippers. A few curve up toward the top of the bag at the hood to make using them easier. Some bags have short central zippers, a style that used to be standard. To prevent heat loss, zippers usually have filled baffles on the inside, though these may be absent in bags for above-freezing temperatures. Unfortunately, baffles snag zippers. A stiffened, antisnag strip will lessen the number of times the zipper catches, though these are far from perfect. When the zipper does jam, as it will, don't try to yank it free—you could tear the fabric and damage the zipper. Gently ease the fabric sideways out of the zipper teeth. Two-way zippers let you open the bottom of the bag so you can stick your feet out to cool off if you overheat. You could even waddle around outside wearing your bag as a somewhat restrictive, but very warm, coat. Some sleeping bags are designed for this purpose and come with sleeves (the down-filled Nunatak Raku Alpine, weighing 32 ounces) or zipper openings for the arms (Feathered

Friends down-filled Rock Wren at 27 ounces, Exped down-filled Wallcreeper at 33 ounces).

Warmth

Rating sleeping bags for warmth is difficult. There's no standard rating system, and even if there were, individuals aren't standard and feel the cold differently. Most companies use *temperature ratings*. These give the lowest temperature at which the bag should keep you warm. Thus a bag may be described as a 40°F (5°C) bag or a 20°F (–7°C) bag. Another figure sometimes given is the bag's loft. What's important is the *loft over the body*, not the total thickness of the bag. Makers usually give the total loft, though some also give the loft for the top half of the bag. Halve the first to see how much loft you'll have around you.

Although there's no standard, bags with comparable weights of the same type of fill should keep sleepers comfortable over roughly the same temperature range. I'd be very suspicious of any maker that rates a bag as vastly warmer than competitors' bags with a similar weight of the same quality of fill.

No rating system, however, can account for the different metabolic rates of different bodies. Warm sleepers, like me, can use lightweight bags below their rated temperatures; cold sleepers may shiver a summer night away in a bag made for polar conditions. I have a friend who sleeps buried in a four-season mummy bag while I'm comfortable in a summer bag with the hood open. Be realistic about how warm you sleep. It's easy to be tempted by a too-light bag in order to save weight. (A friend pointed out that it's just as easy to be tempted the other way and buy too heavy a bag to be sure of sleeping warm.)

Having tested dozens of sleeping bags over the years, I conclude that ratings for down bags are pretty accurate for a warm sleeper like me, while synthetic bag ratings are usually on the optimistic side. I recently tested fifteen bags for a magazine review—eight synthetic, six down, and one a combination down-synthetic. I was chilly in all the synthetic bags at temperatures higher than their ratings but warm at the rated temperature in five of the down bags, the only exception being a bag with no fill on the bottom. The combination bag was also warm at the rated lowest temperature. I measured the loft of each bag. None of the synthetic bags had as much loft as the lowest-lofting down bag; mostly they had half the loft of down bags with the same temperature ratings. Adding five or ten degrees to the rating of a down bag and more to a synthetic one would be wise for many people.

Other factors also influence how warm you'll sleep. Food is fuel is heat, so however tired I am at the end of a long day, I always try to eat something before going to sleep on a cold night; if I don't, I wake up in the early hours of the morning feeling chilly. (If it's warm and I don't eat, I wake up because I'm hungry!) Putting on some clothes is an obvious thing to do when you wake up in the night feeling chilly, but a carbohydrate snack can also help warm you up. If you don't eat, fatigue can keep you shivering long after you expect to be warm. The weather is a factor, too—high humidity means a damp bag (though it may feel perfectly dry), less loft, and conductive heat loss. Thus you may feel colder when the temperature's near freezing and the humidity is high than you do when it's below freezing but dry. Wind reduces a bag's efficiency, as does sleeping under an open sky with no barrier to prevent radiant heat loss. If you regularly sleep under the stars, you'll need a

In cold weather, sit in your sleeping bag to keep warm.

warmer bag than if you always use a tent. Any barrier can make a difference. I've sometimes slept under a tree with the foot of my sleeping bag outside the tree's cover and awakened to find the foot of the bag covered with frost.

Weight

High loft requires more fill, which means more weight. Down-filled bags are much lighter than synthetics across all temperature ranges, from about 1 pound for 40°F (5°C) bags to 2.5 to 3.5 pounds for 0°F (–18°C) models. The lightest synthetic-fill bags start at about 1 pound, 12 ounces for a 40°F bag and 3.5 pounds for a 0°F bag. Based on weight alone, I'd choose a down bag, especially since my experience suggests that synthetic bag ratings are on the optimistic side.

Models and Choices

There are hundreds of sleeping bags—371 from thirty-four companies in *Backpacker*'s 2004 Gear Guide. However, it's fairly easy to reduce the choice to a handful of models that fit your specific criteria. I look for the lightest, least bulky bag—which means one with down fill—that will keep me warm when I sleep unclothed in a tent in the average temperatures for the time and place of my trip. If temperatures are cooler than average, I wear clothes in the bag.

Several years ago the lightest 40°F (5°C) bags weighed about 25 ounces and had 10 ounces of down fill. New lighter shell fabrics and higher-lofting down mean they now weigh 16 ounces and have 8 ounces of down fill. I have two of these ultralight bags, both of them favorites. The first is a British-made 32°F (0°C) Rab Quantum 200, with 7 ounces of 850+ fill-power down, box-wall construction, a hood, and a Pertex Quantum shell.

The weight is 16 ounces. There's no zipper. I took it on a five-week hike in the High Sierra and needed to wear clothes in it only on the five nights when the temperature dropped below freezing. My only complaint is that the lining is white and shows dirt. My other ultralight bag is a 40°F Western Mountaineering HighLite, which also has a Quantum shell and weighs 16 ounces. It has 8 ounces of 850+ fill-power down contained in chambers that are square rather than long and thin and that have sewn-through horizontal seams and baffled vertical seams. There's a half-length zipper and a hood, and the lining is black. Both bags are fine for summer trips when I'm expecting temperatures to be mostly above freezing, and they can be used together, since the Quantum 200 is cut slightly smaller than the HighLite. Similar bags weighing under a pound and a half are sold by Exped, PHD, GoLite, Marmot, Mountain Hardwear, Mountainsmith, Nunatak, Sierra Designs, and Bozeman Mountain Works.

These ultralight summer bags are fine for warm sleepers like me, but many people will find them inadequate in all but the very warmest temperatures (over 45°F [7°C]). Bags in the 15 to 25°F (–9 to –4°C) range are the standard for three-season use. The weights of these have come down as well, with many below 2 pounds, though some weigh as much as 3.5 pounds. The ones at the lighter end (with 16 to 20 ounces of fill) should be adequate for most people. Of the ones I've tried, I like the 1-pound, 11-ounce, 20°F (–7°C) GoLite Feather, which has 18 ounces of 800-fill-power down (700-fill-power in my early model) and a Pertex Quantum shell. There's a quarter-length zipper on the top and an excellent-fitting hood. The Feather has kept me very warm at 28°F (–2°C), and it's now my first choice for trips where temperatures are likely to be between 20 and 32°F (–7 to 0°C), which generally means spring and fall. Most makers have bags like this—it's the closest thing you can find to a general-purpose bag.

My well-used winter bag sees little use these days because I rarely venture into areas where the temperature will be below 15°F (–9°C) on many nights, for which the Feather plus clothes is adequate. In colder temperatures the HighLite and Feather bags combined only weigh 2 pounds, 11 ounces and are warmer, smaller-packing, and more versatile than the winter bag. My bag (the model hasn't been sold for many years) is typical of many winter bags: it weighs 3.5 pounds, with 26.5 ounces of 650-fill-power down. It's rated to 0°F (–18°C) and is warm at 5°F (–15°C) but too hot at 35°F (2°C). Most makers offer similar bags, as well as bags designed for much colder temperatures. If I were replacing my old bag it would probably be with a Marmot Lithium. I borrowed one of these 0°F-rated bags for a spring ski trip and was extremely impressed. It contains 27 ounces of 900-fill-power down, has a Pertex Quantum shell, and weighs 2.5 pounds, less than many 20°F (–7°C) bags. There's a half-zipper and a superbly comfortable hood. Marmot's two other bags in this 900-fill-power series, the 15°F (–9°C), 29-ounce Helium and the 30°F (–1°C), 21-ounce Hydrogen look excellent too.

Combining bags is a good way to increase the warmth while keeping the versatility of two bags. Not all combinations are comfortable, however, and some can be hard to get in and out of, so it's best to check that bags are compatible before trying them in camp. Obviously the outer bag will need to be roomier than the inner one. Some makers offer bags designed to fit inside others, such as Western Mountaineering's 45°F (7°C), 14-ounce LineLite, which has no hood or boxed foot so it will fit easily inside other bags.

I use synthetic bags only when they're sent to me for tests and reviews, but they're the ones most people buy. I find down softer and more comfortable, as well as lighter and more packable. If I were buying a synthetic bag, I'd look for Polarguard or Primaloft, and I'd choose one rated 5 to 10° lower than the temperatures I expected to use it in. I did try a 54-ounce, 20°F (–7°C)-rated Polarguard 3D bag on a nine-day trip and found it warm and quite comfortable, though the coldest overnight temperature was only 36°F (2°C). A down bag half the weight would have been just as warm and much smaller-packing.

Carrying

Sleeping bags are best carried inside the pack, where they are protected from rain, dirt, and damage. I pack my down bag at the bottom of the lower compartment, in an oversized waterproof stuff sack (see page 122). The oversized stuff sack lets the bag mold to the curve of the pack around my lower back and hips and fill the corners. A round stuff sack packed to bursting is very hard to fit in a pack without leaving lots of unfilled space. If I use a synthetic sleeping bag I pack it in an even bigger stuff sack and carry it packed as loosely as possible at the top of the pack, since compression reduces the loft of a synthetic bag. Because they are bulky when packed, many synthetic bags come with compression stuff sacks. These should never be used unless you like replacing your sleeping bag frequently.

Care

In the field, all sleeping bags benefit from being aired whenever possible to let any moisture evaporate. This is especially important with down bags, which can absorb a surprising amount of moisture overnight. It's also a good idea to remove down bags from their stuff sacks a while before you use them to let the fill expand, and to give them a shake before you climb in, which helps distribute the fill. Neither makes the slightest difference to synthetic bags.

Patch small cuts or holes in the fabric with rip-stop nylon tape or duct tape to prevent fill from escaping. You can sew a patch on when you return home—just remember to coat the stitch lines with seam seal to make them downproof. If tendrils of

down start to work their way through the fabric, don't pull them out, which may enlarge the hole. Instead, pull the down cluster back into the chamber from the other side.

At home, always make sure a bag is dry before storing it and *never* store a bag compressed; prolonged compression may damage the fill's ability to recover so it won't loft fully anymore, reducing the warmth. This affects synthetic bags the most; prolonged compression can destroy virtually all the loft. Bags should be stored so that the fill can loft—either flat, hung up, or packed loosely in a large bag. They need airflow round them, too, so don't store them in a waterproof bag; cotton, polyester-cotton, or mesh is ideal. Many manufacturers provide breathable storage sacks with sleeping bags.

Whatever the outer fabric, the shell should have a durable water-repellent (DWR) treatment. As with clothing, this treatment will wear off in time; it can be restored by low-heat tumble-drying, which also helps break up any clumps the down may have formed. Running a warm hair dryer over the bag could help revive the DWR, too. Ironing

ABOVE: Airing a sleeping bag on top of a tent. GoLite Feather. RIGHT: Airing sleeping bags on skis at a spring camp.

should work, but I wouldn't risk ironing a sleeping bag. When the DWR has gone completely, which does happen, you can apply a spray-on DWR treatment (see pages 176–78). Wash-in water-proofing also can be used, though drying the bag thoroughly—which is essential—is said to take a very long time.

Eventually a well-used bag will need washing. With down bags this requires great care. Down loses some of its insulating properties every time it gets cleaned, so you should do it only when the fill is so dirty that it no longer keeps you as warm as it should. If only the shell is dirty, it can be sponged clean. Synthetic fills may be damaged by washing too, so again do so only when absolutely necessary.

When washing a bag take great care. Down absorbs vast amounts of water, and a wet bag is very heavy; if it's lifted when wet, the baffles may tear under the weight of the wet down, so sliding it into a laundry basket is a good idea. Most instructions say bags should be hand washed in a large tub or else washed in a front-loading machine and dried on low heat in a large commercial tumble dryer to keep the down from forming clumps. You need a special down soap such as Nikwax Loft Down Wash, since detergents strip the natural oils from down and shorten its life. I always send down bags out to be washed by professionals. This relieves me of the task and increases the likelihood that my bag will survive. Many experts think that improper cleaning ruins more down bags than anything else, including prolonged use.

If you decide to have someone else wash your bag, ask for recommendations from the store where you bought it or from the manufacturer. Dry cleaning isn't recommended for sleeping bags, since the solvents can remove the down's natural oils. The fumes from dry-cleaning chemicals are poisonous, too, so any bag that is dry cleaned must be aired well before being used.

Reconstruction

The shell of your down-filled bag eventually may become dirty enough that no cleaning company will touch it. This happened with the bag I used on the Continental Divide walk. It had a polyester-cotton inner shell, which was in appalling condition after 157 nights' use. Cleaners I approached wouldn't handle it, saying the inner shell was rotten and would disintegrate during cleaning. Since the expensive goose-down fill still lofted well and kept me warm, I was loath to throw the bag away, so I had it remade. This cost less than half the price of a new bag and included washing the down. The resulting bag not only was a better fit, since I could specify the length, but it weighed just 2 pounds rather than 2 pounds, 12 ounces because the new inner shell was nylon.

Liners

One way to improve the warmth of a sleeping bag is to wear clothes in it. This keeps the bag clean and extends its life too, because it needs washing less often. A liner accomplishes the same thing but adds weight. Clothes you can wear at other times; liners aren't much use for anything else. I don't really like liners because it's easy to get tangled up in them. Liners come in cotton, wicking synthetics like CoolMax, silk, fleece, and coated nylon. I'd disregard cotton entirely because of its weight, absorbency, and slow drying time. Synthetic liners make more sense—Cocoon's CoolMax Mummy Liner weighs 9 ounces. Silk is really light and low in bulk, and I have a 4.5-ounce Cocoon mummy-shaped silk liner that I sometimes use when weight isn't important. It's what I'd recommend if you really want a liner.

Coated nylon liners form a vapor barrier that keeps moisture in and stops evaporative heat loss. A vapor-barrier liner can add a surprising amount of warmth to a bag. Because drying a bag can be almost impossible in extreme cold, they're useful in such conditions just to prevent your body moisture from condensing inside the bag and dampening it. Vapor barrier liners weigh 4 to 8 ounces. Although I've slept in vapor-barrier clothing (see pages 163–64), I've never used a vapor-barrier liner. Makes include Stephenson's Warmlite, Feathered Friends, Western Mountaineering, Integral Designs, and Dancing Light Gear. Because they're waterproof, vapor barrier liners can double as an emergency bivy bag. The converse, of course, is also true.

SLEEPING PADS

No sleeping bag provides much insulation or cushioning from the ground because the fill is compressed under your body weight. In summer weather, some hardy souls manage without a pad, putting clothing or their packs under them if it's cold, but most people, including me, use a pad year-round.

There are two sorts of sleeping pads in general use: *closed-cell foam pads* and *self-inflating open-cell foam pads*, though modern versions of the old air mattress have made a bit of a comeback and there are some noninflating open-cell foam pads. Thickness means warmth, though how much depends on the type of pad. Self-inflating mats are not as warm for the same thickness as closed-cell foam pads. The R-value, which measures the resistance to heat flow, tells you how much insulation a pad provides, though not all makers provide this information. The higher the R-value, the greater

the insulation. The 1-inch-thick Therm-a-Rest ProLite 3 self-inflating pad has an R-value of 2.3; the 0.75-inch-thick Ridge Rest closed-cell foam pad has an R-value of 2.6.

Closed-cell foam pads are lightweight, reasonably inexpensive, and hardwearing, but they're bulky to carry. Although they're efficient insulators, they don't provide much cushioning, and you can feel stones through them. These pads are made from foam that is either pressure blown or chemically blown; the first is warmer, more durable, and resists compression better than the second, but the two types look identical, and manufacturers rarely tell you which is which. Various materials are used to make pads—Evazote (EVA), Ensolite, and polyurethane are common ones. The big advantage of closed-cell foam is that's it's waterproof, since the air pockets in the foam are sealed inside, so it doesn't suck up water the way open-cell foam does. Closed-cell foam is pretty indestructible, too, though it can be torn apart by spiny vegetation (and duct taped back together if necessary). In time the foam compresses and doesn't provide as much insulation or cushioning, though it's still usable.

Closed-cell pads come in different lengths, widths, and thickness, and you can easily cut one down to the shape you want. I find three-quarter-length pads adequate, since I use clothes as a pillow and under my feet if necessary. This saves a little weight and bulk. Weights for short pads start at 3.7 ounces for the 18-by-29-inch NightLight pad from Gossamer Gear. The thickest, longest, widest pads can weigh 20 ounces or more.

Most foam pads have flat, smooth surfaces. But the most comfortable closed-cell foam pad I've used, Cascade Designs' very popular 0.75-inch laminated EVA Ridge Rest, has a ridged pattern that adds softness and traps air for greater warmth. Although it has more bulk than flat-surfaced pads, the 48-inch model weighs only 9 ounces, the 72-inch one 14 ounces. Cascade Designs also makes the 48-inch EVA Z-Rest (R-value 2.2), which has an egg-crate pattern and folds up like an accordion. The 48-inch Z-Rest weighs 11 ounces, the 72-inch full-length one 15 ounces. The Z-Rest is more comfortable than most closed-cell foam pads but in my experience not quite as comfortable or durable as the Ridge Rest. Because of their bulk, closed-cell pads are normally carried on the outside of the pack, wherever there are convenient straps. In hiking through low, dense brush, however, a pad attached to the side or the bottom of a pack is likely to get ripped, as I discovered when bushwhacking down an unmaintained trail in a side canyon of the Grand Canyon. Before it was totally torn apart, I transferred it to the top of the pack, where it was above the bushes. In forests with low branches, of course, the top of the pack is not where you want to put a pad.

Cascade Designs is best known for introducing the first, and in my opinion still the best, self-inflating pad, the Therm-a-Rest, back in 1973, and it has since become the nearest thing there is to a standard pad. I've used one of these for over two decades. Therm-a-Rests have a tough waterproof coated nylon shell bonded to an open-cell polyurethane foam core that sucks in air and inflates when you open the valve at one corner. That's the theory anyway. In reality it takes a few puffs of breath. Once the pad has reached the desired thickness, you close the valve to keep the air from escaping. Self-inflating pads combine the comfort of an air mattress with the insulation of a foam pad and are relatively luxurious to sleep on.

My first Therm-a-Rest, bought back in 1981, was a 48-inch model weighing 24 ounces. Back then the only choice was between two lengths. Now there's a whole family of Therm-a-Rests, with seven models, many in a choice of lengths and with

The Therm-a-Rest ProLite 3 self-inflating pad.

weights up to 8 pounds. I long ago replaced my first Therm-a-Rest with the 47-inch-long, 1-inch-thick UltraLite (R-value 2.6), which weighs 16.5 ounces. This has been replaced by the tapered ProLite 3 Short, which weighs just 13 ounces owing to new materials and construction methods but is still 47 inches long and 1 inch thick. My original 47-inch UltraLite lasted through both the Continental Divide Trail and walks the length of the Canadian

PREPARING FOR BED AND COPING WITH THE NIGHT

There's no right way to prepare for bed, but this is what I do: Once I've selected a campsite and erected my shelter, if any, I lay out my sleeping mat and, if it's a Therm-a-Rest, open the valve. If the ground is cold and I want to sit on the pad, I generally blow it up rather than waiting for it to expand. Then I pull out my sleeping bag and lay it out on the pad. Depending on the temperature, I may lie on or in the bag while I cook, eat, read, make notes, study the map, watch the stars and the trees, daydream, or otherwise while away the evening until I start to feel sleepy. Then I usually strip off my clothes, get in the sleeping bag, arrange a pillow from a fleece or insulated garment, lie down, and adjust the bag until I feel warm enough. Spare clothes go in a stuff sack, which I place on or in the pack, which is either acting as a backrest, if I'm outside or under a tarp, or lying in the vestibule or just outside the tent. My footwear stays nearby too, as do my headlamp, notebook, pens, books, maps, and water bottle, all laid out where I can reach them easily. Except where bears may come around, my stove, pans, and food are on the other side of me, ready for breakfast.

Most nights don't need coping with because I sleep right through. On very, very rare occasions I've abandoned camp in the dark and fled to a more sheltered spot. Usually, though, storms mean only that I don't get quite enough sleep, and I am glad to see the first gray, distorted edges of daylight through the fly sheet.

But what do you do if you wake feeling chilly long before dawn? First, if you haven't done up the hood of the sleeping bag or have the zipper partly open, adjusting those may do the trick. Almost all nights grow colder as the hours go by, so you may need to adjust the sleeping bag a few times to stay warm. I'm so used to doing this that I barely wake at all; I just fumble with the drawcords and sink back to sleep. The next stage, if you're still cold, is to put on some clothes, especially a hat and socks, and have a snack. You could even fire up the stove and have something hot. Clothing such as an insulated jacket or a rain jacket can be spread over the sleeping bag for added warmth. Don't wear so many clothes in your sleeping bag that you compress the fill; that won't keep you warm. If your pad is only a short one and your legs or feet are chilly, put spare clothing under them to insulate them from the ground. If none of this warms you up, then either you've seriously overestimated the capabilities of your sleeping bag and clothing or the temperatures are extremely cold for the area and time of year. In that case, all you can do is shiver until dawn, with the aid of hot food and drink, then hike out and not make the same mistake again.

When temperatures drop below freezing you need to protect gear as well as yourself. Water containers can be wrapped in spare clothing or even stuff sacks and placed on top of the pack to insulate them from the ground. If you turn them upside down, any ice that forms won't be at the top, so you'll still be able to get water out. If you're sure they won't leak, you could keep water bottles in your sleeping bag; if you fill them with warm water, they'll act like hot water bottles. I also fill my pots with water. If it freezes it will soon thaw on the stove.

Rock-hard frozen boots are difficult to get on and awkward to wear. I store wet footwear inside a stuff

Rockies, plus many other trips, a total of well over a year's use in ten years, before finally splitting around the valve, where a repair was impossible (the valves used to be metal; now they're plastic and much better attached). Having found nothing better, I replaced it with a new UltraLite, which is still going strong, though I now also have a ProLite 3. The ProLite 3 has die-cut foam with holes through it, hence the reduction in weight. The warmth is reduced slightly too, but I've still found the pad warm on freezing ground. It also has a base that grips well and doesn't slide about on groundsheets.

sack on top of the pack or other item so they aren't on the ground and cover them with any spare clothing. If the temperatures aren't much below freezing, this is enough to keep them from turning solid. Placing them next to your sleeping bag helps stop them from freezing too. You can store them in your sleeping bag, though I've never done this—it sounds too uncomfortable. Some people use them as pillows, but when I've tried this it feels too unpleasant to persevere with for long. If boots do freeze, placing them

in the sun can thaw them out quickly. Putting a bottle of hot water in each boot is effective too. Otherwise hiking in them will thaw them out eventually, though it's not fun.

Battery-dependent gear—headlamps, flashlights, GPS, altimeters, cameras—needs protecting from cold too. I keep them off the ground, and if it's really cold in the morning I remove the batteries and store them in my pocket for a while.

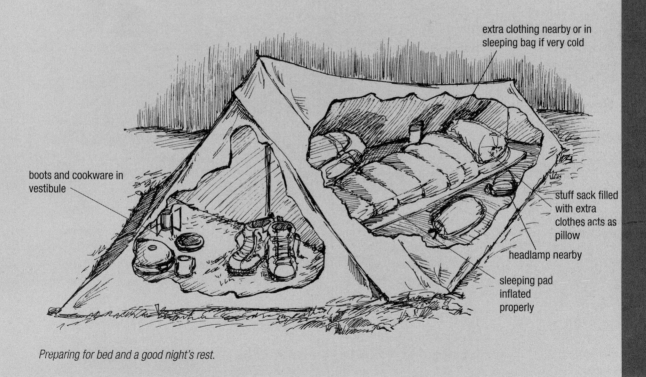

boots and cookware in vestibule

extra clothing nearby or in sleeping bag if very cold

stuff sack filled with extra clothes acts as pillow

headlamp nearby

sleeping pad inflated properly

Preparing for bed and a good night's rest.

Like the UltraLite it's a great three-season pad but for cold temperatures and snow camping I'd supplement it with a foam pad.

Although slightly heavier than many closed-cell foam pads, the ProLite 3 is much less bulky and can be folded and packed inside the pack, where it

is protected from damage. I would never carry a self-inflating pad on the outside of a pack unless it was in an extremely tough stuff sack. To deflate a self-inflating pad you open the valve and slowly roll the pad up, either on a ground cloth or on your thighs, squeezing out the air as you go. Keep pressure on the rolled pad—I kneel on it—while you close the valve. The deflated pad can then be rolled or folded as you choose. Open-cell foam has a "memory." Leave it compressed for a long time and it'll stay compressed. At home, Therm-a-Rests should be stored uncompressed with the valve open. This also allows moisture from breath to escape. Breath doesn't harm Therm-a-Rests. I always blow mine up rather than waiting for it to inflate.

Therm-a-Rests require care. I don't throw mine down on the ground and sit on it without checking for sharp objects that might puncture it. In fact, I don't put it on bare ground at all, I always use a ground cloth. In case the pad does spring a leak, you can get a repair kit containing patches and glue. The HotBond Repair Kit weighs an ounce, and I usually carry it. Sticky-backed nylon repair tape can be used too, or even duct tape as a last resort. Finding a pin-prick-sized leak can be difficult, however. The best method is to immerse the pad in a creek or pool and watch for bubbles. Because of the foam core, self-inflating mats still supply a little insulation if punctured. Look after your pad, and punctures should be rare. I've only had three in twenty-one years, during which I've slept on a Therm-a-Rest at least a thousand nights. DEET-based insect repellent (see page 337) can damage the coating, another reason for not using DEET or at least wiping it off yourself before handling or lying on a pad. Prolonged exposure to ultraviolet light can damage a pad too, as can solvents. Various other self-inflating mats are sold by Slumberjack, Outbound, Artiach, Exped, Big Agnes, and Pacific Outdoor Equipment. POE makes InsulMat mummy-shaped pads, which is a nice idea. I've tried the full-length, 1-inch-thick Insul-Mat Max-Lite 1.0 (R-value 3); it's very comfortable and weighs a reasonable 25 ounces. Perhaps the most interesting alternative to a Therm-a-Rest is Bozeman Mountain Works' tapered 1-inch-thick TorsoLite. It's only 32 inches long, but it weighs just 10 ounces.

Traditional air mattresses are very comfortable but also cold, since there's no fill to hold the air in place, so it moves around and conducts ground cold upward. Few traditional air mattresses are still around, though Big Agnes makes one, the REM (Rest Easy Mama) Air Core. The mummy-shaped version of this weighs 19 ounces and is 72 inches long and 2.5 inches thick. Despite the thickness, however, it's rated only down to 35°F (2°C), and if it punctures it will be much less comfortable than a deflated self-inflating mat.

The most luxurious—and expensive—air mattresses are filled with down. Pump these up (don't use your breath; it will dampen the down), and they form a supportive and warm bed. Stephenson's Warmlite introduced down mattresses way back in 1975 with their DAM (down-filled air mattress) models. The lightest 56-inch one weighs 18 ounces and is 3 to 4 inches thick. Its stuff sack doubles as a pump. Much more recently Exped has introduced its Down Air Mattress, which weighs 32 ounces (plus 6 ounces for the stuff sack, which incorporates a pump), is 70 inches long and 3.5 inches thick, and has an R-value of 9.54, equivalent to over four ProLite 3 Therm-a-Rests. Exped's mattress is filled with 8.8 ounces of 700-fill-power down.

If you want more comfort than closed-cell foam but don't like the idea of a pad that can puncture (my partner, Denise Thorn, won't use a self-inflating pad for this reason), there are pads that provide this. They tend to be heavy and bulky, though, since they use open-cell foam with a waterproof cover, often in combination with closed-cell foam.

Mountain Hardwear pads are such a combination. The cover zips off so the foam can be removed for cleaning and airing. The lightest model is the Superlight 60, at 24 ounces. It's tapered, 60 inches long and an inch thick.

Despite all this choice, I regularly only use two mats, and for many years I used only one. Much to my surprise, after some eighteen years of using a Therm-a-Rest, I have reverted to a closed-cell pad for some trips. During my Therm-a-Rest years I did occasionally use closed-cell pads on short trips, but I never found them very comfortable. However, when I came to hike the Arizona Trail I wanted a pad I could chuck on the ground without bothering about cactus spines or sharp stones, so I took a Ridge Rest. I soon found myself quite happy sleeping on stony ground on this pad, and I've gone on using it—I really like not having to worry about puncturing it and being able to throw it down where I like. It's often said that as you get older you feel the bumps and hardness of the ground more. I seem to be the opposite. When camping on snow, I usually carry both Ridge Rest and ProLite 3, though in spring I sometimes take just one. The combined weight is 22 ounces, still light for a winter pad.

OTHER COMFORTS

Pillows

For a pillow, I simply use a fleece or insulated top stuffed loosely into a large stuff sack (usually the one that holds the sleeping bag). I put this makeshift pillow under my sleeping bag hood so that if I turn over with the bag in the night it stays put. For those who prefer more organized comfort than soft clothing provides, you can get lightweight pillows. Integral Designs make a delightful-sounding Primasilk pillow with Primaloft fill and a silk shell that weighs 4 ounces.

Chairs and Chair Kits

Carrying chairs is unusual in the wilderness, though I did once see two hikers with lawn chairs strapped to their towering packs. Rather than carry these, you can adapt a pad with a chair kit. Cascade Designs makes kits for all their Therm-a-Rests, and they'll undoubtedly work with other pads. I have a 12-ounce Lite Chair that fits shorter pads. It consists of a piece of nylon that slips over each end of the mat, with adjustable straps linking the ends. Tighten these straps and the mat folds up so you can sit in it, adjusting the tension until it feels comfortable. Many years ago my companion and I each took one of these devices on a fairly leisurely eleven-day hike in Yosemite National Park, where weight wasn't paramount. It was very pleasant sitting outside in our chairs each evening. However, we both punctured our Therm-a-Rests, despite the tough nylon base of the chairs. I figured I'd have been as comfortable sitting against a tree, a boulder, or my pack, and I've never taken the chair backpacking again, though I do occasionally use it—with the Ridge Rest—when camping from the car.

Some pads come designed to be used as chairs, or maybe it's the other way around. Crazy Creek was first with these and now offers sixteen models. I have an Original Chair. It weighs 22 ounces and consists of a 15.5-by-33-inch closed-cell foam pad encased in ripstop nylon with carbon fiber stays in the sides and adjustable straps. It's very comfortable as a chair but a bit narrow and short for a sleeping pad. It's good for car camping, but I've

Relaxing in a hammock.

never taken it backpacking. Crazy Creek also makes the Thermolounger Shell (22 ounces) into which you can put your own 48-inch pad.

Hammocks

Hammocks might seem to belong to tropical expeditions rather than most backpacking, but they're gathering a following, mainly owing to one design, the Hennessey Hammock, which was developed for hiking use. The original Hennessey has expanded into nine models, of which the Ultralight Backpacker A-Sym is probably the best for hiking. (I haven't used any of them.) This hammock comes with netting and a silnylon fly sheet and so will keep out bugs and rain. There's a Velcro-closed slit in the bottom for entry, so you don't have to swing yourself in from the side (and maybe rapidly exit the other side, as I've done when trying out hammocks). The weight is 31 ounces. If there are no trees to hang it from (it has extra-wide webbing so it won't damage trees), it can be pitched as a tent using trekking poles. Oh— it can be used with a sleeping pad to make a chair, too! *A-Sym* is short for *asymmetrical*, and it's designed to make it easy to lie diagonally across the centerline, which is supposed to be more comfortable. There appear to be many happy users, and if I were looking for a hammock, this is the one I would choose. There are plenty of others. Hammocks.com stocks more than three hundred—most too heavy for backpacking, of course—while Speerhammocks.com offers hammocks more suited to backpacking along with kits so you can make your own plus a book on hammock camping.

chapter seven

> "I THINK," SAID CHRISTOPHER ROBIN,
> "THAT WE OUGHT TO EAT ALL OUR PROVISIONS NOW,
> SO THAT WE SHAN'T HAVE SO MUCH TO CARRY."
>
> —Winnie-the-Pooh, A. A. Milne

the wilderness kitchen

FOOD AND DRINK

One of the joys of backpacking is taking the first sip of a hot drink at the end of a long day. Often it's the anticipation of that moment that keeps me going for the last hour or so. The tent is up, my boots are off, and I can lie back and start to unwind. I may eat and drink while lying in the tent, a gale raging outside, or while sitting outside, back against a tree or boulder, admiring the view. Either way, this period of relaxation and renewal is a crucial part of living in the wilderness, one of the aspects of backpacking that differentiates it from day hiking.

Food plays a large part in how much you enjoy the outdoors. The possibilities and permutations are endless, so you can constantly vary your diet. Wilderness dining has two extremes: gourmet eaters and survival eaters. The first like to make camp at lunchtime so they have several hours to set up field ovens; they bake cakes and bread and cook multicourse dinners. They walk only a few miles each day

REASONS FOR BACKPACKING

The exact route doesn't matter; we've altered our original plans several times. Time passes. We hear the scolding of squirrels, the screeching of jays, the clicking of deer hooves, the delicate whisper of breezes in the aspens, the trickle of tiny creeks, and the roar of mighty waterfalls. Yes, and the whine of mosquitoes, the buzz of rattlesnakes, and unseen animals in the night that just might be bears. But beyond these sounds—or perhaps beneath them—is a profound silence. When I leave the roaring cataracts of a river to enter a thick grove of massive, ancient conifers, it is as though I've walked under a blanket—so all-embracing, so physical, is the silence.

and may use the same campsite for several nights. Survival eaters breakfast on a handful of dry cereal and a swig of water and are up and walking within minutes of waking. They pound out dozens of miles every day; lunch is a series of cold snacks eaten on the move. Dinner consists of a freeze-dried meal, "cooked" by pouring hot water into the package, or more cold snacks.

Most people, of course, fall somewhere between these two extremes. I lean heavily toward being a survival eater, so you won't learn here how to bake bread or pizza. For that you'll need to turn to an outdoor cookery book, such as Dorcas Miller's *Backcountry Cooking* and *Good Food for Camp and Trail*, Claudia Axcell, Vikki Kinmont Kath, and Diana Cooke's *Simple Foods for the Pack*, June Fleming's *The Well-Fed Backpacker*, and the wonderfully named *Gorp, Glop and Glue Stew*, by Yvonne Prater and Ruth Dyar Mendenhall, in which 165 well-known outdoorspeople give their favorite recipes and tell some kitchen tales. These books are full of mouthwatering recipes and suggestions. I've been meaning to try some of them since I bought *Simple Foods for the Pack* some twenty-five years ago.

Which foods are best for backpacking is debatable. At one hikers' gathering I attended, a speaker denounced a certain popular candy bar as "not food" and said that when they reach town hikers should head for the salad bar, not the all-you-can-eat pizza place. Others demurred, strongly. Pasta keeps me going better than rice, potatoes, or other carbohydrates, perhaps simply because I prefer it. I know other hikers who hate pasta and never eat it. What it comes down to, of course, is personal choice. If a certain food helps you enjoy backpacking, then take it with you, whatever anyone else says.

Here I describe what I eat and why. I prefer less-processed, additive-free whole foods, preferably organic, and I am mostly vegetarian. I've been known to eat candy bars at times, however, and I can't resist pizza.

Much of the information below was derived from *Food Facts*, by David Briggs and Mark Wahlqvist, a fascinating volume published in the UK and Australia in 1988 (it is long out of print, but available online at healthyeatingclub.com), and from the Dietary Guidelines published jointly by the Departments of Health and Human Services and Agriculture (www.nal.usda.gov/fnic/dga).

Hot or Cold?

Hot food provides no more energy than cold food. Cooking food can destroy some vitamins, though some starchy food such as potatoes, beans, and lentils need to be cooked to make them more digestible and, in the case of the last two, to destroy substances that make utilizing their protein difficult. One way to cut the weight of your pack would be to eat only cold food and thus dispense with stove, fuel, and cookware. I've considered this, but I always end up taking food that needs cooking because on short trips the extra weight is so slight that it doesn't matter and on long trips the psychological boost of hot food is wonderful, especially when it's chilly or the weather turns cold and wet.

I certainly wouldn't recommend trying to survive without a stove and hot sustenance in winter, when you may have to melt snow for water and when a hot meal can send waves of welcome warmth through your cold, stiff body. If anyone becomes really cold, perhaps on the verge of hypothermia, hot food and drink are a great help.

Fats, Proteins, and Carbohydrates

Food consists of several components, and the body needs them all. The main ones are fats, proteins, and carbohydrates. All three provide energy but also serve other functions.

Fats release their energy slowly and can be

stored in the body to be used when required. Because fats are digested gradually, they aren't a quick source of energy. Your body can't easily digest fats while exercising, either, so it's best to avoid eating a lot of fat during the day. Eating fats as part of your evening meal, however, enables them to release their energy during the night, which helps keep you warm. Sources of fat include dairy products, margarine, eggs, nuts, and meat. The current standard advice is that you should cut down on foods high in saturated fats (butter, animal-fat margarine, cheese, whole milk, lard, chocolate) and replace them with those high in polyunsaturated fats (vegetable-fat margarine, low-fat spreads, vegetable oil) and monounsaturated fats (olive oil). Nutritionists recommend cutting down the total amount of fat in the diet anyway, since fat can have other unwanted health effects. The body needs some fat, but nothing like the amount most people in developed countries eat. However, fats are an important part of the backpacker's diet, especially in cold weather.

Protein renews muscles and body tissue. During digestion, proteins break down into the amino acids they're made from. The body then rebuilds these into muscle and tissue protein. Complete proteins contain a full complement of amino acids; they're most commonly found in meat, eggs, and dairy products. Incomplete proteins lack one or more amino acids but can be combined to create complete proteins; they're found in grains and legumes. Thus a stew with beans and barley provides all the amino acids. The body either burns protein as fuel or stores it as fat if it isn't immediately used for muscle regeneration, so it's best to eat small amounts of protein at every meal.

The body quickly and directly turns *carbohydrates* into energy, so these are the foods most needed by the backpacker. Carbohydrates may be simple or complex. Simple ones are sugars (sucrose, dextrose, fructose, glucose, and honey); complex ones are starches (grains, vegetables, legumes). Generally you should try to rely more on complex carbohydrates, because they provide more energy over a longer period. They also provide fiber, vitamins, and minerals. Fiber is essential in your diet to prevent constipation—a potential problem for backpackers living on dehydrated food. Sugars give you a quick boost when you're tired, but it won't last and you'll feel tired again when the energy they supply is used up.

Determining what constitutes a proper proportion of these components in your diet is a nutritionist's basic reason for being. The current advice from most experts is to eat less fat and protein and more carbohydrates. Most backpackers, especially those who undertake long hikes, will have come to this conclusion, I suspect, because it's carbohydrates that speed you along the trail and that you crave when food runs low. My backpacking menu is probably 60 to 70 percent carbohydrates, the rest split equally between fats and proteins.

Vitamins and Minerals

Vitamins and minerals are also food components, but not ones you need worry about on trips of less than one month. Even if your diet is deficient in them for short periods, it's not likely to hurt you. But on long trips where you lack fresh food, adding a vitamin and mineral supplement to your diet could mean avoiding a deficiency. I've taken multivitamins on most of my long walks, though I didn't do it on the five-and-a-half-month Continental Divide Trail hike and suffered no ill effects. Now I take vitamin C (1 gram) and vitamin E tablets each day (when I remember). Whether they make any difference I can't tell, but they weigh very little, and they just might prevent a deficiency.

Calories and Weight

A *calorie* is the measure of food's energy value. The calorie measurement used in reference to food is the *kilocalorie* (kcal)—it represents the amount of heat needed to raise 1 kilogram of water one degree Celsius. (Kilocalorie, or Calorie with a capital *C*, is the proper term, but it's often referred to as "calorie" on food packages.) Sometimes kilojoules are used instead of kilocalories. There are 4.2 kilojoules to the kilocalorie.

How many kilocalories a person needs each day depends on metabolism, weight, age, sex, and level of activity. Metabolism is an extremely complex system that is not fully understood, but it defines the body processes that transform foods into usable elements and energy; any surplus is stored as fat. If you eat more kilocalories than you use, you'll put on weight; if you eat fewer, you'll lose it. Putting on weight is not usually a problem for backpackers, but losing it may be. The weight that most concerns us is the weight of the food we must carry in order to have enough energy.

People's metabolic rates differ, though generally the fitter and more active you are, the faster you'll burn up food, whether you're working or at rest. Figures are available for the kilocalories needed for "everyday life" for people of different sizes. For someone of my height (5 feet, 8 inches) and weight (154 to 161 pounds), it's about 2,500 kilocalories a day. Of that, 1,785 kilocalories make up the basal metabolism (the energy required simply to keep the body functioning), based on 1,100 kilocalories per 45 kilograms of body weight. To be able to expend more energy without burning body stores, I need to consume more kilocalories, so it's clear that my backpacking menu must provide more than 2,500 kilocalories a day.

You can roughly calculate your kilocalorie needs based on figures that give kilocalorie demands of various activities (see sidebar). I did this when I wrote the first edition of this book. Before that I had just carried roughly the same

KILOCALORIE DEMANDS OF VARIOUS ACTIVITIES

	Kilocalories per Hour	
ACTIVITY	128-POUND WOMAN	154-POUND MAN
sleeping, resting, fasting	30–60	60–90
sitting—reading, desk work	60–90	90–120
sitting—typing, playing piano, operating controls	90–150	120–180
light bench work, serving in store, gardening, slow walking	120–210	180–240
social sports, cycling, tennis, light factory work, light farm work	180–300	240–360
heavy physical labor, carrying, stacking, cutting wood, jogging, competitive sports	240–420	360–510
very hard physical labor, intense physical activity, heavy lifting, very vigorous sporting activity	600+	720+

weight of food on each walk, assuming it would provide the same number of kilocalories. I made the calculations because I was curious to see how closely my field-based figures compared with scientific ones and because the exercise might be useful for others in planning their food supplies.

If we include walking with a pack at the upper end of category 5 and the lower end of category 6, then men need 360 kilocalories per hour and women 240. If you walk for about seven hours a day, not including stops, as I do, that works out to 2,100 kilocalories for a woman, and 2,520 for a man (five and six per minute, respectively). Splitting up the rest of the day into nine hours of sleeping and resting (category 1), which requires 270 to 540 kilocalories an hour (women) and 540 to 810 (men), and eight hours of category 4 (setting up camp, cooking, packing, "slow walking" around the site), which requires 960 to 1,680 kilocalories (women) and 1,440 to 1,920 (men), we end up with totals of 3,330 to 4,320 kilocalories (women) and 4,500 to 5,250 (men). These figures are very rough, of course, but they seem on the high side. You could argue, however, that a lot of backpacking activity falls into categories 6 and 7 and requires more energy than given here, not less.

Those figures seem high to me, because I need only about 4,000 kilocalories a day on trips that will last no more than a few weeks. But these figures are for "average" people, and no one fits them exactly. Even so, such exercises are useful to those who would like to know how much energy they use and where it comes from.

On longer hikes, my appetite goes up dramatically after the first couple of weeks, and I now plan for more food from that time onward. I estimate that on long hikes I average at least 5,000 kilocalories a day. In bitter weather, I may need more because of the cold, and more again on ski tours, because skiing uses up energy at a far greater rate than walking.

Most foods these days have the calorie content listed on the package, which is useful for making comparisons and compiling menus. I always check labels to see if the kilocalories are listed. Unlike many who count calories, I'm searching for *high-calorie*, not low-calorie, foods. The figures in the table on page 248 are taken from a variety of sources, including the USDA National Nutrient Database (www.nal.usda.gov/fnic/foodcomp); *Food Facts*, by David Briggs and Mark Wahlqvist; and manufacturers' specifications.

Based on calories only, these figures suggest that you should live solely on margarine, vegetable oil, dried eggs, nuts, and chocolate in order to carry the least weight. But you wouldn't feel very well or find hiking easy, since these are all very high in fats (fats contain 9 kilocalories per gram, while proteins and carbohydrates have just 4).

The diet I eat of complex carbohydrates (dried skimmed milk, dried fruit, dried vegetables, pasta, rice, oat crackers, muesli, and granola bars), plus a little fat (cheese, margarine) gives about 400 kilocalories per 3.5 ounces. This works out to 2.2 pounds of food for 4,000 kilocalories per day, which is about what I carry. This diet should also provide enough protein. Only a sugar-based diet runs the risk of being insufficient in protein.

It's worth checking the caloric content of any food you intend to carry—there are significant variations between brands, and high-calorie, carbohydrate-based foods mean less weight than low-calorie ones. For example, I'm glad I don't carry canned fish—as so many backpackers do—since according to the chart the weight per calorie (including the can) is very high. However, I really should give up my coffee in favor of cocoa!

On two- or three-day warm-weather trips, the

NUTRITIONAL CONTENT OF SOME COMMON FOODS

Food	Kilocalories per 3.5 Ounces	% Fat	% Protein	% Carbo-hydrate	Food	Kilocalories per 3.5 Ounces	% Fat	% Protein	% Carbo-hydrate
DAIRY PRODUCTS, FATS, AND OILS					**BAKED PRODUCTS**				
margarine	720	81.0	0.6	0.4	granola bar	382	13.4	4.9	64.4
low-fat spread	366	36.8	6.0	3.0	crispbread, rye	345	1.2	13.0	76.3
vegetable oil	900	100.0	—	—	oat crackers	369	15.7	10.1	65.6
instant dried skim milk	355	1.3	36.0	53.0	bread, white	271	—	8.7	50.5
cheddar cheese	398	32.2	25.0	2.1	bread, wholemeal	243	—	10.5	47.7
Edam cheese	305	23.0	24.0	—	cookies, chocolate	525	28.0	6.0	67.0
Parmesan cheese	410	30.0	35.0	—	fig bar	356	5.6	3.9	75.4
eggs, dried	592	41.2	47.0	4.1	cake, fruit	355	13.0	5.0	58.0
low-fat cheese spread	175	9.0	20.0	4.0					
					MEAT AND FISH				
DRIED FRUIT					beef, dried	204	6.3	34.3	—
apples	275	—	1.0	78.0	beef, corned, canned	264	18.0	23.5	—
apricots	261	—	5.0	66.5	salami	490	45.0	19.0	2.0
dates	275	—	2.2	72.9	salmon, canned	151	7.1	20.8	—
figs	275	—	4.3	69.1	sardines, drained	165	11.1	24.0	—
peaches	261	—	3.1	68.3	tuna, drained	165	8.2	28.8	—
raisins	289	—	2.5	77.4					
					SUGARS AND SWEETS				
VEGETABLES					honey	303	—	0.3	82.0
potatoes, dehydrated	352	—	8.3	80.4	sugar, brown	373	—	—	96.4
tomato flakes	342	—	10.8	76.7	sugar, white	384	—	—	99.5
baked beans	123	2.6	6.1	19.0	chocolate, milk	518	32.3	7.7	56.9
					custard, instant	378	10.2	2.9	72.6
NUTS									
almonds	600	57.7	18.6	19.5	**DRINKS**				
Brazil nuts	652	66.9	14.3	10.9	cocoa (mix)	391	10.6	9.4	73.9
coconut, dried	605	62.0	6.0	6.0	coffee	2	—	0.2	—
peanut butter	589	49.4	27.8	17.2	tea	1	—	0.1	—
peanuts, roasted	582	49.8	26.0	18.8					
					COMPLETE MEALS				
GRAIN PRODUCTS					pasta and sauce	384	4.7	13.1	77.1
oatmeal	375	7.0	11.0	62.4	vegetable goulash and potato mix	375	11.9	15.9	54.4
muesli, sweetened	348	6.3	10.4	66.6	vegetable cottage pie	391	3.0	16.3	66.5
pasta, white	370	—	12.5	75.2	thick pea soup	333	5.3	17.0	58.0
pasta, whole wheat	323	0.5	12.5	67.2	bean stew mix	349	2.9	17.5	67.3
rice, brown	359	—	7.5	77.4	fruit and nut bar	420	28.0	17.0	56.0
rice, white	363	—	6.7	80.4					
flour, plain	360	2.0	11.0	75.0					
flour, wholemeal	345	3.0	12.0	72.0					

weight of food in the pack isn't a major concern, and I sometimes take bread, fresh fruit, canned goods, and anything else I find in the cupboard. But in cold weather and on any trip when I have to carry at least a week's worth of food, weight matters a great deal. Unfortunately, you need less food for short trips and more for long ones. I've read of people who get by on a pound or so of food a day without subsisting on margarine and nuts, but I can't—at least not for more than a few days. Skimp on food and you might find yourself feeling lethargic and irritable. You might even pack in the trip without realizing that your low morale was due to a lack of food.

I need about 35 ounces of food for each day on the trail. Powdered drinks, condiments, and other odds and ends are included in this total, which roughly divides into 7 ounces for breakfast, 14 ounces for dinner, and 14 ounces eaten during the day. The main evening meal usually weighs about 7 ounces, the other 7 ounces being made up of soup, dessert, margarine, herbs and spices, milk powder, coffee, and sugar. These figures yield approximately 800, 1,600, and 1,600 kilocalories for the three meals. If the total weight of my food comes to much more than 35 ounces a day, I know I've packed too much, so I jettison some.

This 35 ounces a day equals 15 pounds a week, a considerable weight. Two weeks' food—30 pounds—is the most I ever consider carrying, and I do that only if there's no other choice. Back in 1982 on the Pacific Crest Trail I foolishly carried *44 pounds* of food on the twenty-three-day crossing of the snowbound High Sierra, which made for a 100-pound load, because I also carried snowshoes, an ice ax, crampons, and cold-weather clothing. My pack was too heavy for me to lift; I had to put it on while sitting down. The weight was ridiculous, and I attempted to carry it only because I had no idea what such a load would feel like. And I *still*

ran short of food—probably because of the extra energy I needed to carry all that weight. Never again!

On long hikes and in cold conditions, I keep the weight down to 35 ounces a day by increasing the amount of fat, usually by adding more margarine and cheese to evening meals. Polar explorers often eat appalling amounts of fat daily, since it's the only way they can consume the 7,000 to 8,000 kilocalories they need. Eating that amount in carbohydrates would mean huge loads and never-ending meals.

Dried Food

How bulky food is doesn't matter much on one- or two-night jaunts, but it can be a problem on longer trips. Fresh, canned, and *retort* (cooked food packed in pouches) goods are bulky and heavy, so dried foods are the backpacker's staple for long-haul hikes. Removing the moisture from food maintains its caloric value while drastically reducing its weight and bulk.

The simplest way of drying food is in the hot sun. Because this doesn't remove as much moisture as other methods, it's not used for many foods, though some fruits, such as bananas, may be sun-dried. Air-drying, where the food is spun in a drum or arranged on trays in a container through which hot air is blown, produces *dehydrated* foods. Reconstituted commercial dehydrated foods have a reputation for being unappetizing, because the cell structure is damaged during the process. In *spray-drying*, food is sprayed at high speed into a hot-air-filled cylinder. (This method is used to dry milk, cheese, and coffee.) The most complex and expensive method of extracting the water from foods is *freeze-drying*, where food is flash-frozen so its moisture turns to ice crystals too small to damage cell structure. The food is then placed in a low-temperature vacuum, which turns the ice directly into vapor without its passing through a liquid state (sublimation), again leaving the cells undamaged. Freeze-dried food is costly compared with dehydrated food, but it tastes better. Because the food can be cooked before being freeze-dried, you often just need boiling water to reconstitute it.

HOME DEHYDRATING Many backpackers dehydrate their own food, everything from dinners to fruit snacks. I haven't done this myself, though I've eaten home-dehydrated food and been impressed enough to plan on doing it myself "one day." Home dehydrators consist of racks of trays through which a fan blows heat from an electric motor. There are several models, or you could build your own or even use the oven on low heat (about 140°F [60°C]) with the door slightly open. I've tried dried fruits—passion fruit is particularly tasty—dried tomato sauce, and dried pasta and lentil meals. All were very palatable and quick to cook as long as they were soaked a little while first. Many outdoor cookbooks have sections on dehydrating. Alan Kesselheim's *Trail Food* has comprehensive details, as does Dorcas Miller's *Good Food for Camp and Trail*.

Cooking Times and Methods

The time food takes to cook affects the amount of stove fuel you have to carry and how long you have to wait for a meal at the end of the day. When you're crouched over a tiny stove, exhausted and hungry at the end of a long day with a storm raging all around, knowing your energy-restoring dinner will be ready in five rather than thirty minutes can be very important. Also, as you gain altitude and air pressure drops, water boils at a lower temperature, so recommended cooking times increase—times listed on food packages are for sea level. The boiling point of water drops 9°F (13°C) for every 5,000 feet in altitude; cooking time doubles for every 9°F (13°C) drop in the boiling point of water. At 5,000 feet, the cooking time is twice what it would be at sea level; at 10,000 feet, nearly four times as long; at 15,000 feet, seven times; and at 20,000 feet an agonizing thirteen times longer. These cooking times are for fresh foods, of course; precooked dried food takes only a little longer to cook at high altitude. For meals above 7,000 to 8,000 feet, you need quick-cooking and precooked foods.

These figures are important because most backpacking foods are cooked in boiling water. Since frying requires carrying oil or cooking fat and cleaning the greasy pan can be difficult, I rarely fry food. You can bake and roast if you have a fire for cooking, but I've never done so. Anglers often carry foil to wrap trout in before placing them in the embers of a campfire—the one type of roasting that makes sense to me. Baking can also be done with lightweight portable devices like the Outback Oven and the Bake-Packer. These are so easy to use that I've baked in camp very occasionally, though only with prepared mixes (see pages 319–20 for more on baking).

Many packaged foods—from soups to noodles—don't require any cooking. Just add boiling water and give a quick stir. They usually don't taste as good as meals that require a little simmering, but I generally carry a few for those times when I want hot food quickly and I'm not too fussy. Most of my meals need five to ten minutes' simmering, a good balance between tasty and fast food.

Cooking times can be reduced by presoaking some foods in cold water. This works with dried vegetables, dried meat, soya products, and legumes, but not with pasta or rice. Some people

Five days' supplies. Items in cardboard containers will be repacked in plastic bags.

soak food in a tightly capped bottle during the day so that it's ready for cooking when they reach camp. You can save fuel—though not time—with most foods that need simmering by bringing the water to a boil, adding the food, and then turning off the heat. As long as a tight lid is used, the food will at least partially, if not completely, cook in the hot water. If necessary you can warm it up again on the stove before eating. I often do this when I make camp with plenty of time to spare, then reheat the food when I'm ready to eat.

What's Available

A list of foods suitable for backpacking would fill a separate book, so here are just a few suggestions heavily biased toward my own diet.

Suitable foods can be found in grocery stores, health-food stores, and outdoor stores. Prices are lowest in supermarkets, which actually have all the foods you need. Quite a few will be processed

A selection of specialty backpacking meals.

foods with additives, however, which may affect your decision. Check cooking times carefully; one package of soup may take five minutes to cook while one next to it on the shelf takes twenty-five. Health-food stores supply unadulterated foods and a wide variety of cereals, dried fruits, and grain bars, though the number of supermarkets selling these items is increasing. Outdoor stores are where you'll find foods specially intended for backpackers and mountaineers. Lightweight, low in bulk, often freeze-dried, and expensive, these are fine if you don't mind the cost.

The best specialty backpacking meals I've found come from AlpineAire (formerly of California but in Montana), whose foods I ate on the Continental Divide walk. Even after five and a half months on the trail, I hadn't grown tired of the food. AlpineAire foods are additive-free, made from wholemeal pasta and brown rice, and include both freeze-dried and dehydrated items. The range includes dishes for breakfast and evening meals, plus soups and light meals for lunch. Recently I've been impressed with MSR's organic Mountain Gourmet food, which comes in brown paper packages that can be burned or recycled, and Backpacker's Pantry. Other brands include Enertia Trail Food, Adventure Foods, Mountain House, Richmoor, Campfood, and Harvest Foodworks.

Some specialty foods are designed for baking devices like the BakePacker and Outback Oven (for more on these, see pages 319–20). Adventure Foods makes a range of meals for the BakePacker. I tried the gingerbread and the honey cornbread and found both delicious. The dry weights are 7 and 9.6 ounces, and there is enough for two. Jean Spangenberg's *The Bake-Packer's Companion* lists many more recipes. For the Outback Oven, Backpacker's Pantry offers a selection of meals. When traveling solo, you can carry surplus baked goods and eat them the next day, something you'd never do with leftover dehydrated food.

The smell of fresh-baked foods emanating from these miniovens is truly wonderful, but cooking times are long, and some preparation is required. These are luxury foods for days when there's time to spare and trips where weight isn't important. (For the addresses of the manufacturers and suppliers listed here, see Appendix 3.)

Basic Breakfast

The only hot sustenance I normally have when I'm still bleary-eyed and trying to come to terms with being awake is a mug or two of decaffeinated coffee with sugar and dried milk (combined weight 0.3 ounce). I eat 4 ounces of muesli or granola with water, dried milk (0.3 to 0.6 ounce) and a few spoonfuls of sugar (about 0.5 to 0.6 ounce) unless the brand is presweetened. I have no preference for any particular brand—there are many good ones. If it's cold enough for the water in the pan to have frozen overnight, I dump the cereal on top of the ice, then heat the lot on the stove to make a sort of muesli porridge.

For those who prefer a hot breakfast, instant oatmeal is popular (and very lightweight), and there are various dried omelet and pancake mixes. Of course, you can eat anything at any time of the day. One of my trail companions ate instant noodles for breakfast—not a food I could face at the start of the day. I traveled part of the Pacific Crest Trail with an experienced hiker who ate trail mix for breakfast, which I've tried but find too dry. Another hiker I met on the same walk ate instant freeze-dried meals three times a day for the whole six-month walk, another diet I couldn't contemplate.

Lengthy Lunch

Walking with a pack requires a steady supply of energy, so I eat several times during the day. I often eat the first mouthfuls of "lunch" soon after breakfast, before I start walking. Some people like to stop and make hot drinks during the day, or even cook soup or light meals. I don't, since I rarely stop for more than ten or twenty minutes at a time, and I'm happy to snack on cold foods and drink cold water. Also, the days when I'd most like something hot are those when the weather's so cold or wet that stopping for more than a couple of minutes is a bad idea. In such conditions I'd rather keep moving and make camp earlier. On days when long stops are pleasant, I don't feel the need for hot food.

Trail mix, or *gorp*, is a staple snack food. At its most basic, it consists of peanuts and raisins (hence gorp—"good old raisins and peanuts"), but more sophisticated and tasty mixes can include bits of dried fruit (my favorites are papaya, pineapple, and dates), a range of nuts, dried coconut, chocolate or carob chips, butterscotch chips, M&Ms, sunflower and sesame seeds, granola, and anything else you fancy. I prefer trail mix to be on the sweet side; others prefer a more savory taste. I plan on 2.5 to 3.5 ounces a day. It soon goes. On stormy days I sometimes carry a bag of trail mix in my jacket pocket so I can snack as I hike.

I used to eat several chocolate bars and other candy bars every day, but following the recommendation to cut down on fat and sugar and increase complex carbohydrates, I no longer do so. Instead, I munch on cereal or granola bars, usually three or four a day.

I also often carry energy bars, or at least a product that has adopted that name since it became popular. Back in 1982 I discovered the California-made Bear Valley MealPack and Pemmican bars, and they've been a favorite ever since. They're filling, packed with energy, tasty, and surprisingly light, at just over 3.75 ounces a bar. They're basically a compressed mix of whole grains, dried fruit, nuts, and soy products with various natural flavorings. They contain all eight essential amino acids, which makes them a good source of protein. I ate at least one every day of the five-and-a-half-month Continental Divide Trail walk, and two or more a day on the three-month Yukon walk, and I never grew tired of them. If I ever do a trip where I eat only cold food, these bars will make up the main part of my diet. There are four varieties: Fruit 'n Nut Pemmican (420 calories), Sesame Lemon MealPack (410 calories), Coconut Almond MealPack (400 calories) and Carob-Cocoa Pemmican (440 calories). Of the other energy bars, I like Clif bars and Balance bars, while Mojo bars are good for a savory rather than sweet bar.

For a contrast to bars and trail mix I usually carry some bread or crackers and cheese or vegetable spread. I like tortillas or pita bread, both of which come in resealable plastic bags. Wholemeal tortillas are best for eating unheated; white-flour tortillas taste uncooked to me. If you carry breads, beware of their going moldy. I took enough pita bread for one a day on a two-week walk in the Grand Canyon. A few days before the end of the trip I was eating one in the dark when a nasty taste filled my mouth—the next day I noticed the green patches of mold on the remaining bread.

Cheese or vegetable pâté spreads that come in squeeze tubes are, for me, a necessity on breads. Meat eaters often carry pâté or salami to go with crackers, while those with a really sweet tooth can take jam or honey, both of which come in plastic squeeze bottles or tubs. I avoid spreads that come in tubs and foil—they ooze around the edges and smear themselves on your clothes and the sides of the plastic bags they have to be kept in.

Dehydrated Dinner

A one-pot dehydrated or freeze-dried meal is the basis of my evening repast. It's possible to concoct such meals at home from basic ingredients, but I prefer to use complete meals, which I doctor to suit my taste. As I mentioned earlier, my favorites come from AlpineAire; all its meals require only boiling water and a seven-to-ten-minute wait. A typical meatless example (the company makes beef, turkey, seafood, and chicken dishes, too) is Mountain Chili (ingredients: cooked freeze-dried pinto beans, soy protein, tomato powder, cornmeal, freeze-dried corn, spices, bell peppers, onions, and salt), which has a net weight of 6 ounces. It makes two servings—maybe: if you're not hungry, haven't been walking all day, and have lots of other food to eat. I have no problem eating all 30 ounces and 680 kilocalories in one sitting. (When searching store shelves for evening meals, I look for dry weights of about 6 to 7 ounces and ignore the number of servings. If the amount is well below 7 ounces, I carry it only if I'm planning on adding extra food.)

When I don't eat freeze-dried meals, I live on pasta-based dinners. Lipton offers a host of pasta-and-sauce meals that are quick cooking and tasty; I know people who've hiked the Pacific Crest Trail using Lipton's meals as their main dinners. The staple outdoor dinner, though, is that perennial hikers' favorite—macaroni and cheese. Kraft Cheesy Pasta is the most common brand (ingredients: pasta, cheese, dried skimmed milk, dried whey, salt, emulsifying salts, lactic acid, color). It

cooks in six minutes and comes in 6.75-ounce packs, just right for a single meal (the pack says "serves 2–3"). The makers advise adding milk and margarine to the dish. I add extra cheese, too.

Asian noodles with flavor packets—usually sold under the name *ramen*—cook in about four minutes and are a good alternative to macaroni and cheese. Westbrae Ramens, made from wholemeal flour and found in health-food stores and some supermarkets, are my favorites. Each of the half-dozen varieties weighs about 3 ounces and makes 9 ounces of cooked food. I use two packages of noodles per meal and add a packet of dehydrated soup mix, cheese, and margarine to make a full meal. Supermarkets sell white-flour versions of these noodles, which I sometimes use.

If I do make up my own meals, they're usually based on macaroni or other pasta as a base, to which I add dehydrated soup mix, such as onion or tomato, plus cheese sliced up with my pocketknife. These are so easy to prepare that I do it in camp rather than at home. Almost every night of the eighty-six-day Scandinavian mountain hike, I dined on quick-cooking macaroni mixed with dried soup, dried milk, and cheese, plus flavorings.

There are various ways to enhance the taste of any meal. Herbs and spices, soup mix, or cheese are popular additions. I carry garlic powder (fresh cloves on short trips), curry or chili powder, black pepper, and mixed herbs (but not salt—there's usually plenty in dried food anyway). Margarine, cheese, and milk powder add kilocalories as well as taste and bulk to meals. Soup mixes can be the sauce for a meal with pasta or rice, with cheese, dried milk, and other ingredients added to increase the food value. I often mix foods on the last few evenings of a long trip, using up whatever I have left. If I'm buying pasta or rice to add to soup, I look for quick-cooking varieties.

I usually eat a bowl of soup before having my

main meal, unless I'm very hungry. The mixes that require simmering for five or ten minutes taste best (I like Knorr), but instant soups require less time and fuel to prepare. The biggest problem with them is the serving size—often a meager 7 ounces when rehydrated, and only 118 kilocalories. I solve this problem by eating two packages at a time (2 ounces total dry weight). Again, adding margarine and cheese increases the energy content.

I always carry dried milk and usually cheese. I used to always carry margarine, usually Parkay or other liquid margarine in a squeeze bottles (weight about 16 ounces), since these are less messy and easier to use than tub varieties, but I stopped taking it several years ago and haven't missed it. With cheese I plan on 2 ounces a day and twice that if it's a main part of a meal. On long trips I use up any cheese in the first few days, so I eat the lowest-calorie meals I'm carrying then. Instant nonfat dry milk adds taste and calories to any dish, and is also good with breakfast cereal and tea or coffee. I think the best is Milkman Instant Milk, which tastes more like fresh milk than any of the others; I prefer brands that contain nothing but milk powder rather than those with additives. A standard 7-ounce pack of instant milk will make 3.52 pints and lasts me at least four or five days.

Coffee and sugar make up the final course of my evening sustenance. Having given up caffeine a few years ago, I now carry only decaffeinated coffee, and I drink much less of it, since I don't need the boost anymore. A couple of mugs an evening means carrying 0.75 ounce of sugar and 0.2 ounce of instant coffee per day. I don't drink tea, but those who do seem to find a large supply of tea bags essential—though an amazing number of mugs can be wrung from just one bag when supplies run low. Hot chocolate supplies plenty of energy—unlike coffee or tea—and comes in convenient envelopes. It's particularly nice on cold evenings as a warming bedtime drink. I've recently taken a liking to hot spiced cider drinks in mug-sized envelopes, and I now often drink one or two of these in the evening instead of coffee.

Variations

There are variations, of course, on what food can be taken on any backpacking outing. On two- or three-day trips, I sometimes pack sandwiches for each day's lunch. Retort foods are feasible then, too—they're lighter and tastier than canned goods, though heavier and bulkier than dried ones.

Cold-weather and winter hikes in northern latitudes call for a big change in my diet. Fewer daylight hours mean more time spent in camp and less on the move, while colder temperatures mean a need for more kilocalories—so I take slightly less food for daytime but more for the evening. In particular, I usually add some sort of dessert as a third course; hot instant custard with dried fruit is a favorite. A 3-ounce package provides 350 to 400 kilocalories even before you add dried fruit. Cold instant puddings are also a good way to pile on calories; preparation time can be speeded up by burying them in the snow to set.

Emergency Supplies

Many years ago I carried a foil-wrapped block of compressed emergency rations, called Turblokken, at the bottom of my pack, assuming that it would keep me going if I ran out of food. I finally ate it once when my supplies ran low and I didn't want to detour to resupply. My journal records that it was "fairly tasteless but kept me going." In case I ran low again, I then started carrying an extra day's worth of food. However, it's many years since I did that. Now I just carry a little extra food, such as an extra Bear Valley bar or two. If you can catch fish or know which insects and plants are edible, you can, of course, try to "live off the land."

I've only once run out of food in an area so remote that I couldn't walk out to a supply point in a day or two. My situation was complicated because I was a bit unclear about where I was (notice I didn't say "lost"). I had to ration my food severely for several days and emerged from the forest extremely hungry, but without having run out of energy. I learned that, if you have to, you can get by on remarkably little food—at least for a short time. I would go to great lengths to avoid another such situation, though. Once is more than enough.

Packaging

Plastic bags are ideal for carrying food. I use them for everything that comes in a heavy container I don't want to carry or that needs extra protection, including coffee, sugar, dried milk, trail mix, muesli, cheese, herbs, spices, and meals such as macaroni and cheese that come in cardboard boxes. If I need the instructions, I tear them off and put them in the bag with the food. The only items I keep in their cardboard containers are crackers, since these break easily. Cardboard gives a surprising amount of protection, but you need to be careful not to crush them. Packages of soup, granola bars, and complete meals in sealed envelopes don't need repacking, but they can be bagged together so that it's easy to see what you have. Bagging also serves as extra protection against tears in the envelopes, which can happen. The best bags I've found are zippered ones like Ziplocs. I always carry a few spare bags in case one splits.

Hiking stores carry many plastic food containers, but I don't use them—they take up as much space empty as they do full and add weight; plastic bags compress to almost nothing and weigh hardly anything. I used to carry herbs and spices in empty plastic film canisters, but now these go in plastic bags too.

Unless I'm using a bear-resistant container (see

By not carrying cans and by repackaging food packed in cardboard in plastic bags, I could fit all my trash from a ten-day trip into these two used food packets.

pages 258–63), I keep my food together in the pack in nylon stuff sacks. When I'm carrying more than a week's food, I use two of them. I put day food, which tends to be the bulkiest of my rations, in one bag, and camp food in the other. Two smaller bags are easier to pack than one large one, and it's easier to find items.

Resupply

On trips of up to a week, resupplying isn't necessary; you can carry all you need unless your route passes through a place where you can buy food. On hikes that last more than a couple of weeks, you have to plan how to resupply. If you're prepared to live on whatever is available locally, you can shop at stores on or near your route. I did this on the Arizona Trail and it worked quite well, though a few times there wasn't much choice. Most small stores stock dried soups, crackers, bread, cheese, candy, chocolate bars, coffee, and tea, but dried meals and even breakfast cereals can be hard to find. This can mean carrying more weight and bulk than you'd like and being prepared to adapt to what you can get.

An alternative is to send supplies to yourself to be collected along the way. This way, you know what's in each supply box and can plan accurately; items such as maps and camera film can also be included in the same boxes. As well as boxes sent out ahead from home a *running supply* or *bounce box* is useful. This is a box you send on to the next post office with stuff you don't need for the next section of trail. If you can only buy larger amounts of foods than you need, the surplus can go in the running supply box, as can extras of any food you really like that you might not be able to purchase again. The obvious places to send supplies are post offices. Boxes should be addressed to yourself *c/o General Delivery* (*Poste Restante* in Europe) in the town scheduled for pickup. They should be marked *Hold for Hiker* and include the intended collection date and a return address. I also write to the post offices to tell them what I'm doing. It's a good idea to phone ahead (if you can) to check that the supplies have arrived; during the Canadian Rockies walk, one box went astray, causing me a week's delay.

Some mail-order food suppliers may drop-ship food to post offices along your route, a service I used on the Pacific Crest and Continental Divide Trails. In remote areas where there are no post offices, you could contact a park or forest ranger's office, or the nearest youth hostel, lodge, or motel, to ask if they'll hold supplies. I've done this several times and never yet been refused, though some of the latter places request a small fee (I always offer payment when I contact them). Rangers or outfitters may also be prepared to take food into wilderness cabins or camps if you're on a long trip. When I walked through the Yukon Territory, I found a commercial tour boat operator who was willing to take supplies down the Yukon River for me, which meant I was able to walk for twenty-three days without having to leave the wilderness to resupply.

You can cache food in advance if you have the time or have someone who can do it for you, though I've never done this. Obviously, cached food has to be stored in an animal-proof container, and you need to be sure you can locate it.

Another resupply alternative is to have food dropped by helicopter or brought in by bush plane. I considered this for the remote northern section of the Canadian Rockies walk but rejected it, mainly because of the high cost, but also because I wasn't happy about bringing noisy machines into the wilderness unless it was absolutely necessary. Instead, I tried to carry all my food for this three-hundred-mile section. I took seventeen days' food but spent twenty-three in the wilderness. Luckily it was hunting season, and the seasonal occupants of several remote outfitters' camps fed me as I passed through. Without them I couldn't have completed the walk. Of course, I could and should have contacted them in advance and asked if they'd take supplies in for me, which is what I would do on a similar venture now.

Food Storage in Camp

On trips where bears aren't likely to raid my camp, I prefer to keep my food beside me so I can cook and eat at leisure and can easily protect it against small animals and birds. Leaving food on the ground away from you, even in the pack, is a sure way to feed wildlife. Sharp teeth will quickly make holes in most materials. The Ursack stuff sack (see page 262) is an exception to this. Although bears are the animals people worry about most, smaller animals—mice, marmots, raccoons—probably make off with more food.

Animals and birds of all sizes like human food.

The worst problems I've had with wildlife occurred on a hike in the Grand Canyon, where deer mice abounded on most sites. One night they kept me awake for hours by running over me and my gear and rustling through the pack, whose pockets and compartments I'd left open so creatures wouldn't rip their way in. My food—inside plastic bags in a heavy-duty stuff sack and hung from a branch—was untouched, however.

Although it's inconvenient for you if animals get your food, for the animals it can be much worse. In the summer of 1995, rangers had to shoot twenty-three mule deer that were starving in the Grand Canyon; autopsies showed their stomachs were clogged with plastic bags, nylon cord, and other indigestible items. On popular backcountry sites in the Grand Canyon, posts are provided for hanging food bags and packs, and park regulations stress that all plastic bags and food must be kept packed away. In other parks there may be similar regulations in some places. When you feel like rebelling against the rules, remember those mule deer.

Hanging your food bags from a low limb may be adequate to keep small animals from getting at them. In areas where animals are likely to raid campsites, I now use an Ursack.

Bears

In bear country you need to take special precautions to keep your food safe, either by hanging it or by using a container bears can't break into. The traditional approach is to hang your food high in a tree, which isn't easy to do effectively. It needs to be at least 12 feet above the ground, 10 feet away from the trunk of a tree, and 6 feet below any branch—bears can climb and reach high. There are various ways of doing this, and all require at least 40 feet of nylon line and a tough stuff sack or two. Gregory makes a 1,300-cubic-inch Bear Bag that looks

Start with two stuff sacks of roughly equal weight. If you don't have enough food, put stones or gravel in one of the sacks. Tie one end of your line to one of the sacks *(1)*. Put a small rock in another stuff sack and tie the other end of your line to the sack. Throw it over a suitable branch and haul the first stuff sack up until it's just below the branch *(2)*. Tie the second stuff sack to the other end of the line while holding it as high as you can. Stuff any spare line into the stuff sack and then throw it up so that the two bags are at an equal height *(3)*. When you need the food, use a trekking pole or stick to pull down one of the bags *(4)*.

good; it weighs 8 ounces and comes with a sewn-in haul loop and a 40-foot length of parachute cord with an attached sack for a rock.

At times hanging food can take a long time. I've spent hours trying and wasted a lot of energy on curses as rocks whirled off into space or spun around branches, leaving a tangle of line to unwind. But whenever I've felt like giving up, I've thought about losing my food to a bear and have gone on until my food was secure. Bearbagging isn't just about protecting food, anyway, it's about protecting bears too, which is more important. A bear that finds food at a campsite may lose its fear of humans and start to raid sites regularly, becoming such a danger that it has to be killed. These are called "problem" bears. Really, though, we create the problem by taking food into the bear's territory and not protecting it adequately.

Having to hang food complicates camping, and

In many areas food must be secured from bears.

there is a tendency to forgo it at the end of a long, hard day or in bad weather. Certainly, when making camp after dark I've sometimes suspended my food in a way I wouldn't be happy with in daylight. I've always hung it though (nowadays I use a canister or an Ursack, which makes life much easier).

The simplest bearbagging method is to tie a rock to the end of the line, throw it over a branch

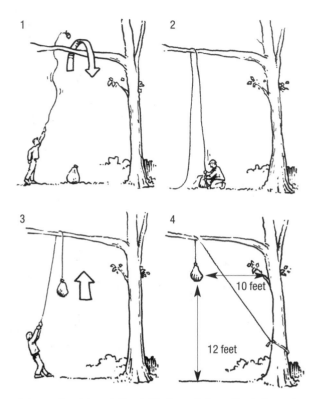

Put a small rock in a stuff sack. Tie the end of your line to the sack and throw it over a branch about 20 feet high. Don't let go of the other end of the rope! If you can't reach the rock, shake the line in a whipping motion to jerk the line over the branch and slowly lower the rock (1). Grab the end of the line and remove the rock (2). Attach your food stuff sack and haul it up (3). Wrap the end of the rope around the tree trunk and tie it off (4).

at least 20 feet above the ground, haul up the food until the bottom of the bag is at least 12 feet up, then tie off the line around the trunk of the tree. Even this is not that easy, since the line can become tangled around the branch. On popular sites in many areas you can see rotting strands of cord dangling from branches. Putting the rock in a small bag and tying that to the end of the line stops the rock from coming untied and shooting off into the distance, as can happen.

Up near timberline trees are usually smaller, with shorter branches. Here it's probably best to suspend food bags between two trees about 25 feet apart, which involves throwing one end of the weighted line over a branch, tying it off, and then repeating the process with the second tree. Keep the line between the two trees within reach so you can tie the food bag to it. Then haul the bag up until it's halfway between the trees and 12 feet off the ground.

In the High Sierra, bears have learned that breaking a line rewards them with a bag of food, so standard hanging techniques don't work. Instead, you should use the counterbalance system, which involves throwing the line over a branch, tying a food bag to the end of the line, and hauling it right up to the branch; you then tie a second food bag (or bag of rocks) to the other end of the line, push any extra line into the bag, and throw the second bag up so that both bags end up at least 12 feet above the ground and away from the tree trunk. If you leave a loop of line at the top of one of the bags, you can hook it with a stick or your staff to pull the bags down the next morning. Counterbalancing is difficult to do correctly, and bears too often get improperly hung food.

A decreasing number of national parks provide high wires between trees or poles with pulleys for hanging food at some campsites. These make the procedure easier, though it can still be difficult if you're alone and have a heavy food bag. Bearproof boxes are provided in some areas too, such as many popular sites in the High Sierra. Always use these if you camp nearby.

When camping above timberline or where there are no large trees, as in the Far North, I used to store food well away from camp in airtight plastic bags. Now I use bear-resistant canisters or Ursack stuff sacks.

In an increasing number of areas, such as Denali and Glacier Bay National Parks in Alaska and many parts of the High Sierra where bears

Left: Packing a bear-resistant container. The plastic liner helps reduce food smells. Right: Closing a bear-resistant container using a quarter as a screwdriver.

regularly get hung food, bear canisters are mandatory. They can usually be rented from park offices. It's wise to check the regulations as to which canisters are approved and where you need one before visiting a park, since they do change.

Bear-resistant canisters are wide and have a smooth surface so bears can't clamp their jaws around one or get their teeth or claws into it. Most have a round lid with recessed catches that can be opened with a quarter or a screwdriver. Canisters are great in camp but a pain on the trail; they're awkward to fit into a pack because of their hard cylindrical shape. I find the best way to pack one is to stand it up in the center of the pack with the sleeping bag below it and stuff soft gear around it. The smallest canisters will hold six days' food for one person, as long as you select low-bulk food and cram it in. Canisters are heavy, too. The original model and the one rented out by national parks is

the Garcia Machine Backpackers' Cache. This weighs 2 pounds, 12 ounces (3 pounds in the first version) and has a capacity of 730 cubic inches. It's made of ABS polymer (plastic). Lighter but vastly more expensive is the Wild Ideas Bearikade, made from composite carbon fiber and aluminum alloy. The Bearikade Weekender weighs 1 pound, 15 ounces and holds 650 cubic inches; the Expedition weighs 2 pounds, 5 ounces and holds 900 cubic inches. Purple Mountain Engineering's aluminum Tahoe Bear Canister is between the Bearikade and Backpackers' Cache in weight and size at 2 pounds, 6 ounces and 8 by 12 inches, which is slightly smaller than the Backpackers' Cache at 8.8 by 12 inches. Perhaps the most interesting canister is the Bear Vault, which is made from transparent polycarbonate and looks like a giant Nalgene bottle. It has a screw-top lid so no tools are needed to open it. The opening is much bigger than on canisters with recessed lids, which should make packing easier, and you can see what food you have left too. It's 8.7 by 12.4 inches and weighs 2 pounds, 6 ounces.

Despite the extra weight and the difficulty with packing, I like canisters. It's wonderful not to have to hang food and great to have easy access to it all the time. You don't have to check that there are suitable trees around before you camp, either, or sleep with half an eye open in case a bear tries to get your food and you have to leap up and try to scare it away (without getting too close, and only try this with black bears, not grizzlies!). Canisters

An Ursack bear-resistant stuff sack.

make good camp stools and tables, but don't use them for stoves or hot pots unless you put something heat resistant, such as foil, on them first. At night it's best to put the canister a short distance away from camp, in the middle of a flat area so a bear can't roll it down a slope.

I used a Backpackers' Cache, rented from Yosemite National Park, on a five-week hike in the High Sierra during which I met a few hikers who'd lost hung food to bears. At one of the rare popular sites I used I woke in the morning to see a bear walk past about forty feet from my camp without even pausing. A few minutes later I heard some pans clattering loudly and then some outraged and urgent yelling. Climbing onto a rock, I looked across a meadow with a small tent in the center to see a bear racing up the mountainside with something in its jaws, pursued by two half-naked campers. I presume they had hung their food with pans attached to act as a warning, but the bear had still gotten it. I'd heard people yelling and banging pots the night before too. My canister sat undisturbed twenty feet from camp.

An alternative that is lighter and easier to pack than canisters would be welcome, though, which is where the Ursack comes in. This is a supertough stuff sack designed to keep animals out, especially bears. The latest model, the TKO, is made from Spectra cloth, measures 8 by 13 inches, holds 650 cubic inches, and weighs just 8.2 ounces. That's almost the same capacity as the Backpackers' Cache canister, which weighs over five times as much. The Ursack can be squashed down when partly full like any other stuff sack, too. Does it work? Evidence from the makers and users suggests it does, though your food may get pulverized if a bear batters it around. Plastic bags inside can burst, so it's best not to pack anything liquid or sticky. It must be used properly to be effective. The mouth must be closed fully so no food is visible, and the bag then tied to a tree trunk or strong branch with a figure eight knot (so it's easy to untie). On a nine-day hike in the High Sierra I used an Ursack and a canister (I was going into an area where canisters were a requirement). I used the Ursack for over three days, after which all my food fit in the canister. As far as I know, nothing even touched it. I now use the Ursack anywhere that animals might try and eat my food, carrying a canister only in areas where they're required. I've had rodents chew through an ordinary stuff sack and into bags of food but fail to make any impression on the Ursack sitting next to it, so it certainly works for small animals.

Bears are attracted to food by smell as well as sight. Double-bagging smelly foods and not carrying really stinky ones in bear country is a good idea. Ursack makes odor-resistant plastic bags that they say are thousands of times more odorproof than standard bags. They weigh 1 ounce, measure 12.5 by 16 inches, and will fit inside an Ursack. Watchful Eye Designs makes a similar product called the O.P. Sak, which they say is odorproof. It comes in two sizes—6 by 9 and 12.5 by 15.5 inches. Bags like this sound sensible for all food storage.

Bears view smelly items such as toothpaste, soap, insect repellent, and sunscreen as food, so store them with your food. Food-stained clothing and dirty pots are best stored away from where you sleep, too.

A good way to keep bears out of your camp is by avoiding popular backcountry sites. Bears frequent those places where there is a regular supply of food. By camping away from such sites on one eleven-day trip in Yosemite National Park, I didn't even see a bear.

If a bear does get your food *don't try to get it back.* The bear will almost certainly defend it. (For more on bears, see pages 394–96.)

"Wild" Food

I'm often asked why I don't "live off the land" during long wilderness hikes. The phrase conjures up the carefree image of a hiker ambling along, munching on nuts and fruits plucked from trailside bushes and scooping tasty trout from every stream.

In fact, unless you hunt or fish, finding enough to eat in the wilderness is very difficult for most people and does not allow time for walking all day. Then too, wild lands are limited and fragile; we should take no more from them than we absolutely must, which means going in with all the food we need. If every wilderness traveler relied on foraging for food, popular areas would soon be stripped bare.

Fishing, perhaps, is an exception. Mountain lakes and streams often seem full of fish (some are restocked regularly, a highly dubious practice environmentally). Anglers often carry light fishing gear (and licenses) in suitable country and thereby supplement their diets with some fresh food. For some, hiking is a means to fish remote waters.

WATER

While you can manage without food for a surprisingly long time, this isn't so for water. Dehydration can kill you in a matter of days—and long before you're in real danger, you'll cease to enjoy what you're doing as your mind dulls and your perceptions numb.

On any walk, you need to know where water sources are and what the condition of the water is likely to be. In many places water is not a

Taking water from a hole cut through the ice of a snow-covered lake.

Fishing water out of a creek with a bottle attached to the end of a pole. Make sure you're standing on secure snow.

problem—unless there's too much of it—but in others, especially desert or semidesert areas, the location of water sources can determine your route. Water supply is one of the first things I want to know about a region new to me.

How much water you need per day varies from person to person and depends on the weather conditions, the amount of energy you expend, and the type of food you carry. I can walk all day without a drink in cool, damp conditions, though I don't recommend this. But I may drink a quart an hour on a very hot day in an area where there's no shade. Estimating needs for camp is easier. With the dried foods I eat, I can get by on 2 quarts a night, but I prefer to have 4 or more—and that's just for cooking and drinking, not for washing utensils or myself. It also assumes I've had enough to drink during the day and either am camping near water or expect to find a source fairly early the next day.

When you have to carry water, these calculations become important, because water weighs more than 2 pounds per quart. In desert areas of the Southwest, I've carried 3 gallons of water—a horrendous 25 pounds. Luckily, it's rare to have to carry that much, at least for a whole day. "Dry" camps (ones away from water sources) may require you to carry 3 or 4 quarts of water, but often this can be picked up late in the day so you only have to carry it for a few hours. Remember that you need enough water to get you to the next reliable source as well as for use in camp.

Snow-covered country is odd—everything is shrouded in solid water, but it's effectively a desert. Walking in snow can dehydrate you as quickly as desert walking, because the dry air sucks moisture out of your body. The thirstiest I've ever felt was when I skied all day in hot sunshine with no shade and not enough liquid. Eating snow cools your mouth but provides little real relief. The answer, easily given but not so easily carried out, is to melt enough snow in camp to keep you well supplied during the day.

Ideally, you should never allow yourself to become even slightly dehydrated. The best way to avoid this is to drink regularly, whether you feel thirsty or not. If you're not careful, though, dehydration may creep up on you, and only when your mouth starts to feel sticky and your tongue swollen do you realize how thirsty you are. Warning signs of dehydration are a reduction in urine output and a change in the color of your urine—the paler, the better. If it's dark, you need to drink a fair amount of water quickly. In order to avoid heat exhaustion, you should eat something as well or add fruit crystals or sports drink powder to the water to ensure that you replace essential electrolytes (sodium and potassium) that are also lost when you become dehydrated.

Sources

Streams, rivers, lakes, and ponds are obvious sources of water, easily identified on a map. In areas with plenty of these features, you won't need to carry much or to worry about running out. Check contour lines carefully, however, to see exactly where the water is. Often the high ridges that make for superb walking are far above any water. In such places it's better to carry full bottles than to make long descents and reascents when you need a drink. Remember, too, that dotted blue lines on the map usually indicate *seasonal* water sources; the rushing stream of June, heavy with snowmelt, may have vanished completely by late September.

Getting water can be as simple as dipping your water bottle into a fast-running river.

Piped springs can provide clean, fresh water if you take it from the inlet.

If water sources are scarce, you may have to hunt out tiny trickles and seeps. To find these, look for areas of richer, denser vegetation and for depressions and gullies where water may gather or run. Pause and listen, too. You can often hear water trickling even when you can't see it.

In deserts, locating water is critical to survival. "Think water" is a valuable mantra. Check guidebooks for information on water sources and, more important, ask rangers and other local people for current information. Sources can dry up quickly, so it's wise to always carry enough water to get to the next reliable source or out to a trailhead if a source isn't guaranteed. In places it may be necessary to place water caches. I did this on the Arizona Trail where there was a 60-mile waterless section across hot Sonoran Desert. My companion and I put out two caches of 9 gallons in gallon jugs and set off with 2 gallons each for the hike of three and a bit days. We simply hid the caches under bushes near the jeep trail we drove in on to place them, then marked them on the map. All were still there when we collected them over the next few days, but plastic jugs aren't the most reliable containers, since animals can bite into them. If you place

caches, it's important to carry out all the water containers. We ended that hike with our packs festooned with squashed empty water jugs.

For those who are intending more serious desert ventures and want to know about natural water sources, solar stills, and other possibilities, I recommend a look at *The Ultimate Desert Handbook* by Mark Johnson.

Safety

A real problem with water is deciding whether what you find is safe to drink. Water clarity is not necessarily an indication of either purity or contamination. Even the most sparkling, crystal-clear mountain stream may not be safe to drink from.

The invisible potential contaminants include a wide variety of microorganisms—protozoans, bacteria, and viruses—that cause intestinal disorders, some mild, some severe. The potential nasties include *Cryptosporidium*, a protozoan, that has gotten much attention recently. This causes

dip a mug in a shallow puddle, then pour into your container

channeling with foil or bark; plastic or stiff paper can also be used

lower a bottle with a rope (rocks inside help the bottle sink)

Water collection methods.

unpleasant watery diarrhea, but once you've had the disorder you should be immune.

Viruses are the most dangerous waterborne organisms—they can cause fatal diseases like polio and hepatitis. But viruses aren't a problem in most of North America. If you visit some other countries, however, they're a real threat. When I went hiking in Nepal, all vegetables and fruit had to be washed in iodine-treated water, and I used iodine to purify all water. Filters, the trekking company told me, were ineffective. If you're going abroad, check with the Centers for Disease Control and Prevention about water there.

The protozoan *Giardia lamblia*, which causes a virulent gut disorder, giardiasis, is the bug that has received most attention. While *Giardia* is indeed found in some wilderness streams and lakes—though not, it seems, in the quantities people think—too many people are far too concerned about it. Giardiasis isn't fatal, and you're unlikely to be incapacitated. Although it makes some people feel quite ill, most don't even have any symptoms and become immune after being exposed to it.

Giardia lamblia lives in the intestines of humans and animals. It gets into water as cysts excreted in feces, which is one reason for always siting toilets well away from water. The symptoms of giardiasis appear a few weeks after ingestion and include diarrhea, stomachache, a bloated feeling, nausea, and foul-smelling feces. However, these symptoms occur in other stomach disorders as well, and only a stool analysis can confirm infection. The chances of catching giardiasis or other illness from water aren't high, despite media coverage to the contrary. To cover themselves, land managers generally advise people that all water needs treating, which adds to concern. People who get a gut disorder then tend to blame *Giardia* in the water because they've been warned about it,

even though the cause is probably not either *Giardia* or the water.

Research published in 1995 in the journal *Wilderness and Environmental Medicine* suggests that giardiasis and other gut disorders are spread "by oral-fecal or food-borne transmission not by contaminated drinking water." Out of 34,348 cases of giardiasis reported to the study's authors, Thomas R. Welch and Timothy P. Welch, by forty-eight state health departments, a mere nineteen were associated with drinking contaminated water, and just two of them were known to be campers and backpackers. The authors compare the likelihood of catching giardiasis from drinking water to the risk of a shark attack and say that it's "an extraordinarily rare event to which the public and press have seemingly devoted inappropriate attention." In a separate study published in the online journal of the Yosemite Association, Robert L. Rockwell comes to a similar conclusion with regard to the Sierra Nevada: "You can indeed contract giardiasis on visits to the Sierra Nevada, but it won't be from the water. So drink freely and confidently." (In the summer of 2002 I did just this on a five-week hike in the High Sierra, never treating any water.)

According to both the Rockwell and Welch studies, *it's far more important to wash your hands thoroughly and keep your cooking pots clean than to treat your water.* Sharing mugs and bowls and bags of gorp is unwise too. Share food by pouring it into people's hands or their own utensils to minimize the chance of contamination.

The most recent study was done by *Backpacker* magazine in the spring and summer of 2003 (reported in the December 2003 issue). Seven backcountry water sources were tested three separate times for *Giardia* and *Cryptosporidium* by a California laboratory specializing in these protozoans. The sources ranged from the Neversink River East Branch in the Catskills in New York

State to the Merced River in Yosemite National Park in California. Only one source had a high enough concentration of cysts (1.5 per liter) for *Backpacker* to advise treating it, though it was still too low to make most people ill. Two had none at all. The other four had no viable cysts. Out of the twenty-one total samples, only six tested positive for *Giardia* and only one for *Cryptosporidium*. Other research also shows such low concentrations of protozoans, when any are found at all, that infection is very unlikely. The *Backpacker* article quotes Robert W. Derlet, a hiker and a professor of medicine who is researching the water sources in the Sierra, as saying that "the warnings about backcountry water quality are vastly exaggerated. Most of them are based on rumor and hearsay, nothing more. The chances of picking up a bug are very slim, and the chances of getting sick are much, much slimmer. If you averaged every drop of water from every lake in the Sierra and put it in a reservoir, you'd have to drink 250 gallons to get enough giardia to make you sick." The evidence suggests most backcountry water is safe, and you are very unlikely to catch anything from drinking it untreated. There are far greater risks in the wilderness. If you're really worried about intestinal illness, you could ease your concerns by treating all water, but the most important thing is to take great care with hand washing and keeping your cooking utensils clean. Even if you treat all your water, it's wise to be careful about sources. No treatment method is foolproof. I treat water only if it's below habitations, including backcountry shelters and popular campsites, and popular trails; if there are cattle or signs of cattle in the area; or if it looks or smells unpleasant. When seeking drinking water I look for springs and fast-flowing streams and take the water from above trails, campsites, and bridges. With lakes I take water from the inlet or the outlet if I can. I love being able to drink deeply from a mountain stream, and I'm very reluctant to give up this wilderness pleasure.

If you do get a bad digestive upset that doesn't clear up in a few days, it's wise to see a doctor just in case it's something serious. In the meantime drink plenty, since diarrhea is dehydrating, and eat plain low-fat foods such as rice and pasta. An upset gut can be debilitating and extremely unpleasant. I once had a very severe bout of diarrhea and vomiting in Nepal (probably contracted in Katmandu) that lasted several days. The cause was undiagnosed.

Treating all water can pose its own dangers. In the Montana Rockies during my Continental Divide walk, I regularly met members of a large party doing the same hike. Most of them were very worried about giardiasis, and they filtered or boiled all water before drinking it. While restocking and resting in the town of Butte after several weeks of very hot weather, I met one of this party walking down the street looking pale and thin. He told me he'd staggered out of the mountains feeling weak and sick. He didn't have giardiasis though—he was suffering from severe dehydration. He wouldn't drink unfiltered water and hadn't filtered the amount he should have been drinking. Dehydration is a serious enough threat, far greater than giardiasis, that drinking enough water is essential whether it's been treated or not.

Treatment

Water can be treated by boiling it, adding chemicals, and filtering. Boiling and chemicals disinfect the water—that is, they kill bugs in it. Filters remove anything too large to pass through the pores, but they don't disinfect water or remove viruses unless they have a chemical component as well, in which case they're described as purifiers. Visibly dirty water can be filtered through a bandanna or a coffee filter, as can glacier meltwater, but this doesn't remove microorganisms.

BOILING Boiling is the surest way to kill dangerous organisms, but it's impractical for all water needs because it uses fuel and takes time. However, it isn't necessary to boil water for the five to fifteen minutes often advised. Just bringing it to a boil will do—harmful organisms, including *Giardia* cysts, are killed at temperatures below the boiling point even at high altitude, where it's lower than at sea level. Boiled water tastes flat. To restore the sparkle, shake it up or pour it from one container into another and back again a few times to aerate it.

CHEMICAL TREATMENT The traditional forms of chemical treatment, iodine and chlorine tablets, are lightweight and simple to use; iodine treatment is regarded as the most effective against *Giardia*, but neither is proven against *Cryptosporidium*. Both chemicals make the water taste foul. Despite what is often stated, iodine isn't highly toxic. Apparently,

Using a coffee filter to strain sediment from pond water.

if you do ingest too much you'll probably vomit, getting rid of most of the iodine. Normal doses of iodine won't harm you. Wilkerson's *Medicine for Mountaineering and Other Wilderness Activities* reports that inmates of three Florida prisons have drunk water disinfected with iodine over a fifteen-year period with no ill effects. Only those with known thyroid problems or goiters need to be careful.

The most common brand of iodine tablets, Potable Aqua, comes in 3.5-ounce bottles containing fifty tablets that will treat twenty-five quarts. You can get neutralizing tablets that remove the aftertaste. These are made of vitamin C (ascorbic acid), so any soluble vitamin C tablets will have the same effect. But don't add them or anything else like fruit crystals until the iodine has had time to work (thirty minutes). I used chlorine tablets on the Pacific Crest Trail and Potable Aqua on the Continental Divide. I drank from filthy

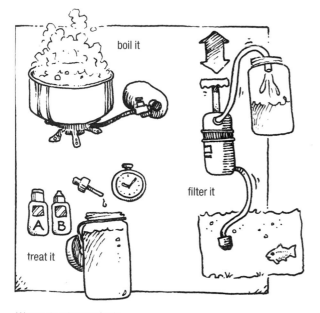

boil it

filter it

treat it

A B

Water-cleaning methods.

Polar Pure iodine water disinfectant.

and you have to carry a glass container with liquid in it. I used it for a while, before I discovered chlorine dioxide.

Chlorine dioxide is meant to kill everything, including *Cryptosporidium*. It's lightweight, easy to use, and in my opinion the best way of treating water. Despite the name, it doesn't kill bugs with chlorine or leave chlorine in the water. When activated, chlorine dioxide releases highly active concentrated oxygen into the water, and it's this that kills bugs. Treated water tastes fresh, with no aftertaste. The treatment comes in two tiny plastic bottles, one containing stabilized chlorine dioxide, the other an activator (5 percent food-grade phosphoric acid), plus a small mixing cap. The weight is 2.8 ounces, and it will purify 120 quarts. To use the treatment you put seven drops from each bottle in the mixing cap for each quart of water, wait five minutes before adding it to the water to be treated, and then wait another fifteen minutes before using the water. (Double the time and dose

stockponds on both walks and never became ill, so presumably both treatments worked. Tablets have a limited life; you should buy a fresh supply at least annually. Once a bottle is opened, it should be used within a few weeks or else discarded.

Iodine crystals, sold in drugstores, are a long-lasting alternative to tablets. These can be held in solution and small amounts poured into water bottles when required, though you need to be sure no undissolved crystals enter the drinking water. Polar Pure (3 ounces dry weight; more, of course, when the crystals are in solution) contains iodine crystals, thermometer (to check water temperature—cold water needs more of the solution), and instructions, and will purify 2,000 quarts of water. It's safer to use than crystals alone, since there's a filter cone inside the bottle that prevents the crystals from accidentally falling into your drinking water. However, it's heavier than crystals or tablets,

Aquamira chlorine dioxide water purification.

for cold or cloudy water and if *Cryptosporidium* is suspected—though how you suspect it I've no idea.) Rather than waiting fifteen or thirty minutes each time you fill up with water, you can simply wait five, add the drops to the water, and then hike on with it in your pack. There are two brands of chlorine dioxide, Aquamira and Pristine, though they seem to be effectively the same. I used Aquamira on the Arizona Trail, when I drank from some really murky cattle ponds at times, and stayed healthy.

Katadyn also offers a chlorine dioxide treatment called MP1 Emergency Drinking Water Tablets. These don't require the use of an activator, which would make them easier to use than Aquamira. You just add one tablet to a quart of water and wait fifteen minutes to kill bacteria and viruses and thirty to kill protozoans. That's if the water is clear and at 68°F (20°C). If the water is dirty and the temperature 40°F (5°C), it takes four hours to kill *Cryptosporidium*. The times remain the same for other bugs. I haven't used MP1 Tablets, but they're lightweight and easy to use and so worth considering. There are thirty tablets in a pack.

The latest method of chemical treatment is the MSR MIOX Purifier, which is unlike anything else. This battery-operated Purifier is a flashlight-like tube measuring 1 inch by 7 inches. To use it you add salt to the unit followed by a tiny amount (¼ teaspoon) of water. You shake the salt and water to create a brine solution and press a button. This sends a small electrical charge through the solution creating a chemical reaction (electrolysis) that produces a "cocktail" of mixed oxidants (MIOX) that when added to untreated water kills any bugs. One dose will purify up to a gallon of water. The whole procedure only takes a few minutes but, as with other purification treatments, you then have to wait to be sure it has worked; thirty minutes for most bugs and a long four hours for *Cryptosporidium*.

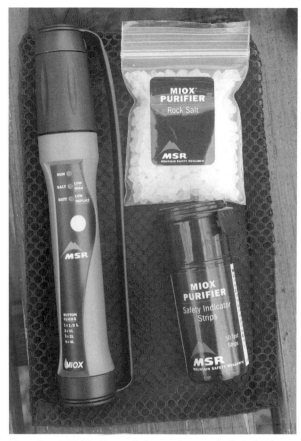

The unique MIOX Purifier works by creating a cocktail of mixed oxidants that kills all bugs.

Purity-indicator strips show the water has been purified. Although there is a strong smell of brine when the solution is added to the water, there is no aftertaste. The MIOX runs off two CR-123 lithium camera batteries and will purify more than two hundred liters on one set. The tube weighs 2.2 ounces without batteries and the whole kit, which includes batteries, salt, purity-indicator strips, instructions, and stuff sack, 8 ounces. It's fairly easy to use, though you have to be careful to follow the sequence of actions correctly. I'd certainly rather use it than most filters, as it seems much more foolproof.

Lightweight, compact water filters (from left): First Need DeLuxe, MSR MiniWorks, Katadyn Hiker, Sweetwater Guardian.

FILTERS Filtration is the high-tech way to treat water and the most common method, though it's not my favorite. Indeed, though I've tested several pump filters over the years, including models from MSR, Sweetwater Guardian, First Need, and Katadyn, I've never taken one backpacking. In my opinion they're all too heavy, too complicated, too inefficient, and too unreliable. I'm unhappy about the need to keep them clean and use them correctly, too. I found this difficult at home; it must be much harder when you're tired, cold, and thirsty at the end of a long day on the trail, yet it's essential if filters are to be effective. I've seen people handling filters with dirty hands, letting the outlet tube dangle in the dirt, allowing water still to be filtered to splash over the filter, and storing filters unwrapped in the pack: I definitely felt safer drinking straight creek water than their filtered supply. Filters can be hard to pump and clog very easily. Carrying a replacement cartridge or a chemical disinfectant as a backup is advisable. Cleaning filters is necessary, too, which means carrying cleaning items on a long trip. Like any piece of gear, a filter isn't magic, despite what some users seem to think. Study the

instructions carefully, practice at home, and make sure you know how to clean and store the filter properly.

The key with any filter is the pore size, since this determines what it will filter out. For *Giardia* and *Cryptosporidium* an absolute (maximum) pore size of 0.5 micron is the minimum needed; smaller pores are better, since pores may enlarge with use. Whether the filter is ceramic, carbon, or fiberglass and exactly how it works are far less important.

Filters come in three forms: bottle feed, gravity feed, and pump. The first are simple filters that substitute for the lid of a water bottle. They're lightweight and easy to use, though you have to squeeze fairly hard to get water out. I wouldn't want to use one if I needed large amounts of water, but for drinking from on the trail they're all right. The tiny TFO Gatekeeper fits into a TFO or Platypus bottle, weighs a minuscule 0.5 ounce, and will filter up to 25 gallons. Other bottle filters are heavier. As an emergency backup, the Gatekeeper could be worth carrying.

Pump and gravity-feed filters are better for camp and group use. Pumping can be slow—a quart a minute is good—and surprisingly tiring, but it can be used for any amount of water. Of the pump filters I've tried, I most liked the Katadyn Hiker (formerly the Pur Hiker—Katadyn took over Pur), which weighs 11 ounces, has 0.3-micron pores, and has a pump rate of 1 quart per minute. The Hiker was easier to use than other models and is quite light and compact. If I carried a pump filter it would be this one.

With gravity-feed filters a bag of water is hung up with the filter unit and a hose leading into a water container below it. The first gravity filter I tried, the 15.5-ounce First Need DeLuxe, (which also has a pump option and is a purifier as well as a filter), took ten minutes to filter a quart of water. Much lighter and faster is Ultralight Adventure Equipment's H2O Amigo, which weighs 8.5 ounces, including 0.9 ounce stuff sack. It takes about 1 minute to filter a quart, depending on how full the water bag is (it holds 1.25 gallons) and how dirty the water is. Sediment settles at the bottom of the water bag and there is a prefilter in the bag to stop larger contaminants from reaching the main

ABOVE: The ULA H2O Amigo, a gravity-feed filter. FAR LEFT: First Need DeLuxe filter/purifier fitted to a Sigg bottle. LEFT: Putting the inlet hose in a creek before filtering water.

filter. ULA says the filter will remove 99.8 percent of contaminants. The filter-unit life is over a hundred gallons. I prefer gravity filters to pump ones as you can do other things while the filter is working and they are generally simpler in design and easier to use. I can see one disadvantage though: you need something to hang them from. In forests this is no problem, but in deserts or above timberlines it could be difficult. I guess you could just hold the filter up, though this would be tiring. If I had to use a filter, the H2O Amigo is the one I would choose . . . as long as there were trees around.

Filters can remove bacteria, organic chemicals, and protozoans, including *Giardia*. They can't remove viruses unless they also include chemical disinfection, in which case you might as well just use chemicals.

Powdered Drinks

Clear, cold mountain stream water is the most refreshing drink there is, the main reason I'm reluctant to treat water unless absolutely necessary. Aquamira doesn't make water taste unpleasant, but the waiting time does remove some of the sparkle. If you like to flavor water, Kool-Aid, Wyler's, and similar fruit-flavored powdered drink mixes are the traditional choice. There are three versions: those to which you add sugar, those containing sugar, and those containing artificial sweeteners. Those presweetened with sugar are the most useful—if you're carrying the stuff, you might as well get a few extra kilocalories.

The modern alternatives to fruit-flavored sugar and chemical concoctions are powdered sports drinks like Gatorade and Gookinaid E.R.G. These contain electrolytes (potassium and sodium chloride) to replace those depleted through heavy sweating, plus carbohydrates and often much

other stuff, sometimes including vitamins and minerals. While such drinks may be useful for athletes, they're not needed for backpacking, even in desert regions. I've drunk them on occasion but never noticed any difference from drinking water and munching snacks, which I find more enjoyable. Such drinks have almost replaced salt tablets, which are no longer recommended because they're too high in sodium and low in potassium. Over twenty years ago on my first desert hike across the Mojave Desert, I followed the current advice and carried salt tablets, though I never used them. Oral rehydration salts, which contain potassium as well as sodium, could be carried as an emergency item, though I've never done so.

Bottles, Bags, and Hydration Systems

Even where water is plentiful, you need some form of water container. In dry, hot country several may be essential, and they need to be of good quality, since a container failure could be serious. For that reason I always carry two or more containers, never just one large one. That said, it's been many, many years since I had a container leak. Water containers used to be simple items. There were rigid ones—bottles or canteens—for carrying water and large, soft compressible water bags for camp use. Now we have hydration systems and reservoirs with drinking hoses, all made from flexible plastic, and the distinction between trail and camp containers has vanished.

Traditional rigid bottles come in a wide variety of shapes, sizes, and makes and in both plastic and aluminum, though the latter are becoming scarce—Sigg is one of the few remaining makes. Aluminum keeps liquids cooler in warm weather than plastic. A lacquered inside stops fruit juice or sports drinks from dissolving the aluminum and tainting the drink. Plastic bottles warm up more quickly. Food-grade ones don't taint water. When you need to carry little water, pint bottles are adequate, but I prefer quarts for general use.

The classic aluminum bottles are the Swiss-made lacquered Sigg bottles, now called Traveler bottles. These come in half-pint, pint, and quart sizes, weighing 3, 4, and 5 ounces. Sigg bottles are durable and have screw tops with rubber seals that don't leak—at least none of mine ever have. But they also have narrow openings, which make them hard to fill from seeps and trickles.

The big name in rigid plastic bottles is Nalgene. They come in rectangular and round shapes, in several sizes, and with narrow and wide mouths. I find the quart wide-mouth round Lexan bottle (5 ounces) the most useful, since it's easy to fill from small trickles. Nalgene bottles are leakproof and hardwearing, unlike some cheaper bottles that leak and crack along the seams after a relatively short time. They're made from high- and low-density polyethylene and more durable but slightly heavier Lexan polycarbonate. The Loop-Top bottles with attached caps are useful if you're careless. (I've twice spent an hour or more searching for bottle caps I dropped in creeks—luckily I found them both times.)

Lighter and less expensive alternatives to the bottles found in outdoor stores are plastic soda bottles. Most of these are tough and long lasting. When I needed extra bottles for a two-week hike in the Grand Canyon, I bought two quart-size bottles of Gatorade, drank the contents the first day out, then used the bottles (3 ounces empty) for the rest of the trip. Ten years later, I'm still using them.

Many bottles have caps with valves so you can drink from them without removing the cap, often by squeezing the bottle. These are convenient if you want to drink while hiking, but I find they leak easily, so I carry them outside the pack in a mesh pocket or external bottle holder. I sometimes carry a 3-ounce polyethylene wide-mouthed GoLite bottle with a 21-ounce capacity that the company describes as a squirt bottle. (This bottle came with a tiny 50-cubic inch lumbar pack called the Quick—there are plenty of similar ones.)

Rigid bottles are heavy and bulky compared with the flexible ones that I now use for amounts larger than a quart and that can be packed flat when empty. I first tried these on the Arizona Trail; I reckoned I needed enough containers to carry three gallons, and I didn't want to rely on just one or two, both in case of failure and because very large bottles are hard to fit in the pack. I also knew that the large water bags I had previously used in camp (see below) weren't comfortable for carrying water. Wanting to keep the weight of the containers to a minimum, I chose Platypus bottles (made by Cascade Designs), the lightest I could find. The quart size weighs just under an ounce, the two-and-a-half-quart size 1.35 ounces. I carried four of the former and two of the latter for a total weight of 6.7 ounces and a capacity of 9 quarts. Because I wasn't totally convinced that such thin, flimsy-seeming containers would survive long, I also carried a quart Nalgene bottle, useful for getting water out of tiny seeps and trickles, for which narrow-necked Platypus bottles are pretty useless, and a 4-quart flexible Ortlieb Water Bag (3 ounces). I'd used the last for years and knew it was tough. My concerns were unfounded, and the three Platypus bottles that did the whole trail survived intact and are still in regular use four years later, though one has started to delaminate around the neck. (I didn't need all these containers, and I ended up putting the Ortlieb and three of the quart Platypus bottles in my running supply box.) Platypus bottles have a triple-layer laminate with food-grade polyethylene as the inner layer plus welded seams. They will stand upright when there's water in them and are the best large flexible containers I've found for carrying water.

The standard Platypus bottles have a narrow neck that makes them awkward to fill in narrow streams or still water and hard to clean and dry. Big Zip Platypus reservoirs open fully at one end, which solves these problems. The zip closures add a fair bit of weight, however, and although they seem secure I don't have the same confidence in them as in a screw-on cap. I'd prefer not to have openings at both ends, either. Other containers, such as those from Vaude and Dana Design, come with roll-down ends that clip in place. The 1-quart Platypus Big Zip weighs 3.5 ounces, the 2-quart 4.5 ounces. Nalgene, seeing the market for rigid bottles dwindling, leaped into the soft bottle fray with products they call Cantenes. These come with wide or narrow mouths. The wide-mouth 1-quart model weighs 2.1 ounces, the narrow-mouth 1.6 ounces.

On most trips I currently carry one wide-mouth rigid bottle, for ease of getting water out of shallow creeks and seeps, plus two 2.5-quart Platypus bottles. The latter are large enough that I only need to make one trip for water for camp, which minimizes impact and means I don't have to leave camp again in stormy weather. When I started backpacking my camp water container was a collapsible water bag that held two gallons and weighed 3.5 ounces. This consisted of a double-layer flexible plastic inner bladder and a nylon cover, with a leakproof spigot and two webbing handles. All the parts were replaceable, and ripstop tape could be used for emergency repairs—and the bags did develop holes rather too frequently. Such waterbags are rare now, having been replaced by tougher single-skin bags that don't need covers or two layers, though Moonbow makes one called the Camp Domo (4 ounces).

I replaced that water bag with an Ortlieb Waterbag, made from a single layer of coated nylon with welded seams. My gallon-size model weighs 3 ounces and has proved much tougher than double-layer ones. Of the other brands of water bags, the best quality and probably the most durable (but also the most expensive) are MSR's Dromedary Bags, made from laminated Cordura nylon with brass grommets laced with webbing along each side. They hold 2, 4, 6, and 10 quarts at weights of 4.6, 5.4, 7.2, and 8.5 ounces. MSR DromLite Bags, made from lighter fabric and without grommets and webbing, come in 2-, 4-, and 6-quart sizes at weights of 3.1, 3.6, and 4.2 ounces.

Other uses of a water bag are as a portable shower and, so I'm told, as a pillow. They aren't, however, very good for carrying water in the pack. The larger ones are especially awkward. I carried my two-gallon one full a number of times, usually strapped to the top or back of my pack, and the water sloshed around, altering the balance of the load in an unnerving way. For short distances I carried the bag in my hand by its strap. The Ortlieb bag isn't much better; it also feels like wobbly jelly in the pack. I find Platypus bottles far more comfortable in the pack, since they'll stand upright and behave much more like rigid bottles. Two bottles are easier to pack and to lift and pour from as well.

Hydration systems are flexible water containers (often known as bladders) with long tubes attached that dangle over your shoulder so you can drink while hiking. I've tried these, and I have to say I dislike sucking on a tube as I hike. I prefer to stop and take swigs from a water bottle. However, my stepdaughter uses one, and they are so popular that many packs come with sleeves for the containers. CamelBak was the first model to appear, but there are now plenty of others from Platypus, Nalgene, MSR, and more. Having quick access is a good idea, of course. I like to carry my water bottle in a mesh pocket or bottle holder on the side of the pack, where I can reach it easily.

In winter a thermos is very useful. By filling it with hot water in the evening, I have warm water that soon comes to a boil in the morning, speeding up breakfast. If I fill it before leaving camp, I can enjoy hot drinks (usually hot fruit juice, sometimes soup) during the day without needing to stop and fire up the stove. The best ones are unbreakable stainless steel. After smashing several glass-lined ones, I purchased a Coleman stainless steel pint thermos, which weighs 18.5 ounces. Each of its many dents shows how many glass-lined ones I would have broken. Steel ones have become lighter since I bought the Coleman, so I retired it to car use in favor of a pint Zojirushi Tuffslim Compact model with push-pour spout that weighs 11.5 ounces.

Another alternative is an insulated bottle cover. I have an Outdoor Research Water Bottle Parka that holds a 1-quart Nalgene bottle. It weighs 4 ounces, so with the bottle the weight is still half that of the stainless steel flask, yet with twice the capacity. The covers won't keep liquids hot for long, so they aren't suitable for coffee unless you like it lukewarm, but they're fine for fruit juice. Platypus makes an insulated bottle holster for their quart flexible bottles that weighs 5.5 ounces.

It's best to store water containers uncapped, so they can fully dry and not become musty. If ordinary washing doesn't clean them fully, soak them in a mild solution of bicarbonate of soda. Iodine, chlorine, or bleach can also be used for disinfecting bottles. Wash containers regularly to prevent the buildup of dirt, especially around the screw threads.

THE CAMPFIRE

Many people find sitting around a campfire the ideal way to end a day in the wilderness. But in too many places badly situated and constructed fires have left scars that will take decades to heal, and too many trees have been stripped of their lower branches, or even hacked down, to provide fuel. Even collecting fallen wood can damage the environment if not enough is left to replenish soil nutrients and provide shelter for animals and food for insects and fungi.

It is far better, and more efficient, to use a stove for cooking and clothing and shelter for warmth. But an essential element of the wilderness experience would be lost if you could never light campfires, and although I cook on a stove 99 percent of the time, I do occasionally light a fire. Fires should be treated as a luxury, however, and lit only where they have minimal impact on the environment. When the risk of forest fires is very high, fires may be banned for short periods. In areas where there has been too much damage or that are environmentally sensitive (often above the timberline), fires may be banned all the time. In national parks you may need fire permits and may be required to carry a stove. Such regulations may seem restrictive, but they prevent further degradation of popular areas.

Fires, officially permitted or not, are inappropriate in some areas, anyway. They shouldn't be lit at and above the timberline, because trees and shrubs grow slowly there and the nutrients from deadwood are needed to replenish the thin soil.

In other areas, fires can sometimes be lit even on pristine sites without significant harm to the environment, as long as you use Leave No Trace techniques. The ideal places for such fires are on mineral soil (sand and gravel) below the high-

RIGHT: The results of poorly sited, misused, and overused campfires. Notice that the ground is trampled and bare, there is an unnecessary rock ring, and firewood and log seats litter the area. A fire should leave no trace. BELOW: No Fires sign in the Grand Canyon.

water mark on the coast and below the spring flood level along rivers—any traces will be washed away, and there is usually plenty of driftwood to burn.

Fires should be built on mineral soil in other pristine places, too, and never lit on organic matter, for both environmental and safety reasons. In particular, meadows and soft vegetation should never be scarred by a fire. Dry vegetation and forest duff—conifer needles—can burst into flame very easily.

Mound fires make the least impact but require the most effort. To build one you first need to find some mineral soil such as sand from a streambed that is already disturbed. Dig up enough soil to fill a large stuff sack, then heap 6 to 8 inches of it on top of a groundsheet, trash bag, or other piece of cloth. The fire can be built in a shallow depression on top of the mound and should always be much smaller than the mound so that hot coals can't fall off the mineral soil. The mound should be built in an area that will stand up to trampling, such as bare rock or earth.

Digging into the ground to create a pit for the fire is destructive and should be done only on mineral soil where there is no organic matter at all. Fires can be lit without a pit, but digging one makes it easier to disguise the site afterward.

Do not build a ring of rocks around a fire on a pristine site. Many people construct a fireplace this way, yet it really serves no purpose, although the concept is that it contains the fire. The best way to prevent a fire from spreading is to clear the area around it of flammable materials; a site 24 to 36 inches across should be big enough. Make sure there are no low branches or tree roots above or below the fire, and pitch your shelter upwind and some distance away, so that sparks can't harm it.

Other gear, especially nylon, also needs to be kept well away from fires.

Leave no sign of your fire. All wood should be burned to a fine ash, then scattered widely before you return the mineral soil to the place it came from. Spreading duff and loose vegetation over the site helps conceal it.

If you camp at a well-used site with many rock-ringed fireplaces, use one of these rather than making a new one, even a minimum-impact one. To reduce the impact it's best to dismantle the least-used fire rings, scattering any ashes and charcoal, in the hope that they won't be used again. Some backcountry sites in national parks have metal fireboxes. Obviously you should use them. Cut wood may also be supplied at such sites to prevent damage to the surrounding forest.

When collecting fuel wood, do so with care. Do not remove wood—even deadwood—from living trees. Snags are needed by wildlife and enhance the scenery and should also be left alone. A campsite surrounded by trees stripped of their lower branches and bare ground picked clean of every twig is depressing. In high-use areas, search for wood farther afield rather than close to the site. Shorelines and riverbanks are good places to scavenge for wood. Collect only what you'll use, and use only small sticks that you can break by hand, since these are easily burned to ash. You don't need axes and saws.

Lighting and Tending the Fire

There's a certain mystique to fire lighting, and survival and woodcraft books devote many pages to describing types of fires. Basically, the secret of fire lighting is simple: start small, with dry tinder. Paper makes good tinder, but I wouldn't carry it just for this purpose. I sometimes lighten my load

sprinkle water on the ashes

stir the coals with a stick and sprinkle again until no more steam rises

feel the ashes to be sure they're cool

scatter the ashes over an unvegetated area

A properly doused campfire leaves no ashes at the site.

by using pages from the books I've read; food wrappings work well, too. If you have no paper, you can use the finest twigs, tiny pinecones, dry leaves, moss, and any other dry plant material. When the weather is wet, look for kindling in dry spots under logs and at the base of large trees. Good kindling can be created by shaving slivers three-quarters of the way off a dry twig to make a

A feather stick.

feather stick. A candle stub or solid fuel tablet can be used, too.

Once you have a small pile of kindling, build a pyramid of small dry twigs around it, making sure there's plenty of air space. Then light the kindling. When the twigs start to catch, add slightly larger pieces of wood. Don't overdo it—it's easy to smother a new fire. At this stage the fire's shape is irrelevant; you can alter it once it's burning well. I try to arrange an area of hot coals at one end of a cooking fire—coals, not flames, provide heat. Small metal grills with short legs make balancing pans over an open fire easy. The Coghlan's Pack Grill (11 ounces) I carried on my long hike in the Yukon was worth the weight, because I often cooked over fires. Cake racks also make good lightweight grills—rest the ends on rocks.

If lighting the fire proves difficult, dismantle it and start over; don't waste kindling by pushing bits of it into the fire and lighting them. People occasionally use stove fuel to get a fire going. This is highly dangerous. *Never throw fuel onto a smoldering fire that won't light properly.* And never do something I once saw in a shelter one damp December night. Having failed to light the pile of damp wood stacked haphazardly in the fireplace, another occupant of the shelter attempted to ignite it with his lit canister stove. I was busy cooking over my stove at the time, so my companion hastily decided to devote herself to getting the fire lit conventionally and took over. Luckily, she succeeded.

Never leave a fire unattended, and make sure the ashes are cold to the touch before you leave the next day—huge areas of forest have burned because of carelessness with campfires. If you're not scattering the ashes to the four winds because they're in a well-used fire ring, douse them with water to make sure they're out. Foil or silver-lined food wrappings won't burn, so don't toss them in the fire unless you're prepared to fish them out and carry them with you when you leave. This applies to hut fires as well; I've spent many hours cleaning out shelter fireplaces blocked by foil.

STOVES

Stoves have replaced wood fires for most backcountry cooking. A stove ensures that you can have hot food and drink quickly whenever you want or need it. I always carry one. In foul weather, a stove enables me to cook in the vestibule or under a tarp while I stay warm and dry inside. When you wake up to the sound of wind and rain on the fly sheet, it's wonderful to reach out, light the stove—on which you'd set a pan of water the night before—and quickly have a hot drink to brace you for the weather outside.

Perhaps it's because they're the modern version of the campfire and represent warmth, sustenance, and safety that stoves arouse such strong passions. Advocates of particular brands or models will argue fiercely that their chosen stoves are best. Some stoves are beautiful pieces of engineering, too—I have an Optimus Svea 123R displayed on a shelf in my study—and some people collect them and like to search out old models. For those interested in this, an excellent resource is the Classic Camp Stoves Web site—spiritburner.com. This is also the site to go to if you're trying to find spare parts for a stove, particularly an old one.

There used to be few stoves to choose from, but the numbers have expanded greatly in recent years. Quality is generally good, although in some situations a malfunctioning stove is merely a nuisance, at other times it could be a serious problem, particularly if you're relying on it for cooking dried food or need to melt snow for water. Some stoves work well in the cold and wind, others don't. A stove that won't produce hot water when you're cold, wet, and tired is at the very least dispiriting. If you're on the verge of hypothermia it could be dangerous.

A good stove should be capable of bringing water to a boil under the most horrendous conditions you're likely to encounter, small and light enough to carry, and reasonably simple to operate. Ideally it should be field maintainable, too. Stability is also important, particularly with stoves that will be used with large pans.

Comparisons and Weights

Charts and tables that compare the weights, rates of fuel consumption, and boiling times of various stoves can be misleading. Many factors that affect a stove's performance in the field can't be duplicated in a controlled environment; moreover, individual stoves of the same model can perform very differently.

Weights aren't always easily comparable either—some models include windscreens and pan sets in the total weight. The amount of fuel you have to carry for a given period and the weight of the fuel container need to be included in the total weight as well. Often the fuel plus its container is much heavier than the stove itself.

I've carried out my own stove tests (see sidebar, pages 282–83), so you can at least compare my findings with others'. Please note all the caveats. My overall conclusions are that all the stoves are efficient and pretty reliable. I wouldn't use boil time as the main reason for choosing a stove; take into account reliability, weight, and type of fuel. In general, any half-decent stove should bring a quart of water to a boil within ten minutes of being lit, as long as the burner is adequately shielded from the wind and the pan is covered; and no backpacking stove should weigh more than 25 ounces, excluding pans and windscreen. Most weigh far less.

Fuels

The availability of fuel may determine which stove you carry, especially on a long hike where you need to resupply with fuel. The choices are solid fuel, alcohol, kerosene, white gas, and butane-propane.

Different areas of the world favor different fuels, which is worth knowing if you range widely, as I do. In Scandinavia, alcohol is the common fuel; in the Alps and Pyrenees, it's butane-propane; in Africa and Asia, kerosene. This doesn't mean you won't find other fuels in those places; but you're more likely, especially in out-of-the-way places, to find the fuels that local people favor. Automotive gasoline can be found everywhere, of course, though obtaining small amounts can be difficult. Filling a quart-size aluminum fuel bottle from a high-pressure pump at a gas station isn't easy, and in my experience the fuel usually sprays everywhere. (Three of us refueled this way during my Pacific Crest Trail hike, and I'd rather not have to do it again. The gas station staff thought the whole episode was hilarious and charged us only for the amount in our bottles rather than the somewhat larger amount vaporizing off our clothes and their bays.)

How much fuel you use each day depends on the type of stove you have, the weather, and the type of cooking you do. If you cook three meals a day, bake foods, or simmer foods for a long time, you'll use more fuel than I do, since I cook just one meal a day and boil water for a hot drink at breakfast. My stove is running for approximately 30 to 45 minutes a day, and my figures for how long fuels last are based on this. If you run your stove for longer or shorter periods, you'll need to adapt my figures. Estimates should be doubled if you're melting snow, because it takes the same amount of energy to produce a given amount of water from snow as it does to bring that amount

STOVE PERFORMANCE

Model	Fuel	Weight (oz.)	Boiling Time (min., sec.)
WHITE-GAS, MULTIFUEL STOVES			
MSR XGK Expedition	Coleman fuel	14.5	5, 30
	kerosene		6, 50
MSR WhisperLite Internationale	Coleman fuel	14	4, 58
	kerosene		4, 30
MSR DragonFly	Coleman fuel	16.5	5, 30
	kerosene		5 min.
MSR SimmerLite*	Coleman fuel	8.5	2, 45
Optimus Nova	Coleman fuel	15	4, 4
	kerosene		3, 47
Optimus Svea 123R	Coleman fuel	19	6 min.
Coleman Apex II	Coleman fuel	18.5	3, 50
Coleman Feather 442 Dual-Fuel	Coleman fuel	24	2, 55
Coleman Multi-Fuel	Coleman fuel	18.5	4, 10
Primus OmniFuel	butane/propane cartridge	19	2 min.
	Coleman fuel		8, 10
	kerosene		7, 54
CANISTER STOVES			
Coleman Xtreme	Powermax cartridge	10.5	1, 30
Coleman Outlander F1 Ultralight	butane/propane cartridge	3.75	2 min.
Coleman Outlander F1 PowerBoost	butane/propane cartridge	4.75	2 min.
Snow Peak GigaPower Titanium	butane/propane cartridge	2.8	3
MSR WindPro	butane/propane cartridge	7	4, 30
Optimus Crux	butane/propane cartridge	3	2, 25
Primus Micron	butane/propane cartridge	3.5	2, 25
MSR SuperFly	butane/propane cartridge	4.5	2, 20
MSR PocketRocket	butane/propane cartridge	3	2, 55
Markill Hot Shot	butane/propane cartridge	4.5	3, 20
Markill Hot Rod	butane/propane cartridge	3	3, 10
Jetboil	butane/propane cartridge	6 burner, 15 whole unit	4, 30

of water to a boil. The figures assume the use of a full windscreen, whether or not it comes with the stove. My figures are for solo use—but don't assume that the amount of fuel per person is the same regardless of group size. I find that larger groups are far more fuel-efficient. On ski tours I've led, groups of ten used less fuel per person—including melting snow for water—than I would expect to use on a solo summer trip. Fuel use also depends on how careful you are to conserve fuel by running the stove only when necessary, using a windscreen, and covering pots. It's also important not to have the stove turned up so high that flames reach around the sides of the pot, which

Model	Fuel	Weight (oz.)	Boiling Time (min., sec.)
ALCOHOL STOVES			
Trangia	alcohol	2.5 burner, 35 whole unit	15, 30
soda can	alcohol	—	8 min.
Brasslite Turbo II-D	alcohol	2.5	8 min.
WOOD STOVES			
Sierra Stove	wood	18.0	3, 30

* The SimmerLite was tested separately from the other white-gas stoves in warmer weather (65°F [18°C]) and with warmer water (52°F [11°C]).

NOTES:
The test consisted of bringing a pint of water to a rolling boil in a covered 1-quart aluminum pan. The test was conducted over several days. The liquid-fuel stoves were tested first, in air temperatures of 38 to 40°F (3 to 5°C) and water at 42°F (6°C). The cartridge, alcohol, and wood stoves were tested in an air temperature of 58 to 62°F (14 to 17°C) with water at 52°F (11°C). The altitude was 1,000 feet. The test was conducted in windless conditions.

Weight does not include fuel bottles, canisters, or windscreens.

Beware! The table shows the results of one set of tests in benign conditions. To relate it to field use a number of factors need to be taken into account:

1. The fast boil time of the cartridge stoves was achieved using full cartridges. As the cartridges empty, boiling time increases. The colder it is, the more quickly this occurs. The performance of the white-gas/kerosene and alcohol stoves stays the same until they run out of fuel, as long as pressure is maintained.
2. Wind can play havoc with stove performance. The MSR stoves, Primus MultiFuel, and Trangia come with adequate windscreens. The others don't—performance declines drastically in wind unless windscreens are added.
3. Other tests give results wildly different from mine. I cannot explain this. I suspect it's both because there are minor but important differences in the testing procedures and because individual stoves of the same model can perform quite differently. Slight design changes can affect performance, too.

wastes fuel. Adjust the stove so the flame just covers the bottom of the pot.

Models

There have been many changes in the world of stoves. A number of interesting new multifuel and white-gas stoves have appeared. One company, Sigg, has stopped producing stoves completely, and stoves that use only kerosene have vanished. Vastly more cartridge stoves have sprung up, most of them ultralight models. At the same time that the choice in the stores has increased and the weight of stoves has come down, there's been a surge of interest in homemade stoves constructed from soda cans.

Different features are needed in different circumstances. No one stove is best for all situations. Good simmer control is essential for those who cook complex meals, but maximum heat output is more important for melting snow, and weight is crucial for ultralight hikers.

Solid-Fuel Stoves

In my opinion solid fuel isn't efficient enough for proper cooking, but it has become popular with some ultralight hikers because of the extremely low weight, ease of use, and lack of anything that can go wrong. Attracted by the very low weight, I tried solid fuel many years ago, but I soon grew tired of the long wait for water to boil, if it did at all. However, hikers have used solid fuel on through-hikes of the Appalachian and Pacific Crest Trails, so it works for some people. If your cooking needs are minimal or you usually use a campfire, solid fuel might be of interest. The Esbit Solid Fuel Stove weighs 3.25 ounces. It's really just a platform for a fuel tablet (0.5 ounce) with two fold-up pan supports. Many people make their own solid-fuel stoves, and there are several Web sites showing you how (see the Wings Homemade Stoves Archive at http://wings.interfree.it). Hexamine tablets (Esbit, Coghlan's) are reckoned by aficionados to be more efficient than trioxane tablets. One advantage of solid fuel is that you can mail it.

Alcohol Stoves

Alcohol in the form of methanol (wood alcohol, methyl alcohol), ethanol (ethyl alcohol, grain alcohol), or isopropyl alcohol (rubbing alcohol, shellac thinner, solvent alcohol, alcohol stove fuel) can be found in drugstores, hardware stores, and outdoor stores, frequently under the names methylated spirits and denatured alcohol. Often the three types are mixed together. Gas-line antifreeze made from methanol can be used in alcohol stoves, though you should check the contents to be sure it is alcohol. Isopropyl alcohol doesn't burn as cleanly or as hot as methanol or ethanol, but it does work, and of course as rubbing alcohol you can use it on your feet! Pure ethanol can be used to make alcoholic drinks and so is expensive because of excise tax. It burns well, though. The type found in paint thinners and methylated spirits has methanol and other substances added to "denature" it and make it poisonous and therefore inexpensive, since it's not liable for duty. Don't drink it! And of course you can burn brandy or rum in an alcohol stove if you run out of other fuel.

Alcohol is the only liquid fuel not derived from petroleum, which makes it more environmentally friendly than other fuels. It's also the only liquid fuel that burns unpressurized, which makes it safer, and thus appealing to those who find most stoves a little scary. It's clean, too, evaporating quickly when spilled. For these reasons, it's a good fuel for cooking in a tent vestibule. It's not a hot fuel, however—it produces roughly half as much heat per fluid ounce as gasoline or kerosene. I use 4 to 5 fluid ounces a day, so a quart lasts about a week, which makes it heavier than other fuels to carry on long trips. Trangia says that a quart of alcohol will boil twenty quarts of water, which fits with my experience, since I boil 2 to 4 quarts a day. As alcohol stoves heat up the output increases, so the first pot boiled will take longer than the second, and that one will take longer than the third. That's as long as you protect the stove from the wind, of course. Strong gusts can blow out an alcohol stove.

Alcohol blackens pans, which many people don't like. This doesn't bother me; in theory, blackened pans should absorb heat faster than shiny silver ones, so I make no attempt to clean off the black. Once pans have cooled, the soot rarely comes off on your hands, unlike the soot from campfires.

One joy of alcohol stoves is that they are absolutely silent—you can hear water coming to a boil and also the wind in the trees, birdsong, the hum of insects, and other sounds that are drowned out by the roar of most stoves. Care is needed when using alcohol in daylight because the pale blue flame is invisible in bright light. Most stoves burn for only half an hour at most on one filling (depending on the wind and the use of any simmer device), so refilling while the stove is in use is sometimes necessary. However, inadvertently refilling a still-burning stove from a fuel bottle because you think it's empty could cause the fuel bottle to ignite. Sometimes there can be a small flame left even if there doesn't appear to be any heat given off. If a stove goes out during use, I refill it by pouring fuel into the burner cover or other small container, then into the burner. If this item catches fire, I simply drop it onto the stove. It is of course important to be sure there are no flammable items near any stove.

When packing an alcohol stove, I pour any unused fuel back into the fuel bottle after the burner has cooled; fuel tends to leak if carried in the burner, though Trangias come with a sealed lid that is effective as long as you don't melt the rubber O-ring by putting it on a hot burner. I also pack the burner in a plastic bag and carry it separately from the pans so that it doesn't dirty them and leave a lingering smell of fuel. Alcohol can be carried in light plastic bottles. Heavy metal ones aren't necessary, which saves a little of the extra weight of fuel needed.

TRANGIA ALCOHOL STOVES Alcohol is very popular in Scandinavia, and the Swedish-made Trangia Storm-Cookers are well made, simple, and almost indestructible.

Trangias come in several versions. Most are complete units, including burner, windscreen/pan support, pans, lid, and pot grab, that nest together for carrying. The excellent little burner itself weighs 2.5 ounces and consists of a short double-walled open brass cylinder with jets around the top, into which you pour fuel—2 fluid ounces fills it. To light it, you simply touch a match to the alcohol. In Trangia 25 and 27 units the burner rests inside a rigid aluminum windscreen, which contains foldout pan supports. With a lid over the top you have virtually a sealed unit, so heat loss is minimal. There are small holes in one side of the windscreen base, which can be turned into the wind to create a draft and make a stronger flame—these are the only stoves I know that boil water more quickly when it's windy. The flame can be controlled somewhat by dropping a simmer ring (0.75 ounce) over the jets so that only the sur-

Trangia alcohol stove with windscreen.

Trangia alcohol stove with windscreen, pans, and pot grab.

face of the reservoir is burning, then partially covering this with a flat metal disk, which you knock into place with a spoon or knife until you achieve the required degree of heat. It's a crude system and awkward to operate, but it does work. One filling burns for 20 to 30 minutes and will boil a couple of quarts.

Trangia 25 and 27 units come in two sizes, each with two pans, a frypan/lid, and an optional kettle. The cook kit comes in plain aluminum, nonstick aluminum, and Duossal (a laminate of stainless steel and aluminum) versions. For solo use, the Trangia 27 is ideal; including two 1-quart pans, lid, and pot grab, it weighs 30 ounces with aluminum or nonstick pans and 32 ounces with Duossal pans (without the pans and pot grab, the unit weighs 15 ounces). Substituting the pint-size kettle for one of the pans brings the weight up by an ounce. The larger Trangia 25 models have 1.5- and 1.75-quart pans and an optional quart kettle. The 25 weighs 38, 45, or 49 ounces, depending on the pan material—too heavy for one backpacker but fine for two or three. There is also a Mini-

Trangia (Trangia 28) consisting of the burner, a simplified windscreen, and a quart pan with frypan/lid that weighs 11.5 ounces, plus the Trangia Westwind, which is just the burner plus pot supports and weighs 6.6 ounces. All the Trangia parts are sold separately, so you could just buy the burner, and perhaps the simmer ring and cover, and construct your own lightweight pot supports and windscreen.

A Trangia 27 was my first backpacking stove. I've had one for about thirty years. For a decade it was my regular stove and has been all over Scotland, Norway in summer and winter, Iceland, and on my 1,250-mile walk from one end of Britain to the other. Although dented, it still works perfectly. There is so little to go wrong that it's just about indestructible. Indeed, I've heard of a Trangia that was run over by a truck; the windscreen was simply beaten back into shape before being returned to use. I haven't taken mine on long trips for many years, though, because of the weight both of the unit itself and of the fuel. Despite what many people believe, the Trangia works well in cold weather, though it can be hard to get the fuel to light. I find the best method is to drop a lighted match into the burner.

HOMEMADE ALCOHOL STOVES Making your own stove might seem a rather difficult and even risky business, but with alcohol stoves it isn't, since they're so simple. The ultralight hiking movement, which seems to harbor a surprising number of innovative and inventive people, has spawned a mass of designs for homemade alcohol stoves. Wings Homemade Stoves Archive lists twenty-eight, most of them alcohol stoves, the others wood and solid-fuel stoves. Many of the alcohol stove designs are similar to a Trangia burner but much lighter because they're made from thin aluminum cans. Some weigh as little as 0.35 ounce. I have one of these stoves, though I didn't make it myself; my friend Jake Schas made it for me. It weighs 1.5 ounces including a wire pot stand. The boil time is surprisingly good. It's not silent like the Trangia; you can hear the alcohol boiling inside once it's very hot. Obviously it's nowhere near as durable as a Trangia burner, but it's incredibly light and inexpensive and would do for simple boiling. If you do make your own stove, I advise testing it thoroughly (outside of course) to check that it's safe and durable before taking it into the backcountry.

BRASSLITE Brasslite stoves (brasslite.com) emerged from the homemade alcohol stove scene. These stoves attracted me as soon as I saw one. They look rather like a miniature Optimus Svea 123R (see below), both because they're made of brass and because of the shape. I found that they not only look good, they work well too. There are two Brasslite models—the 0.8-ounce Turbo F and the 2.5-ounce Turbo II-D. The Turbo F is designed for solo use with pans up to 1 quart. The fuel capacity is just 1 fluid ounce, and on full flame it burns for

Homemade soda-can alcohol stove with wire pot support, made by Jake Schas. While inexpensive and very light, this stove lacks any flame control.

nine and a half minutes. It won't boil more than a quart without refueling. The Turbo II-D, the model I have, will handle pots up to 2 quarts capacity with a minimum base size of 5 inches to prevent flames from spilling around the sides, which wastes fuel. Capacity is 2 fluid ounces, and burn time is twenty minutes on full flame. Both burners have fuel chambers with a hole in the top, air ports with a simmer ring that can be closed for simmering, and wire pot supports. The difference is that the II-D has a double-walled chamber, which Brasslite says makes flame control and simmering much easier. The simmer sleeve is closed by moving a lever, which needs to be done with a metal utensil, since it gets hot.

Brasslite recommends use of a foil heat reflector under the stove and a foil windscreen. I used ones from a multifuel stove. I also used Brasslite's

The Brasslite Turbo II-D is an ultralight, hot alcohol stove with a controllable flame.

1.5 ounce, 8-ounce capacity plastic custom fuel bottle, which makes filling the stove easy and precise. The bottle has a reservoir that takes up to half an ounce of fuel. Measurement marks on it make it easy to see how much fuel you're using. I first used the stove on a two-day trip in temperatures below freezing (the lowest was 26°F [−3°C]). Once I learned to squeeze fuel on the priming pan at the base of the stove and light that, the stove lit quickly. It then boiled a pint of water in about eight minutes, about half the time of a Trangia. The simmer sleeve worked well, and by moving it carefully I could control the flame surprisingly well, certainly better than with a Trangia, though not as well as with a canister stove. I like the Brasslite and will be using it on future trips where I don't have to carry more than a few days' fuel at a time. It's not as sturdy as the Trangia, but it's much tougher than soda-can stoves.

OTHER ALCOHOL STOVES Unsurprisingly, some other makers of homemade stoves started offering them

for sale for those who don't want to make their own. Antigravitygear.com sells a 0.4-ounce Beverage Can Alcohol Stove, and Hike N' Light (hikenlight.com) offers a 2-ounce stove. Mo-Go-Gear's (mogogear.com) Go-Torch stove weighs 1.25 ounces including pot stand. Vargo Outdoors (vargooutdoors.com) has a neat little stove, the Triad Titanium, with fold-out pot supports and legs, which weighs just 1.06 ounces. Since it's titanium, it should be much tougher than soda-can stoves. Slightly more sophisticated though still ultralight at 2.5 ounces is the ThermoJet MicroLite Stove (thermojetstove.com), which claims a very fast boiling time of 3 minutes, 45 seconds for a pint of water. This stove has a combustion chamber that doubles as a windscreen plus a simmer control. These stoves look interesting, but I haven't tried any of them.

White-Gas and Multifuel Stoves

White gas is probably the most efficient stove fuel, lighting easily and burning very hot. Automotive gasoline is a substitute; you can get it everywhere, and for stove use it's very cheap. But it's dirty and smoky, clogs fuel lines and jets, which need frequent cleaning when run on it, and gives off fumes you really don't want to breathe. Stoves run best and cleanest on refined white gas such as Coleman fuel, the most common one. White gas is sold in outdoor, sporting, and hardware stores and often, especially in towns near popular national parks or wilderness areas, in supermarkets. White gas is volatile fuel and ignites very easily. It requires a lot of care but it is very efficient. I use 2 to 3 fluid ounces a day, so a quart lasts at least ten days.

Kerosene is easy to get, reasonably cheap, and burns at least as hot as gasoline. MSR says its stoves boil slightly more water per amount of kerosene than of white gas. Kerosene doesn't ignite easily, so it's relatively safe—far safer than white gas. That means it's harder to light, of course. It won't burn just as a liquid as white gas will, so a wick is needed. Multifuel stoves have a pad or wick for this purpose. I find kerosene messy and hard to work with, so I use it only as a last resort. It also stains badly and takes a long time to evaporate, leaving a strong odor unless you use a deodorized version. Refined kerosene (heater or lamp fuel) is much cleaner than crude versions, which can produce dirty, smoky fumes. I became very familiar with kerosene on an eighty-six-day walk up the length of the mountains of Norway and Sweden when I used it in an MSR XGK Expedition. I've also used it on several ski tours in places like Greenland and Spitsbergen, where it has worked fine at −15°F (−26°C). Kerosene is efficient—I use 2 to 3 fluid ounces a day—but the difficulties with lighting and handling mean it's not my favorite fuel.

White-gas and multifuel stoves burn vaporized fuel, not liquid. The fuel has to be pressurized (these are sometimes called *pressure stoves*) to get it to flow to the burner. Once a stove is lit, the heat from the flames keeps the burner hot so that the fuel vaporizes as it leaves the jet. On many stoves the fuel line runs in a loop next to the burner. This preheat tube heats the fuel before it reaches the jet, speeding vaporization, which is particularly useful when using kerosene. In the simplest stoves, the fuel is transmitted from the tank to the burner by a wick that draws it up to the jet.

Originally white-gas stoves had integral fuel tanks sitting under or next to the burner. This design is still around, but most stoves now connect to a fuel bottle with a long fuel line, giving them a low profile that makes them more stable than taller models. Both types operate best when the tanks are at least half full—they should never be totally filled, because then the fuel can't expand, and you won't be able to pressurize the stove properly.

Built-in fuel tanks are usually small, ⅓- to ¾-pint capacity, so they may need refilling every day or two. I find it best to top up the fuel tank last thing before packing away the stove in the morning. That way I'm unlikely to run out while cooking the evening meal. If you run out of fuel while cooking, you must wait for the stove to cool down before you can refill it.

Stoves have either *roarer* or *ported* burners. In the first a stream of vaporized fuel is pushed out of the jet, ignites, and hits a burner plate that spreads it out into a ring of flame. Roarer burners, as you might guess, are noisy. In ported burners the flames come out of a ring of jets, just like a kitchen gas range. Ported burners are much quieter than roarer burners, though still pretty loud. Neither type seems more efficient than the other.

The main makers of white-gas and multifuel stoves are Primus, Optimus, MSR, Snow Peak, and Coleman.

PRIMING For fuel to flow to the burner and then vaporize, it has to be preheated, known as *priming*. Priming liquid-fuel stoves is quite easy, but it does require a little practice and should always be done with care outside, since the fuel can flare up. It's the trickiest part of using a pressure stove. Pump stoves are all primed in much the same way, though you should always follow the specific instructions. First the fuel is pressurized by pumping, usually for about twenty strokes when the bottle or tank is full. Then you open the valve a little and allow a tiny amount of fuel to dribble out into the priming cup or onto the priming pad or burner, depending on the model. Alternatively, you can use priming paste (such as Optimus Burning Paste, which comes in a plastic bottle), alcohol, solid-fuel tablets, or even bits of paper. These are all less likely to flare than fuel from the

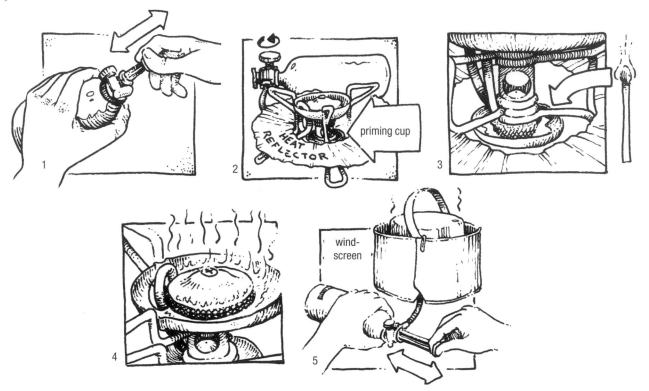

Lighting a white-gas stove. Pump the fuel bottle until you can feel firm resistance when you push the pump in—usually after about twenty strokes when the bottle is full (1). The emptier the bottle, the more pumping is required. It's easiest to do this before you attach the fuel bottle to the stove. When the fuel bottle has been pressurized, open the valve a little until a teaspoon or so of fuel has squirted out and run down into the priming cup or onto the priming wick or pad (2). With stoves without a pump, dribble fuel into the priming cup from a fuel bottle with a pouring spout or an eyedropper filled from the fuel bottle. Light the priming fuel and wait until it has almost burned out (3). Just before it does so open the valve; the stove should roar into life, burning with a blue flame. If the priming flame goes out before you've opened the valve, use a lighter or a match; do this quickly, before the stove cools down. If the stove spurts yellow flames, turn it off; you haven't primed it enough. Wait for the yellow flames to die down, then turn it on again. If it still doesn't light properly, turn it off, wait for it to cool, and then prime it again. Once the stove is lit, let it burn for a minute or so at a low flame and then turn it on full (4). Don't turn the valve more times than recommended in the stove's instructions or you could damage the connection with the bottle. To maintain full power, pump a few strokes every so often (5). If you want a simmering flame, use the stove's simmer control (it it has one), leaving the main valve on full. If there's only one control, turn it down to simmer and don't pump the stove again as it will simmer better with low pressure in the fuel bottle. There will be a short delay between turning a valve on the pump housing and the flame changing. Controls on the burner affect the flame immediately.

stove, but they're something extra to carry. Next you close the valve and light the priming fuel. If you've used too much fuel the stove can flare, so don't have your face over it. As the last flames die away, slowly open the valve again until the burner lights—have a match or lighter handy so you can light the stove if the priming fuel goes out before you open the valve. If you've primed correctly, the flame will be blue. If the flame is yellow you need to turn the stove off and prime it again, after it has cooled down. With stoves that have a control valve on the pump and a flame adjuster at the burner, use the adjuster to control the flow of fuel, leaving the control valve open.

OPTIMUS SVEA 123R The Optimus Svea 123R has been around for over a century and is the classic white-gas stove. (The first Svea stoves were produced by a company called Nyberg and ran on kerosene. Production was three thousand stoves a week in the 1890s.) In the 1960s and 1970s it was one of the most popular white-gas stoves. My first white-gas stove was a Svea that I used on through-hikes of the Pacific Crest and Continental Divide Trails. It performed faultlessly.

The Svea looks like a brass can with perforations; though it doesn't sound attractive, it's aesthetically much more appealing than most stoves. It's made up of a simple roarer burner screwed into a ⅓-pint brass fuel tank and a circular windscreen/pan-support unit that fits around the burner. A small aluminum drinking cup fits over the top to protect the burner when it's in the pack (though I usually leave this at home—it burns your lips). The tank has a screw-on cap with a built-in safety valve designed to release pressure if the tank overheats. (If this happens, the jet of fuel that spurts out will almost certainly become a flame, so it's wise to point the tank cap away from you and anything flammable—like your tent.) The Svea's burner is operated by a key on a chain that fits onto an arm jutting out from the burner and doubles as a maintenance tool. The key is inserted through the windscreen. That and folding out the pan supports are the only setup procedure required, so this stove can be ready to use in seconds.

The Svea doesn't have a pump (though a minipump is an optional extra), so the tank has to be pressurized by priming it. The simplest way to do this is to fill the shallow recess at the foot of the burner tube with about a teaspoon of gasoline

from the fuel bottle (you need a fuel bottle cap with a pouring spout or pouring holes) and light it. Priming paste or alcohol can be used instead, though I don't find them as effective. By the time the last of the flames are dying away, the tank and burner should both be warm enough so that when you turn the key and open the jet the burner lights. If you miss this point, quickly applying a match will usually light the stove. The flame should be blue. If it's yellow, the burner hasn't been primed enough, and the stove is burning semiliquid fuel. Turn it off, let it cool, then prime it again. Once it's lit, you can use the key to control the flame, though the range of control is limited. The key also controls a built-in jet-cleaning needle, operated by turning the key beyond the "on" position. This should be done infrequently to avoid widening the jet hole. The stove will burn at full heat for up to 75 minutes on one filling, according to Optimus,

The Optimus Svea 123 white-gas stove is a classic that has been around for decades.

which seems about right. The Svea is stable enough for small pans, but large ones demand care, because of its tall, narrow shape.

Sveas are tough and long-lived. When I did the burn test for the previous edition, I hauled my blackened Svea—veteran of the Continental Divide Trail but not used for more than five years—out of a jumble of old gear, brushed off the cobwebs, filled the tank, and primed it. It lit straightaway and boiled the water faster than some new white-gas models, which left me wondering why I hadn't used it for so long. I used that same stove for this edition's test.

To make starting the Svea and Hunter (see below) stoves easier, especially in cold weather, there's a pump called the Mini Pump. I've never used one because it can't be fitted to the Svea when the windscreen/pot support is in place. Reports suggest that these pumps can overpressurize the tank and perhaps blow the safety valve, so they must be used with care.

The modern Optimus Nova multifuel stove is easy to light and powerful.

OPTIMUS NOVA While the Svea is a classic white-gas stove, Optimus also make a modern multifuel stove, the Nova, that uses a fuel bottle as the tank and is arguably the most advanced model yet made. In my tests it's certainly the quickest priming and easiest to use. It has a redesigned burner unit with conductor ribs that transfer heat to the fuel tube below the burner much more quickly than traditional designs do. This means that priming only takes 15 to 30 seconds with white gas and a little longer with kerosene, which is much faster than with other stoves. Whichever fuel you use, you don't need to change the jet, an excellent feature that saves time, the hassle of having to take the stove apart, and the risk of losing one of the tiny jets. Once lit, the flame is very powerful but can easily be turned down for simmering. Because the control lever is next to the burner rather than being on the pump, there's no delay when you adjust the flame. One of the aspects of the Nova I like most is the self-purging pump. Instead of depressurizing the fuel bottle by unscrewing the pump slightly, which inevitably lets a spray of pressurized fuel escape, and then detaching the fuel line from the pump, with attendant drips of fuel, you just flip the fuel bottle over and wait (it says *On* and *Off* on the pump). Fuel in the tube then burns off to be replaced by air, which helps clean the jet. As this air is released, the fuel bottle is depressurized, so there's no need to unscrew the pump. Now that I've gotten used to having a clean, nondripping stove to pack I really resent models that drip fuel and leave gas on my hands. The Nova can be turned off with the control lever, so the fuel bottle stays pressurized if you're going to use it again soon. If the jet gets blocked, there's a built-in cleaning needle that you can operate by shaking the stove or by using an included magnetic tool to push the needle into the jet. With this tool you can clean the jet while the stove is lit. The magnetic tool weighs 1.5 ounces and can also be used to disassemble the stove for maintenance, though I've never had to do this. The Nova is very ruggedly built and has a metal pump. It packs up neatly (the legs/pot supports close around the burner) and weighs 15 ounces.

OPTIMUS HUNTER AND HIKER The Hunter white-gas stove (23 ounces) has been around for decades, though it never achieved the popularity of the Svea. It comes in a steel case and is more stable than the Svea because of its lower profile, but keeping the 3-ounce tank pressurized is apparently more difficult because it's next to the burner with a heat shield in between rather than directly below it. The multifuel Hiker also comes in a steel box, but it's a much bigger stove, weighing a hefty 58 ounces, which makes it most suited for expedition and group use.

COLEMAN EXPONENT FEATHER 442 AND MULTI-FUEL Coleman is another traditional stove maker; its first stove appeared in 1923. Its backpacking range used to be called Peak 1 but now is called Coleman Exponent, though the stoves haven't changed. The Feather 442 Dual-Fuel and Multi-Fuel stoves are high-tech constructions bristling with levers and knobs. Both have ported burners set atop 11-ounce fuel tanks and built-in pumps. They need priming only in very cold weather—at least in theory. They're not fully field maintainable, so I wouldn't want to rely on either stove on a cold-weather or remote-country trip.

The Feather 442 weighs 24 ounces and runs on white gas and unleaded gasoline. Lighting it without priming is possible, but the instructions need to be followed precisely, and flaring is likely—my success rate is about 25 percent. I find it easier to light the stove by priming with a little fuel around the burner, especially in cold weather. Once lit, the Feather 442 is a powerful stove with a very fast boil

The Coleman Exponent Feather 442 dual-fuel stove is very powerful but bulky and heavy.

time. Simmering is possible, but it doesn't allow the fine control of some stoves. The Feather 442 is on the heavy side for solo backpacking but would be all right for groups or base-camp use.

The Multi-Fuel Stove is similar to the Feather 442, though slightly lighter at 21.6 ounces. For some reason it lights without priming more easily than the Feather 442, especially in the cold. A tapered plastic ring around the base lets you adjust the short legs to keep the stove level on uneven ground. The weight and bulk make it better suited to group than solo use.

The Multi-Fuel Stove can run on white gas, unleaded gasoline, or kerosene, but to use kerosene you have to change the generator using a small wrench that, together with the generator, adds an extra 2.5 ounces to the weight.

COLEMAN EXPONENT APEX II The third Coleman liquid-fuel stove, the Apex II, also runs on white gas, kerosene, and unleaded gasoline. As with the Multi-Fuel, you have to change the generator to use kerosene, however, and I've always run mine on

Coleman fuel. It's the lightest Coleman model, weighing 18.5 ounces, and the only one that uses a fuel bottle as the tank. Though in theory it can be lit without priming, I've found that this works only when the fuel bottle is full, there's no wind, the temperature is well above freezing, and the instructions are followed precisely. The Apex II was the first stove using a fuel bottle as a tank to have a flame adjuster on the burner as well as a fuel control knob on the pump, which makes fine flame control possible and simmering easy.

I once used an Apex II along with an MSR WhisperLite to cook for ten on a two-week ski trip in the High Sierra. The Apex II was great for simmering sauces, though not strong enough to hold a large pan of pasta, since it's a bit fragile and easily dented. Unlike other stoves that use fuel bottles as tanks, it can't be folded up for packing and so is slightly bulkier. It's not field maintainable, either, which would worry me on a long hike, especially in a remote area.

MSR XGK MSR first came up with the idea of using a fuel bottle as a remote fuel tank back in the 1970s;

its first model, the No. 9, appeared in 1973. This became the GK and then the XGK, which still looks very similar to the original. The MSR XGK deserves the name *multifuel*, since it will run on white gas, leaded and unleaded gasoline, aviation fuel, kerosene, diesel, and more, though you may have to clean it regularly when using anything other than white gas and kerosene. The same jet can be used for white gas and kerosene, though a second one is recommended for diesel and low-grade kerosene and any other fuels that burn with a sooty yellow flame using the standard jet. For remote areas where you don't know what fuel you'll find, this stove is a good choice. I once ran one on something called white spirits for a week when that was the only fuel I could get in a remote part of Norway. The stove gave off appalling dirty fumes but otherwise worked perfectly.

The XGK has a roarer burner (and it does roar!) and a rigid rather than flexible fuel tube. This tube has a wide diameter and is easy to clean if it clogs. Like other MSR stoves it has a Shaker Jet, a weighted cleaning needle built into the burner that cleans the jet when you gently shake the stove. The

The MSR XGK Expedition multifuel stove is probably the best stove to use with dirty fuel.

The MSR WhisperLite Internationale stove is the multifuel version of the popular WhisperLite.

weight is 15.8 ounces including a windscreen and heat reflector, 14 ounces without them. The XGK is field maintainable and comes with a maintenance kit weighing half an ounce.

The XGK is easy to light, but simmering is difficult. It's great for melting snow (for which it was originally designed) and boiling water, however, and a reliable and durable well-proven expedition stove. I previously commented that the then-current model, the XGK II, wasn't as powerful as its predecessors. This has been remedied by altering how far from the burner the pot supports hold the pan, and the XGK is again one of the most powerful stoves.

MSR WHISPERLITE AND WHISPERLITE INTERNATIONALE
MSR's WhisperLite and WhisperLite Internationale stoves are in essence the same, the only difference being that the first burns only white gas while the second has a wider fuel tube and will also burn automotive gasoline and kerosene, though you need to change the jet for kerosene. Both have the same Shaker Jet as the XGK. WhisperLites are small, spidery stoves with ported burners and fold-away legs/pan supports. The weight is 14 ounces

for the Internationale and half an ounce less for the WhisperLite without windscreens and reflectors (which add 1.8 ounces). Both stoves are powerful enough for group cooking. I've used my Internationale to cook for ten for two weeks at a time on spring ski trips, using both white gas and kerosene, and it's worked perfectly with both fuels. Flame control is limited, however, so simmering is difficult. Both stoves are maintainable in the field; maintenance kits, which include spare parts, weigh 0.5 ounce.

For a while the WhisperLite became the nearest thing to a standard backpacking stove. I joined the throng and used a WhisperLite Internationale on my long Canadian Rockies and Yukon walks. It proved very reliable, the only maintenance needed being to the leather pump washer, which dried out. I greased it with margarine, and it worked perfectly.

MSR DRAGONFLY The big complaint with the XGK and WhisperLite stoves has always been that it's difficult to make them simmer even a little. To answer this MSR launched the DragonFly, which has a flame adjuster on the burner so the heat can be easily turned down for simmering. The burner is a roarer, and the DragonFly is one of the noisiest stoves. It has sprung-steel pan supports that fold inward and a pivoting burner and forms a neat unit for packing, though a little bulkier than a WhisperLite. The burner is also suspended above the stove base and so less affected by cold ground. The DragonFly is a multifuel stove and will burn most liquid petroleum fuels. There are

Top: The MSR DragonFly multifuel stove offers separate flame control, which is good for simmering. Above: The MSR SimmerLite white-gas stove is the lightest white-gas stove available.

different jets for white gas and kerosene. The DragonFly is powerful—I've used it for melting snow and cooking for ten on ski tours—and it does simmer well. MSR rates it the most efficient of its stoves, saying it boils more water per volume of fuel. It weighs 14 ounces without windscreen and heat reflector, and there's a 0.75-ounce maintenance kit.

MSR SIMMERLITE Having made a stove that simmers with the DragonFly, MSR's designers turned their attention to weight and came up with the Simmer-Lite, the lightest white-gas stove at just 8.5 ounces without windscreen and heat reflector (2 ounces—there's no hole in the heat reflector, unlike those with other MSR stoves). The SimmerLite looks a little like the WhisperLite, with foldout legs/pan supports and a wide ported burner. The legs are flat rather than round, however, and there's no cup around the burner. Unlike the WhisperLite, the SimmerLite simmers quite well, as the name implies. It's also much quieter. My initial tests—it's new—suggest it's an excellent stove that makes the WhisperLite somewhat redundant, since it performs better and weighs less. Like other MSR liquid-fuel stoves, the SimmerLite has a Shaker Jet and is field maintainable. A maintenance kit weighs 0.5 ounce.

PRIMUS MULTIFUEL AND OMNIFUEL In the late 1990s Primus, once a big name in liquid-fuel stoves but that hadn't made one for many years, introduced the MultiFuel, which looks quite similar to other liquid-fuel stoves. Unlike any of them, however, it also runs on self-sealing butane-propane cartridges, making it extremely versatile. This is achieved by one of those simple but brilliant devices that make you wonder why no one thought of it before; a valve on the pump that's the same as the valve on standard self-sealing cartridges and a fuel line valve that will fit either of them. The

The Primus OmniFuel multifuel stove is the only multifuel stove that works with butane-propane canisters.

OmniFuel has the same valve plus a redesigned burner, rather along the lines of the Optimus Nova, to shorten the preheating time and make lighting the stove easier. The OmniFuel also has a flame adjuster on the burner to aid in simmering. Both stoves have self-purging pumps. To shut the stove down, you flip the fuel bottle over and wait while the fuel line clears and the bottle depressurizes. This means no drips from the fuel line when you detach it from the pump and no need to partly unscrew the pump to release the pressure, allowing a spray of vaporized fuel to escape. The stoves are field maintainable and very ruggedly built. They come with foil windscreens and heat reflectors.

The two stoves look much the same, with three foldout legs/pan supports and a squat profile. The MultiFuel weighs 13 ounces without the pump, the OmniFuel 14.5 ounces. The solid metal pump adds five ounces to both stoves. Both burn very hot and boil water fast with cartridges, but the Multi-Fuel is slower than other stoves with white gas and kerosene. Both stoves also simmer well with cartridges, but again the MultiFuel is not so good with white gas and kerosene. The OmniFuel is bet-ter with white gas but doesn't seem to like kerosene, sputtering and flaring and burning slowly however much it's primed or pumped. I took the OmniFuel and the Optimus Nova on a ski tour in Lapland with two friends and ended up just using the Nova, which worked so much better with the kerosene we were using.

The idea behind these stoves is excellent, and they do work well. But there are disadvantages. With the MultiFuel you have to change the jet if you switch between white gas and kerosene, so it's easier to change from one of those fuels to a car-tridge. With the OmniFuel there are three jets: one for butane-propane, one for white gas, and one for kerosene and other heavy fuels. Changing the jets is only a minor hassle, but I'd rather not have it. The jets are tiny, too, and easily mislaid or lost. The stoves are quite heavy for cartridge stoves—though they support big pans better than most —but reasonable for multifuel ones. I wouldn't want to use either of them with kerosene again because of their poor performance, but if you want one stove to use with white gas and cartridges, the OmniFuel is a good choice.

The Snow Peak GigaPower Titanium is a tiny, ultralight stove.

The VariFuel, which I haven't tried, is the same stove but without the cartridge valve. The weight is given as 14.8 ounces with the pump. Again, there are different jets for white gas and kerosene.

SNOW PEAK GIGAPOWER WG The GigaPower WG is a lightweight white-gas stove that looks a little like the DragonFly. It weighs 12.5 ounces and comes with a foil windscreen. Snow Peak says that no priming is required and that there is precision flame control. *Backpacker* gave it an Edi-

tor's Choice Award in 2001, which suggests it's pretty good. I haven't used it, though, so I can offer no comment other than that it seems worth a look.

Butane-Propane Cartridge Stoves

Light, clean and simple to use, cartridge stoves are excellent for three-season use. The fuel is a blend of butane, propane, and sometimes isobutane kept under pressure as a liquid in a sealed cartridge. Open the stove valve, and the fuel rushes out as a gas, which is then ignited. Pure butane has just about vanished. It performs poorly in cool weather because it doesn't vaporize below 31°F (−1°C) at sea level and is slow to do so below 40°F (5°C). As the altitude increases the boiling point of butane drops, which is the reason butane stoves have been used successfully for Himalayan mountaineering. At 10,000 feet, butane stoves will work down to 14°F (−10°C).

Propane, however, vaporizes at −43°F (−42°C) and so works fine at all altitudes. Unfortunately it's also very volatile, so cartridges have to be strong and therefore heavy. Mix it with a larger amount of butane, and a lighter cartridge can be used, hence blended fuels. Isobutane, which boils at 11°F

Butane-propane cartridges. From left: Coleman Powermax 300, Coleman 250, Campingaz 270, Primus 2207, Snow Peak GigaPower 110.

(–12°C), is sometimes used along with or instead of butane. Coleman cartridges are 70/30 butane/propane; Primus, 70/10/20 butane/isobutane/propane; MSR, 80/20 isobutane/propane; and Campingaz CV, 80/20 butane/propane. I've used all these cartridges, and I can't say I've noticed much difference between them. All are slow in subfreezing temperatures unless the cartridges are warmed. The only exceptions to this are the Coleman Powermax 60/40 butane/propane cartridges, which work well in cold conditions (see below).

The problem is that butane and propane don't bond very well, and the more volatile propane burns off first, giving very fast boiling times with new cartridges. As the cartridge empties there is less propane and more butane left, and performance in the cold declines. This is made even worse because as gas is released the pressure in the bottle falls, and as the pressure drops so does the temperature of the cartridge. You end up with less pressure to force the gas out of the cartridge and a colder cartridge that makes the fuel less likely to vaporize anyway. Thus in temperatures much below freezing cold cartridges don't give out much power. Once they're more than half empty, they may not produce enough energy to boil water at all. To overcome this you have to warm the cartridge, which can be done with gloved hands (bare ones can freeze to the metal) or by stuffing the cartridge inside your clothing. Keeping cartridges in your sleeping bag overnight or bringing them in as soon as you wake up can help too. Insulating cartridges against frozen ground or snow is also worth doing. A piece of foam or even a book makes a difference. Whatever you do it's a hassle, though, and I don't use standard cartridge stoves if the temperature is likely to be below 25°F (–4°C).

The longer you run a standard cartridge stove the more it cools, so running a stove for a long time—often necessary for group cooking—leads to a much more rapid drop in performance than running it in short bursts. This also makes these stoves less efficient for melting snow than stoves that run on other fuels. Overall, most cartridge stoves are best for solo or duo use when the temperature is above freezing. Under those conditions the latest stoves are very powerful, equaling or bettering white-gas boil times. Cartridge stoves are fuel efficient too. In laboratory tests with 70°F (21°C) water, MSR's figures show that its cartridge stoves are up to 25 percent more efficient than its white-gas/multifuel stoves, depending on the model. Their cartridge stoves boil on average 1.9 quarts of water per fluid ounce of fuel, the white-gas/multifuel stoves 1.5 quarts. This is a big change, white-gas stoves always used to be much more efficient than cartridge ones. The weight advantage of white-gas stoves has disappeared for long trips without resupply, when the weight of the stove was more than canceled out by the lower weight of fuel needed.

Most cartridges are vapor feed—the fuel leaves the cartridge as a gas. Powermax cartridges use liquid withdrawal and have a fuel tube inside the cartridge up which fuel is drawn. The fuel then passes through a preheat tube next to the burner head, and it is there that the fuel vaporizes rather than when it leaves the cartridge, so the temperature of the cartridge and the pressure in the cartridge don't have much effect on the vaporization. The fuel tube in the cartridge is weighted so the end always lies on the bottom of the cartridge and fuel is withdrawn at the same rate even when the cartridge is almost empty. This all sounds wonderful, and it is. It works. I've used Powermax cartridges at 20°F (–7°C), and there has been no falloff in performance until the last few minutes' worth of fuel. To see what would happen, I've left the cartridges on frozen ground overnight, too, then fired up the stove when they're covered with frost, and they've worked fine. Coleman says the cartridges will work down to 0°F (−18°C). Powermax cartridges come with a "green key" so that they can be punctured and easily recycled, unlike other cartridges. They're made of aluminum, too, and so are lighter than steel cartridges. There are two sizes: 170 (6 ounces) and 300 (10.5 ounces).

Powermax cartridges can be used only with Coleman X stoves, since they have a nonstandard valve. The industry-standard self-sealing cartridges have a Lindahl valve that most stoves fit. The other nonstandard self-sealing cartridge is the Campingaz CV, which can be used only with CV stoves or the MSR SuperFly. Non-self-sealing cartridges, which can't be detached from the stove until they're empty, are harder to pack, and you can't change the cartridge for a new one when the performance falls off in the cold. They can be discounted for backpacking and anyway have just about disappeared, at least in North America.

Cartridges contain from 3.5 to 21.5 fluid ounces of fuel. The tiniest, lightest ones are all right for one- or two-night trips when you don't need to carry more than one cartridge, but they're not efficient for longer trips because the ratio of metal to fuel is greater than in larger cartridges. Problems with cartridges are rare, but occasionally you get one that doesn't work. This has never happened to me, but I have hiked with people who've found their cartridges wouldn't work and had to borrow fuel. I always check every new cartridge by attaching a stove and lighting it briefly. Stove makers always say you should use only their brands of cartridges with their stoves. In fact, standard cartridges are interchangeable, and when you can't find the same brand as your stove, which often happens to me, a different brand will work just as well.

Whatever the cartridge, I use about 1.5 to 2.5 fluid ounces a day, which means that an 8-ounce cartridge usually lasts me three or four days (though with the Primus Micron stove this increases to five to six days). If you want to know how much gas is left in a cartridge, you can weigh it when new and after each trip, marking the figure on the cartridge. Alternatively, keep a record of how much empty cartridges weigh (each brand is slightly different, but 8-ounce ones weigh about 5 to 6 ounces) and then weigh any partly full cartridge and work out how much gas should be left. I do this occasionally, but mostly I rely on knowing how many days the cartridge has been used or go by the even less reliable method of hefting the cartridge in my hand and guessing.

There's one big problem with cartridges: the empties. Too many lie glinting in the sunlight at the bottom of once-pristine mountain lakes or jut out, half-buried, from piles of rocks in wilderness the world over. I have no solution to this problem. Perhaps mountain stores and cartridge makers could offer a deposit system with a refund for the return of empties. Ultimately, users must be responsible enough to carry out their trash and dispose of it properly. Cartridges can be recycled but need handling as hazardous waste. Don't crush them, since there might be a little fuel left that could explode if there was a spark from anything.

Cartridge stoves generally have ported burners, some noisier than others but quieter than white-gas/multifuel stoves. Heat output is easily adjusted, making these stoves excellent for simmering. Stoves attach to self-sealing cartridges in two ways. The most basic and lightest models simply screw into the top of the cartridge. These are often called *piggyback stoves* and are best used with low-profile cartridges. Heavier but much more stable are stoves with a flexible hose connecting the burner to the cartridge. With these stoves the burner can be safely encircled with a windscreen, something you shouldn't do with screw-in burners because the cartridge could overheat and explode, though you can use a windshield around three sides of a piggyback stove or fit a screen just around the burner (for more, see Windscreens and Heat Reflectors, page 311). Screw-in cartridge stoves are good for solo use and perhaps for duos. They're not very stable with large pans, however, and so are not ideal for groups. Many cartridge stoves come with electric Piezo ignition. Turn on the gas, click the button, and a spark lights the stove. This is great when it works. Spill soup on the igniter or snap the end off, both of which I've done, and it will fail, so I always carry a fire steel, matches, or a lighter as well. Given that, I'm happy to do without Piezo ignition. Cartridge stoves are generally reliable, but if they fail they're not field maintainable. Burner heads can clog if you spill food on them, but wiping them clean usually clears them.

PIGGYBACK STOVES At the time of the previous edition, the lightest cartridge stove was the then ridiculously expensive Primus Titanium at a fraction under 3 ounces. Sensibly priced stoves started at 5.5 ounces. Primus's stove was the start of a rush of ultralight models, however, and there are now many that weigh 3.5 ounces or less and don't cost a fortune. Good 3-ounce models I've used are the MSR PocketRocket, Coleman Exponent F1 Ultralight, Markill Hot Rod, and Optimus Crux. Slightly lighter is the Snow Peak GigaPower Titanium at 2.8 ounces; slightly heavier is the Primus Micron at 3.5 ounces. The differences between these stoves have to do with how they fold up and the size of the burners and in my opinion are not significant. They all perform amazingly well, with fast boil times and good simmer control. The packed bulk is minimal, of course, and many of them can be held in a closed fist. The flame tends to be concen-

Top: The Markill Hot Rod stove is reasonably priced. Center: The Optimus Crux is ultralight and ultracompact and has a folding head. Above: The Primus Micron stove is one of my favorites. It's ultralight and fuel efficient and has a hot flame.

trated, so hot spots in the center of pans are likely, though I've had no problems with burned food. The widest flames are those on the Primus Micron and Optimus Crux. These stoves are best used with small pans anyway, since they're unstable with large ones. While the boil times are similar, the Primus Micron does seem to be more fuel efficient than the others. Primus says a new catalytic burning system is the reason. I took the Micron on a cold fall hike in the White Mountains of New Hampshire and used it in temperatures mostly just below freezing; I was surprised and pleased when a Coleman 7.5-ounce canister lasted for six days— a fuel usage of just 1.25 fluid ounces a day, considerably less than I use with other stoves.

There are plenty of piggyback stoves from the companies named above plus Campingaz (which hasn't entered the ultralight fray) that are bigger and heavier and more suitable for larger pans, but they don't have the stability of hose-connected stoves, which I think are better when cooking for two or more. One model is worth mentioning, though—the 4.5-ounce MSR SuperFly, the only stove that fits both standard self-sealing cartridges and Campingaz's proprietary CV ones. To do this the SuperFly has an aluminum clamp with a plastic collar that slides onto the cartridge valve before the burner is screwed in place. Being able to use different types of cartridges could be useful if you travel widely, particularly to the Alps and Pyrenees, where Campingaz cartridges are all that may be available. On one two-week trip to the Queyras Alps before the SuperFly came along, I took a standard self-sealing stove and four 8-ounce cartridges (which weigh 6 ounces empty, so I had 56 ounces in total), because I knew I probably wouldn't find the cartridges locally. Sure enough I didn't, but there were plenty of CV cartridges, and I could have resupplied several times and carried only one cartridge at a time if I'd been able to use them. Now I would take the SuperFly. It weighs an ounce and a half more than the stove I used, but it would have saved me 42 ounces in cartridge weight.

LOW-PROFILE STOVES Hose-connected stoves are more stable because they sit on the ground and usually have larger pan supports than screw-in models, making them more suited for large pots. The

The MSR WindPro butane-propane stove is the lightest low-profile, hose-attached canister stove.

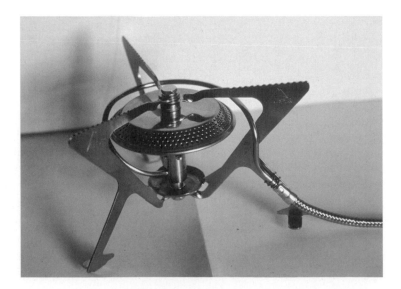

Primus MultiFuel and OmniFuel stoves (see pages 296–97) fit in here and are very powerful when used with cartridges. Without the pumps needed for liquid fuels, they weigh 13 and 14.5 ounces respectively. The same model with no provision for using liquid fuel is called the EasyFuel and weighs 12 ounces. Snow Peak makes an 11.5-ounce hose-connected stove similar to the white-gas GigaPower WG stove called—potentially confusingly—the GigaPower BF (blended fuel); it looks good.

The weights of the stoves described above are fairly typical for hose-connected stoves, but there are some that weigh less. MSR has dropped its 12.5-ounce RapidFire for the 6.8-ounce WindPro, which is the same stove as the white-gas Simmer-Lite except that it has a cartridge connection instead of a pump. It comes with the same MSR 2-ounce windscreen and heat reflector. It's not quite as powerful as some other cartridge stoves, but it's the lightest hose-connected stove. Not quite as light is the 8-ounce, spidery Olicamp Scorpion I, which has been around for many years. I bought one sometime in the 1980s but didn't find it as powerful as other stoves. I didn't like the vulnerable-looking black rubber hose, either. The slightly heavier and larger 9.7-ounce Scorpion III should be a little more powerful. Both stoves are inexpensive.

An unusual hose-connected stove is the Markill Stormy, which comes complete with integrated windscreen and two pots at a weight of 25.5 ounces. It has folding legs but also a chain so you can hang it if required. Wind resistance should be superb—Markill says it's for "extreme conditions."

Trangia 25 or 27 unit owners who want to use cartridges can buy 8-ounce hose-connected burners made by Primus that fit inside the windscreen with the hose running through a cutout in the side. The system works very well, but the weight and bulk are high compared with a cartridge stove

The Coleman Exponent Xtreme stove is the only canister stove that works well in temperatures below freezing.

and foil windscreen. You can also turn a piggyback stove into a hose-connected one with the Markill Sidewinder, a tripod base with a cartridge-type valve and a hose with a cartridge attachment. It weighs 6 ounces and folds up neatly. With one of these a 3-ounce piggyback stove can become a 9-ounce low-profile stove when you want the advantages of the latter and don't mind the extra weight.

The most interesting hose-connected stoves, though, are the Coleman Exponent X stoves, the only ones that will work with the Powermax cartridges described above. There are three models: the 11-ounce Xtreme, the 13.5-ounce Xpert, and the 26-ounce Xpedition double burner. I have the three-legged Xtreme, which is made from magnesium alloy and looks like many other low-profile stoves. The difference is in the performance. This is a very powerful stove, boiling water faster than virtually anything else in warm weather, and as well as anything else when it's cold. In subfreezing temperatures it's the only cartridge stove I've used that works well throughout the life of the cartridge, making it the only one suitable for

Top: The packed Jetboil with a Snow Peak GigaPower 110-gram cartridge. Above: The Jetboil stove.

use year-round. Problems? For a cartridge stove it's expensive, and the cartridges aren't sold everywhere. The legs don't lock, either, so you have to take care that they don't fold in on themselves, or else wedge them in place with tent pegs.

JETBOIL STOVE The Jetboil stove has attracted more attention than any stove for many years. *Backpacker* gave it an Editor's Choice award and *Outside* gave it a Gear of the Year award. However backpacking light.com was more critical. The stove is so new at the time of writing that I've only had it a few weeks, so my comments are tentative. The Jetboil is an integrated canister stove and includes an anodized aluminum 1-quart pot/cup, neoprene pot cozy, and heat exchanger. It all packs together into a neat unit, and 100- or 110-gram canisters can be stored inside the pot.

Jetboil says the heat exchanger doubles fuel efficiency by improving the heat transfer, so a cartridge will last twice as long as with other stoves. The Jetboil runs off standard resealable butane-propane cartridges. One of Jetboil's own 3.5-ounce Jetpower cartridges is claimed to boil 12 quarts. According to MSR their most efficient canister stove, the PocketRocket, would boil 7 quarts with the same amount of fuel. Unable to find any Jetboil canisters, I've used the stove with Snow Peak GigaPower 110 and Coleman 250 canisters. With the GigaPower the stove used 0.2 fluid ounce to boil a quart, which would mean 2.4 fluid ounces for 12 quarts. With the Coleman however it used 0.4 fluid ounce, which would mean 4.8 fluid ounces for 12 quarts. This was in an air temperature of 60°F (16°C), water at 58°F (14°C), and no wind. Boil time for 16 fluid ounces of water was four minutes, twice that quoted by Jetboil, but still perfectly acceptable.

Without fuel, the Jetboil weighs 15 ounces. An ultralight cartridge stove and quart titanium pot weigh around 8 ounces. My brief tests and Jet-

STOVES: MY CHOICES

In order to test them for this book and for magazine articles, I've acquired most of the stoves described here, so I sometimes have problems deciding which to take on a trip. For short ventures in mild conditions, any one will do. Longer walks and stormy weather make me choose more carefully.

For seven years the Optimus Svea 123R was my favorite stove. Then the WhisperLite Internationale replaced it as my first choice because it's easier to prime, lighter, smaller, and more stable and performs better in wind, while being just as efficient and reliable. The Internationale reigned for twelve years but was in turn supplanted in my affections by the Optimus Nova. I'm not constant when it comes to stoves! I've used the Nova on two multiweek hikes, including the Arizona Trail, and many shorter trips, and in my opinion it's the best multifuel stove yet, being easier and quicker to light and cleaner and more compact than the Internationale. If I had only one stove, it would be the Nova.

For most short trips, though, I use cartridge stoves because of their low weight, low bulk, and convenience, though they don't generate the same feelings as multifuel stoves. Somehow they seem characterless. Maybe it's because they're so easy to use. My current favorite is the Primus Micron because it's slightly more fuel efficient than others I've tried, though there's little to choose between all the ultralight models. I now use these stoves on trips where I don't expect temperatures to fall below freezing very often. I wouldn't use a cartridge stove on a long hike in a remote area, however, because they aren't repairable in the field. On short cold-weather trips I often carry the Coleman Exponent Xtreme, since it's much simpler to use than the Nova. Very recently the Jetboil stove has been added to my list, and will undoubtedly get more use in the future.

The Brasslite Turbo II-D has rekindled my interest in alcohol stoves. I'm also inclining more to the attractions of silent stoves that burn nonfossil fuels. For short trips in not too severe conditions I expect I'll be using the Turbo II-D and the Sierra Stove more often.

boil's figures suggest twice as much fuel will be needed with other stoves. For four days I would carry one 9-ounce canister weighing 12 ounces when full, making a total of 20 ounces with the ultralight stove and pan. I could probably get by with a 3.5-ounce canister weighing 6 ounces when full with the Jetboil, for a total weight of 21 ounces. For eight days with a 16-ounce canister weighing 21 ounces when full, the ultralight unit would weigh 24 ounces; the Jetboil with two 3.5-ounce canisters or a 9-ounce canister weighing 12 ounces when full would weigh 27 ounces. These are rough figures that need backing up with some long field tests but they suggest that although certainly very light the Jetboil isn't quite the lightest solution, especially as there are titanium pots lighter than 8 ounces and you might not need quite so much fuel with the ultralight stove as I've presumed. Compared with anything other than a 3-ounce ultralight canister stove the Jetboil is much lighter, however. Weight isn't the only factor in stove choice of course, but Jetboil does claim their stove is the "lightest cooking solution ever."

The efficiency of the Jetboil is probably mainly due to the integrated heat exchanger, which increases the area of the base of the pot, the key area for heating. This more than overcomes the narrowness of the pot, which I find inefficient. The pot cosy helps too. When I didn't use the pot cozy, boiling times increased by nearly 50 percent. When used, the cozy never becomes more than hot to the touch, showing that little heat is being wasted up the sides of the pot. The heat exchanger acts as a partial windscreen too, though I would still use a separate one in anything more than a light breeze. The cosy helps here too by insulating the pot from moving air. I haven't yet been able to test the Jetboil in cold weather but I imagine it should work well, unlike many canister stoves.

The Jetboil isn't perfect, however. It's tall (11¼ inches long with a 100- or 110-gram canister) and narrow (the pot has a diameter of 4 inches), which makes it unstable on rough ground and a little top-heavy. Narrow pots aren't as easy to use or clean as wide ones either. You can't use other pots with the Jetboil and the one provided only holds a quart. Care is needed when the pot is full too, as liquids can easily spill out. The pot/heat exchanger unit should only be fitted to the stove when the stove has been lit, which can be awkward and is best done with a low flame. In wind the stove must be shielded until the pot is in place or it may not light or blow out if it does. Overall, though, the Jetboil is an impressive innovation, and a stove I'll be using in the future.

Natural Fuel

All the stoves described above need fuel that you have to purchase beforehand and carry with you. Not the Sierra Stove. This unique device burns natural materials that can be found around most campsites, such as twigs, pinecones, bark, charcoal, and even dried dung. It consists of a hollow-walled open chamber that sits atop a small battery-operated fan and operates like a miniature blacksmith's forge. Light a small fire in the chamber, then switch on the fan to blow air through holes in the hollow walls, and you get a roaring inferno that quickly brings water to the boil. One AA battery is said to power the fan for six hours, while an adapter with a C cell will run it for thirty-five hours. The fan and battery unit pack inside the chamber for carrying. I hadn't used a Sierra Stove until recently, but I finally succumbed to curiosity and bought the 18-ounce stainless steel version. After brief use I have to say I'm impressed. I have a few caveats, though. I wouldn't like to rely on it in wet country unless I carried a bag of dry fuel, which rather defeats the

Sierra Stove dismantled, showing fan.

Sierra Stove with fire lit and fan on full.

purpose. The battery compartment would need protecting in the wet too, since it's not remotely water resistant. However, in mostly dry places like the High Sierra I can see its working well and allowing you to stay out for long periods without having to carry a great weight of fuel. The weight of my standard version is about the same as an ultralight cartridge stove and one 9-ounce cartridge, which would last me four days. So for trips that long and longer the Sierra Stove would not add extra weight. There's a titanium version weighing 10 ounces if you really want to cut the weight. The stove goes through fuel pretty fast when the fan's on full (the fan has three settings—high, low, and off), so you do need to gather a fair amount before starting it. If you want to use longer sticks there's a Cross Grate (2.5 ounces) that raises the height of the stove. As long as the fire is kept hot there's not much smoke, though pans do turn black, as on any wood fire. If you turn the fan down or off for simmering, more smoke is produced. Light fire tongs (0.5 ounce) let you add and move wood without singeing your fingers. The initial fire can be started with any of the kindling you'd use for a campfire or with Zip Fire solid-fuel blocks from ZZ Manufacturing, which makes the Sierra Stove (otherwise known as the Zip Ztove). A pack of eighteen weighs 3 ounces. One is enough to start the stove with dry fuel. Once you've finished using the stove, leave it to cool down before dumping out any ashes and scattering them widely. Running the fan for a while after the fire is out cools the stove quickly. Some wood sends out sparks, so it's safest to set the stove up on rocks or on bare ground.

A simpler wood-burning stove is F. II. Enterprises' Trekstov, which consists of a base with air holes in the sides, a firebox, and windscreen/pot supports that nest neatly together. The weight is 21 ounces. The flame can't be controlled. There is also a stove you can make yourself, the Nimblewill Nomad, a simple wood-burning box with airholes. The weight will depend on what material you use. Details are on the Wings Homemade Stove site, http://wings.interfree.it.

Safety and Maintenance

All stoves can be dangerous and should be used carefully. The most important safety point: never take a stove for granted.

Before you light a stove, always check that attachments to fuel tanks or cartridges are secure, tank caps and fuel bottle tops are tight, and controls are turned off. Study the instructions that come with all stoves, especially white-gas and multifuel models, and practice using them at home. When you're cold, wet, and tired, it's half-dark, and you desperately need a hot meal, it's important that you can safely operate your stove almost automatically. By testing stoves at home you'll also discover any faults. With one brand-new white-gas stove the pump leaked badly as soon as I started pumping. After I dismantled the pump, checked all the seals, and reassembled it, it still leaked, so I replaced it. In the backcountry I'd have had a useless stove. I also check stoves that haven't been used for a while just in case they need cleaning or maintenance.

Stoves should be refilled carefully, after making sure that there are no open flames such as campfires, burning candles, or other lit stoves nearby. This applies whether you are changing a cartridge or pouring fuel into a tank. Refueling should always be done *outside* for safety.

An overheated cartridge or fuel tank is a hazard. When the burner is directly above or alongside the fuel tank, make sure there is enough air flow around the tank or cartridge to keep it cool. It should never become too hot to touch. Windscreens shouldn't fully surround such stoves. If

STOVE AND FUEL WEIGHTS FOR TRIPS OF DIFFERENT LENGTHS

Model	Stove Weight (oz.)	Fuel Weight (oz.)/Trip Length (days)	Total Weight (oz.)
MSR SimmerLite	8.5	11.0[1]/4	19.5
		21.0[2]/8	29.5
		31.5[3]/12	40.0
Optimus Nova	15.0	12.0[4]/4	27.0
		20.0[4]/8	35.0
		29.5[5]/12	44.5
MSR PocketRocket	3.0	12.0[6]/4	15.0
		21.0[7]/8	24.0
		33.0[8]/12	36.0
Coleman Xtreme	11.0	14.0[9]/4	25.0
		21.5[10]/8	32.5
		29.5[11]/12	40.5
Trangia Westwind	6.0	20.0[12]/4	26.0
		37.5[13]/8	43.5
		57.5[14]/12	63.5
Brasslite Turbo II-D	2.5	18.5[15]/4	21.0
		37.0[16]/8	39.5
		55.5[17]/12	58.0
Sierra Stove	18.0	—/4	18.0
		—/8	18.0
		—/12	18.0

Note: Fuel consumption is assumed to be 2 ounces white gas and butane-propane and 4 ounces alcohol per day.

[1]With MSR 11-ounce fuel bottle
[2]With MSR 22-ounce fuel bottle
[3]With MSR 33-ounce fuel bottle
[4]With Optimus 20-ounce fuel bottle
[5]With Optimus 34-ounce fuel bottle
[6]With Primus 8-ounce cartridge
[7]With Primus 16-ounce cartridge
[8]With Primus 8- and 16-ounce cartridges
[9]With Powermax 11-ounce cartridge
[10]With Powermax 6- and 11-ounce cartridges
[11]With two Powermax 6-ounce and one 11-ounce cartridges
[12]With Trangia 16-ounce fuel bottle
[13]With Trangia 32-ounce fuel bottle
[14]With Trangia 16- and 32-ounce fuel bottles
[15]With Brasslite 16-ounce fuel bottle
[16]With two Brasslite 16-ounce fuel bottles
[17]With three Brasslite 16-ounce fuel bottles

Considerations and Conclusions:

1. These figures are comparative only and are based on my fuel usage. Figures have been rounded to the nearest 0.5.
2. Stove weight counts with white-gas and cartridge stoves. The ultralight PocketRocket is the lightest option even for twelve days, despite the extra weight of the cartridges.
3. Alcohol is heavy even if the stoves aren't. For long trips it is very heavy.
4. MSR Titanium fuel bottles would save weight with the white-gas stoves. A light plastic bottle saves weight with the alcohol stoves.
5. If you're out for more than four days the Sierra Stove is the lightest option.

you use large pans that overhang the burner, periodically check to see if the fuel tank or cartridge is getting hot because too much heat is being reflected off the pans.

Stoves, especially white-gas stoves, can flare badly when being lit. Never have your head over a stove when you light it. Also, don't light a stove that is close to any flammable material. If you need to cook in the vestibule or under a tarp, it's safest to light the stove out in the open, even if you have to stick it out into the rain and then bring it back under cover when it's burning properly. If you do light a stove in the vestibule, leave the door open so you can quickly push the stove out if anything goes wrong (but be careful where you push it if there are other tents around). I was once walking across a crowded campground on a blustery winter day when I saw a bright yellow flash inside a nearby tent. A second later, a blazing gasoline stove came hurtling through the tent fly sheet—leaving behind a neat hole—and landed near my feet. If another tent had been close by, there could have been a disaster.

A threat when using a stove inside a tent is carbon monoxide poisoning, which can be fatal. All stoves consume oxygen and give off this odorless, colorless gas. In an enclosed space they can use up all the oxygen, replacing it with carbon monoxide. There should always be good ventilation when a stove is in use. In a tent vestibule air can usually enter under the edge of the fly sheet, but this can be blocked by snow piling up around the edges of the tent or by a wet fly sheet freezing to the ground. In those cases, if there's no vent, a two-way outer door zipper is useful—the top few inches can be left open to ensure ventilation.

It's best never to use a stove in the inner tent, partly because of carbon monoxide poisoning, but mainly because of fire.

Most stoves need little maintenance. Many white-gas and multifuel stoves have built-in cleaning needles. With those that don't, you may need to clean the jets occasionally with the thin jet prickers (weighing a fraction of an ounce) that usually come with stoves that need them. They should be used only when the stove's performance seems to be falling off, since too much cleaning can widen the jet and lessen the burn rate. If you lose, break, or forget your jet pricker, as I did once on a winter trip, and your soup boils over and blocks the jet, a bristle from a toothbrush makes a good substitute. (This idea was suggested by two walkers in a mountain shelter where I went in desperate search of anything that would restore my stove to working order.)

Check rubber seals and O-rings on tank caps and cartridge attachment points periodically and replace them if worn. I carry spares on long trips. You may need to carry a complete tank cap. On the Pacific Crest Trail I was glad I did so—the original

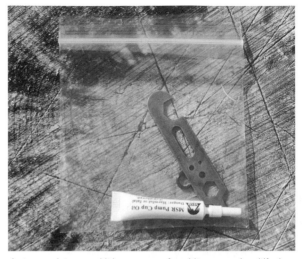

A stove maintenance kit is necessary for white-gas and multifuel stoves. The contents depend upon the model, but a kit usually contains O-rings, a tool for dismantling the stove, pump leather oil, jets, jet needles, and a leather pump cup.

one on my Svea 123R started to leak after four months of constant use.

Fuel Bottles and Tank-Filling Devices

Fuel bottles need to be leakproof and tough. They're best carried away from food, preferably in an outside pocket of the pack, just in case they leak.

Plastic bottles are fine for alcohol. Even empty soda bottles can be used. Brasslite's 8- and 16-fluid-ounce plastic bottles have pouring spouts and reservoirs and weigh 1.5 and 2.5 ounces. Nalgene and Trangia make polyethylene fuel bottles in pint and quart sizes that are suitable for white gas and kerosene as well as alcohol. The Trangia bottles weigh 4 and 5.6 ounces and have safety valves. The Nalgene bottles have pour spouts under the caps and weigh 3.7 and 4.6 ounces.

Metal fuel bottles double as tanks for hose-attached stoves. The standard for decades has been the Swiss-made Sigg bottle. I used the 21-fluid-

NEAR DISASTER

The nearest I have ever come to a serious stove accident was when I was cooking in the vestibule of a tent pitched on snow. A severe blizzard had trapped us at the same site for four nights; during the last night the wind had battered the tents so much that we'd hardly slept at all. I lit the white-gas stove in the vestibule with the door zipped shut to keep out blown snow. The burner caught, but the flame was sluggish. "Pump it some more," suggested my companion. Without thinking, I did so. There was a sudden bright surge of flame, then the whole unit was ablaze as liquid fuel shot out of the jet. Two suddenly energized bodies dived for the door zipper and yanked it open. I threw the stove out and plunged my scorched hands into the snow. Later I discovered that my eyebrows and face were also singed.

In retrospect, we were lucky. One moment's carelessness could have left us without our tent and gear or, worse, badly burned or even dead. My guess is that lack of air was the cause. I should have opened the door and tried to revive the stove outside. As it was, the fly sheet zipper partially melted and wouldn't close, so in subsequent storms we had to cook in the inner tent, which we did with great care, standing the stove on a pan lid to prevent the groundsheet from melting.

On two other occasions I've been present when a stove has caught fire, once outside a mountain hut and once inside. Each time, it was a white-gas stove. As most white-gas stove manufacturers state, these are best used outdoors, not in tents or huts. The safest fuels are solid fuel and alcohol, followed by butane-propane cartridges.

For many years Siggs were the only round fuel bottles—the original MSR stoves were designed to use them. Now MSR, Optimus, Primus, and Snow Peak all make similar aluminum bottles with the same size threads. MSR's 11-, 22-, and 33-fluid-ounce bottles weigh 2.8, 4.9, and 7.3 ounces, Optimus's 20- and 34-fluid-ounce ones weigh 4.2 and 5.6 ounces, and Primus's 18- and 30-fluid-ounce ones weigh 4.2 and 5.8 ounces. Snow Peak's 18.5-fluid-ounce bottle weighs 6 ounces. MSR also makes titanium bottles if you want to shave weight. Titan bottles come in 14-, 21- and 28-fluid-ounce sizes at weights of 3, 3.5, and 4.1 ounces. Coleman's 22-fluid-ounce bottle for the Apex II stove has different-size threads and so isn't interchangeable with the others. It weighs 5 ounces.

It's almost impossible to fill small tanks directly from standard bottles without spilling a little fuel. However, various ingenious devices help. I have a Sigg pouring cap and spout, bought many years ago for filling my Svea 123 tank. This is a standard cap with a small plastic spout inserted in one side and a tiny hole drilled in the other. By placing a finger over the hole you can control the flow from the spout. It's inconvenient to use—you have to remove the normal cap, screw in the pouring cap, fill the stove, and then change the caps again. To avoid losing either cap, I've linked them with a piece of shock cord. The Sigg pouring spout is no longer sold, but REI's 0.5-ounce Super Pour Spout does the same job. Olicamp's Ulti-Mate Pour Spout looks similar but also functions as a standard cap, which is much more convenient. The caps on Optimus and Trangia fuel bottles can also be used for pouring. The Trangia cap is sold separately for use with other bottles.

For filling fuel bottles from larger containers, I use a small Coghlan's polypropylene Filter Funnel (0.75 ounce). I usually carry it on long hikes when

ounce size, weighing 3.5 ounces, for many years for all fuels, and despite getting very battered and dented, the bottles never leaked. Sigg bottles come in sizes holding 10.5, 21, 35, and 53 fluid ounces.

I may have to refill with white gas from gallon cans or use fuel of dubious cleanliness.

Accessories

Windscreens and Heat Reflectors

The one stove accessory that's essential is a windscreen. No stove will function well in a stiff breeze without one. Even if the stove stays alight, it will take a long time and a great deal of fuel to boil water, if it does so at all. In a strong wind an unprotected stove may be impossible to light. MSR's crude-looking but ultralight foil windscreen is arguably one of the greatest advances ever in backpacking stove cooking. If you don't have a windscreen, a foam pad held around the stove at a safe distance works quite well, or you could prop up your pack or boots. These are all a hassle, though, so I always carry a windscreen.

Primus and MSR multifuel and white-gas stoves come with foil windscreens, as does the MSR WindPro cartridge stove, while solid alloy ones come with the larger Trangia models. No other stoves come with adequate windscreens as components. Crosspieces on the burner that stop the flame from blowing out do not count as true windscreens. Foil windscreens, sold by MSR, Primus, and Optimus, are ideal for low-profile stoves with remote fuel tanks. They weigh 1.5 to 2 ounces.

Taller stoves that sit on top of fuel tanks and cartridges shouldn't be completely surrounded by a windscreen; there needs to be some airflow to the fuel container so it doesn't overheat. However, you can protect them on three sides, which is adequate. The tank or canister should always be cool enough to touch. Standard foil windscreens aren't tall enough to protect these stoves, though you can staple two together or make your own from heavy-duty aluminum foil. Taller rigid aluminum windscreens are generally quite heavy. When I used the Svea 123 regularly, my windscreen was a 10-inch-tall folding Coghlan's model made of five sheets of aluminum with anchor rods at each end. This windscreen is efficient and durable and works well with screw-in cartridge stoves, but it weighs 8 ounces. Markill's similar 10-inch-high five-panel windscreen is much lighter at 3.5 ounces. It looks like a good choice, and I'll probably get one. An alternative is a foil windscreen that wraps around the burner only, with another sheet of foil around the base of the burner as a heat reflector. For details, go to the Homemade Canister Stove Windscreen page at backpackinglight.com.

Whatever windscreen you use, it's most effective if it's close to the pan—less than half an inch away—since this traps most heat and minimizes air movement.

Heat reflectors that fit under the burner or the stove speed up cooking times only slightly in my experience. They do protect the ground and fuel tanks and canisters from the heat, however, and can be used as stove stands, especially on snow, when one is essential.

Heat Exchangers, Pot Warmers, and Flame Diffusers

In theory heat exchangers conduct heat from the burner up the sides of a pan, speeding cooking times and reducing fuel consumption. MSR's XPD Heat Exchanger is a corrugated aluminum collar that comes as part of the XPD Alpine Classic Cookset, which consists of two stainless steel pots (1.5- and 2-quart capacities) with frying pan/lid and pot grab. According to MSR, the Heat Exchanger increases heat efficiency by 25 percent. Since the exchanger weighs just 7 ounces, it should save weight overall on long trips. On short trips, the main advantage would be faster boiling times. Although designed for MSR pots, the XPD

Top: Use a Scorch Buster heat-dispersion plate to spread the heat while simmering. ABOVE: MSR XPD Heat Exchanger. Heat exchangers are claimed to increase fuel efficiency.

Exchanger can be used with other brands. It won't work with ones less than 6 inches in diameter, though. I used the heat exchanger on several ski tours with groups and thought it did speed up boiling times, though I never quantified by how much. I did eventually get around to doing some tests, and the results were surprising. A quart of water in an MSR Alpine pan on a Primus OmniFuel stove attached to a cartridge took 3 minutes, 55 seconds to boil. I then fitted the Heat Exchanger so it hung

an inch and a half below the pot and boiled another quart. It took 4 minutes, 40 seconds. Moving the Exchanger so it was level with the base of the pot, I boiled a third quart. It took 5 minutes, 30 seconds. The Heat Exchanger was having the opposite effect from that intended. The OmniFuel has a roarer burner that spreads the flame across the bottom of the pan. To see if there was any difference, I did the test again using an MSR PocketRocket, which has a narrow flame focused on the center of the pan. With the XPD Exchanger hanging an inch and a half below the pot the quart of water boiled in 4 minutes, 45 seconds. With it level with the pot base, it boiled in 5 minutes, 45 seconds. Without the heat exchanger, it boiled in 5 minutes, 30 seconds. These are confusing results—at least they confused me—so I consulted a physicist friend. He thought the heat exchanger was acting as a radiator when used with a stove with a wide flame. The flame was heating the exchanger, which then radiated the heat into the air, slowing heating of the pot. With the narrow flame he thought the exchanger trapped a cushion of hot air below the pot, which speeded up heating of the pot. This effect was lost when the exchanger was level with the base of the pot. In that case, with both flames the heat exchanger absorbed some heat, effectively creating a pot with a larger surface area, and so slowed the heating of the water. My conclusion is that the XPD Exchanger is best used with large pans and stoves with narrow flames. If the XPD gets hot, then it's probably not doing its job. With stoves with wide flames, they could be turned down to prevent the XPD from absorbing heat. My friend thought it wasn't worth using and that a windscreen would be much more effective. Certainly a windscreen and a lid are the two most important items for fuel conservation and fast boiling times. (The heat exchanger on the Jetboil stove sits under the pot, which is why it's so effective.)

The Pot Parka is a soft, aluminized fiberglass dome that keeps pots warm. It weighs 3 ounces for the 8-inch size and 4.3 ounces for the 10-inch. It also forms the main part of the Outback Oven (see below). It saves fuel because when it's in place you can melt snow or warm water with the stove on a low setting. It starts to burn if you use it with a stove on full, however, so it can't be used to speed up boil times. It can also be used to keep food warm when the stove is off—for example, to cook pasta or rice added to boiling water.

Stoves with poor flame control can burn food that needs simmering for any length of time unless you stir constantly and lift the pot above the burner every so often. An answer to this is the Scorch Buster heat-dispersion plate, a ribbed stainless steel disk that weighs 2.8 ounces and is, in fact, the same as the diffuser plate of the Outback Oven described below. It works well and is worth carrying if you tend to burn meals.

Hanging Cook Systems

Hanging cook systems, which can be suspended from pitons or other supports, are designed for mountaineers bivouacking in tight places. Examples are the Bibler Hanging Pot Set, which has a combined windscreen/heat reflector and a 1- or 2-quart pot (20 or 22 ounces), the ultralight 3.5-ounce Primus Suspension Kit, a wire framework that supports both stove and fuel bottle or cartridge, the 9.5-ounce MSR SuperFly Ascent System, which includes the SuperFly stove plus hanging wires and a windscreen/pot holder, and the 17.5-ounce Markill Stormy Hanging, with two pots, windscreen, and hanging chain, which is designed for the Markill Devil stove. You could use one of these in a tent in winter to avoid cooling the fuel by placing it on the snow or suspend it from a tree if you want to cook without bending over. I've never used one.

Stands

Stoves need support on snow and, sometimes, soft ground. They also need insulating from cold ground. You can use a small square of wood, metal, or fiberglass insulation or even a book. On ski tours I usually use the blade of a snow shovel. In the snowbound High Sierra on the Pacific Crest Trail I used my natural history guide to stop my Svea stove from melting down into the snow. MSR makes a flat-folding three-section base called the Trillium that weighs 3 ounces and can be adjusted to fit different MSR stoves, and UCO offers the Mightylite stove stand at 4 ounces that has an elastic cord for attaching the fuel bottle to make a single unit. For piggyback stoves there is the Foot Rest from Primus. This has three folding legs and fits under the cartridge. It weighs 0.75 ounce. Mostly, though, I use a flat rock. I do like the look of the Trangia Multi-Disc, however. This circle of hard plastic with holes in one side can be used as a strainer and a cutting board as well as a stove stand. It could be used as a Frisbee, too. The weight is 3.5 ounces, and I'll probably use one on my next snow-camping trip.

Stove Lighters and Fire Starters

It's best to carry more than one item for lighting your stove. Soaked matches and empty lighters won't help you. I always used to carry a box of strike-anywhere matches (half an ounce) in my food bag, another in the stove bag, and a third in a plastic bag with some toilet paper. I always kept them in Ziploc plastic bags, but waterproof metal or plastic match safes (Coghlan's makes both) provide extra protection and weigh about an ounce. Empty film canisters or other small plastic containers with secure lids can be used too. You can tear the striker off the matchbox and store it inside with the matches. I don't like book matches—the striking strip wears out quickly, and it always seems that half the matches don't work.

The chance that several boxes kept in different places in the pack all will get soaked is remote, but it could happen in a downpour or during a river ford, so carrying an emergency backup fire starter is good for peace of mind. I used to carry a canister of waterproof, windproof Lifeboat matches in my repair kit. The waterproof plastic canister contains twenty-five large matches, has strikers top and bottom, and weighs 0.75 ounce. They work when wet and burn for eleven to fifteen seconds, but beware of the hot embers after one has gone out. You can get other windproof and waterproof matches from companies like Coghlan's.

An alternative to matches is a lighter. Disposable butane lighters weigh less than an ounce, and just a spark from one will ignite white gas and butane-propane, though not kerosene or alcohol (at least not easily). If a lighter gets wet, it's easily dried; a sodden box of matches is useless. Refillable lighters like the classic Zippo (2 ounces) are an alternative. Lighters can be touchy, though, and don't always work. I wouldn't rely on one alone.

Until recently I'd never tried any fire starters

Swedish FireSteel and Tool Logic SL3 knife with FireSteel insert. Fire starters like this one are hot and work in any weather, even rain.

other than matches or lighters, regarding other methods as rather esoteric and complicated—fun maybe, but little practical use. Then I discovered the Swedish FireSteel, a modern version of the old flint and steel. This consists of an alloy magnesium rod with a plastic handle and a small flat steel bar linked by a short length of cord. Striking the rod with the bar produces extremely hot bright white sparks (5,430°F, say the makers). There are two sizes of FireSteel. The smaller Scout weighs 1 ounce and is said to produce at least 3,000 ignitions. The larger Army weighs 2 ounces and lasts for 12,000 strikes. Lighting a white-gas or cartridge stove with the FireSteel is easy, and it really does work when wet. I dunked it in water and struck it while it was still dripping, and bright sparks appeared immediately. I started carrying the FireSteel as a replacement for the Lifeboat matches, but I've ended up using it as my main fire starter. Not having to protect it from damp makes it a great tool. A box of matches or a lighter is now my backup in case I lose the FireSteel.

There are several other fire starters of the flint-and-steel type. The Doan Magnesium Firestarter Tool (1.3 ounces) is perhaps the classic model. To use it you scrape flakes from a magnesium bar, then ignite them by scraping a knife across the bar to create sparks.

Survival manuals describe in detail methods of fire lighting such as bow drills that use natural materials, but these all strike me (on the basis of no experience, I should add) as unworkable in the cold and wet—when you'd need a fire most.

Transporting Stoves and Fuel

If you're planning to fly with your backpacking equipment, check the airline regulations before purchasing a ticket. Federal Aviation Administration regulations say you may carry properly purged stoves and fuel bottles—ones that are well aired and empty with no fuel smell. However, many airlines have much stricter rules of their own. Some won't carry any used stoves or used fuel bottles, some won't carry any stoves or fuel bottles at all even if new, and some won't carry used fuel bottles but will carry purged stoves.

To be sure stoves and bottles are purged, air them, preferably in sunshine, for as long as possible before the flight. Bottles can be washed out with soapy water, too.

You can send used stoves and empty fuel containers as air freight, but this is so expensive and such a hassle that you might as well buy a stove at your destination.

Some airlines will let you carry cartridge stoves but not liquid-fuel stoves. When planning a ski tour to the Yukon, I checked with the airline about stoves and was told that no used liquid-fuel stoves or fuel bottles were permitted but that cartridge stoves were fine as long as I carried no cartridges. We took cartridge stoves and discovered how difficult they are to use at 0°F (−18°C).

Fuel is obviously a hazard, and no airline will carry it. Buying fuel at your destination is the solution.

UTENSILS

Your cooking habits determine what kitchen gear you carry. One advantage of minimal cooking is that it requires minimal tools. For many years my basic kit has consisted of a 0.9-quart titanium pot with lid, a 1-pint stainless steel cup, a small knife, and two plastic spoons—total weight 11 ounces. This serves my needs both on weekends and on long summer trips. When snow camping I carry an insulated 12-ounce mug instead of the stainless steel cup that happens to weigh exactly the same.

Pans

Pots and pans for camping are hardly the most exciting items of gear, and most people give them little thought. I used aluminum pans for well over ten years, then changed to stainless steel, followed by steel-aluminum laminate and finally, for the past decade, titanium. To see how they performed, I've tried a wide selection over the years.

Aluminum, the standard backpacking cookware material for decades, is lightweight, heats evenly without hot spots, and conducts heat quickly, making for fast boiling times. But it pits, scratches, and dents easily, which makes it hard to clean and can give some foods a slight metallic flavor. Concerns that aluminum might contribute to Alzheimer's disease led aluminum pans to lose popularity to stainless steel. Now that these fears have turned out to be groundless, aluminum has had a revival. This has been helped by its low cost and by the introduction of hard-anodized aluminum, which is tough, scratchproof, and hard to dent.

Many aluminum pans, however, are made of soft metal and are poorly designed, low cost being the manufacturers' only concern. Trangia aluminum pans—sold separately from the stoves—are high quality. The 1-quart size weighs 3.5 ounces, the 1.75-quart, 5.5 ounces. I have a 5-quart Trangia pot with a lock-up bail arm that weighs only 18.5 ounces; I use it when cooking for groups (when it makes a good receptacle for packing tortillas). Open Country and Coleman are among other makers of plain aluminum pans. One pan that has become quite popular with ultralight hikers and that is very inexpensive is the Wal-Mart Grease Saver Pot, designed for straining grease. Take out the strainer and you have a 1-quart pot that weighs 2.5 ounces plus a 2-ounce lid with black plastic knob. The pot has black sides with the

RIGHT: Pot selection. Clockwise from top left: Trangia 5-quart aluminum, Olicamp 1.5-quart copper-bottomed stainless steel, MSR Alpine 2-quart stainless steel, Evernew 0.9-quart titanium, MSR DuraLite Mini 1.5-quart hard-anodized aluminum, GSI Bugaboo 1-quart nonstick aluminum. BELOW: Wal-Mart Grease Saver Pot is a budget, ultralight aluminum pan.

word "grease" imprinted and a silver base. It's very light, but the aluminum is soft and easily dented—a pot gripper made marks the first time I used it. There's a lip around the rim that could collect dirt, and the right angle between the base and sides is harder to clean than a rounded edge. For the sake of an ounce and only a small amount of cash, I'd rather have the 1-quart Trangia pan.

Hard-anodized aluminum is more expensive than standard aluminum but should last far longer. MSR, Primus, Outdoor Designs, GSI, and more all make hard-anodized aluminum cookware with nonstick coatings that are meant to be much harder wearing than those found on other metals. Primus's Litech Cook Kit has 2.1- and 1.7-quart pans, a lid, and a pot gripper and weighs 20 ounces. Primus also make the 1-quart Litech Trek Kettle, a tall pot with a pouring spout that weighs 7.5 ounces. MSR makes two hard-anodized aluminum cooksets: the DuraLite Classic with 1.5- and 2-quart pans and the DuraLite Mini with 1- and 1.5-quart pots. Both sets have a lid and a pot gripper and come with a PackTowl cloth for cleaning and to separate the pans when packed. The Classic weighs 18 ounces, the Mini 15.5 ounces. I've used the Litech Trek Kettle and the MSR DuraLite Mini pans, and they do heat evenly and are very easy to clean. The nonstick coating is far tougher than on other pans I've used, too. The 1-quart DuraLite pan weighs 4.75 ounces, comparable with titanium and lighter than steel.

Many standard aluminum pans come with nonstick coatings. These are fine as long as you're prepared to treat them carefully and always use plastic or wooden utensils. I prefer pots I can mistreat and scour with sand or gravel if necessary. (I know this shouldn't be required, but in my experience nonstick means "doesn't stick as badly or as often.") The latest nonstick coatings do seem to be tougher than those in the past, though. I've been using a rather pretty blue GSI Bugaboo nonstick 1-quart pot that weighs 11.5 ounces with lid and have found it surprisingly tough. A neat touch is that the pot gripper fastens to the outside of the pan, not the rim, and so can't scratch the Teflon coating.

Stainless steel is easy to clean, noncorroding, scratchproof, tough, and long lasting, and it doesn't taint food. Unfortunately, it's significantly heavier than aluminum and also conducts heat more slowly, leading to fractionally longer boiling times. Evernew makes excellent stainless steel cooksets, but its smallest set—1- and 0.75-quart pans, frying pan/lid, and plastic cup—weighs 21 ounces, three times the weight of an equivalent-size aluminum set. MSR's stainless steel Alpine Classic Cookset, the same as the one that comes with the Heat Exchanger, with 1.5- and 2-quart pans plus lid and pot grab, weighs 26 ounces. The lightest stainless steel pans I've found are from Olicamp; I have a 1-quart copper-coated pan taken from a larger set that, with its lid, weighs 7.5 ounces. It was my choice for a solo pan until Inoxal (see below) and then titanium came along. The copper-coated bottom is meant to speed up heat conduction. It wears off eventually, however. My pan had a shiny steel base by the time I retired it.

The best qualities of steel and aluminum can be obtained by laminating the two, with steel as the inner surface. Pans made from this are sold by Trangia under the name Duossal. Sigg used to make a fine set under the name Inoxal but these are sadly no longer available, but my usage of them applies equally to Duossal pans. The laminate is lighter than stainless steel, though not as light as aluminum. An aluminum 1.5-quart pan (without lid) tipped the scales at 4.5 ounces, stainless steel at 8.5, and Inoxal at 7.

The first time I used an Inoxal pan, the water boiled so quickly that I wasn't ready for it; during the first few days of use the pan kept boiling over and putting out the stove. I was so used to my standard stainless steel pan that I knew how long soups and meals took to come to the boil without timing them. Clearly, the Inoxal pan was more efficient.

I eventually did a comparison test using aluminum, stainless steel, and Inoxal 1.5-quart pans. I wasn't too surprised when the water took longer to boil in the stainless steel pan than in the Inoxal, though a third longer was more than I'd expected. The real surprise was that water also boiled faster in the Inoxal than in the aluminum pan—one-sixth faster, in fact. I did the test again to double-check, and the results were almost identical.

How much of this performance is due to the Inoxal material and how much to the black exterior (the other pans were shiny silver), I don't know. Duossal pans aren't black, so maybe they

MSR DuraLite Mini Cookset is made with hard-anodized aluminum.

Titanium pan and mug: my favorites.

won't be as efficient. Faster boiling time helps conserve stove fuel, and on long trips it would make a difference to the amount of fuel you had to carry. The difference would be more marked when boiling larger quantities, of course, and I suspect that while large groups might notice it, solo hikers wouldn't. Certainly when I look at my fuel usage on solo hikes over the years when using aluminum, stainless steel, Inoxal, and titanium pans, it hardly varies. It also doesn't vary whether the pans have been silver or black on the outside.

Titanium is my favorite material for pans. It doesn't pit, scratch, or affect flavor, and it cleans easily. It's much lighter than steel—45 percent lighter according to MSR—conducts heat better, and is more durable. I have a ten-year-old 0.9-quart Evernew pan with foldout handles that weighs 5 ounces with lid. It's my most-used pot by far and has had well over a year's worth of use in total, during which it's acquired just one small dent. The latest version of this pan has a nonstick coating, unfortunately from my point of view. However, there are plain titanium alternatives such as MSR's Titan Mini Cookset with 1- and 1.5-quart pans, lid, and pot gripper at 10.9 ounces and

Snow Peak's Multi Compact Titanium Cook Set with 1- and 1.5-quart pans with foldout handles and lids at 11.5 ounces. MSR also makes a 30-ounce Titan Kettle that weighs just 4.2 ounces with lid that looks excellent for solo use. The only downside to titanium is the very high cost. But once you have a pot it will last a very long time.

Whatever they're made from, pans should be simple. Fairly shallow ones with rounded edges are best, because food is less likely to burn in them and they're easy to clean. They also conduct heat more efficiently from the stove to their contents due to their large base area. Rounded bottom edges are also more efficient in theory since heat can more easily travel up the sides of the pot. Tall, narrow pots conduct heat inefficiently. Very shallow, wide pots, such as those found in many traditional-style mess kits, aren't very good for boiling water, though they're OK for frying. Pans that nest are standard. Often, though, cooksets don't contain the mix of pans you want. I like to make my own sets from different pans, checking that they nest together.

Although low weight is welcome, very thin pans can distort, making them hard to balance on stoves, and food tends to burn quickly in them.

Avoid attached handles on aluminum pans because they become very hot, but foldout handles on stainless steel and titanium pans stay reasonably cool unless you use the pan on an open fire. Bails that rise above the pan can get quite hot too. They're useful for suspending a pan above a fire and with large pans that can be hard to lift when full with a side handle or a pot gripper. Check the welds of handles or bails. They can fail, leaving you with a pan that has holes in it and a useless handle.

How big a pan you need depends on how many you're cooking for. I find a 1-quart size is easily large enough for solo cooking. For two I add a 2-quart pan; when I've cooked for ten I've found a 5-

quart pot just big enough for cooking pasta or rice, with a 2-quart pan adequate for the sauce.

Lids are very important for faster boil times and lower fuel use. In strong winds water may not boil at all unless the pan is covered. Good lids should fit tightly. Many are designed to double as frying pans, but people who fry foods tell me that lids don't work very well this way. They're often relatively heavy—the lid for my 1-quart titanium pan weighs 1.5 ounces, the one for the 1-quart Inoxal pan, 3.5 ounces—so I sometimes substitute a piece of heavy-duty foil that weighs just 0.3 ounce.

Pot Grippers

For pans without handles, you need pot grippers, or pot grabs, that clamp firmly onto the rim. I used a 2-ounce Trangia pot grab on almost every trip for nearly twenty years. MSR makes excellent pot grippers too; the 1.6-ounce PanHandler will support up to ten pounds, and the 1-ounce LiteLifter will lift full 4-quart pots. Not all pot grippers are of this quality, though; some thin aluminum ones quickly

A selection of pot grippers for pots of different sizes. You'll need the larger ones for pots that hold more than a quart.

twist out of shape. Now that I usually use the titanium pot with its fold-out handles and a lid with a knob on solo trips, I carry a pot grab only when I intend to cook over an open fire, where the handles get hot.

Ovens and Baking Devices

When I first heard about ovens for backpackers I was highly dubious, suspecting they would be heavy and difficult to use. I couldn't imagine baking anything on a small stove in the wild. However, my assumptions started to waver with reports that the Outback Oven really did work well, so I decided I had to try it. I wasn't disappointed. (Back then the Outback Oven was made by Traveling Light; now it's under the Backpacker's Pantry umbrella—backpackerspantry.com.)

If you're the sort of backpacker who hates dehydrated food and dreams of pizza, fresh bread, or apple pie, you can have them all with one of these ovens, without too much hassle.

The Outback Oven comes in three versions: the 43-ounce 12-inch for large groups, the 26-ounce

Outback Oven with Pot Parka, which can be used on its own to keep pots warm.

10-inch for two to four people (both include a Teflon-coated baking pan), and the 7-ounce Ultralight for one or two. The Outback Oven consists of a foil reflector collar that fits under the burner of your stove and directs heat upward, a stainless steel riser bar and diffuser plate to spread the heat evenly and prevent scorching, a fiberglass convection dome that fits over your pan and concentrates the heat, and a simple thermometer. All the components can be packed inside a small pan.

To use the oven you need a stove with a controllable flame plus pan supports that the heat reflector can be fitted to and that will support the riser bar/diffuser plate unit. Most stoves meet these criteria, but check that the oven will fit your stove before buying one. A windscreen is essential unless it's calm. The Ultralight oven is designed to be used with pans from 6 to 8 inches in diameter and 3 to 5 inches high, which includes most 1.5- and 2-quart pans but rules out smaller ones.

Simpler and lighter than the Outback Oven is the BakePacker. The standard version weighs 8 ounces and the ultralight one weighs 4 ounces. I've tried the latter, which is designed for pots 6 to 7

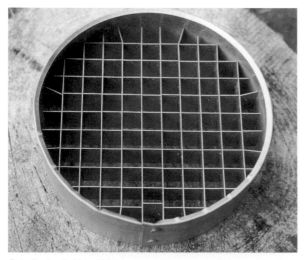

BakePacker baking grid.

inches in diameter. The BakePacker consists of an aluminum grid of heat pipes that sits in the bottom of the pan and conducts heat up through its honeycomb. You put enough water in the pot to cover the grid, then place the food to be baked on top in a plastic freezer bag or oven-roasting bag and spread it out. You then close the bag loosely and put the lid on the pot. Once the water is boiling, medium heat is enough to steam bake the mix in the bag. Because the BakePacker cooks with steam it can't produce crisp crusts, unlike the Outback Oven, and you need a supply of plastic bags. However, it's light and easy to use.

Having eaten freshly baked food on the trail, I can't go back to living on dehydrated meals all the time—or so I thought when my dalliance with baking was new and exciting. For a short while I did bake in camp occasionally. I have to admit, though, that despite my intentions it's now many years since I bothered baking in the wilds. I've discovered I can live on dried food after all.

Plates

I usually don't bother with plates or bowls because I eat straight from the pot, but this is practical only for the solo hiker. Shallow plates spill easily and don't hold much. Deep bowls are a better choice; I carry one when I'm with a group. Plastic is the standard material, with Lexan the toughest type. Plastic bowls weigh 2 to 5 ounces, depending on size. Metal bowls and plates are also available, but are cold in freezing conditions. MSR's steel Alpine Mountain Bowl holds 27 fluid ounces and weighs 3.6 ounces, the Mountain Plate has a 7.5-inch diameter and weighs 4.4 ounces, and Trangia's aluminum 8.5-inch plate weighs 3.5 ounces. Many people eat out of their mugs, but you obviously can't have a drink at the same time, which I like to do, unless you carry two mugs.

Selection of mugs. Clockwise from top left: Aladdin 12-ounce insulated, Aladdin 21-ounce insulated, GSI 32-ounce Fair Share Lexan, MSR double-wall stainless steel, Cascade Cup stainless steel, and polyethylene.

Mugs

A good mug can become a favorite item, perhaps not surprising when it provides that wake-up drink in the morning or warm-up drink after a long cold day. Plastic (usually polyethylene) is light and cheap but not very durable, and it soon develops scratches and cracks. Plastic also retains tastes—last night's tomato soup will flavor the morning's cup of coffee no matter how well you wash the mug. A typical half-pint plastic mug weighs 0.75 ounce. Lexan mugs are better; Lexan is unbreakable and doesn't retain tastes. GSI's 12-fluid-ounce Glacier Ice Lexan Mug weighs 2.9 ounces. If you like large drinks or use your mug for eating, GSI's FairShare Lexan Mug is probably the largest around, with a capacity of 32 fluid ounces. It has a screw-on lid and weighs 7 ounces.

Drinks cool down fairly quickly in a single-walled polyethylene mug, which is fine on a hot summer day but not so good on a frosty morning. The classic foam-insulated mug is the answer. This keeps drinks warm for a long time in the cold, even if you leave the lid off. The main brands are Aladdin and Whirley, which offer a large array of shapes and sizes and also make own-brand mugs for other companies. The nearest to a standard size is probably the 12-fluid-ounce mug. The Aladdin model weighs 5 ounces, including a half-ounce lid. If you want a larger mug there's a 21-fluid-ounce one that weighs 7 ounces. I use the 12-fluid-ounce mug for cold-weather trips. In summer I find it keeps drinks too hot for too long. If you want your drink to stay really hot for a long time, leave the lid on the mug. This really does make a huge difference.

Insulated plastic mugs still hold tastes, though not as badly as polyethylene ones. Metal doesn't. But to drink hot liquids out of aluminum or enamel mugs you need asbestos lips. This means that, except for cold drinks, the cup that comes with the Svea 123R stove and doubles as a burner cover is useless. However, stainless steel and titanium mugs are fine: they don't burn your lips or get scratched and are very durable. I have a pint mug, REI's Cascade Cup, that I bought many years ago; it can be used as a pan on any stove because it has a wide base. It weighs 4 ounces and has a clip-off handle that folds away under the cup. Because I can boil water in it for a drink while I'm eating out of my larger pan, it's my favorite of the ten camping mugs that I'm somewhat surprised to discover I own. It nests neatly inside my 0.9-quart pan. The Cascade Cup is a larger version of the classic Sierra Cup, which holds 10 fluid ounces and weighs 3 ounces. I find the Sierra Cup a little unstable, since the top is much wider than the base. Drinks cool down in it very quickly, too, but many people like it. Olicamp makes a titanium Sierra Cup weighing 1.5 ounces.

To save an ounce, I've sometimes used a 3-ounce MSR 23-fluid-ounce titanium pan with foldout handles as a mug. It's not quite as easy to drink from as the Cascade Cup because liquid can dribble down the sides, though it's fine as a pan. MSR doesn't make this model anymore, but the 23-fluid-ounce pan in Snow Peak's Multi Compact Titanium Cook Set seems effectively the same.

There are conventional tall, narrow stainless steel mugs; I have a pint one that weighs 4 ounces. It can just about be used as a pan on stoves with closely spaced pot supports, such as the Svea 123R, but it's not really the right shape for this. Titanium mugs weigh less (and cost much more). Snow Peak's 21-fluid-ounce single-walled mug weighs 2.9 ounces.

Double-walled stainless steel mugs come in 10- and 12-fluid-ounce sizes if you want to keep drinks hot in a metal mug. They're heavy though, —the 10-fluid-ounce Markill mug weighs 11.5 ounces. Titanium ones are again much lighter and much more expensive. Snow Peak's double-walled 16-fluid-ounce titanium mug weighs 4.2 ounces.

Eating Implements

Lexan plastic works well for cutlery and is very strong. It can be broken, despite claims to the contrary, though this has happened to me only once, and the GSI spoons I now have are over a decade old. A tablespoon and teaspoon together weigh 0.8 ounce. Other plastic spoons break under the weight of a baked bean. If I carried them, I'd take several. Stainless steel cutlery is durable but heavy. Titanium is lighter but pricey. MSR's Titan Spoon weighs half an ounce. Special clip-together camping cutlery seems unnecessarily fussy and always includes forks, which aren't needed in the wilds. Everything can be eaten with fingers or a spoon. If you do want a fork occasionally, you could try a spork—a spoon with tines on the top edge. Snow Peak makes a titanium spork weighing half an ounce. A knife is useful, but I don't bother with a

Wash pots well away from water and pour wash water into thick vegetation or onto bare ground.

Forest kitchen with the stove on a rock to prevent it from scorching the ground or setting the pine needles alight.

cutlery knife when I have a pocketknife anyway. Knives are discussed in the next chapter.

Washing Dishes

Stainless steel and titanium clean much more easily than aluminum. Generally a wipe with a damp cloth is enough, although for hygienic reasons you should sterilize pans and utensils thoroughly every few days. I do this with boiling water.

I don't carry detergent or dishwashing liquid—it's unnecessary and a pollutant, even if it's biodegradable. Nor do I wash dishes directly in a water source or tip food scraps into one. Dirty dishwater should always be poured onto a bare patch of ground or into thick vegetation. To make dishwashing easier, pour cold water into a pan once it's empty to stop food residue from cementing itself to the inside. Some foods are worse than others—oatmeal is particularly bad. Hard-to-clean pans can be scoured with gravel or even snow to remove debris. Mostly I just use a soft dishcloth, which I rinse out regularly and hang on the pack to dry. Scourer sponges are an alternative but are harder to keep clean. A bandanna can be pressed into service if necessary, something I've done on trips where I've forgotten a dishcloth.

Packing

I generally pack my stove, pans, and utensils together in a small stuff sack. I don't pack the stove inside the pans, since this tends to dirty them, although manufacturers tout this packing "convenience" as an advantage of many small stoves. I usually carry fuel bottles in outside pockets in case of leaks or stand them upright at the bottom of the main compartment below my food bag, which is where I keep fuel cartridges, too. The stove and pans also end up there, since I rarely use them during the day. If you cook at lunchtime, you'll need to pack them somewhere accessible.

SITING THE KITCHEN

I like to site my kitchen next to my sleeping bag. That way I can have breakfast in bed—a good way to face a cold or wet morning, and nice any time.

TOP: Kitchen dug out of snow. ABOVE: Melting snow inside a floorless single-skin pyramid tent.

The stove needs to be placed on bare earth or on short, sparse vegetation so that the heat doesn't cause any damage. If the plant growth is long and luxurious, I try to find a flat rock to place the stove on, to avoid singeing the vegetation. You must, of course, return the rock to its proper place when you've finished. I set up the stove, then sort out the food I need for the evening. When all the kitchen items are arranged near the stove and I know where everything is, I start cooking.

You have to modify this pattern anywhere bears are potential visitors. In this case it's advisable to site the kitchen at least 100 yards downwind of where you sleep, because the smell of food might attract a bear during the night. I look for a sheltered spot with a good view, and perhaps a log or tree stump to sit on or lean against. Clean utensils can be left in place overnight. Dirty ones should be hung with the food.

> MAN IS AN ANIMAL WHO MORE THAN
> ANY OTHER CAN ADAPT HIMSELF TO ALL
> CLIMATES AND CIRCUMSTANCES.
>
> —Walden, *Henry David Thoreau*

comfort and safety

in camp and on the trail

To make any walk safe and enjoyable, numerous small items (and skills) are useful. Some are essential, some are never necessary, though they may enhance your stay in the wilderness. I'm always surprised at the number of odds and ends in my pack, yet not one of them is superfluous.

LIGHT

No one goes backpacking in the Far North—Alaska, northern Canada, Greenland, Iceland—during midwinter because there's little daylight —none at all if you're north of the Arctic Circle. In midsummer, however, the Far North is light twenty-four hours a day—no artificial light is needed at "night." Most places backpackers frequent are farther south, though, and some form of light is needed regardless of the time of year. How much you need depends on where you are and when. At Lake Louise in Banff National Park in the Canadian Rockies, there are over sixteen and a half hours of daylight in mid-June, but only eight hours in mid-December; in Yosemite you'll have fourteen and three-quarters hours in June but more than nine and a half in December.

The LED Revolution

The new millennium saw a revolution in lighting with the introduction of lights using *LEDs* (light emitting diodes) rather than incandescent bulbs. My old headlamps are gathering dust at the back of my gear shelves, since LED lights are lower in weight, are much more durable, and use far less battery power, which means batteries last much longer, also saving weight. An LED will last for up to ten years of constant use before burning out, so most people will never need to replace one. LEDs are tough, too, unlike standard bulbs; since there's no thin glass to shatter or thin wires to snap, they're almost unbreakable. There really is no need to carry a spare. Battery life is greatly extended because LEDs don't give out heat, again unlike standard bulbs, so much less energy is needed to

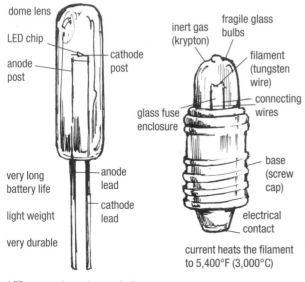

LEDs versus incandescent bulbs.

dome lens

LED chip

anode post

cathode post

very long battery life

light weight

very durable

anode lead

cathode lead

inert gas (krypton)

fragile glass bulbs

filament (tungsten wire)

connecting wires

glass fuse enclosure

base (screw cap)

electrical contact

current heats the filament to 5,400°F (3,000°C)

power a headlamp—some twenty times less, in fact. The Petzl Micro with standard incandescent bulb runs for five hours on two AA alkaline batteries; the Petzl Tikka with three LEDs runs for 150 hours on three AAA alkaline batteries. The Tikka is half the weight of the Micro, too. If an LED light is turned on accidentally in your pack, the batteries are unlikely to be dead when you need it.

LED light is white rather than yellow, so colors appear as in daylight. This is particularly useful when reading maps. LED light is also unbroken, with none of those dark circles found with standard bulbs. I find it excellent for reading. LEDs aren't perfect, however. With most the light is always a flood, which is great for illuminating a small area such as a tent and for close-up use, but it can't be focused to a tight spot, so there's a limit as to how far it can be projected. The number of LEDs doesn't really affect how far the beam goes; it just determines how bright it is within the area it covers. For long distance you still need incandescent bulbs, especially halogen ones, but these bulbs use up batteries very fast and aren't neces-

sary much of the time. To overcome this, hybrid headlamps come with both LEDs and bulbs, so you can use the latter only when necessary. I find these headlamps useful in winter. Otherwise I prefer the lighter, smaller pure LED ones.

This problem is being overcome, however. The first 1-watt LED, said to be brighter than equivalent incandescent bulbs, is used in Princeton Tec's Yukon HL headlamp. The lamp also has three standard LEDs for when you don't need the bright one. The Yukon HL runs on three AA batteries and the burn times are 44 hours with the 1-watt LED and 120 hours with the three standard LEDs. It weighs 8 ounces. Black Diamond has a similar sounding headlamp, the Zenix, with a "Hyper-Bright" LED with five times the light of standard LEDs and a prefocused beam. There are two standard LEDs, too. The Zenix runs on three AAA batteries, which last 12 to 15 hours with the HyperBright LED and 140 with the standard ones. I haven't used either of these lamps but they sound like the future for backpacking lights for dark times of the year.

Wearing a headlamp leaves your hands free for tasks like making camp or cooking.

LEDs fade slowly as battery power declines, so near the end of the batteries' life you might be able to read a book but won't be able to see very far. Batteries that will no longer power a standard bulb will still provide light with an LED. To save batteries, you can turn down the brightness on some lights or switch off some of the LEDs.

Headlamps and Flashlights

Headlamps and handheld flashlights both have advantages and disadvantages. Overall I think headlamps are superior for backpacking. In the past, both were notorious for being unreliable. My field notes from the 1970s and 1980s reflect this: in 1985, two flashlights failed during my Continental Divide hike, and I finished that trek with a large, heavy model, the only one I could buy in a remote country store. By the end of the 1980s, however, tough, long-lasting flashlights and headlamps had swept the market. Many designs don't have on/off switches (which failed so regularly on the older models). Instead, you twist the lamp housing to switch them on. Others have recessed switches that aren't easily damaged or accidentally turned on.

There are a vast number of traditional incandescent bulb flashlights. A classic is the Mini Maglite AA, which runs for five hours on two alkaline AA batteries. It's made from tough aluminum and weighs 5 ounces. It also has an adjustable beam and can be turned into a small upright lantern by using the headpiece as a stand. There's no separate switch; you twist the head to turn it on. Smaller and lighter is the Pelican MityLite, which runs for two hours on three alkaline AAA batteries. It's made of bright yellow polycarbonate (harder to lose than a dark-colored light), has a rotary head switch, and weighs 1.75 ounces. I've used the Mini Maglite and MityLite extensively,

and they are both tough and surprisingly bright for such small flashlights. They tend to be used around the house rather than on the trail, however. Other reputable flashlight makers include Durabeam, PeliLite, Eveready, Streamlight, Tektite, and Princeton Tec.

Tiny LED flashlights may seem like toys rather than serious lights. They're not, as I discovered on my first day out on the Arizona Trail when I ended up following a narrow, snow-covered trail up steep slopes in the dark. Rather than take off my pack and dig out my headlamp, I used a single LED Sapphire Light weighing half an ounce that I happened to have in a pants pocket. You have to keep the switch pressed to get a light, so I just used it every few yards or so to check where the trail went next. It was just adequate. It's guaranteed for life, including the batteries, but it's since disappeared—the only problem with such small lights. I replaced it with an even smaller Princeton Tec Pulsar (it's a touch bigger than a quarter) that weighs a quarter of an ounce and mostly lives on my key ring. The two lithium cells are meant to last twelve to fourteen hours, which is a lot of squeeze time. I wouldn't rely on one of these tiny lights alone, except maybe in the Arctic in summer, but one makes a good backup. Larger LED flashlights are made by various companies such as Streamlight and Lightwave.

Handheld lights are less costly than headlamps, and there's a much wider choice, but they're far less versatile, especially for camping. Many years ago I discovered that a headlamp is much more useful because it leaves both hands free. After having pitched tents and cooked while gagging on a flashlight held in my mouth, stopping every few minutes to recover, using a headlamp was a revelation. First developed for predawn starts on Alpine mountaineering routes, many of the best headlamps come from moun-

HEADLAMPS

Brand	LEDs/ Bulb	Batteries	Weight with Batteries (oz.)	Burn Time (hr.)	Beam (ft.)	Water Resistance
Black Diamond Moonlight	4 LED	3 AAA	4	70	50	waterproof
Black Diamond Ion	2 LED	6 V	1	15	50	waterproof
Petzl Tikka	3 LED	3 AAA	2.5	150	N/A	not completely waterproof
Princeton Tec Aurora	3 LED	3 AAA	3	50-110-160	N/A	waterproof
Black Diamond Supernova	1 LED/ xenon halogen	4 AA/6 V	9	1,000 with 35 LED, 3-5-10 with halogen	35 with LED, 165-230-330 with halogen	not completely waterproof
Petzl Myo 3	3 LED/ xenon halogen	4 AA	8.5	180 with LED, 4 with halogen	50 with LED, 330 with halogen	water resistant
Petzl Duo LED 5	5 LED/ halogen	4 AA	11	160 with LED, 4.5 with halogen	55 with LED, 330 with halogen	water resistant
Princeton Tec Switchback	3 LED/ incandescent	2 AA/4 C with battery pack	7.5 with AA	40 with LED plus AA, 300 with LED plus C, 5-24 with bulb	N/A	waterproof to depth of 33 feet

taineering equipment manufacturers such as Petzl and Black Diamond. In early models, wires trailed from the lamp to battery packs you clipped to your belt or carried in a pocket, and they constantly caught on things. Then came headlamps with the battery case on the headband, a design far more compact, lightweight, and easy to use.

There are various webbing headbands that can adapt a small flashlight for use as a headlamp. I have a Nite Ize headband (1 ounce) that takes a Mini Maglite. It's not as comfortable as a real headlamp, and you can't adjust the direction of the beam, but it does leave your hands free.

For many years I used French-made Petzl headlamps exclusively, since they had the best designs along with superb quality. They always proved very comfortable and reliable. In winter I used the classic Petzl Zoom, a powerful light weighing 11.5 ounces with a flat 4.5-volt battery; in summer I used the lighter Micro, weighing 5 ounces with two AA batteries. These have now been replaced by LED headlamps, both in Petzl's range and in my gear store.

Petzl took the lead with the new LED lights; their tiny three-LED Tikka and Zipka were the first LED headlamps. They're ultralight, too, at 2.5 ounces for the Tikka, which has a wide elasticized headband, and 2.25 ounces for the Zipka, which has a retractable cord. When the Tikka first appeared it immediately became my most-used headlamp, and I've used one for many months in total. It's very comfortable to wear since it's so light, but it doesn't have a swivel head, which can be awkward at times. The switch is recessed and quite stiff; I've never had it turn on by accident. Petzl has followed up these headlamps with the 2.75-ounce Tikka Plus and 2.3-ounce Zipka Plus, each with a tilting head, four LEDs, and four power settings.

The Tikka was soon followed by a growing mass of LED headlamps, several of which I've tried. The lightest by far is the Black Diamond Ion, a tiny but powerful two-LED light that weighs a fraction over an ounce with battery. It has a comfortable headband and a swivel head. I used one as my only light on a five-week hike in the High Sierra one summer and found it adequate even for hiking and making camp after dark. The relatively short fifteen-hour battery life is a downside, though. The 6-volt batteries are quite expensive and hard to find, too. Slightly heavier is the two-LED Princeton Tec Scout at 2 ounces with batteries. This runs off four 2032 lithium coin cells. It has three power levels—high, medium, and low—and two flash modes. Battery

life is twenty-four, thirty-six, and forty-eight hours for the different modes.

The three-LED Princeton Tec Aurora has become my favorite headlamp for summer use. It weighs half an ounce more than the Tikka but has a swivel head and three brightness settings. The only niggle is that the switch is easily depressed, so you have to take care not to switch it on unintentionally. Slightly heavier at 4 ounces but also a bit brighter with four LEDs is the Black Diamond Moonlight. This also has a battery box on the back of the headband rather than immediately behind the LEDs, plus a third strap that runs over the top of the head. This makes it more comfortable to wear for long periods than the smaller headlamps, and it can't slip down. There's no cover over the LEDs; Black Diamond says this isn't necessary. The push-button switch can be protected from accidental pressure when the headlamp isn't in use.

From late fall to early spring, when hiking and camping in the dark is more likely owing to longer nights and a brighter, more focused light can be

The Petzl Myo 3 with three LEDs and halogen bulb (left) is good for when you need a long beam. The Black Diamond Moonlight with four LEDs (middle) and the Princeton Tec Aurora with three LEDs (right) are good for most uses and are very economical with batteries.

useful for selecting campsites and illuminating the route some distance ahead, I carry a hybrid headlamp with LEDs and an incandescent bulb. All these heavier headlamps have straps that run over the top of the head as well as a headband and battery boxes that sit on the back of the head. Of the models I've tried, my favorite is the Petzl Myo, which replaces the Zoom. This comes in three versions. The standard Myo just has a xenon halogen bulb. The Myo 3 has three LEDs as well, the Myo 5, five LEDs. I have the 8.5-ounce Myo 3, and it's an excellent headlamp. It has a swivel head that you twist to turn it on and a zoom function with the halogen bulb so you can spread the light or focus on a specific point. The head can be locked in place so it doesn't turn on accidentally.

Other good LED/bulb headlamps are the 9-ounce Black Diamond Supernova, which has just one LED plus a useful 6-volt backup battery that powers the LED if the main batteries run out. There are three brightness settings with the halogen bulb. It's a good headlamp but would be better with more LEDs. Petzl's Duo comes with three, five, or eight LEDs plus a halogen bulb. I tried the Duo LED 5 and it's fine, though bulkier and heavier than the Myo. The head pivots, with a noisy cracking, and the beam zooms in and out with the halogen bulb. The click switch can be locked in place. Princeton Tec's Switchback has three LEDs and a zoom beam. The main point of interest is the separate battery pack that takes four C cells that will run the standard bulb for twenty-four hours and can be stored in a pocket in freezing weather. The push-button switch is stiff and has to be held down for a while before the light comes on, so it's unlikely to be operated by accident. Other good-looking headlamps come from Tektite and Pelican.

Whatever light you use, it needs to be handy when you need it. I usually carry mine in a pack pocket. In camp I keep it close to the head of my sleeping bag so I can find it without too much trouble if I wake up in the dark.

With an LED light I don't bother carrying spare batteries unless I'm out for several weeks (or can't remember how much use the batteries in the headlamp have had). If you don't have an LED light, it's wise to carry spare batteries and bulbs. Standard tungsten bulbs are fine for camp use and don't use up batteries quickly. With lights that use only a few AA or AAA batteries, the beam is quite weak, however, and not good for walking in the dark. Krypton light is yellow, too, which can make reading maps difficult. Halogen and xenon bulbs (the space-age names refer to the gas they're filled with) are much brighter and throw a whiter light, but they also use up batteries much more quickly. Alkaline batteries are standard. Alternatives are lithium and rechargeable batteries (nickel-cadmium, or nicads, and nickel–metal hydride, or NiMH). Lithium batteries are expensive, but they last much longer than alkaline ones in cold weather; they also maintain a steadier beam until their power is completely drained. Lithiums are slightly lighter as well. Two Energizer 2 lithium AA batteries weigh 1.5 ounces, and two alkaline batteries weigh 2 ounces. Lithium batteries are also available in AAA, but not C or D sizes. In temperatures above freezing, lithium batteries have no advantages over alkalines when used in low-drain items like flashlights or headlamps. I use lithiums on trips where I expect bitter cold, but not on summer hikes.

Rechargeable batteries make environmental sense, since disposable batteries are toxic and require much energy to produce. Early rechargeables were difficult to use; they took a very long time to recharge and needed to be fully drained before being recharged again. The latest ones are much easier to use; they can be recharged in a few hours, and they don't need to be fully drained before recharging. Indeed, NiMH batteries should be recharged before they are fully drained. NiMH batteries are more environmentally friendly than nicads, since they contain no toxic materials, whereas nicads contain the rather nasty heavy metal cadmium, and they're easier to use. They can be recharged hundreds of times—up to a thousand, says Energizer of its NiMH battery. They don't hold a charge very long in warm temperatures, however. If you keep them in a freezer the charge lasts a long time, but that isn't much use on long hikes in anything but winter conditions.

A solar charger seems to be the answer, and there are several portable ones. I have a Brunton Battery Saver AA solar charger that charges four AA cells. It weighs 8 ounces, however, and so far I've used it only on a south-facing windowsill. It takes about twelve to sixteen hours of bright sunshine to charge four batteries, which on my windowsill means at least four sunny days. I live at 58 degrees north, though. Those living farther south should be able to charge batteries much more quickly.

Solar World's SPC-4 at 1.5 ounces looks to be the lightest charger for trail use. It charges four AA or AAA batteries. To use a solar charger effectively you'd have to strap it to the top of your pack or else spend several hours in a very sunny spot. Of course, if you stay in one place for a day you could use it then. I intend taking a solar charger on a hike to see how well it works, but I'll carry some alkaline cells as backup. I suspect that charging batteries at home will be easier.

Candles

Candles give out a soft, pleasant light plus a little heat. I often use one in camp for reading and making notes. On cold, dark winter nights, I'm always amazed at how much warmth and friendliness a single candle flame can give, especially if you put the stove windscreen behind it as a reflector and to keep off breezes. The candles designed for candle lanterns (see below) have fairly wide bases and stand up on their own. Ordinary household candles are less expensive but need to be propped up with a tent stake or small stones or dug into the ground to stop them from falling over. I put a candle on a rock or an upturned cooking pot in a place where it won't land on anything flammable if it falls or is knocked over. I use candles in tent vestibules but never bring one into the inner tent. Used this way a lit candle is fairly safe, as long as you don't leave it unattended. After melting holes in two doors, I also make sure the candle isn't too close to the fly sheet. Because batteries last so long in LED lights, I don't often carry candles in the summer anymore. In winter the warmth is welcome.

Lanterns

Candle and Oil Lanterns

Candle lanterns protect the flame from wind and can be hung up so the light covers a wider area. One will easily light a small tent or the area around the head of your sleeping bag if you're sleeping under the stars. Most come with hanging chains, but these are rather short; I add a length of cord so I can hang the lantern from a branch. The heat from the lantern isn't enough to melt the cord—or at least it hasn't done it yet. The lanterns themselves do get hot, though, and need to be kept away from anything that might melt. If you stand the lantern on the ground there should be enough space for it to topple over without setting anything on fire.

When they work properly candle lanterns are excellent, but problems do arise. The most com-

A candle lantern provides light and warmth.

mon design uses a glass cylinder to protect the flame and a metal or plastic candleholder. The glass slides into the candleholder to protect it when packed. The candleholder has a spring in its base that pushes the candle up as it burns. UCO and Northern Lights are the main brand names. Candle lanterns weigh 5 to 8 ounces, depending on the model and the material (some are aluminum, some brass, some thermoplastic). A candle—they take stubby ones rather than household candles—adds 2.5 ounces. Candles can last eight to nine hours, but in practice I've found that most start to sputter and overflow before they're two-thirds used, leaving the inside of the lantern covered with wax that has to be scraped off—not an easy job, especially in camp in the dark. Part of the reason seems to be that most wicks don't run straight down the middle of the candles but curve off to the side halfway down. Although I used to use one regularly, it's now many years since I used a candle lantern, mainly

because of this problem with the candles. In summer an LED light is adequate, and in winter I carry a plain candle if I want to keep the weight down or a butane-propane lantern if weight isn't so significant. There are lightweight lanterns that burn the little "tealight" tub candles. UCO makes one called the Mini, and Olicamp makes one called the Footprint Lantern. Both weigh 3 ounces. I find tub candles too dim to be useful, however.

For a while I used my lantern with a thermoplastic insert called a Candoil that burns lamp oil via a cotton wick. It can also burn kerosene, though it's very smoky. The Northern Lights Candoil insert weighs 3.5 ounces. It's not as bright as a candle, and the wick has to be adjusted to just the right length to minimize smoking and maximize light output, which is a little fiddly and can take time. The Candoil holds about 1.7 fluid ounces of lamp oil and burns ten to twelve hours. Northern Lights also makes the Ultra Light, an oil-burning lantern that weighs 5.5 ounces and burns for seventeen hours on one fill. Even with lamp oil, I always ended up with greasy fingers after using the Candoil, the main reason I stopped using it.

An interesting new twist is the UCO Duo, which has an LED light in the base so you can use the lantern as a flashlight. You can also remove the LED and attach it to a headband. The batteries are said to last forty hours. The base doesn't add any extra weight, since it replaces the normal one. The LED base can be bought separately if you want to fit one to your lantern.

White-Gas, Kerosene, and Cartridge Lanterns

Lanterns that run off butane-propane cartridges are fine for base camps and for backpacking in winter when a bright light and a little warmth can be welcome. They emit a constant hiss when lit, which can be irritating, though I soon got used to it. They use far less gas than stoves, since the heat output is much less, and will run well on almost empty cartridges that will barely power a stove.

Most lanterns have glass globes that surround and disperse the light from a glowing, lacelike *mantle*, which in turn surrounds a jet. Both the globe and the mantle are fragile, and the lantern must be protected in the pack.

Many lanterns are quite heavy, but a few are light enough for backpacking. I've had a Coleman Peak 1 Micro Lantern for many years and have used it often on winter trips. It weighs 7 ounces and has protective lightweight steel bars around the globe. The output is a bright 75 to 80 watts. It runs off standard resealable cartridges. More recently I've tried Primus's similar EasyLight lantern, which weighs 7.5 ounces and also runs off standard cartridges. The EasyLight has electronic Piezo ignition, which does make lighting it much easier, since you don't have to remove the top and risk burning your fingers when you insert a match. Although I don't like Piezo ignitions with stoves, in lanterns they seem much more durable, since they're protected inside the globe. The 7-ounce Campingaz Lumostar C270 lantern runs off CV cartridges, which could be useful in places where these are sold rather than standard ones. Coleman makes a lantern—the 12-ounce Exponent—that runs off Powermax fuel (see pages 299–300). It doesn't use the cartridges, though. Instead it has a fuel tank that is filled from a Powermax cartridge. Brunton also make a refillable lantern, the strangely named Glorb, that weighs 8 ounces and runs off butane lighter fluid. The Glorb has Piezo ignition, and the light output can be varied for a dimmer or brighter light. The maximum output is 60 watts.

The best-looking lantern for backpacking how-ever is the Primus Micron. This lantern weighs just 4.4 ounces and has stainless steel mesh instead of a breakable glass globe. The Micron lantern uses the same system as the Micron stove, including the Piezo lighter, and is meant to be very fuel efficient. It's also said to be quieter than other cartridge lanterns. Output is 70 watts. I'm looking forward to trying one.

White-gas and kerosene lanterns are heavier; at 30 ounces, the Coleman Peak 1 Liquid Fuel Lantern is one of the lightest. I wouldn't bother with one for backpacking.

Lightsticks

Lightsticks are thin plastic tubes that when bent break an internal glass capsule, allowing two nontoxic chemicals to mix and produce a pale greenish light. To me they seem no more than a curiosity (at least for backpacking). I've never carried one. If you want an emergency light a tiny LED one would be the best choice.

HEALTH AND BODY CARE

First Aid

Basic first-aid knowledge is essential for hikers, since it may be some time before help arrives if there's an accident. Taking a Red Cross, YMCA, or similar first-aid course is a good idea. Many outdoor schools also offer courses in wilderness first aid. There are many books on the subject, too. *Medicine for Mountaineering*, edited by James Wilkerson, is the standard work. It's comprehensive and good for home reference, but at 26.5 ounces it's rather heavy for carrying in the pack. More portable at 6.5 and 7 ounces are Paul Gill's *Wilderness First Aid* and William Forgey's *Basic Essentials:*

Wilderness First Aid. Even lighter at 4 ounces and the only first-aid book I've ever actually carried is Fred Darvill's clear and concise *Mountaineering Medicine.* Be forewarned: a close study of these texts may convince you that you're lucky to have survived the dangers of wilderness travel and that you'd better not go back again! (The antidote to this is a glance through the statistics on accidents that occur in the home and on the road—driving *to* the wilderness is likely to be far more hazardous than anything you do *in* it.)

First-aid basics consist of knowledge, skill, and a few medical supplies. The last are only of use if you have the first two. There are many packaged first-aid kits. Some are very good, some are pretty poor. Outdoor Research, Adventure Medical, and REI are among those that offer good ones. But the problem with even the best ones is that they usually contain items I don't feel are necessary, while items I consider essential are absent. Putting together a kit from the shelves of the local drugstore, as I do, means you get exactly what you want. It also means you know what you've got and are likely to know how to use it. I've been surprised at how many people with packaged kits don't know what's in them, let alone how to use everything.

Every book on wilderness medicine and backpacking features a different list of what a first-aid kit should contain. Many years ago I carried a fairly comprehensive kit (weighing a pound), but in keeping with cutting weight wherever possible, I now take it only when I'm venturing into remote areas where help could be many days away. The total weight has dwindled to 8 to 10 ounces, too.

Mostly I carry a small kit weighing 4 to 5 ounces. The contents vary, but it usually contains:

- first-aid information leaflet
- 1 6-inch-wide elastic or crepe bandage for knee and ankle sprains

- 4 2nd Skin Blister Pads or other gel dressings
- roll of 1-inch tape for holding dressings in place
- 2 2-by-2-inch nonadhesive absorbent dressings for burns
- 2 butterfly closures
- 3 or 4 antiseptic wipes for cleaning wounds and blisters
- 12 assorted adhesive bandages for cuts
- 10 foil-wrapped painkillers—ibuprofen or aspirin
- 2 safety pins for fastening slings and bandages

I keep the kit in a small zippered nylon case marked with a large white cross and the words *First Aid.* Having your first-aid kit clearly identifiable is important in case someone else has to rummage through your pack for it. There are no scissors or tweezers in the kit because I have these on my knife and no large bandages because a bandanna or torn piece of clothing could be used. Other items can be used for first aid too—needles and thread, duct tape, moist wipes, even pack frames, foam pads, or tent poles for splints.

For a larger kit I usually add the following:

- 1 4-by-6-inch sterile dressing for major bleeding
- 2 sterile lint dressings for severe bleeding
- 1 7-inch elastic net to hold a dressing on a head wound
- extra antiseptic wipes
- 4 butterfly closures
- 4 2nd Skin Blister Pads or other gel dressings
- triangular bandage for arm fracture or shoulder dislocation
- 4 safety pins
- 1 4-by-4-inch sterile nonadhesive dressing for burns
- 20 extra painkillers

On long walks in remote country I also carry prescription antibiotics in case of illness or infection and prescription painkillers—ask your doctor about this. If you need personal medication, it will have to be added to the kit as well, of course. Such medicines don't last forever, though—be aware of expiration dates.

Groups need to carry larger, more comprehensive kits. The one I take when I'm leading ski tours weighs 24 ounces. A plastic food storage container keeps a large first-aid kit from being crushed. Nylon pouches are lighter, however, and fine for the smaller kits.

Tooth Care

It's wise to have a dental checkup immediately before a long trip. I can tell you from painful experience that a lost filling or an abscess is to be avoided if at all possible. If your teeth, like mine, are as much metal as enamel, I suggest carrying temporary filling materials such as Dentemp or Cavit. If you're really concerned about tooth problems, you could take an emergency repair kit such as the Adventure Medical Dental Medic kit. This comes in a waterproof case and contains a tube of temporary cavity filling material, a wax stick for filling cavities or stabilizing loose teeth, anesthetic gel for pain, a black tea bag for relief of dental pain and bleeding, 12 yards of dental floss, 3 toothpicks, 5 gauze pellets, 5 gauze rolls, and an instruction sheet for various dental emergencies.

Wash Kit

It's surprising how long you can go without washing your hair or body; I managed twenty-three days in the High Sierra on the Pacific Crest Trail. When every drop of water you use has to be produced laboriously by melting snow, washing—except for your hands—becomes unimportant, though I did occasionally rub my face and armpits with snow. Still, a minimum of cleanliness is necessary. In particular, you should always wash your hands after going to the toilet and before handling food. I usually manage to rinse my face most days as well. When it's cold, I save more thorough washing for when I get home or, on long trips, for a shower in a motel or campground. In hot weather I wash more often, if only to stay cool. Large water containers hung from trees make good showers—if you leave them in the sun for a few hours beforehand, the water is surprisingly warm.

Proper hand washing is essential in a group to avoid spreading stomach bugs, and it's wise for solo hikers as well. There are several phosphate-free, biodegradable soaps, including Coghlan's Plus 50 Sportsman's Soap in small squeeze tubes weighing an ounce, Campsuds in 2- and 4-ounce plastic bottles, Mountain Suds Backpacking Soap in 2-ounce bottles, and Dr Bronner's Soap (various scents) in 4-ounce plastic bottles. Even these soaps can pollute water sources, however, so use a minimum amount and dispose of washing water on gravel or rock at least 200 feet from any lake or stream. I prefer moist wipes, which I drop in my garbage bag after use, or hand-sanitizer gel; neither requires any water. On long trips I've carried a pack of fifty wipes. Mostly, though, I decant two or three a day into a Ziploc bag. Most recently I've been carrying antibacterial Atwater Carey Hand Sanitizer, which comes in 2-ounce plastic bottles, since this leaves no residue or trash to carry out. The main ingredient is ethyl alcohol, so once you've rubbed some on your hands it evaporates very quickly, leaving your hands feeling fresh. Whether I carry sanitizer or wipes, they go in the plastic bag with my toilet paper to remind me to use them immediately after defecating.

If you want to do more than wash your hands

or face, No-Rinse Bathing Wipes are larger than standard ones. They can be useful for removing dirt and sweat at the end of a trip so you don't smell too bad on the journey home or in that first restaurant. No-Rinse also makes 2- and 8-ounce bottles of No-Rinse Shampoo and Body Wash that could be used for the same purpose.

I don't carry a cotton washcloth or towel; both are heavy and slow to dry. A bandanna does for the former, a piece of clothing for the latter. Fleece jackets make particularly good towels. If you don't fancy using clothing to dry yourself, there are small, light pack towels. Cascade Designs' Packtowl is made from a highly absorbent viscose material and comes in several sizes. The smallest 10-by-30-inch size weighs 1.5 ounces, the extra-large 30-by-50-inch weighs 7.5 ounces. The Packtowl works surprisingly well. I've tried the small one, which is fine for hands and face, and it soaks up masses of water—nine times its own weight, according to Cascade Designs—most of which can be wrung out so you don't have to carry it. Tie it on the back of the pack, and the Packtowl dries quickly.

My current wash kit consists of a small toothbrush (without the handle removed), a very small tube of toothpaste (I collect those often provided on long-distance flights, or you can decant some into a tiny plastic bottle), moist wipes, and a comb. The kit weighs about 2 ounces in its Ziploc bag. Like soap, toothpaste should be deposited a long way from water. You can get biodegradable toothpaste, but toothpaste isn't essential anyway; if I run out I do without. I carry a comb so I can look somewhat presentable in towns on long hikes. If I won't be passing through any towns I leave the comb in my car or with any clean clothes I've left to be picked up after the hike.

I don't shave, so I don't carry a razor. Those who do shave carry disposable razors—and usu-

ally curse them and the difficulty of shaving in the wilds—or else a tiny battery-powered shaver, such as Braun's Pocket Twist, which runs on two AA batteries.

Biting and Stinging Insects and Arachnids

If you're unprepared, swarms of biting insects—mosquitoes, black flies, no-see-ums—can drive you crazy in certain areas during the summer. Bites can itch maddeningly for hours, even days. I've yet to meet anyone immune to insect bites, though sensitivity varies and some people suffer much more than others. Biting insects are usually found in damp, shady areas. Camping in dry, breezy places is one way to minimize insect problems, though it's often not possible. Insects are usually less evident when you're walking, but the moment you stop anywhere sheltered they're likely to appear. The increase in West Nile virus, spread by mosquitoes, makes prevention important. West Nile virus affects the central nervous system and can be serious.

Insect repellent and clothing are your main defenses. You can cover up with tightly woven, light-colored clothing (dark colors apparently attract some insects) and fasten wrist and ankle cuffs tightly. A head net (1 to 2 ounces), worn over a hat with a brim or bill to keep it off your face, is extremely useful. It's the only defense I've found against black flies, which seem immune to repellents. If you're likely to need a head net often, Plow and Hearth's 4-ounce cotton Bug Cap comes with a nylon head net that rolls into a pouch on the bill. Any head net needs some form of closure at the bottom or else loops that fit under your arms to prevent it from riding up. Clothing made from no-see-um netting is available, but I've never used any.

Netting clothing needs to be held away from the skin, since insects can bite through it.

Any uncovered skin needs to be protected with repellent if you don't want to be bitten. The most effective is reckoned to be DEET, short for N,N-diethyl-meta-toluamide or N,N-diethyl-3-methylbenzamide, the active ingredient in most insect repellents. Well-known brands include Muskol, Cutter, Ben's 100, Jungle Juice, Repel, Sawyer, Buggspray, and Deep Woods Off! Small bottles and tubes weigh about an ounce. Creams are the easiest to apply, but liquids go further. DEET repels most biting insects, including ticks. It also melts plastic, so it needs to be kept away from items such as watches, pocketknives, GPS units, and cameras.

DEET was developed by the U.S. Army in 1946 and first registered for public use in 1957, so it's been around a long time. It's considered safe by the EPA, which reregistered it in 1998, as long as instructions are followed. These include not applying it over cuts, wounds, or irritated skin, using just enough to cover skin or clothing and not using it under clothing. Wash skin once the repellent isn't required anymore, and wash treated clothing before using it again. The latest DEET repellents feature controlled release and contain about 20 percent DEET. Because the DEET is released slowly, one application can last all day. Sawyer says its Controlled Release Lotion works for twenty hours.

Some people react badly to DEET and feel unwell or nauseated if they use it or even smell it. My partner Denise reacts like this and never uses the stuff. Although I don't use DEET anymore, I did for many years without any adverse reactions—except that Denise wouldn't come near me! However, I was never too happy with the idea of putting something on my skin that could dissolve plastic and make some people feel ill, and since an increasing amount of gear had to be kept away from it, it seemed easier to use an alternative. If you do use DEET, you can keep it off your skin by applying it to clothing.

Oil of citronella (Natrapel is the main brand) is the traditional alternative to DEET. A more recent one is lemon eucalyptus, found in Avon Skin-So-Soft Bug Guard, Repel Lemon Eucalyptus, Badger Anti Bug Balm, and Off! Botanicals Insect Repellent. Most of these come in 4-ounce pump bottles and 2-ounce tubes. My experience is that citronella doesn't work very well and eucalyptus is better. The active ingredient in eucalyptus repellents is citriodiol, which is said to last for six hours before it needs to be reapplied.

Other suggested ways of repelling insects include massive doses of vitamin B or eating lots of garlic. I can't vouch for these.

Repellents do just that. They repel, not kill. Pyrethoids are insecticides and kill insects on contact. The original pyrethrum comes from chrysanthemum flowers, though many pyrethoids are now synthetic. Permethrin is a common one. Pyrethoids can be used for backpacking in two ways: as sprays for tents and clothing and as coils for burning in camp. Sawyer 6-ounce EcoPump Spray and Repel Permanone Trigger Spray are two types of pyrethoid sprays. I've sprayed tents with permethrin and found that it stops insects from landing on the tent so you don't wake up with the fly sheet black with them. You should use these sprays at home and let the tent dry before use. Applications are said to last up to two weeks of exposure to light. When sprayed items are stored in the dark the permethrin doesn't degrade, so items don't need retreating before use if they've had less than two weeks' use. There's no point in putting permethrin on your skin, since it will last only fifteen minutes. It can be used on clothing though, including head nets.

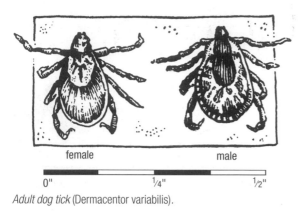

Adult dog tick (Dermacentor variabilis).

In an enclosed space such as a tent vestibule or under a tarp, burning a mosquito coil can keep insects away. On my walk through the Yukon, I often lit a coil at rest stops and found that even in the open it kept mosquitoes away. You can also buy citronella candles, but these are much heavier than coils. Coils come in packs of ten or twelve weighing about 7 ounces. Each coil lasts five to ten hours. When lit, they smolder like an incense stick, sending wreaths of insect-repelling smoke into the air. Remember that the end of a burning coil is hot and can burn you and melt holes in synthetic gear.

Making camp when bugs are biting requires speed and a fair bit of teeth gritting. I pitch the tent as fast as possible, fill my water containers, get in the tent, close the fly sheet door, light a mosquito coil in the vestibule, and stay there until dawn. No-see-ums will enter by the thousands under a fly sheet if no coil is burning, so I set up a coil last thing at night, then sleep with the insect-netting inner door shut. By dawn the inner door is often black with hungry no-see-ums and the vestibule is swarming with them. I unzip a corner of the netting, stick my hand out, strike a match, and light the coil. Then I retreat and close the netting again. Within five minutes most of the insects will be gone or dead, and I can open the inner door and have breakfast in peace. I keep the coil burning

until I leave the tent. The tent often becomes hot and stuffy and stinks of burnt coil, but it's better than being bitten or having to eat breakfast while running around in circles, as I've seen others do. Even if you douse yourself with repellent, no-see-ums will make your skin and scalp itch maddeningly by crawling in your hair and over any exposed flesh, even though they won't bite. You shouldn't use repellent in bear country, of course, so a breezy kitchen site is a good idea. Otherwise you just have to be as quick as possible, perhaps making do with cold food and drink.

Ticks, which are arachnids, not insects, are usually no more than an unpleasant irritant, but they can transmit Rocky Mountain spotted fever (found mainly in the East, despite the name) and Lyme disease. Luckily, both can be cured with timely treatment. Symptoms of Rocky Mountain spotted fever, which include the sudden onset of fever, chills, severe headache and muscle ache, general fatigue, and a loss of appetite, begin to appear two to fourteen days after a bite. A rash will develop within two to five days, beginning first on wrists, hands, ankles, and feet. If untreated, the disease lasts for a couple of weeks and is fatal in 20 to 30 percent of cases, depending on one's age.

Lyme disease also appears a few days to a few weeks after a bite and usually involves a circular red rash, though not always. It isn't fatal, but if not

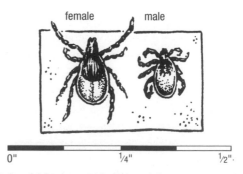

Adult deer tick (Ixodes scapularis/dammini).

treated it can recur years later and lead to bizarre symptoms and severe, crippling arthritis.

A more common, though less serious, tick-borne illness is Colorado tick fever, which appears four to six days after the tick bite. Symptoms are fever, headache, chills, and aching. Your eyes may feel extra sensitive to light. The illness lasts, on and off, for about a week. There is no specific cure, but most victims recover completely.

If you are bitten by a tick and feel ill in the next three or four weeks, consult a doctor.

A sensible precaution is to check for ticks when you're in areas where they occur (local knowledge is useful here) and when you're walking in tick season, usually late spring and early summer. Ticks crawling on your body can be detached with tweezers (found on most Swiss Army Knives)—apply these to the skin around the tick not the tick itself so the head isn't left in the flesh. Pull ticks straight out, along with a tiny bit of skin. *Don't twist or burn embedded ticks*, because the mouthparts could remain in the wound and cause infection. Body searches usually locate most unattached ticks, though some ticks are no bigger than a pinhead. (Searches work better when two people "groom" each other.) Tick kits weighing a couple of ounces consist of a magnifier, curved tweezers, antiseptic swabs, and instructions. The Tick Nipper Tick Remover looks like a pair of plastic pliers and includes a 20x magnifier, while the Pro-Tick Remedy is made from steel. Both items weigh 0.5 ounce.

Ticks live in long grass and vegetation and attach themselves to you as you brush past. A tick then crawls about for a while, possibly for several hours, before biting and starting to suck blood. The bite is painless and doesn't itch, which is why body searches are necessary. Long pants tucked into your socks or worn with gaiters protect against ticks. If your clothing is light colored it's easier to spot the dark ticks crawling around on it.

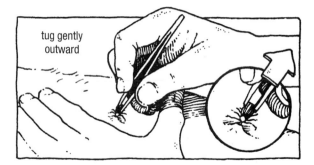

tug gently outward

To remove a tick, grasp it at the mouth end with fine tweezers or a tick removal tool. Tug gently outward until the tick lets go. A tick removal kit containing magnifier, curved tweezers, antiseptic swabs, and instructions can be handy.

Bee and wasp stings can be very painful. There are various remedies. Sting Eze is a liquid antihistamine in a 2-ounce bottle; antihistamines also come in tablet form. (Use antihistamines, however, only when there are signs of an allergic reaction, such as hives, wheezing, or facial swelling.) People who have adverse reactions to stings should carry an EpiPen containing epinephrine (a prescription medication) and inject this as soon as symptoms appear. Bees leave their stingers behind in the wound. A Sawyer Extractor suction pump (3.5 ounces) can be used to suck the stinger out of the skin, or you can scrape it out with a knife blade. A moist aspirin taped over the sting site is said to stop pain.

Sunscreen

Protecting your skin against sunburn is a *necessity*—sunburned shoulders are agony under a pack, and a peeling nose also can be very painful. In the long run, overexposure may increase the risk of skin cancer. To minimize burning, use sunscreen on exposed skin whenever you're in sunlight, especially between 10 a.m. and 4 p.m. when the sun is strongest. Don't forget your feet if you're wearing sandals without socks. Brimmed and peaked hats help shade your face and cut the need for sunscreen, as does long, tightly woven clothing.

All sunscreens have a sun protection factor (SPF); the higher the SPF, the more protection. SPFs of 15 and above are recommended, especially for high altitudes, where ultraviolet light (the part of the spectrum that burns) is stronger. UV light increases in intensity 4 percent for every 1,000 feet of altitude. I burn easily, so I apply a sunscreen of SPF 15 or higher several times a day. Snow reflects sunlight, so when crossing snow-fields protect all exposed skin, including that under your chin and around your nostrils. The best sunscreens are creamy rather than greasy and don't wash off when you sweat—at least not quickly. They should protect against both UVA and UVB rays; both can damage the skin, though it's the latter that cause sunburn. The skin is damaged long before it starts burning. Surveys suggest that most people don't use enough sunscreen (independent surveys, not those sponsored by sunscreen makers). Apply it lavishly and often, starting a half-hour before you venture into the sun. Large bottles are the least expensive. Small amounts can be decanted into smaller containers with secure lids for carrying in the pack. Sunscreen has a shelf life of three to four years, so you don't need to use it up quickly.

If you get sunburned, various creams and lotions will help reduce the suffering, but it's best to avoid the problem in the first place. I don't carry any sunburn treatment.

Lip Balm

Lips can suffer from the drying effects of the wind as well as from sunburn, and they can crack badly in very cold conditions. A tube of lip balm weighs less than an ounce yet can save days of pain.

Sunglasses

Most of the time I don't wear sunglasses, except during snow travel, when they are essential to prevent corneal burning, a very painful condition known as *snow blindness*. This can occur even when the sun isn't bright, as I learned on a day of thin mist in the Norwegian mountains. Because visibility was so poor and wearing sunglasses made it worse, I didn't wear them but skied all day straining to see ahead. Although I didn't suffer complete snow blindness, my eyes became sore and itchy; by evening I was seeing double, and my eyes were painful except when closed. Luckily it was the last day of my trip; otherwise I would have had to rest for at least a couple of days to let my eyes recover. It's my guess that sunlight filtered through the fine mist and reflected off the snow. I should have worn sunglasses with amber or yellow lenses, since these improve definition in poor light, and I now always carry a pair.

The main requirement of sunglasses is that they cut out all ultraviolet light, which cheap ones may not do. Those designed for snow and high-altitude use should also cut out infrared light. Glass lenses are scratch resistant; polycarbonate lenses weigh less. Large lenses that curve around the eyes are best, since they give the most protection. Quality glasses include Bollé, Vuarnet, Ray-Ban, Cébé, Julbo, Smith, Native Eyewear, and Oakley. For snow use, glacier-type glasses with side shields are best. They are essential at high altitudes. I have two pairs of glacier glasses, Julbo Sherpas (1 ounce) with gray lenses for bright light, and Bollé Crevasses (1.5 ounces) with amber lenses for hazy conditions. I always carry both pairs on trips in snow, both to deal with different conditions and because losing or breaking a pair could be serious. On summer hikes where I might encounter snow, pale sand, or rock, I carry the Sherpas with the side shields removed. I rarely wear them, however; I prefer a hat to shade my eyes.

If fogging is a problem there are antifogging products such as the Smith No Fog Cloth. I've never used these, but people who wear glasses all the time tell me they're quite effective.

Keeping glasses on can be a problem, especially when skiing. The answer is a loop that goes around your head or neck. Glacier glasses usually come with these, but many sunglasses don't. Various straps, such Croakies and Chums, slip over the ear-pieces. I've used Croakies, and they work well.

In severe blizzards and driving snow, goggles give more protection than glasses. For well over a decade I've had a pair of Scott ski goggles with amber double lenses, which improve visibility in haze. They weigh 4 ounces. The foam mesh vents above and below the lenses reduce fogging, though the goggles suffer this more than glacier glasses. A wide elasticized, adjustable headband plus thick, soft foam around the rim makes them comfortable to wear. For a few years I stopped carrying them, since I rarely used them. Then I had a horrendous descent down a steep ridge in strong winds and driving, stinging snow that kept blowing behind my glacier glasses so I couldn't see. Every few minutes I had to stop and clear the glasses. Goggles would have made the descent quicker, safer, and more pleasant. Goggles can be worn over a hat or hood and pushed down around your neck when not needed, which is less risky than pushing them up on your forehead and having them fall off. Bollé, Jones, Cébé, Smith, and Scott all make good goggles.

Sanitation

All too often, every rock within a few hundred yards of a popular campsite sprouts ragged pink and white toilet paper around its edges. Aside from

Outhouse sign. Where there are outhouses you should always use them.

turning beautiful places into sordid outdoor priv-ies, unthinking toilet siting and waste disposal cre-ate a health hazard—feces can pollute water sources. As a result, land-management agencies sometimes provide outhouses and deep toilet pits at popular destinations. Mount Whitney, the high-est peak in the lower forty-eight states, has one on its summit.

Outhouses are obtrusive and detract from the feeling of wilderness. Careful sanitation tech-niques can ensure that no more need be built. Good methods prevent water contamination, speed decomposition, and shield humans and ani-mals from contact with waste.

To prevent water contamination, always site toilets at least 200 feet (70 paces) from any water. Heading uphill is usually a good way to achieve this. Look for somewhere comfortable to squat

A pit toilet with a view.

that is out of sight of trails, campsites, and anywhere people might see you. The best way to achieve rapid decomposition is to leave waste on the surface, where the sun and air soon break it down. But this isn't a good idea in popular areas and is now not recommended anywhere. As well as being unsightly, it attracts insects and animals. Instead, dig small individual catholes 6 to 8 inches deep, in dark organic soil if possible, since this is rich in the bacteria that break down feces. After you've finished, break feces up with a stick and mix them with the soil—they decompose more quickly—then fill in the hole and camouflage it. Feces don't decompose very rapidly in catholes, so where they are sited is important. Ideally they should be on a rise where water won't flow and wash the feces downstream. A site that catches the sun is good too, since heat speeds up decomposition.

You need a small trowel for digging catholes. I carry a 2-ounce orange plastic Coghlan's Backpacker's Trowel in a pack pocket. An alternative is the Eastman Outdoors Little Jon Shovel, which weighs 2.8 ounces and has a hollow handle that holds eighty-five sheets of toilet paper. These plastic trowels make digging catholes easy, but they can and do break, especially in rocky ground. Somewhat heavier at 6.5 ounces but much stronger is the U-Dig-It Stainless Steel Hand Shovel with folding handle.

Large groups should not dig big latrines unless there are limited cathole sites or the group is staying at a site for more than one night. The idea is to *disperse* rather than concentrate waste. If you do dig a latrine, it should be sited as for a cathole.

There remains the problem of toilet paper. I use a standard white roll with the cardboard tube removed—3.5 ounces. (Avoid colored paper because the dyes can pollute.) Although toilet paper seems fragile, it is amazingly resilient and shouldn't be left to decorate the wilderness. You have two options—burning it or packing it out. The first should never be used when there is any fire risk, however minute. If you have a campfire, though, it makes sense to burn used toilet paper in it. Mostly you should pack it out in doubled plastic bags. In some areas where campfires are banned, such as Grand Canyon National Park, this is required. As long as the bags are kept sealed, used paper doesn't smell. The paper should be disposed of in a toilet, the plastic bags in a garbage can. Women also should pack out used tampons unless they can be burned, which requires a very hot fire. If tampons are buried, animals will dig them up. More specific advice for women, plus a lot of good general advice on backcountry toilet practices, can be found in Kathleen Meyer's humorous *How to Shit in the Woods*.

For those prepared to try them, natural alternatives to toilet paper include sand, grass, large leaves, and even snow. The last, I can assure you, is less unpleasant than it sounds.

Deep snow presents a problem. Digging a cathole just means the contents will appear on the surface when the snow melts. This is still the best method in little visited areas, however. It's even more important to be sure catholes are sited where no one is likely to find them and in places where no one will camp, such as narrow ridge tops and thick bushes or stands of trees. In really remote areas feces can be left on the surface, since then they'll start to decompose straightaway. In both cases check where water flows in the summer—by observation and from the map—and try to site your toilet well away from any creeks. In popular areas consider packing feces out. If they're frozen, this is less unpleasant than it sounds. The Phillips Environmental Wag Bag, designed for the removal of feces, could make it more acceptable. This consists of a waste bag, a zip-closed storage bag, toilet paper, and hand sanitizer. The biodegradable waste bag is puncture proof and contains an environmentally friendly gelling agent with the wonderful name of Pooh-Powder that turns feces into a stable gel.

Urination is a matter of less concern. Urine is sterile, so it doesn't matter too much where you pee. However, the salts in urine may attract animals, so it's best to pee on bare ground rather than vegetation that could be damaged by animals' licking the salt off the leaves. In snow urine leaves unsightly yellow stains that should be covered up.

The only time urination becomes a problem is when you wake in the middle of a cold, stormy night and are faced with crawling out of your sleeping bag, donning clothes, and venturing out into the wet and wind. The answer is to pee into a wide-mouthed plastic bottle. With practice, men can do this easily. I use a cheap plastic pint bottle (2 ounces) with a green screw top that clearly distinguishes it from my water bottles. I've marked it with a large letter *P* as well. I carry it mainly in winter and spring. A pee bottle could also be useful in summer when biting insects are around, since otherwise you'd have to get dressed before leaving the tent. (Not to do so is to invite disaster. On a course I led, a student left his tent one night clad in just a T-shirt, despite warnings. He was out less than a minute, but in the morning he emerged covered with no-see-um bites from the waist down.)

For women pee bottles clearly present problems. Two devices may help. The Lady J Adapter fits into the mouth of a shaped bottle called the Little John Portable Urinal and can be used in a tent. An alternative is Sani-fem's Freshette, a close-fitting plastic funnel with attached tube that can be used with any bottle.

EQUIPMENT MAINTENANCE AND REPAIR

It's an unusual trip when something doesn't need repairing, or at least tinkering with, so I always carry a small repair kit in a stuff sack. Although the contents vary from trip to trip, the weight hovers around 4 ounces. Repair kits for specific items such as the stove and the Therm-a-Rest travel in this bag.

The most-used item in the kit is the waterproof, adhesive-backed ripstop nylon tape, which patches everything from clothing to fly sheets. You can buy this in rolls, but I prefer the strips that come stapled to a card. Most types have four to six different colored strips of nylon, measure 3 by 9 inches, and

WOLVES

The river is a half mile or so away. I set off toward it to collect water as dusk falls. In the middle of an expansive meadow I suddenly sense that I am watched. Looking toward the forest, I freeze with a mixture of awe, excitement, and fear. A few hundred yards away, on the fringe of the timber, a pack of wolves is watching me. I count six, some of them pale gray, others almost black. After a few seconds they begin to move off slowly in single file, one of them always stationary, watching. When that one falls to the rear another stops, and the pack continues. Eventually they disappear. I do not know how long I have been holding my breath.

weigh about an ounce. There are several brands, including Kenyon and Coghlan's. When applying a patch, round the edges so it won't peel off, and patch both sides of the hole if possible. Patches can be reinforced with adhesive around the edges. I carry a small tube of seam sealant or epoxy for this purpose, or I use the glue that comes with the Therm-a-Rest repair kit.

An alternative to sticky ripstop tape is duct tape, the mainstay of many repair kits. I carry strips of duct tape wrapped around a small piece of wood, and have used it to hold together cracked pack frames, split ski tips, broken tent poles, and other items. On clothing, sleeping bags, and tent fabrics, however, I find sticky nylon tape better because it is more flexible and stays on longer. Duct tape leaves a sticky residue too. Professional repairers and cleaners hate it.

Large pieces of nylon are useful for patching bigger tears and holes. Since repair swatches often come with tents and packs, I've built up a collection from which I usually take two or three sheets of different weights, including a noncoated one for inner tent repair; the biggest swatch measures 12 by 18 inches. They have a combined weight of half an ounce.

Also in the repair kit goes a selection of rubber bands. These have many obvious uses, and some not so obvious. A length of shock cord tied in a loop makes an extra-strong rubber band. Any detachable pack straps not in use also end up in the repair bag—perhaps "oddities kit" would be a better name.

My sewing kit consists of a sewing awl, two heavy-duty sewing machine needles, two buttons, two safety pins, a cotter pin (for rethreading drawcords), two ordinary sewing needles, and several weights of strong thread packed in a small zippered nylon bag. The total weight is only 1.5 ounces, yet with this kit I can repair everything from packs to pants.

For details of how to repair outdoor gear see Annie and Dave Getchell's excellent book *The Essential Outdoor Gear Manual*.

Nylon Cord

The final item in the repair bag—nylon cord—deserves a section of its own because it's so useful. I use *parachute cord* (paracord), which comes in 50-foot lengths with a breaking strength of 350 pounds at a weight of 4 ounces per hank. Over the years I've used it for pitching a tarp, making extra tent guylines, bearbagging food, replacing boot laces, hanging out wet gear, tying items to my pack (wet socks, crampons, ice ax), fashioning a swami belt (made by wrapping the cord around and around your waist) for use with a carabiner and rope for river crossings, lashing a broken pack frame, lowering a pack down and pulling it up short steep cliffs or slopes (with the cord fed around my back, a tree, or a rock—not hand over hand), and anchoring gaiters and hats. The ends of cut nylon cord must be fused with heat or they'll fray.

Paracord has been around for decades. Now there is a lighter and stronger alternative in Spectra cord. Fifty feet of Bozeman Mountain Works' AirCore Plus weighs 1.8 ounces and has a breaking strength of 1,109 pounds. And for real weight cutting, the extremely thin AirCore 1 weighs just 0.2 ounce per 50 feet and has a breaking strength of 188 pounds. Cord this thin is fine for guylines (though it's so thin it can be difficult to knot), but not for bearbagging or other heavy-duty uses. AirCore Plus sounds excellent, though. Next time I buy cord I'll get some.

Knife

A small knife is useful for backpacking, but you don't need a large, heavy sheath knife or "survival" knife for most purposes. I mostly use a blade for opening food packets and slicing cheese, as well as cutting cord and other items. Scissors are the other tool I use frequently, and it's convenient and lighter to have these on a knife.

Victorinox Classic Swiss Army Knife.

Small pocketknives, especially the classic Swiss Army Knife (SAK), are the standard backpacking tools. Beware of inferior imitations—the only genuine brands are Wenger and Victorinox. There's a huge range of models with just about every blade or tool you could want.

For years I've used the Victorinox Climber, which weighs 2.5 ounces and has two blades, scissors, can opener/screwdriver, bottle opener/screwdriver, corkscrew, tweezers, and toothpick, plus a couple of those slightly strange tools whose usefulness is unclear—a reamer/punch and a multipurpose hook. If I'm really trying to keep the weight down I carry a tiny Victorinox Classic, which weighs 0.7 ounce and has a small blade, a file/screwdriver, scissors, tweezers, and a toothpick. I was dubious about such a tiny knife at first but was pleasantly surprised to discover that it did everything I wanted from a knife.

Recently I've been fascinated by the Altimeter model (3.25 ounces). Just when it seemed that Victorinox really couldn't add anything more to an SAK, up pops one with an altimeter and thermometer built into the handle, displayed on a tiny digital screen. (See Chapter 9 for information on altimeters.) It has the same blades as the Climber, though with a third tiny screwdriver but no tweezers (I replaced the toothpick with the tweezers from my Classic).

I have sometimes carried other knives such as the 7.5-inch French Opinel folding knife with wooden handle and single locking carbon steel blade. It weighs just 1.75 ounces, and the blade holds an edge better than the stainless steel Swiss Army ones. Recently I've been tempted by the Tool Logic SL3, which has a 3-inch blade and weighs 2.75 ounces, because it has a FireSteel in the handle and a notch on the blade for drawing it across (see page 314). There are many other small knives and folding multitools around: Gerber, Schrade, Kershaw, SOG, Buck, and Leatherman are some of the other quality ones. Most of the multitools have pliers, which I rarely need, but not scissors, which I use regularly.

Keeping your knife blades sharp is important. I don't carry a sharpener, however, because the best place to sharpen them is at home.

IN CASE OF EMERGENCY

Signaling

If you are injured or become seriously ill in the wilderness, you need to alert other people and rescuers to your whereabouts. Displaying a bright item of clothing or gear is one way to do this. Your headlamp or flashlight can be used for sending signals, in daylight as well as at night. Noise can attract attention, of course, and I always carry a plastic whistle. For years this was a Storm Whistle (0.8 ounce), from the All-Weather Whistle Company of St. Louis, which is said to be one of the loudest, reaching almost 95 decibels. I've passed this whistle on to my stepdaughter and replaced it with a Fox 40 Classic (0.5 ounce with lanyard). I've never used it, but it's always there just in case. Whether you use light or sound, the recognized distress signal is six regular flashes or blasts, pause, then six more.

In most remote areas, initial searches are likely to be made by aircraft, so you need to be seen from above and from afar. A fire, especially with wet vegetation added, should create enough smoke to be easily seen. Ideally, you should light three fires in the form of a triangle, an internationally recognized distress signal. Flares are quicker and simpler to use, and various packs are sold. I've never carried flares, but they would have been reassuring at times during the Canadian Rockies and Yukon walks. Carrying several small flares seems to make more sense than one big one; larger flares last longer, but unless you carry several, you have only one chance to draw attention to your plight. Packs of six to eight waterproof miniflares with a projector pen for one-handed operation weigh only 8 ounces or so. The flares reach a height of about 250 feet and last six seconds.

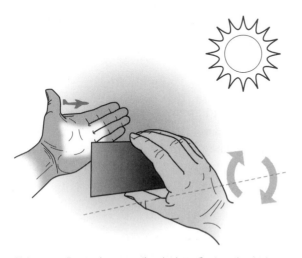

Using an ordinary mirror as a signal mirror. Capture the sun's reflection in your palm, then flick the mirror up and down to send a signal to approaching aircraft.

Signaling mirror with sighting hole.

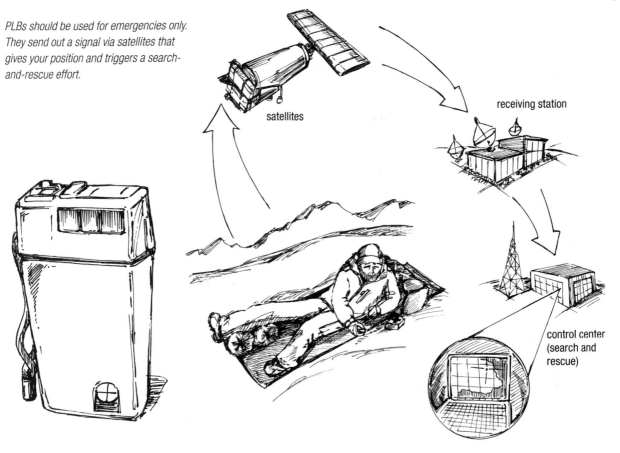

PLBs should be used for emergencies only. They send out a signal via satellites that gives your position and triggers a search-and-rescue effort.

satellites

receiving station

control center (search and rescue)

Flares need to be handled and used carefully. A much safer alternative is a strobe light. Some LED lights can be set to flash regularly.

Mirrors can be used for signaling, though obviously only in sunlight. Plastic ones are cheap and light (0.5 ounce upward). I have an MPI Safe Signal mirror weighing 1.25 ounces. It's made from polycarbonate and is silver on one side and red on the other, for use with a flashlight at night (the effect is very bright). I sometimes carry it in my "office" pouch (see below). Any shiny reflective object, such as aluminum foil (stove windscreen), a polished pan base, a watch face, a camera lens, or even a knife blade could be used instead.

If you are in open terrain and have no other signal devices, spreading light- and bright-colored clothing and gear out on the ground could help rescuers locate you.

Personal Locator Beacons

Personal locator beacons (PLBs) have been around for decades and are standard safety items on boats and planes. They were illegal for land use in the United States until July 2003, however. PLBs send out a signal via satellites that gives your position and triggers a search-and-rescue (SAR) effort. *They are for emergencies only and should never be used unless you're in a life-or-death situation.* I've carried PLBs twice. The first time was on my 1,000-mile solo hike in the Yukon where I was loaned one, unofficially, by local people concerned for my safety in remote wilderness. "If it goes off by accident, jump over a cliff before the rescue teams arrive," I was told, only half jokingly. It lay mostly forgotten in a pack pocket for the next three and a half months. The second occasion was when I led a skiing expedition in Greenland. In this case the PLB was not only official but also a legal requirement. Both these trips were into very remote, little visited country where an accident or illness could have been fatal. Whether PLBs are needed in most backcountry areas, which are much more accessible, is debatable. They will undoubtedly save lives and make the work of SAR teams easier and safer. However, as with cell phones, there is a danger that some people will regard PLBs as substitutes for skill. They could easily be misused too, with people using them for minor inconveniences or concerns that don't warrant calling out a rescue. At present

Cell phone in waterproof Ortlieb case.

the very high cost will probably limit the number of people who carry them but as with all electronics prices are likely to fall. Whether or not to carry one is a personal decision but they should only be used when absolutely necessary.

The PLBs I carried were designed for carrying on aircraft, and were large and heavy. Since their legalization in the United States, lightweight models suitable for backpacking have appeared. The lightest is the McMurdo FastFind PLB, which weighs 9 ounces. The basic unit can locate the signaler to within half a mile. The FastFind Plus has a GPS receiver built in and is accurate to within 100 yards. A little heavier at 12 ounces is the ACR Terrafix. Again there are versions with and without GPS. All PLBs have to be able to broadcast continuously for 24 hours and work down to –4°F (–20°C). This makes for a hefty battery, which makes up most of the weight.

Cell Phones

An increasing number of hikers carry cell phones, though many backpackers feel they have no place in the wilderness and detract from the reasons for being there. Their usefulness in an emergency is undeniable, and many people have been rescued quickly because they had phones. However, too many people use their phones for what can only be regarded as frivolous reasons, such as asking for advice on routes and where to find water to drink. Some people seem to think a phone is a substitute for wilderness skills— if you get lost, you can just make a call. This is irresponsible and puts great pressure on rangers and rescue services. Phones should be used only in real emergencies where you need outside help. Relying on a phone is unwise anyway: they can break, and batteries can fade. Also, they're unlikely to get a signal in remote areas, deep canyons, and dense forests. If you do bring one and want to use it other than in an emergency, do so away from others. It can be very irritating to reach a summit or a pass and hear someone talking on a phone. Think, too, about how much a phone detaches you from the wilderness you've come to experience.

Rescue Procedures

If you're alone and suffer an immobilizing injury or illness, all you can do is make yourself as comfortable as possible, send out signals, and hope someone will respond. In popular areas and on trails, attracting attention shouldn't be too difficult, but in less-frequented places and when traveling cross-country you may be totally dependent on those who have details of your route to report you missing when you don't check in as arranged.

Groups should send for help if they can't handle the situation themselves. It's important that whoever goes has all the necessary information: the location of the injured person(s), compass bearings, details of local features that may help rescuers find the place, the nature of the terrain, the time of the accident, a description of any injuries, and the size and experience of the group. All this should be written down so that important details aren't forgotten or distorted. Once out of the wilderness, the messenger should contact the local law enforcement, park, or forest service office.

Most mountain rescue teams are made up of local volunteers. These people give up their time to help those in need, often at great personal risk and cost. If you need their services, make a generous donation to the organization afterward; they are not government funded.

Rope

Roped climbing is for mountaineers. However, there are rare times when backpackers need a short length of rope for protection on steep terrain. Full-weight climbing rope isn't necessary; I've found quarter-inch line with a breaking strain of 2,200 to 3,400 pounds perfectly adequate. A 60- to 65-foot length (the shortest that's much use) weighs 20 ounces or so. For a rope to be useful, you need to know how to set up belays, how to tie on, and how to handle it safely. This is best learned from an experienced climbing friend or by taking a course. Ropes need proper care. They should be stored out of direct sunlight and away from chemicals. A car seat or trunk is not a good place to keep ropes. Even with minimum use and careful storage, ropes deteriorate and should be replaced every four or five years. I've mostly carried ropes for glacier crossings during ski tours. These have been full-weight, full-length climbing ropes. I haven't carried a rope when hiking for nearly twenty years.

Snow Shovel

In deep snow, a shovel is both an emergency tool and a functional item. The emergency uses range from digging a shelter to digging out avalanche victims. More mundane uses are for leveling tent platforms, digging out buried tents, clearing snow from doorways, digging through snow to running water, collecting snow to melt for water, supporting the stove, and many other purposes. I find a snow shovel essential in snowbound terrain. They come with either plastic or metal blades. I prefer metal; plastic blades won't cut through hardpacked snow or ice. There are many models, usually with detachable blades. Voilé, Life-Link, Backcountry Access (BCA), Ascension, and Safety on Snow (SOS) make good snow shovels. I have a BCA Tour Shovel with a large aluminum blade that weighs 18 ounces.

Fishing Tackle

I once carried a length of fishing line and a few hooks and weights on a long wilderness trip, in case I ran out of food. I duly ran short of food, and on several nights I put out a line with baited hooks. On each successive morning I pulled it in empty. Experienced anglers probably would have more success, and if you're one, I'm sure it's worthwhile to take some lightweight fishing tackle, depending on where you're headed.

Navigation

Route finding as a skill is discussed in Chapter 9, and it therefore makes sense to leave any detailed discussion of equipment until then. Here I will mention the effect navigation can have on your load. On any trip a compass and a map, weighing between 1 and 4 ounces, will be the minimum gear you'll need. On most trips you'll need more than one map, and you may carry a trail guide as well. On trips of two weeks and longer, I usually end up with 25 to 35 ounces of maps and guides. In remote, trailless country, you might want a GPS receiver, which adds at least 3 ounces. Chapter 9 contains details of these.

OFFICE

I carry a notebook, pen, and pencil on every trip. Along with a paperback book, maps, and various papers, they live in a small pouch or stuff sack. There are many suitable pouches, mostly containing several compartments and designed to be fastened to pack hipbelts or shoulder straps. Weights range from a few ounces to a pound or more. I use a simple single-compartment waterproof nylon pouch with a Velcro closure that weighs an ounce. If I have books and maps that won't fit in this flat pouch, I carry them in a small waterproof stuff sack. My office lives in a pack pocket where it is easily accessible.

Writing Paper and Notebooks

Keeping a journal on a walk is perhaps the best way of making a record for the future. I've always kept journals, long before I began writing for anyone other than myself, and by reading them I can spend hours reliving a trip I'd almost forgotten. In order to record as much as possible, I try to write in my journal every day, often making a few notes over breakfast and at stops during the day, then more extensive ones during the evening. This is difficult enough to do on solo trips; when I'm with companions, I'm lucky if I write in it every other day. I use single journals for long trips (over two weeks) and an annual journal for other trips.

There are masses of suitable notebooks. Those with tear-out pages are very light, but I prefer bound ones. I mostly use oilskin notebooks with water-resistant black covers. There are various brands, such as Moleskin Pocket Notebooks from Dick Blick Art Materials and Blueline Memo books, which are made from recycled paper. A 4-by-6-inch notebook with 190 pages weighs about 4 ounces. If you want to make notes when the weather's wet, waterproof notebooks are available from Rite in the Rain. The 4-by-6-inch All-Weather Pocket Journal has 50 detachable sheets and weighs 3 ounces. The bound 4-by-6.5-inch Adventure Travel Journal has 78 sheets plus 15 pages of reference material. To write on the waterproof paper you need a pencil, a Space Pen, or Rite in the Rain's All-Weather Pen. These notebooks are waterproof, but they're also expensive. I have a Pocket Journal, which I use only in really wet weather.

In my notebook I keep route plans, addresses of people at home and people I meet along the way, lists of how far I go each day and where I camp, and any other information I may need or collect along the way. Looking at my Canadian Rockies journal, I see I kept records of my resting pulse rate (which ranged between 44 and 56) and how much fuel my stove used (ten to fourteen days per quart). I also made shopping lists and, toward the end, a calendar on which I crossed off the days. (There was a reason for this—buses at the finish ran only three times a week.) Such trivia may not seem worth recording, but for me they bring back the reality of a trip very strongly.

I usually carry at least two Space Pens, which have waterproof ink in case my notebook gets wet, and usually a refillable pencil as well. They weigh half an ounce each.

Some hikers now use small electronic notebooks, often ones that will connect to a modem so they can send e-mail and update Web logs either via their cell phones or when they reach a standard phone. I prefer my notebook. I did try a PDA to see what it was like, but I found the tiny keyboard difficult to use. Also, I sit in front of a computer for too long at home working. Out in the backcountry I prefer not to do so. But such portable devices are there for those who want them.

Documents and Papers

The documents you need to carry on a trip can amount to quite a collection, though they never weigh much. On trips close to home, you may need none. On any trip abroad you'll need your passport, perhaps a visa and hiking permit, and insurance documents. It's wise to carry airline or other travel tickets too. It's useful to have some form of identification such as a driver's license in case of emergency. While walking I keep my papers sealed in a plastic bag in the recesses of my "office." Trail permits, if required, also go in a plastic bag, but I often carry them in a pocket or my fanny pack so they're ready if I meet a ranger.

In case your documents are lost or stolen or you have an accident or become ill, it's a good idea to carry a list of important information, including who to contact in an emergency, separate from other paperwork. Leave a copy of this at home, too. You should also leave as detailed an itinerary as possible, including dates when you expect to phone home, or send a card, letter, e-mail, or fax. (See Chapter 10 for more on trip lists.)

Wallet and Money

In the wilderness, money serves no purpose, and on short trips close to home I carry very little. On long trips money is essential at town stops. I try not to carry loose coins, which are relatively heavy. It's best to carry small-denomination notes, since in remote places there may be no place that will accept large bills. I also carry a credit card, in case of unexpected larger expenses. I used to carry my wallet—nylon, 1.5 ounces—with me, after removing the extra clutter it somehow generates. But it's not waterproof and it's easier not to remove the clutter. Zippered plastic bags will do, but they don't last long and I hate throwing them away, so now I use an Aloksak from Watchful Eye Designs. Aloksaks are tough, reusable transparent waterproof bags with zip closures. Mine is the smallest one—4.5 by 7 inches. It weighs a quarter of an ounce. Larger ones could be used for books and maps.

Watch

I'm often tempted to leave my watch at home, but a watch has its uses, even in the wilderness. It's helpful to know how many daylight hours are left when deciding whether to stop at a good campsite or push on. When the sun's visible, you can estimate time fairly accurately, but on dull, overcast days it's almost impossible. A watch with a built-in calendar also helps keep track of the days, something that can be confusing on long trips. Checking your watch when you stop for a break may also help get you moving again, especially when you realize that the intended "couple of minutes" has somehow become half an hour. If your watch has an alarm, you can set it to wake you for morning starts. These days I wear a wrist altimeter, the Suunto Altimax, that tells the time and date and has an alarm as well as being a barometer, altimeter, and thermometer.

BINOCULARS AND MONOCULARS

Few walkers carry binoculars, which surprises me. They're practical for scouting the trail or the country ahead and for checking out whether that dark lump under the tree you're approaching is a mossy boulder or a bear (I once changed my route when a dark object in a distant berry patch turned out to be a grizzly). I use mine regularly, and they've often saved me from taking a route that would have led to a dead end or an obstacle when hiking cross-country. I also use them to survey rivers from a high point for possible fords.

Aside from functional uses, binoculars open up the world of birds and wildlife to the walker. Whether it's otters playing in a lake, a grizzly rooting through a meadow, or an eagle soaring overhead, binoculars allow you to watch wild creatures from a safe distance (both for you and for them).

There are a wealth of ultralight minibinoculars. Mine are 8x21—at 5.5 ounces the lightest pair I could find. I've had them over a decade, and the make—Sirius—has disappeared, but there are many similar ones. They're so small I carry them in a shirt or jacket pocket. When selecting binoc-

ulars, note the relationship between the first number, which is the magnification, and the second, which is the diameter in millimeters of the front lens, known as the aperture. The size of the aperture determines how much light the lenses admit. Large figures mean plenty of light but also more weight owing to the bigger pieces of glass. Divide the aperture by the magnification and you can get a figure called the exit pupil. The bigger this is the better the image in poor light. My minibinoculars have an exit pupil of 2.6, which is low so they aren't much use when it's very dull. Again, though, a bigger exit pupil means heavier binoculars.

A monocular is a lighter alternative to a pair of binoculars, of course. I find monoculars harder to hold steady and focus than binoculars and gave up on mine many years ago. However, a reader suggests they are easier to use than binoculars if you wear glasses. There are many models, the lightest weighing just 3 ounces.

PHOTOGRAPHY

Taking photographs is probably the most popular nonessential backpacking activity. Everyone likes to have a visual record of trips. But if you simply point the camera at every scene regardless of the light or viewpoint, you may end up with pictures that aren't very satisfactory. Those who take the time and care to study the details of a place in order to make the best picture, the one that most reflects how they see it, may share my feeling that this gives them a deeper appreciation of the wilderness.

Anyone wanting to pursue the subject of wilderness photography further can learn a great deal from the late Galen Rowell's books and from *Outdoor Photographer* magazine.

Photography is about seeing, not about equipment. No amount of expensive gear will make someone a good photographer. That said, the more ambitious you become, the more gear you end up carrying. I used to carry around 10 pounds of cameras and accessories, which seems an enormous amount to the nonphotographer. But I've become something of a professional over the years, and I go on most walks knowing I have to come back with a set of pictures. Recently I've cut the weight by half, though, and my photos don't seem to have suffered.

Cameras

There are two lightweight choices for backpacking cameras. A compact camera or a single-lens reflex (SLR) with interchangeable lenses. Either may be digital or use traditional film. For similar-quality images you'll pay more for a digital camera, and it will weigh more too, but digital cameras do have the advantage that you can see the picture straightaway and delete it if it's not what you want. Digital images can be downloaded directly to the Internet and displayed on the Web or e-mailed as well. I carried a digital compact on the Arizona Trail—a now-discontinued Ricoh RDC 5000—and some of the images did appear on a Web page.

Most compacts are fully automatic, though a few have manual settings. Weights start at just a few ounces. For those who have no interest in photography but would like to have some pictures of their trips, a fully automatic compact—digital or film—is ideal.

However, even the best compacts cannot match an SLR for versatility. SLRs take interchangeable lenses, so focal lengths are limited only by what you can carry. And with an SLR you look directly through the lens, which helps with composition.

My main camera for more than two decades was a film SLR, with a semiautomatic compact as a backup. Currently I use a Canon Rebel, since it's very light; with a 24-70 mm zoom lens, the total weight is 23 ounces. I now also have a Canon Digital Rebel that weighs 32 ounces with the 18-55 zoom lens and battery. This is 9 ounces more than the film Rebel but image storage cards only weigh 0.2 ounce and 140 top-quality images will fit on one 1 GB card, equivalent to four rolls of film at an ounce each. On trips where weight isn't paramount, I also carry an 80-200 mm lens (10 ounces). Zoom lenses are lighter than the three or four fixed-focal-length lenses they replace, and they aid composition—wilderness pictures are often taken from positions you can't change, like the edges of cliffs and the sides of mountains. As a backup, I carry a Ricoh GR1s compact, which weighs 6.7 ounces and has a superbly sharp 28 mm lens.

There is a wide choice of SLRs, most of them of high quality. Choosing one is really a question of which features, price, and weight suit you. Top names are Canon, Nikon, Pentax, Minolta, Olympus and, if you have the money, Leica. Professional models are heavy and bulky. For hiking lightweight ones are fine.

One big problem with most cameras today is that they're totally dependent on batteries to operate the autofocus, autoexposure, motor-wind, self-timer mechanisms, and in digital cameras, image capture. I always carry spare batteries.

Filters

Filters are often overused, and I carry very few of them. I want the light and colors in my pictures to look natural. For protection and to cut out ultraviolet light, I keep a skylight filter on every lens. I also use a polarizer to cut glare and to darken blue skies. If the sky is bright and the land dark (or vice versa), I use a graduated neutral-density filter in a filter holder. Each filter weighs about 0.75 ounce with case.

Film

I nearly always take color transparencies (slides) because they work best for publications and slide shows. The speed of the film, the ISO, is important. For fine detail and the best colors, 100-speed film or slower is best. I mostly buy film with pre-paid mailers so I can send it home to be developed during a long walk—the results are waiting for me when I get back. With print film, faster speeds—200 and 400—can give good results and are easier to handhold in low light. Fuji Velvia 50 is the outdoor photographer's favorite, but 50 ISO is quite slow for handholding. I use Velvia with a tripod at times, but mostly I use Fujichrome Sensia 100 and Kodak EBX 100.

Individual rolls of film don't weigh much, but a half-dozen thirty-six-exposure rolls with canisters weigh about 7 ounces. I average a roll a day.

Supports

In low light and with slow film (ISO 25 and 50), you need something to steady the camera. (As a rough guide for handheld shooting, the shutter speed should approximate or be faster than the focal length of the lens. For example, a 28 mm lens shouldn't be handheld at slower than $\frac{1}{30}$ second; a 200 mm lens no slower than $\frac{1}{250}$.) A camera support can be as simple as propping your arms on a rock, bracing yourself against a tree, or even lying down.

If you carry a monopod, minitripod or clamp, or tripod, you don't need to rely on natural supports, which may not be in convenient places. My trekking pole has a screw in the handle to which a ball-and-socket tripod head can be mounted, making it a monopod. I use this for wildlife photogra-

phy when I don't have time to remove my pack and set up the tripod. There are many small tabletop tripods and clamps, but the lightest I've seen is the REI Ultrapod (2 ounces), an ingenious little device that can be used as a tripod, and with a Velcro strap, as a clamp. I sometimes use it on ski trips, strapping it to a pole. It's too light for long lenses, but it works well with standard zooms.

I use a tripod most of the time, both for self-portraits and for low-light photography. The problem is finding a lightweight one that doesn't develop the shakes after minimal use. I have several; the one I use most is an old Cullman Backpack tripod that weighs 21.5 ounces and has been held together with duct tape for the best part of a decade. Slik's 26-ounce Sprint Mini tripod looks like a modern equivalent. I usually strap my tripod to the side of the pack so I can get to it easily.

Protection and Carrying

You can protect your camera by carrying it in your pack, but you won't take many pictures that way. I like to sling a camera across my body so that I can get at it quickly. But it's vulnerable there, so I keep it in a foam-padded, waterproof case. There are many such cases sold by Tamrac, Lowe, Crumpler, Tenba, Kinesis, Camera Care Systems (CCS), and others. Weights of padded cases range from 3 ounces for compact cameras or wide-angle lenses to 12 ounces plus for cases for SLRs with telephoto lenses. I attach my CCS camera case to a wide adjustable webbing strap. The compact camera and telephoto zoom also live in padded cases kept, along with filters and film, in a small stuff sack in a pack pocket.

Cleaning

I carry lens-cleaning cloths for removing marks from lenses and a blower brush for puffing out the inside. But the danger of damaging equipment in field conditions makes me keep cleaning and tinkering to an absolute minimum.

Recording

You may think that you'll remember the details of every photo you shoot, but you won't—unless you take very few pictures or have a phenomenal memory. You need some method of recording each roll of film or photo as it's shot. Occasionally I keep a tiny notebook (0.5 ounce) and pen in a pocket and note down when and where I start and finish each roll, plus any particular details I want to remember about the pictures. To relate the film to the notes, I photograph this page on the last frame. Sometimes I mark photo locations on the map in pencil. Most often I photograph trail signs and other identifiable markers so I can relate the photos to them. An advantage of digital cameras is that the time and date of the image are recorded, which can help greatly in identifying it.

ENTERTAINMENT

Reading Matter

Because I'm a book addict, I always carry at least one paperback on every walk. Too often I end up with several. There are three kinds of books that might find their way into your pack: trail guides, natural history guides, and books for pure entertainment. On my 124-day Canadian Rockies walk, I read thirty-six books, an average of one every three and a half days—twenty-four were fiction and twelve were nonfiction. This doesn't include a field guide that I carried all the way, parts of which I read several times, and a trail guide I carried on the first half of the walk.

Natural history guides are a problem because

you usually need several if you want to identify trees, flowers, mammals, birds, and insects. In a group, each member can carry a different volume, but the solo walker has to be selective. I usually carry the smallest bird and tree guides I can find, sometimes adding a flower guide if the weight can be kept down. The lightest guides are the little Finder books published by the Nature Study Guild. The ones for trees are particularly good. I always look for a guide that covers everything, but sadly these are few. The best I've found is Ben Gadd's *Handbook of the Canadian Rockies*, which is a complete natural history field guide and also covers geology, history, weather, and much more. I carried it when I hiked the length of the Canadian Rockies. It weighs a hefty 2 pounds in the latest full-color edition, though. On the Arizona Trail I carried the National Audubon Society's *Field Guide to the Southwestern States* (16.5 ounces).

A planisphere showing the stars in position for each month is well worth carrying if you're interested in identifying constellations and planets. Small ones weigh less than 0.25 ounce and take up no space. I don't use mine often, but when I do, I'm very glad I remembered to bring it.

Radios, CD Players, Etc.

Tiny radios in the 3- to 7-ounce range could be worth carrying if you grow bored with reading or need to rest your eyes. Himalayan mountaineers now regularly take portable stereos or MP3 players for use on the climb as well as in camp. I used to carry a radio now and then (on the pretext that it was for weather forecasts), but I rarely used it because, even in the tent, it cut me off from the world I'd come to experience. Proponents of radios point out that books do the same, but to my mind they don't have the same effect; you can still hear the sounds of nature when reading. Modern devices have many uses. As I write this, a friend is hiking the Pacific Coast Trail with an Ipod, which not only contains his favorite Beach Boys' tracks but is also being used to download and store images from his digital camera. If you use a radio, please use headphones. Sound carries in the quietness of the wilderness. I remember coming off a high Pyrenean peak, my eyes set on a necklace of mountain tarns far below surrounded by green sward ideal for camping, only to be greeted, while still a half mile away, by the tinkling sounds of music coming from the only tent I could see. Once down there, I found the sound permeated the whole basin, so I pushed on into the next valley bottom to camp—much later than I'd planned, but in quiet.

Cards and Games

There are various games that groups can take along for entertainment, and, of course, you can make up your own, but a deck of cards is the most obvious lightweight entertainment to carry. You can buy miniature decks, though a standard one weighs just 3.5 ounces. I've never carried cards, but a companion did on a ski crossing of the Columbia Icefield in the Canadian Rockies, and we played many games during the four days we spent stormbound in the tents. You could carry cards on solo trips for playing solitaire, though I can't imagine wanting to. A hiking book I read many years ago did recommend carrying a deck in case you became lost. Don't panic, the author recommended; just sit down and start playing solitaire, because some damn fool is then bound to pop up behind you and tell you which card to play next!

Thermometer

Few people carry thermometers, but I'm fascinated by the temperature data I've collected over the years. My immediate finding, reinforced whenever I camp with others, was that it's never as cold as people think. Also, I've noted that you really do feel warmer when the temperature drops a few degrees below freezing and the humidity falls than when it's a few degrees above. On the Canadian Rockies walk, I recorded no temperatures below freezing during July and August and only three freezing nights in September; yet by the middle of October it was freezing hard every night. During four days I spent stormbound on the Columbia Icefield, the temperature in the tent ranged, astonishingly, from 28 to 75°F (−2 to 24°C), depending on whether we were cooking and whether the doors were open. Having such data gives me a reference for what temperatures to expect when I revisit an area, which helps with planning.

To entertain myself with such detail, I often carry a Taylor Analog Instant-Read Dial Thermometer, which comes in a plastic case with a pen type clip (0.75 ounce with case). It came as part of a Life-Link Snow Study Kit but is sold separately, mostly from kitchen stores. There's also a digital version. I use it for checking the snow temperature for waxing skis. My altimeter has a thermometer, but this is of use only if I take it off my wrist. There's a thermometer on the SAK Altimeter knife too, and on the Brunton Sherpa Atmospheric Data Center (see Chapter 9).

There are also tiny thermometers, with windchill charts on the back, attached to split rings for hanging on jacket and pack zippers. These come under a variety of labels, and their weight is negligible. They provide only a rough idea of temperature.

THE ABILITY TO ADAPT TO THINGS AS THEY ARE— A PRACTICAL NECESSITY IN WILDERNESS EXPLORATION —ALSO TEACHES US HOW TO LIVE MORE PERCEPTIVELY. IN HIGH AND WILD PLACES, ADVENTURE IS LIFE ITSELF.

—High and Wild, *Galen Rowell*

on the move

skills and hazards

Walking is very easy. Walking in the wilderness with a pack isn't quite so simple. You have to find your way, perhaps in dense mist or thick forest; you need to cope with terrain, which may mean negotiating steep cliffs, loose scree, and snow; and you must deal with hazards ranging from extremes of weather to wild animals. Most wilderness walking, however, is relatively straightforward as long as you're reasonably fit, have a few basic skills, and know a little about weather and terrain.

FINDING THE WAY

Maps

Knowing how to read a map is a key wilderness skill, yet many hikers can barely do so. I have one regular backpacking companion who has little understanding of maps and is quite happy to let me plan and lead. The only solo backpacking he's ever done was on a coastal footpath, where route finding consisted of keeping the sea on the same side. There are also some inland areas where trails are so well posted and trail guides so accurate that you don't need a map. Even in such areas, though, you may find unmarked trail junctions where it's impossible to work out which way to go without a map.

A plethora of signs, indicating a popular place.

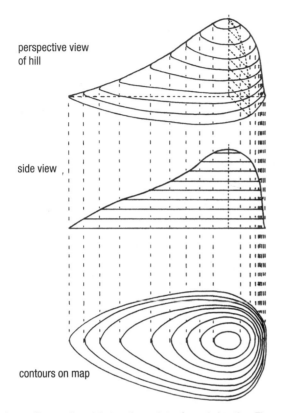

perspective view of hill

side view

contours on map

ABOVE: Contour lines join together points of equal elevation. The patterns they form represent the three-dimensional shapes of features. Once you can interpret them, you can tell what the hills, valleys, and ridges of an area are like (right).

With a map you plan walks, follow your route on the ground, and locate water sources and possible campsites. But maps also can open an inspiring world—I can spend hours poring over a map, tracing possible routes, wondering how to connect a mountain tarn with a narrow notch, speculating whether it's possible to follow a mountain ridge or if it will turn out to be a rocky edge that forces me to take another route.

Every map has a key. Using this key to interpret the symbols, you can build a picture of what the terrain will be like. There are two types of maps: *planimetric* and *topographic*. The first represents

gentle slope

moderate slope

steep hill

mountainside with cliff

gully or couloir

ridge

peak or summit

bowl or cirque

saddle, pass, or col

features on the ground; the second shows the topography, or the shape of the ground itself. Topographic ("topo") maps use *contour lines*, which join points of equal elevation starting from sea level. Contour lines occur at given intervals, usually from 15 to 500 feet. U.S. Geological Survey (USGS) 1:24,000 maps have a contour interval of 40 feet. On most maps, every fifth contour line is thicker and has the elevation indicated, though you may have to trace it for some distance to find this marker. The closer together the contour lines, the steeper the slope. If they're touching, expect a cliff (though cliffs of less height than the contour interval won't show on the map). Some maps mark cliffs, others don't; check the key to see if you might encounter cliffs not shown on the map.

The patterns that contour lines form represent the three-dimensional shapes of features. Once you can interpret them, you can tell what the hills, valleys, and ridges of an area are like and plan accordingly.

The *scale* tells you how much ground is repre-

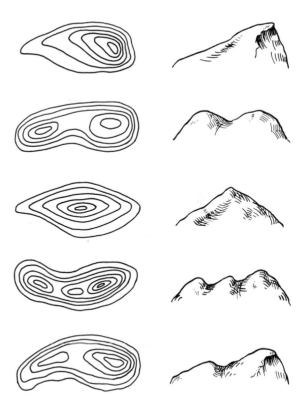

The topo views (left) match the appropriate profiles (right).

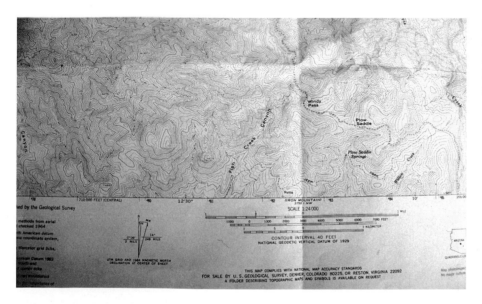

USGS topo map with scale and declination information. These maps cover the whole country but often don't contain up-to-date trail information.

A MOUNTAIN STORM

The wind whipping along the rocky ridge drives sheets of rain into my face. Clouds swirl all around, ripped apart at times to reveal sharp pinnacles soaring above me or the dark outline of a lake far below in the valley. I scramble along the narrow crest, exhilarated by the storm's fury and reveling in the rough rock under my hands. I am at the heart of the world. There is no sense of time; it's a shock when I come to the top of the talus slope that leads safely down into the valley. I hesitate to leave the storm, but the thought of dry clothes and the warmth of camp spurs me into the long descent.

sented by a given distance on the map. The standard scale for USGS topo maps outside Alaska is 1:24,000. These are known as *7.5-minute maps* because of the area of latitude and longitude they cover. On a 1:24,000 map, 1 inch equals 24,000 inches on the ground, which is roughly 2.5 inches per mile. In Alaska, 1:63,360 maps—about 1 inch to the mile—are the norm. These *15-minute maps* are still available for some other areas but are being replaced by 1:24,000 ones—a pity, since the scale is adequate for backpacking and each sheet covers a larger area. USGS topo maps, sometimes known as *quads* (from *quadrangle*), are the standard in the United States.

For most of the world, metric scales are standard, with 1:25,000 and 1:50,000 the most useful for walkers. Smaller-scale maps covering larger areas, such as 1:100,000 and 1:250,000, are helpful for planning. Although the greater detail of large-scale maps is best for walking, it's possible to use smaller-scale ones in the wilderness. In remote areas they may be all that's available. I've used 1:250,000 maps in Greenland and even 1:600,000 in the northern Canadian Rockies.

Most Forest Service maps are planimetric, but there are some topographic ones covering designated wilderness areas, such as the 1:63,360 maps covering the Ansel Adams and John Muir Wildernesses in the Sierra. The Bureau of Land Management also makes an increasing number of metric topo maps at different scales, such as 1:100,000, with contour intervals of 50 meters.

Several companies produce maps for wilder-

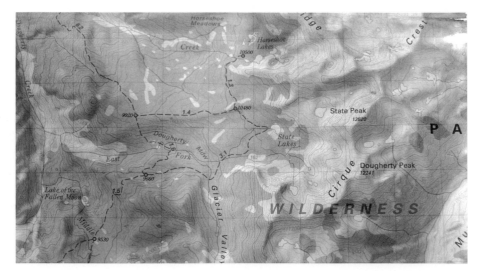

Tom Harrison Trail Map with trails clearly marked, along with distances. Maps like this are excellent for trail hiking but are available only for popular areas.

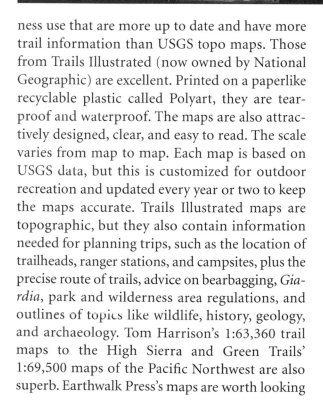

ness use that are more up to date and have more trail information than USGS topo maps. Those from Trails Illustrated (now owned by National Geographic) are excellent. Printed on a paperlike recyclable plastic called Polyart, they are tear-proof and waterproof. The maps are also attractively designed, clear, and easy to read. The scale varies from map to map. Each map is based on USGS data, but this is customized for outdoor recreation and updated every year or two to keep the maps accurate. Trails Illustrated maps are topographic, but they also contain information needed for planning trips, such as the location of trailheads, ranger stations, and campsites, plus the precise route of trails, advice on bearbagging, *Giardia*, park and wilderness area regulations, and outlines of topics like wildlife, history, geology, and archaeology. Tom Harrison's 1:63,360 trail maps to the High Sierra and Green Trails' 1:69,500 maps of the Pacific Northwest are also superb. Earthwalk Press's maps are worth looking

out for, too; I found the 1:48,000 map covering part of the Grand Canyon very good. For the northeast Appalachians, Map Adventures' waterproof topo map of the White Mountains of New Hampshire and Maine is excellent as are the Appalachian Mountain Club's maps.

Maps based on USGS quads are now available on compact disc or can be downloaded from the Internet, from companies like National Geographic Topo!, Topo USA, and TopoZone. You can draw routes on the map and calculate distances and ascents, then print out the results so you have a complete route plan or even download them to some GPS units. Maps can be printed too, though with an A4 printer you'll need several sheets to cover much of an area. You can get waterproof tear-resistant paper such as National Geographic's Adventure Paper for this. Maps can be bought at outdoor stores, bookstores, agency offices, and direct from the publishers. Web sites such as Map Link, Fresh Tracks, and the USGS are very useful. (See Appendix 3.)

For general planning, the state atlases and gazetteers published by DeLorme are useful. The maps are topographic (mostly 1:250,000 or 1:300,000, though national parks may be shown at 1:70,000). They also give a great deal of other information. I've used the Arizona and Utah atlases for planning a thousand-mile walk in the Southwest canyons. I haven't done the walk yet, but the planning has been fun!

Many topographic maps have a grid superimposed on them; each line in the grid may be numbered. If it is, you can record the grid reference for precise location. Also, counting the number of squares a route crosses is a quick way to estimate the distance.

To work out distances on maps without grids, a map measurer is useful. You set this calibrated wheel to the scale of the map and run it along your route. You can then read the distance off a scale on the device. It weighs only a fraction of an ounce, but I've never carried one. You could draw a grid on a map, but I've never done this, either. Laying a piece of string along the route and measuring it is another way of determining distance.

While large-scale topographic maps are the best for accurate navigation, other maps offer information useful to the walker. Land-management agencies, such as the National Park Service, often issue their own maps showing trails and wilderness facilities. These maps are more up to date than the topographic maps for the same area. Forest Service and Bureau of Land Management planimetric maps (usually half an inch to the mile) often show roads and trails that don't appear on topo maps. These planimetric maps don't have contour lines, so they don't tell you how much ascent and descent there is over a particular distance. (The 1:600,000 map I used in the northern Canadian Rockies was planimetric; I worked out when I would be going uphill and downhill by studying the drainage patterns of streams, but I had no way of knowing whether I was headed for a 300- or a 3,000-foot climb.) Some planimetric maps are shaded to show where the higher ground lies, but this gives only a rough idea of what to expect.

Maps normally have the date of publication listed with the key, along with the dates of any revisions. Remote areas are rarely remapped, and you may find that some maps are decades old. Obviously, the older the map, the less accurate the information may be, especially with regard to man-made features like roads. The maps I used in the northern Yukon in the 1990s didn't show the Dempster Highway, built in the 1960s and 1970s. I added it myself from highway maps, which are updated regularly. On one section of the Arizona Trail, which I hiked in 2000, the USGS map I used had last been field-checked thirty-six years earlier in 1964. Features can disappear as well, of course, and trails on maps may be hard or impossible to follow if they haven't been maintained. It's wise to consult current guidebooks and ranger stations if you don't want to risk a nasty surprise.

I am a firm believer in doing virtually all navigating with only a map. As long as you can see features around you and relate them to the map, you know where you are. The easiest way to do this is by *setting*, or *orienting*, the map, which involves turning it until the features you can see are in their correct positions relative to where you are. If you walk with the map set, it is easier to relate visible features to it.

Many people automatically use a compass for

navigating, ignoring what they can see around them, yet even at night you can navigate solely with a map. Many years ago I did a night-navigation exercise on a mountain leadership-training course and was the only person to travel the route without relying on a compass. It was a clear night, and the distinctive peaks above the valley were easily identifiable on the map, while the location of streams showed me where I was on the valley floor. The others in the group navigated as though we were in total darkness, relying on compass bearings and pace counting. If you always depend on such methods, you cut yourself off from the world around you, substituting figures and measurements for a close understanding of the nature of the terrain. I don't like my walking to be reduced to mathematical calculations.

When you're following a trail, an occasional map check is enough to let you see how far along you are. When you're going cross-country, however, study the map carefully, both beforehand and while on the move. Apart from working out a rough route, note features such as rivers, cliffs, lakes, and, in particular, contour lines. Be prepared not to always find what you expect, though. The lack of contour lines around a lake may mean you'll find a nice flat, dry area for a camp when you arrive, or it may mean acres of marsh (as happened to me a few times in the Canadian Rockies). Close-grouped contour lines at the head of a valley may mean an impassable cliff or a steep but climbable slope. You have to accept that sometimes you'll have to turn back and find another route, that sometimes you'll have to walk twice as far as planned to reach your destination and it will take you twice as long. No map will tell you everything. Flexibility in adapting your plans to the terrain is important.

Always keep your map handy, even if the route seems easy or you're on a clear trail. A garment pocket is the obvious storage place. Unless the maps are made of waterproof plastic, it's essential to protect them from weather. Unfortunately, most map cases are bulky, awkward to fold, and hard to fit into a pocket or fanny pack. Those from Ortlieb (a fraction over 2 ounces) are quite flexible and very tough. Mine is a decade old. Plastic bags work well, but they don't last long. An Aloksak bag would be a good, durable alternative. You can cover maps with special clear plastic film, and some hikers use waterproofing products, such as wipe-on Nikwax Map Proof, which I'm told are effective. I don't bother with waterproofing maps. Although some of mine look disreputable, I've never had one disintegrate.

Those who wander widely may be interested in *World Mapping Today*, by R. B. Parry and C. R. Perkins, which describes maps available for each country.

The Compass

Although I prefer to navigate with just a map, I always carry a compass. For trail travel I hardly need it, except perhaps when at an unsigned junction in thick mist or dense forest. For cross-country walking, though, a compass may prove essential, especially when visibility is poor.

The standard compass for backpacking is the *orienteering* type, with a liquid-damped needle and a transparent plastic baseplate. Silva is the best-known brand; Suunto and Brunton are others. Corporate changes have led to some confusion, however. Johnson Outdoors holds the rights to the brand name Silva in the United States and used to distribute the Swedish-made Silva compasses. In 1996 Silva bought Brunton and ended its link with Johnson, but Johnson still had the rights to the name Silva. This has led to the strange situation where the original Swedish Silva compasses

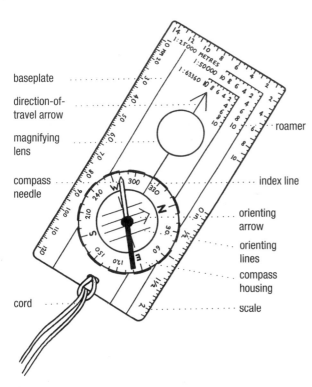

baseplate

direction-of-travel arrow

magnifying lens

compass needle

cord

roamer

index line

orienting arrow

orienting lines

compass housing

scale

The main features of an orienteering compass, including a magnifying lens. The compass housing is a rotating ring, also known as the azimuth.

are sold in the United States and Canada under the Brunton label (though as Silva elsewhere in the world), while compasses sold under the name Silva by Johnson Outdoors are now made in Finland by Silva's big rival Suunto. So there are three brands but only two makers. Luckily both make top-quality compasses.

I mostly use the smallest, lightest model—the Brunton 7DNL Star (Silva Field 7 outside North America), which weighs 0.8 ounce. This is just 0.2 ounce lighter than the Silva Type 3 I used to use. But that's still a 20 percent weight saving. For backpacking, models with sighting mirrors and other refinements are unnecessary.

The heart of the compass is the magnetic needle, which is housed in a rotating fluid-filled, transparent, circular mount marked with north, south, east, and west, plus degrees. The base of the dial is marked with an orienting arrow, fixed toward north on the dial, and a series of parallel lines. The rest of the compass consists of the baseplate, with a large direction-of-travel arrow, roamers for taking grid references, and a set of scales for measuring distances on a map. Some baseplates also have a small magnifying glass built in to help you read map detail.

A compass helps you walk toward your destination, even if you can't see it, without reference to the surrounding terrain. Without a compass, you might veer away from the correct line. The direction you walk is called a *bearing*. Bearings are given as degrees, or the angle between north and your direction, reading clockwise. To set a bearing, you use the compass baseplate as a protractor. Point the direction-of-travel arrow toward your destination, then turn the compass housing until the red end of the magnetic needle aligns with the orienting arrow. As long as you keep these two arrows pointing to the north and follow the direction-of-travel arrow, you'll reach your destination, even if it's hidden. However, you can rarely take a bearing on something several hours away and walk straight to it (although it's possible in desert and wide-open tundra). It's better to locate a visible, stationary feature (a *checkpoint*) that lies along your line of travel, such as a boulder or a tree, and walk to that. You may have to leave your bearing to circumvent an obstruction, such as a bog or a cliff, but that's all right as long as you keep the chosen feature in sight. Once you reach a checkpoint, you can check your bearing and find another object to head for.

In poor visibility, solo walkers may have to walk on their bearings by holding the compass and literally following the arrow. Two or more

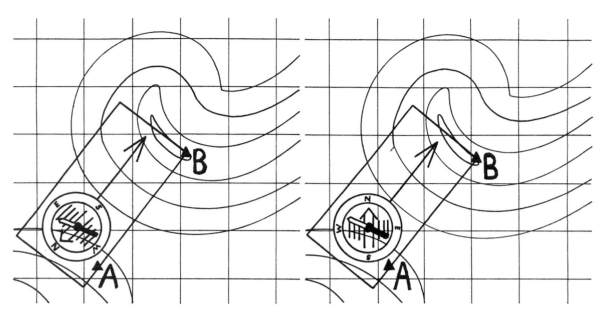

Taking a compass bearing from a map. Align the compass with your objective on the map (left), then rotate the housing to line up the orienting arrow with the north-south grid lines (right).

walkers can send one person ahead to the limit of visibility. The scout stops so another walker can check the position with the compass and direct the scout to move left or right until in line with the bearing. Then everyone else joins the scout and the process is repeated. It's a slow but very accurate method of navigation, particularly useful in whiteout conditions. I've used it many times when skiing.

If you know where you are but not which way you need to go to reach your destination, then you need to take a bearing off the map. To do this,

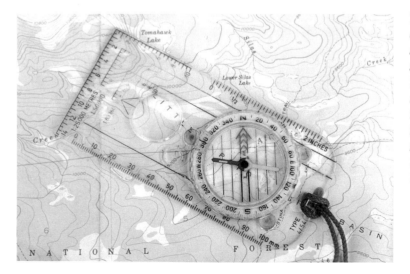

Taking a map bearing with an orienteering compass from the trail to Tomahawk Lake. Place an edge of the baseplate on the point on the trail at your location and line up the edge with Tomahawk Lake. Rotate the compass housing until the orienting arrow is aligned with north on the map. Remove the compass from the map and turn it—without rotating the housing—until the magnetic needle and orienting arrow are aligned. The direction-of-travel arrow now points to Tomahawk Lake.

place an edge of the baseplate on the spot where you are, then line up the edge with your destination. Rotate the compass housing until the orienting arrow is aligned with north on the map. Remove the compass from the map and turn it, without rotating the housing, until the magnetic needle and orienting arrow are aligned. The direction-of-travel arrow now points in the direction you want to go. The number on the compass housing at this point is your bearing.

This process is straightforward, but you must account for magnetic variation. Most topographic maps have three arrows somewhere in the margin showing three norths. *Grid north* can be ignored for compass navigation (though not for GPS navigation—see UTM sidebar, pages 368–70); the other two are very important. One is *magnetic north*, the direction the compass needle points. The other is *true north*. The top of the map is always true north, so if your map has no grid marked on it, you can use the margins. Because compasses point to magnetic north and maps are aligned to true north, the difference between them should be taken into account when using the two

in conjunction. This angle is measured in degrees and minutes (60 minutes equal 1 degree) and is called the *magnetic variation* or *declination*.

Since magnetic north lies in the Far North of Canada, true north can be either east or west of magnetic north. In parts of Michigan, Indiana, Ohio, Kentucky, Tennessee, and North and South Carolina, however, magnetic north and true north coincide. In areas of North America to the east of those states, true north is west of magnetic north, but to the west of them, true north is east of magnetic north. The declination is usually marked on topo maps. For example, the Tom Harrison Trail Map for the Mono Divide High Country in California gives the declination in 2002 as 14.5 degrees east, while the Appalachian Mountain Club map of the Presidential Range in New Hampshire gives the declination in 2003 as 17 degrees west. Just to confuse matters further, magnetic north isn't stationary but moves in a (luckily) predictable pattern. The declination on an old map will not reflect the current position of magnetic north. Some maps list the rate of change so you can work out the current figure. If your map

Aiming off.

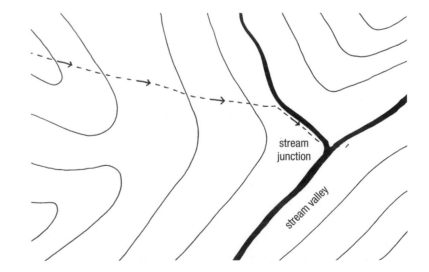

stream junction

stream valley

isn't new and doesn't show the rate of change, you may be able to find it in a trail guide. You also can calculate the magnetic variation yourself by taking a bearing from one known feature to another, recording the bearing (without taking any declination into account) and then taking the same bearing from the map. The difference between the two is the current declination. If you stick a piece of tape on the compass as a declination mark, you won't have to recompute it every time you use the compass. You will have to remember to move it if you visit different areas, though. Some compasses come with adjustable declination marks.

In the eastern United States, because magnetic north lies west of true north, when you take a bearing from the map you add the declination figure. However, if your bearing is taken from the ground and transferred to the map (not something you're likely to do often), you subtract the declination. A mnemonic for remembering this is "empty sea, add water"—MTC (map to compass), add. Of course, in western states the opposite applies; you subtract declination when taking a bearing from the map and add it when taking one from the ground.

There's always an element of error in any compass work. If your bearing is 5 degrees off, then you'll be 335 feet off the correct line of travel after walking 0.6 mile, 650 feet after 1.2 miles, and more than half a mile after 6.2 miles. This makes it difficult to find a precise spot that lies some distance from your starting point unless you can take a bearing on some intermediate feature. One of the few compass techniques I use, other than straightforward bearings, is *aiming off*, which is especially handy in poor visibility. If your destination lies on or near an easy-to-find line such as a stream, you can make a deliberate error and aim to hit a line on one side or the other of your destination. When you reach the line, you know

which way to turn to reach your destination. I used aiming off on a large scale in the Canadian Rockies. I knew that hundreds of miles somewhere to the northwest was the little town of Tumbler Ridge, which I wanted to reach, and that a road ran roughly east-west to the town. By heading north rather than northwest, I knew I'd hit the road east of Tumbler Ridge, and after a week's walking I did—and found myself 46 miles away. But I knew where the town was, and, more important, where I was.

The compass has other, more complex uses; you'll find instructions for them in good navigation books. Don't rely on your compass blindly, though. There are areas high in iron ore where a compass won't work.

Keep your compass where you can reach it easily; otherwise you might be tempted to skip checking it when you're unsure of your direction. As I've learned, this can mean retracing your steps a considerable distance. Like most people, I have a loop of cord attached to my compass (most come with small holes in the baseplate for this purpose), though I don't often hang it around my neck. I may tie the loop to a zipper pull on a garment pocket so that I don't lose the compass and can refer to it quickly whenever I want to.

GPS

GPS (global positioning system) is a government-operated system that consists of twenty-eight satellites 12,000 miles up, four of them used for backup. Each satellite orbits earth twice a day and sends out a continuous signal, giving its position and the time. By locking onto a minimum of four satellites, a GPS receiver on the ground can *triangulate* its position. An accurate fix may not be obtainable if the satellites aren't in the right alignment, however. Also, there must be a line of sight

UTM COORDINATES AND GPS

All GPS receivers give positions as a set of numbers called coordinates. Latitude and longitude is the standard coordinate system. However it isn't the easiest to use. Much simpler and the best for use with GPS is Universal Transverse Mercator (UTM), a metric system that appears on all U.S. topo maps and many other maps. The UTM system divides the earth into sixty zones, each with its own number. Zones 5 to 22 cover North America. Each zone is then divided into a rectangular grid. The UTM grid is superimposed on a flat projection of the earth's surface rather than on a globe like latitude and longitude (which means a degree of longitude varies in size according to distance from the equator). This means the grid squares are identical in size, which makes plotting a position easy. (Using a flat projection does introduce some inaccuracies but these are so small—less than 0.4 percent—that they can be ignored. The discrepancy is marked on topo maps as the difference between grid north and true north.) Using the UTM grid you can give a position in numbers of meters from the horizontal and vertical grid lines on a map. The grid lines are 1 kilometer apart on USGS topo maps. (Always check the map key for the distance between UTM marks—on the Map Adventures White Mountains of New Hampshire and Maine Trail Map and the Trails Illustrated Sequoia and Kings Canyon National Parks map they are 5 kilometers apart for example.)

To plot positions accurately using UTM you need a plastic measuring device called a *roamer*, which is transparent and has sets of lines at right angles to each other for different map scales such as 1:24,000, 1:50,000 and 1:63,500. Roamers are found on many protractor compasses (see illustration page 364) and also separately, such as the UTM Grid Reader and the Topo Companion. Alternatively

USGS topo map with UTM grid penciled in.

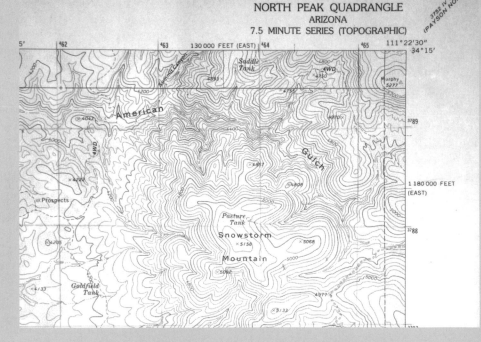

you can use a grid tool, with which you can subdivide a map grid into tenths. As the grid square on a 1:24,000 USGS topo covers 1,000 square meters a grid tool will let you locate a 100-meter square. Grid tools come in different map scales.

Unfortunately on USGS topos the grid is not drawn on the map. Instead blue ticks round the edges of the map mark the position of the grid. To find positions on the map you need a straight edge. Eyeballing positions away from the edge of the map is difficult. Using a straight edge in the field can be hard too, especially when it's windy or raining and there is no level surface on which to place the map, so it's best to draw the grid in place at home with a fine pen or pencil. As the grid may not be exactly in line with the edges of the map make sure you link up the blue ticks on either side.

To plot a position as a UTM coordinate on a map you need to measure the distance from the grid lines that border the position. UTM is designed to be read to the right and from the bottom up so the grid numbers increase from left to right (east to west) and from bottom to top (south to north). The vertical (north-south) grid lines to use are those to the west (left) of the position. The horizontal (east-west) grid lines to use are those to the south of the position. To emphasize: the grid lines to use are those on the left (western) and bottom (southern) sides of the square in which the position lies. Using a roamer you can measure tenths of a square to give a Grid Reference (GR). The distance of a point east of the vertical grid line is called an easting. The distance of a point north of the horizontal grid line is called a northing. Coordinates are always stated with eastings first.

As an example let's take a typical USGS 1:24,000 topo map, North Peak, Arizona, which shows part of the Mazatzal Mountain range (see opposite), with UTM grid lines penciled in. The information in the lower left margin of the map tells us that the map is in UTM zone 12. That will be the figure that first appears on a GPS reading for anywhere on this map (sometimes with a letter after

it—N, S, or U—this can be ignored). Along the sides of the map are the UTM blue ticks, with numbers alongside with the first figure or figures printed small, the second ones printed large, such as ⁴63. The larger printed figures are the ones that mark kilometer distances on the grid, the smaller ones aren't relevant (they refer to the distance from the zone meridian, a line running down the center of each UTM zone, and the equator). Let's say we want to put the coordinates of the Pasture Tank into a GPS receiver (which, as a water source, could

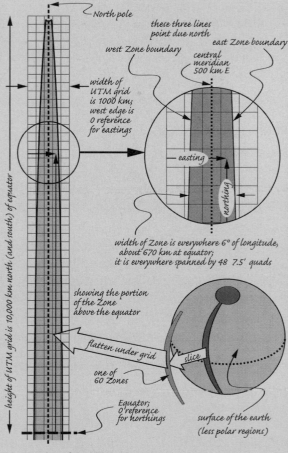

An overview of the UTM grid system.

UTM COORDINATES AND GPS (continued)

be a crucial feature). The Pasture Tank lies in the square 63 (easting) 88 (northing). Using a roamer we can divide the square into tenths. The pasture tank is $^9/_{10}$ of a square east of line 63 and $^1/_{10}$ north of line 88, giving Grid Reference 639 881. Six-figure coordinates like this are for a 100-meter square, normally accurate enough for practical purposes. GPS receivers usually give more precise readings than these, often ten-figure ones accurate to a square meter. However I find six-figure coordinates—three for the easting, three for the northing—accurate enough and easy to use. When entering a coordinate into a GPS receiver, zeros can be used for the final three figures if these are required. Sometimes a GPS receiver shows a zero at the start of a seven-figure easting. This can be ignored.

Further information on using UTM and GPS can be found in Michael Ferguson's *GPS Land Navigation* and Lawrence Letham's *GPS Made Easy* and at the maptools.com website.

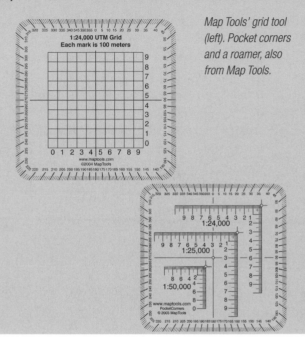

Map Tools' grid tool (left). Pocket corners and a roamer, also from Map Tools.

between the receiver and the satellites; it can be impossible to get a fix in dense forest or below steep cliffs.

Using electronic gadgets like GPS in the wilderness is frowned on by some. Whatever you think about the place of electronics in the wilds, one thing is clear: they won't go away. Indeed, their use will increase as more devices designed for wilderness use are developed. It is futile to debate whether the wilds are an appropriate place for such technology. The point is to look at electronic devices exactly as we would any other new gear: to consider what purpose they serve and just how useful they are. After all, they're only tools, like packs or stoves.

I've tried a number of GPS units, but this is an area of rapid development, so before buying a unit I'd recommend getting up-to-date expert advice. GPSinformation.net is the Web site for such information.

For several reasons, GPS should not be considered a substitute for a map and compass (and the skills to use them) but rather as complementary. On a few occasions I've been unable to confirm my position with GPS because the receiver wouldn't give a reading; each time I was very glad I'd been checking my progress on the map.

Once a receiver has a fix, it will show the position on its screen. This can be in latitude or longitude or UTM (Universal Transverse Mercator), the grid used on USGS topo maps. To translate this reading onto the map, you must be able to plot grid references accurately (see sidebar). All receivers can be set to give positions for the maps of different countries. These are known as *map datums*. It is very important to set the correct map datum, as an incorrect one will result in an inaccurate reading. The most common map datums for North America are North American Datum 1927 (NAD 27) and World Geodetic System 1984 (WGS 84).

Anyone comfortable with computers should have no problem with GPS. Technophobes and those who have trouble programming a video recorder might find GPS receivers difficult. Studying the manuals carefully (which takes several hours) and practicing with the receiver at home are essential if you are to make full use of a unit in the field.

GPS receivers have multiple functions. In addition to showing your position, they tell you the approximate altitude, and they can be programmed to guide you to a specific destination by a series of legs—they can store from dozens to hundreds of locations, called *waypoints*—or take you back to your starting point. They can tell you how far you have to go to reach your goal, which direction to go, how fast you're traveling, how long it will take you to get there, and the estimated time of arrival. If you stray from the route they'll warn you of that, too.

Using all these functions requires power, and that means batteries. Most receivers run off AA batteries, some off AAA; and though figures for battery life are impressive (twenty hours and more), these are usually for temperatures of about 70°F (21°C). In colder temperatures (I've used receivers at 0°F [−18°C]) battery life is much shorter, even when the receiver is kept warm inside your clothes and you use lithium batteries. Carrying spares is advisable.

The most common use of GPS is to guide you toward a destination. To do this you first enter the grid references of the destination and waypoints en route into the receiver's memory (most easily done by downloading them from a computer mapping program), then follow the direction indicators on the screen to each point or transfer the bearings given to your compass. Of course, the receiver can direct you only in straight lines, though most will indicate how far off your line of travel you are.

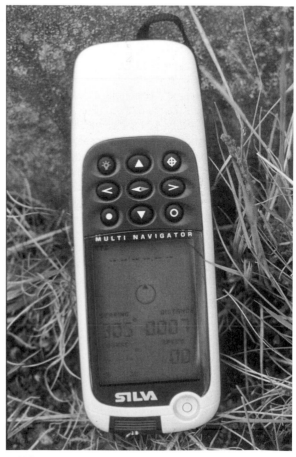

A GPS receiver. Brunton/Silva Multi-Navigator.

Using GPS like this means walking with the receiver in your hand and consulting it regularly. I tried this on a cross-country walk in viewless forest, and it worked well. However, I don't go for walks in order to stare at a screen; I do enough of that when I'm writing. There are times and places—when I was unsure of my whereabouts for nearly a week in the Canadian Rockies, for example, or in a whiteout in winter anywhere—when I could see the usefulness of following a preset course. But for most walking it's unnecessary and a waste of batteries. I think GPS is better used as a means of checking your position when it's important you know *exactly* where you

GPS: MY CHOICE

My current GPS unit is a Brunton Multi-Navigator, a powerful waterproof device that weighs 10 ounces with two AA batteries. The Multi-Navigator has a compass that automatically compensates for local declination and can be used with the GPS turned off, as well as an altimeter/barometer. It can hold ten routes and one thousand waypoints with names of up to eight characters and record tracks for downloading to a computer mapping program. It does far more, but all I use it for on the rare occasions I take it out—mainly on ski tours—is pinpointing my position, usually in a whiteout or dense mist or in featureless terrain. For this a much less sophisticated GPS unit would be fine, and if I were purchasing a new one it would be the tiny Garmin Geko 201, which weighs 3.01 ounces with two AAA batteries. At that weight I might carry it more often than the Multi-Navigator.

are. I've used it for this in trackless, snow-covered terrain in poor visibility and felt reassured when the receiver confirmed that I was where I thought I was. For this a simple tiny, lightweight receiver is adequate, like one of the 3-ounce Garmin Gekos.

The GPS receivers I've tried perform well once you master the necessary procedures and the technical jargon of the instructions. Besides Brunton and Garmin, good units are made by Magellan and Trimble.

Altimeters

Wrist altimeter-watches have become popular in recent years, mainly owing to Suunto and Casio, which make large ranges. For Alpine and Himalayan mountaineers altimeters are important navigational aids. For backpackers, a map and compass have always been adequate. Initially I was dubious about the usefulness of altimeters for backpacking (and I still don't think they're essential), but after using one for over a decade, I now find one very helpful, especially for cross-country travel.

On an ascent, knowing the height and the time means you can monitor progress and work out how long it will take to reach the top. If you know the height at which you need to leave a ridge or start an ascent from a wooded valley, an altimeter will tell you when you reach that point. During a long traverse on steep, difficult terrain during a ski tour in the High Sierra, I could see from the map that the only safe descent to the valley was through a tiny notch that led into a wide, shallow gully. By using the altimeter I was able to ski through trees in growing darkness directly into the notch. It would have been much harder to find by map and compass alone.

Altimeters are barometers—they work by translating changes in air pressure into vertical height. To maintain accuracy, they must be reset at known heights. Temperature changes can cause

A wrist altimeter for navigation. The Suunto Altimax.

inaccurate altimeter readings. The best altimeters are temperature compensated, but the least expensive ones usually aren't. The best way to minimize inaccuracies is to avoid temperature variations by keeping the altimeter at the same temperature as the outside air. For quick reference, you can wear a wrist altimeter on the outside of your jacket.

The altimeter I currently use is the temperature-compensated Suunto Altimax, which will measure the altitude from −500 to over 9,000 feet at a resolution of 10 feet. I wear it on my wrist, though of course the temperature reading isn't accurate if it's worn this way. The Altimax will record the ascent during a trip and the time taken, useful data for future trip planning, and tell you the rate at which you're ascending or descending, which can be useful in timing your progress. Because it's also my watch, I wear the Altimax even when I carry the SAK Altimeter knife, which simply gives the height with no other data. And because the SAK Altimeter is also my knife I carry that when I also carry the Sherpa Atmospheric Data Center to measure wind speed, which includes a barometer/altimeter. This means I'm sometimes carrying three altimeters! I've compared them at times and found that they rarely disagree by more than 20 feet.

Navigating by Natural Phenomena

There are many ways to navigate without a map or compass, but I habitually use only two—the sun and the wind, and then only as backups. Knowing where they should be in relation to my route means I'm quick to notice if their position has shifted. If I've veered off my intended line of travel—easy to do in rolling grassland or continuous forest—I stop and check my location. I also check that the wind hasn't shifted and see what the time is so that I know where the sun should be.

Learning More

There are many helpful books for those who want to learn more about navigational techniques. The classic is *Be Expert with Map and Compass* by Björn Kjellström; a good modern one is David Seidman's *Essential Wilderness Navigator*. To learn more than these books can teach, you'll need to take a course at an outdoor center or join an orienteering club.

Waymarks and Signposts

Paint splashes, piles of stones (called cairns, or ducks), blazes on trees, posts, and other devices mark trails and routes throughout the world. (In Norway, wilderness ski routes are marked out with lines of birch sticks.) These *waymarks*, combined with signposts at trail junctions, make finding many routes easy, but I have mixed feelings about them—part of me dislikes them intensely as unnecessary intrusions into the wilderness; another part of me follows them gladly when they loom up on a misty day. But waymarking of routes doesn't mean you can do without map and compass or the skills to use them. Useful though it is, I would not like to see waymarking increase. I'd rather find my own way through the wilderness, and I don't build cairns or cut blazes, let alone paint rocks. In fact, I often knock down cairns that have appeared where there were none before, knowing that if they are left, a trail will soon follow. Painting waymarks in hitherto unspoiled terrain is vandalism. On a weeklong hike in the Western Highlands of Scotland, I was horrified to discover a series of large red paint splashes daubed on boulders all the way down a 3,300-foot mountain spur that is narrow enough for the way to be clear. There wasn't

RIGHT: Trail markers. Know what they mean, but please refrain from making your own—you might confuse future hikers. BELOW: A cairn or duck marks the line of a trail. BOTTOM: Tree blazes also show the line of a trail.

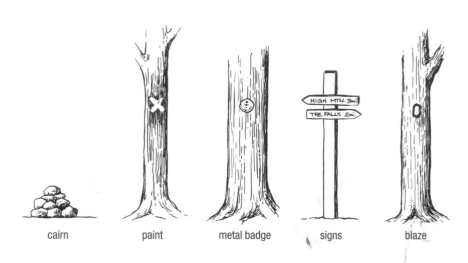

cairn   paint   metal badge   signs   blaze

even a trail on this ridge before. Now it has been defiled with paint that leaps out from the subtle colors of heather, mist, and lichen-covered rock. May the culprit wander forever lost in a howling Highland wind, never able to locate a single spot of paint!

Guidebooks

There are two kinds of wilderness guidebooks: area guides and trail guides. The first give a general overview, providing information on possible routes, weather, seasons, hazards, natural history, and so on. Often lavishly illustrated, they are usually far too heavy to carry in your pack. I find such books interesting when I return from an area and want to find out more about some of the places I've visited and things I've seen. They're also nice to daydream over.

Trail guides are designed as adjuncts to maps. Indeed, some of them include the topographic maps you need for a specific location. If you want to follow a trail precisely, they're very useful, though your sense of discovery is diminished when you know in advance about everything you'll see along the way. Some cover only specific trails; others are miniature area guides, with route suggestions and general information. Most popular destinations or routes have a trail guide, and many have several. Since trail guides frequently contain up-to-date information not found on maps, I often carry one, especially if I'm visiting an area for the first time.

There are a vast number of guidebooks. Good trail guides include the *100 Hikes* series from Mountaineers (mountaineersbooks.com); the *50 Hikes* series from Countryman (countryman press.com); the Sierra Nevada guides from Wilderness Press (wildernesspress.com); the Sierra Club's guides (sierraclub.org/books), which cover areas from the Smoky Mountains to the Grand Canyon; and the hiking guides from Falcon (now part of Globe Pequot, globepequot.com), which cover a selection of states and wild areas. The Appalachian Mountain Club's *White Mountain Guide*, now in its twenty-seventh edition, is a classic for this region. Lonely Planet (lonelyplanet.com) has an increasing number of good hiking guides, including excellent ones to the High Sierra and Yellowstone and Grand Teton National Parks, as well as a good overseas travel guide series. Bradt (bradt-travelguides.com) publishes a series of invaluable trekking guides to remote places, from South America to Spitsbergen.

The big three long-distance trails all have detailed guidebooks. Those on the Appalachian Trail are published by the Appalachian Trail Conference, those on the Continental Divide Trail by the Continental Divide Trail Society, those on the Pacific Crest Trail by Wilderness Press, which also publishes a guide to the John Muir Trail. There are also a couple of very useful annual guides to the AT: Dan "Wingfoot" Bruce's *The Thru-Hiker's Handbook* and the Appalachian Trail Long Dis-

Trail sign at a junction with distances to trailheads and other trails. Mazatzal Mountains, Arizona.

tance Hikers Association's *Appalachian Trail Thru-Hikers' Companion*. (See Appendix 2.)

On Being "Lost"

What constitutes being lost is a moot point. Some people feel lost if they don't know to the yard exactly where they are, even if they know which side of which mountain they're on, or which valley they're in. It's possible to "lose" a trail you're following, but that doesn't mean you're lost.

I think it's very hard to become totally lost when traveling on foot; I've never managed it. I was "unsure of my whereabouts" during the week I spent in thick forest in the foothills of the Canadian Rockies, but I knew my general position, and I knew which direction to walk to get to where I wanted to go. Although I couldn't pinpoint my position on a map (indeed, I couldn't locate myself to within twenty-five miles in any direction, and I've never been able to retrace my route on a map), I wasn't

SORT OF LOST

On the Pacific Crest Trail, two of us mislaid the trail in the northern Sierra Nevada after a "short-cut" took us off the map. The evening this happened we "camped above a river we think may lead to Blue Lake" (journal entry, June 22, 1982), the lake being the next feature we expected to recognize. My rather confused journal entry for June 23 describes what happened next: "Took three hours before we were back on the trail and even then we weren't sure where. We must have been farther north and east than we thought. The hill we thought was the Nipple wasn't and when we'd finally given up trying to reach it we found ourselves traversing the real Nipple just after I'd been talking about Alice in *Through the Looking Glass* only reaching the hilltop by walking away from it."

We didn't know we were back on the Pacific Crest Trail until we found a trail marker telling us so. Once we knew exactly where on the trail we were, all the other features fell into place, and the terrain we'd been crossing suddenly made sense. That's when we realized we couldn't reach the peak we were seeking because we were already on it!

course is to *stop and think*. Where might you have gone wrong? Check the map. Then, if you think you can, try to retrace your steps to a point you recognize or can identify. If you don't think you can do that, use the map to figure out how to get from where you are (you always know the area you're in, even if it's a huge area) to where you want to be. It may be easiest to head directly for a major destination, such as a road or town, as I did in the foothills of the Canadian Rockies, rather than trying to find trails or smaller features. Often it's a matter of heading in the right direction, knowing that eventually you'll reach somewhere you want to be.

I don't mind not knowing exactly where I am—sometimes I enjoy it. There's a sense of freedom in not being able to predict what lies over the next ridge, where the next lake is, and where the next valley leads. I enjoy the release of wandering through what is, from my perspective, uncharted territory. I never intend to lose myself, but when it happens I view it as an opportunity rather than a problem.

lost, because I didn't allow myself to think I was. Being lost is a state of mind.

The state of mind to avoid is panic. Terrified hikers have been known to abandon their packs in order to run in search of a place they recognize, only to die from a fall or of hypothermia. As long as you have your pack, you have food and shelter and can survive, so you needn't worry. I've spent many nights out when I didn't know precisely where I was. But I had the equipment to survive comfortably, so it didn't matter. A camp in the wilderness is a camp in the wilderness, whether it's at a well-used, well-posted site or on the banks of a river you can't identify.

The first thing to do if you suspect you're off

Checking the map on a high point with a good view of the surrounding terrain.

COPING WITH TERRAIN

On and Off Trail

As long as you stick to good, regularly used trails, you should have no problems with terrain except for the occasional badly eroded section. Don't assume that because a trail is marked boldly on a map it will be clear and well maintained. Sometimes the trail won't be visible at all; other times it may start off clearly, then fade away, becoming harder to follow the deeper into the wilderness you go. Trail guides and ranger stations are the best places to find out about specific trail conditions, but even their information can be inaccurate.

Many people never leave well-marked trails, feeling that cross-country travel is simply too difficult and too slow. They're missing a great deal. Going cross-country differs from trail walking and requires a different approach. The joys of off-trail travel lie in the contact it gives you with the country you pass through. The 15-to-20-inch dirt strip that constitutes a trail holds the raw, untouched wilderness a little at bay. Once you step off it, the difficulties you will encounter should be accepted as belonging to that experience. You can't expect to cover the same distance you would on a trail or to always find a campsite before dark. Uncertainty is one of the joys of off-trail travel, part of the escape from straight lines and the prison of the known.

Learning the nature of the country you're in is very important. Once you've spent a little time in an area—maybe no more than a few hours—you should be able to start interpreting the terrain and modifying your plans accordingly. In the northern Canadian Rockies, I learned that black spruce forest meant muskeg swamps so difficult to cross that it was worth a detour of any length to avoid them; if the map showed a narrow valley, I knew it would

TOP: A well-constructed mountain trail. The John Muir Trail below Selden Pass. Note the rocks lining the trail to keep it in place and the smooth tread. ABOVE: A trail through a meadow edged with stones.

A sketchy trail above timberline. Glacier Peak Wilderness, North Cascades. Keep an eye on the map in areas where trails vanish.

be swampy, so I would climb the hillside and contour above the swamps; if it showed a wide valley, I would head for the creek because there probably would be shingle banks I could walk on by the forest edge. It's useful to be able to survey the land ahead from a hillside or ridge—for which binoculars are well worth their weight—and I often plan the next few hours' route from a hilltop.

Compared with walking on trails, cross-country travel is real exploration, both of the world around and of yourself. To appreciate it fully you need to be open to whatever may happen. Distances and time matter far less once you've shrugged off the trail network. What matters is being there.

The Steep and the Rough

Steep slopes can be unnerving, especially on descents. If you're not comfortable going straight down and there's no trail, take a switchback route across the slopes. Look for small flatter areas where

you can rest and work out the next leg of the descent. Making a careful survey of the slope before you start down is always wise. Work out routes between small cliffs and drop-offs.

Slopes of stones and boulders, known as *talus*, occur on mountainsides the world over, usually between timberline and the cliffs above. Trails across them are usually cleared and flattened, though you may still find the going tricky. Balance is the key to crossing rough terrain, and trekking poles are a great help, though you need to be sure they don't get caught between two rocks. Cross large boulder fields slowly and carefully, testing each step and trying not to slip. Unstable boulders, which may move as you put your weight on them, can easily tip you over. The key to good balance is to keep your weight over your feet, which means not leaning back when descending and not leaning into the slope when traversing.

You may go crazy trying not to slip on the smallest stones, known as *scree*, though, so you just have to let your feet slide. Some people like to run down scree—a fast way to descend—but the practice damages scree slopes so quickly that it should no longer be indulged—too much scree

Watch your footing on narrow trails on steep, rocky mountainsides like this one in the Ochil Hills, Scotland.

LEFT: *A ladder takes a trail over a rock slab in the White Mountains, New Hampshire.* MIDDLE: *A line of rocks marking where a trail crosses a large rock slab.* RIGHT: *When descending a steep, rocky ridge—like this one on King's Peak, Uinta Mountains, Utah—take short steps and watch for loose rocks.*

running turns slopes into slippery, dangerous ribbons of dirt embedded with rocks. Be very careful if you can't see the bottom of a scree slope—it may end at the edge of a cliff. Because climbing, descending, or crossing a scree slope without dislodging stones is impossible, a group should move at an angle or in an arrowhead formation so that no one is directly under anyone else. Because other groups may be crossing below you, if a stone does start rolling you should shout a warning—*"Rock!"* is the standard call. If you hear this, *do not look up*, even though you'll be tempted to. Instead, cover your head with your pack or your hands.

Traversing steep, trailless slopes is tiring and puts great strain on the feet, ankles, and hips. It's preferable to climb to a ridge or flat terrace, or descend to a valley, rather than to traverse a slope for any distance. You may think that traversing around minor summits and bumps on mountain-ridge walks will require less effort than going up or down, but in my experience it won't. (Still, I'm frequently drawn to traversing. Heed my words, not my practice!)

In general, treat steep slopes with caution. If you feel uncomfortable with the angle or the ground under your feet, retreat and find a safer way. Backpacking isn't rock climbing, though it's surprising what you can get up and down with a heavy pack if you have a good head for heights and a little skill. *Don't climb what you can't descend* unless you can see that your way is clear beyond the obstacle. And remember that you can use a length of cord to pull up or lower your pack if necessary.

However, it's unwise to drop packs down a slope; they may go farther than you intend. Bad route finding once left two of us at the top of a steep, loose, and broken limestone cliff in Glacier National Park in Montana; foolishly, we decided to descend rather than turn back, and it took us several hours of heart-stopping scrambling to reach

RIGHT: A narrow trail on a steep, vegetated mountainside. Glacier Peak Wilderness, North Cascades. BELOW: "Postholing" through deep snow is slow, hard work. This hiker should be using the trekking pole strapped to her pack for balance and support. BOTTOM: The trail may be buried in snow, but trail signs can still point the way.

the base. At one point my companion decided he could safely lower his pack to the next ledge, even though he would have to drop it the last few feet. The pack bounced off that ledge and a few more before being halted by a tree two hundred feet or so below. Amazingly, nothing broke—not even the skis strapped to the pack. If we'd lost the pack or the contents had been destroyed, we would have had serious problems.

Snow

Much of what I just said about traversing rock slopes applies to crossing snow. However, you may come upon small but steep and icy snow-fields in summer when you aren't carrying an ice ax or crampons. Having a staff or trekking poles makes it easier to balance across snow on small holds kicked with the edge of your boots, though you shouldn't attempt this if there is dangerous ground below the snow slope, since you can't stop a slide with a staff. Without a support, take great care and, if possible, look for a way around a snow slope, even if it involves descending or climbing.

Bushwhacking

"Bushwhacking" is the apt word for thrashing through thick brush and scrambling over fallen trees while thorny bushes tear at your clothes and pack. It's the hardest form of "walking" I know, and it's to be avoided whenever possible—though sometimes you have no choice.

Bushwhacking takes a long time and a lot of energy, with very little distance to show for it; half a mile per hour can be good progress. Climbing high above dense vegetation and wading up rivers are both preferable to prolonged bushwhacking. But if you like to strike out across country, bushwhacking eventually will be essential.

Bushwhacking can be necessary even during ski tours. On one occasion in the Algäu Alps, four of us descended from a high pass into a valley. The snow wasn't deep enough to fully cover the dense willow scrub that spread over the lower slopes and rose a yard or two high. Luckily the scrub didn't spread very far, but skiing through it was a desperate struggle, since the springy branches constantly knocked us over and caught at our poles and bindings.

Unmaintained trails can quickly become overgrown, too. I made the mistake of wearing shorts while descending one in the Grand Canyon; the upper part of the trail ran through dense thickets of thorny bushes and small trees, and my legs were soon bloody. It was quite a relief to reach the desert farther down, where at least the cacti and yuccas were widely spaced.

MINIMIZING IMPACT

A trail is a scar on the landscape, albeit a minor one. But where there is a trail, walk on it. Cross-country travel is for areas where there are no trails. Don't parallel a trail in order to experience

Top: A slightly overgrown forest trail. Glacier Peak Wilderness.
Above: An old trail sign points the way through a trailless meadow. Here it's best to try to follow the line of the original trail.

off-trail walking. Most damage is caused when walkers walk along the edges or just off a trail, widening it and destroying the vegetation alongside. Always stick to the trail, even if it means walking in mud.

On slopes, you should always use the switchbacks. Too many hillsides have been badly dam-

A trail in need of restoration and relocation. Note the multiple channels, eroded ground, and damage to the meadow.

A steep switchbacking trail, High Sierra.

aged by people shortcutting switchbacks, creating new, steeper routes that quickly become water channels. In meadows and alpine terrain, where it's easy to walk anywhere, multiple trails often appear where people have walked several abreast. In such terrain, you should follow the main trail, if you can figure out which it is, and walk single file. When snow blocks part of a trail, try to follow the line where the trail would be; don't create a new trail by walking around the edge of a snow patch unless you need to do so for safety.

When you walk cross-country, your aim must be to leave no sign of your passing—that means no marking with blazes, cairns, or subtle signs like broken twigs unless they're removed later. It also means avoiding fragile surfaces where possible, walking around damp meadows, and staying off soft vegetation. Rock, snow, and nonvegetated surfaces suffer the least damage; gravel banks of rivers and streams are regularly washed clean by floods and snowmelt, so walking on them causes no harm.

It would take a skilled tracker to follow a good solo walker's cross-country route. Groups have a more difficult time leaving no sign of their passage. The answer is to keep groups small and to spread out, taking care not to step in each other's boot prints. As few as four sets of boots can leave the beginnings of a trail that others may follow in fragile meadows and tundra. Where these new trails have started to appear, walk well away from them so you don't help in their creation. The aim should be to use obvious trails but not make new ones or expand signs of faint ones.

In many areas, land-management agencies maintain and repair trails, often using controversial methods. However, wide, eroded scars made

A boardwalk built to allow ground damaged by too many hooves and boots to recover.

LEFT: Boardwalks to protect soft, wet ground on a trail in the White Mountains, New Hampshire. RIGHT: Hiking along the smooth slabs beside a creek when going cross-country in rocky mountain terrain.

by thousands of boots (and sometimes hooves) hardly create a feeling of wilderness either. Unfortunately, some popular trails may be saved only by employing drastic regulations. Walkers can help by following trail-management instructions, staying off closed sections, and accepting artificial surfaces as necessary in places.

Generally, when walking cross-country you should always consider your impact on the terrain and pick the route that will cause least damage.

WILDERNESS HAZARDS

Weather

Most outdoor hazards are caused by the weather. Wind, rain, snow, thunderstorms, freezing temperatures, thaws, and heat waves all introduce difficulties or dangers. Coping with weather is the reason

backpackers need tents, sleeping bags, and other equipment.

With a little knowledge you can often predict the weather at least a few hours ahead, though you can't compete with expert meteorologists using satellite images and computers. For any given trip, knowing in general what weather to expect should be part of your trip planning. Area guides, local information offices, and ranger stations are the places to get details of regional weather patterns. For a specific day, check Internet, radio, television, and newspaper forecasts if you can; park and forest service ranger stations often post daily weather forecasts. If you don't see one, inquire. If you monitor forecasts for an area you visit regularly, you'll soon be able to develop an annual weather overview. If you're going to an unfamiliar area, checking weather patterns for some time in advance can give you an idea of what to expect. Before I hiked the Arizona Trail I followed Web weather reports for several months so I knew that it had been dry even by Arizona standards. I also knew that the first real storm for months was due about the time I reached Arizona, so I wasn't too surprised (though delighted) to land in Phoenix in pouring rain.

Even the most detailed recent forecast can be wrong. Regional patterns can mean rain in one valley and sun in another just over the hill. Mountains are particularly notorious for creating their own weather. Weather has less impact on travel over low-level and below-timberline routes—if it rains, you don rain gear; if it's windy, you keep an eye out for falling trees.

High up, however, a strong wind can make walking impossible, and rain may turn to snow. On any mountain walk you should be prepared to descend early or take a lower route if the weather worsens. Struggling on into the teeth of a blizzard when you don't have to is foolish and risky. It even may be necessary to sit out bad weather for a day or more. I've done so on a few occasions and have been surprised at how fast the time passes.

Weather Forecasting

Observation is the key to short-term weather forecasting. Watch out for slight changes. Which way are the clouds moving? What type of clouds are they? Thickening clouds can mean rain, thinning ones sun. Fast-approaching clouds may mean a storm soon. What direction is the wind blowing? Has it shifted, and if so which way? How strong is it? Any big change in the direction or strength of the wind suggests a change in the weather. Knowing the air pressure can greatly increase the accuracy of your forecasts. If the pressure is rising, dry weather is likely; if it's falling, wet weather is probably on the way. The faster the rate of change, the quicker the weather will change. All altimeters are barometers and so can be used for forecasting. They have to be kept at the same altitude, however, so camp is the best place to do this. I set the altitude when I reach camp, then note the barometer reading on my Suunto Altimax. Next morning I check the barometer again and look at the overnight pattern. It's heartening to see that the pressure is rising after several days of bad weather. Unfortunately, the opposite also is true.

I also have an instrument called the Brunton (Silva outside of North America) Atmospheric Data Center (ADC) Pro. This measures altitude, barometric pressure, temperature, relative humidity, and wind speed, and keeps twenty-four hours of records. The wind speed is measured by a tiny wind vane that you hold into the wind to record the speed. It gives the current, average, and highest speeds. With it you can keep a record of the wind speed and also discover just what various wind speeds mean when hiking and when camping. I now know that wind speeds above 30 mph are uncomfortable to walk in, so if the forecast is for speeds above that I plan on sticking to sheltered ground. I also know that a gusty 20 mph wind can rattle most tents. The humidity and temperature readings are useful, too. (I now know there can be a huge difference in humidity between the floor and peak of a tent, showing that vents should be high up.) By recording data from the ADC I can build up a picture of the weather in areas I visit often and know what to expect at different times of year. Of course, notes can be used for the same purpose, but knowing that the average nighttime temperature was 25°F (−4°C) with a low of 20°F (−7°C) and the average wind speed was 35 mph with gusts to 45 tells me much more than notes that say "frosty" for each morning and "windy" or even "very windy" for each day. The ADC only weighs 2 ounces and runs off a 3-volt lithium battery. It's easily carried in a shirt pocket.

An excellent book on weather in the backcountry is *Weathering the Wilderness*, by William E. Reifsnyder. It describes the weather you can expect in the Sierra, Cascades, Rockies, Appalachians, Olympics, and the Great Lakes Basin at different times of year and includes tables covering temperature, rainfall, and hours of sunshine. It also explains weather patterns and has photographs of cloud types.

Altitude

As you go higher, atmospheric pressure lessens, making it harder for your body to extract oxygen from the air. This may result in *acute mountain sickness* (AMS), typified by headaches, fatigue, loss of appetite, dizziness, and a generally awful feeling. AMS rarely occurs at altitudes below 8,000 feet, so many backpackers never need worry about it. But if you do ascend high enough and experience AMS, the only immediate remedy is to descend. If you don't, the effects usually pass in a few days.

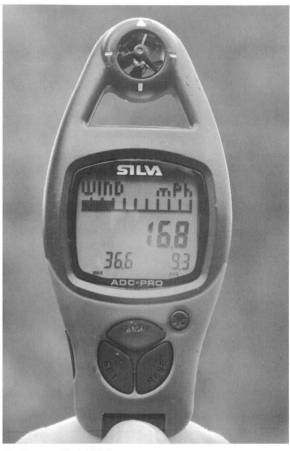

The Brunton (Silva) ADC Pro weather-recording instrument.

To minimize the chances of AMS, acclimatize slowly by gaining altitude gradually. If you're starting out from a high point, you can aid acclimatization by spending a night there before setting off. It's also important to drink plenty of fluids—dehydration is reckoned to worsen altitude sickness. Most backpackers won't get higher than the 14,000 feet of the Sierra or the Rockies; spending three or four days hiking at 6,000 to 8,000 feet should minimize altitude effects, but it's not always easy to do this. The altitude where you sleep is important too; if you sleep below 8,000 feet you can ascend to 14,000 feet without much likelihood of altitude sickness.

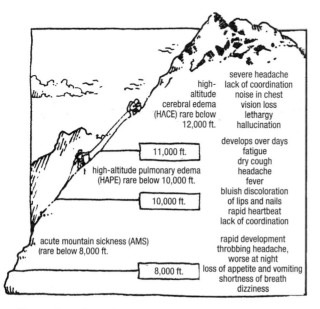

The possible effects of altitude.

The only time I've suffered from mountain sickness was when I took a cable car up to 10,600 feet on the Aiguille du Midi in the French Alps. The moment I stepped out of the cable car I felt dizzy and a little sick and had a bad headache. But we'd gone up in order to ski down, so I was soon feeling fine again.

Much more serious than AMS are *high-altitude cerebral edema* and *high-altitude pulmonary edema* (fluid buildup in the brain or lungs), which can be fatal. Cerebral edema rarely occurs below 12,000 feet; pulmonary rarely below 10,000 feet. Lack of coordination and chest noises are among the symptoms, but you may not be able to differentiate between AMS and edema. Your only course is to descend—quickly.

Medicine for Mountaineering, edited by James Wilkerson, has a detailed discussion of high-altitude illness that is worth studying by those planning treks in high mountains.

Avalanches

Avalanches are a threat to every snow traveler who ventures into mountainous terrain, more so for the skier than for the walker. In spring, great blocks of snow and gouged terrain stripped of trees mark avalanche paths and show the power of these snow slides. Avalanches can be predicted to some extent, and many mountain areas, especially those with ski resorts, post avalanche warnings. Heed them. Anyone heading into snow-covered mountains should study one of the many books on the subject. *Avalanche Safety for Skiers and Climbers*, by Tony Daffern, is one of the best for home study, while *The ABCs of Avalanche Safety*, by Sue Ferguson and E. R. LaChappelle, is light enough at 2 ounces to carry in the pack.

Lightning

Lightning is both spectacular and frightening. Thunderstorms can come in so fast that you can't reach shelter before they break (although I've learned that I can run very fast with a heavy pack when I'm scared enough). If you see thunderclouds building up or a distant storm approaching, head for safety immediately—don't wait until the thunder starts. In thunderstorms, avoid summits, ridge crests, tall trees, small stands of trees, shallow caves, lakeshores, and open meadows. Places to run to include low points in deep forests, near but not

Avalanche debris, High Sierra.

In a lightning storm, beware of ground currents. Don't lie or sit on the ground. Instead, squat on an insulating mat, with your hands and arms off the ground. Put metal gear, such as framed packs and hiking poles, some distance away so they don't burn you if there's a nearby strike.

next to the bases of high cliffs, depressions in flat areas, and mountain huts (these are grounded with metal lightning cables). Remember that, statistically, being hit by lightning is very unlikely, though this may fail to comfort you when you're out in the open and the flashes seem to be bouncing all around.

During a storm, there's danger from ground currents radiating from a lightning strike; the closer to the strike you are, the greater the current. Wet surfaces can provide pathways for the current, which may also jump across short gaps rather than go through the ground. If part of your body bridges such a gap, some of the current will probably pass through it. Your heart, and therefore your torso, is the part of your body you most need to protect from electric shocks, so it's advisable to crouch with just your feet on your foam pad so that any ground current passes through your limbs only. I'd also keep away from damp patches of ground and wet gullies and rock cracks. Groups should spread out.

Metal can burn you after a nearby strike—if you're caught in a storm, move away from pack frames and tent poles. The most frightening storm

I've encountered woke me in the middle of the night at a high and exposed camp in the Scottish Highlands; all I could do was huddle on my foam pad and wait for it to pass, while lightning flashed all around me.

Anyone who is hit by lightning and knocked unconscious should be given immediate mouth-to-mouth resuscitation if breathing or the heart have stopped.

Hypothermia

Hypothermia occurs when the body loses heat faster than it produces it. It can be a killer. The causes are wet and cold, abetted by hunger, fatigue, alcohol, and low morale. The initial symptoms are shivering, lethargy, and irritability, which develop into lack of coordination, collapse, coma, and death, sometimes very quickly.

Because wind whips away heat, especially from wet clothing, hypothermia can occur in temperatures well above freezing. Indeed, it is often in summer that unwary dayhikers get caught, venturing high into the mountains on a day that starts sunny but becomes cold and rainy. Too many people die

RIGHT: A temperature inversion with the valleys full of cloud (cold air) and the summits bathed in sunshine (warm air). BELOW: Cloud hanging on one side of a ridge in the White Mountains, New Hampshire.

or have to be rescued because they weren't equipped to deal with stormy weather.

If you start to notice any of the symptoms of hypothermia in yourself or any of your party, take immediate action. The best remedy is to stop, set up camp, get into dry clothes and a sleeping bag, start up the stove, and have plenty of hot drinks and hot food. Pushing on is foolish unless you've first donned extra clothes and had something to eat. After you're clothed and fed, exercise will help warm you up, since it creates heat. Even then you should stop and camp as soon as possible.

The best solution to hypothermia is to prevent it. If you're properly equipped, stay warm and dry, and keep well fed and rested, you should be in no danger.

Frostbite

When body tissue freezes, that's frostbite. It can be avoided by covering up and by keeping warm. Minor frostbite is most likely to occur on the extremities—the nose, ears, fingertips, and toes. If any of these areas feels numb and looks colorless, it may be frostbitten. Rewarming can be done with extra clothing, by putting a warm hand over the affected area, or in the case of fingers or toes, holding them against someone's armpit, groin, or stomach. I've come across mild frostbite only once, to a companion's nose on a windy mountaintop in February with a temperature about 0°F (−18°C); she pulled a woolen balaclava over her face, and within half an hour the color had returned. Deep frostbite is a serious condition and can be properly treated only in a secure shelter with a reliable source of heat. *Frostbitten areas should not be rubbed; this can damage the frozen tissue.*

Heat Exhaustion

Most walkers are afraid of the cold, but heat can be dangerous too. The opposite of hypothermia, heat exhaustion occurs when the body cannot cool itself sufficiently. Typical symptoms are muscle cramps,

nausea, and vomiting. Because the body uses perspiration for cooling, the main cause of heat exhaustion is dehydration and electrolyte depletion—if you are severely dehydrated, you cannot sweat.

The main way to prevent heat exhaustion is to drink plenty of water, *more than you think you need* on hot days. Don't neglect eating as well; water alone won't replace the salts lost when you sweat, so you could still become ill. If you start showing symptoms, stop and rest somewhere shady—exercise produces heat. If you feel dizzy or weak, lie down out of direct sunlight and drink water copiously. In very hot weather, travel in the early morning and the late afternoon and take a midday siesta in the shade to minimize the chance of heat exhaustion. A sun hat or umbrella also helps.

Fording Rivers and Streams

Unbridged rivers and streams can present major hazards. Water is more powerful than many people think, and hikers are drowned every year fording what may look like relatively placid streams. If you don't think you can cross safely, don't try.

If no logs or boulders present a crossing, wad-

ing a stream or river may be the only option. Whether you prospect upstream or downstream for a potential ford depends on the terrain. If you can view the river from a high point, you may be able to see a suitable ford. Otherwise, check the

spring snowmelt in Iceland, my route was almost totally determined by which rivers I could cross and which I couldn't (which was most of them). During my walk through the northern Canadian Rockies, I spent many hours searching for safe fords across the many big rivers there.

In the end, only experience can tell you whether it's possible to cross. If you decide fording is feasible, study your crossing point carefully before plunging in. In particular, check that the far side isn't deeper or the bank undercut. Then cross carefully and slowly with your hipbelt undone so that you can jettison your pack if you're washed away. If this does happen, try to hang on to the pack by a shoulder strap—it will give extra buoyancy, and you'll need it and its contents later. You should

TOP: *Crossing a small stream. The main aim here is to keep your feet dry.* ABOVE: *A river in spate. Crossing this would be dangerous and foolhardy. Search for an alternative route or turn back.*

map for wide areas where the river channels may be braided. Several shallow channels are easier to cross than one deep one, and wide sections are usually shallower than narrow ones. Check the map for bridges, too—many years ago, after torrential rain had turned even the smallest streams into raging torrents, two companions and I walked many extra miles upstream and camped far from where we'd intended because we didn't notice on the map that there was a bridge not far downstream of where we were.

On a weeklong trip during the height of the

Even small streams can become raging torrents during snowmelt or after heavy rain and be unsafe to cross. If you can't find a safe crossing point, you can camp on the bank and wait for the water to subside or look for an alternative route.

cross at an angle facing upstream so the current won't make your knees buckle. Feel ahead with your leading foot, but don't commit your weight to it until the riverbed beneath it feels secure. One of your trekking poles or a stout stick is essential in rough water. If the water is fast flowing and starts to boil up much above your knees, *turn back*—it could easily knock you over, and being swept down a boulder-littered stream is not good for your health.

If I'm wearing sandals, wet feet are no problem. For shallow crossings, I don't even break my stride. If I'm wearing shoes or boots and carrying sandals, I change into the sandals unless my footwear is already wet. If there are lots of fords, I keep the sandals on, even in cold weather, so I have dry shoes for campwear. If I can see that the river bottom is flat and sandy or gravely rather than rocky, I sometimes cross wearing just a pair of dirty socks.

Mountain water is very cold, and you'll often reach the far side feeling shivery. I find that the best way to warm up is by gulping down some carbohydrates like trail mix or candy, then hiking hard and fast. The best clothes for fording are shorts and a warm top. Long pants can drag in the water and aren't very warm when sodden.

Groups can use various techniques to make fords safer. Three people can cross in a stable tripod formation, or a group can line up along a pole held at chest level. In the past, I've used a rope to belay forders, but the newer thinking is that roped crossings are dangerous—there's too great a chance of someone's slipping and being trapped underwater by the rope.

I have never swum across a river—the water in the areas I frequent is generally too cold, too fast, and too boulder strewn for this to be practical. Bigger, warmer, slower rivers can be swum, however.

If you can't find a safe crossing, you have one

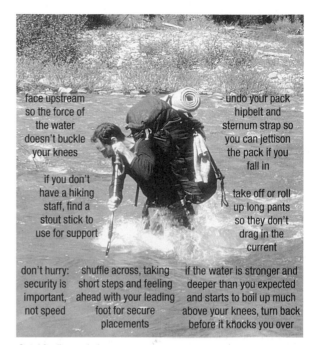

Good fording technique.

final option before you turn back—wait. In areas where mountain streams are rain fed, they recede quickly once the rain stops; a raging torrent can turn into a docile trickle in a matter of hours. (And placid streams can swell just as quickly, so you should camp *after* you've crossed a river, or you may wake to a nasty shock.) Glacier- and snow-fed rivers are at their lowest at dawn. If you camp on the near side, you may be able to cross in the morning. Meltwater streams are the worst to ford because you can't see the bottom through the swirling silt.

Poisonous Plants

There are a few poisonous plants that can harm you by external contact. One is the *stinging nettle*, which has a sharp but transitory sting. Although painful, it's nothing to worry about unless you dive naked into a clump. At low elevations you may find the nastier *poison oak*, *poison ivy*, and *poison sumac*. These closely related shrubs can cause severe allergic reactions, raising rashes and blisters in many people. They have leaves in groups of three that often hang across trails at knee height. If you brush against this stuff, immediately wash the affected area well with water (soap isn't required), if you have any, since the oil that causes the problems is inactivated by water. The oil is also tenacious and long-lived, so also wash any clothing or equipment that has come into contact with the plants. If you still start to itch after washing the affected area, calamine lotion and cool saltwater compresses can help. Some cortisone creams can help with red and itchy rashes where no blisters have yet developed, as well as later when the rash has healed and is scaly yet still itchy.

A final plant to watch out for is *devil's club*, whose stems are covered with razor-sharp spines that can break off and remain in the wound, causing inflammation. It's found in montane forests in the Cascades and British Columbia. I came across large stands of this head-high, large-leafed shrub mixed in with equally tall stinging nettles in the Canadian Rockies, just south of the Peace River. I normally try to avoid any unnecessary damage to plants, but on this occasion I used my staff to beat my way through the overhanging foliage.

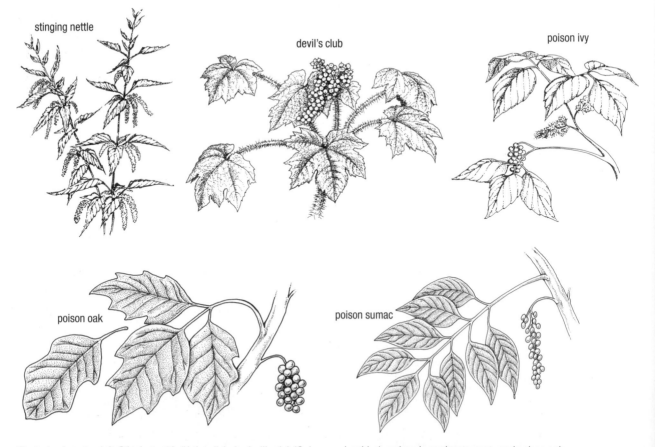

Clockwise from top left: Stinging nettle (Urtica dioica)*, devil's club* (Oplopanax horridus)*, poison ivy, poison sumac, and poison oak.*

high socks and boots are good protection from snakes and scorpions

don't place your hands behind rocks

When hiking in rattlesnake or scorpion country, be wary around bushes and rock piles.

Many agencies, park offices, Web sites, and guidebooks provide identification information; you may also find warning notices at trailheads. If you rely on plants for food, you need to be very sure you know what you're eating, especially with fungi. There are numerous guides.

DEALING WITH ANIMALS

Encountering animals in the wilderness, even potentially hazardous ones, is not in itself a cause for alarm, though some walkers act as if it were. Observing wildlife at close quarters is one of the joys and privileges of wilderness wandering, something to be wished for and remembered long afterward.

You are the intruder in the animals' world, so don't approach closely or disturb them, for their sake and for your safety. When you do come across animals unexpectedly and at close quarters, move away slowly and quietly and cause as little disturbance as possible. With most animals you need fear attack only if you startle a mother with young, and even then, as long as you back off quickly, the chances are good that nothing will happen.

Some animals pose more of a threat and need special attention, however. (Insects, of course, are also animals, and are the ones most likely to be a threat—to your sanity if not your physical health. The items and techniques needed for keeping them at bay were discussed in Chapter 8.)

Snakes

The serpent is probably more feared than any other animal, yet most species are harmless, and the chances of being bitten by one are remote. In the major North American wilderness areas there are four species of poisonous snakes—the *coral snake, rattlesnake, copperhead,* and *water moccasin* (also called a *cottonmouth*). Not all areas have them. They are rarely found above timberline or in Alaska and Maine. Their venom is unlikely to seriously harm fit, healthy persons. In many parts of South America, Asia, Africa, and Australia, much more deadly species exist, and anyone intending to hike there should obtain relevant advice.

Snakebites rarely occur above the ankle, so wearing boots and thick socks in snake country minimizes the chances of being bitten. Snakes will do everything possible to stay out of your way; the vibrations from your feet are usually enough to send them slithering off before you even see them. However, it's wise to be cautious around bushes and rock piles in snake country—there may be a snake sheltering there. At a snake-country campsite, do not pad around at night barefoot or in sandals or light shoes without checking the ground first.

Rattlesnakes seem to strike more fear into people than other snakes do, though I don't understand why. By rattling, at least they warn you of their presence so you can avoid them.

While walking in the cool of the night can be a way to avoid the heat in deserts, it's not a good way to avoid snakes. On the Pacific Crest Trail, I hiked through the Mojave Desert with three other backpackers. Battered by the heat of the day, we decided to take advantage of a full moon and hike at night. However, we quickly found that rattlesnakes, which abound in the Mojave, come out at night, and we couldn't distinguish them from sticks and other debris. Several times we stopped and cast around anxiously with our flashlights for the source of a loud rattle. Once we found a snake, a tiny sidewinder, between someone's feet. We didn't hike at night again.

On that trip, I carried in my shorts pocket a snakebite kit with implements for cutting and sucking the wound. Such kits are frowned on now as being dangerous. Using them could easily cause more harm than the bite itself. The Sawyer Extractor, a suction device that doesn't require cutting the wound, can be used. Otherwise wash the bite with soap and water, then bandage it and keep the limb hanging down to minimize the chance that venom will enter the bloodstream. The victim should stay still and rest while someone goes for assistance. If you're on your own, you may have to sit out two days of feeling unbeliev-ably awful unless you're close enough to habitation or a road to walk to aid quickly. That's if the bite contained any venom anyway—about 25 percent don't.

For those who want to know more about snakebite treatment, I recommend *Medicine for Mountaineering*, edited by James Wilkerson.

Bears

In many mountain and wilderness areas, black bears and grizzly bears roam, powerful and independent. Knowing they're out there gives an edge to your walking; you know you're in real wilderness if bears are around. In many areas though, bears no longer roam. Grizzlies in particular have been exterminated in most of the lower states; there are now just tiny numbers in small parts of Montana, Idaho, and Wyoming (mainly in Glacier and Yellowstone National Parks). They're found in any numbers only in Alaska and western Canada (the Yukon, Northwest Territories, British Columbia, and western Alberta). I like knowing they're there, lords of the forests and mountains, as they have been for millennia.

The chances of seeing a bear, let alone being attacked or injured by one, are remote. In Yellowstone National Park, home to both grizzly and black bears, there were 47 million visitors between 1980 and 1997. Just twenty-three of them were injured by bears. That makes the odds on being injured by a bear in Yellowstone about 1 in 2.1 million. You are at far greater risk from drowning, falling, or vehicle accidents. In about ten thousand miles of walking in bear country, most of it alone, I've seen only eighteen black bears and three grizzlies, and none has threatened me—most have run away.

However, you should minimize your chances of encountering a bear. Dave Smith's *Backcountry*

Bear Basics is recommended reading for anyone venturing into bear country. I also recommend Doug Peacock's *Grizzly Years*, an excellent personal account of two decades of studying grizzlies while living among them.

When you're on the move, you want bears to know you're there so they'll give you a wide berth. Most of the time, their acute senses of smell and hearing will alert them to your presence long before you're aware of them. However, a wind blowing in your face, a noisy stream, or thick brush can all mask your signals. In these circumstances, make a noise to let any bears know you're around. Many people wear small bells on their packs for this purpose, but these aren't really loud enough, and they tinkle annoyingly even when you don't need them, scaring away other wildlife. It's better to shout or sing and clap your hands in thick brush or when you can't see far and the wind is in your face. Don't forget to use your eyes—I once came across a hiker sitting on a log eating his lunch, all the while calling out to warn bears he was there. I walked toward him for several minutes without his seeing me and finally startled him by calling out a greeting when I was a few steps away.

In open terrain and on trails, scan ahead for bears. A pair of binoculars helps greatly with this. They'll help you determine if that tree stump ahead is actually a grizzly sitting by the trail. Look for evidence of bears, too—paw prints and scat (dung) are obvious signs, but also look for scratch marks on trees and mounds of freshly dug earth in alpine meadows where grizzlies have been digging for rodents.

If you see a bear before it sees you, detour away from it quietly and quickly. Be particularly wary of female grizzlies with cubs—70 percent of known attacks are by mothers defending their young. If the bear is aware of you, move away

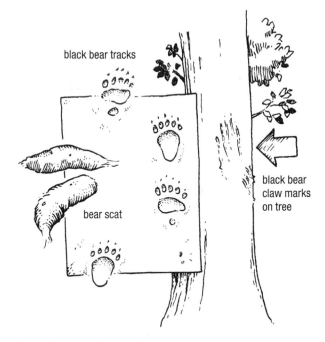

black bear tracks

bear scat

black bear claw marks on tree

Be alert for signs of bears, which may appear on the ground as prints, droppings, or diggings, and on tree trunks as parallel scratches as high as 6 feet above the ground.

from it, perhaps waving your arms or talking to help it identify what you are. Don't stare at it or act aggressively; you don't want to be seen as a threat. The only grizzly I've met at fairly close quarters moved slowly away from me once I'd made a noise and let it know I was there. The nearest it came was about fifty yards.

Many people suggest climbing a tree if a bear charges you. Dave Smith thinks this is a bad idea, since the bear will usually catch you and pull you down. (One bear-country saying is that the way to tell the difference between black bears and grizzly bears is to climb a tree—black bears will climb up after you, grizzlies will knock the tree down.)

Very occasionally, a bear will charge. Advice is mixed regarding what to do if one does. Don't run—bears are much faster than you are. Dropping an object, such as a camera or an item of clothing, may distract it and allow you to escape. Don't drop your pack—if the bear eats your food, it may learn to regard future walkers as food sources. Your pack will also help protect your body if the bear does attack. If dropping something doesn't work, your choices are trying to frighten the bear by yelling, banging objects together (metal on metal may be effective), backing away slowly, or standing your ground while acting non-threatening by talking quietly to the bear (the option Dave Smith advises). If the bear actually attacks you (many charges don't result in physical contact), you can play dead or fight back. The best position for the first is lying on your front with your legs slightly apart, your elbows tucked in, and your hands protecting your neck so the bear can't easily roll you over. Keep your pack on to protect your back and neck. If the bear doesn't leave you alone fairly quickly when you play dead, fight back instead, since it may view you as prey.

You could also use one of the powerful pepper sprays such as Counter Assault. This is a strong version of cayenne pepper–based antidog sprays that has been shown to repel bears both in the wild and in controlled tests. In one case a grizzly that had already knocked a man down and was biting him ran off when sprayed in the face. The manu-facturer stresses that it isn't a substitute for knowing about bear behavior and taking the usual precautions, but—the advertising says—"it's better than no protection at all." It doesn't guarantee protection, however, and isn't a reason to take risks or feel overconfident. Pepper spray is nontoxic (the bears aren't harmed) and comes in an 8-ounce canister. There's also a holster for carrying it on your belt. I've never carried it, though I might if I went hiking in Alaska again.

Bear-country ranger stations and information offices have up-to-date reports on areas that bears are using and whether any have caused trouble. Trails and backcountry campsites may be closed if necessary. For your own safety and that of the bears, obey any regulations that are in force.

HUNTERS

In many areas the late summer and autumn see the backcountry fill up with hunters carrying high-powered rifles. Try to make sure they don't shoot you by wearing something bright, like an orange hat or jacket. In some areas, officials recommend wearing two or more pieces of blaze orange. Hunting season is not the time to be wearing camouflage in the wilderness.

chapter ten

adventure travel

backpacking abroad

North America may well be the best place in the world for backpacking: it's got a good trail network and vast areas of protected wilderness. Ironically, the excellence of the trails and the numerous published trail guides can lessen the adventure.

Trekking abroad can be different. There are few places in the world where hiking isn't possible, though it may be very different from what you're used to at home. In Europe there's a huge network of well-maintained trails; mountain lodges that provide beds, meals, and heating are found in many areas, including the Alps, the Pyrenees, and the Scandinavian mountains, making long-distance walks with very light loads possible. To explore the more remote areas, "primitive" camping is still necessary, of course (and many, including me, prefer it, at least in good weather).

European hikers often carry their own gear, but in many countries porters or pack animals are used, as in that ultimate hiking destination, the Himalaya. Treks there usually involve porters—

one or two for small groups, up to forty for large, organized trips. Tea houses are found on the most popular routes, such as the Annapurna Circuit or the Everest Base Camp Trek, but in most areas all your supplies have to be carried in. The same system is used in Africa for ascents of mountains like Kilimanjaro. Other foreign hiking opportunities range from the rain forests of Costa Rica and other

A mountain hut in the Queyras Alps, France.

397

RIGHT: High on the Hardangerjøkulen ice cap, Norway. BELOW: Charkabhot village, Dolpo, Nepal.

Central and South American countries to the deserts of Australia or Israel.

Not all these areas are "wilderness" by the North American definition; in the Alps, the valleys are cultivated (in fact, *alp* means mountain meadow); in the Himalaya, the hiking trails are highways for the local people, used for trading and travel. Some areas *are* untouched and remote, however: most of Greenland is a mass of uninhabitable ice, as is Antarctica.

Long-distance trails exist in many countries. You can walk from the Atlantic Ocean to the Mediterranean Sea along the spine of the Pyrenees on the 500-mile Pyrenean High Level Route or cross the Arctic Circle on Sweden's 280-mile Kungsleden (the King's Way). Other well-known trails are New Zealand's Milford Track in the Fiordland Mountains, the Tour of Mont Blanc in the French Alps, England's 270-mile Pennine Way, the High Level Route in Corsica, the Concordia Trek in the Karakorum, the Ascent of Kilimanjaro in Tanzania, and the Annapurna Circuit and the Everest Base Camp Trek in Nepal.

Two books with general introductions to these and other international hikes are *Classic Treks: The 30 Most Spectacular Hikes in the World*, edited by Bill Birkett, and *The World's Great Adventure Treks*, edited by Jack Jackson. Where long trails don't exist, it's usually easy to link shorter trails to make through-routes or circuits, just as you would at home.

The problems of hiking in some of these areas mainly concern information and organization. Only the most experienced travelers can set out for unknown foreign destinations on short notice and with minimal planning—and even then chances are something important will be overlooked.

Foreign adventure travel is often considered expensive, but this is true only if you want to visit a place like Antarctica. Indeed, you can visit many places for less than it would cost to hike in some areas of North America. If you live on the East Coast, a visit to Costa Rica or even Nepal may be less expensive than an airline flight to the Southwest—and certainly less than one to Alaska. Although the airfares may be higher, the ground costs are much, much less.

INFORMATION AND PLANNING

It's not difficult to learn what to expect at most hiking destinations. At an outdoor store, bookstore, or library you should find guidebooks to most countries and areas. Many, of course, are designed for auto travelers and "tourists" rather than trekkers. Lonely Planet, Rough Guides, Bradt, Sierra Club Books, and Mountaineers publish books covering areas outside North America that are suitable for hiking. Most include general information about the countries, along with details of towns and popular destinations. Some have details of specific hikes, as well. There are trekking guides for many areas such as Nepal and other Himalayan countries. John Hatt's *The Tropical Traveler* covers everything a first-time traveler could want to know in an entertaining and informative way. Its focus is the tropics, but the general information is just as useful for trips to other areas.

Travel guides can never be completely up to date, however, and they may not include the information you require. Tourist boards can be helpful, as can national parks and other land-management agencies, especially for Europe, Australia, and New Zealand. All this information can be found on the Web, now the main research tool.

Many trekking guides contain maps; some, such as those for many European long-distance paths, may even contain topographic maps. However, for most trips you'll want separate maps. These can be ordered at home from Web sites such as maplink.com or bought at your destination. I prefer to buy maps before the trip so I can use them for planning. Map quality varies enormously from country to country; some are barely more than sketches. I used basic 1:250,000

On a high pass in the Himalaya, Dolpo, Nepal.

TRIP PLANNING

Hiring a Guide

In some parts of the world, such as the Himalaya, hiking without a local guide can be difficult, especially in remote areas, unless you can speak the local language. If you are going to be out for several weeks you may need porters to carry food and equipment too. Joining an organized trek is one way to deal with this but it is possible to hire guides and porters yourself. In cities like Katmandu there are many guiding and trekking companies offering this service. National tourist bureaus, adventure travel and outdoor magazine advertisements, trekking Web sites, and hiking guidebooks are sources of information. To check the reputation of a guide or trekking organization you could put a query on an Internet hiking newsgroup or message board. Nothing beats a personal recommendation.

When hiring guides and porters all the details of their employment should be established clearly at the time. As well as their duties and payment this should include food and equipment, both of which you may be expected to provide (and which can usually be bought or hired locally). Procedures for cooking, sanitation, water treatment, and trash disposal should be established before the hike begins, too. Tipping after the trek is the norm. The booking agency should be able to tell you the standard rate.

Political Instability and Terrorism

The political situation is very volatile in many countries with violent demonstrations and uprisings always possible. Getting caught up in these can be frightening and dangerous, even when visitors are not targeted. Sometimes, though, kidnapping rich Westerners (and even a threadbare hiker living on minimum means is rich in many countries) for ransom or political leverage is a deliberate tactic. Even worse some terrorist organizations target and murder visitors from countries they see as enemies. It is important when planning trips abroad to find out the up-to-date position regarding security in the places you intend visiting. This information is available on the State Department's Bureau of Consular Affairs Web site at travel.state.gov/travel/warnings.html.

Vaccinations

Vaccinations against various diseases—everything from yellow fever to hepatitis—are necessary when visiting many countries. Courses of vaccination can take four to six weeks to complete so you need to contact your doctor well in advance of your trip. Information on what vaccinations are needed plus other health information can be found in the Centers for Disease Control (CDC) biennial Yellow Book, Health Information for International Travel, and on the CDC website (www.cdc.gov/travel).

maps on a trek in the remote Dolpo region of Nepal. We crossed three 17,000-foot passes on that trip, none of which was named or had a height assigned on the map. Adapting to the scale was difficult, and the lack of detail made walking interesting in places—cliffs and gullies appeared in front of us that weren't on the map. Most foreign maps and trekking guides use metric measurements, so you should become familiar with measuring in meters and kilometers before a trip.

Once you have general information and an idea of where you want to walk, you can get to the specifics. Making lists may seem tedious, but I find they're the only way to ensure I don't forget anything. One is a gear list, tailored to the area and weather conditions expected; a separate list covers items you need for travel but that you won't take backpacking, such as extra toiletries and clothes. Perhaps the most important list is for the essentials—passport, airline tickets, foreign currency, and addresses of hotels, contacts, and embassy. (I

Money

When traveling it's best to carry some coins and low denomination notes in the local currency for small value purchases. In some remote areas where only cash is accepted you may need a fair amount, in which case it's best to carry it in small sums in different places on your person and in your pack. It's best to obtain foreign currency in advance of your trip too so you can get the best exchange rate and not end up trying to find an exchange bureau after a long tiring flight. For anything other than small expenses credit cards are ideal, being safer and more convenient than cash. The main brands are usable in a surprising number of places (in Norway, for example, you can pay for accommodation and food in remote unstaffed mountain huts by filling in a credit card slip). In towns credit cards can be used to withdraw more cash from banks or ATMs. Bankcards can be used for this too but only if your bank is part of the same international network. Traveler's checks, the traditional means of dealing with foreign currency, aren't as convenient as credit cards or ATMs but might still be useful at times, though I haven't carried any for many years. If you do use traveler's checks ones from widely recognized brands such as American Express or Visa are best. Dollar checks are welcome in many developing countries, ones in the local currency or Euros are more likely to be accepted in Western Europe.

Web Planning Sources

Finding information for foreign travel used to be difficult and time-consuming. The Internet changed all that. The problem now is the vast amount of information available. Say you are interested in Nepal, a prime destination for overseas hiking. Enter "Nepal" on Google and you get an astonishing 8,980,000 results. Refine the search to "Nepal Hiking" and you still get 161,000 results. Even if you then search for just one popular hike in Nepal, the Annapurna Trek, there are 35,100 results. This overwhelming volume of information can be reduced by using sites that have done the searching for you and which provide links to selected relevant sites. One of the best of these is a Dutch site called Traildata base (traildatabase.org), which claims to be the world's largest such site. Click on "Nepal" on the Traildatabase home page and you get 61 links, a much more manageable number, especially as they are divided into categories. There is also much useful information including links on the now venerable (in Web terms) GORP site (gorp.com) and on Away.com. (Among the material on Nepal on GORP.com you'll find a feature of mine on a hike through the remote Dolpo region.) Most countries' tourist boards have Web sites too. Nepal's can be found at welcomenepal.com.

leave a copy of this list at home, along with an itinerary, in case people need to contact me.) This last list should be kept in a secure place while you travel; I use a small nylon pouch that I can hang around my neck or over my shoulder (under my clothes) for all documents, including passport and tickets. When hiking, I keep it in an internal pack pocket.

A typical information list contains two sublists: information common to every trip and that specific to a particular trip. John Hatt describes a good way to organize this in *The Tropical Traveler*. The list below is adapted from his.

Permanent Trip List

- Passport number with date and place of issue
- Credit card numbers and bank's telephone number and e-mail address
- Home doctor's name and telephone number and e-mail address
- Camera equipment with serial numbers

- Camera insurance policy number and insurance company phone number

Specific Trip List

- Embassy address and telephone number and e-mail address
- Travel insurance number and telephone number for claims
- Medical emergency telephone number
- Plane ticket booking reference number
- Plane ticket serial number and date of issue
- Dates and times of flights
- Telephone and booking numbers of the flight-booking agent
- Phone card numbers
- Telephone code from home
- Telephone code to home
- Traveler's check numbers
- Contact address

ORGANIZED TRIPS

One way to avoid having to do all the trip organization yourself is to go with an adventure travel company. These trips vary from "catered" ones—your gear is carried by porters or pack animals and all the cooking and even tent pitching is done for you—to ones where you carry everything and do most of the work yourself. (The ski tours I led in Scandinavia fell into the latter category.)

Organized trips can be fun and a good way to experience a new country. You do need to be comfortable traveling and hiking with a group and with a specific itinerary, however. Most companies give you all the details, such as how many people will be on the trip, how far you'll walk each day, how difficult the walking will be, how many days will be spent walking and how many in motorized

transport (some trips can involve more motor travel than walking), what to bring, and what type of weather to expect.

IMMUNIZATIONS AND HEALTH

Foreign travel, especially to developing countries, often raises health concerns. The first thing to do is discuss the trip with your doctor to find out what immunizations you'll need. Do this well in advance of the trip—some shots may be necessary weeks before you go. You also need to know what other medication it would be advisable to carry, such as malaria pills. I always take a broad selection of antibiotics, plus a strong prescription painkiller (remember to bring copies of any prescriptions to show officials).

Water can be a problem in developing countries, or in any remote area—some foreign waterborne diseases make giardiasis look like a slight cold. The biggest danger is from viruses—*unless they have a chemical disinfectant built in, filters do not remove viruses*. Iodine is the standard water treatment; I used the Polar Pure Iodine Crystal Kit when I went trekking in Nepal for two weeks and had no problems, though I did come down with a nasty stomach ailment in Katmandu (which I blame on brushing my teeth with unpurified tap water in my hotel). I found being careful much more difficult in the city than in the wilderness.

FOOD AND SUPPLIES

Eating different foods is one of the joys of adventure travel. Finding quick-cooking ones suitable for backpacking can be difficult, though, so I usually carry some dehydrated meals. This applies even in Europe; I've resupplied with some very odd selections from tiny village stores in the Pyrenees and ended up carrying loaves of bread and tins of beans at times because I couldn't find dried items.

Fuel supplies can be even more of a problem. White gas is almost impossible to find outside North America. If this is all your stove runs on, you'll need gasoline (which could cause clogging). Far better is a stove that will run on kerosene, a common fuel in the Third World. (It's usually not very clean, though, so bring a filter funnel.) The MSR XGK II is probably the best stove for international travel because it will run on any type of petroleum, clean or dirty, and is easily maintained in the field. In Europe, butane-propane cartridges are common, and alcohol can be found in many countries, especially Norway and Sweden. By the way, knowing the local name for your fuel is important: In France kerosene is called *pétrole*, but in Britain *petrol* means gasoline (kerosene is called paraffin).

If you plan to take photographs, take along all the film you expect to need when visiting developing countries; carry spare batteries, too. In Europe, film is easy to find but is more expensive than in North America. On long trips, bringing a second camera is a good idea because making repairs or finding spare parts is likely to be impossible in most places. I know people who carry three cameras—the third usually is a small compact, carried "just in case."

INSURANCE

Comprehensive travel and medical insurance is essential. For backpacking, it's important to check that hiking and camping are covered in your policy—many general travel policies don't cover you

A self-catering hut in Norway.

during such activities. Gear and cameras need insurance, too. Carry a list of camera gear serial numbers, both in case of a claim and in case a customs inspector asks you where you bought your gear. If you can't show where you purchased it, you could face hefty import charges.

DIFFERENT CULTURES

Meeting people from different cultures can be one of the great pleasures of adventure travel. But it's important to learn something about their cultures in advance so you can avoid behaving offensively or disrespectfully. Good guidebooks have details for specific countries. Knowing just a few phrases of the local language can help with communication;

Buddhist prayer wheels, Dolpo, Nepal.

phrase books can be useful, but most are geared to general tourism and don't include the words you need while backpacking. Trekking guides are usually better. Stephen Bezruchka's *Trekking in Nepal* has an excellent appendix on Nepali for trekkers.

When employing local people as porters, you have a responsibility if problems arise. You're on a vacation, but they're working. In the fall of 1995, a huge snowstorm swept areas of the Himalaya in Nepal, killing many people—locals and trekkers—and causing serious problems for trekking groups. Some of the stories that came out of this disaster are very disturbing, including tales of trekkers' abandoning porters to die in the snow while they took helicopter flights back to Katmandu or refusing to let locals use tents and other equipment. Some of those involved were trekking companies. I suggest quizzing any company you're thinking of traveling with about how they treat their porters and what provisions are made for them in emergencies. On the other hand, some trekkers went out of their way to assist porters and local people, and some companies treated porters

and clients exactly the same, which is as it should be. I don't want to imply that all trekkers behave badly.

GETTING THERE

Internal travel can be exciting. I've been petrified in a taxi on narrow winding mountain roads in the Spanish Pyrenees, bumped in a car over a potholed highway in Nepal, chugged down an iceberg-dotted fjord in a fishing boat in Greenland, and helicoptered just above glacier-filled valleys in the same country.

The most exhilarating, overwhelming, and downright terrifying journey I've ever made was in a small passenger plane in Nepal, from Nepalgunj in the lowlands to Juphal, high in the Himalaya. The little plane, packed to bursting with people and baggage, flew into a narrow mountain valley with dense conifer forests on each side, the treetops so close it seemed you could pluck cones through the windows. Our altitude was 17,000 feet, high enough to clear most mountain ranges, but here

LEFT: *A traditional Sami hut, Sarek National Park, Arctic Lapland, Sweden.* BELOW: *Monte Viso from the Col de Chamoussiere, Queyras Alps, France.*

the peaks soared to 26,000 feet and more on each side, towering masses of rock and ice. I checked my watch, which indicated we should be landing in a few minutes. I looked down: below, a winding river slid through the dense forest; clearings or flat land were nowhere to be seen. Through the cockpit window I could see a spur of the mountainside cutting across the valley—we were flying straight at the top of it. Surely the pilot would climb, I thought. But no, on we went toward what seemed an inevitable crash. Finally we cleared the rocky edge of the spur, the wheels touched down, and we bumped to a halt on the sloping field that constituted Juphal airport. These are known as STOL airstrips—short takeoff and landing.

In other places, internal travel can be the opposite, a time to relax in comfort. I especially love the train journey through Norway and Sweden to the Arctic, with the big, well-appointed trains drifting north through increasingly wild, snowy northern landscapes. At night there are comfortable beds to sleep in, and for breakfast coffee and donuts are served in the restaurant car.

Whether by car, coach, train, boat, or plane, getting there takes time. Rather than viewing it as a means to reach the mountains or trailhead, it's better to treat it as an element of the adventure, as part of experiencing what a new country has to offer.

a final word

Finishing this edition, I've been surprised at how it's grown and how much more I've had to say. As always, I hope you find my thoughts interesting and useful. I always welcome comments and suggestions.

As I write these last words, the summer sun is shining outside my window and the trees are green and bursting with life. Birds are singing, and a low hum of insects rises from the flower-filled meadows. Beyond the forest, brown hills fade into the sky. It's time to leave the desk and the computer, shoulder my pack, and head out into nature.

As always, I'll see you out there—in spirit, at least.

equipment checklist

This is a list of every item you might take on a backpacking trip. No one would ever carry everything listed below; I select items from this master list to create smaller, specific lists of what I need for each particular trip.

PACKS

- Backpack
- Fanny pack
- Day pack

FOOTWEAR AND WALKING AIDS

- Boots
- Trail shoes
- Sandals
- Footbeds
- Wax (for cleaning and waterproofing boots)
- Socks
- Liner socks
- Fleece socks
- Insulated booties
- Gaiters
- Staff/trekking poles
- Ice ax

- Crampons
- Snowshoes
- Skis
- Ski poles
- Ski boots
- Climbing skins
- Ski wax

SHELTER

- Tent with poles and stakes
- Tarp
- Bivouac bag
- Groundsheet
- Sleeping bag
- Sleeping bag liner
- Sleeping pad
- Pillow

KITCHEN

- Stove
- Fuel
- Fuel bottles
- Pouring spout
- Windscreen
- Pan(s)
- Mug
- Plate/bowl
- Spoon(s)
- Pot grab

- Baking accessory
- Pot scrubber
- Water containers
- Thermos bottle
- Insulating water bottle cover
- Water purification tablets
- Water filter
- Matches/lighter/fire starter
- Plastic bags
- Bear bag and cord
- Bear-resistant container
- Food

CLOTHING

INNER LAYER

- T-shirt
- Shirt
- Long underwear
- Underpants

MIDLAYER

- Synthetic shirt
- Wool shirt
- Cotton shirt
- Wool sweater
- Fleece top
- Insulated top
- Vapor-barrier suit

OUTER LAYER

- Windproof top
- Rain jacket
- Rain pants

LEGWEAR

- Shorts
- Trail pants
- Fleece pants

HEADGEAR

- Sun hat
- Watch cap
- Balaclava
- Neck gaiter
- Fleece-lined cap
- Bandanna

HANDS

- Liner gloves
- Thick wool/fleece mittens
- Shell mittens
- Insulated gloves/mittens

MISCELLANEOUS: ESSENTIAL

- Flashlight/headlamp and spare bulb and battery
- Candles
- Candle lantern
- Oil lantern

- Butane-propane lantern
- First-aid kit
- Compass
- Whistle
- Map
- Map case
- Altimeter
- Map measurer
- Guidebook
- GPS receiver
- Repair kit:
  - Ripstop nylon patches
  - Duct tape
  - Needles and thread
  - Glue
  - Stove maintenance kit/pricker
  - Rubber bands
- Waterproof matches
- Wash kit
- Sunglasses
- Goggles
- Sunscreen
- Lip balm
- Insect repellent
- Mosquito coils
- Head net
- Pepper spray
- Flares
- Strobe light
- Fishing tackle

- Cord
- Knife
- Notebook, pen, and documents
- Watch
- Toilet trowel
- Toilet paper
- Rope
- Plastic bags

MISCELLANEOUS: OPTIONAL

- Binoculars
- Photography equipment:
  - Cameras
  - Lenses
  - Flash
  - Spare batteries
  - Tripod
  - Minitripod/clamp
  - Filters
  - Cable release
  - Lens tissue
  - Film
  - Padded camera cases
- Books
- Cards
- Games
- Radio
- Portable CD player/Ipod/MP3 player
- Thermometer

further reading

This is a list of books I've found inspirational, helpful, or at least interesting. It's by no means comprehensive, and some may be out of print. Check your library or used book stores and Web sites. Many are not backpacking books as such, but all of them are about, or relevant to, wilderness travel. I've also included my other books.

Obviously I hope this book will serve as a guide and inspiration for your wilderness hiking. But it's only one person's view. Many of the books that have influenced me and that I feel are the most useful and enlightening are gathered here.

Colin Fletcher's classic *The Complete Walker* first appeared in 1968. The fourth edition, cowritten with Chip Rawlins, was published in 2002. Two authors mean that it's almost two books with different approaches and opinions, sometimes contradictory, usually entertaining. Fletcher takes what might be called a standard approach to backpacking; Rawlins is much more on the lightweight side. The ultralight manual is Ray Jardine's *Beyond Backpacking*, a provocative, entertaining, inspiring, and sometimes infuriating book. A much lighter and amusing though still informative read is *Allen and Mike's Really Cool Backpackin' Book* by Allen O'Bannon, which contains some excellent cartoon-style illustrations by Mike Clelland. *Allen and Mike's Really Cool Backcountry Ski Book: Traveling and Camping Skills for a Winter Environment* is similarly entertaining about winter camping and ski touring.

Karen Berger is the author of a growing number of backpacking books, all worth consulting. If you're interested in long-distance trails, her *Hiking the Triple Crown* is a great resource. Also useful for long-distance hiking and full of interesting statistics is Roland Mueser's *Long-Distance Hiking*.

For equipment repair and maintenance Annie Getchell and Dave Getchell Jr.'s *The Essential Outdoor Gear Manual* is comprehensive. For people repair and maintenance, otherwise known as first aid, *Medicine for Mountaineering and Other Wilderness Activities*, edited by James A. Wilkerson and now in its fifth edition, is one for the bookshelf, while Fred T. Darvill Jr.'s *Mountaineering Medicine and Backcountry Medical Guide* and Paul G. Gill Jr.'s *Wilderness First Aid* are light enough for the pack. Sanitation is a key health issue, and here Kathleen Meyer's uncompromisingly titled *How to Shit in the Woods* is a key text. More general minimum impact information is contained in Bruce Hampton and David Cole's *Soft Paths* and Annette McGivney's *Leave No Trace*.

Bears are a particular concern for many hikers, and there are several books on this subject. I think the most useful and sensible is Dave Smith's *Backcountry Bear Basics*. A more personal book about bears and about hiking and camping in their country is Doug Peacock's *Grizzly Years*.

Except for the last one, the works above are basically instructional books. Many of them are inspirational as well, but this is not their main purpose. Hiking stories and adventures can inspire and also, by example, give much information about what it's like to hike in a particular area or for months at a time. In my opinion there are two classic hiking books, both by Colin Fletcher: *The Thousand-Mile Summer* and *The Man Who Walked Through Time*. The first tells the story of the author's hike the length of California, the second his hike the length of the Grand Canyon. The other great wilderness writer of the past thirty or so years is the late Edward Abbey. His books aren't specifically about backpacking, though many feature hiking stories, such as the excellent "A Walk in the

Desert Hills" in *Beyond the Wall*, but they are celebrations of wild places and nature and the freedom found there plus a call to defend them from exploitation. His classic work is *Desert Solitaire*, a series of essays based on the time he spent as a ranger in Arches National Park, but all his books are worth reading.

Going further back than Abbey and Fletcher, we come to John Muir, a prodigious hiker as well as a mountaineer, naturalist, and conservationist. There are many collections of his work available. Of the individual books, I recommend *My First Summer in the Sierra* and *The Mountains of California*. There are also many books about Muir and his wilderness philosophy: I think *The Pathless Way* by Michael P. Cohen is the best. A more general and pretty definitive study of the development of wilderness philosophy and conservation is Roderick Frazier Nash's *Wilderness and the American Mind*.

Abbey, Edward. *Abbey's Road*. New York: Plume, 1991.

———. *Beyond the Wall: Essays from the Outside*. New York: Holt, Rinehart and Winston, 1984.

———. *Desert Solitaire: A Season in the Wilderness*. New York: Simon & Schuster, 1990.

———. *Down the River*. New York: Plume, 1991.

———. *The Journey Home: Some Words in Defense of the American West*. New York: Perennial Classics, 2000.

———. *The Monkey Wrench Gang*. New York: Perennial Classics, 2000.

Adkins, Jan, ed. *The Ragged Mountain Portable Wilderness Anthology*. Camden ME: Ragged Mountain Press, 1993.

Alden, Peter, et al. *National Aubudon Society Field Guide to the Southwestern States*. New York: Knopf, 1999.

Annerino, John. *Hiking the Grand Canyon*. Rev. and expanded. San Francisco: Sierra Club Books, 1993.

———. *Running Wild: An Extraordinary Adventure of the Human Spirit*. New York: Thunder's Mouth Press, 1997.

Appalachian Long Distance Hikers Association. *Appalachian Trail Thru-Hiker's Companion*. 11th ed. Harpers Ferry WV: Appalachian Trail Conference, 2004.

Appalachian Trail Guidebooks. Harpers Ferry WV: Appalachian Trail Conference.

Axcell, Claudia, Vikki Kinmont Kath, and Diana Cooke. *Simple Foods for the Pack*. 3rd ed. San Francisco: Sierra Club Books, 2004.

Berger, Karen. *Advanced Backpacking: A Trailside Guide*. New York: Norton, 1998.

———. *Hiking the Triple Crown: How to Hike America's Longest Trails: Appalachian Trail, Pacific Crest Trail, Continental Divide Trail*. Seattle: Mountaineers, 2001.

Berger, Karen, and Daniel R. Smith. *Along the Pacific Crest Trail*. Englewood CO: Westcliffe, 1999.

———. *The Pacific Crest Trail: A Hiker's Companion*. Woodstock VT: Countryman, 2000.

———. *Where the Waters Divide: A 3,000-Mile Trek along America's Continental Divide*. Woodstock VT: Countryman, 1997.

Bezruchka, Stephen. *Trekking in Nepal: A Traveler's Guide*. 7th ed. Seattle: Mountaineers, 1997.

Birkett, Bill, ed. *Classic Treks: The 30 Most Spectacular Hikes in the World*. Boston: Little, Brown, 2000.

Briggs, David and Mark Wahlqvist. *Food Facts: The Complete No-Fads-Plain-Facts Guide to Healthy Eating*. Harmondsworth UK: Penguin, 1988.

Brower, David R., with Steve Chapple. *Let the Mountains Talk, Let the Rivers Run: A Call to Those Who Would Save the Earth*. San Francisco: HarperCollins West, 1995.

Brown, Hamish M. *Hamish's Mountain Walk and Climbing the Corbetts: His Two Acclaimed Mountain-Walking Books on the Munros and the Corbetts*. London: Baton Wicks, 1997.

Brown, Tom, Jr., with Brandt Morgan. *Tom Brown's Field Guide to Wilderness Survival*. New York: Berkley, 1983.

Bruce, Dan "Wingfoot". *The Thru-Hiker's Handbook: #1 Guide for Long-Distance Hikes on the Appalachian Trail*. Updated annually. Hot Springs NC: Center for Appalachian Trail Studies.

Cleare, John, ed. *Trekking: Great Walks of the World*. London: Unwin Hyman, 1988.

Cohen, Michael P. *The Pathless Way: John Muir and American Wilderness*. Madison: University of Wisconsin Press, 1984.

Colorado Trail Foundation. *The Colorado Trail: The Official Guidebook*. 6th ed. Golden CO: Colorado Mountain Club Press, 2002.

Continental Divide Trail Society. *Guide to the Continental Divide Trail*. 7 vols. Baltimore: Continental Divide Trail Society.

Copeland, Kathy, and Craig Copeland. *Don't Waste Your Time in the Canadian Rockies: The Opinionated Hiking Guide*. 5th ed. Canmore AB: hikingcamping.com, 2004.

———. *Don't Waste Your Time in the North Cascades: An Opinionated Hiking Guide to Help You Get the Most from This Magnificent Wilderness*. Berkeley: Wilderness Press, 1996.

Cox, Steven M., and Kris Fulsaas, eds. *Mountaineering: The Freedom of the Hills*. 7th ed. Seattle: Mountaineers, 2003.

Crane, Nicholas. *Clear Waters Rising: A Mountain Walk Across Europe*. New York: Penguin, 1997.

Cudahy, Michael. *Wild Trails to Far Horizons*. London: Unwin Hyman, 1989.

Daffern, Tony. *Avalanche Safety for Skiers and Climbers*. 2nd ed. Seattle: Mountaineers, 1992.

Daniell, Gene, and Steven D. Smith, eds. *AMC White Mountain Guide: Hiking Trails in the White Mountain National Forest*. 27th ed. Boston: Appalachian Mountain Club Books, 2003.

Darvill, Fred T., Jr. *Mountaineering Medicine and Backcountry Medical Guide*. 14th ed. Berkeley: Wilderness Press, 1998.

Dempster, Andrew. *The Munro Phenomenon*. Edinburgh: Mainstream, 1995.

Dudley, Ellen. *The Savvy Adventure Traveler: What to Know Before You Go*. Camden ME: Ragged Mountain Press, 1999.

Fayhee, M. John. *Along the Arizona Trail*. Englewood CO: Westcliffe, 1998.

Ferguson, Michael. *GPS Land Navigation: A Complete Guidebook for Backcountry Users of the NAVSTAR Satellite System*. Boise: Glassford, 1997.

Ferguson, Sue, and E. R. LaChapelle. *The ABCs of Avalanche Safety*. 3rd ed. Seattle: Mountaineers, 2003.

Fleming, June. *The Well-Fed Backpacker*. 3rd ed. New York: Vintage, 1986.

Fletcher, Colin. *The Man Who Walked Through Time*. New York: Vintage, 1989.

———. *River: One Man's Journey Down the Colorado, Source to Sea*. New York: Knopf, 1997.

———. *The Secret Worlds of Colin Fletcher*. New York: Vintage, 1990.

———. *The Thousand-Mile Summer*. New York: Vintage, 1987.

Fletcher, Colin, and Chip Rawlins. *The Complete Walker IV*. 4th rev. ed. New York: Knopf, 2002.

Forgey, William. *Basic Essentials: Wilderness First Aid*. 2nd ed. Old Saybrook CT: Globe Pequot, 1999.

Frazine, Richard Keith. *The Barefoot Hiker: A Book about Bare Feet*. Berkeley: Ten Speed, 1993.

Gadd, Ben. *Handbook of the Canadian Rockies*. 2nd ed. Jasper AB: Corax, 1995.

Getchell, Annie, and Dave Getchell Jr. *The Essential Outdoor Gear Manual: Equipment Care, Repair, and Selection*. 2nd ed. Camden ME: Ragged Mountain Press, 2000.

Gill, Paul G., Jr. *Wilderness First Aid: A Pocket Guide*. Camden ME: Ragged Mountain Press, 2002.

Gorman, Stephen. *Winter Camping: Wilderness Travel and Adventure in the Cold-Weather Months*. 2nd ed. Boston: Applachian Mountain Club Books, 1999.

Hampton, Bruce, and David Cole. *Soft Paths: How to Enjoy the Wilderness without Harming It*. Rev. ed. Molly Absolon and Tom Reed, ed. Mechanicsburg PA: Stackpole, 1995.

Hatt, John. *The Tropical Traveller: An Essential Guide to Travel in Hot Climates*. 3rd ed. London: Penguin, 1993.

Herrero, Stephen. *Bear Attacks: Their Causes and Avoidance*. New York: Nick Lyons Books, 1988.

Heuer, Karsten. *Walking the Big Wild: From Yellowstone to the Yukon on the Grizzly Bears' Trail*. Toronto: McClelland & Stewart, 2002.

Hillaby, John. *Journey Through Britain*. London: Paladin, 1970.

Howe, Nicholas S. *Not Without Peril: One Hundred and Fifty Years of Misadventure on the Presidential Range of New Hampshire*. Boston: Appalachian Mountain Club, 2000.

Ilg, Steve. *The Outdoor Athlete: Total Training for Outdoor Performance*. Evergreen CO: Cordillera, 1987.

Jackson, Jack, ed. *The World's Great Adventure Treks*. London: New Holland, 2004.

Jardine, Ray. *Beyond Backpacking: Ray Jardine's Guide to Lightweight Hiking: Practical Methods for All Who Love the Out-of-Doors, from Walkers and Backpackers, to Long-Distance Hikers*. LaPine OR: AdventureLore Press, 2000.

———. *The Pacific Crest Trail Hiker's Handbook*. 3rd ed. LaPine OR: AdventureLore Press, 2000.

Johnson, Mark. *The Ultimate Desert Handbook: A Manual for Desert Hikers, Campers, and Travelers.* Camden ME: Ragged Mountain Press, 2003.

Jones, Tom Lorang. *Colorado's Continental Divide Trail: The Official Guide.* Englewood CO: Westcliffe, 1997.

Kephart, Horace. *Camping and Woodcraft: A Handbook for Vacation Campers and for Travelers in the Wilderness.* Knoxville: University of Tennessee Press, 1988.

Kesselheim, Alan S. *Trail Food: Drying and Cooking Food for Backpackers and Paddlers.* Camden ME: Ragged Mountain Press, 1998.

Kjellström, Björn. *Be Expert with Map and Compass: The Complete Orienteering Handbook.* Rev. and updated ed. New York: Collier Books, 1994.

Krakauer, Jon. *Eiger Dreams: Ventures among Men and Mountains.* New York: Anchor, 1997.

———. *Into the Wild.* New York: Anchor, 1997.

———. *Into Thin Air: A Personal Account of the Mount Everest Disaster.* New York: Anchor, 1998.

Leopold, Aldo. *A Sand County Almanac: With Essays on Conservation.* New York: Oxford University Press, 2001.

Letham, Lawrence. *GPS Made Easy: Using Global Positioning Systems in the Outdoors.* 4th ed. Seattle: Mountaineers, 2003.

Lopez, Barry. *Arctic Dreams: Imagination and Desire in a Northern Landscape.* New York: Vintage, 2001.

Lynx, Dustin. *Hiking Canada's Great Divide Trail.* Calgary AB: Rocky Mountain Books, 2000.

Macfarlane, Robert. *Mountains of the Mind.* New York: Pantheon, 2003.

Manning, Harvey. *Backpacking, One Step at a Time.* 4th ed. New York: Vintage, 1985.

Matthiesen, Peter. *The Snow Leopard.* New York: Penguin, 1996.

McGivney, Annette. *Leave No Trace: A Guide to the New Wilderness Ethic.* 2nd ed. Seattle: Mountaineers, 2003.

McNeish, Cameron. *The Wilderness World of Cameron McNeish: Essays from Beyond the Black Stump.* Glasgow: In Pinn, 2001.

McPhee, John. *Encounters with the Archdruid.* New York: Farrar, Straus & Giroux, 1971.

Meyer, Kathleen. *How to Shit in the Woods: An Environmentally Sound Approach to a Lost Art.* 2nd ed. rev. Berkeley: Ten Speed, 1994.

Miller, Arthur P., and Marjorie L. Miller. *Trails Across America: Traveler's Guide to Our National Scenic and Historic Trails.* Golden CO: Fulcrum, 1996.

Miller, Dorcas. *Backcountry Cooking: From Pack to Plate in 10 Minutes.* Seattle: Mountaineers, 1998.

———. *Good Food for Camp and Trail: All-Natural Recipes for Delicious Meals Outdoors.* Boulder CO: Pruett, 1993.

———. *More Backcountry Cooking: Moveable Feasts from the Experts.* Seattle: Mountaineers, 2002.

Molvar, Erik. *Alaska on Foot: Wilderness Techniques for the Far North.* Woodstock VT: Countryman, 1996.

Mortlock, Colin. *Beyond Adventure.* Milnthorpe UK: Cicerone, 2001.

Morton, Keith. *Planning a Wilderness Trip in Canada and Alaska.* Calgary AB: Rocky Mountain Books, 1997.

Mueser, Roland. *Long-Distance Hiking: Lessons from the Appalachian Trail.* Camden ME: Ragged Mountain Press, 1998.

Muir, John. *John Muir: The Eight Wilderness Discovery Books.* Seattle: Mountaineers, 1992.

———. *The Mountains of California.* New York: Modern Library, 2001.

———. *My First Summer in the Sierra.* New York: Modern Library, 2003.

———. *Sacred Summits: John Muir's Greatest Climbs.* Graham White, ed. Edinburgh: Canongate, 1999.

Nash, Roderick Frazier. *Wilderness and the American Mind.* 4th ed. New Haven: Yale University Press, 2001.

Newby, Eric. *A Short Walk in the Hindu Kush.* Oakland: Lonely Planet, 1999.

O'Bannon, Allen. *Allen and Mike's Really Cool Backcountry Ski Book: Traveling and Camping Skills for a Winter Environment.* Helena MT: Falcon, 1996.

———. *Allen and Mike's Really Cool Backpackin' Book.* Helena MT: Falcon, 2001.

O'Bannon, Allen, and Mike Clelland. *Allen and Mike's Really Cool Telemark Tips: 109 Amazing Tips to Improve Your Tele-Skiing.* Helena MT: Falcon, 1998.

Parker, Paul. *Free-Heel Skiing: Telemark and Parallel Techniques for All Conditions.* 3rd ed. Seattle: Mountaineers, 2001.

Parry, R. B., and C. R. Perkins. *World Mapping Today.* 2nd ed. München: K. G. Saur, 2002.

Peacock, Doug. *Grizzly Years: In Search of the American Wilderness.* New York: Henry Holt, 1990.

Powell, John Wesley. *The Exploration of the Colorado River and Its Canyons*. New York: Penguin, 2003.

Prater, Gene. *Snowshoeing*. 5th ed. Dave Felkley, ed. Seattle: Mountaineers, 2002.

Prater, Yvonne, and Ruth Dyar Mendenhall. *Gorp, Glop and Glue Stew: Favorite Foods from 165 Outdoor Experts*. Seattle: Mountaineers, 1982.

Reifsnyder, William E. *Weathering the Wilderness: The Sierra Club Guide to Practical Meteorology*. San Francisco: Sierra Club Books, 1980.

Reynolds, Kev. *Walking in the Alps*. New York: Interlink Books, 2000.

Rockwell, Robert L. "*Giardia Lamblia* and Giardiasis, with Particular Attention to the Sierra Nevada." *Sierra Nature Notes*, 2 (2002) (rev. 5/2002): www.yosemite.org/naturenotes/giardia.htm.

Roper, Steve. *The Sierra High Route: Traversing Timberline Country*. Seattle: Mountaineers, 1997.

Ross, Cindy. *Journey on the Crest: Walking 2,600 Miles from Mexico to Canada*. Seattle: Mountaineers, 1987.

Rowell, Galen. *The Art of Adventure*. San Francisco: Sierra Club Books, 1996.

———. *Galen Rowell's Vision: The Art of Adventure Photography*. San Francisco: Sierra Club Books, 1993.

———. *High and Wild: Essays and Photographs on Wilderness Adventure*. Special expanded ed. Bishop CA: Spotted Dog Press, 2002.

———. *In the Throne Room of the Mountain Gods*. San Francisco: Sierra Club Books, 1986.

———. *Mountain Light: In Search of the Dynamic Landscape*. San Francisco: Sierra Club Books, 1986.

Russell, Terry, and Renny Russell. *On the Loose*. Salt Lake City: Gibbs-Smith, 2001.

Schaffer, Jeffrey P. *Yosemite National Park: A Natural-History Guide to Yosemite and Its Trails*. 4th ed. Berkeley: Wilderness Press, 1999.

Schaffer, Jeffrey P., and Andy Selters. *The Pacific Crest Trail*. 5th ed., 2 vols. Berkeley: Wilderness Press, 1990–95.

Schmidt, Jeremy. *Adventuring in the Rockies: The Sierra Club Travel Guide to the Rocky Mountain Regions of Canada and the U.S.A*. Rev. ed. San Francisco: Sierra Club Books, 1993.

Secor, R. J. *The High Sierra: Peaks, Passes, and Trails*. 2nd ed. Seattle: Mountaineers, 1999.

Seidman, David, with Paul Cleveland. *The Essential Wilderness Navigator: How to Find Your Way in the Great Outdoors*. 2nd ed. Camden ME: Ragged Mountain Press, 2001.

Selters, Andy. *Glacier Travel and Crevasse Rescue*. 2nd ed. Seattle: Mountaineers, 1999.

Simpson, Joe. *Touching the Void*. New York: Harper-Perennial, 2004.

Slack, Nancy G., and Allison W. Bell. *AMC Field Guide to the New England Alpine Summits*. Boston: Appalachian Mountain Club Books, 1995.

Smith, Dave. *Backcountry Bear Basics: The Definitive Guide to Avoiding Unpleasant Encounters*. Seattle: Mountaineers, 1997.

Smith, Steven D., and Mike Dickerman. *The 4,000-Footers of the White Mountains: A Guide and History*. Littleton NH: Bondcliff Books, 2001.

Snyder, Gary. *The Practice of the Wild: Essays*. Washington DC: Shoemaker & Hoard, 2003.

Sobey, Ed. *The Whole Backpacker's Catalog: Tools and Resources for the Foot Traveler*. Camden ME: Ragged Mountain Press, 1999.

Soles, Clyde. *Rock and Ice Gear: Equipment for the Vertical World*. Seattle: Mountaineers, 2000.

Spangenberg, Jean S. *The BakePacker's Companion: An Outdoor Cookbook*. 2nd ed. www.adventurefoods.com.

Starr, Walter A., Jr. *Starr's Guide to the John Muir Trail and the High Sierra Region*. 12th ed. rev. San Francisco: Sierra Club Books, 1977.

Steck, George. *Hiking Grand Canyon Loops: Adventures in the Backcountry*. Guilford CT: Falcon, 2002.

Steele, Frederic L. *At Timberline: A Nature Guide to the Mountains of the Northeast*. Boston: Appalachian Mountain Club, 1982.

Stegner, Wallace. *Beyond the Hundredth Meridian: John Wesley Powell and the Second Opening of the West*. Lincoln: University of Nebraska Press, 1982.

Stevenson, Robert Louis. *Travels with a Donkey; An Inland Voyage; The Silverado Squatters*. London: Dent, 1984.

Strauss, Robert. *Adventure Trekking: A Handbook for Independent Travelers*. Seattle: Mountaineers, 1996.

Strickland, Ron. *The Pacific Northwest Trail Guide: The Official Guidebook for Long Distance and Day Hikers*. Seattle: Sasquatch, 2001.

Thoreau, Henry David. *A Week on the Concord and Merrimack Rivers/Walden, or Life in the Woods/The Maine Woods/Cape Cod*. New York: Viking, 1985.

Tighe, Kelly, and Susan Moran. *On the Arizona Trail: A Guide for Hikers, Cyclists, and Equestrians*. Boulder CO: Pruett, 1998.

Tilman, H. W. *The Seven-Mountain Travel Books*. Seattle: Mountaineers, 2003.

Townsend, Chris. *The Advanced Backpacker: A Handbook for Year-Round, Long-Distance Hiking*. Camden ME: Ragged Mountain Press, 2001.

———. *Adventure Treks: Western North America*. Seattle: Cloudcap, 1990.

———. *Backpacker's Pocket Guide*. Camden ME: Ragged Mountain Press, 2002.

———. *Crossing Arizona: A Solo Hike Through the Sky Islands and Deserts of the Arizona Trail*. Woodstock VT: Countryman, 2002.

———. *The Great Backpacking Adventure*. Sparkford UK: Oxford Illustrated, 1987.

———. *High Summer: Backpacking the Canadian Rockies*. Seattle: Cloudcap, 1989.

———. *Long Distance Walks in the Pyrenees*. Swindon UK: Crowood, 1991.

———. *The Munros and Tops: A Record-Setting Walk in the Scottish Highlands*. Edinburgh: Mainstream, 2003.

———. *Walking the Yukon: A Solo Trek Through the Land of Beyond*. Camden ME: Ragged Mountain Press, 1993.

———. *Wilderness Skiing and Winter Camping*. Camden ME: Ragged Mountain Press, 1994.

Townsend, Chris, and Annie Aggens. *Encyclopedia of Outdoor and Wilderness Skills*. Camden ME: Ragged Mountain Press, 2003.

Turner, Frederick. *John Muir: Rediscovering America*. Cambridge MA: Perseus, 2000.

Unsworth, Walt, ed. *Classic Walks of the World*. Yeovil UK: Oxford Illustrated Press, 1985.

U.S. Department of Agriculture, Agricultural Research Service. *USDA National Nutrient Database for Standard Reference, Release 16-1*. www.nal.usda.gov/fnic/foodcomp. 2004.

Vickery, Jim Dale. *Wilderness Visionaries: Leopold, Thoreau, Muir, Olson, Murie, Service, Marshall, Rutstrum*. Minocqua WI: NorthWord Press, 1994.

Waterman, Laura, and Guy Waterman. *Backwoods Ethics: Environmental Issues for Hikers and Campers*. 2nd ed. rev. Woodstock VT: Countryman, 1993.

———. *Forest and Crag: A History of Hiking, Trail Blazing and Adventure in the Northeast Mountains*. Boston: Appalachian Mountain Club, 2003.

———. *Wilderness Ethics: Preserving the Spirit of Wildness*. Woodstock VT: Countryman, 1993.

Welch, Thomas R., and Timothy P. Welch. "Giardiasis as a Threat to Backpackers in the United States: A Survey of State Health Departments". *Wilderness and Environmental Medicine* 6 (1995): 162–66.

Wilkerson, James A., ed. *Medicine for Mountaineering and Other Wilderness Activities*. 5th ed. Seattle: Mountaineers, 2001.

Wilkinson, Ernest. *Snow Caves for Fun and Survival*. Rev. ed. Boulder CO: Johnson Books, 1992.

resources

PERIODICALS

Backcountry Magazine, 888-424-5857, www.back countrymagazine.com
Backpacker, 800-666-3434, www.backpacker.com
Backpacking Light, www.backpackinglight. com/cgi-bin/backpacking light/backpacking_light _magazine_print.html
Explore: Canada's Outdoor Magazine, 416-599-2000, www.explore-mag.com
National Geographic Adventure Magazine, 800-NGS-LINE (800-647-5463), www.nationalgeographic. com/adventure
Outdoor Photographer, 800-283-4410, 310-820-1500, www.outdoorphoto grapher.com
Outside, 800-678-1131, 515-246-6917, www.out sidemag.com
TGO The Great Outdoors, 00-44-141-302-7744, www.tgomagazine.co.uk

ORGANIZATIONS

American Avalanche Association, 970-946-0822, www.americanavalanche association.org
American Hiking Society, 301-565-6704, www.americanhiking.org
American Long Distance Hiking Association–West, www.aldhawest.org
American Mountain Guide Association, 303-271-0984, www.amga.com
American Red Cross, 202-303-4498, www. redcross.org
Appalachian Long Distance Hikers Association, www.aldha.org
Appalachian Mountain Club, 617-523-0636, www.outdoors.org
Appalachian Trail Conference, 304-535-6331, www.appalachiantrail.org
Arizona Trail Association, 602-252-4794, www.aztrail.org
Bureau of Land Management, 202-452-5125, www.blm.gov
Canadian Avalanche Association, 250-837-2435, www.avalanche.ca
Canadian Parks and Wilderness Society, 800-333-WILD (800-333-9453), 613-569-7226, www.cpaws.org

Centers for Disease Control and Prevention, Travelers' Health Hotline, 877-FYI-TRIP (877-394-8747), www.cdc.gov/travel
The Colorado Trail Foundation, 303-384-3729, www.coloradotrail.org
Continental Divide Trail Alliance, 888-909-CDTA (888-909-2382), 303-838-3760, www.cdtrail.org
Continental Divide Trail Society, 410-235-9610, www.cdtsociety.org
Highpointers Club, www.highpointers.org
Leave No Trace, 800-332-4100, 303-442-8222, www.lnt.org
The Long Trail (Green Mountain Club), 802-244-7037, www.long trail.org
National Outdoor Leadership School, 800-710-NOLS (800-710-6657), www.nols.edu
National Park Foundation, 202-238-4200, www.nationalparks.org
National Park Service, 888-GO-PARKS (800-467-2757), 202-208-6843, www.nps.gov
Outward Bound, 866-467-

7651, 845-424-4000, www.outwardbound.org
Pacific Crest Trail Association, 888-PC-TRAIL (888-728-7245), 916-349-2109, www.pcta.org
Pacific Northwest Trail Association, 877-854-9415, www.pnt.org
Sierra Club, 415-977-5500, www.sierraclub.org
Tom Brown's Tracker School, 908-479-4681, www.trackerschool.com
USDA Forest Service, 202-205-8333, www.fs.fed.us
Wilderness Medical Associates, 888-WILD-MED (888-945-3633), www.wildmed.com
Wilderness Medicine Institute, 866-831-9001, 800-710-6657, www.nols.edu/ wmi
Wilderness Society, 800-THE-WILD (800-843-9453), www.wilderness.org
Wildlands Project, 802-434-4077, www.twp.org
Yellowstone to Yukon Conservation Initiative, 403-609-2666 (Canada), 406-327-8512 (U.S.), www.y2y.net

MAPS

Appalachian Mountain Club, 617-523-0636, www.outdoors.org

DeLorme, 207-836-7000, www.delorme.com

Earthwalk Press (available at www.boredfeet.com, www.omnimap.com, and other outlets)

Fresh Tracks Map Store, 303-471-5400, www.freshtracksmaps.com

Green Trails, 206-546-MAPS (206-546-6277), www.greentrails.com

Map Adventures, 207-879-4777, www.mapadventures.com

Maplink, 800-962-1394, 805-692-6777, www.maplink.com

MapTools, 650-529-9410, www.maptools.com

Tom Harrison Maps, 800-265-9090, 415-456-7940, www.tomharrisonmaps.com

Topo!, 800-962-1643, http://maps.nationalgeographic.com/topo

Topo USA, 800-561-5105, www.delorme.com/topousa

TopoZone, 978-251-4242, www.topozone.com

Trails Illustrated, 800-962-1643, http://maps.nationalgeographic.com/trails

USGS Topographic Maps, 888-ASK-USGS (888-275-8747), http://topomaps.usgs.gov

INTERNET NEWSGROUPS

These Usenet groups are open forums; anyone can post to them. The result is sometimes entertaining, sometimes informative, and sometimes infuriating. There are bizarre opinions, turf wars, and endless circular arguments. However, there are many helpful and regular posters. Read the groups for a while and you'll soon work out who these are. Post a query and you'll probably get valuable responses.

alt.rec.hiking
rec.backcountry
rec.skiing backcountry

WEB SITES

American Trails, www.americantrails.org

America's Roof, www.americasroof.com

thebackpacker.com, www.thebackpacker.com

BackpackGearTest.org, www.backpackgeartest.org

Backpacking Light, backpackinglight.com

Classic Camp Stoves, www.spiritburner.com

eBay, www.ebay.com

FitSystem by Phil Oren, www.fitsystembyphiloren.com

Gear Weight Calculator, www.chrisibbeson.com/pages/GearWeightCalculator.html

gpsinformation.net, www.gpsinformation.net

GORP, www.gorp.com

Hammocks.com, www.hammocks.com

Hike N' Light [stoves], www.hikenlight.com

The Lightweight Backpacker, www.backpacking.net

TrailQuest, www.trailquest.net

Wal-Mart, www.walmart.com

Wings, The Homemade Stove Archives, http://wings.interfree.it

EQUIPMENT SUPPLIERS

This is a fairly comprehensive list of backpacking equipment suppliers. Companies move, get taken over, and go out of business, of course, so this list is only a guide.

Aarn Design
U.S. distributor: Brett Malcolm
243 E. Hopkins Ave.
Aspen CO 81611
970-274-1733
Fax: 970-925-1371
www.aarnpacks.com
Natural Balance packs

ACORN
P.O. Box 1190
Lewiston ME 04240
E-mail: info@acornearth.com
www.acornearth.com
Fleece socks

ACR Electronics
5757 Ravenswood Rd.
Ft. Lauderdale FL 33312
954-981-3333
www.acrplb.com
PLBs

Adidas America
5055 N. Greeley Ave.
Portland OR 97217
971-234-2300
Fax: 971-234-2450
www.adidas.com/us/
Footwear

Adventure Foods
481 Banjo Lane
Whittier NC 28789
828-497-4113
Fax: 828-497-7529
E-mail: CustomerService@AdventureFoods.com
www.adventurefoods.com
Food

Adventure Medical Kits
P.O. Box 43309
Oakland CA 94624
800-324-3517
Fax: 510-261-7419
E-mail: questions@adventuremedicalkits.com
www.adventuremedicalkits.com
First-aid kits

Alico Sport
P.O. Box 165
Beebe Plain VT 05823
800-475-4266
www.alicosport.it
Footwear

All-Weather Safety Whistle Co.
P.O. Box 8615
St. Louis MO 63127
314-436-3332
Fax: 314-843-2317
E-mail: storm whistles@storm whistles.com
www.stormwhistles.com
Whistles

Alpina Sports Corp.
P.O. Box 24
Hanover NH 03755
603-448-3101
Fax: 603-448-1586
E-mail: info@alpinasports.com
www.alpinasports.com; www.crispi.it
Footwear; U.S. distributor of Crispi ski boots

AlpineAire Foods
Infinet Communications

8551 Cottonwood Rd.
Bozeman MT 59718
406-585-9324
E-mail: info@
  alpineaire.com
www.alpineaire.com
Food

AntiGravityGear
609 Hollingsworth Dr.
Wilmington NC 28412
E-mail: tinman@
  antigravitygear.com
www.antigravitygear.com
Ultralight gear

**Appalachian Mountain
  Supply**
731 Highland Ave. NE
Atlanta GA 30312-1425
Artiach sleeping pads

Aquaseal
Trondak
17631 147th St. SE, #7
Monroe WA 98272
360-794-8250
Fax: 360-794-9857
E-mail: info@
  aquaseal.com
www.aquaseal.com
Waterproofing products

Arc'teryx Equipment
2770 Bentall St.
Vancouver BC V5M 4H4
CANADA
800-985-6681; 604-451-
  7755
Fax: 604-451-7705
E-mail: bird@arcteryx.com
www.arcteryx.com
Packs

ASC Scientific
2075 Corte del Nogal,
  Suite G
Carlsbad CA 92009
800-272-4327
Fax: 760-431-0904

www.ascscientific.com
Retailer of Brunton,
  Nexus, and Suunto com-
  passes, altimeters, etc.

Asolo USA
190 Hanover St.
Lebanon NH 03766
603-448-8827
Fax: 603-448-8873
www.asolo.com

Atlas Snow-Shoe Co.
115 Tenth St.
San Francisco CA 94103
888-48-ATLAS (888-482-
  8527); 415-703-0414
Fax: 415-252-0354
E-mail: atlas@
  k2sports.com
www.atlassnowshoe.com
Snowshoes

Atwater Carey
c/o Wisconsin Pharmacal
1 Pharmacal Way
Jackson WI 53037
800-558-6614; 262-677-
  4121
Fax: 262-677-9006
E-mail: info@
  pharmacal way.com
www.pharmacalway.com
First-aid kits, hand sanitizer

Avid Outdoors
9 Lake Rd.
Albany NY 12205
518-453-2436
Fax: 518-453-0053
E-mail: mail@
  avidoutdoors.com
www.avidoutdoors.com
Tents

Backcountry Equipment
5419 Bandera Rd., #708
San Antonio TX 78238
800-569-8411; 888-779-

5075; 210-682-9881
Fax: 210-682-9882
www.backcountry
  equipment.com

Outdoor equipment,
  clothing, accessories.

Backpacker's Pantry
6350 Gunpark Dr.
Boulder CO 80301
303-581-0518
E-mail: info@
  backpackerspantry.com
www.backpackerspantry.
  com
Food, Outback Ovens

BakePacker
Strike 2 Industries and
  Wilderness Ventures
P.O. Box 50544
Irvine CA 92619-0544
866-576-0642; 949-679-
  7371
Fax: 949-679-7372
E-mail: info@
  bakepacker.com
www.bakepacker.com
Baking accessory

Baldas USA
1101 Wetherburn
Winston-Salem NC 27104
336-659-9990
Fax: 336-659-0355
www.baldas.com
Snowshoes

Bear Valley
Intermountain Trading
  Co.
P.O. Box 6157
Albany CA 94706-0157
800-323-0042
E-mail: customer
  service@mealpack.com
www.mealpack.com
Energy bars

Bear Vault
5663 Balboa Ave. #354
San Diego CA 92111
866-301-3442; 858-204-
  6164
Fax: 866-301-3442
sales@bearvault.com
www.bearvault.com
Bear canisters

Bergans North America
1934 E. Lynn St.
Seattle WA 98112
206-329-2088
E-mail: info@bergans.com
www.bergans.com
Packs

BHA Technologies
8800 E. 63rd St.
Kansas City MO 64133
800-391-0696; 816-356-
  5515
Fax: 816-246-9592
E-mail: info@
  bhatecnologies.com
www.bhatechnologies.com
eVENT fabric

Bibler Tents
Black Diamond
  Equipment
2084 E. 3900 S.
Salt Lake City UT 84124
801-278-5533
E-mail: tents@bdel.com
www.biblertents.com
Tents, bivy bags, hanging
  stove

Big Agnes
735 Oak St.
Steamboat Springs CO
  80477
877-554-8975; 970-871-
  1480
Fax: 970-879-8038
E-mail: info@
  bigagnes.com
www.bigagnes.com

Sleeping bags, self-inflating pads

Bite
7120 185th Ave. NE
Redmond WA 98052
800-248-3465
E-mail: info@
biteshoes.com
www.biteshoes.com
Sandals

Black Diamond Equipment
2084 E. 3900 S.
Salt Lake City UT 84124
801-278-5552
Fax: 801-278-5544
E-mail: climb@bdel.com;
ski@bdel.com;
tents@bdel.com
www.bdel.com
Megamid tents, waterproof stuff sacks, gaiters, gloves, back-country skis, mountaineering and Nordic ski boots, ski poles

Blue Magic Products
2440 Adie Rd.
Maryland Heights MO 63043
314-997-5222
Fax: 314-432-3542
E-mail: info@boydspecial tysleep.com
www.bluemagic.com
Tectron boot and clothing proofings, cleansers

Bollé
9200 Cody
Overland Park KS 66214
800-22-Bollé (800-222-6553)
www.bolle.com
Sunglasses, goggles

Boreal USA
U.S. distributor: S. W. Partners
P.O. Box 706
Capistrano Beach CA 92624
714-248-5688
Footwear

Bozeman Mountain Works
1627 W. Main St., Suite 310
Bozeman MT 59715-4011
Fax: 406-522-0948
www.bozemanmountain works.com
Stakes, self-inflating pads, tarps, clothing, accessories

Brasslite
267-307-4585
E-mail: aaron@
brasslite.com
www.brasslite.com
Stoves

Brunton
620 E. Monroe Ave.
Riverton WY 82501
800-443-4871; 307-856-6559
Fax: 307-856-1840
E-mail: info@
brunton.com
www.brunton.com
Compasses, Optimus stoves, GPS, weather-recording instruments.

Buff
Calle de França 16
08700 Igualada
Barcelona
SPAIN
34-938-054-861
Fax: 34-938-044-702
E-mail: buff@buff.es

www.buff.es
Headgear

Camelbak Products
1310 Redwood Way, Suite C
Petaluma CA 94954
800-767-8725; 707-792-9700
Fax: 707-665-9231
E-mail: webmaster
@camelbak.com
www.camelbak.com
Hydration systems

Campfood
Backpacker's Pantry
6350 Gunpark Dr.
Boulder CO 80301
303-581-0518
E-mail: info@back
packerspantry.com
www.backpackerspantry.
com
Food

Campmor
28 Pkwy.
Box 700
Upper Saddle River NJ 07458
888-CAMPMOR (888-226-7667); 800-525-4784
www.campmor.com
Outdoor equipment and clothing

Camp 7
3701 W. Carriage Dr.
Santa Ana CA 92704
800-224-2300; 714-545-2204
E-mail: campseven@
aol.com
Packs, sleeping bags, clothing

Camp USA
580 Burbank St., Suite 150

Broomfield CO 80020
303-465-9785
Fax: 303-465-9428
E-mail: tommy@camp-usa.com
www.camp-usa.com
Ice axes

Cannondale Bicycle Corp.
16 Trowbridge Dr.
Bethel CT 06801
800-BIKEUSA (800-245-3872)
E-mail: custserv@
cannondale.com
www.cannondale.com/
clothing/index.html
Ov'r'sox

Caribou Mountaineering
400 Commerce Rd.
Alice TX 78332
800-824-4153; 361-668-3766
Fax: 361-668-3769
E-mail: caribou@
granderiver.net
www.caribou.com
Packs, sleeping bags

Cascade Designs
4000 First Ave. S.
Seattle WA 98134
800-531-9531
Fax: 800-583-7583
www.cascadedesigns.com
Therm-a-Rest and Ridge Rest sleeping pads, sleeping bags, Tracks staffs, Platypus hydration systems, SealLine sacks

Casio
570 Mount Pleasant Ave.
Dover NJ 07801
800-836-8580
www.casio.com
Altimeter watches

Cassin
Via Piedimonte, 62
23868 Valmadreda (LC)
ITALY
39-0341-580352
Fax: 39-0341-200242
E-mail: info@cassin.it
www.cassin.it/uk/
  home.htm
Ice axes

Cébé
UK distributor: Marcolin
  UK
Unit G, Venture House
Bone Lane
Newbury, Berkshire RG14
  5SH
UNITED KINGDOM
44-01635-277-288
Fax: 44-01635-277-298
www.cebe.com
Sunglasses, goggles

Chaco
39955 Hayden Rd.
Paonia CO 81428
970-527-4990
E-mail: info@
  chacousa.com
www.chacousa.com
Shoes

Chuck Roast Equipment
P.O. Box 2080
Conway NH 03818
800-533-1654
Fax: 603-447-2277
E-mail: custserv@
  chuckroast.com
www.chuckroast.com
Fleece clothing

Climb High
135 Northside Dr.
Shelburne VT 05482
802-985-5056
Fax: 802-985-9141
www.climbhigh.com
Full range of outdoor

equipment and supplies

Cloudveil
120 W. Pearl Ave.
Jackson WY 83002
877-255-8345
Fax: 303-296-2577
E-mail: cloud@
  cloudveil.com
www.cloudveil.com
Clothing

Coghlan's
121 Irene St.
Winnipeg MB R3T 4C7
CANADA
204-284-9550
Fax: 204-475-4127
E-mail: coghlans@
  coghlans.mb.ca
www.coghlans.com
Outdoor equipment

The Coleman Co.
3600 N. Hydraulic
Wichita KS 67219
800-835-3278
E-mail: consumerservice@
  coleman.com
www.coleman.com
Stoves, packs, sleeping
  bags, footwear,
  Campingaz cartridges

Columbia Sportswear
P.O. Box 83239
Portland OR 97283
800-MA-BOYLE (800-
  622-6353)
www.columbia.com
Clothing

Conform'able
Sidas SA
ZA le Parvis BP 353
38509 Voiron Cedex
FRANCE
33-0-4-76-67-07-07
Fax: 33-0-4-76-67-03-03
E-mail: info@sidas.com

www.sidas.com
Footbeds

Crazy Creek Products
P.O. Box 1050
1401 S. Broadway
Red Lodge MT 59068
877-835-6200; 406-245-
  2008
Fax: 406-245-1266
E-mail: chairs@crazy
  creek.com
www.crazycreek.com
Chairs and sleeping pads

Dana Design
19215 Vashon Hwy.
Vashon WA 98070
888-357-3262
www.danadesign.com
Packs

Dancing Light Gear
c/o David Mauldin
P.O. Box 428
Clayton GA 30525
E-mail: rainmaker@
  rabun.net
http://trailquest.net/
  dlgc.html
Tarps

Danner
18550 NE Riverside Pkwy.
Portland OR 97230
800-345-0430; 503-251-
  1100
Fax: 503-251-1119
E-mail: info@danner.com
www.danner.com
Footwear

Design Salt
P.O. Box 1220
Redway CA 95560
800-254-7258
Fax: 707-923-4605
E-mail: support@
  designsalt.com
www.designsalt.com

Cotton and silk sleeping
  bag liners

Devold
14800 28th Ave. N., Suite
  100
Plymouth MN 55447
800-433-8653
www.devold.com
Wool underwear, sweaters,
  and socks

**Diamond Brand Canvas
  Products**
145 Cane Creek Industrial
  Park Rd., Suite 1
Fletcher NC 28732
800-258-9811; 828-684-
  9848
Fax: 828-687-0965
E-mail: edarnell@
  diamondbrand.com
www.diamondbrand.com
Packs, tents

Dick Blick Art Materials
P.O. Box 1267
Galesburg IL 61402-1267
800-828-4548
Fax: 800-621-8293
E-mail: info@
  dickblick.com
www.dickblick.com
Notebooks

**Doan Machinery &
  Equipment Co.**
P.O. Box 21334
S. Euclid OH 44121
216-391-7410
E-mail: info@doan
  firestarter.com
www.doanfirestarter.com
Magnesium fire-starting
  tool

Dolomite
1 Sellec St.
Norwalk CT 06855
800-257-2008

www.dolomiteusa.com
Footwear

**Dr. Bronner's Magic
Soaps**
P.O. Box 28
Escondido CA 92033
760-743-2211
Fax: 760-745-6675
E-mail: customers@
drbronner.com
www.drbronner.com
Liquid soap

Duofold
475 Corporate Square Dr.
Winston-Salem NC 27105
800-994-4348
www.duofold.com
Underwear and fleece
clothing

Duracell
Berkshire Corporate Park
Bethel CT 06801
800-551-2355
Fax: 800-796-4565
www.duracell.com
Flashlights

Eagle Creek
3055 Enterprise Ct.
Vista CA 92081
800-874-1048; 760-599-
6500
www.eaglecreek.com
Travel packs, duffel bags,
and accessory pouches

Eastern Mountain Sports
1 Vose Farm Rd.
Peterborough NH 03458
888-463-6367
E-mail: customerservice@
ems.com
www.ems.com
Outdoor gear, clothing

Eastman Outdoors
P.O. Box 380

Flushing MI 48433
810-733-6360
Fax: 810-720-8787
E-mail: info@
eastmanoutdoors.com
www.eastmanoutdoors.com
Trowels

Ecover
P.O. Box 911058
Commerce CA 90091-1058
800-449-4925; 323-720-
5730
Fax: 323-720-5732
E-mail: ecover@pacbell.net
www.ecover.com
Soap

Edko Alpine Designs
P.O. Box 17005
Boulder CO 80308
303-440-0446
Packs, limited-edition
sleeping bags

Energizer
Customer Support
Energizer Headquarters
533 Maryville University
St. Louis MO 63141
800-383-7323
www.energizer.com
Lithium AA and AAA bat-
teries, Eveready flash-
lights

Enertia Trail Food
877-Enertia (877-363-
7842)
Fax: 866-742-1026
http://trailfoods.com
Food

Equinox
1307 Park Ave.
Williamsport PA 17701
570-322-5900
Fax: 570-322-0746
E-mail: explore@
equinox.com

www.equinoxltd.com
Packs; U.S. distributor of
Komperdell trekking
poles

Esatto
866-ESATTO1 (866-372-
8861)
www.esatto.biz
Boots

Eureka!
625 Conklin Rd.
Binghamton NY 13903
800-572-8822
E-mail: camping@
johnsonoutdoors.com
www.eurekatent.com
Tents

Exped
1402 20th St. NW, Suite 7
Auburn WA 98001
888-609-7187; 253 735
6200
Fax: 253-735-6228
E-mail: cb@exped.com
www.exped.com
Bivy bags, etc.

Feathered Friends
1119 Mercer St.
Seattle WA 98109
206-292-6292
Fax: 206-292-6403
E-mail: customerservice@
featheredfriends.com
www.featheredfriends.com
Sleeping bags, down,
fleece, and waterproof-
breathable clothing

Ferrino
E-mail: export@ferrino.it
www.ferrino.it/eng
Ferrino packs, tents, sleeping bags

First Need
General Ecology

151 Sheree Blvd.
Exton PA 19341
800-441-8166;
610-363-7900
Fax: 610-363-0412
E-mail: info@general
ecology.com
www.generalecology.com
Water filters

Fisher Space Pen Co.
711 Yucca St.
Boulder City NV 89005
702-293-3011
Fax: 702-293-6616
E-mail: weborders@
spacepen.com
www.spacepen.com/usa
Pens

Five Ten
P.O. Box 1185
Redlands CA 92373
909-798-4222
Fax: 909-798 5272
E-mail: custserv@
fiveten.com
www.fiveten.com
Footwear

Foam Design
444 Transport Ct.
Lexington KY 40511-2502
859-231-7006 ext. 309
Fax: 859-231-7731
E-mail: info@foam
design.com
www.foamdesign.com
Sleeping pads

Fox River Mills
P.O. Box 298
227 Poplar St.
Osage IA 50461-0298
641-732-3798
Fax: 641-732-5128
E-mail: foxsox@
foxrivermills.com

www.foxsox.com
High-performance outdoor footwear, including X-Static socks

Frogg Toggs
P.O. Box 428/114 Bright Rd.
Guntersville AL 35976
800-349-1835; 256-505-0075
Fax: 256-505-0307
E-mail: froggtoggs@ localaccess.net
www.froggtoggs.com
Clothing

Gabel USA
102 Kimball Ave., Unit 12
South Burlington VT 05403
802-862-3347
E-mail: gabel.us@gabel.net
www.gabel.net
Trekking poles

Gaiam
360 Interlocken Blvd., Suite 300
Broomfield CO 80021-3440
877-989-6321
www.gaiam.com
Soap

Gander Mountain
4567 American Blvd. W.
Bloomington MN 55437
800-282-5993; 952-830-8700
www.gandermountain.com
Packs, tents, sleeping bags

Garcia Machine
14097 Ave. 272
Visalia CA 93292
559-732-3785
Fax: 559-732-5010
www.backpackerscache.com
Backpackers' Cache bear-resistant containers

Garmin International
1200 E. 151st St.
Olathe KS 66062
913-397-8200
Fax: 913-397-8282
www.garmin.com
GPS systems

Garmont USA
170 Boyer Circle, Suite 20
Williston VT 05495
802-658-8322
Fax: 802-658-0431
E-mail: info@ garmontusa.com
www.garmontusa.com
Packs, boots

Georgia Boot
235 Noah Dr.
Franklin TN 37064
877-795-2410
E-mail: info@ georgiaboot.com
www.georgiaboot.com
Footwear

Gerry Sportswear
350 Fifth Ave., Suite 1435
New York NY 10118
E-mail: info@ gerryusa.com
www.gerryusa.com
Down and waterproof-breathable clothing

GoLite
P.O. Box 20190
Boulder CO 80303
888-546-5483
Fax: 303-546-6557
E-mail: info@golite.com
www.golite.com
Clothing, packs, etc.

Gossamer Gear
3764 Cavern Pl.
Carlsbad CA 92008-6585
760-720-0500

Fax: 760-720-2282
E-mail: info@ gossamergear.com
www.gossamergear.com
Packs, accessories

Granger's USA
800-577-2700
E-mail: info@ grangersusa.com
www.grangersusa.com
Waterproofing

Granite Gear
2312 10th St.
Two Harbors MN 55616
218-834-6157
Fax: 218-834-5545
E-mail: info@ granitegear.com
www.granitegear.com
Packs, mittens, gaiters, hats

Gregory Mountain Products
27969 Jefferson Ave.
Temecula CA 92590
800-477-3420; 909-676-5621
Fax: 909-676-6777
www.gregorypacks.com
Packs

Grivel North America
1435 S. State St.
Salt Lake City UT 84115
801-463-7996
Fax: 801-463-1868
E-mail: websales@ grivelnorthamerica.com
www.grivelnorthamerica.com
Ice axes

GSI Outdoors
1023 S. Pines Rd.
Spokane WA 99206
509-928-9611
www.gsioutdoors.com
Cookware

Harvest Foodworks
445 Hwy. 29, RR #1
Toledo ON K0E 1Y0
CANADA
800-268-4268; 613-275-2218
Fax: 613-275-1359
E-mail: thefolks@ harvestfoodworks.com
www.harvestfoodworks.com
Food

Helly Hansen
Kenyon Center
3326 160th Ave. SE, Suite #200
Bellevue WA 98008-5463
800-435-5901
Fax: 425-649-3740
E-mail: customerinfo@ hellyhansen.com
www.hellyhansen.com
Clothing

Hennessey Hammock
637 Southwind Rd.
Galiano Island BC V0N 1P0
CANADA
888-539-2930; 250-539-2930
Fax: 250-539-5390
E-mail: info@hennessy hammock.com
www.hennessyhammock.com
Hammocks

Hilleberg USA
14685 NE 95th St.
Redmond WA 98052
866-848-8368; 425-883-0101
Fax: 425-869-6632
E-mail: tentmaker@ hilleberg.com
www.hilleberg.com
Tents

Hind USA
13 Centennial Dr.

Peabody MA 01961
800-952-4463; 978-532-9000
Fax: 800-797-4248; 978-532-6105
E-mail: hindservice@hind.com
www.hind.com
Clothing

Hi-Tec Sports USA
4801 Stoddard Rd.
Modesto CA 95356
800-521-1698
Fax: 209-545-2543
E-mail: info@hi-tec.com
www.hi-tecsports.com
Footwear

Ibex Outdoor Clothing
2800 Westerdale Cut-Off Rd.
Woodstock VT 05091
800-773-9647
E-mail: info@ibexwear.com
www.ibexwear.com
Clothing

IceBox
Grand Shelters
1327 Sherman Dr.
Longmont CO 80501
866-772-2107; 303-772-2107
E-mail: iglooinfo@grandshelters.com
www.grandshelters.com
Igloo-building tool

Icebreaker New Zealand
64-4-385-9113
E-mail: info@icebreaker.co.nz
www.icebreakernz.com
Merino wool clothing

Integral Designs
5516 3rd St. SE
Calgary AB T2G 5G5

CANADA
403-640-1445
Fax: 403-640-1444
E-mail: info@integraldesigns.com
www.integraldesigns.com
Tents, bivy shelters, sleeping bags, clothing

International Sani-fem
P.O. Box 4117
Downey CA 90241
800-542-5580; 562-928-3435
Fax: 562-862-4373
www.freshette.com
Freshette

Isis
1 Mill St., Suite 126
Burlington VT 05401
866-875-8689
E-mail: info@isisforwomen.com
www.isisforwomen.com
Women's clothing

Jack Wolfskin
Ausrüstung für Draussen Gmgh & Co. KGaA
Limburger Straße 38-40
D-65510 Idstein/Ts.
GERMANY
0049-6126-954-0
Fax: 0049-6126-954-159
E-mail: info@jack-wolfskin.com
www.jack-wolfskin.com
Packs, etc.

Jagged Edge
P.O. Box 2256/223 E. Colorado Ave.
Telluride CO 81435
970-728-9307
Fax: 970-728-9072
E-mail: info@jagged-edge-telluride.com
www.jagged-edge-

telluride.com
Clothing

Jandd Mountaineering
1345 Specialty Dr., #D
Vista CA 92081
760-597-9030; 760-597-9021
Fax: 800-61-JANDD (800-615-2633); 760-597-9022
E-mail: custsrv@jandd.com
www.jandd.com
Packs

JanSport
P.O. Box 1817
Appleton WI 54912-1817
www.jansport.com
Packs, clothing

Jetboil
P.O. Box 173
529 Sunapee St.
Guild NH 03754
603-863-7700
Fax: 603-863-7757
E-mail: info@jetboil.com
www.jetboil.com
Jetboil stove

Johnson Outdoors
555 Main St.
Racine WI 53403
800-572-8822
www.johnsonoutdoors.com
Outdoor equipment, Eureka tents, Silva compasses

Julbo
25 Omega Dr., Suite 150
Williston VT 05495
802-651-0833
Fax: 802-651-0986
E-mail: contact@julboinc.com
www.julbousa.com
Sunglasses

Katadyn North America
9850 51st Ave. N.
Minneapolis MN 55442
800-755-6701
Fax: 763-746-3540
E-mail: outdoor@katadyn.com
www.katadyn.com
Water treatment

Kelty
6235 Lookout Rd.
Boulder CO 80301
800-423-2320
Fax: 800-504-2745
www.kelty.com
Packs

Kenyon Consumer Products
1425 Kingston Rd.
Peace Dale RI 02883
401-792-3705
Fax: 401-792-8093
E-mail: kcp@kenyonconsumer.com
www.kenyonconsumer.com
Underwear and fleece clothing

Kifaru International
15794 W. 6th Ave.
Golden CO 80401
800-222-6139; 303-278-9155
Fax: 303-278-9248
E-mail: cs@kifaru.net
www.tipikifaru.com
Tents

K-Swiss
31248 Oak Crest Dr.
Westlake Village CA 91361
800-938-8000
Fax: 818-706-5390
E-mail: Kscs@k-swiss.com
www.kswiss.com
Footwear

Lafuma America
6662 Gunpark Dr., Suite 200
Boulder CO 80301
800-514-4807
E-mail: lafuma@
lafumausa.com
www.lafumausa.com
Sleeping bags

La Sportiva North America
3850 Frontier Ave., #100
Boulder CO 80301
303-443-8710
Fax: 303-442-7541
E-mail: custserv@
sportiva.com
www.lasportivausa.com
Footwear

Legend Footwear
17930 Rowland St.
City of Industry CA 91748
877-LEGEND8 (877-534-3638); 626-935-0887
Fax: 626-935-0882
E-mail: sales@
legendfootwear.com
www.legendfootwear.com
Footwear

Leki USA
356 Sonwil Dr.
Buffalo NY 14225
716-683-1022
E-mail: service@leki.com
www.leki.com
Hiking poles

Liberty Mountain
4375 W. 1980 S., Suite 100
Salt Lake City UT 84104
800-366-2666
Fax: 801-954-0766
E-mail: sales@
libertymtn.com
www.libertymtn.com
U.S. distributor of Trangia
stoves and Montane
clothing

Life-Link Backcountry Travel
P.O. Box 2913
Jackson WY 83001
800-443-8620
E-mail: Life-Link@
Life-Link.com
www.life-link.com
Backcountry ski accessories

Limmer Boot
P.O. Box 1148
Intervale NH 03485
603-694-BOOT (603-694-2668)
Fax: 603-694-2950
E-mail: info@
limmerboot.com
www.limmerboot.com

Liquipak
Liquid Assets
9493 N. Price
Fresno CA 93720
559-433-1773
Fax: 559-433-1773
E-mail: assetsliquid@
aol.com
http://411hydration.com
Water containers

L.L. Bean
Freeport ME 04033-0001
800-441-5713
Fax: 207-552-3080
www.llbean.com
Outdoor gear, clothing

Lowe Alpine Systems USA
190 Hanover St.
Lebanon NH 03766
E-mail: lowecs@
lowealpine.com
www.lowealpine.com
Packs, clothing

Lynne Whelden Gear
1025 Shaw Pl.
Williamsport PA 17701

E-mail: LWgear@juno.com
www.lwgear.com
Packs, tents, blankets

Magellan
Thales Navigation
960 Overland Ct.
San Dimas CA 91773
800-669-4477; 800-707-9971; 909-394-5000
www.magellangps.com
GPS systems

MAG Instrument
1635 S. Sacramento Ave.
Ontario CA 91761
909-947-1006
Fax: 909-947-3116
www.maglite.com
Maglite flashlights

Manzella Productions
80 Sonwil Dr.
Buffalo NY 14225
800-6GLOVES (800-645-6837)
www.manzella.com
Gloves, oversocks

Marker USA
1070 W. 2300 S.
Salt Lake City UT 84119
www.markerusa.com
Clothing

Marmot Mountain
2321 Circadian Way
Santa Rosa CA 95407
707-544-4590
Fax: 707-544-1344
E-mail: info@marmot.com
www.marmot.com
Sleeping bags, clothing

Masters
Via Capitelvecchio, 29
36061 Bassano del Grappa
(VI)
ITALY
39-0424-524133

Fax: 39-0424-527924
www.masters.it
Trekking poles

McHale Packs
P.O. Box 33672
Seattle WA 98133-0672
206-533-1479
www.mchalepacks.com
Packs

McMurdo Pains Wessex
200 Congress Park Dr.,
Suite 102
Delray Beach FL 33445
800-576-2605; 561-819-2600
Fax: 561-819-2650
E-mail: sales@
mcmpw.com
www.www.mcmpw.co.uk
PLBs

McNett Corp.
1411 Meador Ave.
Bellingham WA 98229
360-671-2227
Fax: 360-671-4521
E-mail: sales@mcnett.com
www.mcnett.com
Aquamira water treatment, waterproofing
products

Medalist USA
1047 MacArthur Rd.
Reading PA 19605
800-543-8952; 610-373-5300
Fax: 610-373-5400
E-mail: info@
medalist.com
www.medalist.com
Base-layer clothing

Mekan Boots
116 E. Helm Ave.
Salt Lake City UT 84115
800-657-2884; 801-293-8135

Fax: 801-293-8181
E-mail: gmekan@
mekanboot.com
www.mekanboot.com
Footwear

Merrell Boots
800-789-8586
www.merrell.com
Footwear

Metolius Climbing
63189 Nels Anderson Rd.
Bend OR 97701
541-382-7585
Fax: 541-382-8531
E-mail: info@
metoliusclimbing.com
www.metoliusclimbing.
com
Sleeping pads

Mo-go-gear
4035 NE Hassalo St.
Portland OR 97232
503-460-3027
E-mail: greg@
mogogear.com
www.mogogear.com
Stoves

Montane
Unit 21
North Seaton Industrial
Estate
Ashington, Northumber-
land NE63 0YB
UNITED KINGDOM
44-0-1670-522300
Fax: 44-0-1670-522400
E-mail: info@
montane.co.uk
www.montane.co.uk
Clothing

MontBell North America
2800 Wilderness Pl.
Boulder CO 80301
866-546-6824
Fax: 720-565-2802

www.montbell.com/
america/index.asp
Packs, sleeping bags, clothing

Montrail
2505 Airport Way S.
Seattle WA 98134-2201
206-621-9303
Fax: 206-621-0230
www.montrail.com
Boots

Moonbow
P.O. Box 25
Glencliff NH 03238
800-MOONBOW (800-
666-6269)
Fax: 801-912-7311
E-mail: info@
moonbowgear.com
www.moonbowgear.com
Tarps, waterbags

**Moonstone Mountain
Equipment**
1700 Westlake Ave. N.,
Suite 200
Seattle WA 98109
800-390-3312
E-mail: info@ moon
stone.com
www.moonstone.com
Sleeping bags, clothing

Mountain Equipment UK
Redfern House
Dawson St.
Hyde, Cheshire SK20 2LA
UNITED KINGDOM
44-161-366-5020
Fax: 44-161-366-9732
E-mail: webenquiry@
mountain-equipment.
co.uk
www.mountain-
equipment.co.uk
Sleeping bags, clothing

Mountain Gear
N. 730 Hamilton

Spokane WA 99202
800-829-2009; 509-326-
8180
Fax: 509-325-3030
E-mail: info@Mgear.com
www.mgear.com
Outdoor equipment

Mountain Hardwear
4911 Central Ave.
Richmond CA 94804
800-953-8375
E-mail: info@mountain
hardwear.com
www.mountainhardwear.
com
Tents, sleeping bags, clothing

Mountain House
P.O. Box 1048
Albany OR 97321
800-547-0244
Fax: 541-812-6601
E-mail: mh-info@ofd.com
www.mountainhouse.com
Food

**Mountain Safety Research
(MSR)**
4000 1st Ave S.
Seattle WA 98134
800-531-9531; 206-505-
9500
Fax: 800-583-7583
E-mail: info@msrgear.com
www.msrcorp.com
Stoves, cooksets, Sweet
Water water filters,
waterbags, Mountain
Gourmet food

Mountainsmith
18301 W. Colfax Ave.
Building P
Golden CO 80401
800-551-5889
Fax: 303-278-7739
E-mail: Service@
Mountainsmith.com

www.mountainsmith.com
Packs, sledges

Mountain Technology
Old Ferry Rd.
Onich, Invernessshire
PH33 6SA
UNITED KINGDOM
44-0-1855-821-222
Fax: 44-0-1855-821-424
E-mail: HughMcNicholl@
MountainTechnology.
co.uk
www.mountain
technology.co.uk
Ice axes

Mountain Tools
P.O. Box 222295
Carmel CA 93922
800-510-2514
Fax: 831-620-0977
www.mtntools.com
Packs

MPI Outdoors
10 Industrial Dr.
Windham NH 03087-2020
800-343-5827; 603-890-
0455
Fax: 603-890-0477
E-mail: info@mpiout
doors.com
www.mpioutdoors.com
Survival bags, Esbit stoves

**Nalge Nunc International
Corp.**
Outdoor Products
Division
75 Panorama Creek Dr.
Rochester NY 14625
800-NALGE-CS
(800-625-4327)
Fax: 585-586-3294
E-mail: nnics@
nalgenunc.com
www.nalgene-outdoor.com
Nalgene products

NEOS Overshoes
208 Flynn Ave., Studio 3F
Burlington VT 05401
888-289-6367; 802-846-8880
Fax: 802-863-6888
E-mail: neos@overshoe.com
www.overshoe.com
NEOS overboots

New Balance Athletic Shoe
Brighton Landing,
   20 Guest St.
Boston MA 02135-2088
800-253-7463
www.newbalance.com
Footwear

Nextec Applications
2611 Commerce Way
Vista CA 92083
760-597-5700
Fax: 760-597-5710
E-mail: info@nextec.com
www.nextec.com
Fabric

Nike USA
P.O. Box 4027
Beaverton OR 97076-4027
800-806-6453
www.nike.com
Footwear, clothing

Nikwax North America
400 N. 34th St., Suite 202
Seattle WA 98103
206-633-0063
Fax: 206-633-1459
E-mail: inquiries@nikwax.com
www.nikwax-usa.com
Waterproofing and cleaning products

No-Rinse Laboratories
868 Pleasant Valley Dr.
Springboro OH 45066
800-223-9348; 937-746-7357

Fax: 937-746-7621
www.norinse.com
No-Rinse wipes, shampoo, body wash

Northern Lites
300 S. 86th Ave.
Wausau WI 54401
800-360-LITE (800-360-5483)
E-mail: snowshoe@northernlites.com
www.northernlites.com
Snowshoes

The North Face
2013 Farallon Dr.
San Leandro CA 94577
800-447-2333
www.thenorthface.com
Tents, sleeping bags, packs, clothing

Nunatak Gear
160 Twisp-Winthrop Eastside Rd.
Twisp WA 98856
866-NUNATAK (866-686-2825); 509-997-0348
E-mail: info@nunatakusa.com
www.nunatakusa.com
Clothing

Olympic Mountain Products
22627 85th Pl. S.
Kent WA 98031
253-850-2343
Fax: 253-850-3545
www.omplabs.com
Mountain Suds soap

Omega Pacific
11427 W. 21st Ave.
Airway Heights WA 99001
800-360-3990; 509-456-0170
Fax: 509-456-0194
E-mail: info@

omegapac.com
www.omegapac.com
Ice axes

Open Country Camp Cookware
Nesco/American Harvest
P.O. Box 237/1700 Monroe St.
Two Rivers WI 54241
800-288-4545
www.opencountrycampware.com
Cookware

Optimus Stoves
Brunton
620 E. Monroe Ave.
Riverton WY 82501
800-443-4871; 307-856-6559
Fax: 307-856-1840
E-mail: info@brunton.com
www.optimususa.com

The Original Bug Shirt Co.
P.O. Box 127
Trout Creek ON P0H 2L0
CANADA
800-998-9096; 705-729-5620
E-mail: bugshirt@onlink.net
www.bugshirt.com
Insect-proof clothing

Ortlieb USA
1402 20th St. NW, Suite 7
Auburn WA 98001
800-649-1763, 253-833-3939
E-mail: info@ortliebusa.com
www.ortliebusa.com
Dry bags, waterbags

OR Women
Outdoor Research

2203 1st Ave. S.
Seattle WA 98134-1424
888-4-ORGEAR (888-467-4327); 206-467-8197
Fax: 206-467-0374
E-mail: info@orgear.com
www.orgear.com
Women's clothing

Osprey Packs
115 W. Progress Circle
Cortez CO 81321
970-564-5900
E-mail: info@ospreypacks.com
www.ospreypacks.com
Packs

Outbound Products
Infinity Sports Imports
E101 19720 94A Ave.
Langley BC V1M 3B7
CANADA
888-718-2288; 604-888-3430
Fax: 604-888-2540
E-mail: info@infinity-outdoor.com
www.outbound.ca
Outdoor gear and accessories

Outdoor Designs
Equip Outdoor Technologies
Wimsey Way, Somercotes
Alfreton, Derbyshire DE55 4LS
UNITED KINGDOM
44-0-1773-601870
Fax: 44-0-1773-607224
E-mail: info@equipuk.com
www.outdoordesigns.co.uk
Cookware

Outdoor Research
2203 1st Ave. S.
Seattle WA 98134-1424
888-4-ORGEAR (888-467-4327); 206-467-8197

Fax: 206-467-0374
E-mail: info@orgear.com
www.orgear.com
Bivy bags, clothing, hats,
   gloves, gaiters, accessories

Overland Equipment
2145 Park Ave., Suite 4
Chico CA 95928
800-487-8851; 530-894-
   5605
Fax: 530-894-1460
E-mail: info@overland
   equipment.com
www.overlandequipment.
   com
Packs

Oware
c/o David Olsen
P.O. Box 548
Truckee CA 96160
888-292-4534; 530-582-
   1843
www.owareusa.com
Tarps

**Pacific Outdoor
   Equipment**
521 E. Peach, Unit 4
Bozeman MT 59715
406-586-5258
Fax: 406-586-5276
E-mail: support@
   pacoutdoor.com
www.pacoutdoor.com
InsulMat pads

**Páramo Directional
   Clothing Systems**
Unit F, Durgates Industrial
   Estate
Wadhurst, East Sussex
   TN5 6DF
UNITED KINGDOM
44-01892-786444
Fax: 44-01892-784961
E-mail: info@
   paramo.co.uk

www.paramo.co.uk
Clothing

Patagonia
P.O. Box 32050
8550 White Fir St.
Reno NV 89523-2050
800-638-6464
Fax: 800-543-5522
www.patagonia.com
Clothing

Pearl Izumi USA
DashAmerica
620 Compton St.
Broomfield CO 80020
800-328-8488; 303-460-
   8888
Fax: 303-466-4237
E-mail: info@
   pearlizumi.com
www.pearlizumi.com
eVENT clothing

Pelican Products
23215 Early Ave.
Torrance CA 90505
800-473-5422; 310-326-
   4700
Fax: 310-326-3311
E-mail: sales@pelican.com
www.pelican.com
Flashlights

PentaPure
1000 Apollo Rd.
Eagan MN 55121-2240
651-554-3140
Fax: 651-554-3164
E-mail: info@
   pentapure.com
www.pentapure.com
Water filters

**Peter Hutchinson Designs
   (PHD)**
Cheethams Mill
Park St.
Stalybridge SK15 2BT
UNITED KINGDOM

44-0161-303-0895
Fax: 44-0161-303-2224
E-mail: contact@
   phdesigns.co.uk
www.phdesigns.co.uk
Sleeping bags, clothing

PETZL America
P.O. Box 160447
Clearfield UT 84016
E-mail: info@petzl.com
www.petzl.com
Headlamps

**Phillips Environmental
   Products**
106 Bartz Lane
Belgrade MT 59714
877-520-0999; 406-388-5999
E-mail: info@thepett.com
www.thepett.com
Wag Bag waste disposal
   bags

Plow and Hearth
800-494-7544
www.plowandhearth.com
Bug Cap

Polar Equipment
408-867-4576
Fax: 408-867-4576
E-mail: questions@polar
   equipment.com
www.polarequipment.com
Polar Pure water treat-
   ment

PolarMAX
Longworth Industries
P.O. Box 968/5417 N.C.
   211
West End NC 27376
800-552-8585; 910-974-
   3068
Fax: 910-974-7379
E-mail: customerservice@
   polarmax.com
www.polarmax.com
Underwear

Polartec
Malden Mills
550 Broadway
Lawrence MA 01842
E-mail: polartec@
   maldenmills.com
www.polartec.com
Fleece

Potable Aqua
c/o Wisconsin Pharmacal
1 Pharmacal Way
Jackson WI 53037
262-677-4121, 800-558-
   6614
Fax: 262-677-9006
E-mail: info@
   pharmacalway.com
www.pharmacalway.com
Potable Aqua water treat-
   ment

Princeton Tec
P.O. Box 8057
Trenton NJ 08650
609-298-9331
Fax: 609-298-9601
E-mail: info.request@
   princetontec.com
www.princetontec.com
Flashlights, headlamps

ProQuip
1 Tantallon Rd.
North Berwick
East Lothian EH39 5NF
UNITED KINGDOM
44-0-1620-892219
Fax: 44-0-1620-892265
E-mail: info@
   proquipgolf.com
www.proquipgolf.com
Rainshield clothing

**Purple Mountain
   Engineering**
813 W. Ave. L 8
Lancaster CA 93534
661-726-1021
Fax: 661-951-5611
Bear-resistant canisters

Pur Water Filters
P.O. Box 340/200 American Way
Windsor CA 95492
877-655-6100
E-mail: pursales@ purwaterfilter.com
www.purwaterfilter.com
PUR water filters

Rab Carrington
32 Edwards St.
Sheffield S3 7GB
UNITED KINGDOM
44-0-144-275-7544
Fax: 44-0-114-278-0584
E-mail: info@rab.uk.com
www.rab.uk.com
Clothing

Raichle
Mammut Sports Group AG
Industriestrasse Birren
CH-5703 Seon
41-0-062-769-81-81
SWITZERLAND
E-mail: info@raichle.ch
www.raichle.ch
Footwear

Rainfair
LaCrosse Safety & Industrial
18550 NE Riverside Pkwy.
Portland OR 97230
800-557-7246
Fax: 800-558-0188
E-mail: info@ lacrossesafety.com
www.rainfair.com
Coated nylon rainwear

Rayovac
P.O. Box 44960/601 Rayovac Dr.
Madison WI 53744
800-237-7000; 608-275-3340
E-mail: consumers@

rayovac.com
www.rayovac.com
Flashlights

RBH Designs
41 Crossroads Plaza, Suite 109
West Hartford CT 06117
860-231-7334
E-mail: info@ rbhdesigns.com
www.rbhdesigns.com
Vapor-barrier handwear and footwear

Redfeather Snowshoes
4705-A Oakland St.
Denver CO 80239
800-525-0081
Fax: 303-375-0357
E-mail: rfsnowshoe@ redfeather.com
www.redfeather.com
Snowshoes

Reebok International
P.O. Box 1060
Ronks PA 17573
800-934-3566
www.reebok.com
Footwear, clothing

REI
Sumner WA 98352-0001
800-426-4840; 253-891-2500
Fax: 253-891-2523
www.rei.com
Outdoor retailer

Reliance Products
1093 Sherwin Rd.
Winnipeg, MB R3H 1A4
CANADA
204-633-4403; 800-665-0258
Fax: 204-694-5132
E-mail: sales@reliance products.mb.ca
www.relianceproducts.com

Pristine water treatment

Richmoor Corp.
6923 Woodley Ave.
Van Nuys CA 91406
800-423-3170
Fax: 818-787-2010
E-mail: mail@ richmoor.com
www.richmoor.com
Food

Rite in the Rain
c/o J. L. Darling Corp.
2614 Pacific Hwy. E.
Tacoma WA 98424-1017
253-922-5000
Fax: 253-922-5300
E-mail: sales@ riteintherain.com
www.riteintherain.com
All-weather writing paper

Rockport Co.
Rockport Customer Service
60 N. Ronks Rd.
Ronks PA 17572
866-290-6431
www.rockport.com
Footwear

Rocky Shoes and Boots
39 E. Canal St.
Nelsonville OH 45764
740-753-1951
E-mail: webmaster@ rockyboots.com
www.rockyboots.com
Footwear, oversocks

Royal Robbins
1524 Princeton Ave.
Modesto CA 95350
800-587-9044
Fax: 209-522-5511
E-mail: rrmail@ royalrobbins.com
www.royalrobbins.com
Clothing

Russi Mountain Works
6654 Gunpark Dr., Suite 101
Boulder CO 80301
720-214-2194
Fax: 720-214-2197
E-mail: info@russi.us
www.russi.us
Packs

Salewa
OBERALP AG/SPA
Via Negrelli, 6
39100 Bozen/Bolzano
ITALY
www.salewa.com
Axes, crampons

Salomon North America
5055 N. Greeley Ave.
Portland OR 97217
800-654-2668; 877-272-5666
www.salomonsports.com
Footwear

Sawyer Products
P.O. Box 188
Safety Harbor FL 34695
800-940-4464; 727-725-1177
Fax: 727-725-1954
E-mail: sales@ sawyerproducts.com
www.sawyerproducts.com
Sawyer Extractor snakebite kits, insect repellents, water filters

Scarpa USA
2084 E. 3900 S.
Salt Lake City UT 84124
801-278-5533
Fax: 801-278-5544
E-mail: scarpa@bdel.com
www.scarpa-us.com
Boots

Schoeller Textile AG
Station Route 17
Ch-9475 Sevelen

SWITZERLAND
41-81-786-08-00
Fax: 41-81-786-08-10
E-mail: info@schoeller-
   textiles.com
www.schoeller-textiles.com
Clothing

SealSkinz
U.S. distributor: Danalco
1020 Hamilton Rd.
Duarte CA 91010
800-868-2629
Fax: 800-216-9938
E-mail: contact@
   danalco.com
www.danalco.com
Socks

Sequel Outdoor Clothing
P.O. Box 409
Durango CO 81302
970-385-4660
Fax: 970-385-4660
E-mail: info@sequel.tm
http://sequel.tm
Clothing

**Serratus Mountain
   Products**
3103 Thunderbird
   Crescent
Burnaby BC V5A 3G1
CANADA
604-444-3348
Fax: 604-444-4011
E-mail: info@serratus.com
www.serratus.com
Packs

Shelter Systems-OL
224 Walnut St.
Menlo Park CA 94025
650-323-6202
Fax: 650-323-1220
www.shelter-systems.com
Tent stakes

Sherpa
P.O. Box 607
Milwaukee WI 53201

800-621-2277
Fax: 414-347-4143
E-mail: kmarkiewicz@
   idealmfgsolutions.com
www.sherpasnowshoes.com
Snowshoes

Sierra Designs
2011 Cherry St., Suite 202
Louisville CO 80027
800-635-0461
www.sierradesigns.com
Tents, sleeping bags, etc.

Sigg
U.S. distributor: Off
   Center Line
12641 N. 65th Pl.
Scottsdale AZ 85254
480-664-3280
Fax: 480-664-3290
E-mail: ronp2@
   mindspring.com
www.off-centerline.
   com
Bottles, etc.

Simon Metals
937 A St.
Fillmore CA 93015
888-638-2599
Tent stakes

Six Moon Designs
16228 SW Ellerson
Beaverton OR 97007
503-430-2303
www.sixmoondesigns.
   com
Ultralight gear

Slumberjack
800-233-6283
www.slumberjack.com
Sleeping bags, self-
   inflating sleeping pads

SmartWool/Duke Designs
P.O. Box 774928
Steamboat Springs CO
   80477

800-550-9665
www.smartwool.com
Socks, clothing

SMC
6930 Salashan Pkwy.
Ferndale WA 98248
800-426-6251; 360-366-
   5534
Fax: 360-366-5723
E-mail: smc@smcgear.com
www.smcgear.com
Ice axes, mountaineering
   gear

Snow Peak USA
P.O. Box 2002
15790 SE Piazza Ave., #101
Clackamas OR 97015
503-697-3330
Fax: 503-699-1396
E-mail: info@
   snowpeak.com
www.snowpeak.com
Stoves, cookware

Solar World
2807 N. Prospect
Colorado Springs CO
   80907
800-246-7012; 719-635-
   5125
Fax: 719-635-5398
E-mail: solar@codenet.net
www.solarworld.com
Battery charger

Speer Hammocks
34 Clear Creek Rd.
Marion NC 28752
828-724-4444
E-mail: info@
   speerhammocks.com
www.speerhammocks.
   com
Hammocks

SportHill
725 McKinley St.
Eugene OR 97402
800-622-8444

www.sporthill.com
Clothing

Stanley Alpine
E-mail: jim@sopgear.com
www.sopgear.com
Alpine axes, tent stakes

Stephenson's Warmlite
22 Hook Rd.
Gilford NH 03249-6745
603-293-8526
E-mail: info@warmlite.net
www.warmlite.com
Tents, sleeping bags,
   down-filled sleeping
   pads, clothing, vapor
   barriers

Streamlight
30 Eagleville Rd.
Eagleville PA 19403
800-523-7488; 610-631-
   0600
Fax: 800-220-7007; 610-
   631-0712
E-mail: cs@
   streamlight.com
www.streamlight.com
Flashlights
.

Stubai
4375 W. 1980 S., Suite 100
Salt Lake City UT 84104
503-685-9600
Fax: 503-685-9400
E-mail: sport@stubai.com;
   LMSABC@aol.com
www.stubai.com/english/
Ice axes

SunDog
700 NW Gilman Blvd.,
   #515
Issaquah WA 98027
206-313-8871
Fax: 253-550-9803
www.sundog.com
Packs, camera bags

Sun Precautions
2815 Wetmore Ave.
Everett WA 98201
800-882-7860; 425-303-8585
Fax: 425-303-0836
E-mail: customerservice@
  sunprecautions.com
www.sunprecautions.com
Sun-protection clothing

Superfeet
800-634-6618; 360-384-1820
Fax: (800) 320-2724
E-mail: here@
  superfeet.com
www.superfeet.com
Footbeds

Suunto USA
2151 Las Palmas Dr., Suite F
Carlsbad CA 92009
800-543-9124, 760-931-6788
Fax: 760-931-9875
E-mail: info@
  suuntousa.com
www.suuntousa.com
Compasses, U.S. distributor of Primus stoves

Swedish FireSteel
c/o Light My Fire Sweden AB
Västkustvägen 7
SE 211 24 Malmö
SWEDEN
46-40-660-16-60
Fax: 46-40-660-16-69
E-mail: info@
  light-my-fire.com
www.light-my-fire.com
Swedish FireSteel

Swiss Army Brands
65 Trap Falls Rd.
Shelton CT 06484
800-442-2706
Fax: 203-926-1505
E-mail: kniferepair@
  swissarmy.com

www.swissarmy.com
Swiss Army and Victorinox
  knives

Tarptent
330 Belmont Ave.
Redwood City CA 94061
650-587-1548
E-mail: info@tarptent.com
www.tarptent.com
Tarp tents

Taylor Precision Products
Customer Service
2220 Entrada del Sol
Las Cruces NM 88001
505-526-0944
Fax: 505-526-4626
E-mail: info@
  taylorusa.com
www.taylorusa.com
Thermometers

Tektite Industries
309 N. Clinton Ave.
Trenton NJ 08638-5122
800-540-2814; 609-656-0600
Fax: 609-656-0063
E-mail: info@tek-tite.com
www.tek-tite.com
Flashlights

**Terramar Sports
  Worldwide**
E-mail: info@
  terramarsports.com
www.terramarsports.com
Silk Skins base layers

Teva Sport Sandals
515 N. Beaver St.
Flagstaff AZ 86001
800-FORTEVA (800-367-8382)
Fax: 928-779-6004
E-mail: customerservice@
  tevasandals.com
www.teva.com
Sandals

TFO
P.O. Box 684
Logan UT 84321-0684
888-463-5394
Gatekeeper water filter

ThermoJet
c/o Tim Huggins
Synergy EC
5215A Fleetwood Oaks
Dallas TX 75235
E-mail: info@
  thermojetstove.com
www.thermojetstove.com
Stoves

Thermo-Serv/Aladdin
3901 Pipestone Rd.
Dallas TX 75212
800-635-5559; 214-631-0307
Fax: 214-631-0566
E-mail: samples@
  thermoserv.com
www.thermoserv.com
Aladdin insulated mugs

Thorlo
2210 Newton Dr.
Statesville NC 28677
888-846-7567
www.thorlo.com
Socks

Tilley Endurables
300 Langner Rd.
West Seneca NY 14224
800-ENDURES (800-363-8737)
Fax: 800-845-5394
www.tilley.com
Hats

Timberland Co.
200 Domain Dr.
Stratham NII 03885
603-772-9500
www.timberland.com
Footwear, clothing

Timberline Filters
P.O. Box 20356

Boulder CO 80308
800-777-5996
E-mail: aew@t-line.com
www.timberlinefilters.com
Water filters

Tough Traveler
1012 State St.
Schenectady NY 12307
800-GO-TOUGH (800-468-6844)
Fax: 518-377-5434
E-mail: service@
  toughtraveler.com
www.toughtraveler.com
Children's packs and sleeping bags

Trangia AB
Trångsviken
83047 Trångsviken
SWEDEN
46-640-681330
Fax: 46-640-681339
E-mail: info@trangia.se
www.trangia.se
Trangia stoves

Trek Sport Outdoors
3068 Covington Pike,
  Suite 7B
Memphis TN 38128
901-888-OUTT
  (901-888-6888)
Fax: 866-388-5700
E-mail: treksportout
  doors@yahoo.com
www.treksportusa.com
Packs

Trekstov
F. H. Enterprises
P.O. Box 36
Iskut BC V0J 1K0
CANADA
250 234-3919
E-mail: traveller@
  trekstov.com
www.trekstov.com
Stoves

Tua Skis
U.S. distributor: Cima
1945 33rd St.
Boulder CO 80301
303-417-0301
Fax: 303-417-0145
E-mail: help@
  cimasports.com
www.cimasports.com;
  www.tuaski.net
Skis

Tubbs Snowshoe Co.
52 River Rd.
Stowe VT 05672
800-882-2748; 802-253-
  7398
Fax: 802-253-9982
E-mail: info@
  tubbssnowshoes.com
www.tubbssnowshoes.com
Snowshoes

UCO Corp.
9225 151st Ave. NE
Redmond WA 98052
888-297-6062;
  425-883-6600
Fax: 425-883-0036
www.ucocorp.com
Candle lanterns, acces-
  sories

U-Dig-It Enterprises
3953 Brookside Lane
Boise ID 83703
208-939-8656; 800-939-
  8656
Fax: 208-939-8656
E-mail: udigit@dmi.net
U-Dig-It trowel

Ultimate Direction
2011 Cherry St., Unit 202
Louisville CO 80027
800-426-7229
www.ultimatedirection.
  com
Hydration equipment

**Ultralight Adventure
  Equipment**
159 N. 200 E.
Logan UT 84321
435-753-5191
Fax: 435-753-5190
E-mail: info@
  ula-equipment.com
www.ula-equipment.com
Packs, Amigo water filter,
  U.S. distributor of Pacer-
  poles

Ursack
P.O. Box 5002
Mill Valley CA 94942
866-BEARBAG (866-232-
  7224)
E-mail: tomcohen@
  ursack.com
www.ursack.com
Bear-resistant sacks

Vargo Outdoors
233 N. 3rd St.
Lewisburg PA 17837
877-932-8546; 570-523-
  9251
Fax: 805-926-4511
E-mail: brian@
  hike-advice.com
www.vargooutdoors.com
Titanium stoves, stakes,
  utensils

Vasque
314 Main St.
Red Wing MN 55066
800-224-HIKE (800-224-
  4453)
www.vasque.com
Vasque footwear

Vaude International
www.vaude.de
Markill stoves

**Voilé Mountain
  Equipment**
2636 S. 2700 W.

Salt Lake City UT 84119
801-973-8622
Fax: 801-973-8918
E-mail: voile@
  voile-usa.com
www.voile-usa.com
Nordic ski bindings, snow
  shovels

Vortex Backpacks
753 W. 1700 S.
Salt Lake City UT 84104
800-386-7839
Fax: 801-978-2249
www.vortexbackpacks.com
Packs

Watchful Eye Designs
P.O. Box 980007
Park City UT 84098
800-355-1126; 435-649-
  9009
Fax: 435-940-0956
www.watchfuleyedesigns.
  com
Water-, odor-, dust-, and
  humidity-proof bags

Wenger NA
15 Corporate Dr.
Orangeburg NY 10962
800-267-3577; 800-447-
  7422
E-mail: custsvc@
  wengerna.com
www.wengerna.com
Knives, watches

Westbrae Natural
Westbrae Consumer
  Affairs
The Hain Celestial Group
734 Franklin Ave., #444
Garden City NY 11530
800-434-4246
www.westbrae.com
Food

Western Mountaineering
1025 S. 5th St.

San Jose CA 95112
408-287-8944
Fax: 408-287-8946
www.western
  mountaineering.com
Sleeping bags

Whirley Industries
618 Fourth Ave.
Warren PA 16365-0988
800-825-5575; 814-723-
  7600
Fax: 814-723-3245
E-mail: info@whirley.com
www.whirley.com
Insulated mugs

Wiggy's
P.O. Box 2124
Grand Junction CO 81505
800-748-1827
Fax: 970-241-5921
E-mail: wiggys@
  wiggys.com
www.wiggys.com
Sleeping bags, sleeping pads,
  packs, tents, clothing

Wigwam Mills
3402 Crocker Ave.
Sheboygan WI 53081
800-558-7760
E-mail: socks@
  wigwam.com
www.wigwam.com
Socks

Wild Ideas
P.O. Box 1575
Santa Ynez CA 93460
805-693-0550
E-mail: info@wild-ideas.net
www.wild-ideas.net
Bearikade bear-resistant
  containers

Wild Things
1618 White Mountain
  Hwy.
North Conway NH 03860

603-356-WILD (603-356-
9453)
Fax: 603-356-0305
www.wildthingsgear.com
Packs, climbing equipment

Wisconsin Pharmacal
1 Pharmacal Way
Jackson WI 53037
800-558-6614; 262-677-
4121
Fax: 262-677-9006
E-mail: info@
pharmacalway.com
www.pharmacalway.com
Potable Aqua water treat-
ment, Atwater Carey,
StingEze, Repel

W. L. Gore & Associates
555 Papermill Rd.
Newark DE 19711
888-914-4673; 410-506-
7787
www.gore.com
Gore-Tex

Wolverine Worldwide
9341 Courtland Dr. NE
Rockford MI 49351
800-789-8586; 616-866-
5500
Fax: 616-866-5550
www.wolverineworld
wide.com
Footwear

Woolrich
2 Mill St.
Woolrich PA 17779
800-966-5372
E-mail: service@
woolrich.com
www.woolrich.com
Clothing

**WTC Industries/
Ecomaster**
14405 21st Ave. N.
Minneapolis MN 55447
PentaPure water filters

ZZ Manufacturing
P.O. Box 1798
Glendora CA 91740
800-594-9046; 626-852-
9690
Fax: 626-852-2428
E-mail: zzstove@
zzstove.com
www.zzstove.com
Sierra Stoves

metric conversions

LENGTH

1 mile = 5,280 feet = 1.61 kilometers
1 yard = 3 feet = 0.914 meter
1 foot = 12 inches = 30.48 centimeters
1 inch = 2.54 centimeters = 25.4 millimeters
0.5 inch = 12.7 millimeters
0.25 inch = 6.35 millimeters

WEIGHT

1 ounce = 28.35 grams
1 pound = 16 ounces = 453.6 grams
2.2 pounds = 1 kilogram

CAPACITY

(U.S. liquid measure)
1 fluid ounce = 2 tablespoons = 29.56 milliliters
1 gill = 4 ounces = 1 cup = 0.1 liter
1 cup = 16 tablespoons = 8 fluid ounces
    = 236 milliliters

1 pint = 16 fluid ounces = 2 cups = 0.5 liter
1 quart = 32 fluid ounces = 2 pints = 0.9 liter
1 gallon = 128 fluid ounces = 4 quarts = 3.8 liters

CAPACITY

(British imperial liquid and dry measure)
1 gill = 5 ounces = 142 cubic centimeters = 0.142 liter
1 pint = 4 gills = 568 cubic centimeters = 0.568 liter
1 quart = 2 pints = 4.5 liters
1 gallon = 4 quarts = 4.5 liters

TEMPERATURE

°F = (°C x 1.8) + 32
°C = (°F–32) x 0.555

index

Numbers in **bold** refer to pages with illustrations

ABCs of Avalanche Safety, The (Ferguson & LaChappelle), 386
Advanced Backpacker, The (Townsend), 19
Adventure Foods BakePacker meals, 252
Adventure Medical Dental Medic kit, 335
aiming off, **366**, 367
Aladdin mugs, **321**
alcohol stoves, 242, 281, 284–85; fuel for, 284, 285; models, 33, 283, **285–88**
Allen and Mike's Really Cool Backcountry Ski Book (O'Bannon & Clelland), 95
Aloksak bags, 126, 351
AlpineAire foods, 252, 254
altimeters, 356, **372–73**
altitude safety, **385**–86
animals, 393; bears, **258**–63, 394–96, **395**; snakes, **393**–94
Annapurna Circuit (Nepal), 398
Annerino, John, 12
Appalachian Mountain Club: maps, 361; *White Mountain Guide*, 375
Appalachian Trail, 11, 15, **16**
Appalachian Trail Conference, 16, 375
Appalachian Trail Long Distance Hikers Association, 375
Appalachian Trail Thru-Hikers' Companion, 375
Appalachian Trailway News, 11–12
Aquamira chlorine dioxide water purification, **270**–71, 274

arachnids, **338–39**
Arc'teryx Bora hipbelt, 107
Arizona Trail, 18, 34–**35**
Ascent of Kilimanjaro (Tanzania), 398
Asolo Approaches shoes, 39
Atwater Carey Hand Sanitizer, 335
avalanches, **386**
Avalanche Safety for Skiers and Climbers (Daffern), 386

Backcountry Bear Basics (Smith), 394–95
Backcountry Cooking (Miller), 244
Backpacker, 31, 47; Gear Guide, 102, 210, 232; water contamination study, 267–68
backpacking: reasons for, 243; training for, 5–7. *See also hiking entries*
Backpacking Gear Weight Calculator, 31
Backpacking Light (Web site), 31–32
BakePacker baking grid, 250, 252, **320**
BakePacker's Companion, The (Spangenberg), 252
baking devices and ovens, 319–**20**
Baldas Matterhorn Trek snowshoes, 93
bandannas, 175–76
Barefoot Hiker, The (Frazine), 39
barometers, 372, 384
Basic Essentials: Wilderness First Aid (Forgey), 333–34
batteries, 330–31
battery chargers, 331
bear-resistant canisters, **261**–62
bears, **258**–63, 394–96, **395**
Bear Valley MealPack and Pemmican bars, 253

Bear Vault, 261–62
Be Expert with Map and Compass (Kjellström), 373
Beyond Backpacking (Jardine), 27, 33, 228
Bibler gear: Hanging Pot Set, 313; snow stakes, 198; Tripod tent, **195**, 208
Big Agnes Horse Thief sleeping bag, 228
bindings, 95
binoculars, 352
Bite sandals, 44, 64–**65**
bivouac bags, **180**–84
Black Diamond Equipment gear: headlamps, 326, 328, **329**, 330; Megamid tent, **203**, 205; Shell Gloves, 174; Zenix headlamp, 326
Blaze Low trail shoes, 65
blisters, 72–**73**
Bollé Crevasses sunglasses, 340
books, 355
"Boot Camps," 47
boots. *See footwear entries*
Bozeman Mountain Works gear: Air-Core Plus cord, 345; sleeping pads, 240
Bradt trekking guides, 375
Brasslite stoves, 283, 287–**88**, 305, 308
breakfast, 252–53
Brown, Hamish, 17, 44
Brown, Nick, 152, 155
Brunton gear: Atmospheric Data Center (ADC) Pro, 384, **385**; Battery Saver AA solar charger, 331; Multi-Navigator GPS receiver, **371**, 372; Sherpa Atmospheric Data Center, 373

Buff neck gaiter, **171**
Bug Cap, 336
bug tarps, 186–87
Bureau of Land Management maps, 360
butane-propane stoves, 281, **298–301**; hose-connected models, **302**–4; models, 282; piggyback models, 300–302, **301**

cairns, 373, **374**
cameras and photography equipment, 353–55
campfires, 277–80, **278**, **279**
camping: coping with the night, 238–**39**; kitchens, siting, **323–24**; making camp, 215–17; preparing a bed, 238–**39**; safety, 213–15; sanitation techniques, **341**–43; striking camp, 217. *See also* campsites
Camping and Woodcraft (Kephart), 25–26
Campingaz gear: butane-propane cartridges, **298**, 299, 300, 302; Lumostar C270 lantern, 333
campsites: minimizing impact on, 212–13; selecting, 210–**13**
candle lanterns, 331–**32**
candles, 331
canister stoves. *See* butane-propane stoves
Canon Rebel camera, 353
Capilene Silkweight, 140
carbon monoxide poisoning, 309
cards, 356
Cascade Cup, **321**, 322
Cascade Designs gear: Lite Chair, 241; Packtowl, 336; Platypus bottles, 272, 275–76
Cascade Designs sleeping pads: Pro-Lite 3 short, 237–39; Ridge Rest, 236–37, 241; Therm-a-Rest, 236, **237**–40, 241; UltraLite, 237–39; Z-Rest, 237
cell phones, **348**–49
chairs and chair kits, 241–42
Charlet Moser crampons, **91**
Classic Camp Stoves Web site, 280
Classic Treks: The 30 Most Spectacular Hikes in the World (Birkett), 398
climbing skins, 95
clothing: carrying, 176; design of garments, 156–60, **157**, **158**, **159**;

down garments, **148**–50; insects and, 336–37; insulated clothing, **147**–51; smell factor, 136–37; underwear, windproof, 140; vapor-barrier theory, 163–64; washing on the trail, 178
clothing, types of: bandannas, 175–76; gloves, 172–**75**; hard shells, 145; mittens, 172–75; pants, 165–68, **166**; ponchos, 156; shirts, synthetic, 139–40; shorts, 164–**65**; soft shells, 145–47; vests, 147–48; wind shells, 144–47. *See also* footwear; headgear; rain gear; socks
clothing layer system, 130–**34**; inner layer, 131, **132**, 134–40; midlayer, 131, **132**, 134, 140–51; outer layer, 131, **133**, 134, **151**–62
Cocoon CoolMax Mummy Liner, 235–36
Coghlan's Backpacker's Trowel, 342
Coleman gear: butane-propane cartridges, **298**, 299–300; fuel bottles, 310; Peak 1 Lantern, 333; thermos bottles, 277
Coleman stoves: Apex II, 282, 293–94; Exponent X, **303**; Feather 442 Dual-Fuel, 282, **293**; Multi-Fuel, 282, 293; Outlander F1 Powerboost, 282; Outlander F1 Ultralight, 282; Xtreme, 282, **303**–4, 305, 308
Colorado tick fever, 339
Colorado Trail, 17
compasses, 363–67, **364**, **365**
Concordia Trek (Karakorum), 398
condensation, **191**–93, 194, 196
conduction, 130
Continental Divide Trail, **16**
Continental Divide Trail Society, 375
convection, 130
cooking and eating utensils: eating implements, 322–23; mugs, **321**–22; packing, 323; pans, 315–19, **316**, **317**, **318**; plates, **320**; pot grippers, **319**; washing, **322**, 323
Cordura, 117
Counter Assault, 396
coyote, o.d., 11–12
crampons, 90–93, **91**, **92**
Crazy Creek chairs, 241–42

cross-country travel, **377–78**, 381–83
Crossing Arizona (Townsend), 18
Cryptosporidium, 266–68, 269, 270, 271, 272
Cudahy, Mike, 12
Custom Fit Superfeet, 49

DAM (down-filled air mattress), 240
Dana Design gear: Astralplane pack, 109, 113, 118, 120; Contour Hip-belt, 107; tents, 204–5; Travel Pocket, 128
Dancing Light Gear tents, 204–5
Dechka, Stu, 162
DEET-based insect repellents, 240, 337, 338
dehydration, 264, 268
DeLorme's Atlas and Gazetteer volumes, 14, 362
dental care, 335
Derlet, Robert W., 268
devil's club, **392**
dinner, 254–55
distance: formula, 8, 9; pedometers, 10; per day, 8–10
Doan Magnesium Firestarter Tool, 314
documents and papers, 351, 400–402
down: care of, 233–34; cleaning, 176, 235; fill power, 149, 221–22; garments, **148**–50; hats, 170; mattress, 240; sleeping bag construction, 225–26, 227; sleeping bags, 221–22, 232
dry bags, 125–26
duffel bags, 127–28
Duossal pans, 317
DuPont Tyvek, 190

Earthwalk Press maps, 361
Eastman Outdoors Little Jon Shovel, 342
eating utensils. *See* cooking and eating utensils
electronic notebooks, 351
emergency situations: cell phones, **348**–49; fishing tackle, 349–50; food and drink supplies, 255–56; PLBs, **347**–48; rescue procedures, 349; rope, 349; signaling, **346**–47; snow shovel, 349
entertainment, 355–56

EPIC (encapsulated protection inside clothing) fabric treatment, 145–46, 223–24

Equinox silnylon stuff sacks, 126

equipment: color considerations, 33–36; cost considerations, 32–33; green gear, 28; making your own, 33; quality of, 32; selecting and buying, 20–22, 31–32; testing, 36; ultralight hiking, 25–28; weight considerations, **22**–25, 29–31

equipment lists: checklists, 29–31, 407–8; eleven-day early summer trip, 23; foreign adventure travel, 400–402; nine-day summer trip, **26**–27; two-month Arizona Trail through-hike, 34–**35**; ultralight overnight summer trip, 30

Esatto boots, 47

Esbit Solid Fuel Stove, 284

Essential Outdoor Gear Manual, The (Getchell), 28, 344

Essential Wilderness Navigator (Seidman), 373

Eureka Timberline tents, 205

evaporation, 130

eVENT fabric: clothing, 153, 154, **159**; sleeping bags, 223

Everest Base Camp Trek (Nepal), 398

Evernew pans, **316**, 318

Exped gear: down mattress, 240; sleeping bags, 223

Explore, 31

fabric choices: cotton, 135, 141; fleece, 141–44; Polarfleece, 141; Polartec fleece, 141, 142; Polartec Thermal Pro, 143; polyester, 137–38; polypropylene, 137; Primaloft, 150, 174, 175, 221; for rain gear, 152–56, **153**; silk, 139, 141; smell factor, 136–37; synthetics, 139–40; synthetic wicking fabrics, 135–36; waterproof terms, 149; wool, 138–39, 141

fabric treatment and care, 176–78

Falcon guidebooks, 375

fastpacking, 12

feather stick, **279**

feet, **37**; alignment of, 47–49, **48**, **50**; blisters, 72–**73**; foot care, 72–**73**; foot casts, 52–**53**; overpronation,

48–49; oversupination, **48**; wet feet/dry feet, 55

F. H. Enterprise Trekstov, 307

Fibraplex carbon fiber poles, 197

Field Guide to the Southwestern States (National Audubon Society), 355

50 Hikes series (Countryman), 375

film recommendations, 354

fire starters, **314**

first-aid supplies, 333–35

First Need water filter, **272**, 273

fishing tackle, 349–50

fitness, 5–7

FitSystem (Phil Oren), 47, 51

flares, 346–47

flashlights, 327

food and drink, 243–44; calories, 246–49; carbohydrates, 245, 247; cookbooks, 244; cooking times and methods, 250–51; daily needs, 249; emergency supplies, 255–56; fats, 244–45; foreign travel and, 402–**3**; hot or cold, 244; nutritional content of, 248; packaging, **256**–57; proteins, 245; storage in camp, **258**–63; vitamins and minerals, 245; warmth and, 231; weight considerations, 247, 249. *See also* meals

food and drink, types of, **251**–52; dehydrated food, 249, 250, 254; dried food, 249–50; freeze-dried food, 249–50, 254; milk, 255; powdered drinks, 274; soup, 254–55; sports drinks, 274; wild food, 263

Food Facts (Briggs & Wahlqvist), 244, 247

footbeds, 49–51, **57**

footwear: ankle-support myth, 39–40; breaking in, 50; changing during a hike, 60; custom-made, 47; light versus heavy, **38**–39; materials, 53–56; purpose of, 37–38; stiffness myth, 40

footwear, care of: drying, 68–69; regluing a sole, **71**; repair, **71**–72; sealing, 67–**68**; washing, 68; waterproofing, 69–71; waxing, 69–70

footwear, fitting, 45–47, **46**, 53; alignment of feet, 47–49, **48**, **50**; footbeds, 49–51, **57**; foot casts, 52–**53**; foot measurements, 49; incline board, **46**, 51; modifications to footwear, 51–53, **52**; right

fit, 51; size comparison chart, 45; toe test, 47–48, 49; tongue depressors, 51; volume adjusters, 51

footwear, types of, 40–45; booties, 82; brands and models, 64–**67**; camp sandals, 82; campwear, 81–84; heavyweight boots, 38–39, 42–43, **57**, **67**; hiking styles and, 39; lightweight boots, **38**–39, 42, **57**, **66**; medium-weight boots, 42, 66–**67**; running and trail shoes, **41**–42, **57**, 65; sandals, 39, **43**–45, 64–**65**

footwear construction, 53–54, **57**–**58**; heel counters, 40, 56, **57**; heel designs, **62**, 63; insoles, **57**, 60–61; lacings, 58–59; lasting, **57**, 60–61; lining and padding, 56–**58**; lugs, **58**, 62; midsoles, **57**, 60–61; outsoles, **57**, 61–63, **62**; rands, 63; removable inserts, 60; scree collars, **58**, 59; seams, 59–60; stitching versus bonding, 63–64; toe boxes, 56; tongue, **57**, 58

fording rivers and streams, **389**–**91**

foreign adventure travel, 397–99; communication, 403–4; food and drink, 402–**3**; getting there, 404–5; guides, 400, 404; immunizations, 400, 402; information and planning, 399–402; insurance, 403; money, 401; organized trips, 402; planning sources, 401; political instability, 400; terrorism, 400; trip list, 400–401; vaccinations, 400, 402; water, 402

Forest Service maps, 360

Free-Heel Skiing (Parker), 95

French Opinel folding knife, 345

frostbite, 388

fuel bottles: filling, 310–11; types of, 309–10; weight, 308

fuel for stoves: choices, 281, 284, 288–89, 298–99, 306; transporting, 314–15; use, estimating, 281–83; weight, 308

gaiters, 80–81

games, 356

Garcia Machine Backpackers' Cache, 261, 262

Garmin GPS receivers, 372

gasoline stoves, 281, 288

Giardia lamblia, 267–68, 269, 272, 274

GoLite clothing: Coal jacket, 150; C-Thru, 140; Phantom jacket, 159; Reed waterproof-breathable pants, 161; Terrain shorts, 165

GoLite gear: Dome umbrella, 163; Feather sleeping bag, 232, 233, **234**; silnylon stuff sacks, 126; SmartFit sleeping bags, 224

GoLite packs, **97**–99; Breeze, **97**, **98**, 100, 105, 118; Gust, **98**, 118, 120; materials, 117; Trek, 100, 120

GoLite tents and tarps: Cave, **185**, 186, **187**, **189**, **204**; Den 2, **196**, 209; Hex 2, **205**; Hex 3, 205; Lair 1 Nest, 187; Lair 2 Nest, 187; Trig 2, 202, **203**, **204**; Tri Trekker Tarp, 202, 204

Good Food for Camp and Trail (Miller), 244, 250

Gore Dryloft fabric, 223

Gore-Tex fabric: clothing, 78, 152, **153**–54; tents, 194

gorp, 253

Gorp, Glop and Glue Stew (Prater & Mendenhall), 244

Gossamer Gear: NightLight sleeping pad, 236; packs, 99, 118

GPS (global positioning system), 367–72, **371**

Grand Canyon Loop Hikes I (Steck), 214

Grand Canyon Loop Hikes II (Steck), 214

Granger's waterproofing products: fabric, 176, **177**, 178; footwear, 70

Gray, Jeff, **52**

green gear, 28

Gregory hipbelts, 107

Grip Clips, 188

Grivel crampons, **92**

Grizzly Years (Peacock), 395

groundsheets, 190

GSI Bugaboo gear: Lexan mugs, **321**; pans, **316**

guidebooks, 355, 374–75, 399–400

Hamish's Mountain Walk (Brown), 17

hammocks, **242**

Handbook of the Canadian Rockies (Gadd), 17, 355

hand hygiene, 267, 268, 335

headgear: choices, 170; hoods, 157–**58**; rain hats, 172; sun hats, 169–**72**; Tilley Hat, 170–71; warm hats, 158, **168–69**

headlamps, **326**, 327–30, **328**, **329**

head net, 336

heat exhaustion, 388–89

heat production and loss, 129–30

heel counters, 40, 56, **57**

Helly Hansen clothing: boot liners, 82–83; fleece, 141, 142; Lifa line, 137, 140; Thin Air Vest, **150**, 151

Hennessey Hammocks, 242

High Level Route (Corsica), 398

hiking: being lost, 375–76; before dawn, 96; distance per day, 8–10; in a group, 7–8; kilocalorie demand, 246–47; pace, setting, 7–8; rhythm, 8; scheduling rest, 6; solo, 10–11

Hiking Grand Canyon Loops (Steck), 214

hiking styles: boot selection and, 39; choosing, 12–13; fastpacking, 12; slackpacking, 11–12; trail running, 12; ultralight hiking, 25–28

Hillaby, John, 5–6, 17

Hilleberg gear: Akto tents, **203**, **209**, 213, **214**; Bivanorak, **183**; Keron 3 tents, **203**; Keron tents, 209–10; Nallo 2 tents, **207**, 209; snow stakes, 198

hipbelts, 21, **99**, **101**, **102**, 105–7

Hi-Tec Sierra V-Lite boots, **66**

homemade alcohol stoves, 283, **287**

hose-connected stoves, **302**–4

How to Shit in the Woods (Meyer), 343

hunters, 396

hydration systems, 276–77

hypothermia, 387–88

Ibbeson, Chris, 31

ice axes, 88–90, **89**

IceBox, **219**, 220

identification, 351

igloos, 219–20

impact on landscape, minimizing, 212–13, 373–74, **381–83**

incline board, **46**, 51

Inoxal pans, 317

insecticides, 337–38

insect repellent, 240, 337, 338

insects, biting, 336–**39**

Internet. *See* Web sites

JanSport packs, 104

Jardine, Jenny, 26–27, 33, 44, 163

Jardine, Ray: books, 26–27; making gear, 33; sandals for hiking, 44–45; sleeping bag recommendations, 228; umbrellas, 162–63

Jetboil stoves, 282, **304**–6

John Muir Trail, **16**, 17, 375, **377**

Jordan, Ryan N., 31

journals, 350

Journey Through Britain (Hillaby), 5–6, 17

Julbo Sherpa sunglasses, 340–41

Katadyn Hiker water filter, **272**, 273

Katahdin, Mount (Maine), 16

Kelty packs, 103, 104, 117

Kephart, Horace, 25–26

kerosene stoves, 281, 288–89

kilocalorie demand, 246–47

kitchens, siting, **323–24**

knives, **314**, **345**–46

Komperdell Guide trekking poles, 85

Kraft Cheesy Pasta, 254

Kungsleden (Sweden), 398

lanterns, 331–33, **332**

LED lights, 325–27, **326**; flashlights, 327; headlamps, **329**–30

Life-Link gear: poles, 85; Snow Study Kit, 356

lightning safety, 386–**87**

lights, 325; candle lanterns, 331–**32**; candles, 331; flashlights, 327; headlamps, **326**, 327–30, **328**, **329**; lanterns, 331–33, **332**; LED lights, 325–27, **326**, **329**–30; lightsticks, 333

Lightweight Backpacker (Web site), 32

Limmer, Peter, 47

lip balm, 340

Lipton pasta-and-sauce meals, 254

Lonely Planet hiking guides, 375

Long Trail (Vermont), **16**, 17

lost, being, 375–76

Lowe Alpine clothing: Mountain Cap, 170, **171**; Power Stretch tights, 167

Lowe Alpine shoulder harness system, 110

lunch, 253–54

Lundhags boots, 47

Lyme disease, 338–39
Lynne Whelden's LW gear, 97, 99

magnetic variation, 366–67
Map Adventure maps, 361, 368
map bearings, **365**–67
map datum, 370
maps, 14, 357–63; availability of, **360**–62; contour lines, **358–59**; distances, figuring, 362; foreign travel, 399–400; navigating with, 362–63; planimetric, 358–59, 362; scale, 359–60; topographic, 358–**59**, 360, 361, 362, **368–69**, 370
Markill mugs, 322
Markill stoves: Hot Rod, 282, **301**; Hot Shot, 282; Stormy, 303; Stormy Hanging system, 313
Marmot clothing: Down Sweater, 149; Evolution garments, 140
Marmot sleeping bags, 222, 233
McHale packs, 112–13; Bypass shoulder system, 108; hipbelts, 105–6; materials, 117
meals: breakfast, 252–53; dinner, 254–55; lunch, 253–54; variations, 255. *See also* food and drink
Medicine for Mountaineering (Wilkerson), 269, 333, 386, 394
Mekan Boot, 47
merino wool socks, 75
Merrell Onos sandals, 64
Milford Track (New Zealand), 398
Milkman Instant Milk, 255
Mini Maglite flashlight, 327, 328
Mini Pump, 292
moist wipes, 335
monoculars, 352
Montane Superfly eVENT jacket, **159**
MontBell sleeping bags, 225
Montrail footwear, 49; Montrail Cristallo, 66, **67**
mosquito coil, 338
Mountaineering Medicine (Darvill), 334
Mountaineering: The Freedom of the Hills (Cox & Fulsaas), 88
Mountain Equipment sleeping bags, 225
Mountain Hardwear clothing: Ascent Ventigaiters, 81; booties, 82; Canyon Shirt, 139, 140; Convert-

ible Pack Pants, **166**–67; Exposure gloves, 174, **175**; Transition, 140; Windstopper Vest, 143
Mountain Hardwear Quantum Expander panels, 225
Mountain Hardwear sleeping bags, 241
Mountain Safety Research (MSR) gear: butane-propane cartridges, 299; fuel bottles, 308, 310; Mini-Works water filter, **272**; MIOX Purifier, **271**; Mountain Gourmet food, 252; mugs, **321**; pans, **316**, **317**, 318, 322; water bags, 276; XPD Heat Exchanger, 311–**12**
Mountain Safety Research (MSR) stoves: DragonFly, 282, 295–**96**; PocketRocket, 282, 308, 312; SimmerLite, 282, **296**, 308; SuperFly, 282, **302**; SuperFly Ascent System, 313; WhisperLite, 295; WhisperLite Internationale, 282, **295**; Wind Pro, 282, **302**, 303; XGK Expedition, 282, 289, **294**–95; XGK II, 403
mountain storm, 360
MP1 Emergency Drinking Water Tablets, 271
MPI gear: Extreme ProTech Bag, 184; Safe Signal mirror, 347; Space Brand Emergency Bag, 183–84
Muir, John, 25
mummy bag, 224, **225**
Munro Phenomenon, The (Dempster), 17
Munros (Scotland), 17, 18
Munros and Tops, The (Townsend), 17
music, 355–56

Naismith, William W., 8
Nalgene bottles, 275, 276
National Geographic Adventure, 31
National Park Service maps, 362
natural fuel stoves, **306**–7
Nature Study Guild Finder books, 355
navigation: books about, 373; with compasses, 364–67, **365**, **366**; with GPS, 367–72, **371**; with maps, 362–63; by natural phenomena, 373; at night, 363; signposts, 373–**74**; waymarks, 373–**74**
neck gaiters, 170–**71**

netting, 186–**87**
night navigation, 363
Nike Reuse-a-Shoe program, 28
Nikwax waterproofing products: fabric care, 176, **177**, 178; footwear, **68**, 69, 70; Loft Down Wash, 235; Map Proof, 363
Nimblewill Nomad stove, 307
Nite Ize headband, 328
No-Rinse Bathing Wipes, 336
Northern Lights Candoil insert, 332
North Face Polarguard 3D-filled Expander Panel, 225
North Face tents: Roadrunner 2, **203**, 207; Tadpole, **203**, 207; VE 25, **203**, 207
no-see-ums, 338
notebooks, 350–51
Nunatak Ghost Blanket, 228
nylon cord, 344–45

Odor Resistant Polartec Power Dry, 137
Olicamp gear: pans, **316**, 317; Scorpion I stove, 303
100 Hikes series (Mountaineers), 375
Optimus fuel bottles, 308, 310
Optimus stoves: Crux, 282, **301**, 302; Hiker, 293; Hunter, 293; Nova, 282, **292**–93, 305, 308; Svea 123R, 280, 282, **291**–92, 305
Oren, Phil, **46**–47, 48–49, 51
orienteering compass, 363–**64**, 365
Ortlieb gear: dry bags, 125; map case, 363; Water Bag, 275
Outback Oven, 250, 252, 319–20
Outdoor Athlete, The (Ilg), 6
Outdoor Photographer (Rowell), 352
Outdoor Research gear: Hat for All Seasons, 170; Modular Mukluks, 83; Water Bottle Parka, 277
outhouses, **341**
Outlast clothing: acrylic garments, 139; socks, 75
Outside, 31
ovens and baking devices, 319–**20**
overboots, 81
overpronation, **48**–49
oversupination, **48**

pace, setting, 7–8
Pacerpoles, 85–**86**
Pacific Crest Trail, **16**, 17, 375, 376

Pacific Crest Trail Association, 16
Pacific Crest Trail Hiker's Handbook, The (Jardine), 26, 162
Pacific Outdoor Equipment (POE): InsulMat sleeping pads, 240; Pneumo Dry Bags, 125–26
pack accessories: covers, 125; duffel bags, 127–28; liners, 125; lumbar packs, 127; pouches, belt and shoulder, 127; stuff sacks, 125–26
packbags, 113–16; floating lids, 115; internal compartments, 114; lids and closures, 114–15; pockets, 115–16; size comparison chart, 113–14; straps and patches, 116; wand pockets, 116
packcloth, 117
pack construction, **101**; adjustable harness, **110**; back bands, **101**, 108; compression straps, **101**, 114; external frame, 100, **101**, 102, 103–4; frames, 103–5; hipbelts, 21, **99**, **101**, **102**, 105–7, 110, 111; internal frame, **99**, **101**, 102, 103, 104–5; load-lifter straps, **101**, 107–8, **110**; lumbar pad, **101**, 106; materials, 116–17; padding, **101**, 108; shoulder straps, **101**, 107; sternum straps, **101**, 108, **110**; suspension systems, importance of, 102; weight considerations, 117–18
packing gear, 119, **121**–22
packs: as a backrest, **124**; care of, 125; choices and models, 120; durability of, 118–19; fitting a, 108–13, **109**, **110**–12; how to pack, 119, **121**–22; putting on, 122–24, **123**; weight of, 25, 96–97
packs, types of: gender-specific, 113; lightweight, **99**–100; standard, 25, 100, **102**; ultralight, 25–28, **97**–99
Paclite clothing, 154
pans, 315–19, **316**, **317**, **318**
paracord, 344–45
Páramo clothing: Alta II jacket, 159; Alta pants, 161; Aspira, 161; Directional Waterproof fabrics, 154, 155; gaiters, 81; pants, 167–68; Parameta S fabric, 137–38, 140; Trail Shirt, 138
passport, 351
pasta, 244, 247, 254
Patagonia clothing, 28; Baggies shorts, 165; Polarfleece fabric, 142;

R1 Flash Pullover, 143
pedometers, 10
Pelican MityLite, 327
Pennine Way (Britain), 17, 398
pens, 351
pepper spray, 396
permits, 15
personal locator beacons (PLBs), **347**–48
Pertex fabrics, 223
Petzl headlamps, **326**, 328–**29**, 330
Phillips Environmental Wag Bag, 343
photography, 352–55
Piezo ignition, 301, 333
piggyback stoves, 300–302, **301**
pillows, 241
planisphere, 355
planning a hike: information gathering, 13–15; long-distance trails, 15–19; permits, 15; route plan, leaving notice of, 11
plants, poisonous, 391–93, **392**
Platypus bottles, 272, 275–76
Plow and Hearth Bug Cap, 336
poison ivy, **392**
poisonous plants, 391–93, **392**
Polarguard fill, 220–21
Polar Pure iodine water disinfectant, **270**, 402
Polartec Power Stretch clothing, 137–38, 140
poles, tent. *See under* tents
poles, trekking. *See* trekking poles
ported burners, 289, 300
postholing, 93
Potable Aqua, 269–70
Pot Parka, 313, **319**
pressure stoves, 289
Primaloft, 150, 174, 175, 221
Primus gear: butane-propane cartridges, **298**, 299, 308; EasyLight lantern, 333; fuel bottles, 310; Micron lantern, 333; pans, 316
Primus stoves: Foot Rest stand, 313; Micron, 282, **301**, 302, 305; Multi-Fuel, 296–97, 303; OmniFuel, 282, 296–**97**, 303, 312; Suspension Kit, 313; VariFuel, 298
Princeton Tec gear: headlamps, 328, **329**, 330; Pulsar flashlight, 327; Yukon HL headlamps, 326
pronation, 48
pyramid tarps, **187**, 189

Pyrenean High Level Route, 398

Rab Carrington gear: Photon Primaloft One smock, 150–51; Quantum 200 sleeping bag, 232; Survival Zone bivouac bag, 182
radiation, 130
radios, 355–56
rain gear, **151**–62; design of garments, 156–60, **157**, **158**, **159**; eleven-day early summer trip, 23; fabrics, 152–56, **153**; hats, 172; hoods, **133**, 157–58; jackets, **133**, **157**, **159**; pants, **133**, 160–62; umbrellas, **162**–63; weight and fit, 160
reading matter, 355
Really Cool Telemark Tips (O'Bannon & Clelland), 95
REI gear: Cascade Cup, **321**, 322; Polarguard Booties, 82
REM (Rest Easy Mama) Air Core, 240
repair kit, 343–44; nylon cord, 344–45; rubber bands, 344; sewing kit, 344; tape, 343–44
repairs: footwear, care of, **71**–72; sleeping bags, 234; tent poles, 197
rescue procedures, 349
resupply methods, 15, 257–58
Reuse-a-Shoe program, 28
rivers and streams, fording, **389**–91
roamer, **364**, 368, 369, **370**
roarer burners, 289
Rockwell, Robert L., 267
Rocky Mountain spotted fever, 338
rubber bands, 344
rubbing bar, 51–52
Running Wild (Annerino), 12

safe camping, 213–15
Salewa Alunal crampons, 92
Salomon XA Pro running shoes, 65
sandals. *See* footwear, types of
sanitation techniques, **341**–43
Sawyer Extractor, 339, 394
Scarpa boots: Delta M3, 66; Manta, 67
Schas, Jake, 228
Scorch Buster heat-dispersion plate, **312**, 313
Scottish Mountaineering Club, 8
SealSkinz socks, 78–**79**

Sequel Solar Shirt, 139–40
sewing kit, 344
Shaker Jet, 294
shelter, 179–80. *See also specific kinds of shelter*
Shelter Systems Grip Clips, 188
Sherlite staff, 84
Sherlock staff, 84
Sherpa Featherweight Sno-Claw snowshoes, 93
shoes. *See footwear entries*
sidecut, 94
Sierra Club guides, 375
Sierra Cup, 322
Sierra Design Flex Bags, 225
Sierra Stove, 283, 305, **306**–7, 308
Sigg bottles, 274–75
signaling, **346**–47
signal mirror, **346**, 347
signposts, 373–**74**
Silva compasses, 363–64
Simple Foods for the Pack (Axcell, Kath, & Cooke), 244
ski backpacking, 93–95, **94**
slackpacking, 11–12
sleeping bag design features: boxed feet, 229; draft collars, 229; hoods, 229; zippers, 230
sleeping bags, 220; bottomless bags, 228–29; care of, 233–35, **234**; carrying, 233; color considerations, 224; construction, 225–28, **226, 227**; covers, 228; down, 221–22, 225–26, 227, 232, 233–34, 235; down-and-feather fill, 222; fill materials, 220–22; gender-specific, 224–25; half bags, 229; liners, 235–36; models and choices, 232–33; Polarguard fill, 220–21; Primaloft fill, 221; shell materials, 222–23; sitting in, **231**; size and shape, 224–**25**; synthetic fill materials, 220–21; warmth ratings, 230–32; washing, 235; weight considerations, 232
sleeping pads, 236–41, **237**
SmartWool clothing, 138, 140; Aero T-Shirt, 140; socks, 76–77
Smith, Dave, 394–95, 396
snakes, **393**–94
snow camping, **217**; making camp, 215; sanitation techniques, 343; snow shovel, 349; striking camp,

217; tent stakes, 198; water, **264**, 265
snow caves, 218–20, **219**
Snow Peak gear: butane-propane cartridges, **298, 304**, 308; fuel bottles, 310; mugs, 322; pans, 318, 322
Snow Peak stoves: GigaPower BF, 303; GigaPower Titanium, 282, **298**; GigaPower WG, 298
Snowshoeing (Prater), 93
snowshoes, 93
soaps, 335
socks, 73–74; caring for, 79–80; choices, 76–77; construction, 75–**76**; fit, 77–78; Gore-Tex socks, 78; liners, 77; materials, 74–75; merino wool socks, 75; Outlast socks, 75; SealSkinz socks, 78–**79**; SmartWool socks, 76–77; waterproof, 78–**79**
soda-can stoves, 283, **287**
Solar World SPC-4 battery charger, 331
solid-fuel stoves, 284
solo walking, 10–11
stabilizing footbeds, 49–51, **57**
staffs. *See* trekking poles
stakes. *See under* tents
Steck, George, 214
Stephenson's Warmlite gear: down mattress, 240; sleeping bags, 228–29; tents, 194–95, 209
sticky-rubber outsoles, 61–62
stinging nettle, 391–**92**
Storm Whistle, 346
stove accessories: flame diffusers, **312**, 313; hanging cook systems, 313; heat exchangers, 311–**12**; heat reflectors, 311; lighters, 313–14; pot warmers, 313, **319**; stands, 313; windscreens, 311
stoves, 280–81, 283; fuel choices, 281, 403; fuel use, estimating, 281–83; fuel weight, 308; maintenance, **309**; packing, 323; performance tests, 281, 282–83; quality of, 280–81; safety, 307–9, 310; selection criteria, 281; transporting, 314–15; weight considerations, 281, 308
stove types, 283–84; alcohol, 284–88; butane-propane cartridge, **298**–306; natural fuel, **306**–7; solid

fuel, 284; white gas and multifuel, 288–98
streams and rivers, fording, **389**–91
sunglasses, 340–41
sunscreen, 339–40
Superfeet footbeds, 49, **65**
supination, 48
supplies: availability of, 88; resupply methods, 15, 257–58
Surveyor overboots, 81
survival bags, 183–84
Suunto Altimax, **372**, 373, 384
Swedish FireSteel, **314**
Sweetwater Guardian filter, **272**
Swiss Army Knife, **345**; Altimeter knife, 356, 373
Sympatex clothing, 153, 154

Tahoe Bear Canister, 261
tape, 343–44
tarps, 184–**86**; netting, 186–87; pitching, **186, 187**–89; pyramid, **187**, 189
tautline hitch, **199**
Taylor Analog Instant-Read Dial Thermometer, 356
tent designs: crossover pole domes, 206–7; floors, 196–97; geodesic domes, **191, 192, 203, 206**–7, **208, 216, 217, 218**; hoops and tunnels, **203, 207**–10; pyramid, **203, 205**–6, **216, 217**; ridge tents, 202–5, **203, 204**; single-hoop, **209**, 210; vestibules, **192**, 200; wedge, 206–7
tents, 190–91; care of, 217–**18**; color considerations, 202; condensation, **191**–93, 194, 196; construction, **191**–93; fabrics, 193–95; guylines, **199**; inner or outer pitching, 201–2; nonbreathable single-skin tents, **195**–96; pitching, 201, 215–16; poles, 197–98; seam sealant, **193**, 194; selecting, 21; size, 200; stability, 201, 207, 209; stakes, **198**–99; waterproof-breathable fabrics, 194, **195**; weight, 200–201
terrain. *See* trails
Terramar merino wool clothing, 138–39
Teva Wraptor 2 sandals, **43**, 44, 64
TFO Gatekeeper water filter, 272
Therm-a-Rest sleeping pads, 236, **237**–40, 241

thermometer, 356
Thorn, Denise, 136, 240, 337
Thousand-Mile Summer, The (Fletcher), 17
Thru-Hiker's Handbook, The (Bruce), 375
ticks, **338–39**
Tilley Hat, 170–71
toe test, 47–48, 49
toilet paper, 342–43
toilets, **341–42**
Tom Harrison Trail Maps, **360**, 361
Tool Logic SL3 knife, **314**, 345
tooth care, 335
Topo! interactive map CD-ROM, **361**
Tour of Mont Blanc (France), 398
Tracks staffs, 84
Trail Crest camp sandals, 82
Trail Food (Kesselheim), 250
trail guides, 355, 374–75, 399–400
trail markers, 373–**74**
Trail Quest (Web site), 32
trail running, 12
trails: bushwhacking, **381**; following, **377–78, 381–83**; scree slopes, 378–79; snow, crossing, **380**; steep slopes, **378–80**
trails, long-distance, 15–19, **16**; failure rate, 16–17; in other countries, 398; preparation to hike, 17; water needs, 18–19
Trails Illustrated maps, 361, 368
training for backpacking, 5–7
Trangia gear: fuel bottles, 308; pans, **316**; stoves, 283, **285–87**, 303, 308
Traveler bottles, 275
Trekking in Nepal (Bezruchka), 404
trekking poles: advantages of, 83–84; materials and designs, 84–**86**; as tent poles, 197–98; using, 86–88, **87**
Triple Crown, 15–16
Tropical Traveler, The (Hatt), 399, 401
Tua Hydrogen skis, 94–95
Tyvek, 190

Ultimate Desert Handbook, The (Johnson), 266
Ultralight Adventure Equipment (ULA) H2O Amigo water filter, **273**–74
Ultralight Adventure Equipment

(ULA) packs, 109–10; Fusion, 105; materials, 117; pack weight formula, 118; ULA P-2, **98, 99**, 100, 109–10, 116, 118, 120
ultralight hiking, 25–28
umbrellas, **162–63**
Universal Transverse Mercator (UTM) system, **368–70**
urination techniques, 343
Ursack stuff sack, 258, 260, **262–63**
U.S. Geological Survey (USGS) topographic maps, **359**, 360, 361, **368**–69, 370

vapor-barrier theory, 163–64
Vibram, 61
Victorinox Swiss Army Knife, **345**
volume-to-weight ratio, 118

wallet and money, 351, 401
Wal-Mart Grease Saver Pot, 315–**16**
Wanderlust Nomad tents, 205–6
washing hands, 267, 268, 335
washing pots and dishes, 267, 268, **322**, 323
wash kit, 335–36
watch, 351–52
Watchful Eye Designs gear: Aloksaks, 126, 351; O.P. Sak, 263
water, 263–65; collecting, **266**; daily needs, 264; foreign travel and, 402; long-distance trails, 18–19; powdered drinks, 274; retrieving, 216; safety, 266–68; sources, **265–66**
water containers: bags, 276; bottles, 274–76; hydration systems, 276–77; storing, 277; thermos bottles, 277
waterproof bags, 125–26
waterproof terms, 149
water treatment, 268–74; boiling, **269**; chemicals, **269–71**; filters, **269, 272–74**; foreign travel, 402
waymarks, 373–**74**
weather forecasting, 384–85
weather hazards, 214, 383–84
Weathering the Wilderness (Reifsnyder), 385
Web sites: barefoot hiking, 39; camp sandals, 82; custom-made boots, 47; equipment, buying, 31–32; fitness, 6; food and drink, 244, 247;

foreign travel, 401; guidebooks, 375; hammocks, 242; maps, 361–62; Nike, 28; Pacerpoles, 85–86; Patagonia, 28; planning, 14; stoves, 280, 284, 288, 307; weight calculations, 31
weight considerations: Backpacking Gear Weight Calculator, 31; durability and, 24; equipment, **22–25**, 29–31; food and drink, 247, 249; fuel for stoves, 308; lightweight, 24; packs, 96–97, 117–18; rain jackets, 160; sleeping bags, 232; standard, 24; stoves, 281, 308; tents, 200–201; ultralight, 24; volume-to-weight ratio, 118
Welch, Thomas R., 267
Welch, Timothy P., 267
Well-Fed Backpacker, The (Fleming), 244
Westbrae Ramens, 254
Western Mountaineering gear: down fill power, 222; Flight jacket, 149–50; HighLite sleeping bag, 232, 233; LineLite sleeping bags, 233; sleeping bags, 223
West Nile virus, 336
white-gas and multifuel stoves, 288–89; lighting, **290**; models, 282, **291–98**; priming, 289–91, **290**
White Mountain Guide (Appalachian Mountain Club), 375
Wilderness and Environmental Medicine, 267
Wilderness First Aid (Gill), 333
Wilderness Press, 375
wilderness shelters, 218
Wild Ideas Bearikade, 261
wildlife, 38. *See also* animals
Williamson, Scott, 44
W. L. Gore Windstopper N2S clothing, 140
wolves, 344
World Mapping Today (Parry & Perkins), 363
World's Greatest Adventure Treks, The (Jackson), 398
writing paper, 350–51

X-Static clothing, 136–37

Yosemite Association, 267